The British Sub-Aqua Club
DIVING MANUAL

A comprehensive guide
to the techniques
of under-water swimming

British Sub-Aqua Club, 16 Upper Woburn Place, London WC1H 0QW

First published in Great Britain in 1959 by the British Sub-Aqua Club, 16 Upper Woburn Place, London WC1H 0QW, 01-387 9302

Copyright © 1977   The British Sub-Aqua Club

1st Edition 1959
2nd Edition 1960
3rd Edition 1962
4th Edition 1964
5th Edition 1966
6th Edition 1968
7th Edition 1972
8th Edition 1975
9th Edition 1976
10th Edition 1977
10th Edition (1st Revise) 1978
10th Edition (2nd Revise) 1979
10th Edition (3rd Revise) 1980
10th Edition (4th Revise) 1982

Printed in Great Britain by Eyre & Spottiswoode Ltd.

ISBN 0 9506786 1 9

CONTENTS

Training Index

The purpose of this index is to provide the reader who is learning to dive with the BSAC, with a quick reference to those parts of the Manual which should be studied prior to or concurrently with training lectures, pool or open-water lessons, and tests. The index follows the normal order of BSAC training which takes him through to Second Class Diver grade. As the student progresses, it is assumed that he has gained an understanding of subjects which precede the one currently being studied.

Lecture/Lesson/Test	Subjects to be studied	Page
Open-water test G	Initial open-water dives	329
Lecture 2.1—Decompression sickness—the condition and its treatment	Decompression	85
	Decompression tables—appendix 1	546
	Recompression treatment—appendix 2	551
Lecture 2.2—Compressors and recharging	Compressors and cylinder filling	157
	Air purity analysis	169
Lecture 2.3—Under-water search methods	Under-water search methods	364
Lecture 2.4—Roped diver operations	Signals and communications	319
	Low visibility and roped diving	358
Lecture 2.5—Low visibility and night diving	Low visibility and roped diving	358
	Night diving	383
Lecture 2.6—Basic seamanship	Small boat seamanship	491
	Appendices 8, 10 and 11	562
Lecture 2.7—Charts and tide tables	Charts and tide tables	522
	Appendix 9	565
Lecture 2.8—Basic navigation and position fixing	Position fixing	535
Lecture 2.9—Expeditions: planning and conduct	Open-water dives	477
	Branch diving expeditions	486
	Scientific expeditions	403
	Appendices 3, 6, 7, 8, 9, 11	552
Lecture 2.10—Expeditions: safe and emergency actions	All medical and organisational subjects	
	Appendix 2	551
Second class drills— Assisted ascents	Ascent procedures	345
Tender to roped diver/roped diver	Low visibility and roped diving	358
Under-water navigation	Under-water navigation	350
Rope search	Under-water search methods	364
Low visibility search	Low visibility and roped diving	358
	Under-water search methods	364
Swim and rescue tow	Rescue and lifesaving	300

Foreword

There are two great adventures for the inhabitants of Planet Earth in the 20th Century: exploration of space and exploration of the world beneath the sea.

The exploration of space is only possible for a few selected individuals with the entire support of government research programmes. The exploration beneath the sea is open to anyone who reads this book!

Beneath the sea you will find a world of extraordinary beauty and excitement. There is a challenge, the need for training and skill, and enormous rewards in terms of enjoyment for those who take the training course available at any of the 1100 branches of the British Sub-Aqua Club. This book contains the concentrated experience of the amateur divers of the British Sub-Aqua Club accumulated over 26 years by hundreds of thousands of divers. Use it as your guide to explore the fabulous world beneath the waves. It will ensure that your dives combine pleasure and safety.

The British Sub-Aqua Club is the governing body for the sport of diving in the United Kingdom, and is a founder member of the World Federation of Underwater Activities. The British Sub-Aqua Club represents sports divers to the Sports Council, and negotiates on behalf of amateur divers with the Health and Safety Executive of the Department of Employment, the Department of Trade, and the Ministry of Agriculture, Fisheries and Food, to ensure that the rights of amateur divers are protected and not reduced by over-strict regulations or restriction of diving areas.

The British Sub-Aqua Club's Diving Manual, now in its 10th Edition, is the standard work for sports divers everywhere. That is the opinion of the Royal Navy. It is also the opinion of amateur divers all over the world. The sensational growth of the British Sub-Aqua Club proves that. There are now some 1100 branches of which about 200 are overseas. The Manual itself is being used more and more internationally.

Many tens of thousands of divers use this Manual. So use it properly. Use it in conjunction with the British Sub-Aqua Club's superb training procedures. Enjoy the world beneath the sea in safety.

Dr. N. C. Flemming
Chairman, British Sub-Aqua Club

Preface to the 10th edition

Underwater swimming has become one of the most popular participation and adventure sports. Although it was once only enjoyed by the most adventurous and extrovert, it is now the chosen sport of many thousands of men and women from all walks of life.

The British Sub-Aqua Club have kept the Diving Manual constantly up-to-date and abreast of changing times, new equipment and improved techniques. Originating from the first 'Training Manual', this 10th edition covers all aspects of free diving and related topics likely to be required by the sport diver. The text has been completely metricated and not only are the RNPL/BSAC sport diving decompression tables included but also the RNPL 1972 Air Diving Tables for Decompression. Most of the chapters in this 10th edition have been completely revised and new illustrations incorporated and the manual is presented in a more logical and progressive order than previous editions.

The members of the BSAC and the many English-speaking divers all over the world who use this manual owe a great debt of gratitude to the numerous authors who are listed elsewhere in this book. The fact that they freely gave their time and expertise is the reason that this manual is in existence today. Special mention should also be made of the considerable work undertaken by Jerry Hazzard and David Sisman.

Alan J. Watkinson,
National Diving Officer, British Sub-Aqua Club

Acknowledgements

This 10th edition of the British Sub-Aqua Club's Diving Manual is the product of many authors, all of whom are specialists in their particular section of the sport, science and profession of Diving.

The British Sub-Aqua Club gratefully acknowledges the efforts of the following persons who have contributed to this and earlier editions of the Diving Manual.

A. Atkinson
The late J. Atkinson

Dr. A. Bachrach
Sgn. Lt.-Cdr.
  P. Barnard, RN
A. Baverstock
Lt.-Cdr. A. Bax, RN
Dr. J. Betts
J. Bevan
Dr. J. Beynon
L. Blandford
B. Booth
The late A. V.
  Broadhurst
A. Brooker
G. Brookes
Dr. R. Brookes
P. Browne
M. Busuttili
Dr. V. Barber

R. B. Campbell
Capt.A.Checksfield, RN
D. Cockbill

R. Darby
P. Dick
Dr. H. Dobbs
A. Double

Dr. G. Egstrom
M. Everard

Dr. N. Flemming
A. Flinder
P. Freeland

W. Gannon
The late M. Goldsmith
R. Goodwin
Sgn.Lt.-Cdr.R.Gray,RN
O. Gugen

J. Hazzard
Dr. V. Hempleman
B. Howitt
P. Hunnam

S. Jones

V. Knapper
R. Knell

R. Larn
Dr. J. Lythgoe

Sgn.Cdr.E.Mackay,RN
K. McDonald
C. McLeod
R. Matkin

J. Meredith
Sgn. Rear Admiral
  S. Miles, RN
D. Moody

J. Newby
G. Oddy

B. Page
J. Phoenix

Q. Reynolds
A. Ridout
D. Robertson

B. Shally
L. Sides
H. Singer
D. Sisman
G. Skuse
J. Stubbs
D. Swales

M. Todd

R. Vallintine

J. D. Woodley

Sgn. Cdr. M. Young, RN

L. Zanelli

The illustrations on pages 475 & 528 are published with the sanction of the Controller H.M. Stationery Office and the Hydrographer of the Navy.

Those on pages 95, 102 and 370 by kind permission of the Royal Navy, and pages 34 & 57 of the *Reader's Digest*.

Other photographs are by Mike Busuttili, Horace Dobbs, Honor Frost, Peter Kerrod, Mike Portelly, David Swales, Richard Taylor, H. S. Usher and Dick Clarke, Geoff Harwood and Flip Schulke, all of Seaphot.

Cover Photograph by Mike Portelly.

An Introduction to the Sport

The Lure of Diving

Some people take up diving for a specific purpose such as scientific investigation, underwater photography or salvage. But for the majority of persons taking up the sport, it is simply the thrill of exploring a new, alien and—from what they have been led to believe —fascinating world that lures them to take up diving. They will not be disappointed.

Almost two-thirds of the world's surface is covered with water. While the abyssal depths account for the greater part of this, there are many millions of square miles of sea-bed which are within reach of the trained sports diver. Most of this is as yet unexplored. Even around the coasts of the densely populated British Isles, there are thousands of square miles of sea-bed which have yet to be visited by the diver. Surely the sea must be the earth's last frontier and any diver who is well-trained and suitably qualified can see a new and exciting realm that can never be adequately described, only experienced.

The pleasure of diving is many-sided and as diverse as the feelings of those taking part, but since it depends upon entry into a new environment, it must first be anticipated, assimilated and understood before it can be enjoyed to the full.

Some aspects of enjoyment spring from the untypical experiences of the human senses underwater. Each time a diver sinks below the surface his whole world changes: the light dims and colours fade as the sun's rays are rapidly absorbed by the water; normal hearing ceases, to be replaced by a vague awareness of slight sounds that cannot be located—sounds of sea creatures, stones rattling in the waves' thrust and surge, the gurgle of a demand valve. Taste and smell are virtually non-existent, and the feel of the water is all-encompassing. The surrounding water imposes its presence in many ways: its coldness and wetness in direct contact with the skin, the increasing pressure as the diver descends and the weightlessness when one is neutrally buoyant.

The experienced diver who is at home in the water has learned to understand these previously unaccustomed and frightening perversions of his senses. He has come to recognise the features of being underwater: the silence, the calm, the caress of the water as it supports his weight-laden body. No longer are his senses distressed. They have re-awakened in a new world with a new set of values and expressions, and they have engendered a self-reliance, an awareness of things and of their significance. The diver has become one with the underwater world and has learned to love it.

On every dive, whether in the sea, rivers or quarries, whether the visibility be good or bad, the current fast or slack, the experienced diver makes renewed contact with a world that he has made—in part —his own. But there is one thing that stands out above all others: the sublime joy that the diver experiences at the instant of breaking surface. The shades of the underwater world are gone, light bursts in on the senses, hearing returns and the wonder, perhaps awe, that compelled creatures to emerge from the seas millions of years ago is experienced.

The aims of diving are, therefore, two-fold: to explore and uncover the unknown, and then to return to the familiar with an added appreciation of its beauties. So that a diver may immerse himself in this new environment, and for a time become part of it, he must first rid himself of cares and worries about the functioning of his diving equipment and of his ability to use it. Of course, the problems of diving, and the fundamental necessity of returning to the surface to breathe when the air supply is exhausted can never be forgotten, but the diver should acquire a complete self-assurance in the use of his diving equipment so that any actions underwater become instinctive. Thought, time and energy spent on the technicalities of diving are then reduced to a minimum, and the diver can devote his energies and interest to other ends.

Such familiarity and confidence in diving equipment can only come after an adequate programme of training and no-one should attempt to explore the seas without first receiving proper instruction and training. The sea frowns on the foolish intruder and although professional divers may undertake deep or dangerous dives under controlled conditions for the sake of their livelihood or the needs of the job in hand, the sports diver has no cause to put his life unnecessarily in jeopardy, and even when fully-experienced with his diving equipment, it should always be used sensibly.

The chapters in this Manual detail how to achieve mastery of the equipment and of diving techniques, instilling a knowledge of the physical factors involved and an understanding of the reactions of the human body to them. Such knowledge is an essential part of the diver's training and the purpose of this Diving Manual is to serve as a reference book for those under training as well as for the experienced diver. Training and knowledge are the passports for entry into the underwater world and with them the diver can make contact with his environment. Building on the foundation stones firmly laid during his training, the diver may then broaden his knowledge and understanding through experience and intelligent observation. It cannot be safely achieved otherwise.

In Great Britain the majority of underwater swimmers learn to dive through membership of one of the many Branches of the British

Sub-Aqua Club. This body is the foremost diving club in Great Britain and is recognised as the governing body for the sport. The Club has a number of overseas Branches and its training programmes and standards are highly regarded throughout the world of diving. With Branches in most towns throughout Great Britain, it is relatively easy to find a Club where divers can receive training, and subsequently take part in exploratory dives at coastal and inland sites. Membership of the British Sub-Aqua Club is open to all who meet the fitness requirements, and carries with it many advantages other than just diver training. While some are mentioned in the following sections, new members of the British Sub-Aqua Club will learn of these during the course of training: the reader who is not a BSAC member is invited to write to the Club H.Q. for further particulars.

During the course of training the diver has to learn many things. It is important that the novice learns the theory as well as the practical aspects of the sport. Since much of the theoretical knowledge falls into natural categories, this Diving Manual has been sub-divided in the same way, and generally closely follows the order in which a newcomer to the sport could learn. For example, a trainee without a knowledge of the effects of pressure would find it difficult to comprehend how an aqualung works or what decompression is all about.

The training index indicates those chapters which should be studied at the various stages of the BSAC diver training programme. The diver under instruction is strongly advised to read up those sections of this Diving Manual which relate to the training, both practical and theoretical, which he has just received, and which he is about to receive. In this way, the diligent student should soon reach a high standard of ability and knowledge.

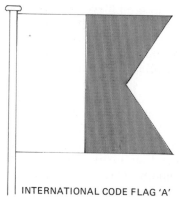

INTERNATIONAL CODE FLAG 'A'
'I have a diver down; keep well clear at slow speed.'

Diving with the BSAC

The sport of underwater swimming began in the years following the Second World War. During that War knowledge and techniques and equipment were developed and with the invention of a functional aqualung by the French pioneer, Jacques Cousteau, equipment was at last available which brought the exploration of the seas within the reach of the layman. The British Sub-Aqua Club was established in 1953 and subsequently Branches were set up in most towns of Great Britain as the Club grew. The BSAC is recognised as the governing body of the sport of underwater swimming in Great Britain and at the time of going to print membership is in the order of 25,000 through some 1000 Branches. Of these Branches, about 150 are overseas Branches and the BSAC is held in high esteem in the world of diving. The BSAC is a founder member of the World Underwater Federation (CMAS) and plays a leading part in the affairs of that world body.

Each Branch is managed by its own freely-elected Committee and conducts its affairs within the framework of Rules set down by the national body. The national body of the BSAC is also managed by an elected Council whose members are nominated by Branches and elected by a postal ballot of membership. The BSAC also has an administrative Headquarters in London where a small full-time staff carry out the day-to-day business of the Club.

The democratically elected Council is responsible for implementing the aims and objectives of the Club. The BSAC National Diving Committee (NDC), chaired by the National Diving Officer, is responsible for all technical matters. The BSAC has an active regional Coaching Scheme, with experienced divers/Instructors serving as Coaches. Their function is to give technical assistance to Branches whenever it is needed; to provide advanced training courses; and to represent the interests of divers within the region. The BSAC publishes a number of Manuals and Handbooks for the benefit of memmers and these are available through the BSAC Shop at Club HQ. On joining a local Branch of the BSAC a new member automatically becomes a full member of the national body and not just of the Branch. The member's subscription provides him with a copy of this BSAC Diving Manual; with monthly issues of the Club journal, *Diver*; with comprehensive Third Party and Public Liability Insurance cover; and many other advantages. A large portion of the member's subscription remains with his Branch and is used to pay for pool hire; to buy and maintain equipment; and to meet the running expenses of the Branch.

Branches of the BSAC provide training in all aspects of under-water swimming and arrange regular diving expeditions for their members. Many Branches provide aqualung sets for the novice diver to use during training and also such things as inflatable boats and air compressors which are used on the open-water diving expeditions.

The BSAC training programme, in accordance with which members are trained, is widely recognised and acclaimed for its thoroughness and safety. It commences with the use of mask, fins and snorkel and progresses to aqualung training in the swimming pool. When ready, the novice progresses to open water where he carries out a number of qualifying dives. This leads to the basic diving qualifications of BSAC Snorkel Diver and BSAC Third Class Diver. A programme of advanced training leads to BSAC Second Class Diver qualifications, and beyond this lies the nationally awarded First Class Diver certificate and a series of Instructor grades. All BSAC diving qualifications are related to those of the CMAS so that BSAC diving qualifications are recognised in many other countries.

Why join a club at all? Apart from the benefit of receiving sound instruction, it should not be forgotten that diving cannot be safely carried out alone, or in very small groups, unless the scope is very limited. Dive partners are required; safety cover; boat crew; shore control, etc.: two or three individuals cannot safely carry out adventurous diving without adequate support. Membership of a diving club provides this sort of support as well as all the facilities of equipment; advanced training; pool sessions to maintain fitness; and by no means least, companionship and an enjoyable social atmosphere.

Add to this the advantages of a regular magazine, comprehensive insurance and internationally accepted qualifications, and the reasons for joining a Branch of the BSAC are clear.

Basic Ability

Whatever the reason they decide to start diving, many will come to the sport with an initial sense of apprehension for water presents a strange and, to some, hostile environment that is not fully understood. In any event, it is certain that most newcomers ask either of themselves or of their instructor, 'Do I have the ability to become a successful diver?'

What might then form an answer to this question? The recent very rapid expansion of professional diving has made necessary research into criteria which might be used to select diving personnel, but so far no positive guide-lines have been published. Nevertheless it is obvious that for the sports diver, for whom the training can be less hurried and the ultimate task less dangerous than that of professional diving, the initial demands on his abilities will be less rigorous. It follows therefore that selection for sport diving begins with the individual himself, for the fact that he has presented himself for training proves that an initial interest exists. However, success depends on more than just an initial interest, no matter how strong, there must also be a sense of motivation, an ability to stick at the task once begun, and to see it through to the end.

Although fins have been designed to increase swimming efficiency, a diver should be capable of swimming confidently and without excessive effort over distances of 2–300 m and should be able to support himself by floating or treading water, without their aid. To determine the trainee's ease and composure in the water therefore, tests of minimum swimming ability without the aid of equipment are taken early in the training programme, and although speed is not important, the trainee diver should have mastered the rudiments of swimming. Unfortunately it is rare that a diving club, engrossed in the detail of its diver training programme, has sufficient instructors to spare for teaching swimming, but those who wish to take up diving and are of moderate swimming ability may improve their personal standards through practice. If truly motivated, with regular attendance at the swimming pool and practice in swimming with a light—then gradually heavier—weightbelt, the swimming standard necessary for diving can be attained.

Although the basic techniques of diving may soon be mastered, safe diving in open waters depends on a period of organised and progressive training. Such a training programme necessitates regular attendance at both the pool and lecture sessions so that the trainee's skills and knowledge can develop together. The trainee diver who lacks enthusiasm and attends the courses irregularly will inevitably find that instruction is disjointed and the resultant erratic progress is unsatisfying.

As with all sports, diving makes physical demands upon the body's resources, and it is therefore essential that the diver be sufficiently fit to meet these demands. It should be remembered that whilst he is underwater the diver is subjected to pressure and that movement under pressure calls for greater exertion than he may at first realise. He must therefore choose his diving activities to match his physical capability; an inability to recognise one's physical limitations is potentially dangerous and may well culminate in an accident.

Diving equipment can be very heavy, and difficult access to some diving sites may necessitate carrying this for some distance, but fitness is a relative term and it is certainly not necessary to be a superman in order to become a good diver, in fact many disabled are able to enjoy the sport. Careful selection of equipment to suit the diver's requirements and physique can keep the weight to an acceptable level, and diving covers a wide range of activities—from the less physically demanding diving in shallow, sheltered waters, to long expeditions and deep dives in tidal waters that can tax the strength of the fittest—so it is possible to find exciting and interesting diving that is within the scope of all ages and physiques.

Basic ability to undertake a particular physical activity can be readily tested, and a person's physical condition can be ascertained by medical examination (see *Fitness and Medical Examinations*). Less easy to define and recognise are those basic mental attributes that contribute to the making of a successful diver, yet these are extremely important. Many of the difficulties that arise as a diver adjusts to the new environment in which he finds himself are frequently a result of temperament. Inevitably it will be necessary to overcome the apprehension that is present when any new activity is undertaken, and this may be even more pronounced in the trainee diver who is also entering a completely strange environment. Frequently enthusiasm and a natural curiosity will overcome this, but far more important in allaying doubts is sound basic training. Under good instruction the learner takes progressive steps, and initial nervousness disappears as success follows success. However, even with the help and careful guidance of an instructor an ability to relax and to adapt to new sensations and changed perceptions is essential: the face mask, whilst permitting underwater vision— which is one of the most exciting experiences in diving—also restricts the total field of vision to a much narrower field; first the snorkel and then the demand valve requires the technique of mouth breathing (which does not always come naturally); correctly weighted, the diver neither floats towards the surface nor sinks to the bottom, but remains in mid-water apparently suspended, and gone are the clues for personal orientation that are available when on dry land. In such conditions the diver must be able to learn to interpret new signals: the way in which pressure builds up in his ears, or the changed feel of his equipment, in order to orientate himself in his environment. Such adaptation does not always come quickly or easily, and a diver needs patience coupled with a placid and imperturbable temperament, for he is not undertaking a sport in which the training can be rushed with safety.

Whilst the ability to remain calm in the face of a crisis is a very necessary part of a diver's make-up, he must also have a developed sense of adventure. Without this there would be no urge to explore a new environment. Diving is not for the unsure or the timid, but rather for those whose sense of adventure expresses itself through a confidence in their ability to face and overcome problems when they arise. Personal confidence grows with experience but must always allow a place for reason, for the diver who is over-confident, who tends to make rash decisions and who takes reckless action out of sheer bravado, will soon place himself and his diving companions at risk.

It must be accepted that in all diving there is an element of risk, and it is often this which, consciously or unconsciously, brings a touch of spice to the activity. However, there is a level of risk acceptance that is permissible in a particular situation and this will depend upon many factors: the skill and experience of the divers, the equipment available and the purpose of the dive. A diver's temperament must be such that he has the ability to exercise a reasoned judgement that is not easily swayed by external pressures, for over-confidence could result in making dives with an unacceptable risk.

In many people a feeling for adventure and excitement is often matched with an independence of spirit and a strong desire to go one's own way. Such a singleness of purpose is a valuable trait, but in diving this must be balanced by a willingness to accept the disciplines that the sport demands. For instance, sport divers should always dive in pairs, each having a conscious awareness of the partner's position and actions, and ready to provide support at all times. This demands an ability to behave unselfishly and to be completely reliable. The individualist who continually wanders off is a danger both to himself and his partner.

Although it may not appear so at first sight, diving is very much a team sport in that it relies upon groups of people working together for the good of the group. A diving expedition is supported by a considerable back-up organisation which involves such activities as site planning, transport, equipment checking, and marshalling and organising at the dive site. Each and every person should be willing to play his part and to make his contribution to the total effort. The ultimate responsibility for safety on an expedition lies with the Expedition Leader, and each member of the diving group must accept his authority and decisions unselfishly. Although initially the diver in training will rely heavily upon the more experienced members of his club, the time will come when he in turn will be ready to step into a position of responsibility. In the first instance this may be as an assistant Marshal or as a Dive Leader—as part of the progressive training programme. Eventually he may find that he has risen to the position of Diving Officer. Any prospective diver should be willing to accept the responsibility of leadership as his experience grows.

Finally, those who wish to take up diving must realise that it is an activity that relies upon more than just a sound physique and an ability to undertake certain skills. To be efficient and safe, diving must be supported by a body of knowledge that forms the basis for many important decisions. A diver must be able to understand sufficient physiology to realise the limitations of his own physique; enough physics to appreciate the effects of a hyperbaric environment, and be sufficiently practical to understand the workings of his equipment.

CHAPTER ONE
PHYSICAL ASPECTS

Physics of Diving

The diver is affected by increasing water pressure as he descends and this manifests itself in several ways. Some will be noticed quickly: others will take longer to become apparent. Both the diver's body and his equipment will be affected. Divers should have a clear understanding of how the laws of physics apply to them and to their equipment. Without this knowledge they put themselves at risk.

Before considering the diving environment, it is necessary to look at the atmosphere in which we normally live and the gases which make up the air we breathe.

Our Normal Environment—Air

ATMOSPHERIC PRESSURE

The earth is surrounded by an envelope of air which we call the *atmosphere*. Air is a mixture of gases, and like all matter, it has mass. A mass exerts a force on those things which lie beneath it, and at sea level the atmosphere presses down with a force of approximately 1 kilogram for every square centimetre of the earth's surface (Fig. 1). Gas pressure is commonly measured in units of *bar* and our own atmosphere exerts a pressure at sea level of approximately 1 bar.

Atmospheric Pressure = 1.02 bar (1 bar approx.)

Atmospheric pressure varies slightly with changes in weather and diminishes with altitude until it reaches zero at the extreme limit of the atmosphere. At about 5000 m above sea level, for example, the atmospheric pressure is about 0.5 bar.

Our bodies do not suffer in any way from this pressure which is applied to every square centimetre of their surface—we are born to it!

GAUGE PRESSURE

When a pressure is to be measured, it is normal practice to relate it to ambient pressure. Thus a simple gauge would read zero at an atmospheric pressure of 1 bar. An aqualung contents gauge would perhaps read 200 bar, but this really means 200 bar above the normal atmospheric pressure of 1 bar. Such a recording would be known as a *Gauge Pressure*.

ABSOLUTE PRESSURE

If the above gauge were related to true zero as found in a vacuum it would read 201 bar—the extra 1 bar being atmospheric pressure. Such a gauge reading would be termed an *Absolute Pressure*.

PRESSURE

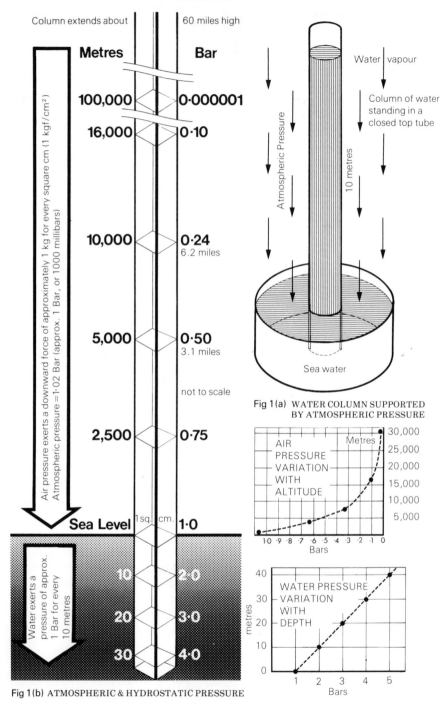

Column extends about 60 miles high

Metres	Bar
100,000	0·000001
16,000	0·10
10,000	0·24 (6.2 miles)
5,000	0·50 (3.1 miles)
	not to scale
2,500	0·75
Sea Level	1·0
10	2·0
20	3·0
30	4·0

Air pressure exerts a downward force of approximately 1 kg for every square cm (1 kgf/cm²). Atmospheric pressure =1·02 Bar (approx. 1 Bar, or 1000 millibars)

Water exerts a pressure of approx. 1 Bar for every 10 metres

1 sq. cm.

Water vapour

Atmospheric Pressure

Column of water standing in a closed top tube

10 metres

Sea water

Fig 1(a) WATER COLUMN SUPPORTED BY ATMOSPHERIC PRESSURE

AIR PRESSURE VARIATION WITH ALTITUDE

Metres: 30,000 / 25,000 / 20,000 / 15,000 / 10,000 / 5,000

Bars: 1·0 ·9 ·8 ·7 ·6 ·5 ·4 ·3 ·2 ·1 0

WATER PRESSURE VARIATION WITH DEPTH

metres: 40 / 30 / 20 / 10 / 0

Bars: 1 2 3 4 5

Fig 1(b) ATMOSPHERIC & HYDROSTATIC PRESSURE

Absolute Pressure = Gauge Pressure + Atmospheric Pressure

In diving physics, it is normal to work in absolute terms, and the reasons for doing so will be soon apparent.

COMPOSITION OF AIR

The air we breathe is a mixture of gases comprising:

Nitrogen (N_2)　　approx. 79%　　(say, 4/5)
Oxygen (O_2)　　approx. 21%　　(say, 1/5)

There are traces of Carbon Dioxide (CO_2) and other rare or inert gases, but in such small quantities that they can be ignored. All gases are compressible, having neither shape nor volume.

On the other hand, liquids have a definite volume and mass and may be considered to be incompressible at the pressures we are to consider.

The Diving Environment—Water

HYDROSTATIC PRESSURE

Water is a dense medium and, therefore, exerts a noticeable pressure upon anything which is immersed in it. Water pressure increases rapidly with depth and a cubic metre of water (1000 litres) has a mass of 1000 kilograms or one tonne. Some fairly simple arithmetic will reveal that, if our cubic metre is divided up into one metre high columns, each of one square centimetre cross section, that the mass of water in each column is 0·1 kg. If each 1 cm^2 column were extended to 10 m in length, the mass would be 1 kg and the pressure exerted by the column would be 1 kgf/cm^2.

But 1 kgf/cm^2 = 1 bar (approx). So, at 10 m beneath the surface the water pressure or *hydrostatic pressure* is equal to the atmospheric pressure at the surface (Fig. 1). 10 m of water is equal to 1 bar gauge pressure or 2 bar absolute, and for every further descent of 10 m beneath the surface, the hydrostatic pressure increases by another bar. Thus at 30 m the absolute pressure is 4 bar.

In a fluid, pressure has the particular property of acting in all directions: thus, 30 m down the body is subjected evenly to 4 bar absolute all over and in all directions. The reader will recognise that this is so when he considers the pressure of the water inside an underwater cave: although it may be largely covered with rock, not water, the pressure inside will exactly equal that of the open sea at the same depth, the pressure being transmitted horizontally.

As the human body consists largely of liquid, it takes up the ambient hydrostatic pressure without any decrease in volume, *but the spaces that contain air (for example the lungs) will be compressed unless they are artificially filled with air of pressure equal to that of the surrounding water.* The aqualung demand valve will supply the diver with air at ambient pressure (see chapter 3), but this subject should be studied further because it affects the body in many ways. The behaviour of gases under pressure needs to be considered.

PRESSURE/VOLUME CHANGES

When a gas is compressed, its volume varies in inverse proportion to the absolute pressure. This is the basis of BOYLE'S LAW—a relationship first recorded by the early physicist of that name.

Thus, an inverted bucket which is full of air at the surface where the pressure is 1 bar will be only half full at a depth of 10 m, where the total pressure is 2 bar, and only a quarter full at 30 m (4 bar absolute). This is illustrated by Fig. 2 where we see that the fractional change in the gas volume for a given change of depth decreases with depth. Thus, a change of 10 m near the surface halves the volume, while the same 10 m drop at 40 m only reduces the volume by a factor of one-sixth.

Divers will encounter the effects of this relationship during training, and several times—and in several ways—on every dive, whether snorkelling or aqualung diving. Ear clearing, mask squeeze, loss of buoyancy, function of a demand valve, ascent risks, air consumption, decompression—ALL are governed and affected by Boyle's Law. Any compressible air space, be it in the diver's body or in his equipment, will change its volume during descent and ascent, and if not equalised or controlled, damage of some sort can occur. The term *barotrauma* is used to describe injuries which result from sudden changes in air pressure: in other words, from failure to allow Boyle's Law to happen safely.

The reader will find frequent references to Boyle's Law elsewhere in this Manual. It is such a fundamental physical relationship to diving that it cannot be avoided.

PARTIAL PRESSURES

It was explained earlier that nitrogen makes up approximately four-fifths of the atmosphere and oxygen the other fifth. If the atmospheric pressure is 1 bar, is it not reasonable to assume that nitrogen is responsible for 0.8 bar and oxygen for 0.2 bar? Correct, and these are known as the *Partial Pressures*. DALTON'S LAW of Partial Pressures states that the total pressure of a gas is equal to the sum of the partial pressures which each member gas has and would alone have if the others were absent. Thus, while at sea level the partial pressure of oxygen is approximately one-fifth bar and nitrogen is approximately four-fifths bar, the air breathed by a diver 40 m (5 bar absolute) below the surface contains nitrogen at 4 bar and oxygen at 1 bar, the total pressure being 5 bar. The importance of this Law lies

Fig. 2. BOYLE'S LAW

The pressure of a given quantity of gas whose temperature remains unchanged varies inversely as its volume

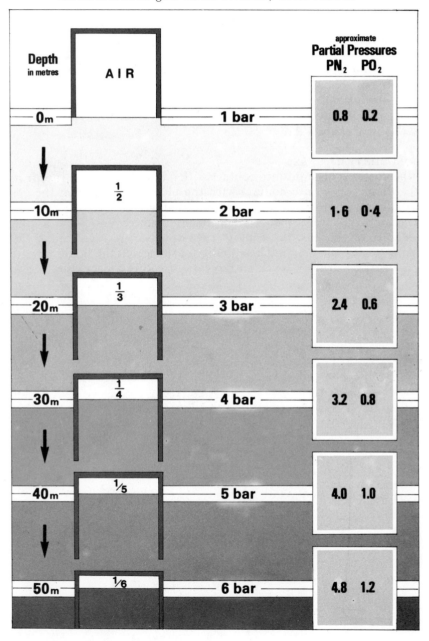

in the fact that the physiological effect of a gas depends upon its pressure or, when in a mixture such as air, upon the partial pressure.

Dalton's Law reveals itself in such conditions as oxygen poisoning, carbon dioxide and carbon monoxide poisoning, and nitrogen narcosis. An understanding of partial pressures also helps in the study of circulation, respiration, hypoxia and decompression.

Later in this Manual, the abbreviation of PO_2 or PN_2 is used to indicate partial pressure of oxygen and nitrogen respectively. Readers are asked to bear this in mind when studying certain sections of chapter 2.

SOLUBILITY OF GASES

When a gas is brought into contact with a liquid (e.g. when the air in the lungs comes into contact with the blood) then some of the gas will dissolve in the liquid. The amount that will dissolve and the rate at which this takes place is dependent upon several factors—the pressure of the gas, the contact area between gas and liquid, the temperature, the maximum solubility of the gas in the liquid. As the gas nears saturation level, so the rate of solution decreases. If gas

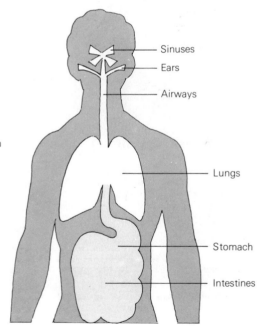

Fig. 3. AIR-FILLED SPACES
IN THE BODY

Air or gas may be present in small quantities in the stomach and intestines which can lead to discomfort due to pressure changes

Sinuses

Ears

Airways

Lungs

Stomach

Intestines

has dissolved in a liquid, and if the prevailing conditions are varied, then the amount of dissolved gas may also vary. This relationship was established by yet another learned scientist of old, and is known as HENRY'S LAW. The fact that gas will dissolve into the bloodstream and be released again when the ambient pressure is reduced, gives rise to the problems of decompression sickness.

TEMPERATURE OF GASES

Temperature affects both Boyle's and Henry's Law, but since temperature variations encountered in diving are very limited, for simplicity, these effects have been ignored. One other gas law which is of interest and which involves temperature is CHARLES' LAW. The volume of a gas varies directly as its absolute temperature if the pressure remains constant. Usually, it is the volume which is constrained to remain constant, while the pressure goes up! For example, an inflatable boat, left in the hot sun, could suffer from expansion of the contained air to the point of explosion. Keep in the shade or the boat partly deflated when not in use.

Water has several other properties: buoyancy: conduction of heat: and transmission of sound. These will now be considered.

Buoyancy

ARCHIMEDES' LAW states that any object immersed in a fluid suffers an upthrust equal to the weight of fluid it displaces, i.e., whose volume it occupies. If the immersed body is that of a diver, he has the facility to vary the volume he displaces by breathing. With full lungs he will displace more water than his body weight and he would be *positively buoyant*. When he breathes out, he may displace less water than his body weight and will sink, being *negatively buoyant*. Somewhere between the two is the desired state of *neutral buoyancy*.

A diver seeks to adjust his buoyancy to suit the varying requirements of his diving. In the vast majority of situations he will try to attain neutral buoyancy, i.e. a precise equality between his total weight and the upthrust due to the displaced water. This is achieved in a simple way. The diver, kitted up as the dive demands, launches himself into the water and exhales hard. By emptying his lungs he is reducing his body buoyancy and he should sink. He inhales from his aqualung, increases his buoyancy and floats upwards. He adds or subtracts weights from his weightbelt until the normal span of breathing bridges the gap between sinking (negatively buoyant) and floating upwards (positively buoyant). He is now *neutrally buoyant*.

However, there are other factors which will affect his state of neutral buoyancy while he dives. These are dominated by two effects, which act quite differently from each other:

CHANGE OF WEIGHT

A 1700 litre compressed air bottle contains about 2 kg of air when full and much less than 1% of this figure when empty. Thus, a diver starting with 1700 litres of air will end his dive some 2 kg lighter. This excess buoyancy can be a considerable embarrassment at the end of a dive, especially if decompressing or returning along the bottom to avoid heavy waves on the surface.

CHANGE OF VOLUME

A rubber diving suit, whether it is a foam wet suit or a dry suit covering woollens, reduces heat loss from the body by interposing an insulating layer of air between skin and water. The volume of this trapped air varies in inverse proportion to the hydrostatic pressure acting on it (see *Hydrostatic Pressure* and *Boyle's Law*) so that at a depth of 30 m the air will occupy only one quarter of its volume at the surface. The average 5 mm thick neoprene suit contains about 6 litres of nitrogen bubbles which makes the diver considerably buoyant on the surface. At a depth of 20 m these bubbles will have been compressed to about 2 litres with a corresponding reduction in buoyancy which will, however, be regained on ascent.

The free diver has a variety of methods of countering these inevitable changes in buoyancy. By swimming downwards if too light, or upwards if too heavy, he can overcome an imbalance of several kilogrammes, but this is extremely tiring and is to be strongly discouraged. A less tiring method of balancing changes of buoyancy is provided by controlling one's breathing. The human lungs contain on average about 6 litres when fully extended and a residual volume of about 1.5 litres after complete exhalation. Thus, the diver can vary his volume by as much as 4.5 litres simply by forcibly breathing in and out; this is equivalent to a change of 4.5 kg of displaced water. The range of normal breathing covers only the middle 20% of this range, so that a neutrally balanced diver breathing normally will experience a regular change of buoyancy from about 0.5 kg too light, when he breathes in, to 0.5 kg too heavy when he breathes out. But by controlled breathing he can maintain an average change in his buoyancy of up to 1½ kilogrammes.

Really deep breaths retained for all but brief periods of exhalation followed by immediate inhalation will make the diver about 1 kg more buoyant than when he breathes naturally. The converse, short shallow breaths designed to reduce one's buoyancy is less easy and may lead to panting, which for a diver is a very inefficient and possibly hazardous way of breathing.

The simplest means of adjusting buoyancy while diving is to use an ABLJ or other buoyancy aid, which can be inflated—by direct feed, cylinder or mouth— to restore neutral buoyancy at will. On ascent, the air can be vented as it expands, thereby avoiding the dangers of a rapid ascent. The use of buoyancy aids for maintaining neutral buoyancy during a dive should be looked upon as a sensible practice. However, it requires a full appreciation of the possible dangers and good technique in handling your equipment. It should NOT be used as an excuse for not being correctly weighted at the start of a dive. The section on *Lifejackets and Buoyancy Aids* in chapter 3 should be studied.

So far, we have considered methods for adjusting buoyancy continually during a dive. Now we must consider how much constant ballast should be carried in the form of lead weights on a quick-release belt. While the basic technique of achieving neutral buoyancy has been explained above, there are occasions when it is desirable to be slightly otherwise than neutrally buoyant. This is really a matter of philosophy based on physics: in general, it is more convenient to be slightly overweight during the early stages of a dive (both to assist the initial descent and to help keep on the bottom once there) than to be too light at the end of a dive, which will probably be in shallow water. So one carries sufficient ballast to ensure neutral buoyancy at a depth of, say, 5 m with empty cylinders. To achieve this, the diver with a 2000 litre cylinder should aim to be about 1.5 kg heavy when on the surface at the start of his dive. Carry out a normal buoyancy check at the surface, then add an extra 1.5 kg to the weightbelt.

THE USE OF BUOYANCY FOR LIFTING

One of the most convenient ways to lift a heavy object from the sea-bed is to fill one or more plastic drums with the exhaled air from one's aqualung. This system has the particular merit of affording a constant-buoyancy system at low cost. An air-filled 12.5 litre drum displaces 12.5 kg of water, so if its mass is 2 kg, the net buoyancy will be 10.5 kg. As the object rises, the air in the drum will expand and the excess will flow freely from underneath, leaving the displacement, and hence the buoyancy, constant. In general, it is best to use slightly too little buoyancy when raising a heavy object by this method, the remainder being supplied by pulling on a rope from the surface. Otherwise, if the buoyancy exceeds the object's weight, it will rise up with increasing speed until the drums break surface, overturn and fill with water, with perhaps disastrous results.

If, on the other hand, it is decided to use closed bags or balloons, they must be provided with an exhaust valve to allow the expanding air to escape as the object rises. These bags should always be blown

LIFTING WITH
THE AID OF
BUOYANCY
BAGS

up taut on the bottom; if an oversize, partially filled bag is used, its buoyancy will increase as it approaches the surface, giving a spectacular, but quite uncontrolled ascent.

Conduction

Water has a colossal capacity for conducting heat away from the body. The high heat capacity and rate of conductivity of water are such that thermal protection is needed in all but the warmest tropical waters. An unclad diver in waters of less than about 21°C will lose heat faster than his body can replace it, and he will become chilled. In extreme cases, hypothermia will follow (see chapter 2). Protective clothing is necessary to avoid chilling (Fig. 5), and the range of diving suits used for sports diving is explained in chapter 3.

Sound

Because water is such a dense medium, sound travels more than four times faster in water than in air. It is anything but a silent world. Since sound travels so quickly it is difficult to determine the exact sound source. However, sound signals made by rapping a stone or knife handle against an aqualung cylinder in a distinct code is a popular way of attracting a dive partner's attention.

Sounds made above water will not penetrate the surface, and neither will underwater sounds pass through into the air.

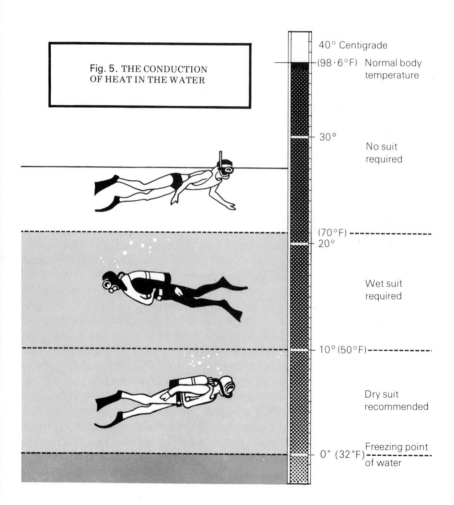

Fig. 5. THE CONDUCTION OF HEAT IN THE WATER

40° Centigrade

(98·6°F) Normal body temperature

30° No suit required

(70°F)
20°

Wet suit required

10° (50°F)

Dry suit recommended

0° (32°F) Freezing point of water

Vision

When a swimmer without apparatus goes under water, his vision becomes inadequate in three distinct ways. Firstly, his eyes are unable to focus and only blurred impressions remain: secondly, it rapidly gets darker as he descends until there is not enough light to see by, and thirdly, visual contrasts are so reduced that even if an object could be brought into focus and even if there were enough light to see it by, it can scarcely be distinguished from the water background. The problem of focussing has been virtually solved by the face mask permitting the eyes to work in their normal medium of air. The reduction of light intensity with depth can also be coped with to some extent, but the loss of visual contrasts under water is a stubborn problem and very little can yet be done about it.

When the eye is working normally in air, light is focussed by the curved cornea and by the lens on to the light-sensitive retina (Fig. 6).

This focussing depends on the fact that a light ray passing from one medium to another is bent or refracted to an extent determined by the difference in the refractive index of the two media. Air has a very low refractive index while the optical media in the eye have rather high ones. Thus, a ray of light entering the eye is refracted at the cornea of the eye and this is where the main focusing power of the eye is found. The partially focused light then passes through the lens which has itself a rather higher refractive index than the media in which it is embedded. Unlike the cornea, the curvature of the lens can be altered, and it is in this that we can focus at will on near or distant objects. As the main imaging power of the eye lies at the air-cornea boundary, the power to focus depends on the difference in refractive index between air and the optical media. The naked eye cannot focus underwater as water and the optical media have rather similar refractive indices and the focusing power of the cornea is much reduced. The lens lacks the power to complete what the cornea has failed to do and the eye cannot focus on any object at all.

The solution is to imprison an air space in front of the cornea and thus allow it to function properly. This is the purpose of the face mask and most types of underwater contact lenses. The slight disadvantage of this system is that light passing obliquely through the face plate will be refracted in its passage from the water, through the glass, into the imprisoned air within. This has the result of making an object in the water appear to be at three-quarters of its true distance (Fig. 7). As the object is optically nearer, a larger

Fig. 6. FOCUSING OF THE EYE IN AIR AND UNDERWATER

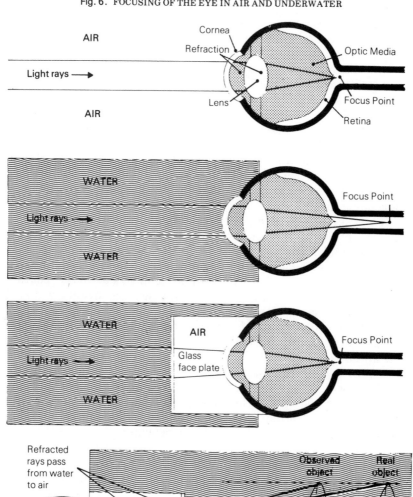

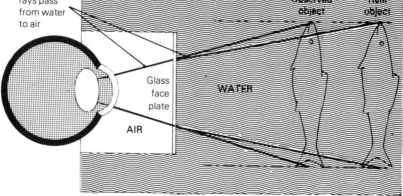

Fig. 7. OBJECTS APPEAR 33% LARGER UNDERWATER

image of it will be projected on the retina, but this does not necessarily mean that it will seem to be bigger. On land a near object is not
judged to be bigger than an identical object further away, because
distance is unconsciously taken into account when estimates of true
size are made. Underwater, the increase in image size should be
offset by a decrease in the apparent distance of the object. An object
underwater should, therefore, appear to be near but not bigger than
on land.

Nevertheless, an inexperienced diver frequently judges things
underwater to be bigger than they really are and this may be because he does not unconsciously compare the size of the retinal
image with the optical distance of the object, but rather because he
compares image size to true distance which he has judged by some
independent means.

Contact lenses are being developed for underwater use although
they are not yet on the open market. They either depend on the air
space principle of the face mask, when a small cap containing air is
cemented to the outside of the contact glass, or they have a small
lens of very highly refractive material embedded in the contact
glass. In its simple form the air space type has the advantage that it
allows equally good vision on land as underwater, but is rather
bulky. The lens type cannot be worn in air but has less bulk. Neither
type has yet been perfected sufficiently to allow extended periods of
wear and they do not give the protection against cold and polluted
water provided by the face mask. Nevertheless, contact lenses do
provide a wider field of view than the standard mask and the
elimination of the inner glass surface of the face plate with its
scratches, condensation and water drops should make a useful
contribution to the clarity of vision under water.

THE REDUCTION OF LIGHT WITH DEPTH AND THE SENSITIVITY OF THE EYE

The rate at which daylight is absorbed by different bodies of water
varies greatly and depends on the amount of dissolved and suspended matter in the water. In Britain it is common enough to find it
too dark to see at 15 metres, whilst in the Mediterranean, this limit
is still far off at the deepest aqualung depth. The eye is able to cope
with great differences in light intensity by switching between its
two visual systems, one adapted for use during the day and the other
at night. In day vision, relatively bright light is needed but colours
can be seen and there is a good perception of contrast and detail.
Night vision is much more sensitive to low light intensities but
colour vision is lost, and there is some reduction in the ability to
distinguish contrasts and detail. It takes between 20 and 30 minutes

for an eye adapted to bright light to achieve maximum sensitivity in very dim light. In diving terms this means that a dive into darker water is usually completed before the eye has had time to reach its greatest sensitivity.

COLOUR UNDER WATER

Pure water absorbs most red and orange light, less yellow, still less green and relatively little blue light (Fig. 8). Therefore, the deeper daylight penetrates into pure ocean water the poorer it becomes in red light relative to blue. Inshore waters, on the other hand, are usually stained by the yellow products of vegetable decay. These substances are very persistent and have the property of absorbing much blue light, less green and very little yellow or red. If these yellow substances are present in quantity they act as such strong light filters as to over-ride the blue filtering properties of pure water, and the reddish-brown colour of freshwater lakes and rivers results. If the yellow stain is rather more diluted, the red and yellow light is absorbed by the water and the blue by the yellow substances and this leaves green as the colour least absorbed. This is the explanation for the green colour of the water around our coasts.

This colour-filter action of a water mass is chiefly responsible for the fact that colours appear different below the surface. An object is coloured because it absorbs some wavelengths more than others. The wavelengths that it does not absorb but reflects are responsible for its colour. For instance, at about 30 m in the Mediterranean, the water has absorbed most of the red light so that an object which is red on the surface because it absorbs all save red light will not be exposed to the only wavelengths it reflects and will thus appear black. In reddish-brown peat-stained water the blue is absorbed more than the red (although both are absorbed more rapidly than in pure water) and it is the blue object which appears black.

SCATTERED LIGHT AND CONTRAST REDUCTION

A distant object under water is usually detected because it is either a little darker or a little brighter than the background it is seen against. Contrasts are low under water because much of the image-forming light from an object is either scattered out of the light path or absorbed by the water before it reaches the eye, whilst daylight is scattered out of its downward path into the eye thus interposing a veil of brightness between the object and the eye. It is this scattered daylight which is responsible for the brightness of the water background. Taking the results of absorption and scatter together, bright objects become darker and dark objects become brighter as they recede until neither can be distinguished from the water background. The rate at which this happens depends upon the rate that a beam of

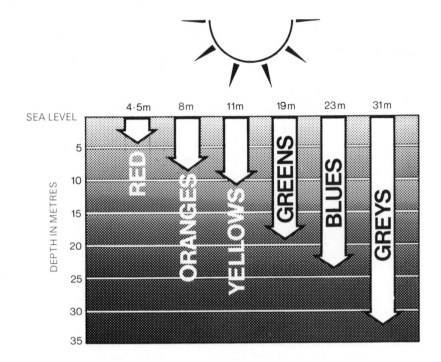

Fig. 8. ABSORPTION OF COLOUR UNDERWATER

light is diffused and attenuated by the water and upon the direction of sight. Obviously—if the rate of contrast decrease remains the same, the distance that an object can recede before it becomes invisible depends on the original contrast with the water background.

PAINTING OBJECTS TO BE CONSPICUOUS UNDER WATER

To begin with a distinction must be drawn between objects which can be seen at a distance under water and those which are conspicuous when seen at close range lying amongst weed or stone on the bottom. In the former case it is the brightness contrast which is much the most important, and in the latter case it is more usually a combination of colour and brightness contrast which renders an object conspicuous.

Safety considerations usually require divers to go down in pairs and it is important for one diver to see the other at the farthest possible distance. It has already been explained why an object presenting the highest brightness contrast with the water background will be visible at the greatest distance. In practice it is white objects which present the greatest contrast with the water background in all directions except directly upwards, when black will be best. This leads to the suggestion that large areas of equipment should be painted white whilst the suit should be black. On the other hand, parts which break the surface whilst swimming should be painted the colour which shows up best against the sea. Fluorescent orange might be the best choice here.

In all except peaty water, fluorescent oranges and reds show up with great brilliance at close range. This is because fluorescent pigments have the ability to absorb the short wavelength light at the blue end of the spectrum and re-emit longer wavelength light at the red end.

Current indications for coloration for all circumstances would be as follows:

> Hood—Fluorescent orange.
> Suit—Black.
> Cylinders, harness straps, etc.—White.

The Sea

What makes the sea behave in the way it does? Why do the tides rise and fall? What are the mechanisms of the currents? The factors covered by these questions, as well as many others, and the complex interactions between all of them go to make up the physical nature of the sea in which we dive. Their study is quite as fascinating as any other aspect of the under water environment: the sea-bed; its animals and plants; the archaeological clues to man's history, and so on. At the same time, the diver with a firm grasp of the mechanisms of the sea—insofar as they are understood—is better able to appreciate the reasons for some of the physical phenomena he encounters on and beneath the surface.

The Tides

First we must consider the forces which produce the rise and fall of level. The British diver is familiar with twice-daily (semi-diurnal) tides whose range varies over a twice-monthly cycle between maximum *Spring* tides and minimum *Neap* tides. The semi-diurnal period of the tide results from the redistribution of the world's surface water caused by the gravitational attraction of the Moon and, to a lesser extent, the Sun. As Fig. 9 shows, the surface of the oceans is raised above the mean level at a point directly below the attracting body and at the corresponding position on the opposite side of the globe. As the Earth rotates about its axis the tidal 'bulge' sweeps round so that every point encounters a high tide twice a day. This process was analysed by Newton some 300 years ago: he was able to explain the monthly cycle of Springs and Neaps by combining the effects of the Lunar tide which has a period of 12 hours 48 minutes and the Solar tide of 12 hours. While in principle these should combine to give Spring tides when the Sun and Moon are aligned at New and Full Moon, in practice there is a lag of, typically, a few days (depending upon the geographical location). The theoretical ratio between the Lunar and Solar tides is about 2:1, giving a ratio of about $2\frac{3}{4}$:1 between the ranges at Springs and Neaps. The reason for the considerable difference between this theoretical value and that found at a given locality will be examined below.

So far we have considered the pattern that tides would exhibit on a featureless, evenly inundated globe. In practice the water is divided into seas and oceans of varying sizes, shapes and depths with the result that the range of tides varies considerably from one place to another. The necessary studies of the response of particular water basins

Fig. 9 THE EFFECT OF THE SUN AND MOON ON THE EARTH'S TIDES

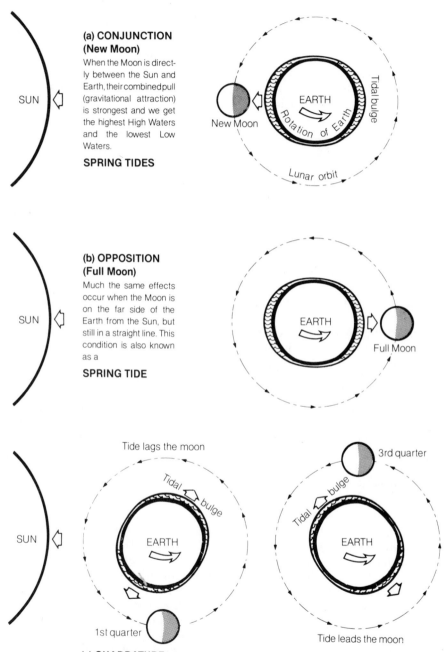

(a) CONJUNCTION (New Moon)

When the Moon is directly between the Sun and Earth, their combined pull (gravitational attraction) is strongest and we get the highest High Waters and the lowest Low Waters.

SPRING TIDES

SUN

EARTH

Tidal bulge

New Moon

Rotation of Earth

Lunar orbit

(b) OPPOSITION (Full Moon)

Much the same effects occur when the Moon is on the far side of the Earth from the Sun, but still in a straight line. This condition is also known as a

SPRING TIDE

SUN

EARTH

Full Moon

Tide lags the moon

Tidal bulge

3rd quarter

Tidal bulge

SUN

EARTH

EARTH

1st quarter

Tide leads the moon

(c) QUADRATURE (1st and 3rd quarters of the Moon)

When the Moon is pulling in a different direction from the Sun, we get a reduction in the range, the least range between High and Low Waters, being known as **NEAP TIDES.**

form the major part of contemporary tidal research. Recently the availability of high-speed electronic computers with large storage capacity has permitted theoretical computations on the tides in actual seas, in contrast to the earlier, rather unrealistic mathematical shapes such as squares and circles.

The problem may best be demonstrated by means of an everyday observation in the home. If a nearly full teacup is tilted, then rapidly replaced on a level surface, the liquid will rock from side to side with a decreasing amplitude, but a constant frequency. If the teacup is now gently rocked from side to side at this 'natural frequency' the amplitude of the sloshing motion will steadily increase until the tea spills over the side. If, however, the experiment is repeated at a different frequency, either faster or slower, the surface of the tea does not slosh so strongly from side to side and may break up into a confusion of waves.

Further experiments will satisfy the reader that there is, in fact, a series of sharply defined frequencies, all multiples of the natural frequency, which also induce a regular tidal motion in the teacup—these are called harmonics. If the experiment is repeated with a larger container, a washing-up bowl for instance, the natural frequency will be lower, while even lower frequencies will be found for the water in a bath or swimming pool. Clearly the natural frequency of the water basin depends upon its dimensions and shape. This phenomenon is called 'resonance'. If the driving force has a frequency different from the natural frequency (or some harmonic) the tide produced will have a reduced range, the value depending upon the difference in frequencies and the strength of the driving force.

The tides in a sea or ocean will depend, therefore, upon how closely the semi-diurnal driving force matches the natural period of the water mass. If the resonant frequency is closer to the 12:48 lunar period than the 12-hour solar period, then the lunar tide will be relatively stronger, and vice versa. This has a corresponding effect upon the ratio of the ranges of Neaps and Springs.

Even quite small features on the edge of the oceans can produce a strong local resonance which gives tides out of all proportion to the oceanic tide. The most famous example is the Bay of Fundy, which resonates almost exactly to the semi-diurnal rhythm to give a tidal range of 17 m at Springs. Other effects can enhance the tides locally; for example, shoaling of the bottom or narrowing of a channel or bay into which the tide floods—both these phenomena contribute towards the very large tides at St Malo (11 m at Springs). More sophisticated theory is required to explain the double tides at Southampton—little did King Canute appreciate that his striking demonstration exploited a unique non-linear phenomenon.

These then are the major principles behind variations in the tides at different places. Several important factors have been left out of the simple description given above; for example, the rotation of the Earth alters the tides from a to and fro motion in each basin to a rotary wave which swings around the basin's edge (this may also be examined at home with the aid of a teacup or washing-up bowl). Nor has mention been made of the tidal currents which transport the great mass of water for every tide, or of the frictional resistance of the sea-bed. These factors must be the subject of further reading in the texts recommended later.

Currents

Although, from the diver's point of view, all currents require precautions, it is the variation of current speed and direction which needs particular attention. The regular cycle of tidal currents are the strongest encountered in British waters, but because they are predictable they do not present too great a problem and are well documented in publications such as Reed's Nautical Almanac.

Waves

The decision whether to dive or not is usually reduced to an assessment of whether it is too rough for the diving boat to put to sea.

Waves are created by the wind and stronger winds give longer and higher waves. A storm in the Atlantic Ocean, for instance. Waves travel out from the storm centre, the longer waves travel fastest across the ocean surface and arrive at Western Atlantic coasts to herald the coming of rough seas and stormy weather. A deep water wave travels by virtue of a circular motion of the water near the surface and its speed decreases with depth. This explains why a diver at, say 30 m can be quite unaware of the development of a rough sea following a change in the weather.

The energy of a wave is spread through a layer of water whose depth is comparable with the wavelength (Fig. 10). When waves approach shallow water this energy is concentrated into the available depth, making the height increase and the speed decrease, both of which increase the steepness of the wave. The increase in wave height is known as *ground-swell*, while the deceleration refracts the waves so that they tend to run up a beach square-on regardless of their original direction. In the end the wave becomes so steep that it breaks, either by plunging over in a graceful arc or in a less spectacular spill down the leading edge.

Density

The diver will encounter variations in the density caused by changes of temperature and salinity (the concentration of dissolved salt). These will be considered in turn.

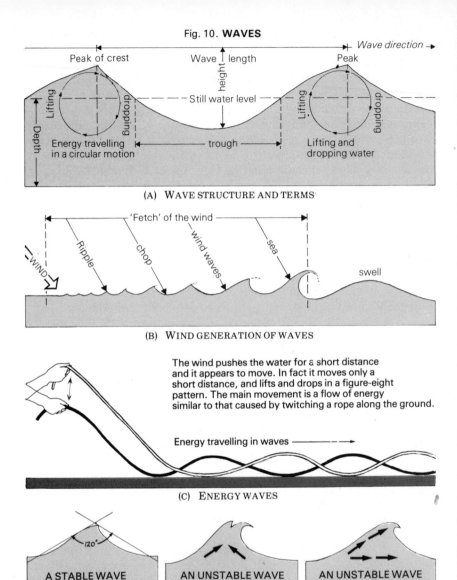

Fig. 10. WAVES

(A) WAVE STRUCTURE AND TERMS

(B) WIND GENERATION OF WAVES

The wind pushes the water for a short distance and it appears to move. In fact it moves only a short distance, and lifts and drops in a figure-eight pattern. The main movement is a flow of energy similar to that caused by twitching a rope along the ground.

Energy travelling in waves ⟶

(C) ENERGY WAVES

A STABLE WAVE
Highest height and minimum wave angle

AN UNSTABLE WAVE
Waves colliding from opposite directions

AN UNSTABLE WAVE
Surface water over-taking a wave

(D) STABLE AND UNSTABLE WAVES

Temperature

Geographical and seasonal differences in sea temperature determine to a large extent where diving is most enjoyable, and the failings of British waters compared with, say, the Mediterranean are well known. However, superimposed upon these broad climatological features there are rapid fluctuations caused largely by changes in the weather over the sea. The most regular mechanism is the diurnal rhythm of heating and cooling, but changes in wind-speed, humidity, air temperature and cloud cover also cause changes in the sea temperature throughout a surface layer whose depth approximately matches that available to the diver.

The most striking feature of the temperature structure in this surface layer is the *thermocline*. There is no really satisfactory theory to explain the development of thermoclines. So, apart from stating briefly that their existence and form depend on the modification of the turbulence in the sea by density gradients, this section will present a description, rather than an explanation, of their principal features.

By definition, a thermocline is any region of the ocean where the temperature changes more rapidly with depth than the water either immediately above or below. A rather weak thermocline exists at a depth of some thousands of metres throughout the oceans of the world, but far stronger temperature gradients develop near the surface during the summer.

A diver can detect the presence of a thermocline by feeling the sharp temperature discontinuity or by seeing the change in refractive index. Usually it is possible to see the two layers of water mixing together in eddies a few centimetres across. When the water masses above and below the thermocline move in different directions, as is often the case, they may carry different concentrations of plankton and other suspended material; often in coastal regions the water above the top transient is heavily contaminated with sewage, while the lower water, which has come from a different direction, is quite clear.

Salinity

With the exceptions considered below, salinity plays a minor role in causing rapid density fluctuations in the surface region of the sea. Because the solubility of salt varies very little with temperature, fluctuations in the sea's temperature structure are not materially modified by secondary changes in salinity. The exceptions all arise from changes at the very surface of the sea.

EVAPORATION

The sea is continually giving water vapour into the atmosphere, but the rate of evaporation is considerably faster when the air is dry and when a wind blows over the sea. The evaporation reaches a peak when white crests develop during stormy weather. Evaporation increases the salinity and hence the density of the surface. In a highly turbulent, well-mixed sea, the extra salt is rapidly diffused into the water below, but when the mixing rate is slow the dense, salty layer

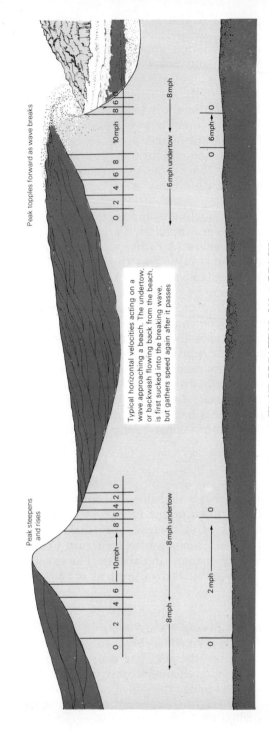

Peak topples forward as wave breaks

Peak steepens and rises

Typical horizontal velocities acting on a wave approaching a beach. The undertow, or backwash flowing back from the beach, is first sucked into the breaking wave, but gathers speed again after it passes

Fig. 11. A WAVE BREAKING ON A BEACH

may accumulate on the surface until there is sufficient to trigger off convection, when plumes of salty water sink down until they meet colder water of equal density. Because evaporation is accompanied by cooling, the surface density reaches this critical value even faster.

FREEZING

When sea water freezes much of the salt in it is rejected by the ice, which is in consequence surrounded by increasingly salty, dense water. Again this may lead to convection, although in this case the latent heat liberated during the freezing process acts against the density rise by warming the sea.

MELTING

When sea ice melts it forms a pool of fresh water, which floats on the sea. Eventually this fresh water mixes with the sea water, but until this happens the two are separated by a *halocline*, which is the salinity equivalent of a *thermocline*.

PRECIPITATION

When rain, snow or hail falls on to the sea a similar layer of fresh water forms on the surface giving a temporary halocline.

OTHER SOURCES OF FRESH WATER

Haloclines are frequently found in estuaries or near sewer outlets, where fresh water runs on to the surface of the sea. A not infrequent phenomenon is the occurrence of fresh-water springs under the surface of the sea. The buoyant fresh water welling up to the surface in a continuous plume can sometimes be spotted from the coast. Occasionally, ships detect these fresh-water plumes with their echosounders—and mistakenly report the presence of shallows.

The reader requiring a more detailed understanding of this subject should refer to one or other of the standard works on physical oceanography. Every keen diver should be familiar with the classic text of oceanography *The Oceans* by Sverdrup, Johnson & Fleming. The non-specialist may prefer the easily-read narrative of King's *Oceanography for Geographers,* while at the other end of the spectrum, Defant's *Physical Oceanography* provides a comprehensive textbook for those with a formal schooling in physics and mathematics. Finally, the diver who is keen to read about the very latest resear·h in oceanography is referred to an exciting three-volume work edited by Hill called *The Sea*. Here we are reminded that our knowledge of the sea is in a state of rapid flux and that each of the topics outlined above forms the subject of current research in laboratories throughout the world.

CHAPTER TWO

MEDICAL

Adapting to the Environment

When a diver leaves the surface, he enters a world which is probably more foreign to him than any other environment he will ever experience. He faces new problems on which his survival may depend, while his perception of the world around him may be impaired and distorted and his capacity for action reduced. Unless he is fully aware of these limitations, a diver will be neither comfortable, efficient nor safe.

The Senses

Man depends on his senses for information about the world around him. When these are required to function in water instead of air, the different physical properties involved may produce an impaired and in some cases distorted picture of his surroundings.

VISION

The effects of diving on the visual senses has been fully described in chapter 1—Physics of Diving. The reader may refer to the appropriate section to see how the sense of vision is affected.

TOUCH

As visibility decreases, touch becomes increasingly important, till eventually it provides the only available information about the diver's surroundings. Even under ideal conditions, however, because of the restriction in visual field, the diver must rely on touch for locating certain crucial parts of his equipment such as the quick-release fastening on his weightbelt. Since his safety may depend on this, it is essential that a diver should be familiar enough with his equipment to locate each item and manipulate it quickly and effectively.

HEARING

At present this is one of the least used of the diver's senses, since for the most part underwater communications still depend on visual signs and rope signals. The ears do, however, function perfectly well under water, and current developments in the field of under-water communications seem likely to increase the importance of hearing to the diver.

SMELL AND TASTE

Since the diver can smell and taste only what is in his breathing set, these senses are of little use underwater. There are two exceptions to this: the tendency of air at depth to have a somewhat metallic taste is a possible though not invariable indication of the onset of nitrogen narcosis; and certain impurities such as oil fumes in the breathing mixture may be detected by smell. If impurities are suspected, the dive must be terminated immediately.

ORIENTATION

Our sense of bodily position depends on the combined effects of gravity and visual information. In conditions of low visibility a correctly weighted diver will be deprived of most of his normal sources of information and may become completely disoriented. In such a situation it is vital that the diver should not panic and swim off in whatever direction he guesses is upwards. There are still several available clues as to the direction of the surface including his rising bubbles, the direction of maximum brightness and the pressure of his weightbelt. Failing this the weightbelt can be taken off and used as a plumb line, and as a last resort, releasing the weightbelt or inflating your lifejacket will at least guarantee that you move up and not down.

Environmental Stresses

The underwater environment is in many ways a hostile one and presents the diver with a number of special problems.

WEIGHTLESSNESS

This, the ability to move freely in three dimensions, is one of the great joys of diving, but anyone attempting to work under water will confirm that it is a mixed blessing. The basic problem is lack of stability, for in the absence of a strong effect of gravity any slight movement is likely to cause the diver to drift away or roll over. This, the ability to move freely in three dimensions in a state of total neutral buoyancy, is one of the great joys of under-water swimming. Initially, trainee divers may find that they lack control and stability but they very soon adapt to the delights of neutral buoyancy. For those who have to work under water, neutral buoyancy is not always an advantage and it is common practice for the working diver to be heavily weighted so that he remains on the sea-bed or at his work site. Under these circumstances the diver would operate on a safety rope from the surface.

COLD

In British waters, cold presents one of the diver's greatest problems. Quite apart from the question of comfort, cold may be dangerous because of both its general effects in reducing the diver's physical and mental efficiency, and its specific numbing effects which may make impossible such vital though apparently simple tasks as operating the quick-release buckle of a weightbelt. In view of this, the importance of protective clothing is obvious and is discussed in detail elsewhere. Ways of somewhat reducing the numbing effects of cold are described under *Protective clothing*, and if exposure to cold is frequent, acclimatisation will occur and circulation improve. In any case it is important to bear in mind when selecting equipment, that it may have to be manipulated with numb fingers. An emergency quick-release device that relies on precise manipulation is worse than useless.

ANXIETY

In view of the potential hazards, it is only natural to feel somewhat apprehensive before a dive, particularly if conditions are not ideal. A moderate amount of anxiety will probably have the desirable effect of ensuring that the diver is particularly careful in checking his equipment and preparing for the dive, and once in the water he will probably feel much less anxious. Beyond a certain point, however, anxiety can become dangerous since it tends to cause a reversion to old-established habits which are unlikely to serve a useful function underwater. Since the more recent, least-practised habits are most likely to be forgotten under stress, it is vital that the basic diving skills should not only be learned during training, but should be practised till they become virtually automatic. If unchecked, anxiety may escalate into panic, the worst possible response to any under-water emergency. It goes without saying that anyone who tends to panic under stress should not dive. This subject is fully documented in the section *Apprehension and Panic*.

NITROGEN NARCOSIS

When breathed at sufficient pressure, air has an intoxicating effect (see *Nitrogen Narcosis*—page 107). The subjective symptoms are in general pleasant, a feeling of relaxation and well-being coupled with a sense of detachment from reality, hence Cousteau's phrase 'the rapture of the depths'. Unfortunately, this feeling of well-being is both illusory and dangerous, since as a diver goes deeper and deeper he will become more and more confident but less and less capable.

   Such narcotic effects can be considerably reduced by breathing a mixture of oxygen and helium instead of air, but since helium is very expensive and presents rather special decompression problems it is not suitable for normal club diving. It seems likely then that nitrogen narcosis will continue to be a problem for the amateur diver.

Apprehension and Panic

All divers at one time or another are apprehensive. Sometimes this may be identified in terms of a specific challenge such as experiencing a new situation—perhaps kelp or cave diving—or at other times it may be a vague, ill-defined feeling about a particular dive.

Apprehension can be defined as a feeling of uncertainty about one's ability to cope with the situation. It's presence should lead the individual to a careful assessment of the new experience in terms of his own ability, preparation, equipment, and the like. Getting as much necessary information as possible about the particular dive, the equipment needed, and the possible problems, is a type of planning that can reduce apprehension. Once the necessary information is at hand, the diver should rehearse any unusual requirements of the underwater task. This rehearsal should, as far as possible, duplicate the elements of the planned dive under nearly ideal environmental conditions, i.e. shallow, clear water. Such rehearsal should lead to the development of skills and techniques that will improve the diver's control over the underwater task requirements.

Panic, on the other hand, is a loss of control. It may be differentiated from apprehension by stating that an individual in a panic situation has perceived that he is losing control and is incapable of extricating himself from the situation he perceives as dangerous. In the apprehension period, if the diver is well trained, there is still time for information gathering, planning and coping. In the panic situation, the likelihood of such coping is severely diminished, if not extinguished. Another most important distinction between apprehension and panic is that panic produces marked physiological changes which, in themselves, have severe consequences, while in apprehension the physiological changes associated with anxiety are usually moderate.

Only in the last few years has the problem of panic been referred to in diving literature. Indeed, panic has been stressed as the possible, even probable, cause of accidents and death in sports divers. This is largely inferential. For example, most of the divers in a series of reported diving accidents were found with their weightbelts on, cylinders still containing an adequate supply of air, masks undamaged, and lifejackets uninflated. In addition, a post-mortem examination of equipment (if such a term can be used) has shown that in the overwhelming majority of cases there was no equipment failure; presumably human error or human incapability was the cause of the accident and death. Finding intact equipment on a victim further suggests that the individual lost control—a loss possibly associated with exhaustion, fatigue and panic. It has also been revealed that the majority of the fatalities have, at some time during the loss of control, been on, or very close to, the surface of the water.

Physiological Consequences of Panic

Let's begin with the diver in a state of panic; evaluate the condition and the consequences of loss of control. An early sign, common to panic situations on land or in water, is an increase in the rate of breathing. Such rapid breathing is a decided indication of agitation, and agitation, which we will consider later, is a major sign of trouble. The physiological consequences are not entirely clear, but if the breathing is shallow as well as rapid, we are aware that it can produce an inefficient exchange of oxygen and carbon dioxide (see *Respiration and Circulation*). This leads to a CO_2 build-up, with a sensation of air hunger, which further exacerbates the feeling of panic and, as a physiological consequence, will also produce hypoxia. The situation could lead to muscle spasms, or loss of consciousness, and drowning. In addition, the lack of adequate inflation of the lungs, which could accompany this rapid shallow breathing, would reduce the diver's buoyancy and this, coupled with fatigue from air hunger, would impair swimming movement and the ability to stay afloat.

A diver in a panic state on the surface struggles with his arms and legs to keep his head above water. (In one Survey, 15 of 18 fatality victims in the Los Angeles area of USA were on the surface just prior to their death.) The struggle results in the head being held higher, but the workload on the body is thereby increased and heart rate and respiration are raised. The struggling diver does not realise that supporting the head (which weighs approximately 8 kg) above the surface of the water increases his workload significantly, and if he raises his shoulders out of the water he can only support this workload for seconds. This severe workload quickly exhausts the diver, and because of the maximal respiration induced, once the head can no longer be maintained above the water, drowning occurs within seconds, or at most within a minute. Heart failure has also been assumed a consequence of some of these physiological events.

Coping Behaviours and Responses

It is apparent that one of the major problems of a distressed diver in a panic situation is his inability to cope with and to solve the problems induced by the stress. The stress itself may come from a myriad of events including novel situations such as the appearance of potentially hazardous marine animals, sudden turbidity, cold or entanglement, to which he is unable to orient himself.

Studies have shown that stress can induce perceptual narrowing in divers—that is, the divers become increasingly less aware of peripheral stimuli, and instead, focus on the immediate narrow solution or event. An example of such a situation is that of a diver whose reserve has been pulled, rendering it inoperative, and who keeps pulling the reserve valve even after he has discovered that no reserve is left. To indulge in such stereotyped, non-problem-solving behaviour is known as a 'non-coping response'. With a coping response (behaviour) he would try several alternative courses of action, such as dropping his weight-belt, air sharing, or attempting to inflate his lifejacket.

A diver in a panic situation is frequently described as a diver who is clawing the air; his mouthpiece spat out; his weightbelt still on; his head held up; his eyes widened, and nearing the point of exhaustion. It should be noted at this point that there is another response to panic, and that is 'freezing', in which the panicked individual simply 'gives up'—an over-simplified description of a very complex event; it appears that there is resignation in the face of fear which completely eliminates any kind of coping, even of the relatively inefficient one of struggling. Freezing is less frequently observed than is struggling in panicking divers, but, nevertheless, it is something to be aware of and may indeed account for some of the very fast sinkings and drownings.

Signs of Panic

We have discussed some of the physiological consequences of panic and have touched upon the possible signs of panic in the diver, most of which can be recognised by other divers in a boat or in the water. As has been mentioned, the first of these is agitation. The diver in control moves along smoothly; his respiration and swimming movements are controlled and regular. Moreover, he is oriented to the front, or toward the bottom, in his diving environment; a diver's posture can be an indication as to whether he is in control. One of the earliest signs as to an agitated diver approaching the panic state is that of rapid breathing and of his frequently checking the surface, positioning his body vertically towards the surface. He may also bring his knees forward, finning with short, jerky movements that start from the knees instead of the thighs.

A diver in control checks his gauges and his equipment to ensure that he has sufficient air, that his dive is carefully timed to avoid decompression problems, and that he is functioning efficiently. An agitated diver over-frequently checks his equipment, almost having a preoccupation with his gauges.

To summarise, the agitated diver who may possibly panic, changes his swimming movements and respiration (readily observed); changes the angle of his body in the water, frequently checking the surface, and over-frequently checks his equipment.

Signs of Apprehension

In as much as apprehension may be a signal of impending panic, it is important to be aware of possible signs in yourself or others on the boat, en route to the dive site; the awareness of the existence of apprehension, even among the most experienced divers, can be a positive move towards eliminating it, for it is critical that divers should not dive when they are uncomfortable about their own ability to cope.

The Diving Officer and Diving Marshal should be alert to signs of agitation, 'gallows humour', and the like, and take action to combat them. For example, proper planning, including discussion of the dive plan and procedures, use of certain kinds of equipment, possible problems and how to handle them, can be initiated or reviewed on the way to the dive site, thus allaying anxiety by focusing attention on competence and coping behaviours.

One of the greatest fears people possess—that of looking foolish—is induced by our culture. However, there are social face-saving devices such as sinus block or a cold, that a diver often uses to avoid a dive about which he is apprehensive. Too often divers are in competition with one another (e.g. by trying to consume less air while going deeper), which can lead to risks not normally taken, and often ends in a crisis situation in which the diver requires assistance. True competition should be a diver competing with himself to improve his skills and techniques. The controlled diver is a conservative diver.

Studies of sky divers some years ago may provide a lesson for sports divers. It was found that experienced sky divers, if they had apprehension about a jump, usually experienced it in the morning before the jump, and if the apprehension was strong enough, they would cancel their participation in the dive. However, novice sky divers' apprehension peaked on the 'plane, just as they were approaching the point of the jump. These documented physiological and verbalised events may have application to divers. It is very likely that a novice diver's apprehension will peak just before the boat arrives at the place where the diver must enter the water, perhaps for the first time since his period of training.

Preventing Panic

It is important that a diver be in good physical condition, and that his training be adequate to develop competence and confidence in his skills. Critical skills should be over-learned prior to the necessity for their use. This is, by far, the best way of preventing panic. The diver who is in good physical shape, who plans well, knows his equipment, knows the water conditions, and who has been thoroughly grounded in the use of the equipment and in the kinds of diving conditions he will meet, is a safer diver, will enjoy his dive more, and will be less likely to panic.

Competence must be built during basic diver training, familiarity with equipment and in the underwater environment itself. The proper sequencing of diver training is critical; effective programmed diver training will proceed in a step-by-step sequence of increasing demands and growing accomplishments. For example, basic diving training will take place in a pool, then when the basics of diving are mastered, the novice diver moves to the open sea, entering from the beach or a shallow cove, and progresses ultimately to a boat.

Competence and confidence are built through a programmed re-petition of each task, with cues and rewards to improve correct responses. It is important that the learning situation be structured in such a way as to maximise the similarities between the training situation and the real one, e.g. training to cope with possible emer-gencies—such as the loss of a mask—is first done in the protected environment, then repeated in open water.

We should also recognise that purposeful interests, such as under-water photography, shell collecting and archaeology, focus a diver's attention away from himself and his equipment and, therefore, may be a means of damping apprehension.

Finally, it has been suggested that there are some measures that may be applied by a companion to aid a diver in panic. In most events, to gain positive buoyancy becomes the first priority for the anxious diver on the surface. The diver who still has a snorkel or demand valve in his mouth (unlikely in most panic situations, when they are spat out) should be made to float on his back and to remove the snorkel or valve in order to permit greater passage of air; there is a danger that holding the valve in his mouth during shallow (panic) breathing may increase the carbon dioxide build-up, rather than aid ventilation. In addition, the panicky diver's lifejacket should be inflated so that he may stop struggling to keep his head out of the water, and rest.

We also suggest that the design of some diving equipment may present problems in a panic situation. The panicking diver who is trying to leave the water has his head up, his hands out of the water, and his arms flailing in his efforts to struggle upwards, and even if he is able to plan and cope at this stage, he may find that to put his hands back into the water to jettison his weightbelt and operate his lifejacket is antagonistic to the psychological need to hold his head up and his hands out of the water. Perhaps a shoulder release or shoulder jacket-inflating mechanism is the answer, as these would not require that the diver again immerse his hands in the water.

To summarise, the one indulgence that a diver cannot afford is the loss of self-control, Thus, the preparation, training and planning for a safe dive should include the evaluation of the specific requirements of that dive and of the diver's capability to meet those requirements in a relaxed, controlled manner. A diver must strive for relaxation and ease of movement as goals for maintaining self-control; he will thus minimise the risk of panic.

Fitness and Medical Examinations

Fitness for Diving

The vague term 'fitness' is often bandied about, yet it is often not fully realised that this may take different forms for different sports. Thus, the lean fitness of a sprinter is not that of the Channel swimmer, whose accent is on moderate obesity and long-term muscular effort; nor yet, to take an extreme, that of the Japanese wrestler in whom immense bulk and muscularity are at a premium. Fortunately, sports diving is compatible with a large number of body builds—with the exception of gross obesity—and, moreover, the individual may limit his diving to areas that are not too physically demanding for him.

Fitness may be considered under three headings. Firstly, the rather negative aspect of ensuring that various diseases or deformities incompatible with diving are absent (this being, to a large extent, the purpose of the medical examination) and, secondly, that of ensuring that the individual can maintain sufficient power output (physical efficiency) to cope with the possible demands upon him. Diving, which involves so much shifting and wearing of heavy equipment, is equivalent in its physical demands to labouring as an occupation, and swimming with equipment in tidal waters requires a work level equal to that of running on dry land. The third component of fitness is the acquisition of the mental and physical reflexes appropriate to the sport concerned. In the case of diving, the appropriate reactions to different situations are acquired as practice drills during the course of the training programme and these skills reinforced by actual diving under supervision.

While an intelligent individual could undoubtedly learn most of the essential drills during a few hours' training, their use will not be automatic when first learnt and they will soon be forgotten unless reinforced by further practice or actual use. Similarly, the more experienced diver may find that his diving technique is rusty after the winter lay-off, and if he has an office job and no alternative winter exercise or sport, his physical efficiency may also have deteriorated. This has proved a constant source of trouble in the past and some form of physical exercise and practice in the basic under-water drills are a good investment before resuming diving activity.

General Medical Examination

A routine general medical examination, with additional attention to the ears and sinuses, is required. The individual's past medical history must be checked, particularly for any major illnesses or accidents involving attendance at or admission to hospital; ear, nose and throat conditions such as otitis media (infection of the middle ear); sinusitis; mental illness; epilepsy; asthma; diabetes; and any drugs regularly taken.

Ideally this examination should be carried out by a doctor conversant with the requirements of diving and in possession of the diver's past medical history, but if this is not possible, his own general practitioner should be asked to give an account of any abnormality found so that its effect on the diver's fitness for diving may be ascertained by a suitably experienced doctor. The BSAC Medical Certificate form (available from Club HQ) tells the GP what to look for during an examination of a diver.

It is impossible in a short chapter to discuss all the effects that every conceivable ailment may have on diving, but in most cases the answers will be self-evident. A few however are particularly important.

The Nervous System

EPILEPSY

Any event producing unconsciousness under water results in high mortality, thus epilepsy, or a history of previous epilepsy, completely debars an individual from diving.

HEAD INJURY

Head injury severe enough to produce concussion, as evidenced by loss of memory and a period of unconsciousness, should normally debar an individual from diving for a period of three months. If, however, it has been found advisable to prescribe anti-convulsant drugs to avoid the development of post-traumatic epilepsy, diving should not be permitted until these drugs have been withdrawn. All drugs of this type tend to be sedative in nature and would predispose the diver to nitrogen narcosis.

Actual post-traumatic fits, other than an isolated fit occurring at the time of injury, must, like epilepsy, debar an individual from diving.

MENTAL ILLNESS

Past mental illness should not debar anyone from diving, although it may raise some doubt as to his motivation for wanting to dive, such as a desire to 'prove' himself.

Current treatment of the milder degrees of depression and anxiety need not prevent training, although open-water diving should be prohibited until three months after treatment has been successfully completed since the illness may affect judgement, and many modern drugs used in treatment can adversely affect the body's reaction to stress and cold.

Respiratory System

It is essential that the diver have both an X-ray and chest examination: active chest disease of any type absolutely precludes diving.

Evidence of healed lung disease does not necessarily prevent diving, but a resultant reduced effort tolerance, or an area of abnormal lung tissue, such as a cyst that may have been present since birth or as a result of disease, must do so. A cyst would fill with compressed air during the dive and, should it prove to have too small an opening to empty sufficiently rapidly during the ascent, the expanding air would be forced into the bloodstream, thus producing air embolism. Similarly, any condition that produces severe narrowing of bronchus or bronchioles may produce the same effect, and would again preclude diving.

ASTHMA

This is most often a problem in a young diver. It may be caused by obvious allergens such as pollen and dust, or be a response to emotional stress.

Although theoretically a hazard, attacks of allergic asthma do not seem to occur in the relatively clean air of the coast or when breathing the highly purified air supplied from an aqualung. Provided that no permanent lung damage has been sustained and that the individual appears perfectly fit between attacks, he may be allowed to dive.

If, however, the asthma attacks develop as a reaction to stress, the individual should not be accepted for diving. Diving is too full of minor incidents and the occasional major one for such a sufferer to be other than at best a liability at times of crisis and at worst the means of converting a minor crisis into a catastrophe.

Some individuals develop asthma when suffering from respiratory infections; provided that they are clinically normal between attacks, there is no reason why they should not dive.

All too often the picture is more complicated than this since individuals may develop attacks from more than one cause. Here, the examining doctor's decision must be based on a careful assessment of the various factors.

Cardiovascular System

Minor degrees of valvular disease of the heart may be ignored provided that the individual's physical efficiency is adequate.

Hypertension (high blood pressure)

Minor degrees are not of importance; probably the dividing line lies at about the level of 140 mm mercury systolic (peak) pressure and 90 mm diastolic (lowest) pressure. Above this no one should be accepted without careful enquiry into its effect on their exercise tolerance and into any associated illness, such as coronary arterial disease.

Certainly, hypertension sufficient to warrant continuous control by drugs should not be accepted. A blood pressure of 160/100 should be regarded as the maximum acceptable level for established divers.

Coronary Arterial Disease

There is considerable evidence, derived from accident statistics, that the exertion and stress of under-water swimming provokes thrombosis in individuals suffering from coronary disease, and that these attacks are generally fatal. Therefore, where there is hypertension, or a history of chest pain on exertion (angina), or heavy smoking, especially in the middle-aged candidate, an electrocardiogram should be taken, preferably during exertion.

No individual with evidence of coronary disease, including previous thrombosis or angina, should be permitted to dive.

Diabetes

The Club no longer admits diabetics although established members may continue. Diabetes is a generalised disease in which the pancreas fails to secrete sufficient hormone-insulin—to keep the blood sugar within normal limits.

Because of the excessively high blood sugar there is increased degeneration of the cardiovascular system, with a liability to sustain strokes and coronary thromboses at an early age, and in the diving context, an increased susceptibility to decompression sickness.

Established divers on insulin may continue to dive provided they satisfy the following conditions:

They must be emotionally stable with a well-controlled diabetes, without any hypoglycaemic attacks in the past two years; the doctor in charge of the diabetes must agree that diving is an acceptable risk; diving activities should be restricted to avoid circumstances in which heavy exertion may be required in the water since this may cause blood sugar to be used up faster than it can be replaced, (attacks may also occur because of omission to eat regular meals, either because of an early start to the day, or through seasickness); the Dive Marshal should always be aware that the subject is a diabetic.

Teeth

These should be adequate to grip a mouth-piece. The wearing of dentures is permitted provided that they will remain in place when the mouth is fully opened and cannot be dislodged by placing the jaws together in any position, or by movement of one denture against the other; they should extend to the junction of gum and cheek.

Although there is some theoretical hazard that, in the event of sudden unconsciousness, dentures may come adrift and block the airway, in practice this seems to be more of a hazard for the professional diver using a re-breathing set with a full face-mask, in which it is possible to remain unconscious under water for some time. Under the same circumstances the amateur diver would quickly lose his mouth-piece and drown, thus rendering the question of whether he would inhale his dentures largely academic.

Ears, Nose and Throat
Attention should be paid to the ears and sinuses since these are a common source of trouble to the diver; in particular, enquiries as to past ear infections and sinusitis should be made. As well as checking that the tympanic membranes are intact, they should be observed while the subject is 'clearing his ears' to confirm that there is no obstruction of the Eustachian tubes.

Otitis Media (inflammation of the middle ear)
Old otitis media which has cleared up and the drum healed over is quite acceptable. However, where there is chronic infection or discharge, diving would almost certainly provoke a flare-up. The problem case is one in which the infection has cleared, but has left the individual with a persistent perforation of the drum. While, undoubtedly many people have successfully dived with such perforations, there is always some danger of starting a fresh attack of otitis media, or even a mastoid infection, and also of provoking uncontrollable vertigo as cold water enters the ear.

Since most of these cases would be suitable subjects for plastic repair of the ear drum, it is far preferable that this be done before making any attempt to dive.

Otitis Externa
This is an infection or dermatitis of the outer ear passage and is not a disqualification except during the acute attack. Affected persons must take additional care over normal hygiene by rinsing the ear with fresh water and by carefully drying it after each dive.

Wax
Apart from making it difficult to examine the ear adequately, wax can cause trouble in two ways. Firstly, if it blocks the external ear

canal, pockets of air trapped between it and the drum have no free communication with the ambient pressure and this may result in damage to the ear drum or external canal. Secondly, after diving, salt water cannot freely drain away from the external canal and the diver is left with what virtually amounts to a salt water poultice in his ear, which can result in a rather unpleasant attack of otitis externa.

At the beginning of each diving season it is a wise precaution to check there is no excess wax in your ears.

Sinusitis

It is difficult to predict how an individual subject to sinusitis will respond to diving: some have small inadequate openings into, or poor drainage from their sinuses and get sinus squeezes or fresh attacks of sinusitis while, on the contrary, others actually benefit from diving, the to and fro movement of compressed air presumably helping to wash mucus out of the sinuses. Thus, cautious experiment may be permitted in the milder case.

Exercise Tolerance

Ideally, the examination should include a physical fitness or exercise tolerance test. Various tests based on the rate of recovery of the pulse after a standard exercise, such as the Harvard step test, have been devised, but they may give misleading results if apprehension has accelerated the heartbeat prior to the test and, in addition, are somewhat time consuming. At present the BSAC swimming tests, particularly those involving swimming 50 m with a 5 kg weight-belt and treading water for one minute with hands above the head, form an effective substitute for a formal test of effort tolerance.

Special Tests

As stated, the chest X-ray is an essential part of the examination. The electrocardiogram should not be undertaken routinely, but only in selected cases, as mentioned.

Lung function tests such as the vital capacity (see *Circulation and Respiration*), the expiratory flow rate and the one-second forced expiratory volume (FEV_1) are used by professional units to assess pulmonary efficiency but are not generally available.

Temporary Unfitness

Any infection of the ears, sinuses, respiratory tract and lungs produces a temporary unfitness for diving.

The movement of compressed air in the ears and sinuses helps to spread any infection far and wide, so converting a mild infection into a serious one. There is also considerable evidence that bacteria and viruses actually multiply far more quickly when, by diving, the oxygen partial pressure is raised.

The same thing occurs when infected lungs are subjected to pressure: bronchitis and pneumonia have been known to become fulminating in their rapid deterioration.

It should not be overlooked that sedative drugs, particularly alcohol, sleeping tablets and some types of seasickness cure, may persist in the body for 12 to 24 hours, and greatly increase nitrogen narcosis or even produce its effects at unexpectedly shallow depths.

Review

Ideally, the individual should be examined prior to diving and then, barring any severe illness intervening, the frequency with which he is reviewed should be related to his age. At present it is recommended that medical examinations be carried out every five years up to the age of 30, three-yearly thereon up to the age of 50 and annually thereafter.

Circulation and Respiration

Metabolism and Respiration

The body is composed of millions of separate cells, each of which carries out a particular function. Some types of cells are widely distributed throughout the body while others are highly specialised and grouped together into organs such as the brain, liver, kidney or lungs. In order to live and grow, each cell needs a steady supply of food and oxygen which it uses to supply energy. This process is called metabolism and in a very simplified form follows the equation:

$$\text{Food} + \text{oxygen} \rightarrow \text{energy} + \text{water} + \text{carbon dioxide}.$$

Not all of the food taken in is used in this process and that which is unwanted is partly released from the body as faeces and partly excreted by the kidneys, together with the water produced in metabolism, as urine. Water is also lost by evaporation of sweat from the skin and as water vapour in the breath.

Respiration is the process whereby oxygen (O_2) is transported from the atmosphere to the cells for use in metabolism, and carbon dioxide (CO_2) is removed from the cells to the atmosphere. Respiration, therefore, includes: the act of breathing; the uptake of O_2 by the blood at the lungs; the transport of O_2 to the cells by the circulation and pumping action of the heart; the uptake of O_2 by the cells from the blood; and the reverse process for CO_2.

The Heart and Circulation

The heart consists of four chambers and can be thought of as two separate pumps. The two chambers on the right side of the heart form a pump supplying blood at low pressure to the lungs via the pulmonary arteries. In the lungs the blood picks up O_2 and releases CO_2 as it passes through the minute capillaries, and is then collected in the pulmonary veins and returned to the left side of the heart.

The two chambers of the left side of the heart form a high-pressure pump which supplies blood via the arteries to the capillaries which supply all other parts of the body, where O_2 is used up and CO_2 is picked up, whence it is collected in the veins and returned to the right side of the heart. Between the two chambers of each side of the heart and on the output side of each lower chamber there are flaps which act as non-return valves. Fig. 12 shows in schematic form the entire respiratory and circulatory system.

The heart is mainly composed of muscle and acts by contraction of this muscle in a rhythmic fashion. Contraction of the heart will squeeze out some of the blood contained within it and the valves will ensure that the expelled blood is pumped into the arteries. On relaxation of the heart muscle, blood will flow into the heart from the veins. The amount of blood pumped out at each contraction will depend upon the volume of the lower chambers and on the strength of the muscular contraction.

Lungs

The lungs are the organ for interchange of gases between the atmosphere and the blood and consist basically of two air-sacs, situated in the chest, connected by the windpipe (*trachea*) to the atmosphere via the mouth and nose. Each lung is enclosed in a membrane (*Pleura*) which protects it and allows it to move freely over a similar membrane which covers the inside of the rib-cage. The space between the two membranes (the *pleural cavity*) is completely obliterated in health except for a small amount of lubricating fluid.

The lungs have elastic properties, like a balloon, and will always tend to contract away from the chest wall but, because of the absence of any gas in the pleural cavity, the lungs cling to the inside of the chest wall in the same way that a rubber suction disc will stick to a flat surface. Contraction of the muscles between the ribs will raise the ribs and swing them outwards while contraction of the muscles of the diaphragm will cause it to be pulled downwards towards the abdomen and both these actions will result in an increase in the volume of the chest (Fig. 13).

The lungs will follow the chest movement and, therefore, there will be a lowered gas pressure within them which will draw air in from the outside atmosphere. Relaxation of this muscular effort will, under normal conditions, allow the diaphragm to rise and the rib-cage to fall passively under the action of gravity, and, aided by the elastic recoil of the lungs, will decrease the volume of the chest, raise the pressure within it and force gas out to the atmosphere again. This is the cycle of inhalation and exhalation.

The pattern of the airways inside the chest can be compared with the branching structure of a tree. As the trachea enters the chest it divides into two, each airway (*bronchus*) supplying one lung. Each bronchus then divides to supply the lobes of the lung and at each division the size of the airway becomes smaller. Further divisions and sub-divisions occur; finally, there are millions of small passages (*bronchioles*) on the end of which bud-like protrusions form the blind end to the airway. These protrusions are known as the *alveoli* and the surrounding tissue of each alveolus is criss-crossed with a net-work of fine blood capillaries which ultimately connect with

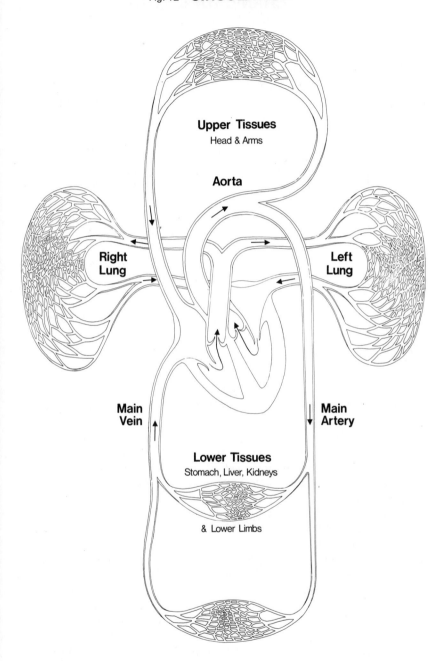

Fig. 12 **CIRCULATION**

Upper Tissues
Head & Arms

Aorta

**Right
Lung**

**Left
Lung**

**Main
Vein**

**Main
Artery**

Lower Tissues
Stomach, Liver, Kidneys

& Lower Limbs

This schematic diagram of the circulatory system shows how the heart — a two-compartment pump — draws oxygen-enriched blood from the lungs as it expands, and pumps it to body tissues as it contracts. The second compartment pumps CO_2-laden blood to the lungs.

c

Fig. 13. THE MECHANICS OF BREATHING

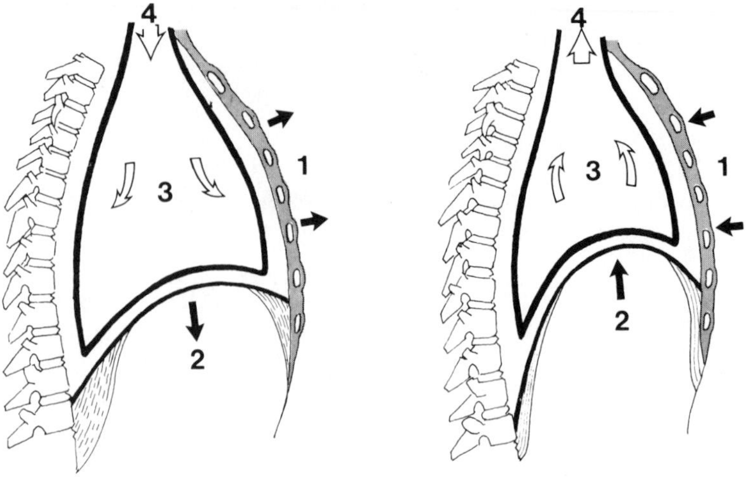

INSPIRATION

1. Ribs raised
2. Diaphragm depressed
3. Lungs expand
4. Air drawn in

EXPIRATION

1. Ribs return
2. Diaphragm relaxes
3. Lungs return to original volume
4. Air expelled

the vein which carries the blood from the lungs to the heart. Gas exchange takes place from the air within the alveoli, through the alveolar membrane and into the bloodstream and vice-versa (Fig. 14). The total surface area of these alveoli in an adult man has been estimated as being equivalent to the area of a tennis court.

In an average man the greatest volume of gas that the lungs will hold when fully expanded (*total lung capacity*) is about 6 litres, but not all of this volume is used in respiration. When at rest and breathing quietly the volume of air moved into and out of the lungs on each breath (*tidal volume*) is about 0.5 litres and at the end of a normal breath out (*expiration*) the lungs still contain about 2.5 litres. During exercise the tidal volume increases, both by having a bigger expiration and a bigger breath (*inspiration*), until it may reach as much as 3 litres with maximum exercise. If you first give a maximum expiration and then measure the volume of a maximum inspiration it will be about 4.5 litres; the value obtained is called the vital capacity and denotes the maximum volume of air that can be moved into or out of the lungs in one breath. The difference between the total lung capacity and the vital capacity—about 1.5 litres—is called the residual volume and represents the gas that cannot be expelled from the lungs, even by a maximum expiration (Fig. 15).

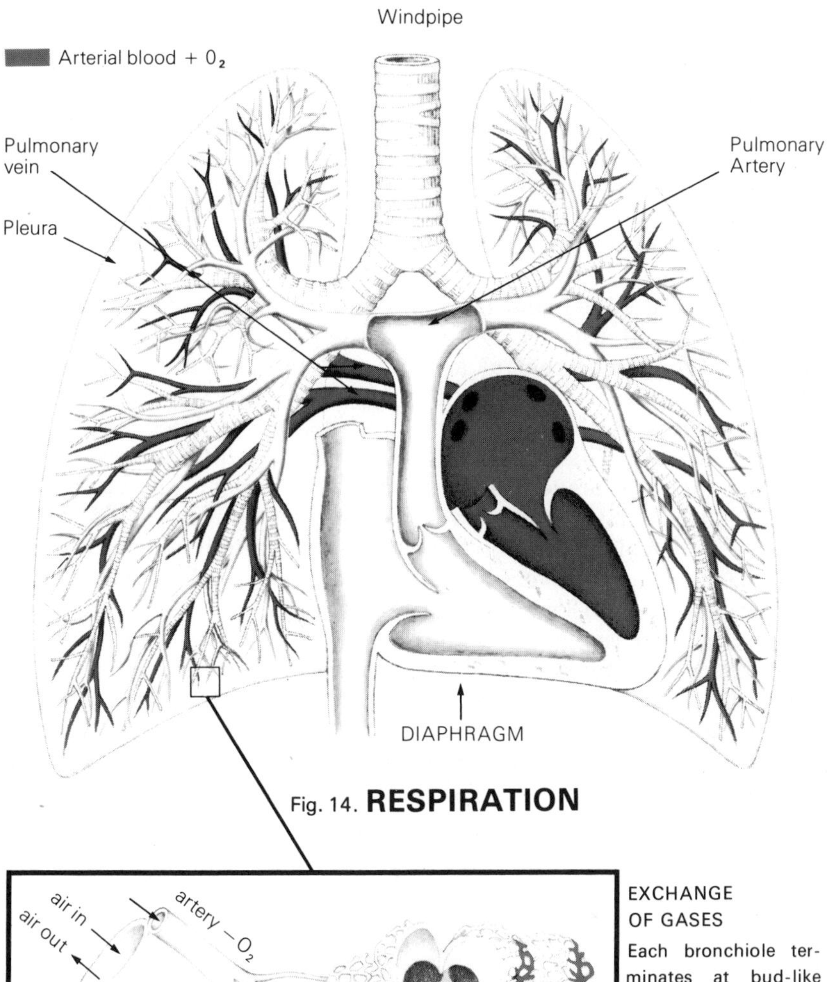
Windpipe
Arterial blood + 0_2
Pulmonary vein
Pleura
Pulmonary Artery
DIAPHRAGM

Fig. 14. **RESPIRATION**

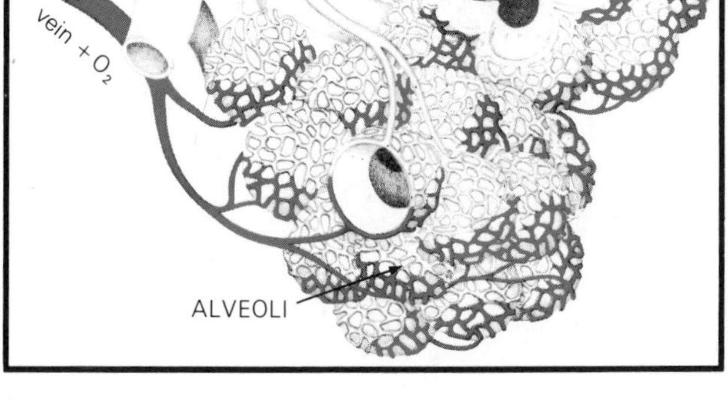
air in
air out
artery $-O_2$
vein $+O_2$
ALVEOLI

EXCHANGE
OF GASES

Each bronchiole terminates at bud-like protrusions called alveoli. Through its membrane oxygen is taken into the blood and carbon-dioxide released. The network of blood capillaries which surround each alveolues, and carries away blood from body tissues, and carries away oxygen-enriched blood. The gases exchange in an effort to equalise their partial pressures.

The residual volume is of great importance when considering the effects of a change in pressure on the lungs. For example, a snorkel diver who breathes in total lung capacity (say, 6 litres) on the surface at 1 bar absolute pressure and then descends to 30 m (4 bar), will have decreased his lung volume to a quarter—1.5 litres—because the pressure has increased fourfold (Boyle's Law). His lungs now only hold their residual volume and, if he descends further, the increased pressure will compress his chest more than nature intended and he could suffer from a thoracic *squeeze*.

Another thoracic squeeze might greet the breath-holding diver who attempts to breathe through a hose pipe from the surface. Chapter 2 explained that at a depth of 1 m below the surface the absolute pressure is 1.1 kg/cm^2 (1.1 bar), and this pressure is applied to the outside of the diver's chest while the air pressure within remains at 1 bar. This apparently small pressure differential is more than enough to prevent the muscular action of inhalation. At greater depths, physical damage—as well as asphyxia—could result. In order to be able to breathe the pressure on the outside of the chest must be the same—or very close to—the pressure of the air within. The limit is about 0.3 m water head difference.

Consider now the aqualung diver, who can fill his lungs from his breathing apparatus, regardless of depth. If he were to commence an ascent from a depth of 40 m (5 bar) say, with empty lungs, i.e. residual volume only, and without breathing during his ascent, the residual air would expand fivefold on the way up. His 1.5 litres residual volume would expand to 7.5 litres by the time he reached the surface.

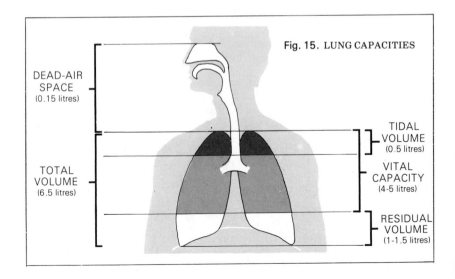

Fig. 15. LUNG CAPACITIES

DEAD-AIR SPACE
(0.15 litres)

TOTAL VOLUME
(6.5 litres)

TIDAL VOLUME
(0.5 litres)

VITAL CAPACITY
(4-5 litres)

RESIDUAL VOLUME
(1-1.5 litres)

This exceeds his total lung capacity, and unless he were to exhale during the ascent, he would suffer severe lung damage—a burst lung.

Blood and Gaseous Exchange

The adult body contains about 5 litres of blood which is composed of a fluid (*plasma*) within which are carried specialised cells. The plasma also contains a substance in solution which forms the main constituent (*fibrin*) of a blood clot. Plasma without fibrin is a thin yellowish fluid (*serum*) and is most commonly seen oozing from a graze.

The majority of cells carried in the plasma are *red cells* which contain within them a substance called *haemoglobin* which has the property of combining chemically with oxygen. There are normally about 5 million red cells per cu. mm of blood. The other cells, which do not contain haemoglobin, are the *white cells* which have special functions concerned mostly with combating infection within the body; there are about 7500 of these cells in every cu. mm of blood.

As the blood passes through the alveolar capillaries of the lungs, oxygen combines with the haemoglobin in the red cells, the amount of oxygen that combines being dependent on the partial pressure of oxygen present in the lungs.

The oxygenated blood coming from the lungs is carried by the circulation, via the heart, to the body capillaries. The tissues of the body will have been using oxygen in metabolism and so the PO_2 in the tissue cells will be lower that in the newly-arrived blood and, as gases always move (diffuse) from an area of high partial pressure towards an area of low partial pressure, the oxygen will diffuse out of the blood capillaries into the tissues. Also because of metabolism, there will be a greater partial pressure of carbon dioxide (PCO_2) in the tissue cells than in the blood, so CO_2 will diffuse into the blood where it is mainly carried as the chemical sodium bicarbonate. As the haemoglobin gives up its oxygen it changes colour and obtains a noticeable blue tint.

This bluish blood will now be collected in the veins and returned via the heart to the lungs; the blood will now have a lower PO_2 and a higher PCO_2 than the air in the alveoli so O_2 will diffuse into the blood from the lungs, and will combine again with the haemoglobin, causing it to change back to the bright red colour of arterial blood. At the same time, the CO_2 is released from its chemical combination and will diffuse out into the lungs, to be expelled from the body during the next expiration, which will usually consist of about 17% O_2, 4% CO_2 and 79% N_2 according to the work done (Fig. 16).

Nitrogen is said to be an inert gas because it takes no part in normal metabolism and therefore, provided the total pressure remains unchanged (i.e. the PN_2 is constant), the amount expired is the same as the amount inspired because the body is already fully

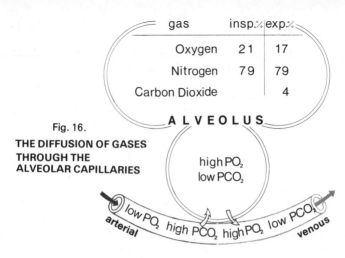

gas	insp.%	exp.%
Oxygen	21	17
Nitrogen	79	79
Carbon Dioxide		4

ALVEOLUS

high PO_2
low PCO_2

low PO_2 high PCO_2 high PO_2 low PCO_2
arterial   venous

Fig. 16.

THE DIFFUSION OF GASES THROUGH THE ALVEOLAR CAPILLARIES

saturated with nitrogen at this PN_2. When air is breathed under pressure, nitrogen does have serious side effects. These will be explained in later sections of this Manual.

Metabolism being a chemical reaction between food products and oxygen, the cells need a supply of food to be brought to them and this is also carried by the blood. The full metabolic reaction takes place by stages and some steps can only be carried out in specialised cells such as those of the liver; it simplifies matters therefore, to say that the blood carries *metabolites* to and from the cells of the body at the same time as it transports O_2 and CO_2.

Effects of Exercise

The rate at which metabolism is carried out in any group of cells depends on the amount of energy being used. Thus, an exercising muscle will use much more energy than one at rest, and the rate of O_2 consumption and CO_2 production will be increased during exercise. If the circulation and respiration remained unchanged in exercise there would again be an increasing lack of O_2 in the cells because oxygen usage would be greater than the supply.

The circulation and respiration rates are, therefore, very finely controlled in the body to ensure that the supply of oxygen and food to the cells, and the rate of removal of CO_2 and other metabolites from them is always sufficient, whatever their rate of metabolism. These control processes are automatic and subconscious but the normal control of respiration can be consciously over-ruled for a short time, e.g. in speaking, eating and breath-holding.

CONTROL OF CIRCULATION

The circulation rate is largely determined by the heart. Like any pump, the output from the heart (*cardiac output*) can be calculated by multiplying the volume ejected from it on each contraction (*stroke volume*) and the number of contractions per minute (*pulse rate*). When exercise occurs, nervous impulses are sent to the heart to increase the pulse rate and this can rise from the average level at rest of 60–70 beats/min to 180–200 beats/min (Table I). At the same time the heart will enlarge slightly and increase its stroke volume so that an overall 4-fold or 5-fold increase in cardiac output can result.

However, the circulation rate can be increased locally by very much more than this by alterations in the distribution of the blood within the body. Not all cells increase their metabolism at the same time and, by contraction or dilation of small arteries, blood can be diverted from those cells at rest to those that are active. Thus, after a heavy meal, the stomach and intestines are very busy digesting food, and blood is diverted from other places—such as the muscles— into the abdomen to increase the oxygen supply. When taking physical exercise, blood is diverted away from non-active muscles such as the intestines and skin, and is concentrated on the active muscles. Thus, the circulation rate to, say, the muscles of the legs, can be multiplied twenty-fold when comparing the resting and exercising states. If exercise is taken after a heavy meal, the circulation finds itself with conflicting needs from two different systems of the body and has to compromise between the two. As with any compromise, the solution must be a less than optimum effort in both directions, so the result in this case is a reduction of physical exercise capability—and indigestion!

CONTROL OF RESPIRATION

The amount of respiration is found by multiplying the tidal volume and the rate of breathing (the *respiratory rate*), and is usually described as the total expired ventilation, measured in litres per minute (l/min). At rest the respiratory rate is normally 12–14 breaths per minute and the tidal volume about 0.5 litres so that the total expired ventilation is 6–7 l/min (Table I). During exercise the respiratory rate and the tidal volume both increase so that expired ventilation may reach 100–110 l/min.

Exchange of gases between the air and the blood in the lungs only occurs in the alveoli but at each inspiration gas has first to fill the airways (the branches and twigs of the bronchial tree) before it can reach the alveoli. Therefore, at the end of inspiration the airways will be filled with gas that takes no part in the gaseous exchange and is expelled, unaltered, on the next expiration. The volume of the airways (the *dead space*) is a nearly constant quantity for an individual but varies, roughly with chest size, between individuals and is of the order of 0.15 litres. The volume of gas per minute available for interchange of gases (the *effective* or *alveolar ventilation*) will, therefore, be less than the total expired ventilation by an amount which is determined by the dead space times the respiratory rate. Any piece of equipment (e.g. a long snorkel tube or full-face mask) which increases the dead space must decrease the effective ventilation and decrease the ability of the body to interchange O_2 and CO_2 at the lungs, causing the PO_2 in the blood to tend to fall and the PCO_2 to rise.

The body contains specialised *receptor cells* which sense any change in blood-gas pressures and which will cause an increase or decrease in the total expired ventilation to return the blood-gas partial pressures to normal values. The most powerful stimulus to breathing is an increase in the PCO_2 and this is monitored by the *respiratory nerve centre* in the brain. This centre keeps the PCO_2 remarkably constant in the body throughout the entire range of body activity. Other receptor cells in the heart and brain are sensitive to an O_2 lack, and cause the body to lapse into unconsciousness when blood O_2 levels reach a critically low level. If the stimulus of an increasing PCO_2 is ignored, the O_2 sensitive receptors say 'Enough —stop everything!' and bring about unconsciousness.

Also, if by deliberate over-breathing (*hyperventilation*) you wash out more CO_2 from the lungs than is being produced by the body and

	Rest	Moderate Work	Maximum Exercise
Pulse rate (beats/min.)	60–70	100	180–200
Cardiac output (l./min.)	4–5	6–8	20–25
Tidal volume (litres)	0·5	1·5	3·0
Respiratory rate (per min.)	12–14	20	35
Total expired ventilation (l./min.)	6–7	30	100–110
Oxygen consumption (l./min.)	0·25	1·2	4·0–4·5
Carbon dioxide production (l./min.)	0·20	1·0	3·5–4·0

Table I. Effects of exercise. All figures are average values, there being considerable variation between individuals. Moderate work may be taken as walking on the flat at 4 mph or swimming at 0·75 knot which is a medium pace for average swimmers.

thus cause a fall in PCO_2, the stimulus to breathe is greatly diminished and breathing may even stop for a while until the PCO_2 is restored to its normal value by continuing metabolism.

The level of ventilation is also affected by nerve impulses from the joints and muscles so that, at the start of exercise, the ventilation is increased almost immediately to cope with the increased amount of CO_2 the body will produce because of the exercise. When this increased PCO_2 appears in the blood some quarter of a minute later, there is a further increase in ventilation because of stimulation of the specialised receptor cells. At the end of an exercise period there is again a very rapid decrease in the level of ventilation, followed by a slower return to normal as the PCO_2 regains its original value. Nerve impulses from the lung tissues, diaphragm and rib cage also affect ventilation, maintaining the regularity of respiration and controlling the relationship between tidal volume and respiratory rate.

OXYGEN CONSUMPTION AND CARBON DIOXIDE PRODUCTION

Oxygen consumption when completely at rest is about 0.25 l/min (Table I). During exercise, as metabolism increases to provide more energy, O_2 consumption must also rise, and the average person will achieve a maximum of about 4.0 l/min when working as hard as possible. The maximum O_2 consumption varies with the degree of fitness and the size of the individual, and consumptions of about 6.0 l/min have been measured in Olympic athletes. During a dive the consumption will be varying with the degree of activity, and the overall oxygen usage will normally be about 1.0 l/min.

Carbon dioxide production is closely linked with oxygen consumption because of the metabolic equation and is measured as the amount of CO_2 breathed out in litres per minute. This amount will be affected by the volume of the total expired ventilation. The ratio between CO_2 production and O_2 consumption will, therefore, vary under different conditions, but as a general rule, CO_2 production can be taken as being 0.8 times the O_2 consumption.

It is important to remember that O_2 consumption and CO_2 production are values which are unaffected by the depth of a dive. If a diver is exercising at a constant rate and has a total expired ventilation of 20 l/min at the surface (1 bar), he will still have a ventilation of 20 l/min at 10 m (2 bar), but this gas volume will be equivalent to 40 l/min when measured on the surface.

Thus, for a constant rate of work, the *surface equivalent* ventilation will increase with depth. However, a constant rate of work will expend energy at a constant rate and, because the production of energy is basically a chemical reaction, this will require a constant number of molecules of oxygen per minute under all conditions. If the work being done requires each minute a number of O_2 molecules which occupy a volume of 1 litre at 1 bar, they will only occupy 0.5 litres if measured at 2 bar, but the 'surface equivalent' O_2 consumption will still be 1 litre/min and thus is independent of depth.

The body does contain a small store of oxygen; in the blood haemoglobin, in the gas in the lungs, and in a special compound found in muscles. This O_2 store is sufficient to support the body for short bursts of exercise and, for example, top-class sprinters rarely breathe during a hundred metre race. The O_2 store can also be used in situations in which the O_2 consumption is greater than the amount of oxygen being taken up by the body, such as in fast swimming in an emergency. However, such exercise will have produced an increase in PCO_2 in the body and decreased the total PO_2 much below normal, i.e. have produced an 'oxygen debt'. The specialised receptors will react to these changed conditions and when the exercise is over will increase the respiration until the PCO_2 has returned to its normal value, the O_2 store has been replenished and the repayment of the oxygen debt has been completed (see *Exhaustion*).

Effects of Increased Pressure

The body is mostly composed of watery fluids and water can be said to be incompressible; certainly it is not affected by the pressures at present foreseen in diving. The air-containing cavities within the body (*lungs, ears, sinuses*) will, however, be compressed with increasing pressure (according to Boyle's Law), and to avoid ill-effects they must be filled with gas at the same pressure as that of the surrounding water.

The effects of pressure on the circulation will vary with the position of the body in the water and are difficult to assess but certainly are less in degree and importance than the effects of exercise. Anyone who is medically and physically fit to take hard exercise will not suffer any circulatory embarrassment in the water.

The effects on respiration arise from several factors. As mentioned above, the supply of air to the diver must be at a pressure close to the water pressure over his chest so that there is no pressure difference across the chest wall. The pattern of respiration tends to change under water because the effect of gravity is hidden amongst the conflicting pressure variations. The act of expiration can no longer be the passive action seen in the normal situation: air has usually to be actively and consciously expressed from the lungs and this skill is sometimes difficult for the new diver to learn as it requires confidence in oneself and one's equipment. Complaints about shortage of air can sometimes be observed as not being due to a lack of air flow from the breathing set, but rather because the diver has not been expiring sufficiently and his chest has become so 'blown-up' that he cannot physically expand his chest any further to breathe in.

As pressure increases so does the density of a gas, and it becomes heavier and more 'sticky' and, therefore, more difficult to move. To obtain the same amount of ventilation as at the surface will, therefore, require more effort under pressure and this can become a serious embarrassment to the diver. For example, experiments show that at 30 m (4 bar) the maximum volume of air that the average man can move into and out of his lungs in one minute (the maximum breathing capacity) is half that which he could attain at the surface. Although at 30 m the O_2 partial pressure is four times normal and, therefore, there is no shortage of O_2, the volume of ventilation required to remove CO_2 from the body is not changed: as the maximum breathing capacity is halved at 30 m so is the maximum amount of CO_2 that can be removed per minute. If the body PCO_2 is to remain at its original value this means that the maximum possible exercise at 30 m will also be half that attainable at the surface. Most types of breathing apparatus cause a mechanical increase in breathing resistance and an increased 'dead space', and this will further restrict respiration as well as increasing the need for respiration. With increasing depth, the maximum breathing capacity and the exercise capacity will be further decreased and this is a major factor in determining the maximum depth to which an air-breathing diver may go.

The solution to this problem is to use a breathing mixture such as oxy-helium (O_2/He), which has a much lower density than air. The work of breathing and the apparatus resistance are much decreased and breathing O_2/He at 90 m is very similar to breathing air at 30 m. However, breathing such an exotic gas mixture is quite beyond the safe practices of sports diving, and is normally unacceptable within the BSAC.

Hypoxia and Drowning

(Study of the previous section—*Circulation and Respiration*—and in particular an understanding of those factors which control respiration is necessary before this section can be fully understood.)

Hypoxia means a reduced amount of oxygen; *anoxia* means total lack of oxygen. Both conditions could result in death or decreased efficiency of the cells of the body. It will be obvious from the description given in the previous section that continuing life depends on the combined reactions of the heart, blood and lungs. If the heart stops, the cells of the body will use up all the O_2 in their immediate vicinity and then die of anoxia. If the heart is inefficient either through disease or inborn defects, it will not be strong enough to pump sufficient blood around the body and the cells will suffer from hypoxia. If the blood volume is decreased because of bleeding (*haemorrhage*), or if the normal quantity of haemoglobin is reduced (as in *anaemia*), the amount of oxygen that can be carried to the cells will be reduced and again, the body will suffer. Some substances, such as carbon monoxide, can poison the blood and interfere with the carriage of O_2.

If the interchange of gases in the lungs is interfered with, either because breathing has stopped or because air cannot reach the lungs, the body will continue to use the O_2 which remains in the bloodstream by metabolism, reducing the blood's PO_2 further. The skin will take on a blue-grey tinge known as *Cyanosis*—particularly noticeable at the lips, ear-lobes and finger nail-beds—which is characteristic of such cases of hypoxia. If normal breathing is not restored, or resuscitation applied, the body will suffer from a lack of O_2 and will surely die.

Lastly, the air inhaled into the lungs must contain a sufficient PO_2 for the body's needs or else again, cyanosis will occur and death of the body cells through anoxia will follow. The air breathed must also contain less CO_2 than is found in the veins of the body so that a pressure difference is still present to cause CO_2 to diffuse from the alveolar capillaries into the lungs. If not CO_2 will accumulate within the body causing adverse effects and eventual death.

The cells of the body vary in their sensitivity to hypoxia and therefore, in the time it takes to cause damage from which they cannot recover. The cells of the brain are the most sensitive and, should the heart stop and the body become hypoxic through the continuation of normal metabolism, the brain is likely to be irrevocably damaged within four minutes. Other tissues are much more resistant and can tolerate an oxygen debt: for example, a muscle will eventually recover its full strength and function, even if its blood supply has been stopped for as much as thirty minutes. However, efficient muscles are useless if the brain is so damaged that it is no longer capable of controlling them properly and, therefore, four minutes must be considered the limit of time available in which to start to restore normal carriage of O_2 to the body.

This then is the general condition of hypoxia/anoxia. Let us now see how the condition applies to the diver. First, the very act of breath-holding whilst carrying out physical exertion brings on a state of hypoxia, so it can be reasonably stated that snorkel diving is a form of calculated hypoxic risk! The aqualung diver, whose air supply fails (rare, and usually because of the diver's inattention) has to make his way to the surface and also risks hypoxia during the ascent. The diver whose aqualung has accidently been filled with pure nitrogen would be a sudden case of anoxia within seconds of breathing from it. But the most common cause is *Latent Hypoxia*.

Latent Hypoxia—Hyperventilation

A snorkel diver takes a full breath and dives. As he swims along underwater, O_2 is being consumed as a result of body activity and CO_2 is accumulating in his bloodstream. There comes a time when the PCO_2 in the bloodstream, and thus passing through the respiratory centre of the brain, stimulates the desire to breathe and the diver returns to the surface. Here he relaxes and restores the normal O_2/CO_2 balance in his lungs and bloodstream.

However, in the excitement of the chase or in an effort to achieve a certain goal, the diver may choose to over-ride this stimulus and this can result in an abnormally low level of O_2 remaining in the bloodstream. When the diver relaxes on returning to the surface, the blood which was supplying his active muscles returns through the circulation and the secondary receptor cells in the heart and brain will notice the abnormally low level of O_2 and will bring about a sudden unconsciousness due to hypoxia. If the diver is in the water at the time he is immediately a drowning victim.

The situation is further aggravated if the diver *hyperventilates* before such a breath-holding dive. The object of *hyperventilation* is to reduce the normal level of CO_2 in the blood and to increase the level of O_2 by taking a series of very deep breaths before commencing breath-holding. While the level of CO_2 can be significantly reduced by this process, there is only a marginal increase in the amount of O_2 taken in. With the diver underwater, finning hard, O_2 is rapidly being consumed, but it takes longer for the CO_2 to reach the level at which it stimulates the desire to breathe. The situation can be reached before the CO_2 sensitive respiratory centre stimulates the desire to breathe, when the secondary receptors in the heart and brain notice the O_2 lack and bring about unconsciousness. Once again, and particularly if under water, the diver is a drowning victim.

The dangers of hyperventilation are graphically illustrated in Fig. 17. Hyperventilation is a practice which should be avoided at all costs. The breath-holding diver is advised to commence his dive in a totally relaxed state and should take no more than two medium-depth breaths before his descent.

The problem of Latent Hypoxia is exacerbated by an increase in depth. If a breath-holding diver descends to considerable depth, for example, 30 m, he will be subjected to a pressure of 4 bars absolute. His lungs will be compressed to one quarter of their volume at the surface and consequently, the PO_2 of the air in his lungs and in his bloodstream will be effectively increased fourfold in terms of surface O_2 pressure. Since the PCO_2 in the lungs is minimal at the surface, considerable quantities of CO_2 can diffuse from the blood into the lungs at depth, and the PCO_2 in the blood and the respiratory nerve centre is insufficient to stimulate the desire to breathe. Also, the underwater effort may be considerable or the rewards of such a dive sufficiently attractive to induce the diver to ignore the first stimulus to breathe when it occurs.

Fig. 17 (a) DIVE WITHOUT HYPERVENTILATION

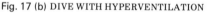

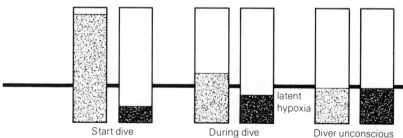

Fig. 17 (b) DIVE WITH HYPERVENTILATION

On his return to the surface, the situation is reversed. The PO_2 of the air remaining in his lungs and, therefore, in his bloodstream falls rapidly and the corresponding drop in the PCO_2 gives a false sense of relief from the urge to breathe. The O_2 sensitive receptors within the heart and the brain will bring about unconsciousness due to hypoxia when the blood O_2 level is insufficient. The diver can become unconscious at some considerable depth beneath the surface. Due to water pressure, his lung volume and, therefore, buoyancy, will be reduced and he will sink, drowning as he does so.

Numerous cases of this latent hypoxia have occurred, particularly among competitive spear fishermen. While the capacity to dive deeper improves with snorkel diving ability, deep snorkel diving for its own sake should be avoided. The risks of latent hypoxia affect the breath-holding diver who takes advantage of the apparent increased duration which he can attain at depth. To avoid this danger, he should spend no more time at great depth than he would normally spend in much shallower waters.

Signs and Symptoms of Hypoxia
These are generally objective, since the subject while under water will have almost no indication of its occurrence.
  (i) Unconsciousness in or under water.
 (ii) Unconsciousness after surfacing, or while surfacing from a long deep snorkel dive, or possibly from a free ascent.
(iii) Strong breathing efforts.
 (iv) Cyanosis (blueness of lips, ear-lobes and finger nail-beds).

Treatment of Hypoxia
Restore normal breathing applying EAR, if normal breathing efforts are not present. Apply pure O_2 if possible, since this will help restore the normal O_2/CO_2 balance. Treat for shock and send to hospital for observation.

Avoidance of Hypoxia
  (i) Never hyperventilate before a dive. Two medium-depth breaths are enough.
 (ii) Do not overwork or linger at depth even though things seem to be going well. As a rough guide, stay no longer than the time you hold your breath at the surface doing the same work.
(iii) If possible, arrange to be buoyant from 10 m upwards.
 (iv) Dive in pairs, one person diving at a time whilst the other observes.

In conclusion, it must be stressed that there is little point in a diver knowing how to treat his own hypoxic condition, but he must know how to avoid it.

Drowning

Hypoxia can bring about unconsciousness of a diver in or under water and unless he is quickly rescued, he will drown.

While unconscious, respiratory effort will take water into the upper breathing tract—the mouth and throat—but *laryngeal reflexes* will divert the water into the stomach. (This is why drowning victims frequently regurgitate water during recovery.) This reflex or spasm occurs also when food or drink 'goes down the wrong way'. As the victim becomes more hypoxic he will lapse into unconsciousness and muscular activity will diminish. The laryngeal reflex will relax and permit water to enter the passages to the lungs and ultimately, it will reach the alveoli.

In many cases of drowning the laryngeal reflex is so strong that almost no water enters the lungs. This is known as 'dry drowning' and is present in the majority of drowning cases. Shock may also bring about the sudden death of the subject before flooding of the lungs can occur. Consequently, since the majority of cases do not involve significant quantities of water reaching the alveoli, the prospects of recovery are good if the subject is resuscitated promptly. Also, it underlines the need not to waste time trying to drain water from the lungs before applying resuscitation.

In those cases where water does reach the alveoli, the effects it has upon the lungs will depend on whether it is fresh water or sea water. Fresh water entering the lungs will quickly be absorbed through the alveolar membrane diluting the blood to a massive extent. A volume equal to half that of the bloodstream can be absorbed within 2 or 3 minutes. This *haemodilution* causes chemical changes in the blood which bring about a heart attack and death in about 2 minutes.

The situation with sea water drowning is different. The salt concentration of sea water being greater than that of the blood causes water from the bloodstream to pass through the alveolar membrane in an attempt to dilute the sea water within the alveoli. This causes the concentration of the blood remaining in the circulation and imposes a progressively greater load on the heart. The *haemoconcentration* causes the heartbeat to slowly fade away and death is complete in about 8 minutes.

Because any drowning condition, whether in fresh water or sea water, brings about chemical changes within the blood, it is vital that anyone who is recovered from a drowning situation is rushed to hospital for observation and subsequent treatment if necessary. Numerous cases have been recorded of death occurring some hours, or even days, after an apparently normal recovery was made following prompt rescue and resuscitation. These delayed complications are the result of chemical changes within the blood which can only be diagnosed and rectified by specialist treatment in hospital.

If the victim can be recovered in the brief interval between the commencement of drowning and its completion (2 minutes in fresh water; 8 minutes in sea water), the prompt and effective application of resuscitation may result in a life being saved. Speed of action is vital, particularly in fresh water drowning accidents, and EVERY SECOND COUNTS. Chapter 5 *Rescue and Lifesaving* explains the techniques which may be used when effecting a rescue.

In underwater swimming other diving-related injuries may complicate or be masked by the more obvious drowning condition of the subject. This fact should be born in mind by all rescuers. With an apparently drowned diver, consider also possible complications brought about by vertigo, decompression sickness, burst lung, hypothermia, etc.

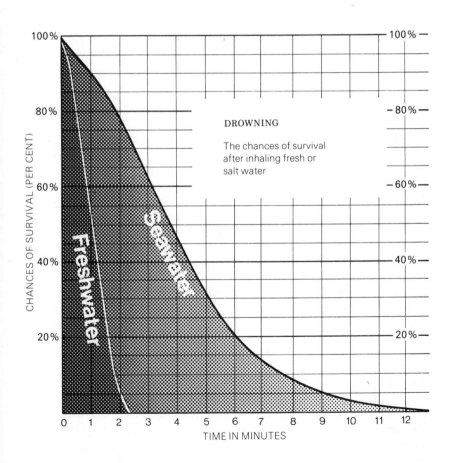

DROWNING

The chances of survival after inhaling fresh or salt water

Ears and Sinuses

In chapter 1 the section dealing with the effects of pressure explained how increasing water pressure affects flexible air spaces. The human body contains a number of such flexible air spaces and all are subjected to changes in pressure and volume as the diver goes under water. The novice diver will encounter the effects—even in the shallow water of the training pool—and will notice them first on his ears and sinuses. Before considering how pressure affects the human ear and sinus cavities, their anatomy should be studied.

The Ear
The ear is the organ of hearing and is also concerned with balance and position sense. It can be described as having outer, middle and inner portions and is shown diagrammatically in Fig. 18.

The outer ear consists of the externally visible ear and the *external auditory canal* which is closed off at its inner end by the *ear drum*. This portion is open to the air and its purpose is to collect sound waves and direct them to the cone-shaped ear drum which will, as a result, be made to vibrate.

The *middle ear* is an air-filled space mostly surrounded by bone. Part of its outer wall is formed by the ear drum, and the air-space is connected by the *Eustachian Tube* to the air passages which lie behind the nose (the *naso-pharynx*). Running across the centre of the middle ear is a chain of three small bones (the *ossicles*) which transmit the vibrations of the ear drum to the inner ear.

The inner ear is filled entirely with fluid and is embedded in the bone of the skull. The *cochlea* receives vibrations from the ossicles and converts them into nerve impulses which are sent to the brain and there perceived as sounds.

The semi-circular canals are usually considered as part of the inner ear although they take no part in hearing. They are of major importance for a sense of balance and enable one to determine one's position in space, but their function can be upset by factors which affect the middle ear (see *Vertigo and Disorientation*).

The Sinuses
The sinuses are air-filled spaces within the bones of the skull and are mostly connected to the inside of the nose (the *naso-pharynx*). The largest are the *frontal sinuses,* in the bone over the eyes, and the *maxillary sinuses* in the cheek bones. Others, which are shown in the illustration (Fig. 20), occupy positions in the mid-line of the skull

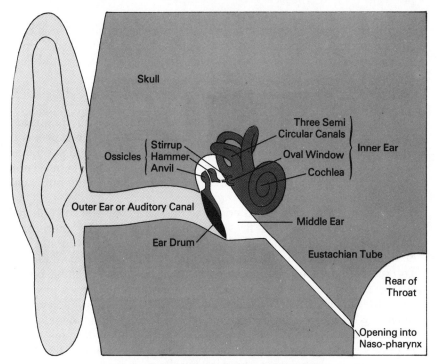

Fig. 18. **DIAGRAM OF THE EAR**

The Ear Drum separates the Outer Ear Canal from the Middle Ear. Sound waves reaching the Ear Drum cause minute movements of the Ossicles, which transmit impulses to the brain where they are interpreted as sounds. The organs of the Inner Ear are responsible for balance. The Middle Ear Cavity is connected to the throat by the Eustachian Tube.

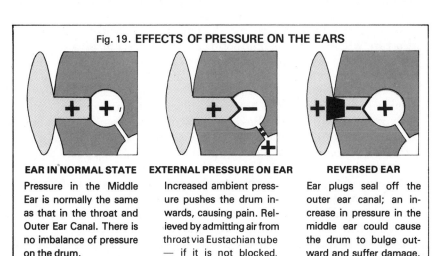

Fig. 19. EFFECTS OF PRESSURE ON THE EARS

EAR IN NORMAL STATE

Pressure in the Middle Ear is normally the same as that in the throat and Outer Ear Canal. There is no imbalance of pressure on the drum.

EXTERNAL PRESSURE ON EAR

Increased ambient pressure pushes the drum inwards, causing pain. Relieved by admitting air from throat via Eustachian tube — if it is not blocked.

REVERSED EAR

Ear plugs seal off the outer ear canal; an increase in pressure in the middle ear could cause the drum to bulge outward and suffer damage.

behind the root of the nose. The mastoid bone, which is the hard protruberance behind the ear-lobe, also contains a number of small air spaces which connect with each other and with the middle ear air space.

The Effects of Pressure

The outer ear is normally in easy communication with the atmosphere via the external auditory canal, and therefore pressure in it will remain equal to that of the surroundings. If the canal should be blocked with wax this must be removed (under medical supervision only) and no ear-plugs or anything that may obstruct the outer ear should ever be worn while diving.

The middle ear is an air-filled space and will therefore be affected by pressure changes. On first descent into water the increasing pressure will be transmitted throughout the outer ear to the eardrum which will tend to be pushed inwards towards the middle ear. To counter-balance this, air at the increased pressure must be admitted to the middle ear via the Eustachian tube. As shown in Fig. 18 the Eustachian tube opening into the naso-pharynx is normally closed so that air cannot pass up to the middle ear unless some positive action is taken to open the tube. This is a knack which is easy for some people but which requires much practice by others and is commonly brought about by swallowing, or by the *Valsalva manoeuvre* (holding the nose, shutting the mouth, and gradually increasing the air pressure within the naso-pharynx by forced expiration). When the Eustachian tube has been opened, air will rush into the middle ear and the ears will be felt to 'pop', this process being called *clearing the ears*. Fig. 19 illustrates the pressure changes during this 'ear-clearing' sequence.

When pressure is increasing, the ears must be repeatedly cleared at a rate which will depend upon the rate of descent into the water and the actual depth. If clearing is not carried out, the difference in pressure across the ear drum will cause it to stretch and ache, and will eventually burst the drum. (Cases have been recorded where the pressure at a depth of 3 m has been sufficient to burst an ear drum.)

Experience will soon tell a diver how often to clear his ears but it is important to clear them before descending to a depth at which pain occurs: pain is a danger signal and signifies that some damage has already been caused. If pain does occur the diver must ascend until the pain is relieved, and then must clear his ears. Descent can then be continued, the diver clearing more frequently than on his first attempt. If the diver is unable to 'clear' ears, or if pain returns on the continued descent, the dive must be abandoned.

During an ascent, the decrease in water pressure will cause the air in the middle ear to expand and, if the pressure is not relieved,

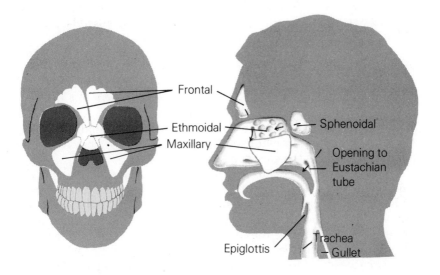

Fig. 20. FRONT AND SIDE VIEWS OF THE SINUSES

the ear drum could again be burst. The anatomy of the Eustachian tube is such that its connection at the middle ear is permanently open and so air has no difficulty in passing down the tube and equalising pressure. This act is helped by swallowing but will occur passively. The Valsalva manoeuvre should not be performed during the ascent as this will hinder ear clearing.

The inner ear contains no air space and is therefore not directly affected by pressure changes.

The sinus ducts are tubes which run in bone and are always open in health and thus no positive action is required to clear the sinuses. The diver usually has no sensation of the passage of air into or out of the sinuses.

The Effects of Disease

The Eustachian tubes and sinus ducts are all lined with living membranes. When any cells are subjected to disease or irritation they become inflamed and swollen, hence the membranes of a person suffering from a cold or hay-fever will become swollen. The degree of swelling is often sufficient to block the sinus ducts completely and to make it impossible to open the Eustachian tubes, hence giving rise to the 'blocked-up' feeling and headaches that are common in the early stages of a cold.

No person should ever attempt to dive when they cannot clear their ears easily as even a shallow dive with blocked ears or sinuses can cause severe pain, rupture of the ear-drum and possible vertigo, and even loss of consciousness.

The anatomy of the Eustachian tube (described above) is responsible for the fact that 99.9% of all cases of blocked ears give trouble on the descent, with increasing pressure. Most cases of sinus pain (67%) also occur on descent; 33% of cases who have got to depth without trouble have pain on the ascent. A quick 'trial dip' is therefore no sure guarantee of fitness to dive after a cold, especially if the diver has had previous sinus trouble, but in most cases the sinuses will clear if the ears can be cleared.

A blocked sinus duct causes pain and often local tenderness of the bone over a sinus. If a duct blocks during the ascent the diver should, if his air supply and decompression time allow, descend again until the pain goes, and then re-ascend more slowly. If the diver must continue to the surface, the air in his sinus will continue to try to expand, causing further pain and an increasing force which will usually succeed in blowing the obstruction out of the duct. This will immediately allow the pressures to equalise and will ease the pain, but usually the diver will find blood-stained fluid coming out of his nose; any such occurrence should be followed by a lay-off from diving until sinus symptoms have disappeared.

Tablets, nose drops or sprays to aid clearing of ears or sinuses during open-sea dives should not be used, except under medical advice —firstly because the effect of the drug may wear off during the time at depth and the diver may have trouble on the ascent and, secondly, some such drugs have side-effects and may cause drowsiness. The appearance of side-effects varies markedly between individuals and from day to day in the same individual and can never be predicted.

The outer ear may become infected causing soreness and a fluid discharge from the external auditory canal, in which case diving should not be undertaken until medical advice has been sought. This infected condition is commonly brought about by not drying the ears properly after a dive, with the result that the lining of the canal becomes saturated and 'soggy' and loses its natural protective qualities. It is not advisable to push anything into the canal deeper than a finger will normally reach, but all excess moisture must be shaken out as soon as possible after leaving the water.

Vertigo and Disorientation

Vertigo and disorientation are the names for the conditions in which the world appears to be spinning around and all sense of position or direction is lost. These symptons are brought about by a disturbance of the semi-circular canals of the inner ear.

If the ears have become partially blocked, the sudden large pressure change on clearing can cause vertigo which, although usually momentary, can be very disturbing. Sudden temperature changes in the ear can give the same effect and this can happen at any time during a dive when cold water gets to the ear-drum. The same condition might occur if the ear drum should rupture, allowing cold water to enter the middle ear. However, the water will be rapidly warmed by body heat and the vertigo will usually disappear in 30–60 seconds. Following a rupture of the ear drum, there is a risk of middle ear infection.

Cases have also been reported of vertigo occurring some time after a dive. The probable cause is a slightly 'sticky ear' which has prevented one or both middle ear cavities from equalising with sea-level pressure. When the pressures do equalise, momentary discomfort and vertigo may occur which could be distracting and possibly dangerous if, for example, it happened while driving. It is important, therefore, to ensure that the ears have been properly cleared after surfacing.

There are other causes of vertigo and disorientation and the advice of an experienced diver or of a doctor should be sought if it occurs.

Burst Lung

There is no medical mystique about the basic cause of burst lung. Burst lung is always caused by a relative excess of air pressure within the lungs. A relative excess of air pressure in the lungs can be brought about if the pressure in the lungs remains constant when the surrounding pressure falls. This is the situation that would arise if air at 'bottom pressure' was retained in a divers' lungs during his ascent.

The mechanics of burst lung are simple. If the pressure of air within the lungs is allowed to become greater than the surrounding pressure, it will cause the lungs to distend and stretch to their limit of elasticity. Once this point is reached any further increase in relative pressure within the lungs will build up sufficient force to burst the lung and allow the air to spill out (Fig. 21). *Pulmonary Barotrauma* (Pulmonary—of the lungs, Barotrauma—pressure damage) is the medical name given to this condition. When the point of maximum stretch has been reached—this point is beyond that which can be achieved by a normal maximum inhalation—the additional pressure the lung can tolerate unaided is equivalent to the pressure of about 1.5 m of water. It follows, therefore, that burst lung is always a risk when compressed-air breathing apparatus is used underwater at almost any depth.

Situations in which burst lung is a risk occur frequently in sports diving; the diver must be aware of these situations and familiar with the procedures necessary to reduce the risk to a minimum.

A diver coming up from depth in a controlled manner and breathing naturally from his aqualung is not usually troubled by air at 'bottom pressure' being retained in his lungs while his surrounding pressure is decreasing; normally there is plenty of time and opportunity for the expanding 'bottom pressure' air to escape with exhaled air during the diver's natural breathing cycle. If, however, the diver was suffering from a lung disorder that resulted in 'bottom pressure' air being entrapped in a small diseased section of the lung, then even a normal ascent would present an unacceptable risk—in spite of the fact that the major part of his lungs could vent unhindered. This is one of the reasons why a diver should keep in good physical condition, undergo regular medical checks with chest X-ray, and avoid diving when suffering from any temporary respiratory infection such as a cold or bronchitis.

A burst lung can happen to anyone ascending more than a few metres, irrespective of the maximum depth and duration of the dive, but when making a normal ascent at 15 m/min the risk, given healthy lungs, is very small indeed. Of course, any increase in the rate of ascent or enforced variation to the natural breathing rhythm during ascent increases the risk of burst lung.

All emergency ascent procedures (see chapter 6) expose the diver to a more-rapid-than-normal decrease in surrounding pressure or to an alteration of his breathing rhythm, or both. If, before discarding his aqualung to make a solo emergency free ascent, a diver fills his lungs with air from the breathing apparatus, he must consciously and continuously exhale during the ascent. He must exhale to allow the 'bottom pressure' air expanding in his lungs to escape. If the diver makes the ascent at a constant speed he will need to allow for the fact that the air in his lungs will expand at a greater rate as he nears the surface, and will therefore need to be forcibly exhaled at a greater rate to avoid a pressure build-up.

Theoretically, if an emergency ascent were made from a depth of 30 m and the diver forcibly exhaled to the fullest extent possible before commencing the ascent, and then held his breath, the residual 'bottom pressure' air left in his lungs would only be sufficient to fill his lungs completely when the surrounding pressure was reduced to surface pressure. Under these circumstances any over-distention of the lungs would be impossible. As a technique this would only be valid for depths of up to 30 m and even then would leave the diver with a strong desire to breathe and a general feeling of discomfort during the ascent. It also imposes upon the diver the additional burden of assessing his depth accurately in relation to the 30 m limit, an assessment he may not be able to give the necessary attention to in an emergency situation. If he should misjudge the depth and attempt to use this technique from a depth greater than 30 m, then the chances of his being aware that his lungs are 'full to bursting' during the latter stages of the ascent are small. This is because the 'full to bursting' signal (known as the *Hering–Breuer reflex*) is very weak in man.

Faced with an emergency ascent, the diver must remember that as the pressure surrounding him is reducing during the ascent, the air in his lungs will expand and must be allowed to escape. This can be comfortably accomplished if he purses his lips in a 'whistling position' and consciously and continuously blows out, increasing the exhalation as the surface is neared. If the expanding 'bottom pressure' air is vented off in this manner no discomfort will be felt during the ascent; since the expanding air being 'whistled' away carries with it any excess carbon dioxide produced in the lungs, there will be no desire to breathe in.

A complete understanding of the technique and, through this understanding, personal confidence in the ability to carry it out, are the most important factors in achieving a relaxed, comfortable, safe emergency ascent without breathing apparatus, should the situation ever arise.

An assisted ascent, during which two divers ascend sharing one breathing apparatus, need not expose the divers to a much greater risk of burst lung than does a normal ascent, provided the assisted ascent is made at the normal rate (15 m/min), and that the divers are competent and sufficiently relaxed to be able to establish a shared breathing rhythm close to their natural rhythm.

Even so, in the special circumstances of an assisted ascent there is a tendency for each diver to take deeper than normal breaths before handing the mouthpiece to his partner. Because of this deeper cycle and, because the ascent is continuing and the surrounding pressure falling during this delay, the air in the lungs will expand and should be consciously vented-off between mouthpiece exchanges to reduce the risk of a dangerous pressure build-up.

The snorkeller who attempts to prolong his dive by taking a breath from the aqualung of a diver under water puts himself at the same risk as a diver making a solo emergency ascent. This risk is *not* acceptable under normal conditions and the practice should be avoided.

By the same token, a diver in a swimming pool breathing from under-water breathing apparatus at a depth of more than a few metres is not exempt from the dangers of burst lung. If a trainee, having swum down to a breathing set on the pool attempted to fit his equipment, but failed, after taking one good breath from it, then decided to surface for a repeat attempt, he could be starting the ascent with his lungs already expanded beyond the normal maximum. This would be the case if at the time he took the breath the demand valve diaphragm was at a greater depth than his lungs. If the pool was a deep one and the trainee did not exhale on the ascent, the risk of burst lung would increase from the possible to the probable.

To reduce the risk of burst lung when a diver ascends with 'bottom pressure' air in his lungs the rule is always the same, whether the ascent is made in the swimming pool or in open water: the *'bottom pressure' air in the lungs must be allowed to expand and escape during the ascent.* This venting, which occurs naturally with the breathing cycle during a normal ascent, will have to be made by the conscious effort of the diver 'whistling' air out continuously during the ascent. The symptons of a burst lung differ according to what has happened to the air that has burst through the lung tissues.

SIGNS AND SYMPTOMS OF BURST LUNG

Air Embolism is a condition that arises if air from the ruptured lung finds its way into the blood circulatory system. Bubbles of air

Fig.21. **BURST LUNG**

AIR EMBOLISM

Excessive stretching of the alveolar membrane can allow minute bubbles of air to enter the capillaries and thus the bloodstream. The circulation would carry these bubbles — which unite into larger bubbles — to the brain, heart and other vital organs where they could lodge, blocking further blood flow and thus oxygen supply. All manner of neurological disorders will follow, and in severe cases, death can occur within seconds.

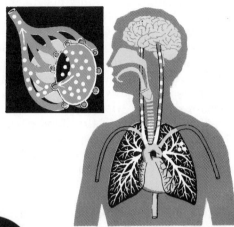

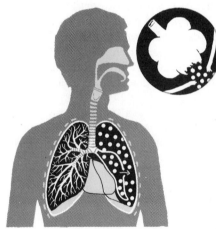

SPONTANEOUS PNEUMOTHORAX

In some cases, the alveolar tissue may suffer a major tear, allowing considerable quantities of air to escape outwards and become trapped between the lung sac and chest wall. As the ascent continues, the pressure of the trapped air will be greater than that of the air in the lungs, and this will cause the lung sacs to collapse. The lung will then be unable to perform its function, and the subject will be starved of oxygen.

INTERSTITIAL EMPHYSEMA

On the other hand, the air may escape inwards and become trapped among the tissues and organs between and above the lungs. It can apply abnormal pressures on airways, blood vessels, heart and lung sacs, with consequent difficulties.

Lung tissue will normally stretch before it tears, and therefore it should be remembered that air embolism may also be present in cases of Pneumothorax and Emphysema.

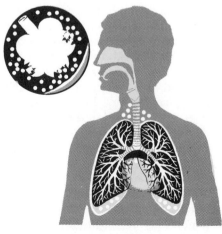

(*emboli*) form in the bloodstream and where they become lodged, prevent further supplies of blood, and therefore essential oxygen, from being carried to any dependent tissues beyond that point.

If the blood supply to the heart muscle is blocked the result can be a heart attack. If the blood supply to the brain is impaired, dramatic symptoms may develop quickly: the diver may lose consciousness upon reaching the surface, or shortly afterwards, and suffer irreversible brain tissue damage and subsequent death unless compressed (usually 6 bar absolute) in a recompression chamber within seconds—within minutes will be too late.

Almost any part of the blood circulation can be affected by an air embolism and, in consequence, any of the body systems or functions which rely upon an unrestricted blood supply can undergo partial or complete failure. The range of symptoms presented is wide, including giddiness (vertigo), patches of numbness, partial paralysis and defects in speech or vision. So wide is the range of possible symptoms that *any abnormal behaviour by a diver upon, or shortly after, surfacing—particularly if he has just completed an emergency ascent—must be taken as the symptom of an embolism.* Even in the case of the less dramatic symptoms it may prove necessary to commence treatment by means of recompression in a recompression chamber within a matter of seconds if permanent disablement or death is to be avoided.

Spontaneous Pneumothorax is a condition that arises if air bursts through the lung lining and collects between the lungs and the chest wall (pleural cavity). If this occurs when the diver is at depth the entrapped air expanding during the ascent may collapse the lung. The symptoms present in the surfaced diver may be: shortness of breath; a cough, perhaps with a small amount of blood from mouth or nose; or he may complain of a pain in the chest. In severe cases extensive collapse of the lungs, perhaps aggravated by the physical displacement and consequent embarrassment of the heart, can cause death. Treatment by a doctor using a hollow needle (*cannula*) and syringe may be needed to withdraw the entrapped air although small quantities of air can be left to reabsorb naturally. (Note: the entrapped air is often under negative pressure and without a syringe more may enter.) Further hospital treatment will be necessary to deal with the collapsed lung. Symptoms may only become apparent during therapeutic decompression of a suspected case of air embolism or serious decompression sickness (*bends*).

Interstitial Emphysema is a condition that arises if air from the ruptured lung gets into the mass of tissues within the chest cavity. Air may spread under the skin at the base of the neck giving a crackling effect (*crepitation*) if the skin is touched. Symptoms, which may be slight, can include shortness of breath and difficulty in swallowing due to pressure on the trachea, blood vessels and oesophagus and, as with the symptoms of pneumothorax, may only become apparent during the therapeutic decompression of a suspected case of air embolism or serious decompression sickness (bends). Recompression in a chamber may be necessary, but the difficulty of removing the air by surgical means coupled with the slow natural absorption and dispersal rate from these tissues may make the therapeutic decompression a slow procedure.

Treatment of Burst Lung

A diver showing any symptoms of burst lung must undergo immediate compression in a recompression chamber. Although subsequently it may become apparent that the condition did not need recompression, the fact that symptoms of burst lung were present meant that lung tissues had been ruptured and that air might have been present in the bloodstream—making seconds vital. Medical advice should also be sought in those cases where pneumothorax or emphysema are suspected in the absence of embolism, even if treatment does not appear to be necessary.

When the diver has been compressed in a recompression chamber to a depth at which all symptoms are relieved, or to a maximum of 6 atmospheres absolute, expert medical advice can be sought to identify the exact problem. If the original diagnosis of burst lung is proved to be wrong, no harm has been done and the diver can be brought back to surface pressure on a regular repeat dive decompression schedule. If the diagnosis was correct, or if the symptoms proved to be those of serious decompression sickness, prompt recompression could well have saved a life.

If no recompression facilities are available and a diver has surfaced showing symptoms of burst lung, the situation is grave. Recompression by sending the diver down again in the water is not recommended. The effects of cold and the limits imposed by the equipment usually used by the sports diver make the procedure impracticable, apart from any other medical considerations. The only answer is recompression in a recompression chamber and all effort should be directed towards this end.

During the delay in getting specialist medical advice or the diver to a recompression chamber he should be positioned comfortably, resting on his left side with the head slightly lower than the feet— in the hope that any free air bubbles in the blood will tend to rise away from the heart and brain. Oxygen may be beneficial if there is respiratory distress or irregularities in the blood circulatory system.

Practising emergency free ascents as part of the normal diving training for a sports diver is not permitted within the BSAC. The dilemma to be resolved is whether more divers would be lost practising the correct emergency free ascent procedure than by using the established but unpractised procedure when the actual emergencies arise. Current medical opinion opposes such practice unless recompression facilities and qualified medical assistance are immediately available at the surface, and for this reason, BSAC is not willing to allow its members to practise emergency free ascent.

Decompression

Definition
Decompression means a reduction in ambient pressure, such as that which occurs when a diver ascends from depth.

Gaseous Exchange in the Body
The lungs may be regarded as two elastic bags containing air passages communicating with millions of tiny distensible air sacs. Air enters the lungs due to chest expansion and eventually reaches air sacs (*alveoli*). Each of these consists of an extremely thin transparent membrane and this is surrounded by a network of very small blood vessels (*capillaries*). This capillary bed of the lungs is responsible for supplying fresh arterial blood to the tissues of the body.

It is very necessary to appreciate the remarkable efficiency of the lungs in promoting rapid exchange of gas between the surrounding air and the capillary bed. If the whole of the area of the lining of the alveoli and capillary bed were to be spread out flat on the ground it would cover an area about 10 m by 10 m, or 50 times the surface area of the skin. This enormous area with air on one side and blood on the other separated by a very thin membrane is capable of promoting very rapid exchange of gases between the blood and the air. In fact, only fractions of a second are necessary to alter the gas composition of the blood leaving the lungs when the gas composition of the alveoli is changed. From the diver's standpoint this is a crucial factor as it means that the moment descent into the sea commences and he starts breathing compressed air, then the body is being supplied by blood from his lungs with a full quota of air dissolved in it. There is very little delay in transmitting the effects of a gas change to the arterial blood supply. Similarly, on decompressing the diver, there is almost no delay in losing excess gas dissolved in the blood passing through the lungs.

When the blood leaves the lungs it flows through the heart and is pumped out via the main arteries to all parts of the body. The pulsation of these thick elastic-walled pipes can be felt where they near the body surface. The arteries diminish in diameter as they approach a particular area of the body to which they are bringing fresh blood. Eventually they become very thin-walled tubes with non-elastic walls and their diameter has been reduced to the order of 1/100 of a millimetre. These very thin-walled vessels are blood capillaries, and across their walls the exchange of gases takes place.

The fresh arterial blood changes its composition and acquires the tissue waste products and becomes venous blood, i.e. O_2 depleted and CO_2 rich. After passage through the capillary bed nearly all the arterial driving pressure is lost and the blood is collected into the veins and returned to the heart where it is pumped through the lungs, and the cycle commences again.

From this outline picture of the circulation it is necessary to emphasise several points of importance to the diver and to his safe decompression. Firstly, all tissues are supplied directly by arterial blood, which has come straight from the lungs, via the heart. Secondly, the number of capillaries in a tissue varies very considerably with the type and activity of the tissue. Taking muscle as an example, it has been established that a resting muscle has 200 capillaries open per square millimetre but that an active muscle has as many as 2500 capillaries open per square millimetre. The tissues depend upon the density of the capillary network for their nutriment, and active tissues such as the brain, the kidneys, and the heart, have very dense supplies, whereas tissues such as cartilage, tendon and fat, are only poorly supplied. Thirdly, as with the lungs, it must be noted that the passage of blood through a capillary takes the order of one second, but that the time for the complete exchange of the dissolved gases between the blood and tissues takes only fractions of a second. Thus, one of the principal factors determining the amount of dissolved gas delivered to a tissue is the rate of blood-flow through the tissue and this is dependent upon the number of open capillaries. If a tissue with a poor blood supply is adjacent to one with a very good blood supply, then some exchange will occur between the two. Thus, the circulation of the blood is not the sole factor determining the distribution of dissolved gases—the location of the tissue is also important.

The Causes of Decompression Sickness
If a diver descends to 30 m under the sea he commences breathing air at this very increased pressure. Almost immediately blood with a full quota of dissolved gas in it is pumped from the lungs to the tissues of the body. These various tissues all have different numbers of open capillaries and, therefore, they all saturate with dissolved gas at different rates. Those with a good blood supply saturate rapidly, and those with a poor blood supply saturate slowly. If, after a few minutes at 30 m, it was possible to examine the gas content of the tissues of the diver's body it would be found that such parts as the kidney, heart, and lungs had a very large amount of gas dissolved in them, whereas cartilage, tendon, and other such tissues had a comparatively small amount of gas. Now, allow the diver to stay at 30 m for a further hour and imagine re-examining the state of his tissues.

All those organs with a good blood supply, the kidney, heart, etc., would have the same dissolved gas content as on the previous analysis performed after only a few minutes, but those that are poorly supplied with blood would have gained an appreciable amount. Eventually, after many hours of exposure, all tissues would reach a new level of gas saturation.

Tissues which absorb gas slowly also release it slowly, and if our diver returned to the surface after a long stay at depth, the reverse situation would apply. Gas at high pressure would remain in the 'slow' tissues and, as experiment has clearly shown, if the drop in pressure exceeded the ratio of 2:1, the gas would form bubbles within the tissues. In severe cases, bubbles might also form in the bloodstream. It is the presence of such bubbles of gas within the body tissues that gives rise to the varied physical and neurological disorders known as *Decompression Sickness* or *'Diver's Bends'*.

Once it had been realised that the nitrogen content of the air was the main cause of the bubbles seen during severe attacks of decompression sickness, it became of importance to discover the speed with which nitrogen entered and left the body. This problem was approached in two ways. Firstly, nitrogen gas elimination from the body was measured in the following manner. A man at atmospheric pressure was fitted with an oxygen-breathing apparatus. As he breathed pure oxygen from his apparatus his exhaled breath contained nitrogen gas which was being washed out of his body. The nitrogen had been acquired through previous living at one atmosphere pressure in ordinary air comprising 79% N_2, 21% O_2. Measurements, at convenient intervals, were made of the nitrogen content of the exhaled breath. In this way the speed of removal of nitrogen from the body was obtained (Fig. 22). Secondly, nitrogen uptake was estimated by actually decompressing men and plotting a graph showing their sensitivity to the adverse effects of too rapid a drop in pressure. This was carried out as follows. For example, a dive duration of 25 minutes was chosen. Divers were then rapidly compressed in air to, say, 24 m and kept there, working hard, for the agreed period of 25 minutes after which they were rapidly decompressed at 18 m per minute back to the surface (atmospheric pressure). When this proved to be a perfectly safe procedure for a group of healthy young men, the pressure was raised the next time they tried this 25 minute dive. So they all now performed a dive of 25 minutes at 27 m with no stops on the way back to atmospheric pressure. Again this proved to be safe. The next dive was 25 minutes at 30 m which gave marginal trouble in a small percentage of men, i.e. mild transient disorders. This was an indication that after 25 minutes at 30 m most normal men had acquired just sufficient nitrogen to be tolerated on immediate return to atmospheric pressure. Having established this point, another time was chosen, say 60 minutes. Here it was found that most normal men would tolerate this exposure at a depth of 18 m before coming close to trouble. Thus, it is now possible to say that 60 minutes at 18 m also gives just sufficient nitrogen to permit rapid safe return to atmospheric pressure. A curve can be constructed showing the various pressures one can go to safely and how long one can stay there without causing any decompression problem. This is called the 'NO-STOP' curve (Fig. 22). The shape and time-course of this curve and the nitrogen elimination curve can be shown to be identical within the experimental limits. Thus, there is obtained data showing the connection between the rate of uptake of gas by the body and the decompression performance. All the main facts are now available for calculating a decompression procedure.

Further similar experiments in recompression chambers indicated that, for exposures beyond the No-Stop curve, a return to the surface in a series of controlled steps—*stage decompression*—avoided the unpleasant physiological problems which would have occurred during an immediate return to the surface. In this way, Decompression Tables were produced.

Divers employ Decompression Tables during the ascent from a dive which has taken them beyond the No-Stop curve in order to avoid the problems of decompression sickness or 'diver's bends'.

It is at this point that a digression must be made to assess the position regarding the various Decompression Tables available throughout the world. Suppose a diver wishes to go to 30 m and stay at this depth for the maximum length of time which just allows him to return to the surface without decompression, he will see the following different international calculations. The RNPL/BSAC Air Diving Table (Appendix 1) will allow a 20 minute dive, the United States Navy will allow 25 minutes and some Italian tables will allow 30 minutes. The diver may then decide to use that routine which allows him to stay 30 minutes and apparently surface in safety. Why not? The answer is fivefold. Firstly, it very much depends where the constructor of a decompression schedule sets his safety limits; secondly, what sort of men he has used to obtain his basic data; thirdly, the sort of work they performed whilst at depth; fourthly, the water conditions (temperature, etc.) and, finally, the way the decompression procedure was performed.

It can be seen that the RNPL/BSAC Air Diving Table is the most conservative, and for hard under-water work in northern waters is undoubtedly the best proposition. Even so, a word of warning is necessary. If the diver is in a position to do dives beyond the limiting

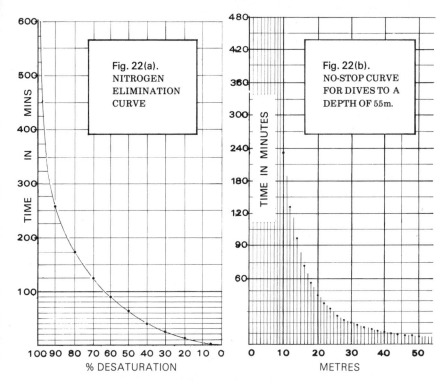

Fig. 22(a).
NITROGEN
ELIMINATION
CURVE

% DESATURATION

Fig. 22(b).
NO-STOP CURVE
FOR DIVES TO A
DEPTH OF 55m.

METRES

line of the table he risks mild decompression sickness.

Repetitive dives are a difficult problem. The number of possible combinations available concerning depth and time of the first dive, the time interval on the surface, and the depth and time of the second dive, is enormous. Therefore, the rules adopted must err on the safe side, giving too much decompression rather than insufficient. For several hours after his first dive, a diver will be releasing from his tissues the dissolved gas acquired during his exposure to pressure. If he wants to dive again soon after the first dive (within 6 hours if the first dive did not exceed 40 m: within 16 hours if it did), there is residual gas in his body tissues which will be added to the gas he acquires on his second dive. This means that the second dive must have a decompression which takes this into account. Traditionally the rule was to add together the duration of both dives, and to decompress for a dive of this combined duration at the maximum depth achieved. Clearly this technique was over-safe and the RNPL/BSAC Table includes a very simple, easy to apply system of surface interval credits. These permit double dives to be made without the penalty of excessive decompression. This system is valid for TWO dives only; if a third, or fourth dive is to be made to a depth greater than 9 m, then the older rule of 'combined times at maximum depth' should be used.

Manifestations of Decompression Sickness

THE BENDS

This is by far the most common form of decompression sickness. 'The bends' are *pains in or around a joint* or sometimes deep within a muscle. They are *most commonly felt around knee or shoulder joints* and can vary in intensity from *excruciating pain to transient mild aches* which have been given the name of 'niggles'. Bends very rarely attack a diver immediately he has finished his dive. There is a delay period of anything between a few minutes to several hours after the dive before any pains begin. A delay of 20 to 60 minutes accounts for the great majority of the bends. Many of the aches and pains of low intensity, i.e. niggles, are tolerated and ignored by most divers. In fact it is quite possible for the amateur to confuse niggles with the muscle aches and pains which may follow hard physical effort by a man not in training. There is, however, no possibility of ignoring a severe attack of the bends. Immediate recompression is the only effective form of treatment.

ITCHES, RASHES AND PRESSURE BRUISING

In addition to the bends described above, there are certain after effects of excursions to depth which are collectively referred to as 'skin bends'. These are *itches*, which can be mildly itchy to intensely irritating for up to an hour or so: *rashes which can appear on almost any part of the body*; and pressure-bruising and *skin mottling* which have the appearance, to the untrained eye, of ordinary bruising. All these effects are usually self-correcting without recompression but should be regarded as warning signs of a more serious manifestation.

CARDIO-VASCULAR AND CENTRAL NERVOUS SYSTEM
INVOLVEMENT

Shortly after a dive, or sometimes during decompression, the diver may find *acute difficulty in breathing*, accompanied by a *tight feeling across the chest*. This is called the 'chokes' and the name is very descriptive. It is an extremely serious form of decompression sickness that is seldom seen nowadays except as a result of a diving accident or a gross mismanagement of a decompression. Immediate treatment is imperative or death rapidly ensures. The chokes are *caused by bubbles appearing in the blood in large numbers*. They block the circulation to the lungs, preventing effective breathing, and they accumulate in the heart as a froth with the result that the heart cannot pump correctly.

Also very serious but fortunately fairly rare are cases where divers surface and then shortly afterwards begin to complain of *weakness in their limbs*, particularly the legs, and then find they *cannot move the affected limbs.* There is generally no pain with this form of de-compression sickness, but the diver is obviously a very sick man judging by his *pallor and the shocked appearance* that accompanies his *limb paralysis.* Here again, as with the chokes, immediate recompression is the effective answer. To delay treatment is to risk permanent damage to the central nervous system which will leave permanent after-effects. There are sometimes *other forms of central nervous system involvement* such as *'tunnel' vision,* the *loss of certain nerve reflexes, partial temporary blindness,* and indefinable *'woolly' or 'fluffy' feelings in limbs.* In all these cases there is no pain present normally, but the man does not feel right in himself and he usually *looks pale and shocked.* Recompression as soon as possible is essential to avoid the risk of permanent after-effects.

It must be emphasised that the chokes and central nervous system decompression sickness are only seen after gross departures from normal diving practice, but a word of caution is necessary: diving accidents do occur in the best regulated circumstances, as when someone gets fouled up at depth or attacked by a sea creature. In these emergency situations, it is as well to know the risks involved in the various alternative procedures that may present themselves.

AIR EMBOLISM

This is the condition in which *air bubbles reach the circulation* via some direct mechanical rupture in the lungs. Holding one's breath at, say, 30 m (4 bars absolute) and then rising towards the surface with the breath still held back will cause expansion of the gas contained in the lungs. Ascent to 10 m (2 bars absolute) would double the air volume. If there are not sufficient empty lung alveoli to take up this extra gas then pressure will be brought to bear on the delicate *lung lining which will easily tear and rupture.* This gas now finds its way into *blood vessels and it often tracks between the lungs inside the chest cavity* (see *Burst Lung*).

Note that air embolism can occur during ANY ascent diving ANY dive, and not only after dives which exceed the No-Stop times.

BONE NECROSIS

A long-term condition which, it is generally assumed, is caused by the blockage of the nutrient vessels of the bones by bubbles formed during decompression, and can result in a weakening in the mechanical strength of the affected bone. This is unlikely to cause any real trouble to a person unless the affected area is in a bone joint when collapse of the surface may occur. Bone necrosis hardly ever occurs in sports divers and has been noticed mainly amongst caisson and tunnel workers who work under pressure of compressed air for many hours a day, five days a week.

Treatment of Decompression Sickness

The only effective treatment is to submit the subject to pressure once again in the hope that the offending bubbles will be reduced in size, thereby relieving the symptoms. The diver is then slowly decompressed in accordance with special tables. During this controlled decompression process, which can take many hours, the excess nitrogen in the diver's body has plenty of time to be safely released.

Treatment can only be safely applied in a recompression chamber as medical attention is frequently needed as part of the treatment. In-water therapy is out of the question.

In the UK, HMS *Vernon* serves as a 'clearing house' for those in need of recompression treatment (see *Appendix 2*).

Practical Decompression

Controlled stage decompression should be carried out in accordance with Decompression Tables by any diver returning to the surface after a dive which has taken him beyond the safe limits of the No-Stop curve, i.e. beyond No-Stop times.

Nitrogen absorption commences at the moment the diver begins his descent: nitrogen release commences when he starts his ascent. Thus, for the purposes of safe decompression, *the time base upon which both the tables and all calculations should be made is the time between leaving the surface and the start of the ascent* (this period is known on the tables as *Bottom Time*) and NOT just the time spent at maximum depth. Once begun, the ascent should not be unduly delayed and should ideally be made at the rate of 15 m per minute. This rate of ascent itself represents a safe decompression.

It is possible to plot a dive in graphical terms. Fig. 23 illustrates this, and is known as a Dive Profile. When the Bottom Time of a dive exceeds the No-Stop limit for the maximum depth reached, decompression stops must be made during the return to the surface. During these stops, the excess nitrogen in the tissues is being released.

It is important that Bottom Time is accurately recorded. The bezel of a diver's watch permits the diver to 'mark' the start of his dive, and to monitor his elapsed Bottom Time during the dive. Ideally, dives should be made within the No-Stop limits. Decompression stops require both careful planning and control and are best carried out deliberately, and not as an unexpected necessity at the end of an ill-planned dive. Divers are advised to carry a waterproof Decompression Table or calculator so that, in the event of an unplanned stop being necessary, they can at least do it properly. Use of an under-water writing slate permits the accurate recording of time in: time of leaving the bottom (and thus, by difference Bottom Time); and surface interval between dives, etc., so that

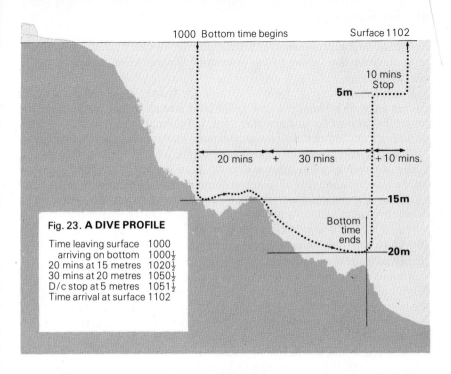

1000 Bottom time begins   Surface 1102

10 mins
Stop
5m —

20 mins   +   30 mins   :+ 10 mins.

Fig. 23. A DIVE PROFILE

15m

Bottom
time
ends

20m

Time leaving surface   1000
arriving on bottom $1000\frac{1}{2}$
20 mins at 15 metres $1020\frac{1}{2}$
30 mins at 20 metres $1050\frac{1}{2}$
D/c stop at 5 metres $1051\frac{1}{2}$
Time arrival at surface   1102

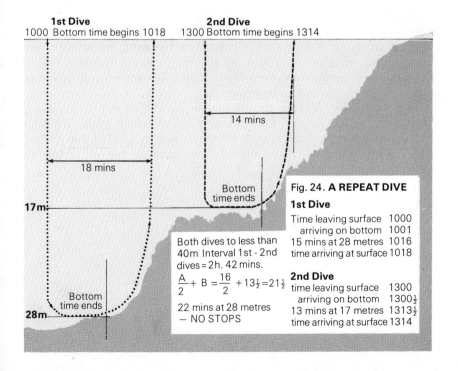

1st Dive   **2nd Dive**
1000 Bottom time begins 1018   1300 Bottom time begins 1314

14 mins

18 mins

17m

Bottom
time ends

28m

Bottom
time ends

Fig. 24. A REPEAT DIVE

1st Dive

Time leaving surface   1000
arriving on bottom   1001
15 mins at 28 metres   1016
time arriving at surface 1018

Both dives to less than
40m Interval 1st - 2nd
dives = 2h. 42 mins.

$$\frac{A}{2} + B = \frac{16}{2} + 13\frac{1}{2} = 21\frac{1}{2}$$

22 mins at 28 metres
— NO STOPS

2nd Dive
time leaving surface   1300
arriving on bottom $1300\frac{1}{2}$
13 mins at 17 metres $1313\frac{1}{2}$
time arriving at surface 1314

accurate decompression requirements can be calculated. Do not try to remember the tables or the essential times: make a note of it—it is safer.

Where stops have to be made, they are best carried out on a fixed datum such as a shot-line (q.v.), the boat's anchor line, or by holding on to the face of an underwater cliff. It is important that the correct level for the stop should be maintained. The time of each stop begins on leaving the previous one: for example, if a diver has to make a 5 minute stop at 10 m after a dive to 40 m, he will take 2 minutes to reach 10 m (ascent rate—15 m/min) and needs to spend only 3 minutes at 10 m. Stop times should not be skimped: when the effects of decompression sickness are considered, is it really worth it?

It is a sensible policy to 'take five' at 5 m after any dive for which the Bottom Time closely approaches the No-Stop limits, and certainly after repeat dives within No-Stop limits.

Repeat dives made after a short surface interval require particularly careful planning. It is so easy to go over the No-Stop limits during a second (or subsequent) dive. The Bottom Time of a second dive should perhaps be deliberately limited to avoid the risk, if stops cannot be carried out in safety (Fig. 24).

The RNPL/BSAC Table appears in Appendix 1 of this Manual, together with several worked examples of decompression calculations. Study these, and practice others so that you are totally familiar with the use of the table. Bear in mind that, if doubt exists over the exact depth or time, the next greater increment should be used. It may mean an extra stop, but at least it is 'fail safe'. Remember also that diving at altitude; flying after diving; and any ascent after surfacing from a dive can possibly bring on decompression sickness. This, too, is explained in Appendix 1.

Decompression Meters should not be used as a substitute for a watch and depth gauge. They are not calibrated to tables used by BSAC, and may be irregular in their performance. They have their uses as an indicator of the need to decompress, but adherence to tables is safer.

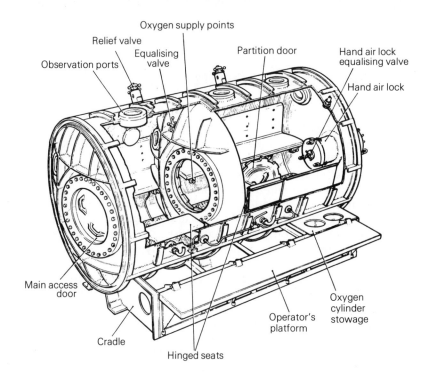

Oxygen supply points
Relief valve
Observation ports
Equalising valve
Partition door
Hand air lock equalising valve
Hand air lock
Main access door
Cradle
Hinged seats
Operator's platform
Oxygen cylinder stowage

Fig.25. GENERAL VIEW OF A RECOMPRESSION CHAMBER

Fig. 26.

INTERIOR OF A RECOMPRESSION CHAMBER

No time should be wasted undressing a diver in need of recompression, which can be done when inside the chamber. Note the Oxygen supply points near the diver's right shoulder.

Oxygen Poisoning

Oxygen is essential to our lives. We must have an adequate supply of oxygen in order to carry on living and there is absolutely no substitute for it. How, then, can oxygen, on which we depend so completely, ever be regarded as a poison? Perhaps the simplest answer is that you can have too much of a good thing.

This section is concerned with explaining how, when and where oxygen can be a poison to us. What is more important, it will show that so long as we use only compressed air in our aqualungs we will be completely free of any possibility of oxygen poisoning in all normal club diving.

Now, even though we will never really meet with oxygen poisoning (or oxygen toxicity, as it is often called), there are two good reasons why it is very important to be able to understand the problem. First, it will allow us to see for ourselves why the Club prohibits the use of oxygen or oxygen-enriched re-breathing equipment in conventional Club diving. Second, once we know how a very rich oxygen supply affects our bodies, we will understand several other important aspects of a diver breathing under water.

Types of Oxygen Poisoning
There are two basic types:
Acute and chronic
'Acute' means a short-term effect whilst 'Chronic' means a long-term effect.

Acute Oxygen Poisoning
This is the more relevant type to the diver because he would seldom —if ever—be exposed to a high enough oxygen partial pressure for a sufficiently long period to suffer from chronic oxygen poisoning.

The following is a list of possible symptoms of acute oxygen poisoning which may be experienced by a diver:
(a) Lip twitching and twitching of other facial muscles
(b) Dizziness (*vertigo*)
(c) Feeling sick (*nausea*)
(d) Unusual tiredness
(e) Disturbances of breathing, e.g. overbreathing (*hyperpnoea*), temporary stoppage (*apnoea*) or difficulty in breathing (*dyspnoea*)
(f) Unusual mental states, e.g. euphoria
(g) Disturbances of sight, e.g. 'tunnel vision'
(h) Unconsciousness and general convulsions similar to a major (*grand mal*) epileptic fit

By far the most dangerous symptoms to a diver are the unconscious-ness and convulsions, since such conditions could easily lead to his losing the mouthpiece and drowning. The other symptoms may or may not occur prior to the onset of convulsions, and experience shows that in the case of divers there is most often no warning whatsoever before convulsive seizure and unconsciousness inter-rupts their dive.

OXYGEN CONVULSIONS

A diver succumbing to oxygen convulsions would become uncon-scious and enter the 'tonic phase'. During this phase, which lasts some half to 2 minutes, the diver would arch backwards as all his voluntary muscles contracted simultaneously and completely, his body thus becoming quite rigid. Following immediately after the tonic phase would come the 'clonic phase' which is the familiar con-vulsive stage. This is when the diver would jerk violently and spasmodically perhaps for two to three minutes. As the clonic phase subsided the diver would pass into a relaxed, though exhausted and unconscious, stage called the 'post-convulsive depression'. Thus, three distinct phases are experienced by the unsuspecting diver:

(a) Tonic phase (rigid)
(b) Clonic phase (convulsive)
(c) Post-convulsive depression phase (relaxed)

Once the series is begun there is no means of stopping the natural progression through to the post-convulsive depression phase.

The next events could depend on what had happened to the diver during his preceding performance. First, if he had lost his mouth-piece he would most certainly have drowned without a chance of recovering consciousness.

Second, if he had retained his mouthpiece and continued oxygen-breathing at the same, or an even deeper depth, he would have undertaken an 'encore' or perhaps several 'encores', before death by oxygen poisoning brought down the final curtain. The diver's 'encores' would consist of clonic phases of increasing frequency interspersed by post-convulsive depression phases.

Third, if the diver was fortunate enough to be accompanied by a buddy diver who was able to bring him to the surface before he drowned, he would have a good chance of surviving. The rescuer should return the stricken diver to air breathing as soon as possible, and then support the unconscious diver on the surface until he was either picked up or the rescuer himself landed the subject. Once the stricken diver has been returned to air breathing he may or may not have another convulsion. In some cases, however, it has been observed that the return to air breathing or even reduction of the partial pressure of oxygen (for example, by ascending) has apparently induced worsening of symptoms and even precipitated convulsions but, nevertheless, this is an acceptable risk, since no alternative method of rescue or revival is obviously available to the buddy diver. The diver should slowly recover consciousness over 5 to 30 minutes after returning to air breathing, but he should not be regarded as having revived since he will be in an exhausted state, mentally confused and likely to become unconscious or fall asleep without warning.

No permanent neurological injury would be expected to have occurred as a direct cause of one or two convulsions. However, the violent muscular contractions which occur during the tonic and clonic phases are so complete (a condition which would never occur in normal life) that the forces exerted occasionally tear the muscle tissue itself, tear its tendons from their bond insertions or even break the very bones to which they are attached.

After such strenuous, though unconscious effort, it is no wonder that the body is so physically exhausted after a convulsion. In fact, there is often a strong desire to fall asleep if the diver had regained consciousness shortly after returning to air breathing. In other cases, the diver may pass from the unconscious depression phase straight into the sleeping phase. There is no harm in this and it is even beneficial so long as he can be kept warm and safe from further accidents.

When he regains consciousness he should be talked to calmly, reassuringly and in simple terms; warm clothing should be provided as soon as possible. He will not have any recollection of his previous experience (*amnesia*) from the time when he became unconscious, or perhaps even a little while before that.

One important item remains to be noted: the diver would be automatically holding his breath (*apnoeic*) during the tonic phase and consequently it would be hazardous to try and bring him to the surface during this brief period due to the danger of burst lung (pulmonary barotrauma). Even though it would be more difficult to surface a convulsing body rather than a rigid one it would be safer to await the onset of the clonic or convulsing phase before ascending. However, the tonic phase is rarely noticed under water and the buddy diver's attention will probably be first drawn by the convulsions, so it is unlikely that the necessity of waiting before surfacing will arise. It should not require emphasis here that great care would have to be exercised whilst in the proximity of a convulsing diver since his movements would be most violent and unpredictable.

WHEN MIGHT A DIVER SUFFER ACUTE OXYGEN POISONING?

Acute oxygen poisoning occurs when a particularly high concentration of oxygen appears in the blood and the brain. This is brought about by breathing a gas mixture with a particularly high partial pressure of oxygen. From many years' experience, the Royal Navy has established a maximum permissible partial pressure for oxygen in breathing gas for divers (1.75 bars absolute). Thus the depth to which a breathing gas may be used will depend on its concentration of oxygen. A high oxygen concentration will have a shallow limit as follows:

100% oxygen limited to 8 metres
60% oxygen limited to 21 metres
40% oxygen limited to 37 metres

It is interesting to note that for a mixture of 21% oxygen in nitrogen (that is air) the partial pressure of oxygen at 80 m is the same as in 100% oxygen at 8 m, so that the possibility of oxygen poisoning can be added to nitrogen narcosis as a barrier to diving deeper than 80 m with air.

Certain types of modern deep-diving breathing equipment automatically change the oxygen concentration in the breathing gas mixture as the diver varies his depth, thus maintaining a constant and safe partial pressure of oxygen.

Oxygen poisoning does not occur immediately the diver goes to depth; there is a delay or 'latent period' whilst the oxygen reaching the brain gradually builds up. Logically, the higher the partial pressure of oxygen (due to greater depth or richer gas mixture) then the shorter the latent period. It is unfortunate, however, that it is impossible to predict the latent period or even an individual diver's susceptibility to acute oxygen poisoning. This is because of the enormous variation which one finds in most physiological functions. Both susceptibility and latency vary widely from individual to individual and even in a single individual from day to day. Certain broad generalisations can, however, be made in some cases. For example, it is known that fatigue, stress, hard work, high carbon dioxide concentrations, cold water, 'hang-over' and poor physical condition increase susceptibility and reduce the latency to acute oxygen poisoning.

Chronic Oxygen Poisoning

This form of poisoning can be suffered at a lower partial pressure of oxygen than that which produces 'acute' oxygen poisoning, and the time taken to onset of symptoms is generally much longer. This particular type manifests itself initially as soreness of the upper respiratory tract. As the lungs themselves become further irritated by the high level of oxygen, there develops a condition similar to pneumonia, with congestion, coughing and considerable discomfort.

In conventional club diving (that is, using compressed air) there is no risk whatsoever of suffering from chronic oxygen poisoning. Even if a diver used pure oxygen there would be no real risk if normal diving practice was employed. It is unlikely that chronic oxygen poisoning would be observed in any but certain clinical conditions when, say, hospital patients breathe oxygen or oxygen-rich mixtures for very long periods, perhaps days.

More pertinent to the diver would be the case of a saturation dive involving perhaps living in an underwater habitat; in which case the diver would be exposed to a high-pressure gas environment for days or even weeks. Thus, if the oxygen partial pressure of the gas were too high, he would be a likely candidate for chronic oxygen poisoning.

If 100% oxygen is breathed at atmospheric pressure (that is, at a partial pressure of 1 bar absolute) the irritation would probably be experienced within 24 hours. However, breathing 60% oxygen at atmospheric pressure (partial pressure of 0.6 bars absolute) for an indefinite period appears to result in no ill effects to most people.

The mechanism of chronic oxygen poisoning is basically similar to that of acute oxygen poisoning. However, in the chronic form where the tissues of the body are having to function in an abnormally high concentration of oxygen over a long period it appears that the most sensitive tissue is the delicate lining of the air pathways within the lungs and throat. Other tissues such as brain, kidney, liver, etc., would eventually suffer if the exposure was not terminated.

Advantages of Pure Oxygen or Oxygen-Rich Breathing Equipment
(i) Construction of the breathing equipment is simple and the set is easy to produce.
(ii) The set is relatively light and compact.
(iii) Longer duration. The limitation is usually imposed by the 'life' of the carbon dioxide absorbent rather than the compressed gas supply.
(iv) Closed-circuit breathing equipment does not produce any bubbles. This is essential when dealing with acoustic mines, and for other military purposes.

Disadvantages
(i) Severely limited in depth (8 m for pure oxygen).
(ii) Danger of acute oxygen poisoning with probable lethal consequences.
(iii) Danger of 'dilution hypoxia' (unconsciousness followed by asphyxia or drowning). This insidious danger occurs when,

due to its accidental dilution, usually by nitrogen, the breathing gas provides too low a partial pressure of oxygen to sustain consciousness. Nitrogen can easily 'contaminate' the breathing gas because insufficient gas was flushed out of the set before use, or by gradual diffusion out of solution from the body into the lungs during the course of a dive. Since the body cannot adequately detect an insufficient supply of oxygen, the unsuspecting diver might become unconscious without warning due to lack of oxygen (*hypoxia*).

(iv) Danger of oxygen fires and explosions. Oil explodes spontaneously in the presence of high-pressure oxygen.

(v) Danger of receiving a 'cocktail'. If water enters the expiratory tube and reaches the soda-lime carbon dioxide absorbent there is an instantaneous reaction producing a highly caustic foam which immediately froths up the breathing tube and can severely burn the mouth, lungs, stomach, etc., perhaps with lethal consequences.

In conclusion it would be pertinent to include another item of information derived from the diving experience of the Royal Navy. The Royal Navy has a definite requirement to use pure oxygen and oxygen-rich breathing equipment and thus has vast experience in most forms of breathing equipment. The men who use this type of equipment are professionals in every sense of the word supported by the very best standards of training. Nevertheless, about 70% of the diving accidents within the Royal Navy, excluding decompression sickness, occur to divers using pure oxygen or oxygen-rich breathing equipment. Thus it can be seen that use of this equipment can only be justified in very special circumstances (i.e., when dealing with acoustic mines), and then only when extra-special organisation and facilities are available to cater for a possible diving accident. Consequently, the use of such equipment is not permitted in the BSAC (see Fig. 27).

Summary
The main points to remember are as follows:

(i) Oxygen poisoning does not occur when using compressed air for breathing—that is in normal Club diving.

(ii) Oxygen poisoning is a problem associated with the use of pure oxygen or oxygen-rich breathing equipment.

(iii) There are two types of oxygen poisoning—acute oxygen poisoning and chronic oxygen poisoning.

(iv) Acute oxygen poisoning is the more dangerous form to the diver since, without warning, it can induce unconsciousness, convulsions and therefore, very probably, drowning.

(v) Acute oxygen poisoning is brought about by breathing oxygen partial pressures in excess of approximately 1.75 bars absolute for a short time (minutes).

(vi) Chronic oxygen poisoning only occurs in people exposed to high oxygen partial pressures, say in excess of 0.6 bars absolute, for very long periods which are well beyond the range of normal dive durations.

(vii) Chronic oxygen poisoning produces symptoms similar to those of pneumonia.

(viii) Having considered both the advantages and disadvantages of oxygen and oxygen-rich breathing equipment the British Sub-Aqua Club has banned the use of this type of equipment for all normal Club diving.

Fig. 27. A ROYAL NAVY CDBA SET, view of a set connected in Mode II for Oxygen re-breathing

Carbon Dioxide Poisoning

Carbon dioxide (CO_2) is a waste product of the body and if it cannot be eliminated through the lungs, it will accumulate in the body and its concentration in the blood will increase. A rise in the PCO_2 will first stimulate the respiratory centre and cause an increase in the depth and rate of respiration. Further accumulation may cause a headache and, if it continues, the sensation of breathlessness may become greater and greater, until confusion occurs and, in an extreme case, consciousness is lost.

A period of heavy work or vigorous swimming can soon cause breathlessness which may lead to exhaustion, 'beating the lung', and may also induce the early onset of nitrogen narcosis during a deep dive. The accumulation of CO_2 is aggravated if attention is not paid to respiratory dead-space. A certain amount of gas from the lungs never leaves the body at the end of expiration but is drawn back into the lungs with its content of CO_2 at the beginning of the next breath. When the volume of the airway is increased by addition of a long snorkel tube or an inferior full face-mask, a greater tidal volume, a deeper breath in, is needed to obtain the usual amount of fresh air. Fortunately, modern diving equipment minimises dead air space and in aqualung diving CO_2 poisoning is unusual.

A 2% level of CO_2 causes little disturbance to the diver. Levels up to 5% will cause increased breathlessness and a feeling of discomfort. Levels of CO_2 up to 10% will cause a marked increase in breathing effort plus mental confusion and headaches. Levels in excess of 10% will be accompanied by marked mental effects and eventual unconsciousness. Higher percentages will cause a rapid convulsion and unconsciousness.

Signs and Symptoms of CO_2 Poisoning
Increasing breathlessness.
Mental confusion.
Headaches.

Treatment and Avoidance of CO_2 Poisoning
Relax and restore normal breathing, preferably by abandoning a dive and returning to the surface. CO_2 build-up can be avoided by breathing steadily and deeply. Avoid shallow panting which is very inefficient at eliminating CO_2 from the bloodstream.

The more severe manifestations are not likely to occur with an aqualung set, but are a hazard of pure oxygen apparatus.

Closed circuit oxygen re-breathing sets have a chemical which extracts CO_2 and if this is exhausted, the CO_2 levels in the breathing system will increase rapidly. The only action is to flush the apparatus through with fresh O_2 and to surface immediately. Because of the potential dangers of this type of breathing apparatus its use is not permitted within the BSAC.

Carbon Monoxide Poisoning

Carbon Monoxide (CO) is the most common lethal contaminant of breathing air. This colourless, odourless gas is produced by incomplete combustion within petrol and diesel engines; in cigarettes; and forms an important constituent of town gas but not of natural gas. It can be lethal even at atmospheric pressure.

The danger arises from CO's affinity for haemoglobin, the oxygen-carrying pigment of the blood, which is 300 times greater than that of O_2 itself. Breathing air contaminated with 500 parts per million (0.05%) of CO will put about half the blood's haemoglobin out of action. In the process, it forms a cherry-red pigment, carboxy-haemoglobin, which is incapable of carrying oxygen within the bloodstream. As a result, insufficient O_2 can be carried by the blood to the tissues which are thus starved of O_2 resulting in tissue hypoxia.

When under pressure during a dive the PCO is increased in proportion to the absolute pressure. The rate at which CO is absorbed into the blood is also greatly increased, and on a 30 m dive it will be absorbed approximately 4 times as quickly as on the surface. The onset of symptoms of CO poisoning will be correspondingly accelerated.

Symptoms of CO Poisoning

These are, in order of severity:

Dizziness, headache and malaise.
Staggering, mental confusion and slurred speech.
Exhaustion.
Flushed lips, cheeks and mucous membranes.
Coma and death.

Death is likely to occur when about two-thirds of the haemoglobin has been combined with CO. Of course, death might occur sooner by some other cause if the earlier symptoms of CO poisoning caused the diver to lose control of himself and his equipment or to perform ineffectively.

Headaches after diving appear to be the most sensitive warning of CO contamination in breathing air and if more than one diver using the same air source has this symptom, the air in their cylinders and the compressor output should be tested for CO contamination.

The BSAC, in its Air Purity Standard (see *Air Purity Analysis*) recommends a limit of 5 parts per million for CO in breathing air.

Treatment of CO Poisoning

If allowed to breathe pure uncontaminated air, the victim's lungs will slowly eliminate the CO over a period of six hours or so, but in all but the most trivial cases, more energetic measures must be urgently employed because of the dangers of heart failure or coma. Principally, the victim should breathe pure oxygen, preferably under pressure in a hospital hyperbaric unit or recompression chamber. The high initial PO_2 produced in this way both speeds up the elimination of CO from the blood and at the same time pushes extra O_2 into simple solution in the blood, thus keeping alive otherwise hypoxic tissues, until adequate haemoglobin function has been restored.

Prevention of CO Poisoning

Since there is no convenient absorbent capable of filtering out CO, prevention of this hazard lies in the proper maintenance and operation of the air compressor. In particular, care should be taken to ensure that the compressor intake does not draw in its own exhaust fumes, if driven by an internal combustion engine, or the fumes from other motor vehicles. Information on the correct siting and operation of air compressors is given in the section: *Compressors and Cylinder Filling.*

The habit of smoking a cigarette just prior to diving leaves an abnormally high level of CO in the diver's lungs, and if the dive is to be a short deep one, the diver might suffer the milder symptoms of CO poisoning. Once the cigarette is smoked, sufficient time should be allowed for the CO to be expelled through the normal cycle of respiration before the diver enters the water.

Nitrogen Narcosis

The two basic components of compressed air are oxygen (21%) and nitrogen (79%). At sufficiently increased pressures, the nitrogen component is responsible for the production of a form of narcosis similar to that produced by alcoholic intoxication, the early stages of oxygen lack or to being anaesthetised by the dentist with nitrous oxide. The condition is commonly known as the *narks*.

The signs and symptoms are characterised by feelings of elation and well-being associated with a sense of detachment from reality with a dangerous over-confidence, an uncontrolled desire to laugh and a tingling numbness of the lips, gums and legs. Sight, sound and smell perception may be affected. More commonly there will be an inability to make correct and rapid decisions or to concentrate. Errors may be made in writing information or reading, accompanied by memory defects and dizziness. Intellectual functions are affected most and manual dexterity to a lesser extent.

The effects of nitrogen narcosis have been shown to be appreciable at a depth of 30 m and are probably present to a lesser extent at shallower depths. There seems to be a fairly general reduction in efficiency extending from an impairment in reasoning ability to slowing down in speed of reaction and a decrease in manual skill. At depths of 30 m and less, nitrogen narcosis is a problem mainly because it reduces the working efficiency of a diver. At rather greater depths it begins to become a real danger since by impairing the diver's judgement it increases the risk of accident while decreasing his ability to cope with an emergency. Finally, at depths exceeding 60 m nitrogen narcosis becomes extremely dangerous, producing bizarre behaviour, stupor and ultimately loss of consciousness.

Narcosis is a significant danger to the diver since it increases the risk of accident and at the same time decreases the ability to cope with emergencies. Many fatal accidents have occurred to divers who chose either to ignore its dangers or foolishly attempted depth records.

The onset of narcosis is rapid, usually reaching a maximum in a few minutes and there is, as with alcohol, a wide variability of sensitivity between different individuals. Frequent exposure to narcosis does not build up immunity to the effects. However, the diver will be better experienced to make allowances for it.

Recovery also is rapid, the extent of the narcosis decreasing as the diver ascends. There are no after effects, except possibly an inability to remember what occurred while narcotised.

Generally the narcosis is more severe when under water than in simulated pressure-chamber diving and is made worse by alcohol, fatigue, ill health, apprehension and hard work.

The narcosis may be prevented by substituting helium for nitrogen in the breathing mixture but this gas has disadvantages of its own such as expense, body temperature regulation and special decompression requirements which make it unsuitable for club use.

Symptoms of Nitrogen Narcosis

30 m—45 m	Narcosis first encountered. Light headedness, dizziness, loss of fine discrimination.
45 m—60 m	Greater dizziness, carelessness.
60 m—80 m	Poor concentration and co-ordination, hysteria.
80 m +	Total lack of concentration and co-ordination. Close to unconsciousness.

Treatment

Return to shallower water, where the symptoms will be relieved.

Narcosis must be recognised as a significant danger and could be minimised by the following rules:

1. Restrict diving to less than 30 m unless, at the instigation of the Branch Diving Officer, special preparation and precautions have been taken. Even then it is not to be recommended, except for the fit, very experienced and well-trained individual.
2. If affected, return immediately to a shallower depth.
3. Take as many decisions as possible prior to the dive, e.g. maximum time permissible on the bottom, decompression required, minimum air required for the ascent and action to be taken in an emergency. Work out a dive plan in advance and adhere to it.

Exhaustion

Exhaustion is a symptom more easily recognised than defined, but may be described as a condition in which the diver or individual has reached a point where he is unable to respond adequately either physically or mentally to further demands on him. In its physical form, it is usually characterised by deep, laboured breathing. It is dangerous because any inability to respond to the demands of diving is liable to result in drowning.

The most common cause of exhaustion is physical exertion, but in diving, and when considering the way the average diver carries out his sport, other factors may be involved. These will include mental fatigue; decompression; breathing resistance at depth; and second only to exertion, the effect of cold.

Causes

PHYSICAL EXERTION

Swimming at a moderate pace, even with the assistance of fins, is equivalent to running or heavy work on land. As explained in an earlier section, muscular exertion results in an increased blood flow to the muscles actually at work to carry oxygen to them and remove waste products. Efficient as this mechanism is, it is unable to provide sufficient oxygen for heavy exertion, and once a muscle has used up the small store of oxygen contained in its own haemoglobin-like pigment, myohaemoglobin (responsible for the reddish-brown colour of muscles), it has two methods of continuing to function for a short time without an oxygen supply. Firstly, there are special phosphate compounds which store rapidly available energy in small amounts and can be used for muscular contraction. These can be quickly reformed when once again sufficient oxygen is available. Secondly, there is a much larger reserve, provided by the breakdown of glucose into lactic acids, an energy-giving process which does not require oxygen at the time, but which eventually requires oxygen to consume the lactic acid produced, a comparatively slow process compared to the first. In the meantime, the lactic acid appears in the bloodstream, producing an acidosis which stimulates the respiratory centre in the brain and causes a great increase in pulmonary ventilation—the deep laboured breathing referred to as being characteristic of physical exhaustion.

It follows from this that the most efficient technique both from the point of view of avoiding exhaustion and minimising air consumption is to swim at a moderate rate, thus avoiding running into severe oxygen debt and incurring the distress and unnecessarily high air consumption produced by the accumulation of lactic acid in the blood. If heavy exertion should be unavoidable, then short bursts of activity with frequent rest periods are the best technique.

HYPOTHERMIA (LOWERED BODY TEMPERATURE)

Loss of body heat, from inadequate or poorly fitting diving suits, results not only in physical discomfort but also in slow mental reactions and loss of ability to think clearly, loss of muscle power in chilled limbs and if allowed to continue, eventually ends in severe hypothermia. In a lesser degree, it is an important but often un-recognised cause of exhaustion and a silent, contributing factor in many accidents. To press on and disregard the physical discomfort of feeling chilled is thus not only foolhardy but also dangerous. (For a detailed study of hypothermia, see the next section.)

MENTAL FATIGUE

A diving week-end may entail a combination of physical and mental work that will tax the strength of even the fittest. An early morning start, followed by a long drive to the coast, the assembly of boats and other equipment on site, and the organisation of diving in addition to the normal exertion of the dive itself, all combine to produce fatigue. Particularly at risk are dives later in the day and the return journey home. The diver who is fit, well rested and well nourished is unlikely to suffer from mental fatigue: it usually afflicts those who burn the candle at both ends, as well as in the middle!

DEPTH

As depth is increased, the density of the air breathed increases, as does the work involved in breathing. At 30 m the diver's maximum ventilation rate is halved, and at 45 m it is down to about one third, and his work capacity correspondingly reduced because of in-ability to eliminate sufficient carbon dioxide. Also further restric-tions on breathing are imposed by the inadequacies of demand valves.

At depth, then, it becomes increasingly essential to swim slowly and easily, and avoid heavy exertion in any form, which not only will be wasteful of air but in addition also lead to exhaustion under water. There is also considerable evidence that if early symptoms of this are ignored, then the accumulated carbon dioxide not only aggravates nitrogen narcosis, but also increases the probability of decompression sickness.

DECOMPRESSION

Fatigue and mental tiredness is a well-recognised symptom of decompression sickness, and may be the only symptom resulting from a dive which was near or just exceeded the No-Stop limit, or in which the recommended rate of ascent was exceeded, or in which decompression was inadequate.

Treatment of Exertion Exhaustion

This is the type of exhaustion most likely to produce a crisis while diving and is recognised by a great increase in the rate and depth of breathing, sometimes to the point at which the demand valve is unable to cope, 'beating the lung'. This situation can occur as the result of poor dive planning, leaving the diver downstream of his boat or other point of return and necessitating a heavy swim upstream against the current, at a time when his air supply is running low. It is essential in this predicament to reduce one's effort, and consequently the demand for air. This can only be achieved by physical rest and relaxation, while at the same time taking such steps as are possible to minimise the danger involved. The technique is to:

1. Stop finning and any other activity, and rest with the demand valve below the level of the chest, i.e., in normal swimming position with mouth-held single-hose valves and lying on the back with twin-hose valves. This ensures that air is supplied at positive pressure and lessens the work of breathing. Give 'I am out of breath' signal to diving partners, who should be ready to offer further assistance as required.
2. Grab hold of some stationary object in order to avoid being swept further away from safety. If this is not possible, perhaps because the divers are in mid-water or at the surface, relax and drift with the current. If in mid-water the divers should ensure that they do not sink.
3. Concentrate on controlling the breathing rhythm, which ideally should be deep and slow.
4. Once breathing is under control the diver may elect to continue the dive, but should ensure that he does not repeat the same sequence of activities which caused him to be exhausted in the first place. Alternatively, it might be wise to abandon the dive and ascend to the surface using normal surfacing procedure.
5. If breathing cannot be controlled under water, an early return to the surface is indicated. The distressed diver should achieve positive buoyancy by lifejacket inflation or his weight-belt should be jettisoned, and his partner may have to assist him to the surface.
6. At the surface, inflate lifejackets fully, remove masks and mouthpieces, relax until composure is recovered. Give 'OK at surface' or 'Distress' signals as indicated by the severity of the situation.

7. In the event of the subject not having a lifejacket, the aqualung mouthpiece should be retained while there is air available. Mismanagement of a change to snorkel breathing by an exhausted diver could initiate drowning. Summon help or tow the subject ashore.

The degree of self control required to cope with this state of exhaustion is considerable and every effort should be made to prevent the exhausted diver bolting for the surface. It is imperative that a diver should stop and relax at the first sign of increased breathing effort on his part.

Avoidance of Exhaustion

A good diving technique demands that diver exertion be minimised, both to avoid exhaustion and to conserve air supplies. In particular the effects of tide and current should be taken into account.

Physical fitness is important, as fit divers need less air for a given amount of exertion. Conversely illness, particularly coughs and colds, may considerably reduce physical efficiency and increase the liability to exhaustion.

When diving from a moored boat, a floating safety line should be trailed astern, so that divers in difficulty will be able to avoid being swept farther away while they relax to regain their breathing rhythm.

AFTERCARE

Shock may follow exhaustion and need treatment with rest, warmth, hot drinks, and if chilled, a hot bath later.

Hypothermia

Body chilling is something which British divers know well. The waters around the British Isles seldom reach temperatures in excess of 16°C in summer and can be as low as 4°C in winter. Water temperatures at depth are usually a degree or two colder than at the surface. In fresh water, such as in rivers, lakes and quarries, the temperatures can be as low as 0°C.

Water is 25 times a better conductor of heat than air, and can hold 1000 times more heat than air. It is, therefore, a formidable adversary to anyone who is forced or chooses to immerse themself in it.

The Effects of Hypothermia

Normal human deep body temperature is 37°C. The body is extremely sensitive to changes in deep body or core temperature, and a drop of as little as 1°C causes shivering and discomfort. A 2°C fall causes the body to maximise its efforts to prevent further heat loss, and shiver- is extreme. Any further drop in deep body temperature will be accompanied by reduced efforts by the body to protect itself, and the drop in core temperature accelerates.

The following schedule tabulates the progressive symptoms and effects of a fall in deep body temperature.

Deep Body Temperature

°C.	*Effect*
36–35	Rise in metabolism and respiration, sensation of severe cold, toes and fingers become painful, then numb.
35	Metabolism begins to decrease.
34.5	Respiration begins to decrease.
34	Heart rate begins to decrease, blood pressure falls.
33	Amnesia begins, shivering gives way to muscle rigidity, mental confusion, semi-consciousness, communication becomes difficult to impossible.
32	Increasingly somnolent and pain resistant, aggravation of epilepsy.
30	Unconsciousness, pupils dilate, no tendon reflex, cardiac arythmas begin, respiration becomes irregular.
28	Respiration ceases, ventricular fibrillation.
25	Death. (Failure to revive.)

This list of symptoms/effects indicates that even a small drop in core temperature can cause serious consequences. A fall of more than 2°C is accompanied by progressive loss of control by the body, and such a condition is known as *Hypothermia*.

Hypothermia occurs to anyone who is exposed to cold, and is by no means a condition met only by water sportsmen in cold climates. Anyone who is inadequately protected from cold is a potential victim; the arctic explorer; mountaineer; shipwreck survivor; through to the old-age pensioner who cannot afford adequate heating. The effects are the same, though the rate of body heat loss will differ.

Influencing Factors

Since water is such a good conductor of heat, the diver is foremost among those who could succumb to hypothermia. We shall now consider why divers require protective clothing by explaining the effects of immersion on an unprotected (naked) diver in UK waters.

It is most important that the unprotected diver/swimmer keeps his movements to a minimum. Lowering of body temperature is accelerated by movement, which allows cold water to come into contact with the skin. There will be an increase in blood circulation to the surface of the body in an effort to warm it, and cold water will cool the blood before it returns to the body core. Even if light clothing is worn, movement as in swimming will flush away the layer of water close to the skin which might otherwise warm up slightly and reduce conduction.

Insulation of the head is also very important. The brain must maintain the deep body temperature of 37°C, and the skull lacks the insulative properties of other parts of the body. Thus, there can be a considerable heat loss from the head. Experiments have indicated that if the back of the head and neck are immersed in cold water, a very rapid and usually irreversible fall in deep body temperature will occur.

Body fat helps in protecting a diver against hypothermia. Subcutaneous fat has good insulating properties, and research has indicated that body core temperatures will fall more rapidly in a thin person than in a fat one. However, fatness is usually associated with lack of physical fitness, and it would be unwise to sacrifice fitness for fatness. The shape of the body comes into this, too. A fat person resembles a sphere more closely than a tall slim person, and a sphere represents maximum volume for minimum surface area. Thus, the tall slim diver is at a disadvantage. Children, who have a high body surface area in relation to volume, and only a thin layer of subcutaneous fat, are much more difficult to keep warm.

The Need for Protection

Fig. 28 indicates the likely survival times for an unprotected body in water for a range of water temperatures, compared with likely survival times for persons wearing wet-suits. Clearly, protective clothing of this sort increases the prospects of survival by tenfold or more.

Thus, to enjoy any watersport, and particularly under-water swimming, some form of protective clothing is necessary, and ideally, the protection should reduce to an absolute minimum the heat lost from the body during immersion.

For some sports such as canoeing or sailing, sweaters may be sufficient to keep the wearer warm—until he becomes wet. *Wind Chill* is another factor which has to be considered. A wet body— even wearing a couple of thick wet sweaters—will quickly lose body heat if exposed to wind. A wet-suited diver can get very cold sitting around after a dive for just the same reason. A windproof garment should be worn over woollen sweaters, and after a dive to prevent wind chill.

The wet-suit has other advantages. It has buoyancy as well as thermal protection, and bearing in mind the survival time available to him, the wet-suited diver who 'misses his boat' and goes adrift on the ebb tide need not battle against it to reach the shore: he can afford to wait and catch the flood tide back! Indeed, this has been done in UK waters!

There is also a case for suggesting that the wet-suited diver SHOULD exercise himself since a wet suit is most effective if the layer of water trapped against the wearer's body is warm. Body activity will keep it warm.

The diver's hands and feet should also be protected, since they have a high surface area to volume relationship.

The wet-suit, and other forms of protective diving dress, are fully explained in chapter 3, *Protective Clothing*.

Treatment of Hypothermia

Let us first review the symptoms, in order of severity. The following are the most common, but may not all be present at the same time:

Complaints of cold.

Mental and physical lethargy.

Mental confusion (so that the symptoms escape notice in oneself).

Slurred speech.

Shivering.

Stiffness and/or pain, and/or cramp in the muscles.

Abnormal vision.

Collapse and unconsciousness. } VERY SERIOUS SYMPTOMS.

TREATMENT

Treatment of hypothermia commences by removing the subject from cold and preventing further heat loss. This can be achieved by placing the subject in an 'exposure bag', a sleeping-bag-size plastic bag or by wrapping him in a 'space blanket'—a metallised plastic sheet. (A well-equipped diving boat should carry one of these.) This will protect the subject from rain, spray, wind chill, etc. and will allow some passive rewarming.

Rewarming in the exposure bag will be increased if warm bodies climb into the bag on each side of the victim. Where practical to do so, the subject should be stripped of wet clothing, dried and dressed in dry clothes.

The subject should then be taken ashore as quickly as possible, and if possible taken to hospital for subsequent treatment. In mild hypothermia cases, the treatment could be applied without hospitalisation, but is best done under medical supervision. Severe cases of hypothermia MUST be handled in hospital.

The treatment which is given is to immerse the trunk of the subject's body in hot water (42°C) until deep body temperature improves. Monitoring of this really requires special equipment, hence the need for medical care. The arms and legs are not immersed in order to prevent a rush of cold blood from these extremities to the body core. This could cause an *After Drop*, in which the core temperature drops further: in extreme cases, by as much as 2°C. If the victim's core temperature is already critically low, the after drop could be sufficient to bring about death. So, if possible, leave the treatment of severe cases to specialists.

The rewarming process must be gradual and overall. The application of local heat (e.g. hot-water bottles, rubbing to stimulate circulation) must be avoided. Giving alcohol to a hypothermic subject is like putting a nail in his coffin—alcohol opens up the blood capillaries and encourages cold blood from the body surface to return to the core.

Once the subject has responded to the immersion treatment, he should be put into a warm bed and allowed to recover fully. Warm high-energy food and drink may be administered at this stage—or at an earlier stage in cases of mild hypothermia.

Hypothermia is clearly a condition to avoid, and one which, with forethought, IS easy to avoid.

The use of adequate protective clothing for the exposure being undertaken is vital, whether it be sailing wear; climbing dress; or diving dress. Out of the water, wind-chill is a major hazard, and can be reduced by use of a windproof coat worn over a wet-suit before and after the dive. The extremities (hands, feet and head) should be adequately insulated.

Abandon the dive when shivering commences. You are then down by 1°C, and wind-chill during the boat trip home could reduce your core temperature by another 1°C.

After the dive, warm up as quickly as possible—don't stand about getting colder. Take a hot bath or shower. Change into warm clothes. Have a hot high-energy drink, and at all costs, avoid alcohol before and immediately after a cold water/cold weather dive.

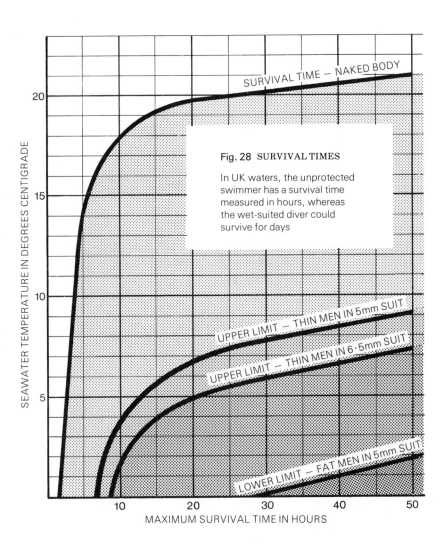

SURVIVAL TIME — NAKED BODY

Fig. 28 SURVIVAL TIMES

In UK waters, the unprotected swimmer has a survival time measured in hours, whereas the wet-suited diver could survive for days

UPPER LIMIT — THIN MEN IN 5mm SUIT

UPPER LIMIT — THIN MEN IN 6·5mm SUIT

LOWER LIMIT — FAT MEN IN 5mm SUIT

SEAWATER TEMPERATURE IN DEGREES CENTIGRADE

MAXIMUM SURVIVAL TIME IN HOURS

CHAPTER THREE
EQUIPMENT

Basic Equipment

The term *basic equipment* is the name given to those items of equipment which are required to allow the swimmer to become a snorkeller—mask, fins and snorkel tube. There are many different types, designs and makes available and an appreciation of the function of basic equipment will help the beginner to make a more reasoned choice. Where possible, he should try as many different types as he can and should also seek the advice of more experienced divers before making his choice and his purchase.

Fins

Fins are used to improve the propulsive power of the legs and so eliminate the need to use the arms for swimming. Fins should have a braced blade which is angled slightly downwards and may have built-in flaps or slots, all of which improve the propulsion of the fin. Fig. 29 illustrates a typical range of fins. There is even one type of fin which has a steel bracing attached to the legs to prevent the ankles from tiring, but these are not advised for the novice.

Fins are secured to the feet in two ways. The simplest way is to have a strap round the back of the heel and ideally, this strap should be adjustable. A better means of fitting is the shoe or slipper-type fin, where the foot fits into a pocket shaped like a shoe or slipper. Fins of this type are made in a range of foot sizes.

When selecting a pair of fins, remember that you may want to wear them over a pair of neoprene wet-suit bootees eventually, and therefore, try to allow for this when selecting the size. If this makes the fins rather loose for pool training, a pair of socks or the neoprene bootees themselves may be used or, alternatively, the fins may be secured by 'fin retainers' (see *Diving Accessories*).

Most modern fins are manufactured from two separate types of rubber—a stiff one for the blade and a softer one for the foot pocket, thereby giving efficiency without having to sacrifice comfort. Some manufacturers produce floating fins which will return to the surface if they come off the foot. However, it would be much wiser to try to ensure that the fins stay on the feet!

Mask

The eyes can only focus properly when looking through air and the mask provides a pocket of air in front of the eyes while the head is submerged. The nose must be included within the mask for a number of reasons. First, as the depth increases so does the ambient water

E

Fig. 29. SWIM FINS

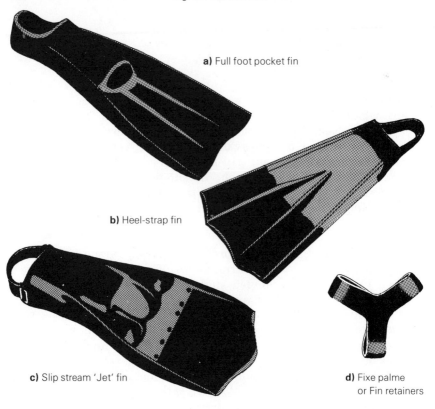

a) Full foot pocket fin

b) Heel-strap fin

c) Slip stream 'Jet' fin

d) Fixe palme
or Fin retainers

pressure, and it is necessary for the air pressure within the mask to be equalised. This is achieved by blowing gently through the nose into the mask. Only with the nose inside the mask can this be accomplished and therefore, goggles or masks which do not include the nose should not be used. Failure to equalise will lead to mask squeeze. Secondly, most divers find that ear-clearing (Chapter 2, *Ears and Sinuses*) is simplified if the nose can be pinched. A face-mask usually provides for this by having pockets in the rubber of the mask on either side of the nose, enabling the mask to be pinched from the outside. Some masks have a moulded nose shape which protrudes forward of the mask glass for the very same purpose. It is advisable that every mask should be fitted with some form of ear-clearing compensator pockets. The third reason for inclusion of the nose is to permit water, which may flood the mask, to be expelled by displacing it with air exhaled through the nose.

A wide range of different face-masks are available (Fig. 30), and the 'window' of the mask should be made from tempered or toughened glass and never from ordinary glass which could splinter and cause serious injury. Clear plastic is sometimes used, but it does tend to scratch rather easily and can also be difficult to prevent from misting up. Misting up occurs due to the presence within the mask of a warm face while the glass is in contact with cold water. Condensation occurs on the inside of the glass. It may normally be prevented by the old-fashioned but effective expedient of rubbing the glass with saliva prior to the start of the dive—but don't forget to rinse with clean water before wearing it. Persistent misting up can usually be defeated by one of the following methods:

(a) Rub the glass with a slice of raw potato.

(b) Rub with French chalk.

(c) Rub with methylated spirit.

(d) Wash with neat detergent.

(e) Use a proprietary demister.

The glass must be firmly fixed to the mask and this is usually achieved by means of a metal or plastic retaining band. It is essential that the glass cannot be dislodged accidentally and neither should there be any leaks between the glass and the rubber body of the mask. Drain valves may be fitted but are not really necessary.

It is essential that the mask should be a comfortable, water-tight fit on the face. Different masks can be checked by placing them on the face without using the retaining strap and holding them there by suction through the nose. At the same time, check that the nose can be pinched through the compensator pockets. The mask is a good fit if it stays on the face with no leakage of air. There are many different designs of masks to choose from, all of which have the aforementioned characteristic. A further characteristic which some divers consider worthwhile is that of 'wide-angle' vision. This is sometimes achieved by utilising a large window and therefore, the mask suffers from having a large air volume. The advantages of wide-angle vision compared with the disadvantages of large air volumes have to be considered. A 'wrap-round' window might be used, but this can be expensive and the curved glass produces distortion. Side windows can be employed, but again, there are blind spots and care is needed in the design of such a mask to minimise these and also to maintain low volume. Try several types of mask before finally deciding on the one which best suits your face and your pocket.

For those who have to wear spectacles, special face-masks are available with separate removable lenses which can be ground to your individual prescription. Alternatively, a spectacle frame can be fitted to most diving masks using rubber suction caps, epoxy resin adhesives or copper wire. A reputable dive shop should be able to give you advice on this type of mask.

Fig. 30. FACEMASKS

a) Simple mask
with finger wells
for ear-clearing

b) Reduced internal
volume, nose pocket
for ear- clearing

c) Semi-goggle
minimum internal
volume

Full face-masks which include the mouth are not favoured for sports diving since they represent a considerable increase in the respiratory dead space and ear clearing during a dive may not be possible. Also a full face-mask does not permit use of a separate snorkel tube and sharing is impossible. Masks of any sort with built-in snorkel tubes should be avoided.

Snorkel Tube

The snorkel tube enables the diver on the surface to breathe without having to lift his head out of the water, as an ordinary swimmer might do. There are many types of snorkels available to the diver but probably the simplest are the 'J' or 'L' type snorkels (this representing their shape) which have proved to be the most satisfactory. The tube should be just long enough to clear the surface of the water—if it is too long, it is unwieldy, uncomfortable and may be difficult to clear. As an average recommendation, a tube with a total

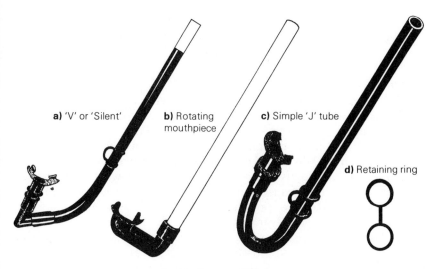

a) 'V' or 'Silent' **b)** Rotating mouthpiece **c)** Simple 'J' tube

d) Retaining ring

Fig. 31 . SNORKEL TUBES

length from mouthpiece to upper end of 40–45 cm is sufficient. The bore of the snorkel should be large enough not to interfere with easy breathing, but not so large that blowing water from the tube becomes difficult. A bore of about 20 mm is suggested. Ideally, the mouthpiece should be capable of swivelling slightly on the end of the tube, which may be made of plastic or hard rubber. A band of fluorescent red tape around the top end of the snorkel makes it a little more conspicuous. Some typical examples of good snorkel tubes are shown in Fig. 31.

Avoid tubes that have unnecessary complications, such as double bends or fitted valves at either end, for these have no distinct advantages and, in fact, may be a source of trouble. The mouthpiece of the snorkel tube has two rubber stumps which are gripped by the teeth, and snorkels are available with mouldable plastic stumps into which you can impress your own dental pattern to give a very comfortable fitting, but at a price. Non-allergic rubber mouthpieces are also available in this form. To prevent the snorkel from being lost and to stop it from pulling excessively on the mouthpiece, it will be provided with a retaining band which enables the tube of the snorkel to be secured to the face-mask strap. Alternatively, some divers prefer to tuck the tube under the mask strap while in use and a number of aqualung divers like to have the snorkel tube on a neck lanyard so that it can be removed from beneath the mask's strap whilst aqualung diving. The neck lanyard prevents the snorkel tube being lost. Such things are a matter of personal preference.

124

Principles of the Aqualung

History

The first regulator for diving was designed in the 1860's by two French engineers, Benoit Rouquaryol and Auguste Denarouze. It is a great credit to these two pioneers that their regulator contained virtually all the basic design details that we still use today. What was lacking in 1860 was the availability of lightweight cylinders of adequate capacity to give the diver a useful under-water endurance; Rouquayrol and Denarouze had to make do with cylinders of only 30 bars pressure rating, a pressure at which we now consider our cylinders to be virtually empty! To boost the endurance of the 'Aerophore' as it was named, an air line from the surface kept the cylinder topped-up. Having little advantage over the copper-helmet diving suit, development of the system did not proceed.

By the 1930's fins and goggles had appeared, but the swimmer's under-water endurance was still limited to his own breath-holding capacity. It was at this stage that Jacques Cousteau became interested in the sport of under-water swimming, and began experimenting with under-water breathing apparatus. In company with Frederic Dumas he tried several systems, from a simple hand-pumped air line to a rudimentary oxygen re-breathing set; the air line was very restrictive and the oxygen set unreliable and dangerous.

However, by the 1940's manufacturers of gas cylinders had at last produced cylinders that could contain a useful supply of air and were sufficiently light to be carried on a man's back.

Another Frenchman, Commander Le Prieur, designed a free diving set, the air being supplied from cylinders. This fed the air to the diver in a continuous flow and had to be manually regulated. Cousteau tried this set but realised that there was still much room for improvement; what was needed was a Demand Valve (or Regulator)—a valve that would supply air to the diver only when he required to breathe in. It was to shut off while the diver breathed out; be automatic in operation, and cope with changes in pressure due to depth.

How was this achieved? In 1943 Cousteau's research led him to Emile Gagnan. Gagnan was already working on the design of gas regulators, some of which were used to enable the war-time Paris taxi to run on coal gas. Gagnan studied Cousteau's problems and produced a demand valve that worked well on the surface, but gushed continuously when submerged.

Experiment continued and the secret of success was eventually discovered: Cousteau and Gagnan had succeeded in producing the true demand valve; sub-aqua diving was born and a new name coined—the *Aqualung*. Since then, the Cousteau–Gagnan partnership has produced other demand valves and, strictly speaking, the term 'Aqualung' should only be applied to these Cousteau–Gagnan team products, but the name is now in general usage. This should not be regarded as plagiarism but rather, a tribute to their pioneer work which helped to create a new sport.

Basic Principles

What were the secrets that the early experimenters had to uncover, facts which today we take for granted? Attempts to breathe surface air through elongated tubes had soon proved that man himself could not draw air down to any significant depth; it was necessary to pump the air down to him until its pressure equalled that of the surrounding water. Such is the principle of the standard diving suit. As the diver descends so he is subjected to increased water pressure, and the pressure of the air that he breathes must be increased so that equilibrium is maintained. Conversely, as the diver ascends and the water pressure decreases, so it is necessary that the regulator adjusts the air to match the lower pressure.

With an increase in the pressure of the air delivered at depth also comes an increase in its density. At a depth of 30 m the absolute pressure is 4 bars, i.e. four times the pressure of the atmosphere on the surface; the density of the delivered air will also be four times greater than surface air, and the regulator must allow this 'thicker' air to flow through its various passages without restriction.

At 50 m which we may accept as the maximum safe depth for sports diving, air should be delivered at 6 times the surface pressure and density. To give a margin of safety, the demand valve must be capable of functioning at even greater pressures, but not all types are recommended for use at such extreme depths.

For economy the air has to be delivered to the diver only when he requires it—hence the term (on) *Demand Valve*. The valve must be automatic in operation, triggered off by the initial suction of the diver's inhalation: nothing is quite so tiring as having to breathe against a restriction, so the action of the demand valve should be initiated by only a very slight inhalation, equivalent to sucking half an inch of water up a straw. The onset of the air flow must be gentle and match the diver's natural breathing rhythm, starting slowly, reaching a maximum about half-way through the breath, then decreasing to zero again. Air should not be forced down the diver's throat, and yet, for ease of breathing, the air flow should be self-sustaining all the time the diver is inhaling.

When the diver stops breathing in, the air delivery must also stop and remain so whilst the diver pauses and then exhales. There should be little resistance to the exhalation for this can also prove to be very tiring. The air delivery must begin again as soon as the diver starts his next inhalation.

Cousteau and Gagnan discovered that their demand valve was sensitive to the relative positions of the exhaust valve and demand diaphragm, and that these two components must be positioned immediately adjacent to each other for correct operation of the device.

Another important factor is the positioning of the demand valve relative to the diver's lungs. Ideally, both should be subjected to identical water pressure although it is not possible to achieve this at all times; luckily, the diver can cope with the variations provided they are kept within reasonable limits. The correct positioning of the demand valve will be discussed later in this section.

Types of Demand Valve

Demand valves may be divided visually into two types: the twin-hose cylinder-mounted valve and the single-hose mouthpiece-held valve. The original Cousteau–Gagnan design demand valve was a twin-hose valve and this set the pattern for development in the early days of the sport. Single-hose demand valves were introduced in the late 1950's and have been progressively developed ever since. By modern standards, the twin-hose demand valve is obsolescent, though it still has its devotees.

Twin-hose demand valves may be of either the *single-stage* or *twin-stage* type while the single-hose demand valves are normally *twin-stage*.

Single-stage and twin-stage are terms describing the number of steps by which the high-pressure air stored in the cylinder is reduced to the lowest ambient pressure breathed by the diver. In the single-stage valve the air pressure is reduced in one step, i.e. there is only one valve and valve seat. A twin-stage valve reduces the pressure in two steps: at the first stage, air pressure is reduced from cylinder pressure to an intermediate pressure—usually approximately 7 bars above ambient pressure—and this is then reduced at the second stage to the breathing pressure required by the diver.

All demand valves must operate satisfactorily over the complete range of cylinder pressures, i.e. from 200 bar—even 300 bar nowadays—down to virtually empty. In general all demand valves cope adequately with this pressure range, but the *unbalanced* valve is more sensitive to changes in cylinder pressure; some becoming free whilst others stiffen. The *balanced* valve is, therefore, an additional refinement to valve design for it sets out to eliminate this variation in sensitivity and to give a constant breathing characteristic regardless of the state of charge of the cylinder. (The terms 'unbalanced' and 'balanced' will be explained a little later on.)

The terms *upstream* and *downstream* refer to the position of the valve and valve seat in relation to the direction of air flow. An *upstream* valve is one in which the valve seat faces towards the on-coming air stream, the sealing face of the valve head preventing the air from entering the orifice until the valve is lifted off its seat. The valve head is in fact on the upstream side of the orifice. The air pressure tends to force this type of valve to shut and when used as the second stage of a two-stage valve, an interstage relief must be provided to protect the valve in case of leakage of high-pressure air passed the first-stage valve seating. A *downstream* valve is one in which the valve seat faces away from the on-coming air stream, the sealing face of the valve preventing the air from leaving the orifice, i.e. the valve is downstream of the orifice. The air pressure tends to open this type of valve and it is kept shut by means of a spring. When used in a two-stage valve, inadvertent over-pressurisation will cause the valve to lift and so act as its own relief valve.

A useful analogy when considering the difference between *upstream* and *downstream* is to consider a spring-loaded door closing against its door frame. If you push the door closed against its frame, you are applying an upstream closing action; if you push the door away from its frame, you are applying a downstream opening action which can only be overcome by a powerful door-closing spring.

The first stage of a twin-stage demand valve may be either *diaphragm* or *piston* action, the latter now superseding the former in most modern single-hose demand valves. With the diaphragm type the first-stage pressure is controlled by a thick laminated rubber/fabric diaphragm which bears down, via a push rod, on the valve. With the piston type the diaphragm and its associated components are replaced by a single metal piston, the large diameter head of which senses the interstage pressure and the end of its stem forming the valve face. The function of all these various components will be explained as we consider each type of demand valve in detail. The early single-hose demand valves had an 'upstream' tilt valve in the mouth-held second stage, and a diaphragm action first stage. The more modern single-hose demand valves have a 'downstream' second stage with a piston action first stage. There is no fundamental reason for this since either type of first or second stage will function with the other—with due regard to the provision of relief valves with 'upstream' second stages.

Twin-Hose Single Stage Demand Valve
Figure 32 shows diagramatically the construction of a twin-hose

single-stage demand valve which represents only a simple development from the original Cousteau–Gagnan design. The main casing comprises two chambers separated by a thin rubber diaphragm. One chamber is open to the water; this chamber also contains the exhaust valve. The other chamber contains a system of levers and a push rod which transmit the movement of the diaphragm to the main valve. The valve is contained in the high-pressure body which clamps directly on to the aqualung cylinder pillar valve. A corrugated hose leads from the air chamber to the mouth-piece, and a second corrugated hose carries the exhaust air back to the non-return valve in the water chamber.

When the pillar valve or shut-off valve on the cylinder is turned on, air flows into the valve through a fine filter—usually a porous sintered bronze disc—and into the high-pressure body. For the moment, the high-pressure air cannot pass the valve which is being held shut by a spring. A small push-rod pin is located into the top of the main valve body, and the lever system rests on top of the pin; to open the main valve the levers must be depressed. When the diver starts to inhale, a very slight suction is created in the air chamber; this pulls down the diaphragm thus compressing the levers and causing the valve to open. Air now flows into the chamber and along the hose to the diver's mouthpiece.

For ease of breathing, the air flow from the demand valve should be self-sustaining, so that the diver may breathe without any tiring respiratory effort. To minimise effort, valves are so constructed that the in-coming air is blown into the delivery hose as a fast-moving jet, thus creating a venturi effect. The velocity of the air causes a partial vacuum which sucks more air from the chamber, thus keeping the diaphragm depressed and the main valve open, and so sustains the air flow. Without this venturi effect the diver would have to suck for the entire inhalation.

When the diver completes his inhalation, the pressure in the air chamber rises slightly, lifting the diaphragm. This relaxes the levers, allowing the spring to close the main valve and shut off the air delivery until the next inhalation.

As well as being sensitive to pressure changes caused by breathing, the demand diaphragm is also sensitive to changes in pressure caused by variations in depth. When the regulator is submerged, the water chamber floods. The pressure of the water depresses the diaphragm, causing the levers to open the main valve. The in-coming air will raise the pressure in the air chamber, and when the air pressure equals the water pressure, the diaphragm moves back to its neutral position and the main valve will close. This action takes place automatically—without any interference to the breathing action of the diver.

Non-return valves are fitted on either side of the mouthpiece of twin-hose demand valves. These simple rubber 'mushroom' valves prevent water entering the delivery hose should the mouthpiece become flooded; they also prevent any water or stale air in the exhaust hose from flowing back or being drawn into the mouthpiece. The original demand valves did not have this facility and both hoses could flood completely, but with the incorporation of the non-return valves it is only necessary to blow the small amount of water from the mouthpiece, into the exhaust hose, before starting to breathe. However, even non-return valves do fail, so do not neglect your flooded hose drills!

The exhaust hose leads from the mouthpiece back to the demand valve casing and vents the expired air through another non-return valve into the water chamber, where it escapes through the same holes that admit the water to the chamber.

It was explained earlier than Cousteau and Gagnan during their research discovered that their demand valve was sensitive to the relative positions of the exhaust valve and demand diaphragm. The question may be asked: why is the exhaust tube necessary? Why cannot the diver exhale directly into the water from his mouthpiece? The answer is simple. If the diver were lying on his back his mouthpiece would be at a lower hydrostatic pressure than the demand valve diaphragm and the latter would remain depressed, causing a continual flow of air which would be wasted through the mouthpiece. The act of holding a twin-hose demand-valve mouthpiece above the level of the diaphragm of the valve will cause a continuous flow of air (see chapter 4, *Aqualung Training—Basic Skills*). The circuit of breathing hoses must be completed so that the exhaled air is exhausted at a pressure equal to that applied to the diaphragm.

Twin-Hose Two Stage Demand Valve

The single stage twin-hose demand valve contains all the essential features of an under-water breathing apparatus but is sensitive to changes of air pressure in the cylinder. Two-stage valves, whether of twin-hose or single-hose type reduce this sensitivity. The function of the second stage of a two-stage valve is in principle similar to that described above for the single-stage valve. However, instead of drawing air directly from the cylinder at a steadily decreasing pressure, the second stage is supplied with air at constant reduced pressure. This intermediate pressure is usually controlled at around 6–8 bars. The reducing valve which controls the pressure is the first stage of the demand valve.

To say that the intermediate pressure is constant is an over-

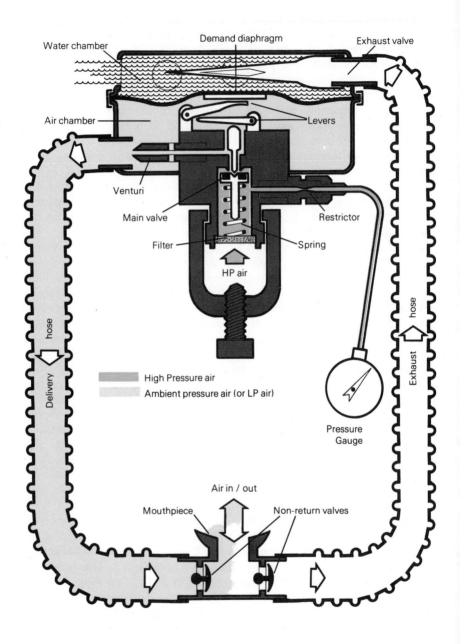

Fig. 32. **A SINGLE-STAGE TWIN-HOSE DEMAND VALVE**

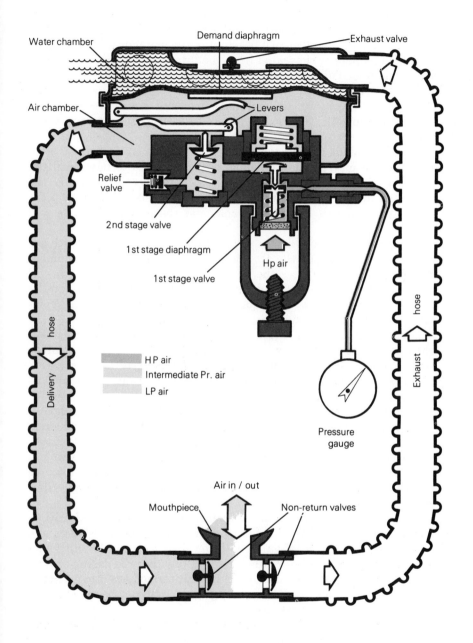

Fig. 33. A TWO-STAGE TWIN-HOSE DEMAND VALVE

simplification: the pressure is actually held at a constant pressure above that of the surrounding (ambient) water. The pressure in the second stage air chamber will be equal to the ambient water pressure and this chamber is separated from the intermediate pressure chamber by a thick rubber/fabric diaphragm (Fig. 33). One side of the diaphragm bears on the first-stage valve, the other side of the diaphragm is open to ambient pressure, and has a heavy spring bearing against it. This spring tends to keep the first-stage valve open.

When the air is turned on, it flows past the open first-stage valve and into the intermediate chamber. Air continues to flow until the pressure in the chamber has risen sufficiently to overcome the combined force of the spring and ambient pressure, at which point the diaphragm will be pushed back, and the first-stage valve will close.

When the diver inhales, the second stage opens (as it did with the single-stage valve) and the air pressure in the intermediate chamber starts to fall. This causes the first-stage valve to open and air will flow from the cylinder to the diver. The second stage closes when the demanded flow ceases, and the intermediate pressure rises to its predetermined level, when the first stage closes.

Some form of relief valve must be fitted to the intermediate chamber to vent off any excess pressure should the first stage fail to seal correctly. If an upstream demand stage is used then a separate relief valve is necessary, but a downstream demand stage will act as its own relief valve.

The double-stage twin-hose demand valve is very similar in appearance to the single stage version, with the first-stage (reducing) valve contained in the same casing as the demand stage.

The relief valve may be arranged to vent overboard, or possibly to vent into the main air chamber, where the vented air may be breathed by the diver. Ordinarily the relief valve leakage—if it exists at all—will be very slight.

Perhaps this is a good point to mention that if the relief valve is found to be leaking, then the fault lies with the first-stage valve, and screwing down the relief valve will not cure the trouble—although it may hide it for a while. Whilst it is unlikely that the casing around the first-stage valve will burst, even if the intermediate pressure rises to cylinder pressure, the demand-stage valve will not be able to open against the excessive pressure.

From Fig. 33 it will be seen that the first-stage diaphragm does not necessarily have to have direct contact with the water, since the demand-stage air chamber automatically equalises to the water pressure, and this air pressure may also be used to actuate the first-stage diaphragm.

Single-Hose, Two-Stage Valves

With this type of demand valve the two stages are separated. The first-stage (reducing) valve clamps directly to the cylinder pillar valve. A smooth bore hose carries the air to the second stage which is built into the mouthpiece, the hose acting as the intermediate pressure chamber. The exhaust valve is also contained in the mouthpiece adjacent to the demand diaphragm. There is no need for an exhaust hose.

Relief valves—when needed—are fitted at the first stage, and vent overboard. Here again, a warning about leaking relief valves: in this case, screwing down the relief valve will not hide the excess pressure for long—the hose will burst! These hoses are of medium-pressure rating and, while they will withstand pressures several times greater than the predetermined first stage pressure, they will not withstand full cylinder pressure.

Fig. 34 shows an early type of single-hose demand valve, with a diaphragm-action first stage and an upstream—tilt valve—second stage. The tilt valve is so named because movement of the second stage diaphragm does not lift the valve head off its seat, but instead, tilts it to one side.

Fig. 35 shows another design of single-hose demand valve which is now widely used. This has a piston action first stage with a downstream second stage. The piston is the only moving part within the first stage: the spring plus water pressure pushes on the underside of the piston head and lifts the stem—which forms the main valve face—off the valve seat. Air then flows through the orifice and into the hose. The piston stem is hollow and so air pressure is also transmitted to the top of the piston head. When this air pressure has reached preset level, it will overcome the combined spring and water pressure and the piston will move down to close the valve. (Note that the intermediate pressure working over the large diameter of the piston head will easily overcome the much higher pressure of air trying to flow through the small diameter orifice.) The piston head and stem are sealed with O-rings and may also incorporate plastic wiper rings to keep the sliding surfaces free of silt.

The downstream second stage consists of a spring-loaded valve sealing against the valve seat. Usually a single lever bears against the diaphragm, and movement of this lever, initiated by the diaphragm, lifts the valve to admit air to the mouthpiece.

Venturi action is achieved in mouthpiece regulators by deflecting the air flow from the inlet orifice to the mouthpiece by means of baffles.

UNBALANCED DEMAND VALVES

All the valves so far described have been of the 'unbalanced' type.

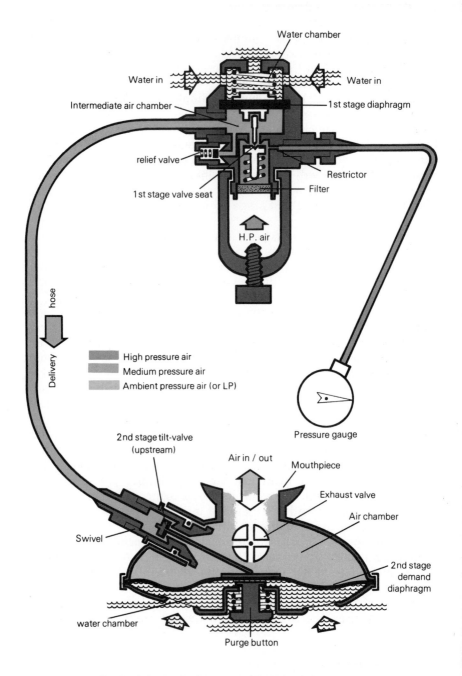

Fig. 34. A TWO-STAGE SINGLE-HOSE DEMAND VALVE

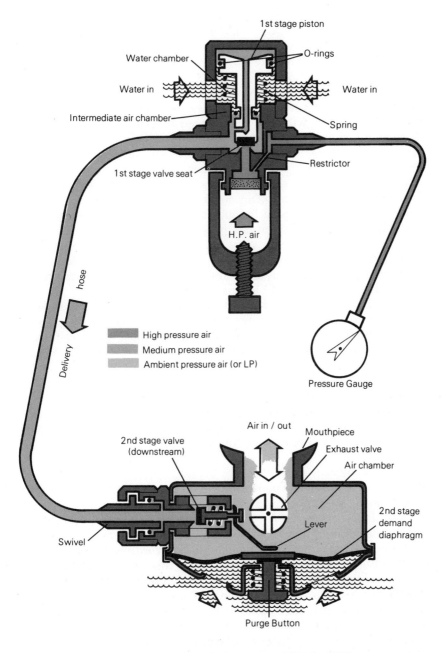

1st stage piston

Water chamber

O-rings

Water in   Water in

Intermediate air chamber

Spring

1st stage valve seat

Restrictor

H.P. air

High pressure air
Medium pressure air
Ambient pressure air (or LP)

Pressure Gauge

hose

Delivery

Air in / out

Mouthpiece

2nd stage valve
(downstream)

Exhaust valve

Air chamber

2nd stage
demand
diaphragm

Swivel

Lever

Purge Button

Fig. 35. A TWO-STAGE SINGLE-HOSE DEMAND VALVE

Fig. 32 showed a single-stage demand valve. The main valve is upstream of the orifice and the cylinder pressure tends to keep the valve shut; the higher the cylinder pressure, the tighter the valve shuts. The breathing on this valve is stiff to start with, and eases off progressively as the cylinder empties. At very high cylinder pressure —such as 300 bar—a single-stage demand valve would probably be too stiff to breathe from.

Figs. 33, 34 and 35 show twin-stage valves, the descriptions given assuming that the interstage pressure remains constant at around 6–8 bar. However, with the unbalanced demand valves illustrated, this is not accurate: the interstage pressure DOES vary according to the state of charge of the cylinder; whether it increases or decreases depends on the construction of the first stage.

The demand valves shown in Figs. 33 and 34 have first stages of 'upstream' configuration. The controlling spring tries to hold the valve open and is opposed by both the cylinder pressure acting on the valve, and the interstage pressure acting on the first-stage diaphragm. As the cylinder pressure falls, so the interstage pressure must rise to maintain equilibrium with the spring. Typically, the interstage pressure on such demand valves could vary from 8 bar on a full cylinder, rising to 12 bar as it empties.

Fig. 35 shows a first stage of downstream configuration. Here, the cylinder pressure acts in conjunction with the spring, and is opposed by the interstage pressure. As the cylinder pressure falls, so the interstage pressure also falls. The variation in interstage pressure is of similar order to the other demand valves: starting at 8 bar and decreasing to around 4 bar.

These variations of interstage pressure can be felt by the second (demand) stage, but the effect is not so marked as with the single-stage demand valve. So, having explained the 'unbalance' of demand valves, how do we create a balanced version?

BALANCED DEMAND VALVES

To achieve a balanced condition it is essential that both ends of the valve head be exposed to identical pressure. Fig. 36 shows a balanced first-stage valve. Cylinder pressure is introduced at the side of the controlling valve. The valve head seals against the orifice, and that portion of the valve head actually over the orifice is exposed to the interstage pressure. To counteract this, the stem of the valve head is led back into a small chamber which is also open to the interstage pressure. The diameter of the stem is exactly equal to the orifice diameter, thus, the valve head is held in balance by the interstage pressure acting simultaneously on both ends. The effect of cylinder pressure on the valve head has been neutralised: any tendency for the cylinder pressure to push the valve head forward, into the orifice,

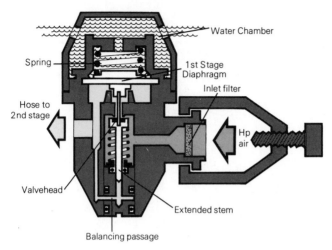

Fig. 36. A BALANCED (diaphragm) FIRST STAGE

is opposed by an equal tendency to push the stem backward. If this seems difficult to grasp, then imagine the effect of cutting the stem in half: the cylinder pressure would push the two halves in opposite directions. It no longer matters if the cylinder pressure varies for there is no resultant force on the valve, and the interstage pressure remains constant at a value determined solely by the control springs.

'BALANCED' PISTON FIRST STAGE

Several manufacturers now use balanced piston first stages for their high-performance regulators. A particularly popular form of balanced piston is one where the whole air delivery flows through the piston itself and the hose is attached to the intermediate air chamber at the top of the piston.

Fig. 37 shows a typical construction for a 'through-piston', balanced first stage. Characteristically the high-pressure air from the cylinder enters at the side of the piston stem, rather than end-on as in the unbalanced version already described. Before the set is first turned on there is no pressure in the intermediate chamber or hose and the spring has pushed the piston to the top of the chamber raising the tip of the stem off the valve seat. The valve seat is a large plastic plug, sometimes nylon, sometimes PTFE.

138

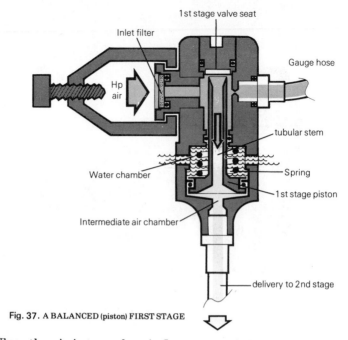

Fig. 37. A BALANCED (piston) FIRST STAGE

When the air is turned on it flows around the knife edge tip of the piston stem, up through the tubular section, to the intermediate chamber and air hose. As the pressure in the chamber and hose rises it pushes the piston back against the spring until, finally, the stem tip seals against the valve seat and stops the air flow. The interstage pressure of this type of regulator can be as high as 10 bar.

When a breath is taken from the second stage (nowadays this will invariably be a downstream type), the interstage pressure drops, the piston moves up and the first-stage valve opens. Air now flows from the cylinder, through the regulator, to the diver. When inhalation ceases the interstage pressure rises again and the first-stage valve closes until the next inhalation.

Auxiliary Pressure Tappings
Although only one delivery hose has been shown in the diagram, it is usual for two or sometimes three hose outlets to be tapped into the chamber cap to supply intermediate pressure air to ancillary devices such as the octopus rig, direct feed to ABLJ's or dry suits or for air-driven tools. For those earlier valves which do not have auxiliary tappings, swivel pieces are available which give two extra take-off points.

OCTOPUS RIG
This piece of equipment has evolved from the need to be able to assist

your companion diver from depth to the surface in the event of a failure of his air supply. Sharing one demand valve during an ascent is not without risk to either diver and the octopus rig overcomes the sharing problems simply by connecting a further hose and second-stage demand valve unit to the existing first stage. The assisting diver may now offer the companion diver the spare demand-valve mouthpiece and both divers may breathe normally throughout the ascent. The first stage of modern single-hose demand valves is well able to cope with this increased flow of air.

DIRECT FEED TO LIFEJACKETS AND DRY SUITS

The majority of these buoyancy compensating devices are designed to be supplied with air by means of an intermediate pressure take-off from the demand valve first stage. The supply hoses will have some form of quick-release coupling which operates successfully even though the hose is pressurised and these couplings will obviously be in reach of the diver so that he may, for example, remove his aqua-lung set complete with its auxiliary hoses whilst retaining his ABLJ.

The amount of air used for buoyancy compensating or suit in-flation purposes is very small and in no way reduces the diver's duration. In fact, the added insulation of a dry suit or the effort saved by being neutrally buoyant could mean that the diver is not con-suming so much air as he might otherwise do.

Twin-hose demand valves do not usually have auxilliary tappings of this sort but a two-stage twin-hose demand valve could be modi-fied to incorporate such an intermediate pressure take-off point. This could not be done on a single-stage twin-hose demand valve.

High-Pressure Auxiliary Tappings

All demand valves have a high pressure auxiliary tapping which is normally used to supply air to a cylinder contents gauge. In the past certain manufacturers have used high-pressure air to supply ABLJ's and dry suits, but the current practice is to feed these devices with intermediate-pressure air only. Do not attempt to connect the demand valve's intermediate-pressure hose to the high-pressure take-off for this will achieve nothing other than bursting the hose.

Cylinder Contents Gauges are fully described in the section deal-ing with *Diving Accessories*.

Positioning of Demand Valves

TWIN-HOSE

Ideally, the demand valve should be sensing exactly the same pressure as that on the diver's lungs. With twin-hose demand valves the height of the cylinder in the harness should be adjusted so that the demand valve is level with the diver's shoulder-blades, just below the nape of the neck.

In this position the demand valve is level with the diver's lungs in the vertical position, and when the diver is swimming normally, face down in a horizontal plane, the demand valve is only at a slightly lesser pressure than the diver's lungs. The very slight drag that this produces on the air delivery is of no significance—it might be noticed at the initial intake of breath, but will be eliminated by the venturi action as soon as the air starts to flow.

If the diver lies on his back the demand valve is subjected to a greater pressure than his lungs. In this position the regulator will deliver air very readily, but not so forcibly that the diver cannot control it. This effect may be used to advantage if the diver has become short of breath.

SINGLE-HOSE

The reaction of single-hose demand valves is different: they are not sensitive to the positioning of the cylinder.

With the demand stage just in front of the diver's mouth, it is in the best position when the diver is swimming horizontally, face down. The natural tendency is for the diver to tilt his head slightly upward, and the demand valve and the diver's lungs are then substantially on the same level. If there is any bias it will be for the demand valve to be at a slightly greater pressure, and delivering air readily. This is the most noticeable difference between single and twin-hose demand valves.

When standing vertically, the mouthpiece demand valve is subjected to slightly less water pressure than the diver's lungs, but, as with the twin-hose demand valve the difference is not so great as to make any significant alteration in the performance of the demand valve.

The trick of swimming on one's back produces no advantage when using single-hose valves.

Future Trends in Demand Valve Design

There have been no developments to twin-hose demand valves during the past 10 years or so but that period has seen tremendous improvements in single-hose demand valve design. The balanced piston first stage is generally superior in performance to other first stage designs and has the additional advantage of being mechanically simpler. It is difficult to foresee how the balanced piston first stage can be improved upon. Meanwhile developments continue on the single-hose demand valve second stage unit, and already a number of superior (though expensive) servo-operated units of this sort are available. Breathing resistance is negligible and the potential air flow from the valve is such that *beating-the-lung* will soon be a thing of the past.

Demand Valve Maintenance

A diver's life depends on the efficient performance of his demand valve. This finely engineered device is sensitive to wear and tear, incorrect lubrication, and corrosion of its internal parts. It is, therefore, important that for dependable service, demand valves should be overhauled regularly and a 12 monthly service is strongly advised. The work should only be carried out by the manufacturer's recognised service agent. 'Do-it-yourself' servicing should be avoided (except, perhaps by those who are professionally engaged in the maintenance of precision equipment), because pressure gauges and flow meters are required to set up the demand valve's first stage. The best maintenance which the owner can give is to ensure that the demand valve is washed thoroughly in fresh water after each use, whether in the sea or in the swimming pool. Demand valves which are used consistently in the swimming pool should be serviced more regularly since the chlorine used to purify pool water dispels the silicone grease lubricant, and ultimately attacks the neoprene O-ring seals which play a major part in the correct function of the valve.

Air Cylinders

The high-pressure cylinder gave diving its freedom—freedom from lines and hoses to the surface; freedom to range over the sea-bed at will. The growth of our sport probably owes as much to the development of the high-pressure air cylinder as to the invention of the demand valve, and yet, how much regard do we give to this vital reservoir?

Apparently inert and yet potentially hazardous. That is the diving cylinder. With correct usage no problems need arise; but abuse will lead to the creation of severe risks. High-pressure air has the qualities of an explosive! It is essential, therefore, that proper safeguards be adopted to prevent any disaster.

Safety is never bought cheaply and divers who will not invest in proper equipment, nor carry out or ensure its correct care and maintenance, put themselves and their fellow divers in jeopardy. The prime safeguard is to use only those cylinders that were designed specifically for use with aqualing sets. Conversion of cylinders intended for other uses is dangerous and illegal because the specifications to which they were manufactured were never intended for under-water use.

All countries have regulations affecting the use of high-pressure cylinders, and it is unfortunate that these vary from country to country, anomalies arising where a cylinder is perfectly acceptable in its country of origin but not in another. Whilst international discussions are being held to rationalise this situation, it will be some time before a state of uniformity is reached and, in the meantime, the BSAC advises its members to abide by the regulations of the country in which they are diving.

UK Regulations

In the United Kingdom, the Health and Safety Executive (HSE) (Explosives Branch) is responsible for the approval of specifications to which all types of gas cylinders are manufactured, and for regulations concerning their use. The regulations affecting the use of diving cylinders are:

'The Gas Cylinder (Conveyance) Regulations' Nos. 679 (1931), 1594 (1947), and 1919 (1959).

These regulations permit only cylinders manufactured to the following specifications to be used for the conveyance of compressed air in the UK:

(i) British Standards Institute Specifications 399, 400 and 1045.
(ii) Air Ministry Specifications 0.133 (exemption order).
(iii) HSE Specifications—HOS and HOT (steel cylinders).
(iv) HSE Specifications—HOAL 1, 2, 3 and 4 (aluminium cylinders).

The three British Standards Institute Specifications (i) are intended for heavy industrial cylinders and are not likely to be encountered in diving sets, although they may appear in storage banks. The exemption order on Air Ministry Specification 0.133 is a wartime relic, and although cylinders to this specification, i.e. the 'Tadpole' and 'Dumpy 80', were in common use in the early days of the sport, the HSE no longer approves their use for diving, and BSAC endorses this opinion.

Acceptable specifications for steel diving cylinders are the HSE Specifications HOS and HOT. Aluminium diving cylinders are covered by HSE Specifications HOAL 1, 2, 3 and 4.

Confirmation that a cylinder has been manufactured to an approved specification is a guarantee of its soundness at the time of manufacture. These specifications stipulate the composition of the metal and define the minimum wall thickness of the cylinder in relation to the pressure and diameter. Stringent tests are laid down, which must be carried out during the manufacture of each batch of cylinders, culminating in an hydraulic stretch test for every cylinder.

All cylinders carry markings to show:

(i) Manufacturer's marks and Serial Number.
(ii) Specification (e.g. HOS or HOAL 2).
(iii) Date of Manufacture and test.
(iv) Water Capacity (WC) and Cylinder weight. (Not normally shown on aluminium cylinders).
(v) Working Pressure (WP) and Test Pressure (TP).
(vi) Marks and dates of subsequent tests.

These markings may be on the shoulder of the cylinder or on a brass collar around its neck (Fig. 38). The charging and testing pressures are determined at the time of manufacture of the cylinder, and cannot be altered subsequently. The water capacity is a measurement of the internal volume of the cylinder expressed as the weight of the water it will contain.

Steel Cylinders

The maximum charging pressure to which HOS or HOT cylinders may be designed is 207 bar (3000 psi). However, most cylinders are designed for lower pressures. The HOT specification cylinders are

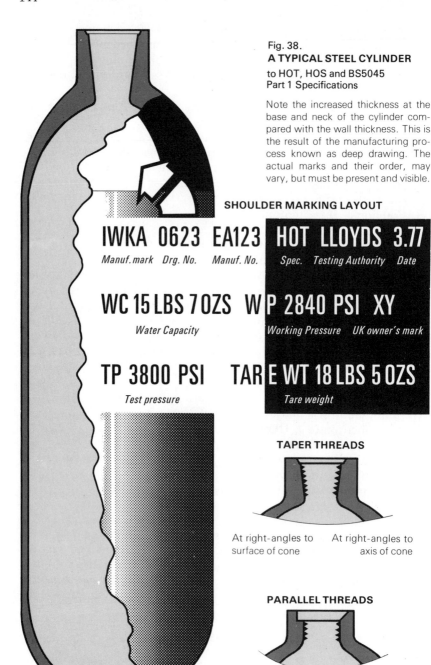

Fig. 38.
A TYPICAL STEEL CYLINDER
to HOT, HOS and BS5045
Part 1 Specifications

Note the increased thickness at the base and neck of the cylinder compared with the wall thickness. This is the result of the manufacturing process known as deep drawing. The actual marks and their order, may vary, but must be present and visible.

SHOULDER MARKING LAYOUT

IWKA 0623 EA123 HOT LLOYDS 3.77
Manuf. mark   Drg. No.   Manuf. No.   Spec.   Testing Authority   Date

WC 15 LBS 7 OZS WP 2840 PSI XY
Water Capacity   Working Pressure   UK owner's mark

TP 3800 PSI TARE WT 18 LBS 5 OZS
Test pressure   Tare weight

TAPER THREADS

At right-angles to   At right-angles to
surface of cone   axis of cone

PARALLEL THREADS

Chamfer or recess for 'O'-ring seal

lighter than the HOS, but are limited to a maximum water capacity of 25 lb (not yet metricated!), which gives a theoretical capacity limit of approximately 2265 litres.

The British Standards Institution is revising the specifications for all types of transportable steel cylinders and after the introduction of the new Standard (BS 5045 Pt. 1), the HSE will require all new cylinders to be manufactured in accordance with it. Although continued use of existing HOS and HOT cylinders will be permitted, manufacture to these specifications will cease, the HOS and HOT Specifications being replaced by a single new specification. The new specification will produce a cylinder midway in weight between the two that are being phased out.

Care and Maintenance of Cylinders

Corrosion is the arch enemy of cylinders and yet simple precautions will avoid most of the ill-effects. Most diving is carried out in salt water—a corrosive liquid—and it would seem obvious that all diving gear should be washed clean of salt water after use. Yet how often is this advice ignored! Cylinders probably suffer most in this respect.

The obvious course is to wash cylinders with fresh water after use; this also applies to swimming pool use when the water is chlorinated. Remove cylinder boots periodically and wash out the accumulated salt and silt; do the same with the harness. Both of these items can cause localised corrosion to the cylinder by trapping mineral particles in contact with the cylinder. Aluminium cylinders are especially susceptible to electrolytic corrosion if a stainless steel or brass harness band is left in place for long periods. Often boots and harness are only removed at the time of the statutory test. This is not enough. When a cylinder is laid-up for the winter these fittings should be removed and the cylinder washed and dried.

Keep cylinders painted. Grey with black and white quarters is the colouring specified by the HSE but, whatever the colour scheme, it is essential that the coating should be coherent and intact. If needs be, repaint each year. Zinc spraying of steel cylinders is a very good pre-treatment for painting; some American cylinders are even hot-dip galvanised. The zinc forms a sacrificial coating and the salt water attacks this in preference to the steel. However, it should not be sacrificed needlessly—a good coat of paint is the first line of defence.

Of the paint treatments, stove enamelling is the most robust. Plastic coatings have been used on steel cylinders, but should not be used on aluminium. When intact they are very good but inevitably puncture and then salt water creeps in between the coating and the cylinder surface. This sets up very severe localised corrosion which may escape detection until it is too late.

Cylinder markings should not be obscured; the compressor operator will need to read the pressure rating, and check the test date, before re-charging. So, ensure that all the markings can be read; pick them out in a contrasting colour if you like and highlight the current test date. It is also helpful to paint the owner's name on the cylinder, for one 1700 litre looks very much like another when placed in a heap at the compressor.

Internal corrosion is not easily controlled by the owner: filling only with dry air is the essential requirement and this rests on the competence of the compressor operator. Branches that operate compressors should ensure that all operators know their job! It should not be regarded as a tedious chore to be palmed-off on the least complaining member! Compressor interstage drains and water separator should be blown down between each filling, and the air delivered should be to the requisite standard of dryness (see *Compressors and Cylinder Filling*).

Tell-tale signs of internal corrosion to the cylinder are:

(i) Rust deposit on the demand valve filter.

(ii) Rustling noises in the cylinder.

If either of these symptoms is discovered, the pillar valve should be removed, and the cylinder inspected internally. In the first instance fine rust dust will get past the filter and may cause malfunction of the demand valve; it will certainly need stripping for cleaning. Remedial action can be taken if the situation is dealt with promptly; ignore the symptoms and the cylinder may be scrapped. A more serious situation is suggested by the second symptom: it may be loose rust in the cylinder, which implies that an advanced state of corrosion has been reached. Still worse, it may be a significant quantity of water—quantities exceeding 0.25 litres have been discovered. This can swamp the anti-debris tube and cause water, instead of air to be delivered to the diver. Choking may ensue and this may have fatal consequences.

Aluminium, of course, does not rust and serious internal corrosion is unlikely to occur. However, being a softer metal, the aluminium cylinder can suffer deep scratches and pitting if mishandled. A 2 mm deep score on the outside can be enough to fail the cylinder on inspection prior to periodic testing.

Dry, pure air and regular inspection are the surest safeguard to combat internal corrosion. It is recommended that all cylinders be opened up each year for visual internal inspection. Cylinders should not be stored in a fully charged state for long periods. The high partial pressure of oxygen in the compressed air can lead to accelerated corrosion if there is any water present. Neither should they be left completely empty for, if the valve is left open, the cylinder will 'breathe' and any changes in temperature will result in condensation inside the cylinder. Store cylinders at a relatively low pressure—say, 10 bar—with the driest air available. For extended storage, inspect the cylinder BEFORE laying it up, and ensure that there is no water, even dampness, inside. Internal corrosion will only take place in the presence of water. Eliminate the water, including water vapour, and the corrosion will be defeated.

Cylinder Testing

In the United Kingdom it is a Health and Safety Executive requirement that all cylinders used for the conveyance of high-pressure gases be subjected to periodic inspection and hydraulic testing. While the law requires tests at five-year intervals, in the case of aqualung cylinders, the HSE recommends a test interval of three years from the date of manufacture, and every two years thereafter. The BSAC further recommends that steel cylinders be given an internal inspection every year.

The test pressure for a cylinder is determined at the time of manufacture and is stamped on the cylinder. The precise value varies according to the specification, type and size of the cylinder but is approximately $1\frac{1}{3}$ (steel) to $1\frac{2}{3}$ (aluminium) times the working pressure. Once determined by the manufacturer, the test pressure cannot be subsequently up-rated.

During its statutory test the cylinder is first inspected externally for damage, corrosion, or unauthorised repair—such as welding. The cylinder markings are checked to establish the specification of the cylinder and its correct test pressure. It is also necessary to confirm that the markings have not been falsified, as has been found on some aluminium cylinders.

After removal of the pillar valve, the cylinder is inspected internally. This is necessarily a subjective test and relies heavily on the skill of the inspector. A light bloom of rust in a steel cylinder is not a serious problem, but heavy rusting or localised pitting may be cause for rejection. Light rusting may be removed by 'rumbling', i.e. partially filling the cylinder with cracked shot and then rotating it continuously for several hours. If this treatment is necessary it must be done before proceeding to the hydraulic test.

The Hydraulic Stretch Test

For the Hydraulic Stretch Test the cylinder is completely filled with water and connected to a high-pressure hydraulic pump. It is then pressurised to its stamped test pressure, and its volumetric expansion is measured. The pressure is released and if the cylinder is in good condition it will return to its original size. As the cylinder ages the metal becomes less elastic and does not return to its original size. This residual expansion—known as 'permanent set'—is also measured, and the HSE regulations state that the permanent set must not exceed 10% of the expansion measured at the test pressure. If it exceeds this it indicates that the metal has lost its ductility, or perhaps because of corrosion, has developed a thin patch. In any case, the cylinder must be rejected.

The measurement of the cylinder expansion needs to be taken very accurately. There are two methods of hydraulically testing a cylinder and the measurement of the expansion varies slightly from one ot the other.

'NON-JACKET TESTING'

The commonest test procedure is the non-jacket method. Here, the water-filled cylinder is connected directly to an hydraulic pump which draws the extra water needed to pressurise the cylinder from a calibrated sight tube. When the cylinder has reached its test pressure, the amount of water drawn from the sight tube is noted, the pressure is released, and the water flows back into the tube. If the cylinder is in perfect condition the water in the sight tube will return to the original level, but if the cylinder has undergone some permanent set (expansion), the level in the sight glass will fall short of the original mark. The amount of water drawn from the sight tube is often regarded as equalling the expansion of the cylinder, but this is not accurate. Just as the cylinder expanded under pressure, so the water inside it compressed, and a correction factor for this compression should be applied before assessing the permanent set. It must be admitted, however, that this correction is not often made by testing stations, but this omission does not appear to allow many suspect cylinders to pass the test, probably because doubtful cylinders are rejected during the preceeding internal inspection.

'JACKETED' TESTING

A more precise test procedure is the 'jacketed' method. In this case the water-filled cylinder is immersed in another water-filled container. This is the 'jacket'. The jacket is not pressurised and, although sealed with a lid, is open to atmospheric pressure via a calibrated sight tube.

The cylinder is pressurised in a manner similar to the previous method: as the cylinder expands it displaces water from the jacket, and the level of water in the sight tube rises. This is a direct measurement of the cylinder expansion and will not require subsequent correction. When the pressure is released, the sight tube level will fall. Any residual reading is the permanent set of the cylinder, and an immediate comparison with the expansion under pressure may be made.

After completion of a satisfactory hydraulic test, the cylinder must be drained of all water and positively dried internally, before the valve is refitted and the cylinder charged.

Certificate and Stamping

The inspecting company should issue a Test Certificate for each cylinder. This certificate should identify the cylinder by Specification and Serial No. It should show the relevant charging and testing pressures, the amount of permanent set encountered, and a comment on the internal condition of the cylinder.

The inspector must stamp the cylinder with the date of the test and an identifying mark of the testing company. The date may be shown as month and year, or quarter and year. The stamping should be on the shoulder of the cylinder, or on the collar ring if fitted. Cylinders should not be stamped on the sides.

British Standards Institution

At the time of writing the British Standards Institution is preparing a Standard for the periodic inspection and testing of cylinders. The HSE will ultimately define this Standard as being the statutory test procedure to be followed by all testing stations.

ABLJ Cylinders

Compressed-air cylinders used on adjustable buoyancy lifejackets have a hard life! Filled by rapid decanting, they are also discharged quickly, often to a completely empty state. Seepage of water from the jacket into the cylinder is common in spite of the non-return valve at the cylinder-to-jacket connection. All these factors contribute to a high corrosion risk in the cylinder.

External corrosion is also a problem, especially with those cylinders covered with a plastic coating. These impervious coatings are very effective when intact, but once they are punctured, salt water will seep between the plastic and the cylinder. This salt cannot be washed out and severe localised corrosion of the cylinder will occur. Abrasion of a painted surface does not produce such a critical condition, and is to be preferred as a protective treatment.

Lifejacket cylinders do not come within the scope of HSE regulations (as yet), so there is no statutory requirement for their inspection and test. However, in view of the severity of the conditions of use, the BSAC recommends that they be hydraulically tested on the same basis as the aqualung cylinders, i.e. three years from the date of manufacture/test, and every two years thereafter, with an internal inspection every year.

Precautions in the use of Lifejacket Cylinders

1. DO NOT OVERCHARGE THE CYLINDER. Most lifejacket cylinders have a charging pressure of around 200 bar, and up to the present time few aqualungs have exceeded this, so the chances of over-filling the lifejacket cylinder when decanting from an aqualung have been remote. However, aqualung cylinders are now being manufactured to specifications that permit charging pressures of up to 300 bar—and this is the TEST pressure for existing lifejacket cylinders! So, in future, care must be taken to ensure that these cylinders are not overcharged.

2. AVOID EMPTYING THE CYLINDER COMPLETELY. It is the empty or near-empty cylinder that is most vulnerable to ingress of water: water seepage through the non-return valve is possible at very low rates of air flow. In addition, closure of the control valve may well be overlooked during an emergency ascent. In any event, if the cylinder does become completely empty, it should be checked for ingress of water.

3. BLOW DOWN THE CYLINDER REGULARLY. Detach the cylinder from the lifejacket, hold the cylinder upright with the valve bottom-most, open the valve and discharge a short burst of air. These cylinders do not contain anti-debris tubes, so by this method any accumulated water will be blown out. Of course, if it becomes obvious that a quantity of water has in fact entered the cylinder, it should be de-valved for inspection and washing out.

4. DO NOT STORE LIFEJACKET CYLINDERS IN A CHARGED CONDITION. The rate of internal corrosion may be accelerated by the presence of high-pressure air. Water traces in the life-jacket cylinder are likely to be salty and this makes the situation even worse. The ease with which these cylinders may be charged removes any disadvantage of not having the cylinder at instant readiness; in fact it ensures that the cylinder is definitely re-charged prior to the dive!

5. CHECK THE JACKET NON-RETURN VALVE. Disconnect the cylinder from an inflated jacket. There should be no leakage of air from the exposed jacket connection. Some early jackets did not incorporate non-return valves, and very great care must be taken with these jackets to avoid completely emptying the cylinder, otherwise water will drain into the cylinder.

Pillar Valves

A pillar valve is more than a mere tap that turns your air supply on and off, and it deserves better treatment than it usually gets. For a start, it should be washed with fresh water after each dive. There is an advantage in leaving the demand valve in place, attached to the pillar valve, and in hosing down the demand valve, pillar valve and cylinder all in one go: the pillar valve can then be left open, thus exposing more of the spindle stem than would otherwise be possible.

If a pillar valve cannot be turned readily by hand then something is wrong with it. Dried salt may have accumulated in the spindle gland, and salt being very abrasive, it will cause the spindle to become stiff in operation. Pillar valves should, therefore, be lubricated periodically—at least once a season. Silicone grease only should be used for this purpose to avoid the dangers caused by mineral greases reacting with the oxygen content of high-pressure air from the cylinder.

Stiffness in operation may also be caused by lack of lubrication or damage to the spindle threads, in which case the valve should be stripped, repaired and re-lubricated. If this point is ignored, the screw thread will ultimately seize up and strip, which may mean the replacement of the whole pillar valve. All pillar valves will suffer damage if unnecessarily overtightened. Use finger pressure only.

The Unbalanced Valve

The commonest pattern of pillar valve is the 'unbalanced' type as shown in Fig. 39a. With this type the spindle and valve head are in one piece and the spindle screws directly into the valve body, thus, the nylon valve pad rotates against the valve seat as it seals, and is, therefore, liable to wear, particularly if screwed down hard.

The term 'unbalanced' means that the thrust of the high-pressure air is attempting to blow the valve head through the valve body. This force has to be resisted by the actuating thread; there is always an extra frictional load on the thread and in consequence it will wear relatively quickly. Lack of lubrication will aggravate the condition. Once the screw thread in the valve body is worn there is no alternative but to replace the whole pillar valve.

The spindle assembly can be removed from these valves by backing off the gland nut, unscrewing the spindle at the same time. The condition of the screw threads can now be seen. The spindle assembly should be taken apart; this necessitates removal of the finger knob. The assembly will now pull apart so that the components can be washed, dried and lightly lubricated.

To re-assemble the pillar valve, first screw the spindle into the valve body; slip on the metal spacer ring, then the O-ring and, using a blunt rod to avoid cutting the O-ring, push the spacer and O-ring down into the recess around the spindle. Now screw home the gland nut and finally re-pin the finger knob in position.

Glandless Valve

Although still an unbalanced valve, this type (see Fig. 39b) is more

F

complex, and has some advantages over the simpler variety. In the first place, the valve head does not rotate with the spindle, so there is less wear on the valve pad because it is not dragged around the valve seat. Secondly, the high-pressure air is prevented from escaping up the spindle by a bell-shaped diaphragm which is attached to the valve head. The actuating screw thread is contained in the cap nut and, being of larger diameter than in the design described previously, is not so prone to wear. Even if the thread did seize it would only be necessary to replace the cap nut and spindle, not the whole valve. Thirdly, the top O-ring does not seal hp air, but serves as a wiper ring to prevent ingress of salt and sand to the screw thread. However, periodically it should be inspected closely, and replaced when worn.

To strip this type of valve: first, close the valve lightly, then remove the cap nut and withdraw the whole spindle and valve head assembly. (A sharp tug may be necessary if the rubber diaphragm proves to be stuck.) Now screw in the spindle so that the valve head may be disengaged from the 'key-hole' slot. Continue screwing the spindle into the cap nut until the plastic finger knob is pushed off; the spindle may now be separated from the cap nut. Clean and re-lubricate all the components, and have a look at that wiper ring.

Re-assemble the components into the cap nut, taking care not to forget the large metal washer between the cap nut and rubber diaphragm. Bring the diaphragm back into contact with the cap nut, but do not squeeze it. Now insert the assembly back into the valve body and lightly tighten the cap nut; 'open' the valve to lift the valve head clear of the valve seat, and then complete the tightening of the cap nut.

Balanced Valves

Fig. 39c shows the third variety, the 'balanced' valve. The valve head, although separate from the spindle, still rotates with it, being driven by a tongue and groove connection. This rotates the valve head but also allows it to move axially along the screw thread, without the spindle following it. When the valve is 'open', the hp air flows past the thread of the valve head so that it is completely surrounded, with the result that there is no extra thrust exerted on the thread. Instead, this thrust is taken on a PTFE (Poly Tetra Fluoro Ethylene) washer, situated behind the shoulder on the spindle. Since there is no axial thrust on the valve head it is considered to be in a 'balanced' condition.

Balanced valves are also made in a pattern known as 'cross flow'. The tap is on the side, and the orifice to which the demand valve is attached is on the top. This reduces the overall height of the shut-off valve, which with the tap NOT on top, is less vulnerable to damage.

While the valve head moves axially, independently of the spindle, it cannot move so far as to come out of engagement. The fact that the operating spindle does not move in or out when the valve is used indicates that it is a balanced type of pillar valve.

Unscrewing the gland nut will allow the whole spindle assembly to be withdrawn; the valve head remaining in the valve body. Dismantle the spindle assembly by removing the little nut inside the finger knob—watch out for the spring! Having separated these components, use the spindle to withdraw the valve head from the body. Wash and clean all components, particularly the spindle and gland nut as these have no wiper ring and will, therefore, be coated with a heavy salt deposit.

After re-lubricating the components, replace them, in order, in the valve body. Insert the valve head, followed by the spindle, thrust washer, gland nut, anti-friction washer, finger knob, spring and nut. The spring nut should be two turns short of coil-binding the spring.

Aluminium cylinders are usually fitted with a special type of pillar valve. The configuration of the spindle and valve head is the same as for the steel cylinder valve already described. The body of the valve is made of aluminium alloy so that it is compatible with the cylinder. Because of the softness of this metal, a separate screwed insert is used for the valve seat. This insert is not normally removable since the 'anti-debris' tube is clenched into the body, thus preventing access. These too are available in 'cross flow' pattern.

The valve for an aluminium cylinder has a large diameter, parallel thread, connecting it to the cylinder. This thread is sealed with an O-ring instead of the PTFE tape used on the taper threads.

The spindle assembly may be removed by unscrewing the gland nut. The valve head may then be removed separately. To dismantle the spindle assembly: first, punch out the spring pin in the finger knob. This should be done with the correct diameter punch, and care should be taken not to get the punch stuck in place of the pin: rest the knob on a small block of wood with a hole beneath the pin, and knock it through. The knob will probably still be tightly fitted on to the spindle so loosen it by grasping the spindle tongue firmly, whilst twisting the knob to and fro. Now separate the knob from the spindle, taking care not to lose the spring that it encloses. Push the spindle out of the gland nut, collecting the spring, wiper O-ring and anti-friction washer in the process.

A shoulder will be seen on the extracted spindle, this rests against a small thrust washer inside the gland nut. Extract the thrust washer from the gland nut carefully: it is very small. If the valve has been leaking up the spindle, it will be because this thrust washer is worn and is in need of replacement.

Fig. 39. **PILLAR VALVES**

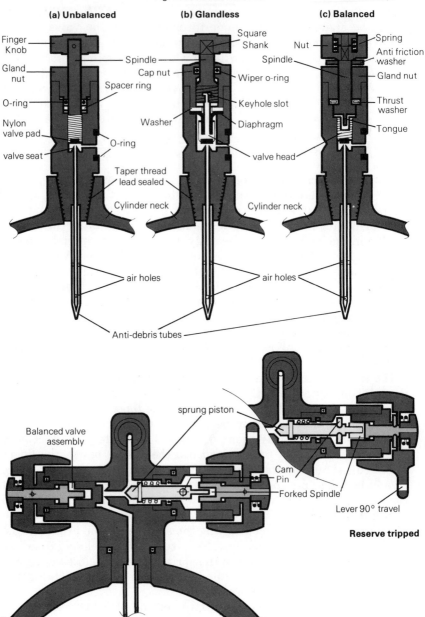

(a) Unbalanced

Finger Knob
Gland nut
O-ring
Nylon valve pad
valve seat
Spindle
Cap nut
Spacer ring
O-ring
Taper thread lead sealed
Cylinder neck
air holes

(b) Glandless

Square Shank
Spindle
Wiper o-ring
Keyhole slot
Washer
Diaphragm
valve head
Cylinder neck
air holes

Anti-debris tubes

(c) Balanced

Nut
Spring
Anti friction washer
Spindle
Gland nut
Thrust washer
Tongue

Balanced valve assembly
sprung piston
Cam
Pin
Forked Spindle
Lever 90° travel

Reserve tripped

(d) Reserve valve

After cleaning all components, lightly lubricate them with silicone grease and reassemble the valve. Fit the thrust washer to the spindle and insert into the gland nut. Fit the wiper O-ring, anti-friction washer and spring over the spindle. Push on the finger knob, holding it against the spring compression, and align the pin holes before trying to tap in the pin. Screw the valve head into the body until it is just below the top. Fit the sealing O-ring. Engage the tongue of the spindle with the valve head, and screw the gland nut, together with the valve head, down into the body until it seals on the O-ring. A few more turns of the spindle will close the valve.

Reserve Valves

On the Continent, and in North America, reserve valves on the cylinder or twin cylinder manifold are commonly used instead of a cylinder-contents gauge. With the reserve valve set in the 'dive' position, the flow of air will be restricted when the cylinder pressure falls to a low level—about 30 to 50 bars. The restriction warns the diver that he is low on air and he can by-pass the restriction by pulling a rod, stowed beside the aqualung cylinder, which opens the air-reserve valve.

Fig. 39d shows such a cylinder shut-off valve. With a charged cylinder the pressure on the face of the valve is sufficient to overcome the force exerted by the spring. There comes a time as cylinder pressure falls when the air pressure on the valve is close to that exerted by the spring, and this is when the diver notices a restriction to breathing. Operation of the mechanism draws the valve face clear of its seating (by compressing the spring) and allows free flow of the remaining air to the demand valve.

The diver has received his warning and commences his ascent. The disadvantages of the system are:

(a) The mechanism can be knocked on by accident during the dive; or not reset. When the restriction comes, it is because the cylinder is empty.

(b) The diver does not have a precise knowledge of air available; something which a cylinder-contents gauge DOES offer.

Anti-Debris Tubes

A small tube extends from the base of all pillar valves, into the cylinder. This is an anti-debris tube, its purpose being to prevent any loose debris in the cylinder—perhaps particles of rust, remnants of tape or lead foil, and even water—from being drawn into the pillar valve. Without the tube it will readily be seen that as soon as the cylinder is inverted all loose debris, especially water, would be funnelled into the pillar valve. The anti-debris tube allows this foreign matter to lie harmlessly in the shoulder of the cylinder, while the air is drawn from a point above it.

Cylinder Threads

The inlet to most steel cylinders is still a tapered thread, and it is not advisable for unskilled mechanics to attempt to remove the pillar valve. Although excessive tightening is not necessary when fitting pillar valves, it still often takes considerable effort to remove them from the cylinder after a couple of seasons' use. The chromium finish of the valve is slippery and will cause a spanner to skid, and it is all too easy to crush the metal around the washer groove and ruin the sealing face. It should also be noted that in many cases the shape of the pillar valves does not permit the use of normal spanners.

The taper thread is made pressure tight by wrapping it in a lead foil cup, or with PTFE tape, prior to screwing it into the cylinder. As the pillar valve is tightened down, the foil (or tape), flows around the threads, completely sealing the mating halves.

The torque required to fit the pillar valve is no more than that needed to tighten an ordinary nut of comparable size. If excessive torque is applied there is a danger that the neck of the cylinder will be strained, or the thread damaged. Extra long spanners may be needed to extract an old pillar valve, but they should not be used to insert new ones.

Siebe Gorman cylinders have a different taper thread from others, and care should therefore, be taken to ensure that an incorrect valve is not fitted to the cylinder.

Aluminium cylinders, and some of the new steel cylinders, have a parallel threaded neck. The corresponding pillar valve has a shoulder which screws down on to the neck of the cylinder. Sealing is achieved by an O-ring placed between this shoulder and the cylinder neck. There is less strain on the necks of such cylinders, hence its use on aluminium cylinders.

The compression of the O-ring acts as a friction grip between the two components and when the cylinder is charged the frictional force on the O-ring and thread is such that it cannot be unscrewed unwittingly. The great advantage of a parallel-threaded cylinder is that it allows a larger diameter hole through which the internal condition of the cylinder may be inspected.

Compressors and Cylinder Filling

High-pressure air cylinders used by divers can be recharged in two ways: from a suitable air compressor; or by decanting from large storage cylinders. The ideal system would incorporate both methods, thereby ensuring a ready supply of air at any time.

While it is desirable that a knowledge of the fundamentals of cylinder-recharging techniques should be imparted to all Club members who dive regularly, it must be stressed that the actual operation and maintenance of air compressors and decanting systems is highly specialised. Compressed air, even at pressures far lower than those charged into aqualung cylinders, is lethal if misused. The high investment made by a Branch in an air compressor should be sufficient justification for careful control over those allowed access to it.

Simple Compressor Theory

'The operation of compressing air produces heat.' This statement describes the fundamental problem of maintaining high efficiencies in air compressors, i.e. the more this compression heating can be reduced, the higher will be the efficiency.

Air can be compressed in many ways, the two most relevant systems being isothermal and adiabatic compression:

1. ISOTHERMAL COMPRESSION

An isothermal air compression is one in which all the heat of compression is dissipated and the final temperature is equal to the initial value. This type of compression is only possible if the cycle of time is extremely slow. (See the dotted line 'ab' of Fig. 40a.)

2. ADIABATIC COMPRESSION

An adiabatic air compression is one in which the majority of the heat of compression is contained within the air itself. This is the type of compression encountered in practical air compressors, and is represented by the full line 'ab1'.

This graph is known as a P–V diagram for a compressor cycle; 'da' represents the suction stroke; 'ab' or 'ab1' represents the compression stroke and 'bc' or 'b1c' represents the constant pressure discharge. As the work required to produce such a cycle is proportional to the area within the curve 'abcd', it will be seen that an isothermal compression requires less work and is therefore more efficient. When the air is eventually cooled after an adiabatic compression, the volume will be reduced and hence, the nearer a compressor can approximate isothermal conditions, the more air it will deliver.

In order to achieve conditions approximating to isothermal compression, modern compressor units pump air in a number of stages. The P–V diagram for a three-stage compressor is shown in Fig. 40b. The dotted line 'bf' is the isothermal: the object is to keep the compression as near to isothermal as possible. In the first stage the air is compressed adiabatically to 'c', it is then cooled at constant pressure by an intercooler until the temperature is reduced to the initial value if possible; this is represented by the constant pressure line 'cd'. For complete intercooling, the point 'd' is on the isothermal line 'bf'. The air is then drawn into the next cylinder for the second stage of its compressions and the process is repeated. Thus it will be seen that each stage increases the pressure of the air whilst the initial temperature is maintained at the end. Throughout the whole process the isothermal line has been approximated to in steps. If the compression reached by all these stages had taken place in a single stage, the compression line would have followed the adiabatic line 'be'; hence the work saved is that shown by the shaded area.

Basic Compressor Design

1. THE COMPRESSOR

An air compressor suitable for charging diving cylinders basically consists of a crankshaft which drives a number of pistons dependent upon the number of compression stages (usually three or four). The reciprocating motion of each piston pumps air through inlet and outlet valves at the end of each cylinder. These valves are simple, air-flow operated, poppet types.

2. COMPRESSOR LAYOUT AND CHARGING CIRCUIT

Fig. 40c shows a simple layout for a three-stage air-cooled compressor. The air enters at the *filter* and is drawn into the *first stage cylinder*. At first stage pressure, the air is pumped through *intercoolers* and the *water separator* and thence to the *second stage cylinder*. At second stage pressure, the air is then pumped through a further intercooler and water separator to the final *third stage cylinder*. Air at the final outlet pressure then passes through the final *water separator* and then through the *composite chemical filter*. The last passage of the air is through the *manifold* to the *high-pressure hoses and 'A'-clamps* to the diving cylinders.

The intercoolers are usually made from coiled copper pipes situated in an external air stream which is derived from a fan mounted on the end of the unit's crankshaft. The water separators

COMPRESSORS

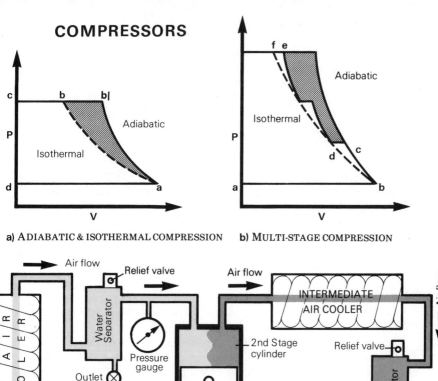

a) ADIABATIC & ISOTHERMAL COMPRESSION   **b)** MULTI-STAGE COMPRESSION

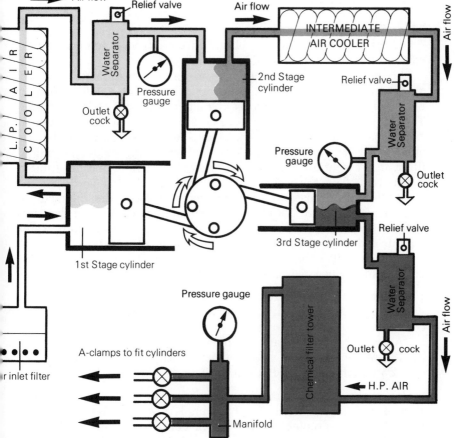

Fig. 40 (c) A THREE-STAGE AIR-COOLED BASIC COMPRESSOR LAYOUT

are usually simple cylindrical chambers in which the air flow changes direction, thereby letting any water vapour condense on to the walls and drain down to the outlet cock where it is periodically discharged to atmosphere. The chemical filter usually contains Silica Gel or Activated Alumina and Activated Charcoal separated by a thick felt pad.

In order to prevent damage to the compressor by over pressurisation, *relief valves* are situated at the entry to the second and third stages. Another relief valve is situated in the final pressure line which is set to the final pressure desired in the diving cylinders.

Although the above description is for a three-stage air-cooled unit, the same type of circuit with minor differences is used in all compressors, e.g. with a water-cooled unit, intercoolers will usually be in part of the main block casting and thus cooled by the same water that flows around the cylinders.

Filter Systems

To maintain a consistent supply of pure air from a compressor, an efficient filtering system should be employed.

The most efficient air-filtering media are manufactured from absorbent materials, that is, materials whose granular form has an extremely high surface area to attract particles of contamination. The most common materials used are Silica Gel or Activated Alumina for removing moisture and Activated Charcoal for removing oil mist and odour. When constructing or recharging a filter, it is essential that the Activated Charcoal should be situated downstream from the desiccating material in order to ensure efficient absorption of oil mist, etc. A rather more efficient filtering medium than those described above is Molecular Sieve (Activated Zeolites) with a granule type 13X. This material will remove both water vapour and oil mist but has the disadvantage of high cost.

The composition of a typical filter for an average-size compressor could be described as follows and is shown in Fig. 41.

12.5 mm thick felt pad at inlet; and separating each chemical.
Silica Gel (self-indicating type) at least 100 mm depth;
OR Activated Alumina, at least 100 mm depth;
Activated Charcoal, at least 100 mm depth;
13X Molecular Sieve, about 50 mm depth;
12.5 mm thick felt pad at outlet.

One of the most important points concerning filtering systems is that of regular maintenance. The simplest way to assess the time interval between replacing the filter elements is to use self-indicating Silica Gel which changes colour as it becomes saturated with water. With a new compressor, the filter life can be established by repeated

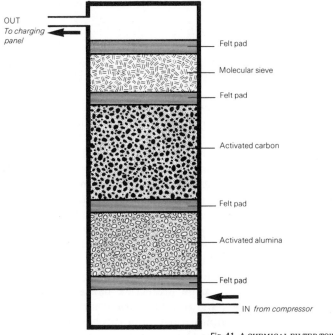

OUT
To charging panel

Felt pad

Molecular sieve

Felt pad

Activated carbon

Felt pad

Activated alumina

Felt pad

IN *from compressor*

Fig. 41. A CHEMICAL FILTER TOWER

inspection (approx. every 10 hours running time) of the Silica Gel—the whole element including felt pads should be replaced immediately a definite colour change is observed.

Lubrication

In order to ensure that a compressor is satisfactorily lubricated it is essential that any manufacturer's recommendations should be followed. In general, most compressors used for filling diving cylinders are lubricated with mineral-based, medium-viscosity index oils which are not prone to emulsification. Liquid paraffin, vegetable motor and medical oils should normally be avoided.

Choosing a Compressor

When selecting a compressor, a consideration of the following points will be useful:

1. The compressor must supply air free of oil, water, dust and contamination by other gases and exhaust fumes. A reputable make originally designed for this purpose should be chosen.
2. It should be capable of supplying air up to the maximum working pressure of cylinders used, or likely to be used.

3. Its output rate should be such that filling does not occupy an unreasonable time.
4. It should be so designed and constructed that it will run for reasonably long periods between overhaul, and be inherently safe.
5. The system of drive should be simple and safe.
6. It should have a high efficiency, and spares and service should be readily available—another reason for selecting a well-proven brand.
7. If portability is required, the output rate is not likely to be more than 200 l/min (7 cu ft/min). Larger machines can be trailer mounted if equipped with a petrol or diesel prime mover.

If considering the purchase of a second-hand machine, the buyer would be well advised to seek the independent opinion of a specialist before confirming the purchase. It is best to buy only a machine built expressly for the purpose of charging breathing air cylinders. 'Bargains' are not always what they seem.

If the machine is for static use (as is the case with a large installation) electric drive is to be preferred, being in the long-term more efficient and cheaper, and free of contaminating exhaust gases. Portable machines must employ a petrol or diesel engine and, in use, care must be taken to prevent the prime mover exhaust fumes from being drawn into the compressor air intake. Diesel engines produce less toxic fumes than petrol engines. All portable machines are relatively noisy, and consideration should be given to operating the machine away from the public, thereby avoiding annoyance.

Siting the Compressor

Portable machines should be used out of doors, and preferably in an open place where there is a wind blowing. The air intake to the compressor—usually on a 3 m long flexible hose—should be situated well up-wind of the engine exhaust.

Avoid having to operate a petrol/diesel driven compressor in a confined space on a windless day. Under these circumstances it is almost impossible to avoid the risk of exhaust fumes being drawn into the compressor.

Portable machines are often noisy and may create a public nuisance. For the good name of the sport, avoid this.

For a permanently installed compressor, an electric motor is quieter as well as being free of toxic exhaust gases. If the compressor has a petrol or diesel engine the foregoing comments apply; have the engine exhaust remote from, and down-wind of the compressor air intake, which should be directly from outside the building if possible.

All compressors should have a simple felt or paper air intake filter, to prevent dust particles entering the machine.

There should be a NO SMOKING Rule if there is a chance that tobacco smoke could be drawn into the compressor air intake.

Layout of Compressor Control or Charging Panel

For the purposes of explanation, two types of compressor charging panel are shown. Compressor operating procedure is virtually common to either.

In Fig. 42 air comes from the compressor's air filter, through a non-return valve, past a main shut-off valve 'A' and into the charging manifold. A high-pressure gauge indicates the pressure within the system and thus in the aqualung cylinders being filled. Each flexible charging hose has its own shut-off valve, and a bleed valve to allow the air in the hose, between the closed charging hose shut-off and cylinder pillar valve, to be vented. A further spur from the manifold leads to the air-storage cylinders via the shut-off valve 'B'. A manifold bleed valve allows the system to 'blow off' or to be drained of air. It is closed during all charging operations.

With shut-off valve A open and B closed, aqualungs connected to the charging hoses can be filled directly from the compressor. With A closed and B open, aqualungs can be filled from the storage cylinders or 'bank' as it is sometimes known. The bank can be refilled by the compressor with A and B open, and all charging hose shut-off valves closed. A single cylinder may be filled off one charging hose with the others closed.

The non-return valve in the supply line prevents reverse pressurisation of the filter and compressor. The NRV is often built into the filter to serve also as a filter pressure retaining valve.

In the case of the smaller compressor layout (Fig. 43), it is common to have a single lever multi-way valve, which directs the air into one of two charging hoses, or allows the entire system, charging hoses as well, to bleed off. A variety of control systems are employed by different manufacturers, and the control panel of each machine should be figured out before use.

Compressor Operation

Anyone wishing to learn the correct operation of an air compressor should receive sound instruction from a competent operator. The Manufacturer's Handbook should also be studied. The trainee operator should realise that a compressor is a costly item— probably one of the Branch's most valuable assets—which, if immobilised by misuse, will mean no training and no diving for want of air, and a big repair bill. It should be operated with care for pure air is vital to the well-being of all divers.

First, learn the layout of the machine: the location of water drains,

COMPRESSOR LAYOUTS

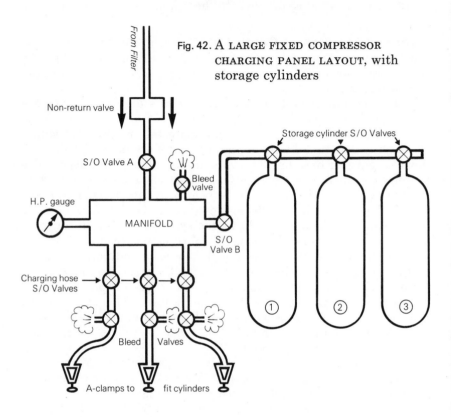

Fig. 42. A LARGE FIXED COMPRESSOR CHARGING PANEL LAYOUT, with storage cylinders

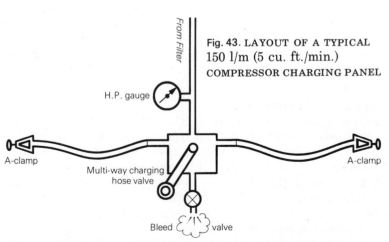

Fig. 43. LAYOUT OF A TYPICAL 150 l/m (5 cu. ft./min.) COMPRESSOR CHARGING PANEL

control valves, sump oil levels (compressor and prime mover), etc. Learn how to start and stop the machine, and how to strip and refill the all-important air filter. This learning should be gained at the hands of a competent operator, by example and supervised practice.

Adopt a set routine when filling. The following procedure is recommended:

1. Check oil levels in compressor and prime mover. Check cooling water levels (where applicable) in compressor and prime mover. Top up as necessary. Fill prime mover fuel tank with the correct fuel. Check that all drains and valves are open so that when the machine is started it is 'blowing off'. (Fig. 42—Valve A open: B closed; manifold open, etc.; charging hose valves open, and no cylinders connected.) Check in the compressor running Logbook (all good compressor houses should have one!) the hours run since the last filter change. If close to the limit, change the filter (see page 160 and BSAC Paper No. 1).
2. Start the prime mover and thus the compressor. Allow the machine to warm up and its lubricating oil to circulate before starting to charge cylinders. Record the start time in the Log. Allow the compressor to blow off while warming up; this will clear any condensates that have accumulated while not in use. While this is happening, sort the empty aqualung sets to be filled into working pressures, checking to see that the cylinders are currently in test. Out of test cylinders should not be filled. It is the right of a compressor operator to refuse to fill any cylinder about which he has doubts.
3. Connect empty aqualung cylinders to charging hose A-clamps— as many as there are—and try to have all the cylinders of the same working or charging pressure. If one cylinder has a lower pressure than the others it will have to be shut off at its pillar valve and charging hose valve when its working pressure is reached, while the other sets are filled to their higher pressure.
4. With cylinders connected, shut off the compressor drain taps, and the manifold vent valve—or whatever valves are open to allow the system to blow off. With all valves closed, the compressor is now filling the system. Allow the pressure to build up—in a large installation it will do so quite quickly—and at about 50 bar pressure on the main hp gauge, open up aqualung pillar valves, then the charging hose shut-off valves. The sets are now filling.
5. Every 10 minutes running time (more frequently in humid or damp weather) crack open the compressor water drains to allow the oil/water condensate—a creamy-looking liquid—to be blown clear. Close each drain cock only when all condensate is removed. (The action of compressing air causes moisture in the air to be

precipitated. It mixes in the machine with the lubricating oil to form this condensate. If it is not cleared regularly, it will be carried over into the chemical filter, rapidly destroying the latter's effectiveness, and allowing wet, unfiltered air to enter the aqualung set.)

6. When the correct aqualung working pressure is reached, shut off the pillar valve; then the charging hose shut off valves; open up the manifold vent valve so that the filling system is blowing off. Bleed the air from the cylinder charging hoses; remove the filled aqualungs and connect more empty ones. Repeat processes 3 to 6 to fill them.

7. When all aqualungs have been filled, allow the machine to run with all drains and valves open for a minute or two before shutting down. Enter the shut-down time in the Log, with particulars of the sets filled and any other information that may be required. Leave drains and valves open when the machine is not in use.

8. Aqualung cylinders will warm up during charging. This is quite normal, but if the increase in temperature is rapid or excessive it can be harmful, The aqualung should then be submerged in a cold-water tank during filling.

9. Keep filled cylinders separate from empty ones to avoid the chance of an empty one being missed. A strip of masking tape round the pillar valve is a useful safeguard and indicator.

Filling from Storage Cylinder (Decanting)

In the early days of the sport in Britain, when compressors were not so readily available, it was common practice to acquire a number of industrial storage cylinders filled with compressed air from industrial gas suppliers, from which aqualungs could be filled by the decanting process. This is seldom done these days, but such storage cylinders may be incorporated into a permanent compressor set-up to provide an instantly available reservoir of air.

In Fig. 42, such a storage 'bank' is shown. It can be filled directly from the compressor, as has been explained, and if the bank is fully charged, a number of aqualung sets can be filled from it without need to run the compressor. Ideally, the working pressure of the bank will be equal to, or greater than that of the aqualung cylinders to be filled. The basic principle of decanting is this:

With an empty aqualung connected through the charging system to the bank, the air in the storage cylinder is able to occupy a greater space. It flows from the storage cylinder into the aqualung until such time as the air pressure is equal. If the bank and aqualung to be filled had a working pressure of 200 bar, and the former was fully charged, the final balance of pressure after decanting might be 170 bar—it all depends on the volume of air in the storage cylinder. To increase the pressure further in the aqualung, the first storage cylinder should be shut off, and a second opened up. Air will again flow into the aqualung, to balance at a pressure of say, 195 bar. This would probably be near enough—after all no 'fill' is ever spot on.

The next aqualung to be filled from storage cylinder 1 will of course balance out at a pressure much lower than 170 bar. Likewise number 2 will not put enough air into the aqualung for it to be considered full; a third storage cylinder will have to be employed to do so. Obviously there comes a time when the bank pressure is low, when an aqualung can only be partly filled, and the compressor would then be used to top up the aqualungs. If the bank working pressure is greater than that of the aqualungs several sets can be completely filled before the bank pressure falls below the working pressure of the aqualungs. The danger here is of over-filling the aqualungs. The pressure gauge must be watched closely.

The procedure for filling from a bank of storage cylinders as in Fig. 42 is as follows:

1. Sort the aqualungs into ascending order of pressure. Chalk their pressures on them for easy reference. Check the storage-cylinder pressures one at a time, and again chalk up on the cylinders their order of pressure, from lowest to highest, using numbers 1/2/3/4.
2. Always start with the highest aqualung pressure and lowest storage cylinder pressure. In this way every available 'drop' of air is utilised to the full. Using a different order will be less efficient.
3. Connect the first aqualung. Close shut-off valve A; open B. Open the charging hose shut-off valve and aqualung pillar valve.
4. Open storage-cylinder No. 1 SLOWLY, allowing air from it to flow into the aqualung cylinder. Watch the gauge carefully to avoid rapid filling. Use the cold-water tank to keep aqualung cylinders cool during filling.
5. There will come a time when the flow of air can no longer be heard. Pressures in the storage cylinder and aqualung are now equal, and the gauge will show the pressure at which they have balanced. Shut off cylinder 1 and open up 2. Air will flow again until a new equilibrium of pressure is reached. Close 2 and if necessary open 3, to reach the aqualung working pressure.
6. Close No. 3, the aqualung pillar valve and charging hose shut-off. Bleed the hose and connect the next aqualung. (The air in the manifold should not be vented; it can be put into the next set!) Repeat the process, taking care to shut off each storage cylinder before opening the next.
7. It is wise to chalk up the final pressure in each storage cylinder after each fill, so that the exact 'status' of the system can be watched. When the last storage cylinder is opened, and is unable

to fully charge the aqualungs, the compressor should be used to top them up. It is quite safe to fill from both a storage cylinder and the compressor in the early stages of filling an aqualung. For instance, a set can be quickly filled to say, 100 bar, from a storage cylinder containing that pressure, after which the bank is shut off while the compressor fills the aqualung to 200 bar. To leave the storage cylinder open would mean that it is being filled too! That takes time.

A high capacity, high-pressure storage bank used in conjunction with a compressor results in 'instant air' for the diver. Such a system is costly, but well worth while in the long-term for a large Branch. A bank can be set up and filled from a small compressor, thereby easing the rush for air on Branch filling nights.

Maintenance of Compressors and HP Air Installations
A few Golden Rules:
1. Leave maintenance to the manufacturers' approved agents, or in the hands of an engineer who is used to such systems.
2. Use NO OIL or GREASE on pipework, shut-off valves, etc.— anywhere on the installation.
3. Avoid stopping the compressor under load, i.e. while it is charging. Do this only in an emergency. At other times vent off the system first by opening drain cocks.
4. Do not allow untrained operators to use the compressor without supervision.
5. Compressed air can be lethal: respect it.

FILLING CYLINDERS ON DIVE SITE FROM PORTABLE COMPRESSORS

Air Purity Analysis

It is desirable and sometimes essential to have a quick and easy but accurate method of checking the purity of compressed air supplied for diving. Such a method should be adaptable to on-site testing of air supplied by portable compressors, or by commercial air suppliers, as well as to the periodic testing of air supplied by static compressors, whether club or commercially owned. Air purity must relate to a standard, and the BSAC Air Purity Standard should be followed.

BSAC Table of Air Purity Standards—1971

Nitrogen	As atmospheric air
Oxygen	21% ±0.5%
Carbon dioxide	0.03% (300 ppm)
Carbon monoxide	5 ppm
Oil	1 mg per m³
Water	As dry as possible and not give rise to condensation at temperatures above 40°F.
Solid particles, dust, etc.	Lack of residue on a Millipore filter after passing 5 litres of air†
Odour and taste	Freedom from both
Nitrogen dioxide and nitrous oxide	Nil (under 1 ppm)

†Millipore filter, rated as fast and of mean pore size 3.4 to 5 microns.

Portable gas-detector kits can be obtained and are simple to operate, the most common being the Draeger Multi-Gas Detector and the MSA–Auer Toxic Gas Detector. (As both the Draeger and MSA kits have the same size detector tubes, and as the bellows have a capacity of 100 ml, they are interchangeable.)

These kits, which are operated by means of a hand pump, draw a volume of air from a sample bag, through a calibrated glass tube containing reagent chemicals. If the contaminant for which the air is being tested is present, it reacts with these chemicals to produce a coloured stain. After drawing the correct volume of air through the tube, achieved by operating the bellows the number of times indicated on the instructions, the length of stain thus produced is read-off against the appropriate calibration marks on the tube, to give the concentration of the contaminant.

The kits are designed to test air at atmospheric pressure; consequently, it will be necessary to reduce the high pressure air produced by the compressor to atmospheric pressure. This is most conveniently achieved by carefully filling a Draeger Alcotest bag from a cylinder containing the high-pressure air to be tested, and by then drawing the air from the bag; refilling as necessary until the correct volume of air has been drawn through the detector tube. A bag can be re-used many times provided care is taken not to overfill it, and it is flushed out to remove any trace of previous contaminants.

Detector tubes that will measure carbon monoxide, carbon dioxide and nitrogen dioxide at the levels required by the BSAC Air Purity Standard are available. However, the water vapour tubes at present available are only capable of giving accurate measurements at concentrations greater than 1 mg/l, whereas the BSAC requirement is 0.02 mg/l. Oil vapour is another contaminant which cannot be determined at the levels required, i.e. 1 mg/m³. However, a Draeger Poly-Test tube will give a positive reaction when 50 mg/m³ of oil vapour is present. These two tubes are therefore only useful as an indication of gross contamination.

Solid contamination is measured by passing 5 litres of air *at a slow rate* through a 0.45 micron Millipore filter, and examining the upstream face of the filter for dust particles; a ×60 magnification microscope should be used, but if one is not available the highest magnification—up to ×60—should be used.

It should be remembered that none of the less expensive Millipore filter holders can withstand pressure, and great care should therefore be exercised when using them.

To measure the 5 litres of air, allow the air from the Millipore holder to fill an Alcotest bag 5 times.

It is possible for all manner of contaminants to be taken into the air inlet of a compressor and to end up in the air supply. The following are some contaminants that have been detected in compressed air cylinders, together with their possible sources of contamination:

Trichloroethylene	The solvent used to remove oil and grease from cylinders
Chlorine and/or Bromine	From swimming baths or local factories

Mesitylene	From a wall painted with a cement
(Tri-methyl-benzene)	stabilising solution
Alcohol	From a beer store
(Ethyl alcohol/ethanol)	
High or Low Oxygen content	From liquid nitrogen or liquid oxygen being used in laboratories or local factories

CAUTION—Oxygen detector tubes become red-hot when in use and care must be taken to prevent burns and fires.

These and other contaminants can be directly attributed to particular localities, and a thorough examination of the conditions in which the compressor is to be run should be made before deciding which, if any, detector tubes are required in addition to the basic set of five.

Collection of Air Sample for Testing

The condition of the cylinder used to collect the air sample for testing is important. It must be clean and dry inside, with no trace of the previous contents. Aluminium cylinders are preferable since they do not have the thin coating of porous rust that is found in most steel cylinders.

Cleanliness is very important when determining low levels of oil and water vapour using the methods described in Appendices II, III and IV of the Revised BSAC Paper 1. Consideration should be given to using a specially prepared cylinder which is charged only from the air supply being tested, or which is vacuum-evacuated before a sample of the air supply is taken.

The air sample should be taken at the end of a long charging run, and tested as soon as possible after the cylinder has cooled. This also applies to air tests following a complaint about the air, or an incident, as dust and oil or water droplets settle out if the cylinder is left standing for any length of time, thus lowering the apparent contaminant level.

Air-Testing Method using a Gas-Detecting Kit

1. Flush out a Draeger Alcotest bag with the air to be tested in order to remove any contamination in the bag; take care not to burst the bag's seams by overfilling it.
2. Using the Alcotest bag to contain the sample, test the air with the carbon monoxide, carbon dioxide, nitrogen dioxide and water vapour detector tubes, following the instructions supplied with each packet. Refill the Alcotest bag as necessary.
3. Test the air with any other detector tubes that have been added to the kit, following the instructions supplied with each packet.

4. Without touching the faces of the filter discs, fit 2 Millipore filters into the filter holder; connect the filter holder to the cylinder via an A-clamp and a short length of polythene tubing (purchased perhaps from Boots or a home-made wine store), and SLOWLY pass 5 litres of air through both filters. The 5 litres can be measured by allowing the air which has passed through the filters to fill an Alcotest bag 5 times.

Remove both filter discs and examine them under × 60 magnification. The second filter acts as a control, allowing for any dust. etc. which has settled from the atmosphere on to the discs—any dust or oil stains on the first disc that are not duplicated on the second (control) disc are contaminants from the air being tested.

5. If no contamination has been detected, it is possible to ESTIMATE the oil vapour concentration using a Draeger Poly-Test tube. This tube will also indicate the presence of a contaminant not already tested for, with the exception of methane—natural (North Sea) gas—ethane, hydrogen and carbon dioxide. Follow the instructions supplied with the tubes, but keep drawing air through the tube and examine for a stain after every 5 pump operations.

No stain after 5 pump operations = less than 50 mg/m³ of oil vapour

10	25
15	17
20	13
25	10

If a stain appears at or before 5 operations of the pump, the air is contaminated and *unfit for use*. Further testing will then be necessary to determine the nature of the contaminant.

If no stain is seen after 25 pump operations, the tube may be tested by drawing tobacco smoke through it; this should produce a green/brown stain covering most of the tube. Attempting to extend the range of the tube below 10 mg/m³ is not recommended due to the time required and the uncertainty of the results obtained.

It is possible to use the Poly-Test tube for a quick air test by following the instructions supplied with the tubes, but if any stain is produced a full air test must be carried out to determine the nature of the contaminant.

After an air test it is advisable to operate the pump several times without fitting a tube—to remove the caustic dust given off by the detector tubes.

The results of the air test should be noted in the Compressor Logbook, or on the Dive Incident Sheet, even if the contamination is of an acceptable level and within the BSAC limits; a low level of contamination produced by a compressor that previously produced pure air is an indication of a possible malfunction of the compressor or its operation.

The following metric equivalents may be useful since the detector tubes are often calibrated in units that are different from those used in the BSAC air purity standard.

1 milligram/litre	(1 mg/l) $=1$ gram/cubic metre (1 g/m^3)
1 milligram/cubic metre	(1 mg/m^3)$=1$ microgram per litre (1 μg/l)
	0.01% $=100$ ppm (parts per million)
	0.001% $=10$ ppm

Shopping List for an Air Test Kit

1. A portable gas detector from Draeger or MSA.
2. 1 pkt Draeger Alcotest bags—Order Code CH 8585. (There are 10 bags in each packet.)
3. Millipore filter disc holder, the least expensive being SXOO 01300. (These are supplied in packets of 10, and cost about £6.00 per packet.)
4. 1 pkt of the following Millipore filter discs:
   (a) White plane discs (Order Code HAWP 01300); *OR*
   (b) White discs with a grid marked on them (Order Code HAWG 01300); *OR*
   (c) Black discs with a grid marked on them (Order Code HABG 01300).
   (These are supplied in packets of 100 discs, costing between £7 and £9.)
   If you can obtain or make filter holders, the following information on the diameters of available Millipore filters for white plane discs will be useful:
   13 mm diameter, Order Code HAWP 01300
   25 mm diameter, Order Code HAWP 02500
   47 mm diameter, Order Code HAWP 04700
5. The following detector tubes, one packet of tubes for each contaminant; each packet contains 10 tubes:

	Manufacturer's Order Code	
Tube Name	**Draeger**	**MSA**
Draeger Poly Test	CH 28410	—
Carbon Monoxide (CO)	CO 5/C CH 25601	CO–10–GT 5085–820

Tube Name	Manufacturer's Order Code	
	Draeger	MSA
Carbon dioxide (CO_2)	CO_2 0.1%/a CH 30801	Not suitable
Nitrogen Dioxide Nitrous fumes (NO_2, NO)	NO_2 0.5/c CH 30001	NITR–0.5–GT 5085–960
Water vapour (H_2O)	H_2O 0.1 CH 23401	Not available

For other tubes, the relevant manufacturer's catalogue should be obtained, and the detector tube with the highest sensitivity ordered. *NOTE*—Always quote the full order code for each item.

ADDRESSES:

DRAEGER   Draeger Safety Limited, Draeger House, Sunnyside Road, CHESHAM, Bucks.

MSA   Mine Safety Appliances Limited, Londford Trading Estate, Stretford, MANCHESTER M32 0LA.

MILLIPORE   Millipore (UK) Limited, Millipore House, Abbey Road, Park Royal, LONDON NW10 7SP.

The BSAC Technical Paper No. 1 (Revised) 'Breathing Air from Oil Lubricated Compressors' gives full information on good compressor management as well as details of air purity testing. Study of that publication is advised.

Protective Clothing

One of the most important factors contributing to the great popularity of diving and ranking alongside the invention of the aqualung, is the development of relatively inexpensive, comfortable and effective protective clothing. This is true even in waters which are definitely warm by British standards. The proper use and treatment of this clothing requires knowledge of certain extra skills; this section attempts to describe these skills, the suits themselves and their various advantages and disadvantages. But before we look in detail at the various suits available today, it is worth considering why they are worn in the first place. What form of protection do they provide and how important are they?

Types of Protection

1. THERMAL PROTECTION
Perhaps the main reason for using a diving suit. The suit reduces the amount of body heat lost to the water and enables the body to maintain a comfortable temperature even in cold water, thus providing an extremely effective survival aid in the event of accidentally prolonged immersions.

2. ABRASION PROTECTION
The risk of sustaining physical damage from accidentally colliding with or grazing against various objects is considerably reduced.

3. BIOLOGICAL PROTECTION
Although often overlooked, this type of protection is occasionally of primary importance in reducing the risk of being stung, bitten or otherwise attacked by living organisms in the water. This is really a form of mechanical protection as the suit provides a tough second-skin between the diver and an offending organism such as, perhaps, a coral or jelly-fish.

4. POLLUTION PROTECTION
Some types of suit prevent the diver from coming into contact with biological or chemical contaminants in the water. This form of protection is more usually associated with commercial diving in polluted water, but occasionally the more dedicated sports diver may also need this type of protection.
    The 'ideal' diving suit would provide protection in all these spheres and at the same time be comfortable to wear, impose no

restriction on movement, and be easy to put on and take off. We can now take a look at the different types of suit that are available and compare the degree and nature of protection that each affords.

Ordinary Clothes

Pullovers, jeans and overalls are amongst the items that can be used in the absence of any more suitable alternatives. Certainly they provide the cheapest form of protection, but unfortunately they are very limited in efficiency. They are perhaps better than nothing, providing as they do a certain amount of warmth and mechanical protection, but in no way can they compare with a specially designed diving suit. They may, however, provide adequate mechanical protection against coral abrasion and strong sun when diving in tropical waters.

The Wet Suit

This is undoubtedly the most widely used diving dress in sports diving today (Fig. 44). It is a relatively inexpensive, rugged, close-fitting garment which is comfortable to wear, and provides sufficient thermal protection for most types of sports diving. As its name implies, it is not a waterproof suit.

In Mediterranean waters, a wet suit jacket is frequently sufficient. In colder UK waters, a full suit comprising trousers (with 'long john' extension to cover the chest if desired), jacket, hood—sometimes built in—bootees and gloves, is necessary. Water enters the suit at its edges, cuffs, neck, etc. and is retained against the wearer's skin by the close fit of the suit. Body heat warms this film of water which assists in providing insulation.

THE MATERIAL

The material from which wet suits are made is called 'closed cell, expanded foam Neoprene'. It is a synthetic rubber-like material having elastic properties, which is full of minute 'closed cells' of nitrogen gas. Its cellular structure can be likened to a sponge, except that the cells are *not* interconnected, and therefore the material does *not* soak up water. It is this closed cell structure which provides the greatest part of the material's insulative properties—the neoprene and trapped water between the suit and the wearer's skin provide only a token amount of insulation.

In general, therefore, the thicker the suit material, the greater is the insulative capacity of the suit. On the other hand, the cellular structure of the material means that it is inherently buoyant so a thicker material creates buoyancy problems, and may be more restrictive to movement. Expanded foam neoprene sheets, used for

Fig. 44. **NEOPRENE WET SUITS**

the manufacture of wet suits, are made in thicknesses from 4 mm to 8 mm, the former being suitable for subtropical and U.K. summer waters; the latter for use in all seasons around the British Isles. 6 mm is a popular compromise. Thinner materials are available for gloves, undervests, etc.

LININGS

Expanded foam neoprene, in the above thicknesses, has a low tear resistance. To give it strength, a multi-way stretch nylon fabric is bonded to the sheet neoprene during manufacture. This lining may be applied to one side (single lined) or to both sides of the material (double lined). The lining can be made in a variety of textures and colours, patterns and prints, which can be applied to give aesthetic appeal and for safety reasons, a bright orange exterior lining being far more conspicuous than a plain black neoprene.

Nylon linings on the inside of the suit make dressing easier (unlined suits require the use of talc as a lubricant); linings on the outside reduce abrasion damage to the soft neoprene. Linings do have disadvantages: the elasticity of the material is reduced and it takes longer to dry the suit after use. The lining may retain bacteria and may become smelly if the suit is not rinsed in fresh water containing disinfectant at regular intervals.

Few suits are made these days from unlined neoprene. The majority of popular wet suits are made with the lining on the inside. The top quality suits are usually double lined and use colour on the outside for fashion appeal or safety, according to the use to which the suit is to be put.

THE FIT

It is important for a wet suit to fit comfortably and correctly if it is to be effective. It should fit snugly around those parts of the body which it is intended to cover, with no stretch along the limbs or trunk and minimal stretch around the limbs. It should cling by its own elasticity without any feeling of tightness, especially around the chest.

If the wet suit is too tight, it may impose an added effort to breathing; restrict circulation and movement, any or all of which can reduce the wearer to a state of extreme discomfort and distress— if not danger—very quickly. On the other hand, if the suit is too loose, water will flow freely through it, flushing away the layer of warm water and with it insulation. Wearing a correctly fitting suit is a delight which has to be experienced to be appreciated.

SEAMS AND ZIPS

The seams of a wet suit are potentially its weakest points. During manufacture the neoprene is glued together and a nylon tape is frequently stitched down on to the seams during this operation. The seams on the neoprene side of a single lined suit may be covered with a glued-on neoprene tape.

Care should be taken when donning or removing a wet suit, not to put undue direct strain on the seams. A well cut suit will be shaped so that seams are avoided at natural stress points of the garment.

Most wet suit jackets have a nylon zip on the front to simplify dressing. Zips do allow water to pass freely through so an adequate backing strip should be provided. Zips on cuffs, ankles, and bootees are not really necessary with modern neoprene and can be a source of trouble.

SWIMMING RESISTANCE

Because of their flexibility, smooth profile and freedom from loose folds of material found in dry suits, the wet suit offers the lowest resistance to movement through water. They are therefore the obvious choice if the diving activity involves swimming long distances or in currents—which is often the case in sports diving.

BUOYANCY OF WET SUITS

Since there is a large quantity of gas trapped in the neoprene, a wet suit is inevitably very buoyant in water. Most of them will have about 5–7 kg of positive buoyancy in sea water. To compensate for this, a weight-belt has to be worn. Ideally this weight, together with that of all the other pieces of equipment, should be exactly equal to the total buoyancy, so that the diver is neutrally buoyant. Thus, in an emergency when the diver may wish to reach the surface quickly or to remain on the surface for a considerable length of time, he can jettison his weight-belt and take advantage of the positive buoyancy of his wet suit.

There is, however, one potential problem associated with the buoyancy of these suits. The pressure of water at depth compresses the gas-filled neoprene, and this results in a reduction in its buoyancy (Archimedes' Principle). Therefore, a diver who is weighted for neutral buoyancy on the surface will become negatively buoyant at depth.

In the absence of an adjustable buoyancy lifejacket (ABLJ), the diver must decide how to arrange his weight. To be neutrally, or just slightly negatively, buoyant at the depth to which he intends to go, this may lead to problems of control on his ascent! Great care should be taken in determining the optimum level at which a state of neutral buoyancy should be achieved. Loss of buoyancy through wet suit compression is a fundamental argument in favour of using an ABLJ or other system for buoyancy compensation at depth.

THERMAL PROTECTION

Wet suits are worn in waters from the Tropics to the Poles and their thermal efficiency is undisputed. However, it is important to appreciate their limitations. The following factors significantly reduce the thermal protection afforded by wet suits:

(i) *Compression with depth* (See above): At 20 m a diver's wet suit is about half its original thickness and its insulative quality is also approximately halved. It is little wonder therefore, that divers wearing wet suits tend to get cold very quickly during the deeper dives.

(ii) *Flushing*: This term derives from the action of pumping out the layer of water between suit and skin. It is initiated by frequent flexing of the body, particularly at the waist, and is at its worst when the suit is loose-fitting; consists of separate parts; or has many tears, zips and leaky seams. Flushing can reduce the usefulness of a wet suit to virtually zero, but steps can be taken to reduce this loss of insulation to a minimum: in suits with a separate hood, place the lower edge of the hood over the collar of the jacket; flushing around the foot is lessened if the boot is placed under the lower trouser leg; likewise, the gloves should be worn outside the cuff.

(iii) *Age*: Frequent use of a wet suit, particularly to the deeper regions, eventually causes collapse of the many gas cells in the neoprene, with consequent loss of insulation. The cells can develop connections with each other, lose gas, and soak up water. Generally, the better the quality of the material, the longer it will survive this problem. As a rough guide, a wet suit will last for up to 5 years, depending almost entirely on the quality and the use to which it is put; longer time-spans can occur in more unusual circumstances.

(iv) *Efficiency in air*: Wet suits are not as effective in air as might at first be expected, and divers often get very cold on the way to or from a dive because they are unprepared for this fact. Air temperatures can often be considerably colder than water. For example, around Britain they vary over a range of 40°C between winter and summer, whilst the water temperature may only vary by about 10°C. Add to this the wind-chill factor and the relative ease with which air can whistle around under a suit (air flushing) compared with water, and it becomes clear why divers feel cold under such circumstances. Fortunately there is a simple and very effective solution to this little problem: any wind-proof garment worn over the wet suit will cut down air flushing; even a plastic raincoat would be effective in this role.

MECHANICAL PROTECTION

The diver is shielded by his wet suit from many of the day-to-day grazes that usually give rise to painful bruises and skin cuts; glancing collisions with another diver, rocks or wreckage are often effectively cushioned by the suit. Wet suits with an outer nylon lining can withstand much more of this type of abuse than can an unlined suit, but the main problem occurs with sharp or pointed edges that can pierce or tear the material; in this case only a limited degree of protection is provided. Any tears or holes that appear in a wet suit should always be repaired at the first opportunity.

BIOLOGICAL PROTECTION

Compared with most countries, British waters are fairly free of dangerous animals: the rare and small octopus is not a problem; the weaver fish appear more friendly than their Mediterranean counter-parts; the Portuguese-man-o'war jellyfish are thankfully very rare, and the more common sting-ray will remain quite passive unless stamped upon or otherwise assaulted! The shark communities around the British coasts are exemplary in their conduct: no authenticated record of a true shark attack on a swimmer or diver has been recorded in the entire maritime history of the country.

The wet suit will afford virtually complete protection against any animal that cannot bite through the thickness of the suit. This includes the very poisonous sea snakes of the Pacific, whose teeth are very short and set far back in their mouths; or whose teeth or stings are less than the suit thickness. It also includes all the jellyfish, anemones, corals and small fish. Neverthe-less, scorpion fish, weaver fish and other, similar bottom-living offenders should be treated with respect. Certain types of marine worms will jettison many small sharp spines if tampered with, but these should not be a problem to the wet-suited diver. Sea urchins come in all sorts and sizes and their brittle spines easily penetrate wet suit material, so heavy contact with these otherwise inoffensive animals should be avoided. Neither wet suits nor any other type of suit afford any protection from a shark attack, and even the claws of small crabs or lobsters can make their presence felt through a wet suit, so it is advisable to approach these with caution. Always seek local advice as to the presence of dangerous animals when diving in unfamiliar waters.

POLLUTION PROTECTION

Since, by definition, a wet suit allows water to come into contact with the skin, this type of suit cannot be regarded as affording any protection against water-borne pollution.

CARE AND MAINTENANCE

Just a little care and effort devoted to looking after one's wet suit during use will increase its durability considerably. Some elementary guidelines to using a wet suit to the best advantage are given below:

DRESSING

There is an art to putting on a wet suit, particularly if it is com-pletely unlined. Apart from the obvious problem of having to wriggle into a fairly tight-fitting garment, the rubber-like material of an unlined suit does not slide easily over the skin. Fortunately French chalk (talc) will provide the necessary lubrication at very little expense. Always err on the generous side when using the powder; it can be very frustrating to get half-way into a suit and come to a sticky stop! Unlined suits are also extremely fragile and will tear badly with remarkably little effort, especially when assisted by a small tear triggered by a sharp finger-nail.

A lined suit slides more easily over the skin and, because of its extra strength, greater force can be safely used to haul it on; usually no talc or alternatives are required. Lined suits can be difficult to put on when still wet so, if you can arrange to do so, dry your suit before you use it again.

Treat all zips with respect, and when dressing, try to avoid pulling across seams; when gripping the material, try to pick up a large fold so that the stress is spread over a large area.

Remember that if the hood is separate, it should be worn outside the collar of the jacket; bootees should be worn inside the trouser leg, and gloves worn over the cuffs.

DURING THE DIVE

You can best preserve your wet suit by treating it with the same respect as you would accord your own skin; do not expect it to be as indestructible as its thickness or snug fit might suggest—there are some pretty sharp and pointed edges to be found on the sea-bed! Remember that one of the consequences of being over-weighted—if that is the case—is that you are more liable to damage the knees, elbows and gloves of your suit; sea urchins, barnacles, rocks and metal wreckage being amongst the worst offenders.

One of the very basic advantages of a wet suit is that if it becomes an urgent necessity to urinate during a dive—perhaps in cold water— this does not present a problem, and the sea exerts a washing action that has already been aptly described as 'flushing'. Of course extra care in washing the suit will be necessary, especially with lined suits as they take longer to dry out. Mild disinfectants can be added to the washing solution in small quantities, and the suit should be thoroughly rinsed in fresh water afterwards.

AFTER THE DIVE

Undressing should be carried out with the same degree of care as was the dressing procedure. If the suit was damaged during the dive, special care must be taken to avoid causing further damage, particularly to unlined suits. The sooner a suit is removed after a dive, the easier it will be, as the retained water will provide some lubrication. Wet it before attempting to remove it. If the jacket and hood are made all-in-one, assistance may be required to take it off.

Always wash your suit in fresh water—a mild disinfectant may be used, but this should always be thoroughly rinsed off in fresh water before the suit is allowed to dry. Avoid drying your suit in direct sunlight, and never use strong artificial heat to force-dry the suit as this can cause rapid deterioration of the neoprene. Zips and 'Tenax' fasteners may be very lightly lubricated with silicone oil or grease.

PACKING AND STORING

Suits should be stored with a mininum number of folds and creases. Hanging the suit from a well-padded coathanger is one of the best methods, or alternatively, try to find somewhere where it may be laid flat, without folds. The problem with folds is that the neoprene becomes permanently creased, with consequent crushing of the gas cells and loss of insulation. Do not place heavy items on the suit as this will also cause collapse of the cells. A dry, cool place, away from direct sunlight, makes an excellent storage place.

REPAIRING

Wet-suit material is quite easy to repair and, like most things, the better the job you make of it, the longer the repair will last. For simple tears you should clean the edges and glue them together, but if the tear is rough-edged, it should be trimmed before glueing, and if a large area has been damaged, a whole section should be removed; the cut-out neoprene can then be conveniently used as the pattern for a patch.

The nylon lining can be carefully stitched together, using a nylon thread rather than sewing cotton which will rot. Patches on knees or elbows can be easily glued on to prolong the suit's life.

Always follow to the letter the instructions provided with the adhesive, and use the adhesive recommended by the suit manufacturer: there is considerable variation in the efficiency of different makes of neoprene adhesive and the wrong choice could mean having to repair your suit yet again.

OFF-THE-PEG AND MADE-TO-MEASURE WET SUITS

There are a considerable number of wet suit manufacturers in the British Isles—indeed, throughout the world—all of whom make quality products. The cut of the suit, the material used, and the final finishing serve to give each manufacturer their own distinctive styles.

Wet suits come as shorty suits for pool use or warm waters; economy three-piece suits—waist-length trousers, jacket and detached hood; up to a full 'long john' trouser-suit with hard-soled bootees and hood-attached jacket in 'double lined' for the expert. Prices vary according to quality and to suit all pockets. Savings can be made with D-I-Y kits, but a professionally made suit usually stands out that little bit more.

Most dive shops can supply a range of suits from stock and if it is a good fit, fine. For a perfect fit, with perhaps your own little extras, a made-to-measure suit can be supplied. A considerable number of measurements have to be taken to ensure a good fit and the customer should be clear as to the type and colour of material he wants, the style of suit, zip options and so on. Your suit has to last you for a few years and you want to be warm and comfortable so choose carefully.

MAKING YOUR OWN WET SUIT

Basically, a do-it-yourself kit comprises foamed neoprene sheets and a pattern drawn on paper, which can be modified to fit anyone before the sheets are cut out, or ready cut-out panels according to a range of pre-determined sizes; a tape measure; some seam tape; any zips (as necessary); fasteners for the jock strap; a tin of adhesive with a brush and corresponding cleaning solvent. Easy-to-follow instructions are usually included and it should be possible to make a very satisfactory wet suit in two evenings.

To make strong, glued seams it is essential that the two surfaces are neatly cut and thoroughly cleaned with glue solvent and that the smooth surfaces have been slightly roughened, before the glue is applied. Remember too that, as with all contact adhesives, you must leave the two glued surfaces for a pre-determined time before bringing them together and pressing firmly. Leave the completed suit for at least 24 hours before trying it on.

Home-made suits can be made to fit perfectly, and if they ever do need modification, the owner should have no qualms about getting out the scissors and performing the necessary surgery. Only when the suit fits comfortably should the seams be taped or sewn. A seam-sewing facility is provided by some wet suit kit dealers.

Dry Suits

These are available in two types: the modern 'Variable Volume Dry Suit'—sometimes referred to as a 'Foam Neoprene Dry Suit (Fig. 45a)—and the more traditional 'Navy' pattern dry suit (Fig. 45c). As the name implies, the diver remains dry within the suit—so long as it is in a good state of repair—and thus may spend several hours in the water without becoming chilled. Dry suits of both types are widely used in professional diving activities and offer excellent protection against all the points listed at the beginning of this chapter. Normally they are of one-piece construction with built-in bootees, and an entry zip (VVDS) or neck entry aperture (Navy type). Seals are provided at the neck and cuffs.

Variable Volume Dry Suit

(Also known as Foam Neoprene Dry Suit)

This relatively modern innovation is rapidly finding favour among professional divers and the more dedicated sports diver because of its superior insulation and ease of buoyancy control. They are the most expensive type of diving dress suitable for free diving because the suit incorporates a number of fittings not found on wet suits or Navy pattern dry suits, and because they are made from a top quality material. However, once converted to this type of dress, the user quickly realises that the expense is justified in terms of comfort and ease of control.

Variable Volume Dry Suits are intended for use in cold water. Such a suit would be far too warm if used in the tropics, but for regular diving throughout the year in latitudes above 50°, they are ideal.

The suit may be manually inflated by means of a direct-feed system from the diver's demand valve to provide additional comfort, insulation, buoyancy control or emergency buoyancy. A dump valve is fitted to permit venting of the suit for buoyancy control.

THE MATERIAL

VVD Suits are made from closed-cell expanded neopr e, usually double nylon lined, such as is used for wet-suits. Normal thicknesses are 6 mm and 8 mm. Sometimes, single-lined material is used in 'economy model' VVDS made for sports diving.

Using expanded foam neoprene in this way, the suit has inherent buoyancy and good insulation since heat loss through the material is minimal. The same comments concerning use of bright colours on nylon linings, made with respect to wet suits, applies for the VVDS.

THE FIT

The singular advantage of all types of dry suit is that insulating undergarments may be worn inside the diving dress to give as much insulation as the diver and diving conditions demand. To accommodate such undergarments, the dry suit must be relatively loose fitting. To some extent this increases drag as the diver moves about in the water, but seldom to the point that it becomes a problem.

Because dry suits are relatively loose fitting, various sizes of diver can be fitted into a given suit! Dry suits of both types are normally made to a limited range of standard sizes, and the diver picks the size which he finds most comfortable. Obviously, if the suit is far too large or far too small, he will have problems, so the selection of size should be tempered with common sense.

SEAMS, ZIPS, SEALS AND FITTINGS

To ensure waterproofing, all joins in the neoprene from which the suit is made are glued, and the nylon facing/lining fabric stitched together without penetrating the neoprene. Excessive strain on seams should be avoided since failure of seams is the usual cause of leakage.

VVD Suits have an entry zip, the position of which varies with each manufacturer's design. One leading make has an entry zip which runs from the middle of the back, between the legs and up to chest level at the front. Others have shoulder entry zips or zips running from waist level up the chest, behind the neck and back to waist level. The zips are very special and quite unlike those used for wet suits. When closed, they are both waterproof and pressure-proof. They are expensive, and represent a significant part of the high cost of the suit. If handled with respect and care, the zip should last the life of the suit.

Another critical part of the suit (though one which can easily be replaced if damaged) is the neck seal. All VVD Suits employ what may be described as a 'reverse polo neck' seal. The diver pulls the seal over his head as he dons the suit and then must invert the seal so that it fits without creases. With a shoulder entry suit, assistance may be needed to achieve a good seal.

The seal is effective only if air is present in the suit. Air pressure at the neck seal—the highest point of the suit in most situations—will press it against the neck, and the greater the air pressure within the suit, the more effective is the seal. The pressure is, of course, never enough to cause discomfort to the diver.

Sealing at the cuffs is achieved either by having a tight-fitting cuff end to the sleeve, or by inverting the cuff on the forearm rather like the neck seal. The latter is the most effective.

Cuffs and neck-seals are usually made with a smooth neoprene skin, which when the seal is made, is in contact with the diver's skin.

The VVD Suit is fitted with an inflation valve and a dump valve, both normally situated on the upper chest of the suit. The inflation air supply comes by direct feed from the demand valve first stage low pressure take-off; via a quick-release connector to the suit. Inflation is either by a press-button or by turning a tap.

A press-button suit-vent permits careful control during ascents, and some vent valves can be preset to maintain a constant volume of air in the suit at working depth. Such vent valves will blow off automatically on ascent.

Some American VVD Suits have a mouth-inflation hose which serves also as a means of venting as in many ABLJ's. While the diver could economise on air by exhaling exhaust air into the suit, use of such a system tends to allow water into the suit.

Fig. 45. DRY SUITS

(a) This VVDS has a body entry zip and direct-feed inflation.

(b) An alternative model has a shoulder entry zip and inflation cylinder

(c) The Navy Dry Suit has a neck entry aperture, which is sealed with a neck seal and clamp band. An inflation cylinder can be fitted just above waist level.

SWIMMING RESISTANCE

Any dry suit has greater drag than a close-fitting wet suit, and long swims in dry suits should be avoided.

BUOYANCY OF VVD SUITS

It has been explained that the material from which the suit is made has buoyancy, and also that the suit needs to be inflated to achieve insulation and for buoyancy control. Like a wet suit, the material will compress with depth, and lose buoyancy. So too, the entrained air will be compressed. However, a touch on the inflation valve will admit more air and the desired state of buoyancy can be recovered or maintained. On an ascent, the expanding air can be vented easily; so at all times the diver is in full control of his buoyancy through manipulation of inflation and vent valves.

Considerably more weight has to be worn by the diver using a VVDS because of the air entrapped within the suit and undergarments. Once in the water, however, this presents little problem. In an emergency, the shedding of this weight will take the diver very quickly to the surface! It would be very hazardous to deliberately dive over-weighted and to compensate by inflation of the suit. Cases of uncontrolled buoyant ascents have been recorded—in two cases the divers ascended feet first!!

THERMAL PROTECTION

The thermal protection afforded by the VVDS is superior to both wet suits and Navy pattern dry suits. Air is obviously far less conductive of heat than water, and foam neoprene retains heat better than the rubberised fabrics from which the Navy pattern dry suits are made.

There is a slight loss of insulation due to compression of the neoprene but this is balanced by providing more air space within the suit. Likewise, deterioration of the material with age is barely noticeable in terms of insulation, but leakage through the seams or damaged areas of a VVDS could represent a problem as the suit ages.

The efficiency of the VVDS depends largely on the insulative undergarments used. The suit is still much warmer than a wet suit if only swimming trunks are worn, and this may be enough if the suit is being used in UK waters during the summer. A T-shirt or thin woollen jumper is desirable to absorb perspiration—it is not difficult to be too warm! During winter months a track-suit makes a good undergarment, but for prolonged diving during cold weather, or for instance in Arctic conditions, the special woollen or nylon fur undersuits or full-length 'thermal underwear' are to be advised. Whatever undergarments are used, they should be as form fitting as possible.

ABRASION PROTECTION

Better than a wet suit, but not as good as a Navy dry suit. Foam neoprene, even if nylon faced and lined, is still delicate material, and care should be taken to avoid unnecessary abrasion. Knees and elbows are usually reinforced on the outside.

BIOLOGICAL PROTECTION

Again, very good, except for attack by large marine animals, against which no diving dress can claim to be proof.

POLLUTION PROTECTION

If full face-masks and waterproof gloves are used, both the VVDS and Navy type dry suit can protect the diver totally from polluted water.

USING A VARIABLE VOLUME DRY SUIT

A training programme which teaches the correct use of VVDS is given in the BSAC Diving Officer's Handbook (1976 edition), and the advice therein applies also to a large extent to Navy type dry suits. Those wishing to learn how to use such a suit should consult that publication.

A VVDS represents a major investment, costing as it does almost as much as the total cost of all the other diving equipment including the wet suit! Consequently the owner will want to get as long a life out of it as he can, and this can be achieved by careful use at all times.

DRESSING

Prepare the suit by opening the zip fully and by lubricating the zip, neck seal and cuffs with silicone grease from a tube or aerosol. This lubricant makes the zip and seals slide more easily and helps to achieve total waterproofing. Be generous with the lubricant.

The diver should dress in the undergarments he is to use, and then don the suit in the manner which will either be obvious, or as recommended by the manufacturer. For example; with a shoulder entry suit the diver puts his feet in, pulls up the legs of the suit until his feet are firmly in the bootees and he can stand. The rest of the suit is drawn up the body until the arms can be put into the sleeves. Next the head is pushed through the neck seal.

On the other hand, one leading make, fitted with a zip from back to front, requires that the upper part of the suit is put on first; then, by squatting down, the legs can be put into the lower half. With feet in the bootees, the diver can stand and the zip be closed.

With the suit on, the neck seal should be achieved. Initially, the seal should be pushed down from above, the fingers used to feel around the neck for a correct fit. With shoulder entry suits, assistance may be needed to pull the edge of the seal down correctly. It is vital that there are no creases or tracks in the seal, through which water will enter and air escape.

With a good seal made, zip up to close the suit, checking that the zip is clean, unobstructed and closing properly. Do not tug at the zip. If all is well it will close smoothly; if undue effort is needed, something is wrong. Check again. With the zip fully closed, another quick spray of silicone does not come amiss.

Invert the cuff seals, then test for leaks by partly inflating the suit (do not over-inflate as this may stretch the seams) paying particular attention to the neck seal. If it is obviously leaking, correct the fault. Diving with a badly leaking seal is both uncomfortable and potentially dangerous since the suit could flood and/or buoyancy not be contained. The testing operation also checks out the inflation and venting valves.

DURING THE DIVE

The same parameters as for the wet suit apply: avoid abrasion and unnecessary wear and tear. The VVDS permits accurate buoyancy control, which should be used.

A normal buoyancy check should be carried out with the suit fully vented in shallow water. Then a further 3–4 kg should be added to the weight-belt so that, to regain neutral buoyancy, some air has to be admitted to the suit. Some air must be present within the suit to make the neck seal work effectively.

One problem of the suit—of all dry suits—is air migration. When in a normal swimming attitude, the feet are lower than the head and the entrapped air is in the upper part of the suit. When making a head-first descent, or when otherwise inverted, the air will migrate to the feet. If the suit contains a lot of air, this migration can lead to loss of fins, and—what is worse,—inability to regain a head up position. A suit which fits closely about the lower limbs will minimise this risk, but the way of avoiding this awkward situation is to weight correctly.

Descents are best made feet first, and if inversion is necessary, give a quick thought to the volume of air in the suit before inverting.

As the diver descends he should valve in air to maintain a state of near neutral buoyancy. A feeling of squeeze will be noted during the descent if this is not done, and the rate of descent will progressively accelerate.

Once at working depth, trim out to the desired state of buoyancy. Adjustments will only be needed if the diver's level fluctuates. During ascent, control buoyancy by use of the vent valve, at all costs avoiding an uncontrolled buoyant ascent.

AFTER THE DIVE

The suit should be removed in the reverse order of dressing. If the suit has not leaked, why not wash it off on the the outside in fresh water before you take it off? It will save getting the inside wet!

Once off, close the zip and drape the suit carefully where it can drain and dry.

From time to time, the whole suit should be allowed to soak inside and out in fresh water to which a small amount of disinfectant has been added—to leech out salt and to keep it fresh.

Check and lubricate valves and store away. VVDS's are usually quite heavy and to hang on a coat hanger or tube through the sleeves can strain the collar and sleeves. The suit is best laid out flat on a clean surface.

REPAIRS

Apart from routine care of zips and valves, repairs to the fabric of the suit are best left to the manufacturer. While wet-suit repairs can be rough and ready, such repairs to a dry suit can be dangerous.

Navy Pattern Dry Suits

Much of what has been said about the VVDS applies to the Navy-type suit, except that the latter does not normally have direct-feed inflation and venting systems. Suit inflation from an ABLJ-size cylinder is available as an extra. However, many users modify these suits by adding direct-feed inflation and vent valves, giving them the same degree of buoyancy control as an orthodox VVDS.

THE MATERIAL

Unlike the wet suit and VVDS the material from which the Navy dry suit is made is not thick, does not contain trapped gas, and is, therefore, not in itself a particularly effective insulation against cold water.

The suits are made of rubber or neoprene-impregnated fabric. The modern material used is a multiway stretch nylon fabric, faced on the outside with a bonded layer of neoprene. This material has elasticity and considerable strength and is relatively unreactive to oils and greases, whereas rubber will perish quickly in their presence.

Insulation is gained by use of undergarments of the polyamid/nylon fur type previously mentioned—'woolly bears' as the Navy affectionately call them.

THE FIT

The suits are of one-piece manufacture with a neck entry aperture and are sufficiently loose-fitting to allow variable thicknesses of undergarments to be used. They are made in a limited range of standard sizes to fit average adults. The panels of the suit are vulcanised together during manufacture with reinforcements at the seat, knees and elbows.

SEALS AND FITTINGS

Entry to the Navy-type dry suit is made through the neck yoke aperture, which is made from a thinner, unreinforced neoprene material. The hole has to be stretched so that the diver may enter; hence a more flexible material is used. Once in the suit, and with his hands through the cuffs (also made from the thinner more flexible material) the diver puts on a rubber latex seal around his neck. This is clamped to the neck yoke with an inner neck ring and outer clamp band. The photograph on page 187 (Fig. 45c) shows this sealing method. It should be noted that the neck and cuff seals are NOT inverted as they are with the VVDS.

Cuffs should be sealed above the wrist, where clenching of the fist or a hard grip does not cause channels at the tendons. Additional or improved cuff seals can be achieved by using 'greys'—broad, tight-fitting rubber bands over the edge of the dry suit's latex cuff seal. These latex seals are easily damaged and so require careful handling. The use of silicone or soap as a lubricant is beneficial.

SWIMMING RESISTANCE

As already mentioned, and like the VVDS, there is greater drag than with a wet suit.

BUOYANCY CONTROL

Many aspects of dry-suit buoyancy are directly comparable with those of wet suits and the VVDS, but there are some fundamental differences:

Deep diving in a Navy-pattern dry suit can lead to loss of buoyancy and the 'squeeze'. 'Squeeze' is best described as a feeling of being compressed all over by the water pressure acting on the suit, and this is accompanied by a widespread and painful pinching. Because of the folds, the suit presses unequally on the body and the skin is pinched in the small spaces under the folds. This can be quite a painful experience at depths in excess of 10 m and may result in a characteristic pattern of red weal marks on the skin, corresponding to the pattern of folds on the suit. This discomfort can be avoided by simply adding air to the layer between skin and suit as the depth is increased by means of a small suit inflation bottle worn around the waist and fitted with a hand-operated valve or by direct feed from the demand valve low-pressure stage. In certain specialised commercial suits, this function can be performed automatically on a demand system. Such suits are called *constant volume suits*.

Whilst inflating the suit will prevent a squeeze, to do this in safety requires practice to ensure that the suit is not over-inflated and that it is vented sufficiently during an ascent to prevent the expanding air inside the suit increasing the diver's buoyancy so much that he would surface out of control and at considerable speed, so risking decompression sickness and burst lung.

Venting is achieved by inserting a finger under one of the cuffs to break the seal of the suit at the wrist, and by holding the wrist higher than the shoulder so the air can escape. With this technique the suit inflation bottle can serve the same function as the bottle of an ABLJ since it provides air for buoyancy adjustment, and can also be used to give buoyancy for rapid emergency ascents. Where a dump valve is fitted, this may be used to vent the suit during ascent.

(A 'squeeze' is seldom encountered in a VVDS because the correct operation of the suit involves regular inflation with increases in depth.)

THERMAL PROTECTION

It has already been pointed out that the main insulative property of the suit is not provided by the material from which it is made but by the layer of air it encloses, and that the thickness of this layer is dependent on the amount of clothing worn beneath the suit: the thicker the layers of clothing then, generally, the warmer the diver will be. The fact that the diver can regulate the amount of heat he wishes to derive from his dry suit according to the amount of clothing he wears beneath it gives the dry suit a distinct advantage over the wet suit. Nevertheless, as with a wet suit, the dry-suited diver experiences a loss of insulation as the gas trapped beneath his suit is compressed at depth, and in the absence of a suit inflation system, the use of dry suits is usually restricted to about 10–15 m. Usually the effects of the squeeze at depth will return a diver to the surface before the reduced insulation and resultant cold has had time to take effect, but in shallow water the suit is quite acceptable, even without the inflation facility.

With an inflation device the diver can maintain the air layer thickness down to virtually any depth that the sports diver would wish to go to. This means that the dry-suited diver could remain comfortably insulated when the wet-suited diver would be feeling the cold, and is one of the main reasons why dry suits are used for commercial and military diving operations.

Obviously, if the air in the dry suit is replaced by water, the suit will have lost virtually all its insulating ability. This could happen, to a greater or lesser extent, for several reasons: a tear may occur; a wrist or neck seal may leak due to improper dressing or damage;

the diver may sweat a great deal and condensation appear on the inside of the suit; the diver may even be obliged to urinate in the suit because of an enforced, protracted period in cold water. The problem of flooding, and the resultant loss in insulation (and buoyancy, if extensive) is a disadvantage of the dry suit which is not experienced by the wet-suited diver.

In the very unlikely event of a dry suit being completely flooded, as much as 10 kg positive buoyancy could be lost during a dive. However, dropping the weight-belt (if worn) would restore neutral buoyancy and swimming ability.

In the case of a surface swimmer wearing a dry suit which has completely flooded, the problems are minimal since the only additional weight that the diver has to support is that of the dry suit itself. Nevertheless, he will discover that it is quite difficult to climb out of the water on to rocks or into a boat because he will now be carrying the water trapped in the suit. This water will of course, sink down to the legs and will impede their movement. The diver might have to cut the suit at the feet to allow water to escape. For this reason it is best to avoid flooding a dry suit!

When wearing any dry suit near the water it is considered wise practice to keep the suit sealed at all times so that in the event of an accidental fall into the water, none would enter the suit and full buoyancy would be maintained. Another method of avoiding at least part of the problem is to wear a wet suit under the dry suit; then, in the event of flooding, some of the buoyancy and insulation would remain. (If a wet suit is being used for this purpose, it can be fairly loose-fitting as water flushing is no longer a problem. However, wearing a wet suit in the dry role for long periods can be irritating to the skin; this would not occur with a lubricating layer of water for which it was originally designed.)

Like the VVDS, the Navy pattern dry suit offers excellent protection against wind chill once out of the water.

MECHANICAL PROTECTION
The material is far more resistant to abrasion than foamed neoprene. Mechanical protection could be further improved for this and any other suit by wearing overalls or a boiler suit over the diving dress for working dives.

BIOLOGICAL/POLLUTION PROTECTION
See these headings for the VVDS.

USING A NAVY-PATTERN DRY SUIT
All that has been said about the use of a VVDS applies to the Navy dry suit and there is almost nothing else to add; other than pointing

out the differences in dressing.

The diver, wearing his diving undergarments, draws the suit on up to chest level, after which he will require assistance to get his arms in place and the suit over his shoulders. The diver should stand with his feet apart in order to brace himself while an assistant holds one arm of the suit in one hand and takes a firm grip of the neck yoke at its shoulder. At a given word, the attendant pulls, stretching the neck entry aperture so that the diver can put his arm through and down the sleeve. The process is repeated for the other side, and the entry yoke is then drawn right up and stretched over the neck ring. A latex neck seal is then put on, fitting closely around the diver's neck to seal the suit and stretched over the neck ring. A screw clamp band which is then clamped around the neck ring ensures no leaks at this point. A free-flooding wet suit hood is usually employed, but modern commercial diving helmets may themselves be clamped up to the neck yoke without need for a separate neck seal.

The same sort of assistance is needed when removing a Navy dry suit to get the upper part of the body through the yoke.

AFTERCARE AND REPAIRS

Rinsing off in fresh water, with internal washing as required, is sufficient. The suit may be stored on a pole through the arms.

Small repairs can be mended with motor puncture repair kits. The cuffs and neck yoke can be closed off with bottles and a large ball and the suit inflated. Soapy water spread over the inflated suit will reveal the small puncture. Larger tears should be repaired by the manufacturer or other specialists.

The latex cuff and neck yoke can be quickly replaced. Users of these suits are advised to keep a spare set of cuff and neck seals, which can be cemented into place with neoprene cement.

ACQUIRING A DRY SUIT

Because the market for dry suits of either type is specialised and limited, they are not often seen for sale in sports diving shops, except for those which also cater for the commercial diving field. Several suppliers should be approached if you wish to make a comparison of those available, since shops tend to supply the goods of only one manufacturer. If possible, listen to any advice offered by divers who have actual experience in using different types of dry suit—experience of one type will give you some ideas as to its pros and cons, but is of limited value in providing comparative information. Naturally many divers are biased in favour of the equipment they learnt on or have owned since they first started diving, but as a prospective buyer, take any opportunity to try out different equipment so that you can judge for yourself.

Dry suits are usually available in just six sizes which basically break down to thin and fat versions of a short, medium and tall man. If one of these does not afford a perfect fit, it is no great detriment to wear the next size up; the extra folds will be lost amongst the many normal folds that the suit assumes when it is worn in the water. From the point of view of warmth and compliance, it is better to err on the side of too large a suit than one that is too small.

The capital outlay for a dry suit, and particularly for a VVDS is considerable, so it is worth getting the best while you are about it. Unless it is an obvious bargain, buying second hand is fraught with risks of buying a suit which is not 'dry'!

At the time of writing, kit form dry suits are not available, but it is probably only a matter of time before kits for VVDS's are on the market. A simplified kit form suit, using single lined material with taped seams, separate wet suit type hood and bootees, would bring VVDS diving within the reach of many sports divers.

Finally, it should be accepted that the principle of a dry suit attempts to defy the laws of physics by keeping water out! Consequently, leaks are not uncommon and are not always due to a defect in the suit. Hurried dressing without sufficient attention to seals can lead to almost unnoticed leakage. Vent valves are inclined to let water in if the suit is fully vented: leakage can occur at neck or cuff seals if head or hands are moved awkwardly. So long as leakage is not excessive to the point of flooding, the diver can be damp but remain warm for long periods while working in cold water.

A Training Programme in the correct use of a Variable Volume Dry Suit, leading to a BSAC Logbook Endorsement is published in the BSAC Diving Officer's Handbook (1976 Edition).

Lifejackets and Buoyancy Aids

Lifejackets

A diver enters the water in a much encumbered state with perhaps 20–50 kg weight of equipment, yet once below the surface he can attain neutral buoyancy. At the surface he may have to tread water vigorously to keep his head clear, and when he descends into deeper water he becomes heavy again.

The diver's lifejacket is designed to solve these problems by allowing him to increase his buoyancy at will. In this way he can make himself buoyant at the surface, so that he can rest, or adjust his buoyancy to a neutral state while below the surface.

Many factors affect a diver's buoyancy; first of all his build will determine whether he will float or sink when he enters the water without equipment. A small percentage of the world's population are not naturally buoyant and will sink if they stop swimming. However, most of us are naturally buoyant with our lungs full of air, but it is important to note that we vary in the extent to which we are buoyant. If the mass of water that we displace when immersed is greater than our own body weight, then we float; if it is less, we sink (Archimedes Principle).

Being made from a buoyant material, a diver's wet suit is bulky but not very heavy, so it floats in water. However, when we put it on and descend into the sea the pressure of the surrounding water compresses the suit material, reducing its volume and, therefore, its buoyancy. Beyond a certain variable depth the suit will no longer be buoyant, yet as the diver returns to the surface the buoyancy returns as the pressure drops. The diver who needs 5 kg of lead to give himself neutral buoyancy at a depth of 5 m may find himself 3 kg heavy at 30 m.

Most other items of diving equipment are non-compressible and their buoyancy is not affected by depth. Divers in warmer waters may not need to wear wet suits and will not, therefore, experience this problem.

The problems of buoyancy, or the lack of it, are overcome by the use of the lifejacket or buoyancy aid, which may be classified as follows:

1. Surface lifejacket	SLJ	⎫
2. Oral buoyancy compensator	OBC	⎬ Lifejackets
3. Adjustable buoyancy lifejacket	ABLJ	⎭
4. Buoyancy compensator pack	BCP	⎱ Buoyancy Aids
5. Variable volume dry suit	VVDS	⎰

1–3 are in the form of a bag or collar worn around the diver's neck and chest, and are inflated either orally by the diver, by a carbon dioxide (CO_2) cartridge, by a mini-bottle of compressed air, or via a hose connecting the jacket with the diver's breathing set.

The Buoyancy Compensator Pack has many of the features of an ABLJ, but the buoyancy bag is BEHIND the diver—in effect, worn on his back. Inflation is by a supply from the breathing set. Any dry suit capable of being inflated can also serve for buoyancy compensation.

Surface Lifejacket (SLJ)

This type of jacket, although it has the obvious advantage of being lowest in price, has only a restricted use for divers. It consists of a suitably shaped bag, which may be inflated either orally by the diver or by means of a cartridge of CO_2. Clearly if the diver is in a calm, relaxed situation, oral inflation is quite simple, so the CO_2 cartridge is only for use when swift emergency inflation is necessary.

The CO_2 cartridge is compact and contains a measured charge of gas that is just sufficient to inflate the bag at the surface. This is useful in the case of a snorkeller who plans to stay on or near the surface anyway, or in the case of a diver who perhaps gets cramp after surfacing from a dive; the jacket will support them safely on the surface.

However, a diver must be aware that this jacket will only inflate fully at the surface and that if he should attempt to 'crack' the cartridge at a depth of, say, 30 m, he would only get a quarter of the buoyancy from his jacket—and experience tells that it may not inflate at all. It can be seen, therefore, that it will only help the diver who is close to the surface: but after all, this is when many incidents occur.

Although the jacket may be inexpensive, the CO_2 cartridges can be costly and, unfortunately, this factor sometimes delays the decision to use them in an emergency. Cartridges should ALWAYS be treated as expendable, and should ALWAYS be checked for satisfactory functioning before each dive. The cartridge will be marked with the weight of CO_2 it should contain, so it is quite a simple matter to check whether the cartridge is charged by comparing its weight with that of a spent cartridge. A further check is to examine the threaded end of the cartridge to see whether the metal seal has been pierced. If in doubt, discard it.

On no account attempt to breathe from a CO_2 inflated lifejacket as this will induce CO_2 poisoning, possible black-out and even drowning.

Oral Buoyancy Compensator (OBC)

This type of jacket is designed as a diver's aid for use in adjusting buoyancy during the course of a dive. It is fitted with a mouthpiece and a hose than enables the diver to breathe his expired air into the jacket and to exhaust air from the jacket. It may also be fitted with a CO_2 cartridge for emergency inflation at the surface.

During the course of a dive the diver can take a breath, remove his demand valve mouthpiece, and exhale into the jacket mouthpiece. He will do this until he has adjusted his buoyancy to a neutral state. If he over-inflates, he can release a little air until he attains the state of buoyancy he requires.

As already explained, the diver wearing a wet suit will find his buoyancy decreasing with depth, and without the means of compensating for it he will have to use more effort to propel himself through the water: a heavy diver will first of all use energy to raise himself clear of the bottom and, secondly, to propel himself horizontally. This extra effort will cause him to use up more air, thus limiting the duration of his dive. So we can see that the OBC is a real aid to diver efficiency and comfort.

However, it does not really deserve the term 'lifejacket' since, usually, it has no provision for emergency inflation, other than by a buddy, or on the surface if a CO_2 cartridge is fitted. It is, therefore, a useful aid, but not yet a lifejacket in the fullest sense. Yet its contribution to reducing diver fatigue—by giving him neutral buoyancy, and by allowing him to inflate on the surface after the dive—deserves credit.

Adjustable Buoyancy Lifejacket (ABLJ)

At the upper end of the scale, we have the all-round diver's aid, which provides buoyancy compensation, buoyant ascent from depth, surface inflation, and emergency breathing. These jackets tend to be larger and more robust than the previous two.

This category of lifejacket incorporates at least two methods of inflation: one oral, the other(s) automatic. The automatic (non-oral) inflation by air is provided either by a mini-cylinder attached to the jacket, or via a direct feed hose connecting the jacket with the diver's breathing set. Some jackets offer all three systems. A valve allows excess air to escape once the bag is full, and there is provision for the controlled venting of the bag (Fig. 46).

CYLINDER-INFLATED LIFEJACKET

The mini-cylinder, which is carried in a pouch attached to the jacket, is fitted with a manually operated tap which controls the flow of air into the jacket. To recharge the mini-cylinder, the diver decants high pressure air from his aqualung, either through the yoke attached to the cylinder, or via a charging clamp supplied with the jacket. The decanting should be carried out slowly to avoid overheating which would hasten corrosion inside the cylinder.

The quantity of air contained within a fully-charged mini-cylinder depends on the pressure of the air in the Aqualung from which it was filled. Typically, an ABLJ cylinder has an 'empty' capacity of 0.4 litres and a working pressure of 200 bar; therefore, when fully charged it would contain 80 l of 'free' air. The capacity of an ABLJ bag is about 18 l, although models vary between 12 and 24 l. From this we can see that a fully charged ABLJ cylinder will inflate the bag almost 4.5 times at the surface, or will inflate it fully once at a depth of 35 m. It is unlikely that a diver would require the buoyancy of a fully inflated bag even in an emergency since a positive buoyancy of 10 kg would be more than sufficient to lift the diver from 70 m—the air in the partly inflated bag would, of course, be expanding and further inflating the lifejacket during the ascent, thus affording increasing buoyancy.

However, we must bear in mind that this sort of performance assumes that we are using the ABLJ at its full working pressure, but if your aqualung has only been charged to 120 bars (which is still the maximum pressure delivered by some older compressors), then you have only filled the mini-cylinder with 48 l of air, and your maximum depth for full inflation is, therefore, reduced to 17 m. This factor should not be overlooked when planning a dive.

The simplicity with which the ABLJ can be orally inflated and de-flated has made partial inflation during a long surface swim a routine measure, and one which can only be looked upon as sensible for safety.

The ABLJ can also be used for buoyancy compensation at depth either by inflation with expired air (in exactly the same way as with the OBC), or by using compressed air from the mini-cylinder. But if you use air from the ABLJ cylinder you must accept that you are reducing the amount held in reserve for an emergency. Generally speaking, you should avoid using a cylinder-fed ABLJ in this way since it is impossible to predict what your emergency needs may be. However, if on a deep dive you find yourself excessively overweight it is probably better to adjust your buoyancy in this way than to struggle on, using more and more air for breathing and becoming more tired. And, of course, any air put into the jacket is held there, and will be available to assist the ascent if necessary (but this should be vented-off before reaching a shallower depth).

Should your main breathing supply fail, the ABLJ cylinder offers an intact air reserve which can be breathed from the jacket via the oral inflation mouthpiece—but only if you have not already used it all for buoyancy compensation!

Make a regular practice of charging your ABLJ cylinder before every dive. This is the only way that you can be sure it is full: do not convince yourself that you only used a little puff from it last time—that 'little puff' may be critical on the next dive.

DIRECT-FEED SYSTEM

This type of ABLJ is fitted with a hose that ends in a tap which controls the flow of air fed into the bag directly from the diver's main breathing set. The other end of the hose will be connected to the demand valve and may supply medium-pressure air, or occasionally high-pressure air, if the contents gauge hose is used. The system is known as a *direct feed* and may be built into the ABLJ, or bought as a conversion kit for an OBC, SLJ, or a cylinder-fed ABLJ.

The advantage of this system is that the bag is inflated with air supplied directly from the aqualung, and that the diver therefore has far more air available for buoyancy compensation and, should he use up a lot of air, his gauge or reserve system will warn him. In any event, the amount of air needed to adjust buoyancy is far less than the overweight diver would use up in the extra effort of keeping himself clear of the bottom and propelling himself through the water.

In addition, a failure in the demand valve need not incapacitate the diver since he will still be able to breathe all the air in his set via the direct feed, bag, and inflation mouthpiece (providing the fault is not within the main cylinder tap or the valve first stage).

The case of buoyancy adjustment by this method is an important aid to the diver since he does not need to remove his mouthpiece to carry out oral inflation, which can be tricky at depth. However, a problem arises at the end of a dive for, if the diver has exhausted his aqualung, he will have no air available for jacket inflation. In practice there is usually a little air left in a cylinder even after the demand valve has stopped supplying it for breathing, but it flows slowly and cannot really be relied upon in an emergency.

If a high-pressure direct-feed system employing the contents gauge hose is used, the flow restrictor must be removed from the demand valve take-off point to allow a swift enough flow of air. Whether high or medium pressure, the hose connection to the jacket should be fitted with a quick-release coupling so that in an emergency the set can be removed from the diver without delay.

Lifejacket Design

In all three types of lifejacket the shape and design of the bag is important. You should look for a bag which when inflated will float the fully-equipped diver face upwards, with his head well clear of the water. This means that the major areas of buoyancy will be high on the chest and behind the neck. If the jacket is also wide, and has additional buoyancy at the side of the head, then this will further reduce any tendency to roll over.

In practice a diver with a weight-belt around his waist and a set on his back will tend to float face upwards and will be very stable. Removing his weight-belt will, if anything, make him less stable, so this is not advisable, unless the jacket is giving insufficient buoyancy.

The harness attaching the jacket to the diver must be sturdy, comfortable, and properly adjusted, for the diver will be suspended from the jacket by means of the harness. For best support the harness should include both crotch and chest straps; make sure these are properly adjusted by fully inflating the jacket on land and then adjusting the straps for a firm fit.

When deflated the bag should fold flat and not offer much water resistance. Large capacity bags will have a gussett construction to allow them to expand like a concertina. A large bag may seem an encumberance, but is necessary to achieve the recommended buoyancy of about 18 kg, which will allow the wearer to support a second diver on the surface.

Remember that a fragile bag which can be punctured easily is useless; such a bag may well leak and fail when you most need it. If you choose a bag which has pockets fitted to the front, avoid collecting sharp items in them for this will cause a leak where you may not detect it.

Consider also the side on which the inflation hose is fitted: if you use a single hose demand valve which comes over the right shoulder then it is preferable that the inflation hose is on the left, since the two may well become entangled. As a general observation most European ABLJ's have right shoulder inflation hoses since they were designed with left shoulder demand valves in mind. American ABLJ's are generally the other way about. If you do not use the hose for deflating the jacket this will not be an everyday problem, but this is only the case in jackets which have a separate 'dump valve' for venting off air.

There are advantages and disadvantages to the ABLJ's ability to fully inflate at depth. In an emergency it may be desirable to get to the surface by the swiftest possible means, and there is no doubt that the ABLJ will achieve this. At the same time, this introduces a considerable risk of bends or air embolism if carried out at the wrong time or in the wrong way. Therefore, never practice, or carry out buoyant ascents unless in a real emergency in which the risks may be acceptable alternatives to black-out or drowning. Make sure that you can control your rate of ascent and can even stop at any desired level by use of the vent valve. It is possible to rise at the prescribed rate of 15 m per minute by use of the ABLJ if, for example, you are unable to swim, but this requires care and practice. It is even possible to lift heavy objects with the aid of an ABLJ but, once again, care is required; incidents have occurred when divers attempting such a lift have lost contact with the object and have ended up making uncontrolled fast buoyant ascents. An ABLJ can lift a

a) SPIROTECHNIQUE

On this Adjustable Buoyancy Life-Jacket the emergency inflation is by the front-mounted air cylinder. The excess pressure valve at the top of the jacket can be operated manually by the pull-cord to act as a rapid 'dump' system.

b) FENZY

This ABLJ has an air cylinder mounted behind the jacket. An automatic mouthpiece enables the air from the cylinder to be breathed in an emergency failure of the main air supply. A direct-feed can easily be fitted for routine buoyancy adjustment.

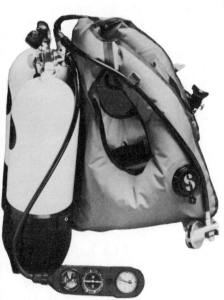

c) SCUBAPRO

This is a 'combined' system having an adjustable buoyancy system with a direct-feed; emergency inflation is by firing one or two CO_2 cartridges. The whole assembly is mounted on an aqualung backpack thereby reducing the number of straps required.

Fig. 46. THREE EXAMPLES OF ABLJs

diver to the surface at a speed of about 90 m per minute; this is unacceptable for safe diving since it does not permit the normal
decompression allowed for in the 15 m per minute rate.

Rules for Use for the ABLJ

1. Always charge the ABLJ cylinder before each dive to ensure
   maximum reliability. Check the charging pressure and determine
   potential buoyancy.
2. Always wear your lifejacket so that the harness is *beneath* the
   breathing set and weight-belt so that these can be jettisoned
   while leaving the lifejacket secure.
3. If starting a dive on snorkel, inflate jacket orally, and deflate by
   venting before diving. Never use the ABLJ cylinder for inflation
   before the dive.
4. If air has been passed into the jacket for buoyancy compensation,
   remember to vent this air during the ascent, in order to avoid too
   rapid an ascent.
5. Unless in an emergency, open cylinder tap or direct-feed slowly.
   Always shut off after use; never leave open.
6. Never use the lifejacket for a fast buoyant ascent, except in an
   emergency. Never practice buoyant ascents.
7. Avoid using air from the ABLJ cylinder for buoyancy compensation since this reduces the amount held in reserve for
   emergencies.
8. Take good care of your jacket and its cylinder, or direct-feed
   system; after all it is a life-saving piece of equipment. Regular
   servicing and examination are vital, and particular note should
   be taken of the cleaning and suitable lubrication of cylinder
   valves and quick-fit connections. One must ensure that the item
   always functions correctly and immediately.

Training in the Use of ABLJ's
Before diving in the sea with an ABLJ the diver should practise the
following drills in order to achieve proficiency. Ideally, this training
should follow his aqualung training and should be carried out in a
pool or sheltered, shallow open water. An instructor or companion
should be close at hand at all times.

1. Enter the water wearing a breathing set and ABLJ. Adjust your
   weights as necessary to achieve neutral buoyancy on the surface
   (ABLJ cylinders weigh a kilo or so). Practise standard surfacing
   drill and oral and mechanical inflation of the lifejacket at the
   surface. Practise surface swimming on the front and back with
   the jacket inflated. Practise deflation by venting.

2. Practise surface rescue tows with the rescuer wearing an inflated jacket. Repeat with the subject's jacket inflated. Practise
EAR with the jackets inflated, then partially deflated, to find the
most comfortable system.

3. Enter the water wearing 2–3 kg excess weight; adjust buoyancy
to neutral by slowly leaking the air mechanically into the jacket.
Vent air completely on the bottom. Adjust buoyancy by oral
inflation; vent; swim to surface. Inflate the jacket on the surface.

4. To practice breathing from the lifejacket, sit on the pool bottom
wearing an aqualung and ABLJ; drape a weight-belt with 5 kg
excess across your lap, making sure that assistance is at hand.
Take a breath from the aqualung; remove the mouthpiece. Place
the ABLJ mouthpiece in position and clear; release a small
amount of air into the bag from the ABLJ cylinder or direct-feed
system; inhale. Breathe out through nose. Release more
air and repeat cycle. Ideally the air should be breathed in as soon
as it reaches the top of the bag so that changes in buoyancy are
kept to a minimum. Repeat the exercise decreasing the excess
weight until normal weighting is reached. (Fitting an 'automatic'
demand mouthpiece to the lifejacket makes this procedure far
simpler, since it is no longer necessary to breathe out via the nose;
the practice session will also be less limited in duration.)

5. Practice in rapid buoyant ascents is not recommended, but ABLJ
users should be instructed to exhale forcibly before and during
such an ascent.

Ideally, most of these training exercises should be repeated under
supervision in open water. The ability to orally inflate an ABLJ
underwater is a very useful skill which requires progressive and
regular practice for success and safety.

Buoyancy Compensator Pack (BCP)

The BCP is a system which is popular in North America, and is now
being seen in Britain. It comprises a horseshoe-shaped buoyancy bag
attached to the periphery of an aqualung harness back-pack. Inflation is either by direct-feed or mouth, and the buoyancy bag has a
pressure relief valve. The unit may be housed in a plastic shroud
which encloses the aqualung cylinder as well.

Most BCP's have an integral weight system, which does away with
the conventional weight-belt. Weights are carried either in a
'locker' which is built into the back-pack, or in tubes attached to the
air cylinder. Both systems have effective quick-release methods of
dumping weights.

The BCP system does all that an ABLJ can do in allowing adjustment at the surface or at depth; the fact that the buoyancy is

BEHIND the diver rather than round the neck means that the diver adopts a more natural head-down position while swimming. The BCP can be breathed from in an emergency. Also, some divers find an advantage in the 'unity' of the system—cylinder, lifejacket, weight-belt and harness are all integrated into one unit. Certainly the BCP leaves the diver with a very clean front—advantageous to the photographer.

On the other hand, the bulk and weight of the system has its drawbacks. It is not easy to pick the set up and sling it over a shoulder because of its weight. It might take up an unacceptable amount of space in a Branch inflatable boat and it would be difficult to lift inboard after a dive. With the buoyancy behind the diver, the BCP could possibly put him into a face-down attitude at the surface if he were unconscious and if the weights had been jettisoned. The trend is to extend the buoyancy bags round to the chest to eliminate this risk. It should be realised that the BCP was never really intended to be a lifejacket—only a means of providing correct and natural trim through buoyancy adjustment at depth.

Variable Volume Dry Suit (VVDS)

This type of diving dress is fully explained in the section on *Protective Clothing*. When used by an experienced diver buoyancy adjustment and control present few difficulties. The great danger is that of air migration to the legs and feet of the suit when the diver is inverted. In an extreme case, the diver might make an uncontrolled buoyant ascent to the surface, where he could still remain inverted.

Inflation is by direct-feed from the breathing set, and the suit is fitted with a vent valve. Readers are referred to *Protective Clothing* for further information concerning the use of the VVDS.

Diving Accessories, Safety Equipment

The term *accessories* covers any item carried by the diver besides his basic kit, aqualung and suit. It has been the practice in the past to regard lifejackets as accessories, but as they are now considered to be such important items of equipment they are dealt with elsewhere. Accessories must be of the best possible quality and reliability, but this does not mean that they must be expensive, nor that they must be purchased ready-made. Some of the items lend themselves to 'do-it-yourself' manufacture, individual ingenuity having full rein—a fact that will become readily apparent in this chapter.

Just how many accessories the diver will wish to possess will depend on the individual, his interest and finances, but those included in the first group—the major accessories—are necessities rather than accessories. The major accessories include:

Weight-belt	Depth-gauge
Knife	Watch
Compass	Contents gauge

All of these must be treated with respect for they are each in turn liable to be responsible for your life—or its loss.

The minor accessories include, but are not limited to:

Torch	Specimen containers
Slate and pencil	Carrying-bag
Decompression meter	Crab-hook
Instrument panel	Lifting bags
Fin retainers	

Major Accessories

Weight-belt

The buoyancy of protective clothing is such that some form of weighting is needed if the diver is to obtain neutral buoyancy under water. This is usually achieved by wearing a weight-belt. Lead weights are added to the belt until the correct buoyancy is arrived at. It is impossible, by this means, to be correctly weighted at all depths as the suit's buoyancy varies with depth. In any case, experienced divers have individual preferences; some prefer to be

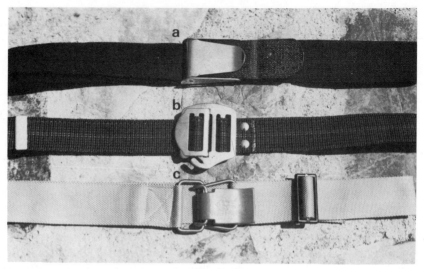

Fig. 47. WEIGHT BELT QUICK-RELEASE BUCKLES
(a) Cam plate type (b) Spirotechnique type (c) Flick-over type

slightly buoyant, some neutral, and some prefer to be slightly heavy. For the novice, however, heavy weighting is dangerous.

It is important that a weight-belt should be comfortable. Make sure that the belt is reasonably wide—a narrow belt cuts in and can be very uncomfortable. Likewise the weights should be fitted flush with the inside and protrude outside so that there is nothing pressing into the diver's body.

The main function of weights is to assist the diver to descend. So it follows that if he should wish to surface in a hurry, or be exhausted on the surface, he must be able to dispense with them quickly. A weight-belt should possess an efficient *quick-release*. An ordinary belt strung with lumps of lead is potentially lethal. The belt must be able to be released in a single movement, and the release mechanism should be easy to locate with bulky gloves on. A small spring or tape is of little or no value in this case if it cannot be found and grasped easily with gloved, frozen hands. A weight-belt should fit snugly—if it doesn't it is likely to 'revolve' round your waist; and when you want to get rid of your weights in a hurry the release mechanism might be located somewhere around your back and inaccessible. It must be worn so that it will come away freely when released—i.e. there must be no harness or other strap over it.

If you have need to get rid of your weight-belt, don't just pull the

Fig. 48. A DIVER'S KNIFE AND SHEATH

release and let the belt drop—it might snag in your knife or some other item of equipment. When you have released the belt, keep hold of it, then throw it away. In other words, hold it at arm's length before dropping it, so that it does not snag on anything.

The weights should be able to be fitted, or removed, easily; otherwise there might be a tendency to leave them on when they should be removed, leaving the diver dangerously heavy. The weight-belt may be made from nylon or rubber webbing, and some of the quick release systems used are shown in Fig. 47.

Knife

Every diver in open water must carry a knife, its main purpose being that of cutting entangling nets, line or rope. Lesser uses, although more frequently employed, include levering off shellfish, hammering or screwdriving, etc. However, it should be remembered that a knife is a dangerous thing and must be treated with respect.

A good knife will be of solid construction and quite heavy. The blade is usually of stainless steel despite the fact that stainless steel does not hold a good edge for long; if a good knife steel were used it would be unable to stand up to the highly corrosive conditions that are met with in diving. Hidden corrosion of the tang inside the handle is very likely. Even stainless-steel will corrode if not properly cared for and the blade benefits from oiling, especially for the first few dives, and at regular intervals thereafter. In any case, knives need sharpening regularly, and this provides an opportunity for cleaning and oiling as well. By the way, it pays to keep your knife clean since this minimises possible corrosion. The blade should have one ordinary cutting edge, often needed for fine lines, and one saw-edge, of more use on larger lines and ropes. A sharp point at the end is usual, although some divers prefer a screwdriver or chisel point. The blade must be thick enough to withstand the heaviest use to which it may be put, without bending (Fig. 48).

The handle may be made of metal, plastic or hard rubber, with a cross hilt to protect the hand. Floating knives have a use in boats, but they are not recommended for divers—imagine yourself trapped on the bottom by a line, and you let the knife go . . .! Diving knives should be made with divers in mind.

At all times the knife must be sheathed when not actually in use. The habit of carrying your knife at the ready throughout the dive is strongly advised against—both for your own safety, and for that of your buddy: remember, skin becomes softened during immersion. The sheath must be manufactured of a material and to a design that is not cut when removing or replacing the knife. Removal should be easy and quick, but at the same time, the knife should be secure against accidental loss. Manufacturers provide some form of neoprene or rubber ring attached to the sheath, which secures the knife when slipped over the handle. The sheath itself should not be attached to any equipment that is liable to be jettisoned in an emergency. Usually, it is strapped to the calf of the leg, or to the thigh: or it may be attached to a special belt, the belt being worn under the weight-belt and *all* other harnesses; it does not have a quick-release buckle.

The Magnetic Compass

One's sense of direction is easily lost underwater and although it may be possible to surface and to return with your destination in view, there are a number of occasions when relying solely on vision may be dangerous, i.e. when decompression is necessary, or when the surface is being churned up by myriads of water-skiers.

In sight of the bottom the experienced diver will navigate by noting the ripples in the sand, or the way the weed is moved by the tide, or merely by noting familiar 'landmarks' etc., but eventually only the possession of a suitable compass will provide the necessary measure of safety.

MAGNETIC VARIATION AND DEVIATION

Let us be quite clear as to what a compass is and what it can do. The earth acts as a giant magnet attracting to its poles other freely swinging magnets. The magnetic compass is, therefore, attracted to the earth's north magnetic pole, which is different from the true navigational/geographic pole, the amount by which the compass varies from True North being known as *Magnetic Variation*. This variation is different all over the earth's surface and, since the degrees of variation are known, correction from what the compass reads (Magnetic North), to the True North can be calculated.

The presence of any stray iron and steel in the boat or on the diver, or undiscovered underground, causes *Magnetic Deviation* by an unknown amount. By a process of 'swinging the compass' it is possible to find out just how much magnetic deviation there is at each point of the compass, due to iron etc. on the boat.

Both variation and deviation are vital factors in boat navigation, but it is customary for divers to ignore them, simply using the compass on one bearing in order to keep to a straight line—for which purpose it is perfectly accurate. But, bear in mind that because of deviation the opposite bearing may not be different by exactly 180°!

From the above it can be concluded that a magnetic compass permits a diver to swim a straight line, but that only with specialist knowledge can it be used to obtain an actual bearing, or for real navigation (see chapter 6 *Underwater Navigation*).

A wrist compass must not collapse under pressure, nor must it swing too freely. Since it is pressure-proof and excessive swinging from the needle is damped down, the oil-filled compass is ideal. The compass needle should still register the direction of Magnetic North and swing freely when the compass has a slight tilt on it, because it is not always easy to keep the compass absolutely level while under water. The compass should have a clearly marked *direction of travel* line on its face and as implied, the diver using a magnetic compass to navigate under water should ensure that this line and his course are one and the same. A compass should also have some means of ensuring that a pre-determined heading is followed and this facility is usually provided by means of a rotating bezel with two prominent marks between which the compass needle should be held to ensure that the pre-determined course is followed. If the needle is not held between these two points, then the diver is swinging off course.

Most under-water navigation using a magnetic compass is carried out by taking a relative bearing to an object or landmark sited in advance. The compass lubber line is set to this bearing and the diver simply swims holding the compass needle on the lubber line. Alternatively, he may calculate from maps or charts his actual heading or bearing in terms of an angle relative to Magnetic North using the 0–360° notation. Magnetic compasses usually have an outer scale which is calibrated through 0–360° and the practised under-water navigator can usually follow a course to an accuracy of ±5°. It should be noted that on some compasses the calibrations are sometimes reversed, i.e. instead of going clockwise from 0° round to 360° the figures are set anti-clockwise. Thus, the Magnetic North pointing needle will indicate the bearing ON which the diver is travelling, rather than the bearing FROM which he is travelling (see Fig. 49). This method generally reduces the chance of making mistakes when using the compass.

Depth Gauges

On the face of it a depth gauge is often only used to satisfy our curiosity, provide some information to boast about, or to ensure that we have achieved the depth specified for a particular test. However, there is a much more serious aspect: maximum depth must be accurately recorded, together with time, to enable us to avoid running into decompression time, or to ensure correct decompression stops at specific depths at the end of extended dives. Our lives and health depend on this. (Nevertheless, new depth gauges have been known to show considerable inaccuracies.)

Three types of depth gauge are most commonly available: the so-called capillary gauge or bathymeter; Bourdon Tube gauge; and diaphragm gauge.

CAPILLARY (Fig. 50a)

A capillary gauge or Bathymeter is the simplest of all the gauges. It is a thin column of air, sealed at one end with the other end open to the water. When the gauge is submerged, water enters the tube and progressively compresses the column of air with increasing depth. Applying Boyle's Law to this, you know that at a depth of 10 m the water will occupy half of the tube and the air will be compressed into the remaining half. At 20 m the water will occupy two-thirds of the tube and at 30 m, three-quarters of the tube and so on.

The scale on the gauge is, therefore, non-linear and the graduations at depth become very small and difficult to read. It is a useful gauge in shallow water but becomes less useful the deeper you go.

If you are making a bathymeter out of glass tube, for example, the diameter of the bore should be about 2–3 mm. It does not matter whether the tube is straight, U-shaped or circular. However, the positioning of the markings along its length is critical. Whatever the length, the column of air will contract to:

One half its original length at   10 m—2 bar absolute
One third its original length at   20 m—3 bar absolute
One quarter its original length at 30 m—4 bar absolute

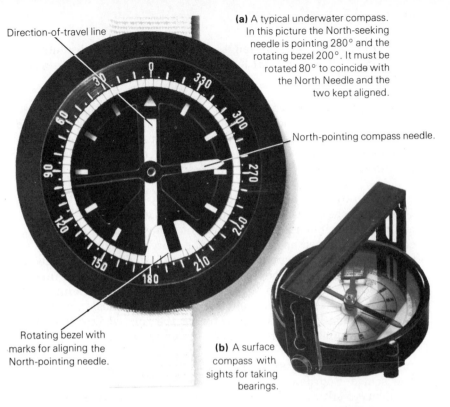

Direction-of-travel line

(a) A typical underwater compass. In this picture the North-seeking needle is pointing 280° and the rotating bezel 200°. It must be rotated 80° to coincide with the North Needle and the two kept aligned.

North-pointing compass needle.

Rotating bezel with marks for aligning the North-pointing needle.

(b) A surface compass with sights for taking bearings.

(c) By rotating the bezel to coincide with the North-seeking needle, and keeping them together by turning the body, the Compass Course in this example shows 300°; as long as the direction of travel line (0°) is in the same line as the diver's body.

(d) To swim on a reciprocal course, it is only necessary to rotate the bezel 180° (to 120° in this example). To swim at right angles to 300° such as on a square search, the bezel should point to either 030° or 210°, and the body turned until the needle coincides.

Fig. 49. **MAGNETIC COMPASSES**

One fifth its original length at   40 m—5 bars absolute
One sixth its original length at   50 m—6 bars absolute
etc., etc.

Several gauges incorporate a *Bourdon Tube*. This is a curved metal tube, sealed at one end, which attempts to straighten itself as pressure is increased within it. A linkage is attached to its closed end, thus moving a needle over the dial to indicate pressure and therefore, in this context, depth.

OPEN BOURDON TUBE (Fig. 50b)

This is the cheapest form of Bourdon Tube gauge where the tube is mounted in a rigid and sealed case. The Bourdon Tube is fixed to the case and this fixed end is open to the water. The other end is free to move and as the water pressure tries to straighten the tube the movement of this free end is transmitted through the connecting link and toothed quadrant to the pinion which holds the pointer. This type of gauge was quite common initially but corrosion and silting which is caused by the water entering the tube, makes it prone to malfunction and necessitate periodic maintenance.

SEALED BOURDON TUBE (Fig. 50c)

The sealed Bourdon Tube gauge was developed to overcome the problems of silting and corrosion that were being experienced with the open tube variety.

This gauge is fundamentally the same as the former but the tube is oil-filled and separated from the water by a rubber diaphragm. The pressure from the water is transmitted through the diaphragm into the oil and the pressure of the oil in the tube begins to straighten it and moves the pointer. This type of gauge is sometimes mistaken for a diaphragm gauge because it uses a small rubber diaphragm as part of its mechanism. It is primarily a Bourdon Tube gauge.

ENCLOSED BOURDON TUBE GAUGE (Fig. 50d)

This gauge is sometimes referred to as an 'oil-filled' gauge and is probably the most popular type currently in use. With both the previous gauges the pressure of the water was applied directly to the inside of the Bourdon Tube but with the oil-filled gauge the operation is quite the reverse.

The Bourdon Tube is air-filled at atmospheric pressure and is sealed at both ends. The tube and mechanism are mounted in a pliable case which is filled with oil. When the gauge is submerged the water pressure is applied to the case which, being pliable, transmits it to the oil, and the oil squeezes the Bourdon Tube causing it to curl further and move the pointer.

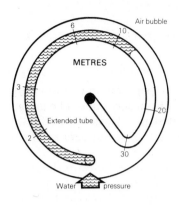

(a) **Capillary gauge**

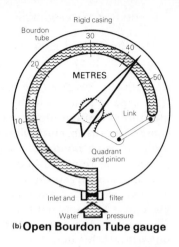

(b) **Open Bourdon Tube gauge**

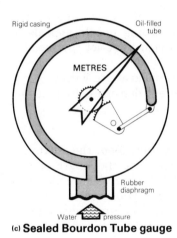

(c) **Sealed Bourdon Tube gauge**

(d) **Enclosed Bourdon Tube gauge**

(e) **Diaphragm gauge**

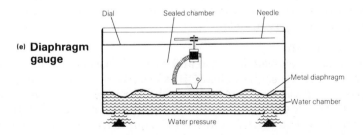

Fig. 50. **TYPES OF DEPTH GAUGES**

H

This fluid-filled capsule is maintenance free and, of course, the mechanism is at all times well lubricated.

DIAPHRAGM GAUGE (Fig. 50e)
This type of gauge which is becoming very popular now is the only mechanical gauge which does not utilise a Bourdon Tube. The gauge comprises a thin metal diaphragm mounted in a rigid hermetically sealed case with most of the air surrounding the mechanism and face having been removed to create a partial vacuum.

When submerged the water enters through large holes in the back of the case and presses on the diaphragm. Movement of the diaphragm is transmitted through the toothed quadrant to the pointer. The back of the water chamber is normally removable for cleaning out silt but this does not present the same problem as the silting and corrosion which occurs with the open Bourdon Tube gauges.

In any depth gauge, large clear luminous markings are essential for low to nil visibility diving, and a recording needle appeals to many divers. However, if a magnet is carried to re-set this needle, beware its effect on your compass!

Finally, note that few depth gauges are accurate to within $\pm 2\%$. Remember too that because of their different densities, 10 m of seawater is equivalent to 10.4 m fresh water.

Watches
Each dive should be planned before it is undertaken: the maximum depth should be agreed within defined limits and the length of stay at a specified depth must be pre-arranged. Whether you are planning your dive within 'No-Stop' limits, or whether you wish to make an extended dive at depth that will necessitate decompression stops, a watch is essential for recording the dive time elapsed and for ensuring that any decompression stops are carried out accurately.

Diving watches must fulfil two basic requirements—they must be waterproof and they must incorporate some method of recording elapsed time. Accuracy is a poor third—even the cheapest watch will not lose as much as a minute an hour, which is the minimum degree of accuracy required.

IS IT WATERPROOF?
If a watch has been well designed and correctly assembled, it will not leak. Why then DO so many leak? It is usually because of damage to the crown (winder) or crystal (glass), and the precautions necessary to prevent this are obvious: do not apply undue pressure or force to either the crown or crystal at any time. Your diving watch should be covered by a guarantee which specifies the test pressure or its depth equivalent; this should be at least 90 m. Some watches are designed

such that the crown is securely 'home' when not in use. Automatic winding mechanisms are an advantage: they reduce the usage of the crown and possible wear on the seal.

ELAPSED TIMING

Recording elapsed time is usually achieved by means of a movable bezel situated at the outer edge of the watch face. On some cheap watches this can rotate without check and can, therefore, be accidentally re-set under water . . . choose a watch that has a positive method of preventing accidental rotation, other than straightforward stiffness. All the figures on the bezel should be clear and easy to understand; at the very least, the zero mark should be large and unequivocal, and the figures/marks on the watch dial should be easily legible. A good luminous paint is now used on most diving watches, so a black dial gives the greatest contrast under water.

Fancy watches with a multiplicity of markings on the dial and/or bezel should be avoided—they can cause confusion in the dark, or when the diver is experiencing symptoms of nitrogen narcosis. A diving watch could be the most expensive piece of diving equipment that you purchase, but it need not be: very many of the cheaper watches may prove adequate.

STRAPS

A leather watch strap will not last for many dives. A plastic one, like those designed for tropical use, is much better. Stainless steel sprung bands are very good, although on some the catch is a weak point, and on others the springs in the links are weak. On the whole then, stainless steel spring straps are preferable; they are more comfortable to wear but it is a case of personal preference.

Contents Gauge

Unless you calibrate your gauge to suit the cylinder you are using, 'contents gauge' is a misnomer. The gauge only indicates the *pressure* of the contents, and only by deduction can the actual contents be assessed. For example, any cylinder at half its working pressure is only half full; at one quarter pressure it is one quarter full, etc.

Contents gauges work on the Bourdon Tube principle, already explained in this section under *Depth Gauges*. The gauge is attached to the demand valve by means of a flexible high-pressure hose (this is British practice; continental divers rely more on a cylinder shut-off valve that incorporates a reserve air supply in the cylinder—See *Cylinders*). Thus, should the gauge or tube fracture, a rapid and possible dangerous loss of air would result. It is, therefore, essential that a narrow-bore restrictor valve be fitted at the demand valve end. This is usually built into the demand valve itself, but if it can be removed, make sure that it is always replaced. This restrictor will have no effect on the pressure recorded, but would considerably reduce the volume of air escaping after damage, so enabling the diver to surface before all his air vanishes.

When opening the cylinder, the sudden surge of high pressure air could fracture the Bourdon Tube or its connections, allowing high pressure to enter the gauge body. This might cause the gauge glass to explode, with consequent danger to the diver and his companions standing nearby. Therefore, you should not look directly at the gauge, or point it at anyone else, until *after* you have turned on the air supply from the cylinder and the pressure in the gauge has risen to its maximum. To prevent such an accident the better gauges incorporate a pressure relief valve or blow out plug set into the back of the case—don't look at this either when cracking the cylinder!

Some gauges are filled with glycerol to damp needle movement. Never remove or replace this with anything else, especially not oil. Pressure gauges are not items of equipment that the ordinary diver should attempt to service or repair, nor should pressure gauges that are designed for surface use be adapted for use under water—even if they are the right size and fitting and cover the correct pressure range.

Minor Accessories

Torches

Essential for night diving, when at depth or in dark water, a torch is also useful on brighter days when investigating nooks and crannies in reefs and wrecks when it will reveal the true colours of marine life at depth, even on the brightest of days, It is also a very effective means of signalling whilst under water, particularly at depth. The variety of diving torches available these days is considerable (Fig. 51) and excellent torches are available at very competitive prices. Torches vary in size and also in their means of power supply. The majority employ the common U2 dry cell in quantities ranging from 2 to 8, depending upon the size of the torch. Under-water lanterns employ the 6-volt lantern dry cell, and a number of under-water torches with rechargeable batteries can be bought.

Some diving lanterns are positively buoyant and will float to the surface if released, whilst other torches have a removable ballast weight which allows the diver to choose whether he wants a torch to be buoyant or otherwise. Diving torches are provided with some sort of lanyard so that they may be secured to the wrist. In this way,

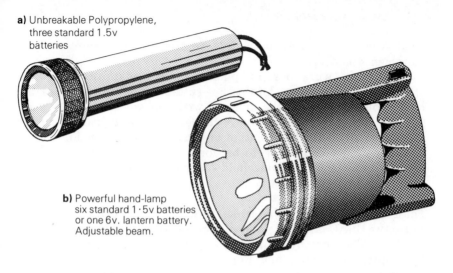

a) Unbreakable Polypropylene, three standard 1.5v batteries

b) Powerful hand-lamp six standard 1·5v batteries or one 6v. lantern battery. Adjustable beam.

Fig. 51. UNDERWATER TORCHES

it is possible to let go of the torch without risk of loss whilst using that hand for other things.

Sealed dry cells should be used in under-water torches and the torch should be stripped and inspected after each dive. Leakage of salt water into the torch will quickly cause harmful corrosion. Do not attempt to conserve batteries. If in doubt, replace the batteries with fresh ones before the dive. There is nothing so frustrating (or potentially dangerous on a night dive) as a battery failure while under water. The diver is then deprived of his only means of signalling. Sometimes the torch switch is affected by increasing pressure and, thus, divers are advised to switch on at the surface and leave the torch on throughout the duration of the dive.

Slate and Pencil

This is a means of recording or exchanging information under water. Any piece of perspex or rigid plastic, roughened with wet-and-dry sandpaper, will take an ordinary lead pencil underwater. Even better is an opaque white plastic such as formica, which does not need roughening. Useful sizes, depending upon the amount of writing you intend to do, are 15 × 20 cm or 20 × 30 cm. For the major under-water survey job a plastic A4 size clip-board and a number of sheets of 'ozalid' water-proof plastic paper are ideal. For specific surveys these sheets of plastic paper can be pre-printed with spaces and columns into which information is written.

The BSAC produces under-water slates which carry the RNPL/ BSAC Abbreviated Decompression Table on one side. These are an ideal way of recording both dive details and decompression requirements on deeper dives.

Soft pencils work best on plastic slates and these should be attached to the writing slate with a suitable length of light string, long enough to permit the diver to write on any part of the slate without running out of string. A rubber can also be carried in the same way, and it is advisable that at least one spare pencil is carried if there is a lot of writing to be done. Slates are best cleaned off using white spirit, or a household scouring powder.

Decompression Meters

These are relegated to the ranks of 'minor accessories' simply because the BSAC does not advise its members to place great reliance on them. They are by no means as accurate as correctly applied Decompression Tables and Repeat Dive Rules, because the only decompression meters available are calibrated to either Italian or US Navy Tables.

A decompression meter comprises basically a gauge employing an open Bourdon Tube into the mouth of which is fitted a special filter element. A sealed flexible bladder containing a special gas is then attached to the mouth of the Bourdon Tube so that as ambient pressure increases this gas is forced through the filter element into the Bourdon Tube (Fig. 52). The rate of gas passage through the filter element is slow so that more gas passes with an increase in pressure or passage of time. The Bourdon Tube is connected through linkage systems similar to those of a depth gauge to a dial which records against the specially calibrated face of the instrument. The object of the decompression meter is to simulate the absorption of nitrogen into the tissues and for this reason, the rate of gas flow through the filter element attempts to match the average rate of nitrogen absorption into a human body.

On reduction of pressure the gas in the Bourdon Tube passes back through the filter element into the sealed flexible bag. This too, takes time and the face of the instrument will indicate the amount of gas released during a surface interval. If the diver decides to do a second dive, the instrument may well show residual gas remaining in his body and during that repeat dive will move more rapidly into those zones of the instrument face which indicate the need for decompression.

The principle of the decompression meter is good, but unfortunately, experience shows that in addition to being calibrated to a table which the BSAC does not recommend, it cannot exactly simulate nitrogen absorption and elimination in the human body—for all tissues and for all times and depths—it can only 'average'. Some instruments, in the past, have been quite variable in per-

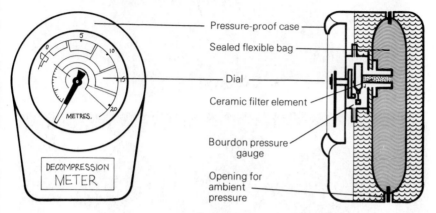

Pressure-proof case

Sealed flexible bag

Dial

Ceramic filter element

Bourdon pressure gauge

DECOMPRESSION METER

Opening for ambient pressure

Fig. 52. A TYPICAL DECOMPRESSION METER

formance. The Decompression Meter could have its uses for those divers who are regularly ascending and descending in the water (e.g. the diving school instructor or the diver scientist who has to make several short but deep descents in the course of a day to monitor scientific equipment), the instrument does indicate when he has reached a certain danger level, and the BSAC recommends that the instrument be used as a 'no-stop' indicator rather than for controlling decompression.

Perhaps the future will see considerable improvement in decompression meters to the point that they will be individually calibrated to suit each diver, thereby superseding the need for Decompression Tables. However, that time is still far off.

Instrument Panels

Where to put all these instruments is sometimes a problem. Usually, the cylinder-contents gauge is tucked under the aqualung harness out of the way, while depth gauges, wrist watches and compass are worn on the wrist. There is much to be said for having some form of instrument console and two sorts are available. Fig. 53a shows a contents-gauge hose mounted instrument console which not only includes the cylinder contents gauge, but also has room for a depth gauge, a compass, and sometimes a decompression meter. It is also possible to have a Decompression Table on the reverse of this console. Fig. 53b shows a typical home-made instrument panel which can house the depth gauge, watch and compass side by side on a board or slate, and which may be worn round the neck. It is sometimes useful to have all instruments in an array of this sort and if an elastic neck-cord is used, this instrument panel does not hang down and drag along the sea-bed. Care should be taken to ensure that the depth gauge and diving watch do not affect the magnetic

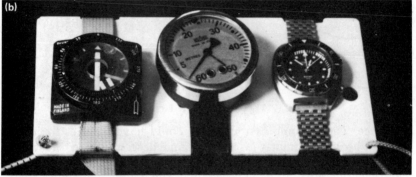

Fig. 53. A COMMERCIALLY PRODUCED (a) & A HOME MADE (b) INSTRUMENT PANEL

compass in any way. Brief notes or dive details can be written on the slate if necessary.

Fin Retainers or 'Fixe Palmes'
These are 'Y-shaped' rubber straps which are slipped over the fin and ankle to secure the fin and prevent loss. They may be purchased, or made from old motorcycle inner tubes (Fig. 29d).

Diver's Hold-all
The diver has to carry his gear somehow, and it is usual practice to put everything except the cylinder, harness and weight-belt into a hold-all or kit bag. (The cylinder is transported in its harness on the diver's back; the weight-belt around his body.) Most equipment manufacturers produce hold-alls, though any large nylon hold-all or kit bag will suffice.

It is a good idea to have a smaller kit bag in which to put mask, fins, snorkel and other items when boat diving (see chapter 6, *Diving from Small Boats*).

Specimen Containers
Generally speaking, long clear polythene bags make the best containers for small specimens taken under water. The bags are more easily opened if a little water is introduced into each bag before

leaving the surface. When the specimen has been captured and placed in the bag, the neck may be knotted, or doubled over and closed with an elastic band. For larger specimens, a nylon mesh shopping bag is ideal, and inexpensive.

Carrying Bag

This 'goody' bag is a bag for crabs, lobsters, small trophies, etc. For the usual few specimens a nylon mesh shopping bag, or an onion bag will do. A draw-string will help secure the mouth. An angler's folding keep-net is also effective if more expensive, no draw-string being necessary. A snap-hook is a useful addition to this piece of equipment: worn on the knife belt, the bag may be hitched on to it, so leaving both hands free for diving.

Lifting Bags

Used for lifting heavy objects from the sea-bottom, this item of equipment is only taken on specific salvage projects and is not commonly used on diving expeditions, unless heavy objects have to be recovered.

They must be strong enough, and attached sufficiently securely to their lines, for their lifting capacity. Remember that 1 litre of water weighs 1 kilogram. Displace that water with air and 1 kilogram of buoyancy is gained. This also gives a clue as to the method of testing the strength of a lifting bag: it should be possible to fill it to capacity with water, and then to suspend it by its lines without it breaking in any way. This is exactly the strain to which it will be subjected when filled with air under water. An open-necked bag which is strong enough will do, and if it does not have adequate lines attached, it can be held in a net bag of proportions sufficient to encompass the lifting bag when inflated.

If the bag is not totally air-tight, a large plastic bag may be used as a liner. Ex-army kit bags make ideal medium-sized lifting bags when a polythene liner is employed. For the small job, an inverted bucket or plastic chemical drum with a stout handle can be used.

Taken down empty, the lifting bag is attached to the object to be raised, and is then filled with air—either from a spare cylinder or from the diver's mouthpiece. If the calculations have been correct, once he has filled the lifting bag(s) to capacity, the object that is to be raised will be neutrally or slightly positively buoyant on the bottom; the bag(s) and object will ascend at a steady rate, the air within the bags expanding and venting off through the opening at the bottom of each. However, if the object is already neutrally buoyant when the bag is—say—only half full of air at ambient pressure, the air will not vent from the bag until it has expanded during the ascent to fill it to capacity. Thus, the buoyancy and, correspondingly, the rate of ascent, will be increasing all the time. This could be dangerous, so it is safer to have several small bags each filled to capacity, rather than one enormous bag only partly filled.

Sealed bags with pressure relief valves, rather like constant-volume lifejackets, are often used commercially. Industrial-sized oil drums may be used for lifting purposes but, of course, are not so easily transported. Wire strops should be used to link the drums together and this requires careful advanced preparation. In any under-water lifting task the use of prepared strops and slings using shackles and snap-hooks saves considerable time and effort. Don't waste time tying knots under water—many divers find this hard enough at the surface, let alone at great depth!

This section has not attempted to introduce the wide range of accessories which are sometimes employed by divers for specific purposes. The following section deals with those accessories which may be looked upon as desirable safety equipment

Safety Equipment

Safe diving procedure has one important requirement—that the position of the diver is known, initially to his companion and secondly to the surface party.

Vision is our usual means of maintaining contact with the other member or members of our diving party, but in conditions of darkness or low visibility this becomes unreliable. In darkness, that is to say at night or in an enclosed space such as a cave or a wreck, we still have clear water but may be suffering from lack of ambient light.

Torches

The easiest way to re-establish visual communication is by means of an under-water lamp carried by each diver. Apart from allowing the diver to observe the terrain and its life it also allows the divers to see each other, sometimes more clearly than in daylight. The lamp can be used for signals, by illuminating the standard hand signals or by a pre-arranged set of flashing signals. Make flashing signals by covering and uncovering the light rather than switching the lamp on and off. It is bad practice to turn the lamp off in dark conditions; the switch may get stuck in the 'off' position.

Emergency lighting incorporating a salt-water activated battery is also available and can be used as a standby or emergency system. However, it is relatively costly to run and for this reason would not be practicable for every-day sports diver use. Remember, too, that this type of lighting employs sea-water as the electrolyte in the battery and will not, therefore, operate in fresh water.

Buddy Lines

When low visibility reduces the effectiveness of visual contact a 'buddy line' should be used. This is a length of strong rope finishing at each end in a loop, which each diver in the pair attaches to his wrist or arm. This can be anything from 1 m to 3 m in length depending on the purpose of the dive. The length of the line should allow one diver to swim behind the other—along a narrow gulley, for instance—without the leader kicking his 'number 2' in the face!

If low visibility is predicted then the divers should enter the water already connected by the 'buddy line'. If the water is acceptably clear but there is a chance of visibility worsening, the dive leader should carry a buddy line so that he can use it as the occasion demands. Signals are given by the agreed code of rope signals.

A variation on the buddy line is an item which was first introduced in the USA as the 'Florida Divers' Belt'. This is a length of stout rope, either manilla or a synthetic fibre, which has a spliced loop at one end and a non-corrodible spring clip at the other. It is from 90 cm to 1 m in overall length and can, therefore, be worn around the diver's waist, ready for use, or stowed in a pocket ready and accessible for many situations. It serves well as a buddy line and if both divers have one they can be linked to form a longer buddy line. When descending or ascending a shot line in a current, the snap hook can be attached to the line; when returning to a boat after a dive you can use it to hang your camera or 'goody bag' from the ladder while getting out of your gear; it can also be used as a rescue towing aid or as a lifting strop.

Fluorescent Hoods

The increasing use of inflatables and other boats with the safety party at sea-level has brought home to many the difficulty of seeing black-helmeted divers on the surface. This difficulty might not arise if divers were to dive with surface marker buoys, but the fact remains that they don't. One answer to this is to use a wet-suit hood made with a 'day-glo' red nylon facing. Another answer is to use overhoods made of a fluorescent material. These hoods may be purchased ready-made, or made at home. They fit loosely round the neck and are fixed with 'pop-fasteners' or 'velcro'.

Surface Marker Buoys

One of the chief communication problems is between the divers and the surface party, and in anything but the most still and limpid waters this is a source of danger. The surface party or cover boat can only offer support to the divers if they know where they are or where they will appear and this calls for some form of marker at the surface. This had led to the evolution of the *Surface Marker Buoy*.

Fig. 54. SURFACE MARKER BUOYS & REELS

a) An inflatable bladder float of a bright colour attached by a stout line to a hand-made wooden reel. Details of how to make this type of reel may be found on page 229 (Fig. 55)

b) Another bright inflatable float attached by a light line to a commercially manufactured fishing-reel type of hand-reel. Note the wrist-strap, essential if the diver wants to keep both hands free during a dive.

c) A different type of inflatable float with a diver's flag A attached. The hand-reel has a long lanyard ending with a clip so that it can be attached to the body during the dive or to an object underwater that needs marking.

Now let us consider the ideal specification for this item. First of all, the surface buoy must be instantly and clearly visible to the surface party or any other water users, and should indicate that there are divers below; this calls for the use of the International Diving Flag displayed in such a way that it will stand out from the mast even in windless conditions; it should also be sufficiently large to be clearly visible at a range of between 100 and 200 m. The floating buoy must be able to support the weight of the flag, the mast and a sinker at the lower end of the mast which keeps it upright, and then give sufficient additional buoyancy to allow for the divers pulling on the line—and using it for support on the surface after the dive. Thus, it needs about 15 kg of buoyancy (Fig. 54).

This surface marker will be connected to the divers by a length of line which will comfortably reach to the deepest point of their dive with an additional margin of 10–15% to allow for currents or tidal flow. If the line were exactly equal to the depth then the current might cause the buoy to sink—or at least impede the activity of the divers on the sea-bed. The line should be conspicuously coloured, strong, yet thin enough to wind easily on to a compact reel.

This long length of line (as much as 50 m in practice) needs to be handled properly to avoid entanglement. The line is best wound round a ratchet reel which allows the diver to pay the line out automatically as he descends, fix the length when he arrives at the bottom, and wind it in as he ascends, thus keeping it reasonably free of slack at all times. A simpler device is a 'winder' frame, which is easier to make or improvise but requires more work on the part of the diver. Wood is the most suitable material for these items since its buoyancy allows it to float at the end of a lanyard, and clear of the diver as he swims along the bottom.

Avoid systems in which the line is paid-out by twining it around the buoy, since these can only be used at a fixed constant depth, incorporate no method for taking up slack, and once more leave you with a length of trailing line at the end of the dive.

The night diver will need to attach a lamp to his surface marker buoy so that the surface party can follow it. For maximum visibility this should be omnidirectional and reasonably clear of the surface. A good alternative to a lamp is the electronic flashing emergency beacon which has very good long-distance visibility due to its high power. The flag/buoy arrangement may also be replaced with a lifebuoy light—this is a purpose-designed battery-driven light in the shape of a buoy. An additional emergency flashing beacon may be carried by the divers for use in an emergency, i.e., should they lose both their buoy and the surface party.

Detailed instructions for making your own Surface Market Buoy and Reel are given on the following pages.

INSTRUCTIONS FOR MAKING A
SURFACE MARKER BUOY REEL
(as illustrated in Fig. 55)

To make the Reel you will require:

12.5mm Marine Plywood. A piece about 30 cm square will be enough for all wooden parts.
Thicker plywood may be used for the handle, and thinner ply for the Outer Wheel.
One brass hexagon headed bolt, 75mm long x 10mm diameter.
Two brass hexagon nuts; four brass washers to fit this bolt.
Two brass countersunk fully threaded screws, 5mm diameter x 50mm long.
Four brass hexagon nuts and washers to fit these screws.
Two brass round head wood screws, No. 6 x 12.5mm.
Two brass countersunk wood screws, No. 6 x 40mm.

Instructions

Cut out the wooden parts to the patterns shown. The shape of the Handle can be varied to suit personal preferences if desired.

Drill 5mm holes in the Handle for the Lanyard: the Pawl pivot: and as a pilot hole for the Spindle.

Drill 5mm holes in the centre of the Ratchet Wheel; Boss Pieces; and Outer Wheel. In the Outer Wheel, also drill 5mm holes for the Winder Knob. Countersink this hole on the inner face of the Wheel. Drill a 3mm hole for line anchorage.

Drill a 5mm hole in the Pawl.

Cut a slot about 5mm wide in the Line Guide, so that the slot lines up with the Drum of the S.M. Reel.

Using a marine quality glue, glue up the Ratchet Wheel, Boss Pieces and Outer Wheel to make the Drum. Use a spare 5mm bolt to align the parts, and to clamp them together while glueing. (If the Drum can also be screwed together, it will be stronger. Use suitable countersunk screws).

Once the Drum is assembled, drill through the 5mm pilot hole to give a clearance hole for the Spindle Bolt. If possible, counterbore the drum on the Ratchet Wheel side to make a recess for the locking nut, so that there is the minimum gap between the Handle and Drum.

Make up a Winder Knob from scraps of plywood (or hardwood): it may be round or square. Drill through 5mm and counterbore slightly to fit the locknut.

Varnish all wooden parts with three coats of Polyurethane Varnish.

Fit the Spindle Bolt through the Drum, with a washer under the bolt-head: put another washer on the inside of the drum and fit the locknut. This should be run on so that the drum rotates freely but has almost no lateral play. Put another washer on and fit the Handle. Yet another washer on the outside, then tighten up the outer nut. Once tightened, the drum should spin freely without binding on the face of the Handle. Adjust as necessary to achieve this. Saw off any surplus bolt, and lock the outer nut with a centre punch.

The Pawl and Winder knobs are fitted on much the same way, taking care to achieve free movement with the screws securely tightened. Fit the two round headed screws at points 'y' on the Handle and Pawl, and wrap an elastic band between the two screws. This serves as a Pawl Spring.

Fit the Line Guide so that the slot covers only the width of the part of the Drum where the line fits. (Use No. 6 x 40mm.)

Splice or tie on the Lanyard — length to suit: snap hook if required.

Wind onto the drum the light cord chosen, using the line anchor hole to secure the inner end. Fit a small snaphook onto the end of the line so that it can be clipped to the Surface Marker Buoy.

Fig. 55. A SURFACE MARKER BUOY REEL CONSTRUCTION

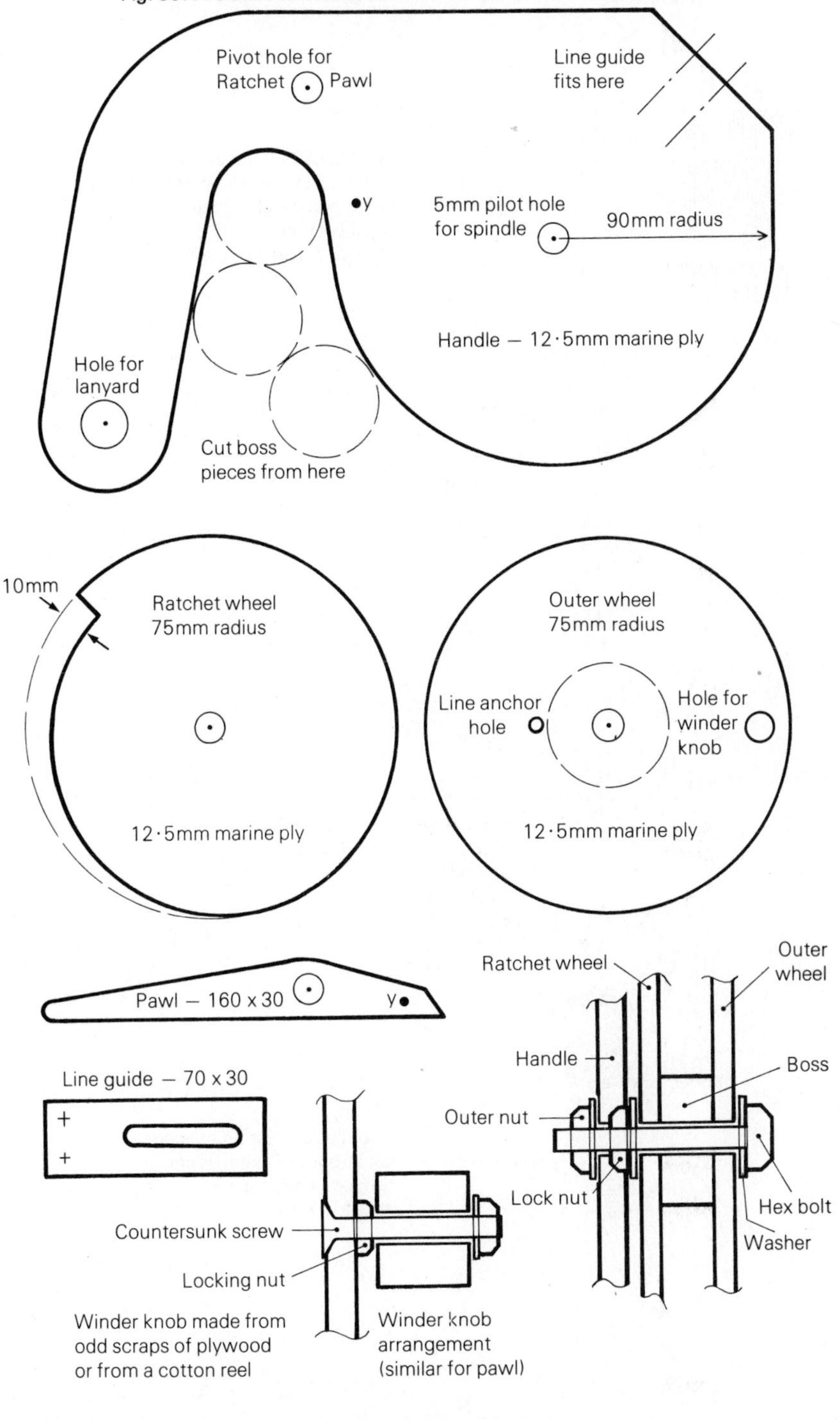

Pivot hole for
Ratchet Pawl

Line guide
fits here

•y

5mm pilot hole
for spindle

90mm radius

Handle — 12·5mm marine ply

Hole for
lanyard

Cut boss
pieces from here

10mm

Ratchet wheel
75mm radius

Outer wheel
75mm radius

Line anchor
hole

Hole for
winder
knob

12·5mm marine ply

12·5mm marine ply

Pawl — 160 x 30   y•

Ratchet wheel

Outer
wheel

Handle

Boss

Line guide — 70 x 30

Outer nut

Lock nut

Hex bolt

Washer

Countersunk screw

Locking nut

Winder knob made from
odd scraps of plywood
or from a cotton reel

Winder knob
arrangement
(similar for pawl)

Fig. 56. MAKE YOUR OWN SURFACE MARKER BUOY

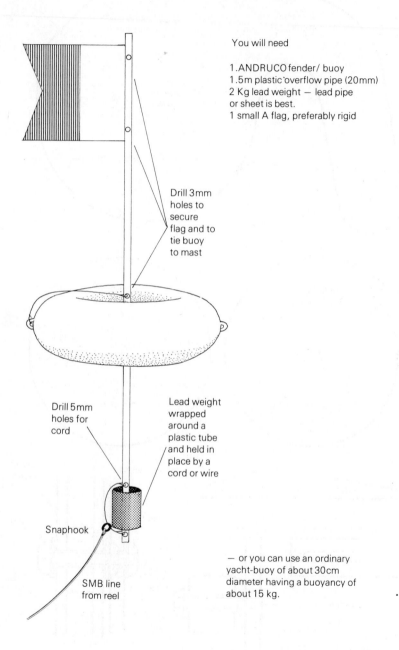

You will need

1. ANDRUCO fender/ buoy
1.5m plastic overflow pipe (20mm)
2 Kg lead weight — lead pipe
or sheet is best.
1 small A flag, preferably rigid

Drill 3mm
holes to
secure
flag and to
tie buoy
to mast

Drill 5mm
holes for
cord

Lead weight
wrapped
around a
plastic tube
and held in
place by a
cord or wire

Snaphook

SMB line
from reel

— or you can use an ordinary
yacht-buoy of about 30cm
diameter having a buoyancy of
about 15 kg.

CHAPTER FOUR

TRAINING

Branch Training Organisation

Introduction
The purpose of this chapter is to explain to new members how Branch training is organised. It will be appreciated that every Branch of the British Sub-Aqua Club is different and therefore the contents of this chapter must of necessity reflect general principles and common practice rather than the actual situation in individual Branches.

Those Responsible for Organising the Training
The structure of a Branch is explained elsewhere in this manual. It is sufficient here to mention that the Diving Officer (DO) holds ultimate authority within the Branch for the diving activities and the training of Branch members. The DO is of course an elected member of the Branch committee. In most Branches it is found that the DO's job is so large that delegation of his responsibilities is necessary. In most Branches, therefore, a Training Officer (TO) is either elected to the Branch committee by the members, or is appointed by the DO. The particular job of organising the Branch training can be said to rest jointly with the Diving Officer and the Training Officer. It is likely that these two in conjunction with the other Branch instructors will devise the training schedule for the Branch.

Areas of Responsibility
When the DO and the TO, in conjunction with the other Branch Instructors, begin to devise the training schedule they will have particular areas in mind. These can be summarised as follows:

Pool Training	Snorkel and Aqualung
Theoretical Knowledge	The lecture programme
Open-Water Training	With emphasis on open-water tests
Further Training	ABLJ training, Training drills, Sub-Aqua bronze, Deep rescue, etc.

The DO and TO who devise the training schedule will concentrate on logical progression from one skill to the next. It cannot be too strongly emphasised that learning to dive is a 'building block' process; it is pointless trying to work on a particular skill if earlier skills have not yet been mastered.

Those Responsible for Training

We have so far considered the people who are responsible for producing a training schedule; we should now spend a little time in considering the people who are actually going to instruct the trainees in the Branch. These people are, of course, the Branch Instructors. Each Branch will have its own method of selecting Branch Instructors, however, and it is important for the beginner to realise that the instructors will have been selected with some care and because they display such qualities as diving proficiency, enthusiasm and teaching ability. Ideally, Branch Instructors should be qualified with a nationally-awarded instructor qualification such as Club Instructor, Advanced Instructor or National Instructor. It is realised, however, that it is not always possible for every Branch Instructor to be so qualified, particularly in newly-formed Branches. However, to have all Branch Instructors qualified as Club Instructors is a goal worth striving for as the benefits to the Branch will be very considerable. In certain countries it will be obligatory for anyone engaged in instruction to hold an instructor qualification.

The Training Schedule

The importance of a logical progression in training has been stressed earlier. The training should, of course, reflect this logical progression.

The divers under training, the instructors responsible for their training and all other Branch members should be made aware of what training is going on, and where and when it will take place.

To this end the training schedule is published, and if possible, duplicated so that all members may have a copy. There are several additional benefits derived from the publishing of a training schedule. These are:

1. It impresses on divers under training the need for regular attendance, and indicates the progression of their training.
2. If the time at which the event starts is quoted, it is more likely that the diver under training will arrive promptly at the training session.
3. Since instructors are likely to be named in the schedule, it improves the attendance and punctuality of that instructor. The divers under training know who has let them down when deficiencies arise!

Content of the Training Schedule

The Training schedule should be a detailed diary of events concerning training and should be published in advance of the period to which it relates. The trainee will then be able to consult the Training schedule, in order to find out where, when and with whom his next training session will occur. The schedule should include all pool training, open-water training, theoretical knowledge and further training.

The Organisation of Pool Training

In this section we are concerned with pool use and with the reasons for certain restraints on the use of particular areas of the pool. Trainees should consider the following comments carefully for they will then realise why they are asked to co-operate by confining themselves to certain areas of the pool.

The first thing that needs to be said is that 'pool time' is valuable (it can cost up to £20 per hour); it is also much in demand so it is easy to see why it should be used carefully and efficiently.

The user should also realise that each group under training has a different requirement. For instance, there may well be two groups under snorkel training, one of which may require to swim lengths, whilst the other needs deep water; and two groups under aqualung training may require deep water. An area may well also be needed for people doing advanced training (e.g., ABLJ course, Training Drills, Sub-Aqua Bronze course), and a separate area is needed for the 'free swimmers' of your Branch.

No one pool is likely to be large enough or sufficiently adaptable to cover all the above requirements and so a compromise has to be made. The Branch Instructors responsible for training will decide how best to use the available space and will divide off areas of the pool for each group of users.

It is worth mentioning here that the pool users' requirements will vary from week to week and it may be necessary to change the areas allotted to each group accordingly.

Again, there will be differences from Branch to Branch depending on local conditions. For example, some Branches allocate pool time rather than space, so that all those requiring to do lengths will use the pool for, say, half an hour and other users with a different requirement will take the next half hour. However, whilst this might be necessary for clubs using small pools it is not a particularly efficient method of allocating the expensive facility of a pool.

At the beginning of a pool training session the instructor and his trainees should be ready for a prompt start in the area of the pool given over for their use as, obviously, this will make the best use of available pool time and it may even enable a second later group to use the particular facility of, say, deep water.

In summary then, the pool is a valuable resource which should be sensibly apportioned and efficiently used for the benefit of all Branch members.

Organisation of Lecture Programme

Where Branches hold their lectures can vary from a member's sitting-room at home, through upstairs rooms in pubs, up to lecture theatres in colleges and universities. Clearly, local conditions dictate what facilities are available. However, trainees may be sure that their instructors will do everything in their power to obtain the best possible facilities.

Detailed listings of lecture content will be found in the Diving Officers' Handbook and it is sufficient here to point out that as far as possible the lecture schedule should be in step with the pool training. Clearly it is of great value to a trainee to have heard the lecture 'Choice and Use of Basic Equipment' *before* he purchases his own equipment. Similarly the lecture 'The ABLJ, Its Use and Application' would be valuable to the student just before he begins his practical training in the use of an ABLJ.

Although it may not be possible to keep pool training and lectures exactly in step, trainees may be sure that their instructors will endeavour to keep them as closely in phase as possible. Where this is not possible a careful study of the subjects in this Manual is commended, as shown in the Training Index.

Organisation of Open-water Training

After the relevant pool training, lectures and tests, the trainee will move to the open-water situation *to continue his training*. Ideally the instructor with whom he has done all his snorkel training so far will be the one who introduces him to the open water on his first snorkel dive, during which, training and possible parts of 'D' Test may take place. Later, after completing aqualung training and tests in the pool and having attended the relevant lectures, the trainee will be ready for his first open-water dive with an aqualung. Again it would be ideal if the instructor with whom he has been through his training so far could be the one to take him into the water.

It cannot be too strongly stressed that the novice diver still has a tremendous amount to learn and that his instruction will continue in open water. The trainee now starts on a schedule for Open-Water Training which begins with training for 'D' Test, continues through 'G' Test and up to the Training Drills for Second Class and, further still, to the more advanced training that experienced divers will wish to have, such as Deep Rescue, Boat Handling, Seamanship, Navigation, etc. It should be mentioned in this connection that the BSAC, through its Coaching Scheme, runs courses for many of the training requirements of the more experienced diver. Interested divers should contact their nearest Coach, and watch the Club journal *Diver* for details of such courses.

Trainees should bear in mind that in producing the Open Water training programme the Diving Officer and Training Officer will have borne in mind the need for a logical progression from early pool training right up to the more advanced training drills and it cannot be too strongly emphasised that such a logical progression is the basis of a good, reliable diver.

Organisation of Further Training

Trainees who have completed their pool training as far as 'E' and 'F' Test will have only just begun their open-water training, but it is important that they maintain their interest in pool training whilst their open water training progresses.

Most Branches ensure that interest is maintained by the provision of suitable courses in skills for which the pool is necessary. Clearly a course on the ABLJ would be extremely valuable at this rime since novice divers will soon be using the ABLJ in the open-water situation. Similarly, Rescue and Life Saving skills need to be improved and an ideal way of doing this is to provide a course leading to the Sub-Aqua Bronze Award of the Royal Life Saving Society. In addition, some of the training required for Second Class drills would be best begun in the pool; for example, drills such as Underwater Navigation, Tender to a Roped Diver, Planning a Search, etc.

Clearly, trainees who have maintained their keenness and enthusiasm throughout their pool training so far are potential Branch Instructors. It may be that at this stage in their training some time could be devoted to a short course intended to put over basic principles of instructing. Such a course could also feature as part of further training.

The Responsibilities of the Trainee

So far in this chapter we have spent some time detailing the considerable amount of organisation that is done by senior Branch members for the benefit of the trainees of that Branch: clearly a great deal of time and effort is spent in the organisation of training schedules. In the conclusion of this section the trainees' responsibilities should be mentioned.

Obviously, if a trainee is to benefit fully from the training arranged for him he must attend regularly and be punctual. Irregular attendance or late arrival are not only going to slow his own progress but may well also slow down the progress of other trainees in his class.

The trainee has responsibilities to the other trainees in his group. He also has responsibilities to his instructor. The instructor has a right to expect loyalty and co-operation from the trainees in his care. He has given up a considerable amount of his own time in organising and operating Branch training for the benefit of the trainee.

Conclusions

It is hoped that after reading this chapter newer members of a Branch will have a better understanding of how the training in a Branch takes place.

The importance of Branch training cannot be too strongly emphasised. In every location throughout the world where branches of the BSAC exist, members meet together regularly as a group for the purpose of Branch training. It can truly be said that training is the backbone of the BSAC. Good training produces good and safe divers which is in everyone's interest for the furtherance of this great sport of ours.

Snorkelling Training—Basic Skills

Learning to dive is similar to building; by laying a foundation and then carefully placing blocks one on top of the other, a safe structure can be completed. With weak foundations and carelessly laid blocks, the structure is unsafe. In the sport of under-water swimming, the diver who does not pay attention to mastering basic skills will find difficulty in later stages of training, and his overall technique will be poor. He is the sort of diver who is most likely to have an accident.

Learning to snorkel dive should not be looked upon as something totally divorced from learning to aqualung dive. The sport is 'diving', and snorkelling is an ideal way of exploring shallow waters, while aqualung diving is better for greater depths. Both are essential aspects of the sport, and snorkel diving skills must be learned before the novice progresses to aqualung diving. In order to progress to your ultimate goal of becoming a proficient diver, it is essential that you master the use of all items of equipment and the face-mask, fins and snorkel will play a vital role in your diving career and your progress and enjoyment of the sport will depend upon the ease and efficiency with which you use them.

Using a Face-mask

To prevent the inside of the face-mask from misting up apply a liberal coating of saliva to the inside of the glass and then rinse off with water. Now put the mask on to your face offering it up with one hand while the other keeps your hair out of the way (Fig. 57a). Hold the mask in place by suction through the nose while drawing the strap around the back of your head just below the crown (Fig. 57b). The strap should hold the mask firmly but should not be uncomfortably tight: if it is it will cause the bottom edge of the mask to press uncomfortably against the underside of the nose.

Standing in the shallow end of the pool, hold your breath and put your mask and face into the water. Provided you have selected your mask carefully, and fitted it correctly there should be no leakage. Get used to the feel of the mask against your face; you may also notice the effect of magnification and refraction, which was explained in chapter 1.

While continuing your study of the pool bottom or sea-bed, you will soon appreciate the value of a snorkel tube, which enables you to continue breathing without having to raise your head.

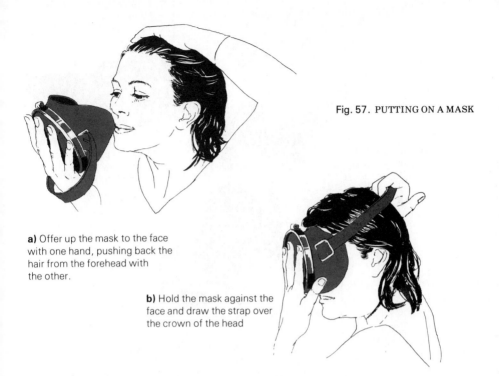

Fig. 57. PUTTING ON A MASK

a) Offer up the mask to the face with one hand, pushing back the hair from the forehead with the other.

b) Hold the mask against the face and draw the strap over the crown of the head

Using a Snorkel Tube

The snorkel may be held in place either by slipping it under the mask strap or by using the retaining loop provided with most makes. Insert the mouthpiece: the seal goes between the lips and the gums and the rubber lugs are generally bitten by the teeth. Do not bite too hard because this will cause jaw-ache fairly quickly. It is advisable to take the first few breaths with your head out of the water until you are able to breathe normally and feel relaxed and comfortable using the snorkel tube.

With mask and snorkel fitted, and again, in shallow water, put your face under water. Practice breathing while in this position. Assuming that the snorkel mouthpiece is being held correctly and that the upper end of the tube is not allowed to sink beneath the surface, no water should enter the tube or your mouth. Again, continue this surface breathing exercise until you are comfortable and confident.

Now comes the time to deliberately flood the snorkel tube and learn how to blow the water clear from it. The object of our sport is to get under water and whenever you do with basic equipment, the snorkel tube will flood and this water must be blown clear when you return to the surface. So, back you go to the pool-side rail and,

a) Holding onto the side of the pool, sink a little and allow snorkel to flood

b) Rise to the surface and blow the water out of the snorkel

Fig. 58. CLEARING A SNORKEL TUBE

holding on to the rail, take a medium breath and push your whole body under water so that the snorkel tube is flooded. While you can hear·the air bubbling out of the tube, the easiest way to ensure that it is completely flooded is to stay down for a count of five seconds or so (Fig. 58a). Allow your body to float up to the surface and, without lifting your head from the water, give a short sharp puff into the snorkel mouthpiece. The force of this exhalation should be similar to that required to blow out candles on a birthday cake. This action should expel the water in one go (Fig. 58b). You will soon discover that a forceful puff is required to clear all the water from your snorkel and it is, therefore, advisable to take a very tentative breath immediately after tube clearing, otherwise you risk an unplanned gargle. Repeat this exercise until you are able to flood and clear the tube time after time without lifting your head from the water. Do take care not to fall into the common trap of exhaling partly through your nose whilst attempting to clear the snorkel tube.

Here are a couple of exercises which will help you to perfect your snorkel-clearing technique:

Still by the pool-side and keeping your face submerged, remove the snorkel tube from your mouth. Pass around your back or exchange snorkels with a companion. Replace the tube into your mouth and clear.

You can extend the same exercise having learned how to use your swim fins by removing the snorkel as you swim along and passing it from hand to hand behind your back; replace; clear and carry on breathing. Repeat as often as possible, at no time lifting your head from the water.

Another snorkel-clearing technique, used when surfacing from a deep dive, will be explained later.

Using Fins

To put fins on, sit on the edge of the pool at the shallow end, wet both feet and both fins and slip them on. (They go on better if both fins and feet are wet.) If they are slipper fins, pull back the heel pocket as you push your foot in; if they are heel-strap type, put your foot in and draw the heel strap up around the heel. With slipper fins you can turn the heel pocket inside out if you wish and with the foot hard in to the fin, pull the back of the fin up, just as if you were pulling a heel strap up.

Now, carefully lower yourself into the water. Your finning skills will first be developed while holding on to the side of the pool. Subsequently, you should attempt to swim breadths across the pool, finning in the normal frontal position. Good finning technique will take time to develop, but concentration on the following points will help.

Keep your legs straight, toes pointed and swing from the hips, using all the leg to power the fins with deep steady strokes. The knees should be thought of as shock absorbers and should neither be kept rigid nor allowed to bend excessively. The fins should not break the surface of the water behind you. If splashing takes place, then the action is incorrect. However, a head-up position, looking ahead, rather than directly down, will tend to keep the legs lower in the water and will prevent the fins breaking the surface (Fig. 59a). At this stage hands and arms should play no part in the fin swimming and should be kept firmly to your side or clasped behind your back.

Using fins increases the power and ease of swimming. Use this power wisely to conserve your energy and increase range rather than speed. Speed potential should be reserved for emergencies.

Remember one golden rule: fins are for finning, not for walking, and they should be fitted as near as possible to the point of entry into the water. Likewise, they should be removed as soon as you leave the water: or before doing so, if you have to climb up steps or a ladder. A number of unpleasant accidents have been caused by walking around in fins, so, if a short walk in fins is unavoidable, walk sideways or backwards, not forgetting to look over your shoulder!

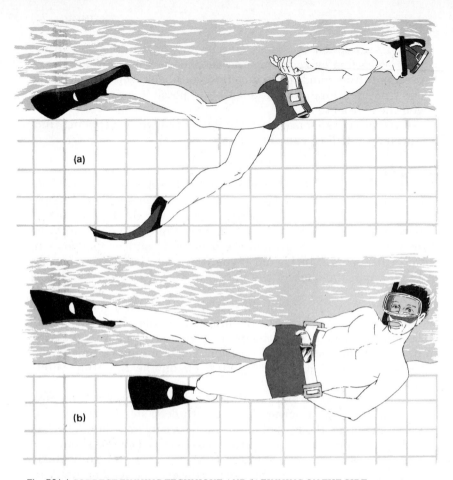

Fig. 59(a) CORRECT FINNING TECHNIQUE AND (b) FINNING ON THE SIDE

Having achieved an acceptable performance in finning in the face-down position, it is worth trying variations of this style by developing your ability to fin on your back and on your side. Finning on your back is straightforward because you can watch what your legs are doing, and in that way make sure that your toes are pointed and your knees are kept reasonably straight. Finning on your side requires no change in technique, but you can take a wider sweep with the legs. Do make sure when you swim on your side that you have the snorkel tube uppermost and that you look ahead of you from time to time (Fig. 59b). These finning variations can be employed simply by way of a change or to ease tiring muscles during a long snorkel swim.

(Although the text has introduced basic equipment in the order of mask, snorkel and fins, there is no reason why the correct use of fins should not precede the use of mask and snorkel tube. There is also a case for teaching divers how to breathe from and clear a snorkel tube even before they use a face-mask. The diving instructor will have his own views as to the order of things, but by the end of the first lesson, the novice diver will be using mask, fins and snorkel tube altogether.)

Treading Water

Divers spend a lot of time at the surface treading water while waiting to be picked up after a dive, or if it is necessary for them to surface to exchange information or instructions. Treading water is nothing more than finning in a vertical direction and is best performed by concentrating on keeping the toes pointed down and the legs straight. Take wide 'strides' for best results. From a treading water position it requires no more than leaning forward to go into a face-down forward finning position and backwards to fin on your back.

Surface Diving

The next phase in your initial training is to perfect the surface dive, and as the head-first dive is the most common means of getting under water, used by snorkellers and aqualung divers alike, we will consider how best to perform it. The aim should be to get under water as effortlessly as possible with minimum disturbance to the surface. To practise a reasonable surface dive, you need slightly deeper water—2 m depth will do nicely.

Kit-up with your mask, fins and snorkel and lie face down on the surface of the water, arms stretched forward, and legs out straight. Now, bend from the waist, point your arms down towards the pool bottom, lift both legs together, straight up into the air, and at the same time, sweep the arms into a wide breast stroke pull. At this instant your legs will be up in the air above you and the weight of them out of the water will be sufficient to drive your body right down to the bottom of the pool (Figs. 60 a, b, c). A well-executed surface dive will push the diver down 4 or 5 m before he needs to fin. In kicking your legs up behind you you may find it easier to draw the knees in towards the chest slightly as you bend forward from the waist, and then kick them out straight behind you. If you find this method easier, fine: it is the end product—a clean, quiet and efficient dive—that really matters. When practising a surface dive in shallow water, you should not need to fin in order to surface. As you pull out of a dive, face your head upwards and watch the surface during the ascent. A second downward push with your arms will carry you up to the surface where you blow the water clear from your snorkel.

At this stage in your snorkel training, you will be experiencing the

Fig. 60. SURFACE DIVES

a) Flat on surface, bend from waist, point arms down-wards to bottom

b) Lift both legs together straight up into air and sweep arms in a breast-stroke pull

c) Weight of legs will carry body down. Do not fin until whole body is submerged

first practical effects of pressure. Even at 2 m you may have felt a slight ear discomfort and you will certainly have felt your mask press on to your face. These are the first signs of the need to clear ears and to prevent mask squeeze. A little air breathed out through the nose will equalise pressure in the mask and use of the compensator pocket of your face-mask will help in ear-clearing (see chapter 2, *Ears and Sinuses*).

A second method of getting under water is to perform a feet-first dive. This is done from a treading water position. Stretch out your arms to the sides with the palms facing downwards and while making a violent finning action, push up strongly on your arms. This should lift your body chest high out of the water and as your arms come down to your sides, stop finning and keep the body in a rigid 'attention' position. The body will drop back into the water and will sink a metre or so beneath the surface, and bending your feet back as you sink will cause your body to topple forward, so that by the time you stop sinking you are in a near horizontal position from which you can move forward into an under-water swim.

Forward and Backward Rolls

A surface dive is easily developed into a forward or backward roll, which are good tests of control and mobility. To perform a forward roll:

Make a surface dive and, once below the surface, tuck your chin into your chest, draw your knees up and keep your legs and feet together. Extend both arms out sideways, palms open, fingers together. Now roll yourself into a ball and swing your arms round so that they brush your hips and legs with even balanced strokes, scooping the water up towards you. This action, if properly executed, will produce a quick, clean forward roll (Fig. 61a).

To make a backward roll, perform a surface dive and once underwater throw your head back and arch your back. Extend your upper arms sideways from the shoulders, and forearms vertically— a 'hands-up' attitude— and this time sweep them forward as if pushing the water away from you. This will spin you in to a neat backward roll (Fig. 61b).

Another method of performing a backward roll is to swim on your back at the surface, with the body as flat as possible; take a breath with your head forward and then bend your head right back, at the same time arching your body back so that your head and shoulders submerge. You should keep finning while you do this, because if you have sufficient 'way on', your momentum will turn your body through the first 90° of the roll. Then, put your hands in the 'hands-up' position; give a good even pushing sweep, and round you will go. Let your legs trail along: do not fin after pushing with your hands.

It is important with both forward and backward rolls that your arms are moved in unison and with equal pressure, otherwise you will twist out of the roll. It is a good idea when practising rolls to line yourself up along some conspicuous datum line, such as one of the lane marks in the swimming pool, and to watch this datum all the way round. This will help you to keep in a perfectly straight line whilst you perform the roll.

Finning Under Water: Surfacing Drill

A few points should be borne in mind when swimming under water. The section on *Hypoxia* in chapter 2 explained the dangers of hyperventilation before a breath-holding dive and this practice should be avoided at all costs. The breath taken to be held whilst

(left) Fig. 61 **(a)** A FORWARD ROLL

Fig. 61 **(b)** A BACKWARD ROLL

under water should not be an excessively deep one because this will be uncomfortable to hold. Take care to ensure that the breath is held, for some beginners have a tendency to exhale slowly while under water and at the end of their swim, have insufficient air remaining in the lungs to clear the snorkel tube.

Look ahead whilst you swim along and use a wider more powerful swimming stroke. Look up as you approach the surface at the end of your dive to ensure that you surface in unobstructed water. Be ready to stay down, or dive again if you face a hazardous situation.

If you are ascending in a near vertical position, your head should be quite well back looking towards the surface. During such an ascent the snorkel tube can be cleared during the last metre or so before you break the surface. This is called *displacement clearing*: it is sometimes easier, neater, and saves the odd second or so when you desperately need a breath. As soon as your head breaks the surface you can roll it forward and inhale.

The technique is shown in Fig. 62. So long as the snorkel tube is pointing 'downhill' water cannot enter it once you have emptied your lungs. The exhalation requires timing and the head MUST be held well back. Clearing becomes part of the ascent procedure, and you have no excuse for not looking where you are going!

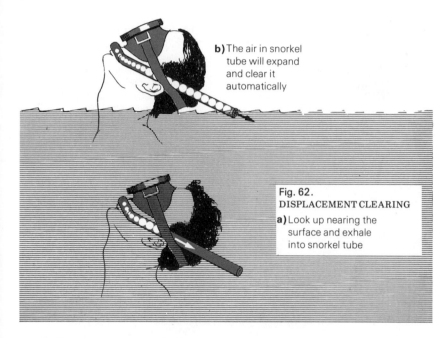

b) The air in snorkel tube will expand and clear it automatically

Fig. 62.
DISPLACEMENT CLEARING

a) Look up nearing the surface and exhale into snorkel tube

Clearing a Flooded Mask

When a face-mask floods, the simplest way to clear water from it is to tread water with the head above the surface and lift the bottom edge of the mask away from the face, allowing the water to drain. Alternatively, the face-mask may be cleared while under water and this exercise is a good preparation for the mask-clearing drill which forms an essential aqualung training skill. The procedure is as follows:

Tilt the head back, so that you are looking towards the surface through the lens of your face-mask. Apply gentle finger pressure to the upper part of the mask and while doing so, commence a steady exhalation through the nose (Fig. 63). The air expelled through the nose will displace the water in the face-mask while the finger pressure at the top of the mask prevents the escape of air at the top. If performed well, two or three seconds of steady exhalation through the nose will clear the flooded mask. The cycle of actions: head back, finger pressure, exhale—should be carried out as a smooth sequence and not as separate steps.

To practise mask-clearing drill, find a place at the edge of the training pool where the water is about 1 m deep. Take a breath and while holding yourself under the water by means of the pool rail or

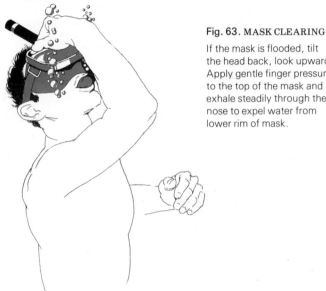

Fig. 63. MASK CLEARING

If the mask is flooded, tilt
the head back, look upwards.
Apply gentle finger pressure
to the top of the mask and
exhale steadily through the
nose to expel water from
lower rim of mask.

ladder, draw the top of the mask away from the face in order to allow
water to flood the mask. Once it is flooded, change over to finger
pressure on the top of the mask and go into the clearing cycle explained above. Do commence the exhalation through the nose as
soon as you start to tip your head back and thereby avoid the discomfort of water running into the nose, causing irritation, spasm
and, perhaps, abandonment of the exercise. Repeat the flooding and
clearing cycle several times until a good technique is acquired.

Fitting Equipment in the Water

There are times when the snorkel diver's basic equipment may become dislodged during the course of his activities. Face-masks may
be flooded and fins may slip off the feet. It is important, therefore,
that the snorkel diver should be capable of removing, clearing and
refitting any item of equipment without having to return to shallow
water to do so.

The reader has already been introduced to the exercise of removing and refitting the snorkel tube, so this skill should by now be
mastered. Fitting of fins whilst in deep water presents little problem
so long as the snorkeller realises that this can only be done if he
doubles himself up into a ball and sticks his face right under water

whilst putting his fins on. It is virtually impossible to fit fins in the water by any other means.

During BSAC training and tests, the novice will have to pick all his basic equipment up from the bottom of the training pool and fit it while treading water. The order in which it is fitted is unimportant and some prefer to recover and fit the face-mask first so that they can locate the other items. On the other hand, swim fins are usually more conspicuous and if these are recovered and fitted first, the diver is able to move around under water further and more quickly whilst seeking his mask and snorkel; and can tread water at the surface more easily whilst fitting them.

Swimming Without a Face-mask

Another item in the BSAC Snorkel Diver Tests requires that the diver swims with his face submerged, breathing through the snorkel tube, but without a face-mask. (This simulates loss of the face-mask when aqualung diving.) Many people find this difficult, and initial experience of breathing through the snorkel tube only without a face-mask is a good way of avoiding this problem at a later stage. Those who do have difficulty in performing this exercise should gain further practice at breathing from a snorkel only in the safety of shallow water. It is important to concentrate on the breathing cycle while performing this exercise, during which one hand holds the snorkel tube against the head while the other is held out in front to ward off any obstruction.

Entries into the Water

Seldom does the diver, whether a snorkeller or an aqualung diver, enter the water as he might initially enter the training pool. More often than not, he will roll off the side of a boat, or jump off rocks, pier or quay. The various methods are shown in Figs. 64a, b, c, d, and e.

The Stride Entry can be used when the height difference between point of entry and water is not great—up to a metre or so. The fact that the legs are apart helps to break the fall.

From greater heights, a Vertical Entry should be used. In this method, the feet are kept together or better still overlapped, with the toes pointed down. The body enters the water vertically and with some impact if entering from a great height. In both the Stride and Vertical entries, the mask should be held firmly against the face with both hands.

Forward and Backward Roll Entries are used when the difference in level between entry stage and water is not more than 0.5 m. Either way, the diver squats down, holds his mask in place and falls in—backward or forward as the case may be.

The forward roll can be embellished by springing up from the

Fig. 64. ENTRIES INTO THE WATER

(a) Vertical entry

(b) Stride entry

(c) Silent entry

(d) Forward roll entry

(e) Backward roll entry

knees as the body loses its balance. This flicks the body over quickly so that the diver lands more on his arched back rather than neck and shoulders. If performed well, the mask does not have to be held in place: the diver might choose this method of entry when carrying a camera or tools.

Finally, there is the Silent Entry. There may be occasions when it is necessary to enter the water without a splash, and this is done by sitting with the feet in the water, and turning the body so that the weight can be taken on the arms while the diver slowly slips into the water (Fig. 64c). This can only be carried out from a shallow height.

All these entry techniques can be carried out by aqualung divers, as those under training will ultimately learn.

When entering the water, by whatever method, ENSURE that there are no obstructions or other swimmers beneath you, and keep a firm hold of the mask in (almost) every case.

Weight-belt Release and Refit

Snorkel divers should be well practised in removing and refitting their weight-belt whilst under water and this action should be done entirely by feel. When practising the release of the weight-belt, the quick-release coupling should be unfastened and then the belt drawn off the body and held to one side before it is released. It is not enough just to undo the buckle: if the swimmer is in a prone position, the weight-belt will remain draped about his body. It should be deliberately drawn clear before being jettisoned.

Lifesaving

The snorkel diver is better equipped and trained than many others to carry out rescue and lifesaving activities. These skills warrant an entire chapter elsewhere in this Manual and the reader is referred to chapter 5 for full particulars of lifesaving techniques which should be learned during Snorkel Diver Training.

BSAC Snorkel Training programmes take every opportunity to relate skills to aqualung diving, so that the novice is better prepared when he reaches that stage. The programme will give the snorkeller a high level of skill and stamina in preparation for open-water snorkelling and aqualung diving. Maintenance of snorkelling skills leads to safe diving, so keep in practice.

Aqualung Training—Basic Skills

We have already learned that the aqualung allows us to breathe normally under water and automatically compensates for depth: it also enables us to carry with us a supply of air sufficient for our needs during a dive.

During the training for aqualung diving we must become completely familiar with this piece of equipment and proficient in its use. We must practise the techniques that will be needed during our open-water diving and also prepare ourselves for any emergency situations which may arise.

The Training Programme

The transition from snorkel diver to aqualung diver covers the important step between relying basically on one's own physical ability, and relying on a piece of mechanical equipment. This transition must be gradual and must fulfil certain requirements.

1. The total length of a course must allow for the trainee to build up sufficient experience in the use of the aqualung. A shortened course may give the impression of covering the ground, but will not allow time for the techniques to become second nature.
2. All the necessary techniques and exercises must be covered and repeated until a high standard of proficiency is reached. Good preparation in the protected waters of a swimming pool will mean that the trainee can pass on to open-water diving with confidence in his ability.
3. Attention must be given to practising emergency techniques so that the correct reaction will come automatically should an emergency arise. Many accidents and incidents would be avoided if every diver knew what to do and how to do it in the various emergency situations that can be predicted.
4. Ideally—the equipment used during training should be similar in type to that which the trainee hopes to own. Although there are several types of aqualung in use, it is of prime importance that the trainee becomes familiar with the more common models, rather than a highly specialised or out-dated set of equipment.
5. Most of all, the objective of the early aqualung training should be to make the trainee at ease in the under-water environment and confident in his ability.

The First Step—Assembling and Fitting the Aqualung

The equipment that the trainee will use during his training has four components: an air cylinder; demand valve; harness; weight-belt. In addition he will also wear his snorkelling equipment of mask, fins and snorkel.

The diver should first ensure that the aqualung is fitted either with a pressure gauge or with a reserve system, otherwise he will have no means of knowing the state of the air supply during a dive. More particularly, he will need to know when the cylinder has only a limited amount of air (usually 50 bars) remaining.

Before entering the training pool, or the sea, he must check that the cylinder he intends to use is charged with compressed air. A pressure gauge is necessary for this. The demand valve may be fitted with its own pressure gauge, in which case the cylinder pressure will·register automatically when testing the demand valve; otherwise a separate test gauge should be used to determine the state of charge of the cylinder, prior to fitting the demand valve.

To fit the demand valve to the cylinder, first check that the O-ring is in position in the cylinder shut-off valve, or pillar valve, and that it is in good condition. If there is a chance that some dust or foreign bodies have been allowed to enter the pillar valve since charging, open the tap momentarily to blow this clear. Now slide the demand valve fixing clamp over the cylinder shut-off valve, making sure that the air outlet of the pillar valve faces the air inlet on the demand valve. Locate the clamp correctly by placing the point of the screw into the small depression at the back of the pillar valve, then tighten up, making sure that the O-ring mates cleanly with the demand valve seat.

On a single-hose demand valve, check that the mouthpiece lies the right way up and that the hose passes over the correct shoulder (Fig. 65). With a twin-hose demand valve it is also necessary to check that the hoses are not punctured; squeeze the hose near to the exhaust and blow hard through the mouthpiece, then suck in hard and see whether either movement produces a hissing sound. In both types of demand valve it should not be possible to draw in any air from the mouthpiece when the cylinder is turned off.

The shut-off valve can now be opened gently to allow air to pass into the demand valve. Listen for a hissing that would indicate a leak, and if you hear this, identify its source and either re-fit or tighten up as necessary. As the air flows into the demand valve, the pressure gauge (if fitted) will register the cylinder pressure. Check that pressure remains constant; turn off the cylinder and check that it is still constant, thus indicating that there are no further leaks.

If you are using a single-hose demand valve· you may find that it has a neck strap attached to the mouthpiece, but unless the strap

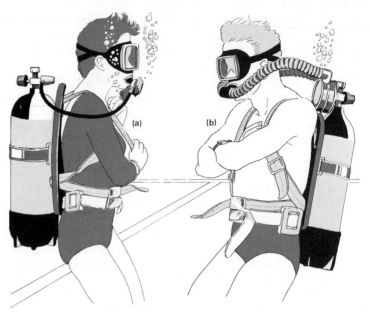

Fig. 65 (a) A SINGLE HOSE   (b) A TWIN HOSE AQUALUNG

releases from the mouthpiece quickly and easily, it is more likely to hinder than help, and should be removed. However, a strap that remains around the neck after release, leaving the mouthpiece clear, is recommended, and may be used during training.

The cylinder should be fitted with a rubber or plastic 'boot' which serves to protect it and to cushion its impact with other objects. Although this boot makes it possible to stand the cylinder upright, resist the temptation to leave the cylinder unattended in this position: it may easily be knocked over, or fall, giving rise to injury, or damage to the demand valve—as well as to the training pool deck. Some cylinders have flat bottoms, and the same caution applies; the aqualung is safe and stable lying on its side in a protected place.

We rely on a harness to hold the heavy cylinder and demand valve in a comfortable position and in order to do this effectively it has to serve two functions: while on dry land it has to support the aqua-lung in such a position that the main weight is taken on the shoulders, but when submerged, the weight is transferred to the back. Alternatively, when swimming on the back, or if using a buoyant cylinder, the harness must hold the cylinder close to the back in a firm position. When fitting the harness we will therefore require a firm but comfortable fit that spreads the weight.

The harness should allow for adjustment on each strap—both

shoulder straps, and the waist belt and/or crotch strap, since these will allow a snug but comfortable fit. The waist/crotch straps must be fitted with quick-release buckles so that the aqualung and demand valve can be removed instantly and easily with one hand. If you are wearing a wet suit you will probably need to tighten the harness again when diving, at depth, due to compression of the suit.

When adjusting the harness on the cylinder make sure that it is in such a position that the shut-off valve and demand valve come below the level of the diver's head. Test for this by bending your head right back to make sure that you do not touch them. The correct position for a twin-hose demand valve is between the diver's shoulder blades, and therefore level with the top of the lungs.

When the harness has been properly adjusted, check that the demand-valve mouthpiece reaches your mouth and is comfortable. If a pressure gauge is fitted, it should be passed beneath the arm and under a shoulder strap to hold it within reach, and to avoid damage or snagging on any under-water obstruction.

BUOYANCY ADJUSTMENT

A weight-belt is worn to counteract any positive buoyancy that the diver may have when submerged; the amount of weight required will vary from person to person and with the equipment used. To check the amount of weight required, the diver descends to the pool bottom, exhales, and lies there on his stomach, if he can. If he is too light, and has to fight to stay down, he should add weight to his belt until he is able to lie flat. On inhaling, he should slowly lift off from the bottom of the pool, to sink again with the next exhalation. The quantity of weights carried on his weight-belt should be adjusted until this can be achieved. The diver is then weighted for *neutral buoyancy*.

In effect a diver increases his volume, and therefore displaces more water, every time he takes a breath, and reverses this as he exhales. If the total weight of the diver and his equipment is less than their combined displacement, he will float; the addition of lead, which has low displacement but high weight, will reverse this process.

The weight-belt is worn around the diver's waist in such a position that he can jettison it quickly in an emergency. This means that it must not be covered by any other straps or harness, or obstructed in any way. The exact method of fitting will vary with the type of harness used but it must always meet this requirement. It is also of vital importance that it is fitted with a quick-release buckle that can be released instantly with one hand. Arrange the weights equally to left and right, and avoid placing them underneath the cylinder, as this is uncomfortable.

Before entering the water, check all your equipment to ensure that it is intact; in good working order; that buckles release; that the cylinder is charged and turned on; and that the demand valve is functioning correctly. And then check that your companion's equipment is in similarly good order.

Swimming Under Water

The fin stroke used by the aqualung diver is different from that used by the snorkeller since the problems of alignment with the surface and of fin splashing no longer exist. The stroke is deep, slow and steady, aiming to get the maximum forward motion from the minimum muscular effort. This economy of effort is most important and will be improved by maintaining a streamlined form. Reduce to a minimum the amount of loose equipment carried and keep your arms to your sides when they are not actually in use or carrying something. The hands play no part in your propulsion and should be used only for balance or intricate manoeuvres.

If your weight has been correctly adjusted to neutral buoyancy, you should find that when swimming slowly through the water you will rise slightly as you inhale and sink as you exhale. Fast forward movement will tend to overcome these variations in level since the speed of your finning will overcome the gravitational forces. A fine control over your state of buoyancy will assist you in performing manoeuvres such as swimming through holes (as in the side of a wreck) or standing on your head (to look at a lobster in a hole) and these are usually simulated in pool training by forward and backward rolls.

Clearing the Mouthpiece

We expect only to get air from the demand-valve mouthpiece, but during certain exercises it is necessary first to clear water from it. The modern demand valve is designed such that water will not leak into the mouthpiece while we are breathing from it, and the actual space which could be occupied by water is kept to a minimum. Nevertheless, there will be occasions, i.e. during air sharing, or at the surface, or when inflating an ABLJ/OBC (see chapter 3 *Lifejackets and Buoyancy Aids*), when the mouthpiece will become filled with water.

Single-Hose Valves: In single-hose valves the part between the diaphragm and the mouthpiece—the second stage—will flood when not held in the mouth. In most cases the exhaust valve is fitted at the bottom of this section, and therefore the diver has only to insert the mouthpiece and blow for the water to leave via the exhaust valve. In some models the exhaust valve may be to the side of the mouthpiece, in which case a slight inclination of the head in its direction will assist evacuation of the water.

Should the diver find himself in a situation in which he is unable to blow to clear the mouthpiece, the demand valve can be made to clear itself by applying pressure to the *purge button*, which is generally found in a central position on the front of the second stage and which acts directly on the diaphragm.

In normal use, however, it is seldom necessary to use the purge button in this way as the mouthpiece clears very easily with a simple blow. But it is worth mentioning that the demand valve is not designed to clear when in an upside-down position, and should you find yourself in this situation, you will need the assistance of the purge button.

Practise mouthpiece clearing by simply taking the mouthpiece out of your mouth, returning it, and blowing it clear. Also practise using the purge button to assist clearing. Some single-hose demand valves are adjusted so that the air flows freely if the mouthpiece points upwards, but this can be stopped by pointing it downwards. Avoid any tendency to waste air by free flowing; you never know when you may value those extra few breaths.

When not in your mouth the second stage will hang free and its location can usually be predicted. However, if you should lose it, roll forward and on to the shoulder over which the hose passes. It will then lie ahead of you, and as you return to a vertical position it will fall across your chest and can be easily retrieved. Alternatively, you can wear the type of retaining strap already mentioned, but only if you are sure that it can be released instantly and, preferably, if the strap remains around the neck rather than attached to the mouthpiece; any such encumbrance could become an unnecessary hazard during emergency air sharing.

Twin-Hose Valves: With this type of demand valve the air arrives at the mouthpiece from one side, is breathed by the diver and expelled via the other side, the direction of flow being controlled by one-way valves at each side of the mouthpiece. It follows then that any water in the mouthpiece must be expelled in the same direction as expired air—via the one-way valve. Here again, the space which could become flooded is kept to an absolute minimum.

The flooded mouthpiece can be placed in the diver's mouth and cleared with a blow, possibly assisted by tilting the head so that the exhaust hose is in the lower position.

This type of demand valve has no purge button so if a free flow of air is required to assist clearing, it is obtained in a different way. Whenever the mouthpiece is in a higher position than the diaphragm (found in the main body of the demand valve), the difference in water pressure will cause air to flow freely from the mouthpiece. We make use of this phenomenon in the following way: the diver adopts a vertical position, holding the mouthpiece until it bubbles; he inverts the bubbling mouthpiece so that the orifice faces downwards; then lowers the mouthpiece—still bubbling—into his mouth. There should be no water in the mouthpiece, so he can breathe in immediately.

Some older types of demand valve which are not fitted with one-way valves still exist, and in newer models these valves have been known to fail. It is therefore necessary for the diver to be able to clear tubes that are completely flooded.

First of all, when using the older type of demand valve, the diver must check which hose leads to the exhaust. This can be easily done at any time by pinching one of the hoses to shut it off, and by then blowing into the mouthpiece: if you can still blow, you are pinching the inlet; if you cannot blow, you are pinching the exhaust. The diver can now clear his tubes in the following way: he starts from a lying face-downwards position; he then rolls over in the direction of the exhaust tube until the demand valve is almost directly beneath him, thus causing the water to flow down this hose. He then blows into the mouthpiece and forces the water out through the exhaust valve in the demand valve. The hoses are then clear of water and he can breathe normally.

If you lose the mouthpiece of a twin-hose demand valve, remember that it will tend to float upwards, and can be found above your head, bubbling. Lean backwards until you can see the mouthpiece and regain it.

Mask Clearing

The air space in the mask allows us to see clearly, and must be kept free of water. Any water in the mask must be displaced by air, and to do this we make use of the simple fact that water is heavier than air.

If leakage or dislodging has allowed water into the mask, put the mask in such a position that the 'open' side (that part which fits against the face) is in the lowest position, with the glass face-plate uppermost. The water will then settle in the lower part of the mask, and if you then exhale steadily through the nose, the water will be expelled past the flexible rubber seal. It will be easier if you press gently on the face-plate to hold the mask firmly against the face; this will prevent the mask from moving too much as the water is blown out, but will still allow the water to escape (Fig. 63).

This can be easily practised in the pool: kneel on the bottom and remove the mask completely, blowing out through the nose slightly as you do so. You should be able to continue breathing from the mouthpiece quite happily even though you have the mask in your hand. To replace and clear the mask, follow these steps:

1. Check that you are holding the mask the right way up, locating the nose pockets at the bottom.
2. Bring the strap in front of the face-plate.

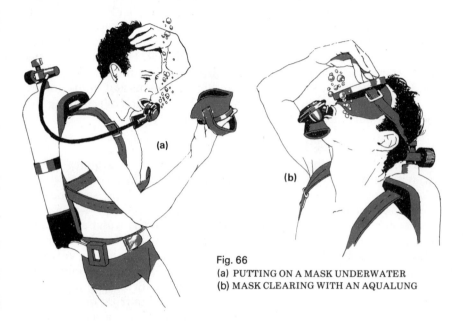

Fig. 66
(a) PUTTING ON A MASK UNDERWATER
(b) MASK CLEARING WITH AN AQUALUNG

3. With one hand, clear your hair away from face and forehead, and with the other, place the mask in position.
4. Fix the strap snugly at the back of the head.
5. Look up towards the surface, trying to get the face-plate almost horizontal.
6. Press gently against the face-plate and blow firmly through your nose. The water should be displaced, but if some remains, give a second blow.

As you become more experienced you will adjust this technique to suit the requirements of your own mask, but these principles will still apply.

Some masks are fitted with drain valves in their lower edge, or at the bottom of the face-plate, and these make the clearing process a little easier. The position for clearing is different from that detailed above since the drain valve must be in the lowest position; it is then only necessary to hold the mask firmly and blow. Drain valves often clear more slowly than when using the 'head-back' technique, and do not always offer any real benefit.

Removing and Refitting the Aqualung

There are occasions when a diver might be forced to remove his aqualung underwater; or might choose to do so for some purpose.

When diving from small boats, it is common practice to remove the set in the water and pass it aboard before getting back into the boat. During pool training, all divers carry out 'Ditch and Retrieve' drill—removing the set under water, surfacing, diving down again and refitting it.The object of this exercise is to acquaint the diver with the correct method of removing the aqualung quickly under water; and it builds up the novice's confidence in his equipment and in his ability to use it. The techniques of 'Ditch and Retrieve', and of removing the set at the surface, will be described separately.

DITCH AND RETRIEVE

Except when getting rid of the aqualung in an emergency under water, the diver normally performs this exercise in a static position on the pool bottom, either sitting or kneeling. The sequence of actions is thus:

Slacken the harness shoulder straps, release the waist strap (and crotch strap if fitted). Reach your hands over your head and grasp the upper part of the aqualung set—by the harness, pillar valve or demand valve. Pull the set upwards and over your head, keeping the elbows forward and together while doing so. Bring the aqualung right over into your lap: it will then be inverted in front of you, with the harness backpack uppermost and pillar valve towards you. This technique works equally well with single or twin-hose demand valves. Place the set on the pool bottom, and after ensuring that your arms and hands are clear of the harness straps, take a final breath from the demand valve, turn off the pillar valve, spit out the mouthpiece and leave the set. As you surface, exhale steadily to avoid baro-trauma.

If the aqualung set employed has a buoyant cylinder, the chances are that you will be using a weightbelt to achieve neutral buoyancy. The weightbelt should be removed and draped over your legs while removing the set, and draped over the cylinder to hold it down before you take the final breath.

To refit the aqualung you simply reverse the procedure. Fig. 67 illustrates the sequence of refitting. After taking a breath at the surface, dive down to the aqualung and, according to whether the set is buoyant or otherwise, either hold on to the heavy set with one hand; or pick up the weightbelt and drape it over your body as you lie on the pool bottom facing the pillar valve end of the set. Once held down, the other hand turns on the air, picks up and fits the mouthpiece which is purged to ensure a flow of air when you take the first breath. Depending on the type of aqualung harness used, the weightbelt can now be secured, or draped over your thighs as you adopt a sitting or kneeling position, with the set picked up and placed in your lap. The harness straps can now be sorted out, arms

Fig. 67. **DITCH AND RETRIEVE—REFITTING**
(Single Hose)   261

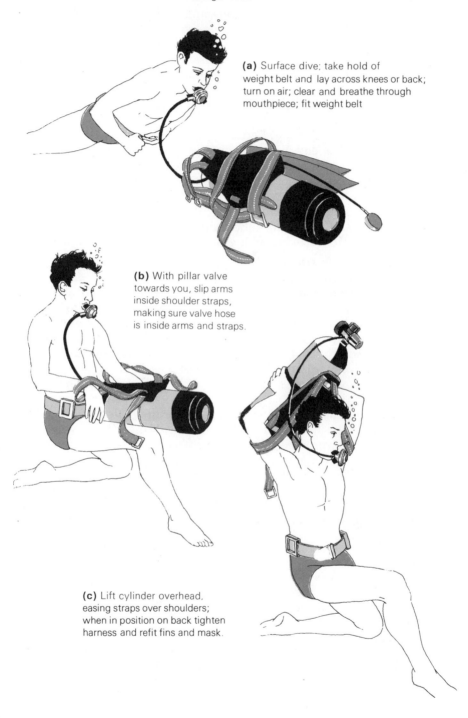

(a) Surface dive; take hold of
weight belt and lay across knees or back;
turn on air; clear and breathe through
mouthpiece; fit weight belt

(b) With pillar valve
towards you, slip arms
inside shoulder straps,
making sure valve hose
is inside arms and straps.

(c) Lift cylinder overhead,
easing straps over shoulders;
when in position on back tighten
harness and refit fins and mask.

passed through the shoulder straps and the aqualung lifted over your head and allowed to drop in place on your back. (Buoyant cylinders will have to be pushed/pulled into place.) Care should be taken when using a single-hose valve, not to pass your arm through the loop of hose coming from the first stage to the mouthpiece. The harness straps can now be secured and adjusted. If the weightbelt has not already been fitted, it should be secured now outside all aqualung harness straps.

During the 'Ditch and Retrieve' exercise, the trainee will have to remove all his equipment including basic equipment, and after surfacing, dive to refit it all. If a good ditch and retrieve technique has been mastered using basic equipment, this usually presents little difficulty.

Novices should look upon the 'ditch' part of this drill as an emergency skill requiring a slick performance. The 'retrieve' part has limited practical use, but adds greatly to the trainee's confidence.

REMOVAL AT THE SURFACE

During Third Class qualifying tests, the novice has to demonstrate ability to remove the aqualung while treading water at the surface. This has considerable practical application when diving from small boats. It is important that the diver is able to do this quickly and efficiently, even in a rough sea. In the pool test, weightbelts if worn should be retained in place: in the open-water application, they should be removed and handed into the boat before the set is taken off. The following notes apply to both the pool test drill and to open water situations.

On the surface, establish snorkel breathing. Remove and hand over the weightbelt (open water). Release Single Hose valve neck straps: pass Twin Hose tubes over your head. Release harness waist straps and crotch strap. Slacken shoulder straps, and slip an arm out of one shoulder strap so that the set is hanging on the other shoulder. Slip the set off the shoulder, using the other hand if necessary. Turn off the air and pass the set up to the boatman. (When returning to a small boat, the set can be removed in this way using one hand only while, with the other, you hold on to the boat.)

Sharing Air

It is most important to practise emergency drills, and thus to ensure that a situation which could turn into an emergency remains a mere incident. If one member of the diving party loses his air supply—for whatever reason—it is quite a simple matter for him to signal to his companion that he needs air, and then to start sharing his companion's air supply. This technique will be most successful if it has been practised thoroughly in the pool and in shallow water during training.

AIR-SHARING

Fig. 68. AIR SHARING WITH A SINGLE HOSE D/VALVE
Notice that the donor does not hold her breath
during the ascent

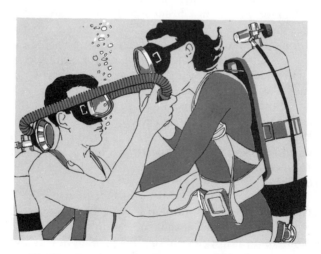

Fig. 69. AIR SHARING WITH A TWIN HOSE D/VALVE
The donor must be positioned below the recipient
to ensure mouth-piece clearing

The procedure is quite different for single and twin-hose demand valves, and we will consider only the type of demand valve being used by the *donor*—the diver whose air supply is being shared.

Single Hose: When sharing a single hose, the victim (the diver who needs air) should position himself level with, and his chest at right-angles to, the donor's. Each diver should grip the other's cylinder neck with his nearest hand. Thus, if the donor's hose passes over his right shoulder the victim must position himself so that his right shoulder touches the donor's left, and will grasp the donor's cylinder neck with his right hand. This position guarantees that both divers are as close together as possible; have a firm grip on each other; can see each other clearly; and reduces to a minimum the distance that the mouthpiece has to travel while passing from mouth to mouth.

Once in position, the donor takes a breath, grips the demand valve second stage, removes the mouthpiece from his own mouth and places it close to the victim's.

The victim places his hand on the donor's hand (which is holding the demand valve) and guides the mouthpiece into his own mouth. He must then clear the mouthpiece, with the assistance of the purge button if necessary, and take *two* good breaths. So the sequence is OUT, IN, OUT, IN, and then releases his grip. The donor then takes two breaths and the cycle recommences.

As this technique is intended primarily as practice for an assisted ascent, the diver who is not breathing from the shared mouthpiece should breathe out, so simulating the exhalation of expanding air from his lungs which would be necessary during such an ascent.

Twin Hose: The positioning of the donor and victim is quite different when sharing from a twin-hose demand valve: in response to the 'I need to share air' signal, the donor approaches the victim face to face. Since the twin hose has no purge button, the only way he can assist the victim's mouthpiece-clearing is by making sure that the mouthpiece is bubbling air when it is handed over. This he does by positioning himself slightly *lower than the victim*, and by passing the mouthpiece *up* to him; the donor's face level with the victim's chest (Fig. 69).

The donor grasps the victim's weight-belt or waist belt while the victim grasps the donor's shoulder straps. The breathing cycle and procedure is then the same as that for a single-hose demand valve.

BSAC tests of aqualung skills require proficiency at swimming on the surface in full kit; of exchanging from demand-valve mouthpiece to snorkel tube: of swimming with a blacked-out mask and in life-saving. The latter is explained in chapter 5. The other items are quite straightforward to the competent snorkeller undergoing aqualung training, who has taken care to adjust buoyancy correctly.

Progressive Open-water Training

Diving is a sport in which training is never really completed. Even the most experienced diver can learn something new; or can practise and improve his skills. In particular, safety skills, such as mask clearing or aqualung sharing, require regular practice to maintain optimum levels of safety.

The novice should not consider himself to be anything like fully trained on completion of Tests through to E, F, and G. His initial open-water dives are TRAINING dives as much as they are experience dives. After gaining BSAC Third Class Diver Qualifications, the novice will hopefully continue with TRAINING to gain Second Class Diver grade; and thereafter, the road is open to First Class Diver and a range of instructor qualifications for all of which TRAINING is required. There are also a range of optional 'Logbook Endorsement' courses, for which TRAINING is given. Training is a continuous and progressive process: the standard may be higher, but it is all training.

There have been those, and no doubt there will be others, who consider that they can take short cuts in pool and initial open-water dive training. Sometimes they get away with it: sometimes they pay dearly for their shortsightedness. It must be admitted that learning to dive with a diving club does take time: it is unlikely that Third Class grade could be reached in much less than six months in the average club. Some novices are unwilling to wait for this length of time, and having gleaned a little knowledge, buy their own gear and learn the rest for themselves. The result is—all too often—a diver lacking in general skill and in the knowledge and ability to deal with the unexpected. The diver who has learned progressively will not lack these things.

Records clearly show that accidents are most likely to happen to the poorly trained and the inexperienced diver who is taking on more than he can handle. If you want to avoid being involved in an accident, DO NOT take short cuts, and do not be talked into joining a dive which you know is beyond your abilities. You would be a fool to do so: the diver who tried to talk you into it would be an even greater fool.

For the diver who does not wish to gain the highest qualifications, there is no obligation to do so. Many are content to reach Third Class Diver standard and to remain there. After all, they can do the sort of diving they want, with their club, so why go on? On the other hand, progression to higher qualifications brings with it a greater range of skills, knowledge and, not least, satisfaction.

Training Programmes leading to BSAC qualifications require that the novice is introduced progressively to more demanding skills, and types of diving, as his experience broadens. Just as snorkel diving precedes aqualung diving, so a basis of carefully planned and controlled introductory dives must be carried out before the diver can progress to more advanced activities, where his diving ability enables him to perform useful work under water.

The dives which have to be carried out in order to obtain BSAC qualifications contain a number of options, some of which have to be met to ensure a breadth of experience. Ten dives at different sites under differing conditions leads to a wider experience than ten dives at the same site. Make sure that you gain new skills and experience with each of your early dives. Diving is a means to an end, and the sooner you achieve mastery of yourself and your equipment, the sooner you can put your diving abilities to use. Second Class Diver open-water drills equip the diver with valuable skills which enable him to navigate accurately and to search effectively. These should be acquired as quickly as possible, and not left until the last minute before gaining that grade. Practise these drills in the pool or on dry land before attempting them in the sea. Iron out all the problems before adding the complications of low visibility, cold, currents, etc. That is what progressive instruction really means.

Every dive represents a learning opportunity, and the word 'dive' is used in the broadest sense. The novice can learn a great deal about a great many diving-related topics simply by watching and asking his mentors as they plan, prepare and conduct the day's diving. For their part, the diving marshals, instructors and experienced members should be willing to accept a novice diver's enquiring mind as eagerness to learn, and not as nosiness or a nuisance. The novice is advised, therefore, to learn from watching others; by offering to help; and by asking to be taught things. For example, a novice could assist in the preparation and operation of the boat used for cover duties: or, under supervision, help with the recharging of cylinders. Even the boat ride home can be used to practise knots or to learn about transit marks and seamanship. Every opportunity to learn should be offered and taken.

CHAPTER FIVE

SAFETY AND LIFESAVING

Accident Avoidance

The Incident Pit

The word 'accident' has been defined as 'an unforeseen event without apparent cause'. On analysing reports of diving accidents it is clear that the word accident is a misnomer; it is usually quite easy to analyse the accident and its causes. By far the greatest number of diving accidents are caused by human error. More often than not, the divers involved blithely put themselves into a hazardous and sometimes tragic situation without any prior consideration of the possible consequences of their action.

Many accidents start in a small way and failure to cope with simple problems—through inexperience or lack of practice—causes the incident to accelerate down the slippery and increasingly steep sides of the Incident Pit (Fig. 70). The safe diver considers the consequences of a course of action BEFORE he instigates it, thereby saving a considerable toll of anxiety and distress on his companions and family. Very few other recreational sports are as intolerant of a careless participant. The chances of survival are more than 100:1 when a person becomes unconscious on land, but that ratio falls dramatically to 1:1 (or less) under the water. Thus, it becomes clear that all accidents under water must be considered as potentially fatal.

Elsewhere in this Manual a series of recommendations and procedures are given to cover various sports diving techniques and situations. These recommendations are based on a vast amount of experience gained over the last quarter century. Abide by them. Do not take short cuts through them. In this way you will avoid repeating the mistakes which were the cause of these recommendations in the first place.

To avoid accidents under water, the diver needs to fully understand the basic principles of the factors affecting him and to be constantly aware of the way he interacts with his surroundings. He should be constantly correcting any faults as they occur before they have a chance to develop into a serious incident. Safety consciousness should be part of the sensible diver's character. Some specific aspects of accident avoidance are now considered.

Know your own Limitations

Never allow yourself to be challenged or goaded into diving situations which you know are likely to overtax you; and equally, do not do this to others. Diving in marginal conditions is foolhardy and has

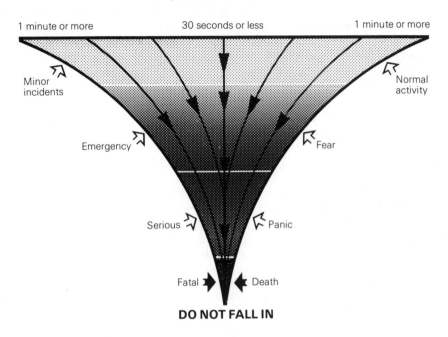

Fig. 70. THE INCIDENT PIT

1 minute or more · 30 seconds or less · 1 minute or more

Minor incidents · Normal activity

Emergency · Fear

Serious · Panic

Fatal · Death

DO NOT FALL IN

little to do with recreational diving. If you know the conditions are going to be poor, call off the dive. Be fit, well rested and well nourished before a dive. Diving with a cold, headache or hangover is just asking for trouble. Drinking until 4 a.m. followed by a dive five hours later is a formula for disaster. Days of under-water searching have been spent looking for the bodies of those who attempted such a feat. Beware of large meals, especially of rich food, shortly before a dive. There have been a number of incidents, some fatal, where divers have vomited under water. Seasickness is very effective for dulling one's sense of awareness and thus, putting the diver at risk. Some anti-seasickness medications bring on drowsiness and may be as much a danger to the diver as the seasickness itself. Keep yourself physically fit. Diving can be a strenuous sport and a person who is easily exhausted is a danger to himself and his companions. Do not get involved with attempts to break under-water records and be especially aware of the newly qualified diver's syndrome—rapture of the depth gauge, i.e. diving ever deeper for its own sake. Learn to use your new-found skills as a means to an end, not to your end.

Never Dive Alone

A diver with a problem he cannot solve himself will generally require immediate help from his buddy. The person who dives alone, other than as a roped diver, can quickly find himself in a perilous situation. Dive in pairs, and remember, *you* are personally responsible for the safety of your companion. Stay together, especially when descending and ascending, when the risk of separation is greatest. Try to avoid groups of three divers if possible; the risks of one diver getting separated are increased.

Never Ascend with Empty Cylinders
By far the greatest number of under-water incidents occurring in sports diving are primarily due to divers running out of air. This is sometimes due to equipment failure, but much more frequently due to poor diving practice. Dives should be planned in advance, an adequate reserve of air being calculated for the ascent plus a safety margin. The dive should be terminated when the first diver reaches this predetermined remaining cylinder capacity. Far too often dives are conducted on the assumption that the ascent is started when one diver's contents gauge reaches the red sector. This has no real meaning in itself unless the gauge reading is related to the volume of air left in the cylinder and the time it will take to reach the surface safely, allowing for any unforeseen delays during the ascent. The experienced diver is aware of how much air he and his companion has left at all times throughout the dive, by regularly checking cylinder contents gauges. (Refer also to chapter 6, *Air Endurance.*)

Always Check Equipment before Diving
Never dive with faulty or suspect equipment. You are entrusting your life, and possibly that of your companion, to the efficient operation of diving equipment. Have it serviced regularly and check that it is complete and functioning correctly before you enter the water. Check your companion's equipment carefully; he may not notice that he has fitted his weight-belt beneath his lifejacket, or that he cannot reach his cylinder-contents gauge. Be sure that *you* can operate his lifejacket and quick releases, should the need arise. Do not waste vital time fumbling with unfamiliar buckles—check and practise in advance.

Keep in Training
The BSAC has evolved a very comprehensive and progressive training schedule for recreational diving. The purpose of this training is to give the diver a number of skills in the correct use of his equipment and to enable him to become conversant with emergency procedures. Thus, should an emergency arise, both he and his companion will know exactly what to do and how to do it. This will only occur if the training has been adequate in the first place and the

divers have also kept in practice. So often emergency procedures are only practised in the pool or 'for the test' and then never used again until a real emergency comes along. This is too late to realise the difference full diving equipment makes to the technique tried in the pool, or to learn the idiosyncrasies of your partner's equipment/ technique. There are more than enough problems at this stage as it is. Training and practice for the emergency drills, particularly sharing and assisted ascents should be regular. Reactions should be instinctive if these drills are to have a chance of success in a real emergency. It takes little effort to practise mask and mouthpiece clearing on every dive, or to spend a minute on aqualung sharing towards the end of a dive.

Never dive without having first received adequate training, and having been trained, keep in practice. In this way, you will be prepared for the unexpected.

Dive Planning

'In all things success depends upon previous preparation. Without such preparation there is sure to be misfortune.' (*Confucius*)

As stated previously, diving accidents do not just happen, they are CAUSED. Consequently, often they can be AVOIDED by considering the hazards involved before the dive, and planning the dive so as to minimise the risks.

It is essential that a Dive Marshal is appointed in order to get coordinated activity towards a common plan. The Marshal should know what is happening at all times and will recognise any anomalies as they occur. He can then take immediate effective action to correct anything which is undesirable. The Dive Marshal needs to keep all of his party informed as to the plan and its progress, and he must appoint INDIVIDUALS to their various duties. For example, if he assumes a group of people are acting as lookout, they will in turn assume that someone else has that responsibility and no one will be really aware should a diver surface in trouble. Appoint individuals, not groups.

The dive should be planned to coincide with the required tidal conditions. Do not dive at 10.30 a.m. just because that happens to be the time everyone turns up! Consider the likely conditions both above and below the water due to the natural effects of winds and tides—ebb tides near estuaries, for example, tend to give poor visibility. If it is a recreational dive, the enjoyment will diminish with the visibility while the risks of diver separation will greatly increase. Plan your dives to coincide with as many favourable conditions you can predict, and if the visibility is poorer or the current stronger than you predicted, be prepared to call off the dive. Sports diving should be fun. Leave the marginal conditions to the commercial divers who have to dive, come what may. If you are planning a deep dive consider the current experience of your divers. There is ample evidence to indicate that the human body gradually adapts to pressurisation after a number of dives. Work up your team to greater depths over a period of time. Do not involve people in deep dives if they have not dived regularly, recently. They may have a greater tendency to suffer a bend, even though they may be diving according to the decompression tables, and may also be more susceptible to narcosis at depth.

Shore Diving

Diving from a beach has much to recommend it for introducing new divers to the sport. However, without taking into account some basic considerations some beach entries can be fraught with danger.

At low tide, access is frequently over weed-covered rocks which are extremely slippery. Divers with equipment on their backs are very unstable out of water and some have sustained serious injury by falling heavily on to boulders. Time the dive to coincide with high water if there is no alternative access point, and carry the equipment so as to maintain maximum stability.

Entry into the water can also have its problems especially on shingle beaches where quite small waves have knocked divers over and rendered them helpless half in and half out of the water. Unable to regain a firm footing, the diver can soon become exhausted in this situation and is at risk. Choose an access point for ease of both entry and exit.

Some inland diving sites are polluted and have caused infection and illness in divers foolhardy enough to dive in them. If you have to dive in suspect water have it analysed first, and make sure you receive the requisite immunisation before diving.

Boat Diving

Much Club diving takes place from small inflatable boats. These vessels offer a fast, highly manoeuvrable and very stable platform for diving. They also offer a minimal amount of shelter from the elements and may be powered by temperamental outboard motors. Each time you go to sea, make sure you have with you ALL of the ancillary equipment necessary (chapter 8 *Small Boat Seamanship*). A boat is not safe or seaworthy if this gear is not in the boat. Make a checklist of all the essential items and fix it to the boat. You can then make sure everything is on board before you set off.

In the event of an engine failure in an open boat, it may be that divers are at sea for an extended period. In such conditions it may be a short time before divers clad only in wet suits will become chilled. Continual evaporation on the surface of the wet suit, accelerated by any wind, will drain body heat quite quickly. Make sure all the boat's occupants take a wind-proof jacket with them each time they put to sea.

With divers under water, it is necessary to consider how the boat can follow them, recall them, or render them immediate assistance at the surface should it be required. Following bubbles just will not work in anything other than a mirror-calm sea and then there is still the problem of communicating with the divers. An obvious solution is to use surface marker buoys (SMB) attached to the divers (chapter 3, *Equipment*). With the divers clearly marked by a SMB, consider whether the boat should remain mobile or at anchor. If the divers are remaining in a confined area in still water there may well be a good reason for anchoring the boat. With mobile divers in a current, an anchored boat will not be able to monitor the divers or render immediate assistance. In this case, it is recommended that the boat is also kept mobile. Far too often Branches are seen taking their boat out to a site, anchoring, putting their divers in and remaining at anchor awaiting the return of the divers, regardless of the currents prevailing. The divers may be lost in this situation and will spend a long, lonely time at sea where they are at considerable risk. The sport receives bad publicity whenever the emergency services are called out due to such thoughtless behaviour.

Wreck Diving

A large number of wrecks around the UK were sunk during the two World Wars. The structure of these vessels has been deteriorating since that time and is consequently weakened and could collapse at any time. Beware of jagged metal if the vessel was sunk by enemy action, cleared by explosives, or is broken up. Be particularly careful of snagged fishing lines and nets, which are often made of tough synthetic materials and may be difficult to cut should a diver become entangled in them. If you enter the hull of a wreck, make sure you have a clearly defined return route. Lay a safety rope and take a good torch. It is easy to become lost inside a wreck especially after sediment has been stirred up, possibly reducing the visibility to zero. If you find ammunition or the like, leave it well alone; make a note of its position or mark the area with an SMB—then report it to the police. They will arrange for it to be disposed of safely.

Finally, be aware of the hazards to which you are exposing yourself and your companions, and plan your actions accordingly. In all things, THINK BEFORE YOU ACT. It is all too easy to slide into the Incident Pit—don't let it happen to you. PLAN your dive.

First Aid

Don't leave it until too late to learn first aid—until a crisis situation occurs—NOW is the time to learn how to save life and prevent suffering, which is what first aid is about.

When presented with a casualty who is obviously in need of your attention, it does not really matter *how* you save his life or relieve his pain, but the following guide-lines, in descending order of importance, will prove helpful.

1. Remove the casualty from danger.
2. Check his pulse. Restore heart-beat.
3. Check his breathing; restore as necessary.
4. Stop major bleeding.
5. Treat any other conditions.
6. Treat for shock (shock and fright are not the same thing).
7. Send the casualty for further treatment.

1. REMOVE FROM DANGER

In the diving context, removal from danger is largely a matter of deep rescue and/or lifesaving. Because EAR can be administered in the water (see *Rescue and Lifesaving*), resuscitation, or at least some part of it, may be administered *before* the patient is removed from danger. However, as a general principle, removal from danger must take a priority that should only be delayed by the obvious necessity of giving treatment to prevent imminent death. Bear in mind at all times that where resuscitation is necessary, *SECONDS COUNT*. Delay in starting resuscitation while removing the patient from danger may result in permanent brain damage, or in his being beyond recovery by the time you start EAR.

It should not be forgotten that while removing the victim from danger, the rescuer or first-aider is himself at greatest risk. The rescuer should not put his own life in jeopardy.

2. RESTORE HEART-BEAT

If the patient is breathing, his heart will also be beating. If he is not apparently breathing, but is bleeding heavily, it is probable that his heart is still beating—check this on the carotid pulse in the neck.

The method of restoring the heart-beat is described in the section on *Resuscitation*.

3. RESTORE BREATHING

For details of the expired air method of resuscitation (EAR), which is now the only method recommended by the BSAC, see *Resuscitation*.

Remember, if you are in doubt as to whether the patient is breathing, start EAR; it will do an adult no harm, even if he is breathing.

If the victim is bleeding heavily, AND his respiration has ceased, both conditions will require immediate attention. The procedure is rapidly to place a dressing or thick pad of cloth firmly over the wound—even if only crudely held in place—and, within seconds, to start EAR.

4. STOP BLEEDING

Remember that even a little blood makes a considerable mess, and this will frighten the patient who may in fact have lost relatively little blood.

Severe bleeding can be stopped by applying direct pressure to the wound or, if there is a foreign body in the wound, pressure as near to the edges as possible. (Don't remove a foreign body that is plugging the wound and reducing the bleeding.)

Blood escapes less quickly if the patient is sitting or lying down, and also if the injured limb is raised. A dressing may be applied instead of, or as soon as possible after this.

Dressings: The best dressing is known as a Standard Dressing, which consists of a sterile pad of gauze-covered cotton-wool firmly attached to a bandage, and wrapped in such a way that it remains sterile even when applied with filthy hands. Dressings may be bought medicated, but these are no longer recommended as the medication may adversely affect subsequent medical treatment. The most useful sizes of Standard Dressing are Medium and Large (Numbers 8 and 9).

In the absence of proper dressings, substitute materials, including most woven materials, especially cotton or linen, and paper tissues or handkerchiefs, can be used in an emergency. Obviously, the cleaner the material the better, but do not allow dirt to deter you from using the only available material while the patient bleeds to death! If any dressing fails to stop the bleeding, do not remove or replace it, but add further dressings on top, and bind them securely in position.

The Tourniquet: There is little doubt that the most effective method of stopping bleeding is the tourniquet. However, it is so efficient at closing off the circulation that the death of some or all tissues beyond it is probable. Tourniquets must therefore be loosened every 20 minutes to allow some blood to pass into the blood-starved tissues, even though some blood may escape. Because of the risks involved, it is now believed that tourniquets should not be applied by first-aiders, except, perhaps, in instances of amputation through shark attack or boating accident. If this is the case, the medical attendant MUST BE TOLD of the tourniquet immediately he arrives. Write the word 'tourniquet' on the patient's forehead with ball-pen or lipstick.

Self-adhesive Dressings: These will not stick to wet skin and may therefore be of little use to divers. They are however popular for minor cuts, blisters, etc. sustained before or after diving, so some should be carried, preferably in a container separate from the rest of the first-aid kit—so that clean dressings, etc. are not spoilt when hunting through them for a 'plaster'.

Individually-wrapped sterile dressings are recommended.

5. TREAT OTHER CONDITIONS

Decompression Sickness: In 90% of cases, symptoms will have appeared between 5 minutes and 3 hours after surfacing. Whereas with pneumothorax, air embolism and emphysema, symptoms occur within seconds of surfacing.

IMMEDIATE RECOMPRESSION in a chamber is necessary for each of the above, with the possible exceptions of emphysema and pneumothorax. During transport, do not exceed 300 m altitude. The patient should be placed in the left coma position, with the head kept low; or if conscious, on his back with the feet slightly elevated. An attendant *must* be present.

Foul-Air Poisoning: Whether due to carbon monoxide, other gas or oil vapour, or any combination of these, the patient will probably complain of a foul taste to the air. He will almost certainly suffer nausea, vomiting and/or headache.

Remove from exposure. Administer oxygen if necessary, especially in the case of carbon monoxide poisoning (apparent by the patient's cherry-red lips). Retain the air-cylinder and its contents for later air-analysis.

Fractures: If in doubt as to whether an injury is a sprain, disloca-tion or fracture, treat it as a fracture. The patient will be in pain; the limb may be deformed, and some use will be lost; there will also be some swelling.

There is a danger that movement of the broken ends may cause further damage, so it is best to immobilise the limb to reduce this movement. Remember that immobilisation should be comfortable as well as effective, and that if a long or rough journey is contemplated, a greater degree of security will be necessary.

Immobilisation may be achieved by the use of well-padded splints, or by strapping the broken limb to the trunk, or to a healthy limb (i.e. finger to finger). Triangular bandages are particularly useful for bandaging fractures and making slings.

Exactly where to place the splints, bandages and padding depends on the exact location of the fracture but, broadly speaking, bandages are applied: to secure the ends of the splints; at each side of the fracture; at each side of any nearby joint. For comfort, padding should be applied between two limbs and between the injured limb and the splint. If no splints are available, use cushions, rolled-up clothes, etc., to support the limb in a comfortable position from which it will move as little as possible. For all injuries of the pelvis and lower limbs, the feet must be tied together.

Burns and Scalds: By their nature burns and scalds are sterile. Make every effort to keep them so by covering them with sterile dressings, but do not apply lotions, ointments, etc. which will only have to be removed later as they can hinder subsequent treatment. Do not prick blisters. Pain will be lessened if the affected part can be cooled rapidly, e.g., with plenty of cold water.

Be ready to treat for shock; it can be severe. Seek medical attention.

Sunburn: Make the patient rest in the shade, and give him fluids to drink. Seek medical attention. Serious cases should be treated as burns and scalds.

Hypothermia: Symptoms of a serious fall in the inner core temperature of the body include:
complaints of cold
mental and physical lethargy
mental confusion (so that the symptoms escape notice in oneself)
slurred speech
shivering
stiffness and/or pain and/or cramp in the muscles
abnormal vision ⎫
collapse and unconsciousness ⎬ VERY serious symptoms

As in the treatment of shock which is dealt with under item 6 of this section, it is *vital* that any increase in the blood supply to the surface of the body be avoided—it could prove fatal.

In general, the fit young adult may be treated (when possible) by immersing the trunk (not legs or arms) in a bath of water at about 42°C. Note that as the circulation returns to normal there may be an initial drop in the patient's temperature as cold blood returns to the core. Be prepared to administer resuscitation if necessary.

PREVENT FURTHER CHILLING. This means changing wet clothing for dry. If no dry clothes are available, do *not* remove his wet ones, but wrap him in plastic sheeting or a rescue blanket or survival bag. Keep the patient out of the wind and rain. If he is conscious and able to swallow, give him tepid or warm food or drink, but do *not* offer him alcohol or spiced foods; nor should you massage him. All these actions will actually draw blood AWAY from the core, and any increase in surface blood supply in these conditions is always at the expense of the heart and brain, and is therefore a danger to life.

CARRY the patient to safety and medical aid.

Hypothermia is reviewed further in chapter 2.

Cramp: Fear of cramp and its associated pain is perhaps more dangerous than the cramp itself. Treatment consists of stretching the affected muscle. Keeping fit and warm are perhaps the best way of avoiding cramp.

Headache: A headache is always a symptom of something else. Alleviating the pain with drugs does not remove the cause and does not make a man fit to dive again; most pain-killing drugs also lower the body temperature, which is not desirable either. Therefore, a diver with a headache, or a diver treating a headache, should not be allowed in the water again that day.

Stings and Bites: There is no universal antidote; one merely treats whatever symptoms appear: if there is pain, ease the pain; if there is swelling, reduce it, etc. If the effects of the sting are very severe, be prepared to carry out EAR with or without cardiac massage, as appropriate.

Syncope (Fainting): In divers, syncope is due to the simultaneous occurrence of one or more of the following:

hyperventilation

after-effects of alcohol

emotional disturbances, anxiety, etc.

fatigue

hunger

breathing pure oxygen

incubating a febrile (feverish) illness

poor vaso-motor tone (susceptible persons commonly faint at the thought of receiving an injection, etc.)

increased intra-pulmonary pressure (holding the breath during physical exertion)

In every case, the result is an inadequate supply of blood to the brain. Treatment consists of lying the patient flat and, if possible, raising his legs above the level of his head. Loosen but do not unnecessarily remove any tight clothing.

Sea-Sickness: The probability of a person becoming sea-sick is increased by:

sitting in a stationary boat in a swell

cold

apprehension

unpleasant smells, such as exhaust fumes

the sight of another person being sick

the after-effects of alcohol

Treatment consists of returning the affected person to shore as soon as possible. Meanwhile, lay him down and keep him warm. If he vomits, give him a drink of cold water, this will help to remove the unpleasant taste, even though it may be brought up almost immediately.

Once sea-sickness has started, drugs by mouth are totally ineffective as, obviously, they will be vomited out again. Sea-sickness pills should be taken at least half an hour before embarking. However, nobody should be allowed to take such pills unless he has taken them before on a non-diving occasion and has thus proved that they have no side-effects *on him*. The side-effects and aftereffects which may be encountered include serious drowsiness and narcosis, which would be additive to nitrogen narcosis or alcohol.

If there is any doubt about the suitability of any pill, consult your doctor; do not dive on it. Each sea-sickness pill has a different effect, and success or failure with one particular brand does not necessarily mean that another brand will have the same effect.

6. TREAT FOR SHOCK

Shock is a state of collapse *which can be fatal*. It follows severe bleeding, severe or extensive burns, fractures, severe abdominal emergencies, excessive sea-sickness, severe decompression sickness, and certain emotional situations.

Symptoms are apparent as follows:
the patient breaks out into a cold sweat
he is very pale
his breathing is shallow and rapid
he may be gasping and suffer 'air-hunger'
his pulse rate increases (except in emotional shock)
the pulse becomes weaker
the patient is worried and often confused
he may become unconscious and die

The patient should be reassured, made to lie down, and steps should be taken to prevent chilling. Note that 'prevent chilling' does *not* mean making him warm—refer to items on *Hypothermia*. Remove the patient to hospital at once.

7. CONVEY THE PATIENT TO HOSPITAL

An ambulance obviously provides the best mode of transport; if the casualty is to be carried in any other vehicle there *must* be an attendant as well as the driver. If the patient has to wait for treat-treatment the attendant should stay with him both for comfort and to provide the authorities with background (possibly vital) information. He will also be able to take or telephone the latest information to the patient's family. The attendant should leave only when dismissed by the hospital or recompression authorities. In

K

view of the possibility of a long wait the attendant's gear will also have to be cleared up, and his family informed as to his whereabouts.

Even when an ambulance is being used, someone from the casualty's diving party should accompany him, if possible. Remember that an unconscious patient must be transported in the coma position, even on a stretcher.

First-Aid Kit

All first-aid kits should include simple instructions so that anyone can use them in an emergency. After all, the only person who knows any first-aid may be the very one who is lying there unconscious.

The following instructions, numbered 1 to 6, are intended to be copied and included in the First-Aid Kit which accompanies any diving party.

Alternative instructions of value, although not aimed at divers and their peculiar accidents, are published in:

Department of Employment and Productivity Form 1008.

Reed's Nautical Almanac; the section 'First-aid at Sea'.

The First-Aid Manual.

INSTRUCTIONS FOR INCLUSION IN THE FIRST-AID KIT

1.

If there is *massive* external bleeding:

(a) Stop the bleeding.

(b) Check the respiration and give EAR as necessary.

(c) Treat burns, fractures, etc. Add further dressings if the bleeding continues.

(d) If unconscious, place the victim in the coma position.

(e) Treat for shock.

(f) SEND FOR HELP—A LIFE IS IN DANGER.

(g) Convey the casualty to shore/hospital immediately.

2.

If there is little or no bleeding, but the patient does not appear to be breathing:

(a) Check respiration and give EAR if necessary.

(b) Check pulse and restore heart-beat if necessary.

(c) Stop any bleeding.

(d) Treat burns, fractures, etc.

(e) If unconscious, place in the coma position.

(f) Treat for shock.

(g) If any of the above are serious, SEND FOR HELP—A LIFE IS IN DANGER.

(h) Convey the patient to shore/hospital immediately.

3.

If there is evidence of internal bleeding *after a dive*, e.g. the casualty is coughing up blood, has a rapid feeble pulse, shows air-hunger, or lapses into a coma:

(a) Move the patient as little as possible and make him rest.
(b) Check respiration and give EAR as necessary.
(c) Stop any external bleeding.
(d) Treat burns, fractures, etc.
(e) Place the patient in coma position, *whether unconscious or not.*
(f) Treat for shock.
(g) SEND FOR HELP—A LIFE IS IN DANGER. Contact HMS *Vernon**.
(h) Convey the patient to shore/recompression chamber /hospital immediately.

4.

If the patient is convulsing after a dive:

(a) Check severe bleeding, see 1.
(b) If he is not breathing, see 2.
(c) If he is coughing up blood, has a rapid, feeble pulse, is unconscious, see 3.
(d) Use the minimum of restraint to prevent the casualty damaging himself further.
(e) When the casualty is quiet, place him in the left coma position, *whether unconscious or not.*
(f) SEND FOR HELP—A LIFE IS IN DANGER. Contact HMS *Vernon**.
(g) Convey the casualty to shore/recompression chamber/hospital by the fastest possible means.

5.

If the patient is acting in a drunken manner and/or has severe pains in the chest after a dive:

(a) Check severe bleeding, see 1.
(b) If he is not breathing, see 2.
(c) If he is coughing up blood, has a rapid, feeble pulse, is unconscious, see 3.
(d) If the patient is convulsing, see 4.
(e) Constant supervision is essential—his condition may worsen, and resuscitation may become necessary.
(f) Place the patient in the left coma position, *whether unconscious or not.*
(g) SEND FOR HELP—A LIFE IS IN DANGER. Contact HMS *Vernon**.
(h) Convey the patient to shore/recompression chamber by the fastest possible means.

6.

If the patient complains of other severe pains, especially in the shoulder, knee or other joint, after a dive:

(a) Check severe bleeding, see 1.
(b) If he is not breathing, see 2.
(c) If he is coughing up blood, has a rapid, feeble pulse, is unconscious, see 3.
(d) If the patient is convulsing, see 4.
(e) Place the patient in any position which is comfortable for him, unless he becomes unconscious, in which case he should be placed in the coma position.
(f) Keep the patient under constant close supervision; his symptoms may worsen.
(g) Contact HMS *Vernon**.
(h) Convey the patient to shore/recompression chamber by the fastest possible means.

*Portsmouth (0705) 822351 Extension 872375 and ask for the Superintendent of Diving by day, and for the Duty Officer Extension 872413 if it is after working hours.

The following three first-aid kits are recommended, each suitable for different situations.

1. THE SMALL KIT

This contains the absolute minimum and is suitable for carrying in a diver's kit-bag, or on an inflatable which is never more than half an hour from medical assistance. It could be included in the 'boat box'.

1 waterproof plastic bag or other container
First-Aid Instructions
3 large Standard dressings (Number 9)
2 triangular bandages
4 medium safety pins
1 large polythene bag/rescue blanket/survival bag

When in doubt about the size of dressing to be included in the first-aid kit, choose the larger: a large dressing will cover a small wound, but a small dressing is useless for a large wound. For the sake of simplicity therefore, the small kit need only contain large dressings.

A large polythene bag (2 m × 1 m), or a piece of polythene tubing taped up as a bag (any gauge polythene) will retain as much body heat as a rescue blanket, and affords the same protection against wind and rain. Rescue blankets are of aluminised melanex and therefore reflect radar (a useful property on a small boat), as well as the sun's heat (useful in the tropics). They may be coloured orange which would, of course, attract the attention of rescuers. A survival bag is a rescue blanket taped-up as a sleeping bag.

2. THE LARGE KIT:
This would be kept at base, i.e. on shore or on a large diving boat. It can cope with a greater number and a wider variety of accidents. A first-aid box complying with the requirements of the Factories Act for 10–15 persons would make a good foundation for this kit.

1 polythene box, tin or other suitable container
First-Aid Instructions
6 small Standard dressings (No. 7)
6 medium Standard dressings (No. 8)
6 large Standard dressings (No. 9)
a minimum of 24 assorted sterile adhesive dressings
4 triangular bandages
12 medium safety pins
1 roll zinc oxide plaster 25 mm × 5 m
2 ½ oz packs of sterile cotton-wool
1 50 mm or 70 mm crepe bandage
1 pair of scissors
1 large polythene bag/rescue blanket/survival bag

The cotton-wool is for miscellaneous wounds; it is better to have several small packs rather than one big one so that the whole stock is not rendered unsterile for one small wound.

3. THE MEDICAL KIT:
This is intended for use on more ambitious expeditions, holidays or voyages. It caters for more than first-aid treatments as it contains drugs, etc.; the more remote the expedition, the wider the range of drugs which may be carried.

1 large box or case with compartments
First Aid Manual
12 small Standard dressings (No. 7)
12 medium Standard dressings (No. 8)
12 large Standard dressings (No. 9)
4 eye pads (Standard dressing No. 16)
a minimum of 48 assorted sterile adhesive dressings
8 triangular bandages
24 assorted safety pins
2 rolls zinc oxide plaster 25 mm × 5 m
4 ½ oz packs of sterile cotton-wool
1 lb pack of sterile cotton wool
2 50 mm or 70 mm crepe bandages
1 pair of scissors
1 pair of splinter forceps/tweezers
1 eye bath
100 soluble Aspirin tablets
500 ml Kaolin/morphine mixture and/or 100 Enterovioform tablets

100 ml Cetrimide antiseptic concentrate
25 gms antiseptic ointment (e.g. Dettol ointment)
1 bottle of Milk of Magnesia
a selection of sea-sickness pills
25 gms of bicarbonate of soda
250 gms glucose sweets

Aspirin is for headache and pain generally. If you are planning an expedition to very remote areas you may consider including stronger drugs; the expedition doctor will make recommendations.

The Kaolin/morphine mixture is for diarrhoea.

Cetrimide is for skin cleansing and disinfection. It is also useful for sterilising instruments. Antiseptic ointment is for stings, sores, etc.

Milk of Magnesia is for indigestion; it is also a laxative.

Bicarbonate of soda dissolved in 1 teaspoon per half litre is useful for severe burns. It may also be used for indigestion and bathing the eyes.

Glucose is for hypoglycaemia in diabetics.

The most highly recommended method of learning first-aid is to study and take the First-Aid Certificate of the Red Cross, St John Ambulance Association, or the St Andrew's Ambulance Association. Courses consist of ten or twelve lectures in theoretical and practical first-aid, but it is not necessary to join any of the above associations in order to attend. Enquiries should be made at any of their local headquarters. (The certificate awarded also covers the requirements for first-aiders under the Factories and Shops Acts, etc. and is valid for three years.)

Although some amplification of methods of treatment is included in this section (Ref. Nos. 1 to 6, Instructions to be included in the First-Aid Kit), of necessity these instructions cannot be complete, and those who do not wish to attend any of the courses sponsored by the first-aid associations, should study the First-Aid Manual which is produced jointly by the above organisations. It is reasonably priced and it is recommended that every first-aid kit should include a copy.

Courses in First-Aid for Divers are available through the BSAC Coaching Scheme. Attendance leads to a Logbook Endorsement.

The aim of First-Aid is to:

1. Sustain life (resuscitation, control bleeding, etc.).
2. Prevent the worsening if any condition (cover wounds, immobilise fractures, coma position, etc.).
3. Promote recovery (reassure, relieve pain, prevent chilling).

The old image of first-aid as a formal drill, rigidly tied to fancy methods of bandaging, etc. should be discounted and the above aims kept in mind.

When tackling a situation in which first-aid is needed, it is helpful to follow a 'check-list' of priorities so that the more serious threats to life are dealt with first. Such a list of priorities is:

1. Remove the patient from danger.
2. Restore breathing.
3. Restore heart-beat.
4. Stop bleeding.
5. Treat other conditions.
6. Treat for shock.
7. Convey the patient to hospital, etc.

No list of priorities can cover every eventuality, but the most likely deviation from the above list is when a person has a major haemorrhage AND has stopped breathing, in which case the bleeding should be dealt with first, *but quickly*.

Always carry printed instructions with the first-aid kit. Make sure everyone knows where the kit is, and can get at it.

LEARN RESUSCITATION THOROUGHLY.

Resuscitation

The section on *Circulation and Respiration* in chapter 2 explains the function of metabolism and the need for oxygen by all body cells. It also explains that if the body is deprived of oxygen, permanent damage to cells will quickly occur. When a person stops breathing for any reason some artificial means of providing him with oxygen is urgently required if he is not to die within a few minutes. This process is known as *Resuscitation* or artificial respiration, and it will be appreciated that speed in initiating treatment is the essence of all the techniques to be described.

This section will explain how to assess the need for resuscitation; the techniques of doing so; how to recognise whether your efforts are succeeding; and the need for subsequent care of the victim. The general principles will be described as for the dry-land situation. The next section of this chapter explains 'in water' rescue and resuscitation methods.

Assessing the Need for Resuscitation

In chapter 2 respiration was defined as the entire process of breathing and blood circulation. For the purposes of this section, it will be more convenient to consider respiration as the breathing cycle only.

Signs of Respiratory Arrest

(i) The subject is not breathing.

(ii) The subject's skin has a blue-grey appearance (*cyanosis*), particularly noticeable at the lips, ear-lobes and nail-beds.

(iii) The pulse rate is erratic and usually slow.

The causes of respiratory arrest include:

(i) Asphyxia due to drowning.

(ii) Obstruction in the airway.

(iii) Gas or chemical poisoning.

(iv) Heart attack.

(v) Electrocution.

It should be realised that there may be other causes of respiratory arrest. In diving, cause (i) may mask other factors which lead to drowning, such as vertigo (result of a damaged ear-drum), embolism or burst lung, decompression sickness, gas poisoning, hypoxia, etc. It is important, therefore, that when treating a drowned diver, consideration is given to other possible factors and complications.

In many cases, such as heart attack and electrocution, both breathing and circulation will stop at the same instant. Failure of the heart and circulation always follows soon after the cessation of breathing and this is known as *Cardiac Arrest*.

Signs of Cardiac Arrest
(i) The subject has no detectable pulse (this is best sought at the carotid artery of the neck).
(ii) The subject's eyes have widely dilated pupils.
(iii) The subject will not be breathing.
(iv) The subject will have the overall pallor of death, i.e. cyanosis.

In considering how to resuscitate an unconscious victim, one must think of two things:
(i) How to provide adequate ventilation of the lungs.
(ii) How to stimulate the heart and to provide an artificial blood circulation whilst the heart is stopped.

There are four essentials for the success of emergency resuscitation:
(i) It must be started at the earliest possible moment.
(ii) The airway to the lungs must be kept clear.
(iii) Artificial respiration must be continued until normal breathing is restored.
(iv) An artificial circulation must be maintained if the heart has stopped.

It is vital that the rescuer determines as soon as possible whether cardiac arrest has occurred. Ventilation of the lungs will be ineffective if there is no circulation and the presence of a circulation will do little good if ventilation is not taking place. Prompt action by the rescuer may catch the victim in the brief period between respiratory arrest and before cardiac arrest. In this case the ventilation of the lungs by artificial respiration may be sufficient to bring about recovery of the victim.

Before considering how treatment can be given to a subject who has suffered from cardiac arrest, the procedures for resuscitating the subject who has suffered respiratory arrest only will now be given. However, it must be stressed once again, that the rescuer *must* first look for signs of cardiac arrest and must satisfy himself that circulation has not stopped before treating respiratory arrest.

The following instructions also presuppose that the subject has been removed from danger in accordance with the advice given in the sections on *Rescue and Lifesaving* and *First Aid*.

The Treatment of Respiratory Arrest

OBSTRUCTION OF THE AIRWAY

There is an important distinction between a person in whom breathing has ceased and one with an obstruction in his airway. In the first case, the chest will not be moving; in the case of an obstruction, initially there will be violent movements of the chest wall as the victim attempts to breathe, but no air will be able to get into his lungs unless the obstruction is cleared. After a while these violent movements will cease and then it will be impossible to distinguish between the two by just looking at the subject.

Obstruction to breathing is most commonly caused by:

(i) The tongue falling back and blocking the air passage in the throat (probably the commonest cause).

(ii) Materials such as blood, vomit, water, or even seaweed in the throat.

(iii) Spasm of the vocal cords shutting off the airway, which occurs in many cases of drowning.

For this reason the first essential in resuscitation is to clear the airway. Open the mouth and with a finger remove any solid matter from the throat. Any vomit, blood, or water in the throat is best drained by turning the patient on his side, head down. Contrary to popular belief, in many cases of drowning there is little or no water in the lungs, and draining of the lungs before instituting artificial respiration is probably of little benefit and is time-wasting. If the victim is making violent breathing efforts, it may be sufficient simply to extent the neck so that the tongue does not obstruct the throat. The victim's natural breathing efforts will then be rewarded and consciousness should soon be regained.

Methods of Artificial Respiration

Artificial respiration may be applied in one of two ways: air may be blown into the chest via the nose and mouth, as in Expired Air Resuscitation (EAR), or external forces may be applied to the outside of the chest, as in the Sylvester-Brosch method (page 292).

Expired Air Resuscitation (EAR)

Movements of the chest can be induced by altering the internal pressure of the airways. By forcing air down the airway to the lungs, they will expand; when the pressure is released, the chest returns to the resting position and the air is expelled. EAR employs these principles, and is the most satisfactory form of artificial respiration for normal use.

Its main advantages are:

(i) Easy and effective to apply, and can be done with little training.

(ii) Can be used in situations where other methods cannot, for example, in the water, on rocks, or in a small boat.
(iii) Gives much greater and more controlled ventilation of the lungs than do other methods.
(iv) The operator can assess the degree of inflation of the lungs by observing the movements of the chest.
(v) Less tiring to perform, and does not require strength of the operator.
(vi) Can be used on persons of any age, including newborn babies and infants.

Before commencing resuscitation, it is essential to remove any respiratory obstruction, and to maintain a clear airway. This must be checked first.

Mouth-to-Mouth Method (on land)

First, the operator should lay the subject on his back and take up a convenient position at one side, level with the subject's head. With one hand he should then tilt the head backwards to extend the neck, and squeeze the nose closed between thumb and forefinger. This prevents leakage of air through the nose.

At the same time, with the operator's other hand, the lower jaw should be pushed forward and upwards. This prevents the tongue from falling back and obstructing the air passage in the throat. Occasionally this manoeuvre may prove difficult, in which case a clear airway may often be obtained by putting the forefingers of each hand behind the angles of the jaw and pulling steadily and firmly upwards and forwards. This provides better leverage. Once this is done one hand can be transferred to the point of the jaw, whilst maintaining the position with the other, and then this hand is moved to the nose as described (Fig. 71a).

The operator should open his mouth wide, take a deep breath, seal his lips around the subject's mouth and exhale positively into his lungs. If the airway is clear, air will enter the subject's lungs with little feeling of resistance, and the chest wall will rise (Fig. 71b).

The operator then removes his mouth from the subject and turns his face towards the subject's feet. In this way he can observe the fall of the chest, and, at the same time, can bring his ear over the victim's mouth and nose to listen for exhalation of air. Gurgling or noisy breathing indicates that the airway is not properly clear. (Fig. 71c).

Initially, four quick breaths should be given to inflate the subject's lungs, and thereafter EAR should be continued at a normal breath-

Fig. 71. **APPLYING E.A.R. ON LAND**

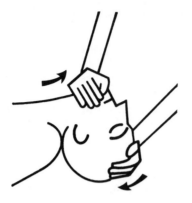

a) Put one hand on the crown of the head, the other underneath the chin, and gently bend the head of the unconscious patient well backwards

b) Apply the Kiss of Life
Take a deep breath and, with your mouth wide open, exhale without force into the slightly opened mouth of the unconscious patient, pinching his nostrils gently

Alternatively you can blow into his nose, making sure his mouth is closed (mouth to nose artificial respiration)

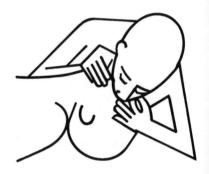

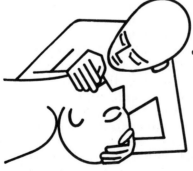

c) Take another deep breath and while doing so observe the patient's breathing (rise and fall of the chest and sound of breathing)

Repeat again and again, at the rate of 14 breaths a minute, until such time as the patient breathes of his own accord.

ing rate of 14 per minute. Do not blow too forcibly, but rather, gently and steadily, otherwise air will be forced into the stomach, which may cause a recovering subject to vomit. Observe for signs of response to EAR.

Mouth-to-Nose Method (on land)

If the patient's mouth is damaged or cannot be opened, or he has no teeth, then the mouth-to-nose method can be used. It is similar to the mouth-to-mouth method except that the operator seals his lips widely over the subject's nose and closes the mouth by placing the thumb on his lips. The lower jaw must be pulled forward, as described in the mouth-to-mouth method.

This method may be more effective in those whose airway is difficult to maintain clear. It is also stated that there is less risk of inflating the stomach with this method.

With small children it is best to seal both mouth and nose with one's lips, and in older children either method may be used. There are no hard and fast rules; the best guide is to use the method which seems to work best at the time.

Manual Methods of Artificial Respiration

The resting position of the chest is between full inspiration and full expiration. You can test this for yourself by holding your breath in inspiration or deep expiration for a few seconds, then releasing it, when, without any effort on your part your chest will return rapidly to a more comfortable position. This is because the chest wall and the lungs act as opposing forces, the former tending to spring outwards and the lungs tending to collapse. At the resting position these two forces equal each other and so no effort is required to maintain the chest in that position. Thus, if external pressure is applied to the chest wall the lungs tend to deflate, and when the pressure is released, the chest will spring back to the resting position, pulling the lungs out with it and drawing air into them. Inspiration may be further increased by movements that expand the chest wall. The Silvester–Brosch method employs these principles.

The Silvester–Brosch Method

This method should only be used if, for any reason, neither of the Expired Air Resuscitation methods (EAR) can be used.

1. Lie the casualty on his back and quickly place suitable padding *under the shoulder blades* (if immediately available). This should be thick enough to raise the shoulders so that the head just rests on the ground with the neck extended to open the airway.

Fig. 72. **THE SILVESTER-BROSCH METHOD OF ARTIFICIAL RESPIRATION**

This method should only be used if, for any reason, the Expired Air method cannot be used.

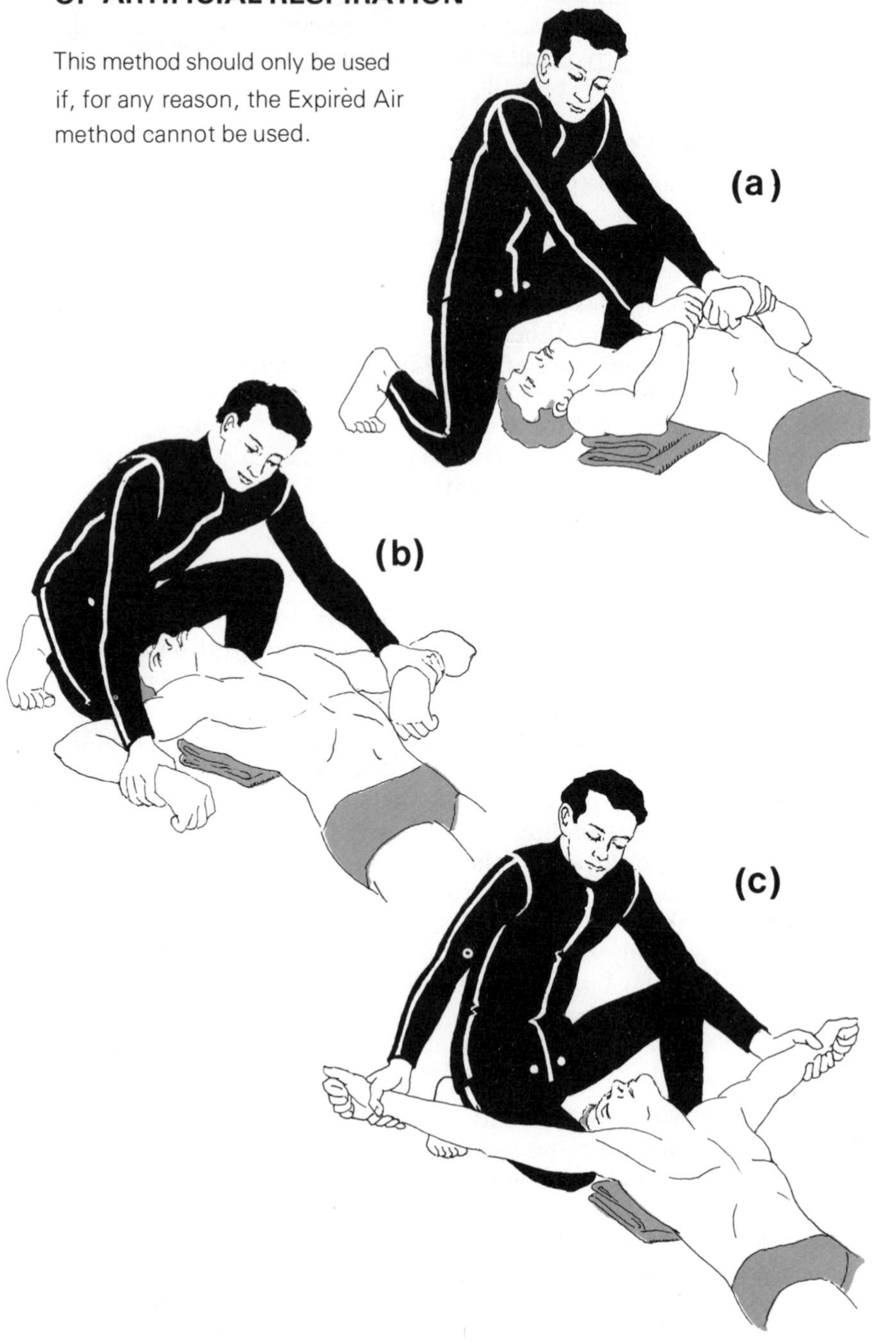

(a)

(b)

(c)

2. Check for any obvious restriction or obstruction and keep the airway clear throughout.
3. Kneel on one knee just clear of the top of the casualty's head and to one side. Place the other foot beside his shoulder.
4. Grasp the casualty's wrists and cross them over the lower end of his rib cage.

5. To compress the chest cage, rock the weight of your trunk forward with straight arms until they are vertical, exerting a smooth, evenly increasing pressure 10–15 kgs for an adult: 5–6 kgs for a slight woman and children: 1–2 kgs for infants.
6. Rock back, releasing the pressure, and move the arms with a smooth semi-circular sweep parallel to the ground, until the casualty's arms are extended above his head.
   Stop when slight resistance is felt and do not force the casualty's arms to the ground in the extended position. Watch for the chest cage to lift as the extended position is reached.
7. Return the arms along the same route and place them in the original position on the casualty's chest, ready for the next compression.
8. The whole cycle should take about 5 seconds: 1 second for compression: 2 seconds for extending the arms: and 2 for their return, i.e. about 12 cycles per minute.

Treatment of Cardiac Arrest
If the heart has stopped, efforts must be made to induce an artificial circulation immediately. First strike the lower part of the breast bone (the sternum) with a single sharp blow using the side of your clenched fist. Occasionally, this measure alone will be sufficient to start the heart beating again and if so, the victim's condition will show signs of rapid improvement, provided the lungs are being properly inflated at the same time. Do not waste more than a few seconds for this initial action. If the heart does not appear to have started again, External Cardiac Massage (ECM) should be performed. (The terms, Closed Chest Cardiac Massage, Closed Chest Cardiac Compression and External Cardiac Compression are alternative titles for the same treatment.) ECM is applied in this way.

First, for effective ECM, the victim must be laid face up on a firm surface. If the person is lying on a soft surface, for example, a bed, effective compression will not be achieved. Locate the sternum (Fig. 73a). Place the heel of the palm (where the hand joins the wrist) on a point about 3 cms from the tip of the sternum and place the heel of the other hand over the first (Fig. 73c). With the arms straight, apply a downward pressure with a sharp movement sufficient to depress the sternum about 4 cms. Release the pressure

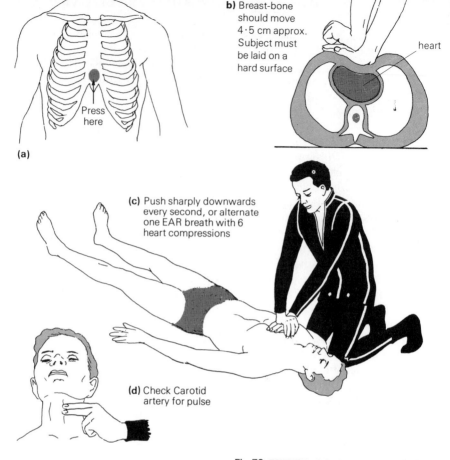

b) Breast-bone should move 4·5 cm approx. Subject must be laid on a hard surface

heart

Press here

(a)

(c) Push sharply downwards every second, or alternate one EAR breath with 6 heart compressions

(d) Check Carotid artery for pulse

Fig. 73. EXTERNAL CARDIAC MASSAGE.

and allow the sternum to spring back. Repeat the cycle for 6 compressions and then seek a pulse at the carotid artery (Fig. 73d). If no pulse is detected, apply a full breath of EAR and then a further 6 compressions of ECM. Repeat this cycle of EAR plus ECM until a pulse is restored, after which EAR *only* should be continued (further ECM, after the detection of even a faint pulse, could cause the heart to stop again). While continuing EAR, monitor the pulse. If the pulse should fail, ECM should then be reapplied.

The heart lies behind the sternum, between it and the spine (Fig. 73b). When the sternum is depressed in the manner explained, the large chambers of the heart are squeezed and blood is thus forced out into the blood vessels. A remarkably effective artificial circulation can be provided if the method is done properly. Care must be taken not to press too hard, too sharply or in any direction other than vertically, for there is a risk that the inexperienced operator might cause ribs to be fractured. On the other hand, the possibility of fractured ribs in the process of saving a life is an acceptable risk.

It will not normally be possible—and neither is it advisable—to practise ECM on a conscious subject because of the possibility of injury. A resuscitation training manikin is the best means of practising and perfecting the technique. However, you can be assured that the sternum will depress freely in the unconscious person.

Combined EAR and ECM

In many cases cardiac arrest and respiratory arrest will both be present, and it is then necessary to combine EAR and ECM. It is advisable to give 6 cardiac compressions to every breath of air; that is, at the rate of 14 respirations and 60 compressions per minute. Preferably, two operators should execute these actions, but it can just be managed with one rescuer. If a third person is present, then he should time the actions, and the three rescuers should rotate positions every ten minutes or so, since the application of combined EAR and ECM is very exacting and tiring for long periods.

Assessment of Resuscitation

People complain that they are not taught how to assess their efforts at resuscitation. This is because assessment is extremely difficult, and can easily be misleading to the layman (and to medical attendants). However, the following points may be helpful:

  (i) Return of spontaneous respiration, a good pulse, and recovery of consciousness are obvious indications of success.

  (ii) Change of colour from blue to a more normal colour (best seen on the lips, especially the inner surface and inside the mouth) indicates an improvement. Conversely, a deepening purplish appearance shows that for some reason one's attempts are not adequate, which may be due to:

    (a) Inadequate ventilation of the lungs due to a blocked airway (usually by the tongue);

    (b) Ineffective cardiac massage;

    (c) Severe irreversible damage due to delay in commencing resuscitation.

(iii) Return of a pulse shows that the efforts are successful. Unfortunately, a pulse at the wrist is very often not easy to detect under these circumstances (especially in a cold subject), and is therefore, not a good guide. If heart-beats can be heard in the chest when the operator's ear is placed against the front of the chest wall, this can be taken as an indication that at least some effective pumping is occurring. Alternatively, movements of the chest wall may indicate that the heart is pumping.

(iv) When the victim is first seen his pupils may be open very wide, and do not contract down when the lids are opened suddenly (fixed dilated pupils). This is a bad sign and, should it persist, indicates severe brain damage caused by lack of oxygen. Pupils which do react to light when the lids are opened, or when a light is shone into the eye, or which are small, are signs that your efforts are probably being effective.

Aftercare

Whilst artificial respiration is taking place, the subject should be covered with a blanket or other convenient covering, but do NOT apply artificial heat to his body. With any form of artificial respiration, as soon as there are signs of breathing, the operator's rhythm should be adjusted to synchronise with the subject. One of the biggest dangers is the risk of the patient vomiting during resuscitation, or after recovery. If vomit goes down into the air passages—which can easily happen in an unconscious person, without your being aware of it—dire consequences may result. Therefore, the back of the subject's mouth should be checked periodically since stomach contents may well get up into the throat. If vomiting occurs, tip the head well over to one side, turning the patient on the side, and clear out fluid and solid matter with the fingers. For the same reason, the subject should NOT—under any circumstances—be given fluids or food for at least two hours after fully regaining consciousness, except under the direction of a medical practitioner.

Even though the subject has gained consciousness and is breathing normally he or she should not be allowed to sit or stand up, but should be kept warm with coverings and laid on the side in the Coma Position (Fig. 74). In this position, the tongue cannot fall back to obstruct the airway, and should the subject vomit, the vomitus will drain from the subject's mouth without hampering breathing. He or she should be watched carefully and the pulse checked at intervals. If the breathing fails again, EAR and, if necessary ECM, must be recommenced immediately.

In all cases medical aid should be summoned at once because, even after normal breathing has returned, serious complications may arise—particularly in cases of drowning. Even if recovery is rapid and appears to be complete, every case should ALWAYS be seen by a doctor at the earliest possible opportunity, preferably at a hospital, where the subject can be admitted for further observation if necessary. The reasons for this are several.

Firstly, one of the greatest dangers after apparently complete initial recovery from salt-water drowning is the development of congestion of the lungs (pulmonary oedema), which, unless rapidly and vigorously treated, may be fatal within a few hours. Secondly, residual damage to the heart, kidneys or brain due to the period of anoxia may necessitate an extended period of hospital care. Thirdly, acidosis occurs rapidly during respiratory and cardiac arrest due to accumulation in the body of carbon dioxide, lactic acid, and other acids produced by metabolism (see chapter 2, *Exhaustion*). If resuscitation is successful these will rapidly correct themselves, but special therapy in hospital may be necessary for those subjects who survive the initial mishap but whose condition remains critical. Fourthly, pneumonia is a common sequel to near-drowning. Finally, additional injuries received at the time of the accident may require treatment.

The decision to discontinue efforts at resuscitation should only be made by a qualified medical practitioner—unless geographical reasons or the fact that you are alone makes this absolutely impossible. This is for two reasons: firstly, it is a difficult decision to make, even for the medically qualified, let alone the layman; secondly, such a decision taken by a layman may present legal problems afterwards—doctors are legally covered (in the U.K.) to make such decisions—you are not.

If you do have to take this responsibility the signs described above may help to guide you.

If there is *any evidence at all* of an improvement in the victim's condition, then resuscitation efforts must continue, if need be, for hours.

Aids to Artificial Respiration

There are several different methods of artificial respiration and ways in which these can be applied. Certain of these employ some form of aid to simplify or assist the work of the operator. Whilst in the hands of a person experienced in their use and fully conversant with their purposes and limitations, aids can be extremely useful. But it is not recommended that they be used by Club members unless they have this special training.

Moreover, it is not wise to place reliance solely upon methods that require the use of an aid for it is probable that on the very occasion it is required for use it may be lost, not available, or involve a delay in applying respiration. For this reason, only those methods of respiration which require no aids, and which can easily be taught and used by Club members, are described here. It is obvious, however, that constant practice is the surest aid to speed and efficiency in starting and maintaining artificial respiration until a successful outcome is achieved.

Resuscitation Training Manikins

The best way of obtaining practice at the lifesaving skills of EAR

Fig. 74.
THE COMA POSITION

An unconscious,
but breathing
subject must at
all times be
placed in this
position, even
during transport
to hospital

and ECM is by the use of a training manikin such as 'Resusci-Anne' or 'AMBU'. These manikins simulate in a most realistic way the problems of maintaining a clear airway, achieving a good seal over the mouth or nose, and require realistic pressure during practice of ECM.

Summary

(i) Get to know the signs of both respiratory and cardiac arrest and how quickly to determine them.

(ii) EAR by the mouth-to-mouth or mouth-to-nose method is by far the most effective and efficient means of getting oxygen into the lungs of a victim requiring resuscitation.

(iii) The Sylvester–Brosch method of 'mechanical' resuscitation should be employed if EAR cannot be used—for instance, in a case of severe facial injury.

(iv) Nothing should delay the application of resuscitation. EVERY SECOND COUNTS.

(v) Seek a pulse at the earliest possible moment. If absent apply ECM in conjunction with EAR. Do not attempt ECM if any detectable pulse can be found. Monitor the pulse continuously and once a natural heart-beat is restored, discontinue ECM whilst continuing EAR.

(vi) Seek help with your efforts at resuscitation and summon a doctor or medical assistance at the earliest moment.

(vii) Continue resuscitation until the subject responds or is handed over to medical specialists.

(viii) Look for improvement in the skin colour of the subject and for a return of his own breathing efforts. If ECM is applied, check regularly for restoration of a natural pulse and for the other signs of response to resuscitation.

(ix) Once the victim recovers, place him in the coma position until he can be transported to hospital.. Hospitalisation is VITAL after any situation in which the subject has been saved by prompt resuscitation.

(x) Practice lifesaving skills regularly. Use training manikins for this purpose if available. (Often, local Red Cross or St John's Ambulance Corps will provide one. The BSAC Coaching Scheme can also provide one.) Gain RLSS lifesaving awards, such as the Sub-Aqua Bronze Medallion.

(xi) EAR can be messy and aesthetically unpleasant, but to save a life is something to be proud of.

Rescue and Lifesaving

The section on *Resuscitation* explained clearly the techniques of Expired Air Resuscitation (EAR) and External Cardiac Massage (ECM) and mentioned briefly that EAR can be applied while in the water—something which cannot be done with other methods of resuscitation.

This section explains the various methods of rendering assistance to those in difficulty in the water, ranging from giving a helping hand to a fatigued swimmer to the application of EAR to an unconscious subject.

Divers should bear in mind that the subject of their lifesaving efforts may not necessarily be a diver. Indeed, it is hoped that a well-trained diver would not get himself into trouble. It is clearly the duty of every Club member to prevent the occurrence of dangerous incidents, and, if they should occur, also to know how to deal with them effectively. In this respect the Club co-operates closely with the Royal Life Saving Society, whose teachings are the result of much research and evaluation. It is obvious that the use of diving equipment and swimming aids such as fins and a face-mask introduces both advantages and disadvantages in a lifesaving situation. Even so, the basic RLSS teachings are essential working foundations for swimmer and diver alike. Lifesaving classes instituted within Branch training programmes stimulate considerable interest among members, and are instructive and necessary for general watermanship.

Before any details of possible rescue techniques are studied, the following points should be fully appreciated:
1. The snorkel diver has very great advantages of mobility, vision and ease of breathing over any 'steam' swimmer.
2. Offsetting the difficulties of wearing a weight-belt and cylinder, the aqualung diver has the advantage over the 'steam' swimmer of fins, face-mask, air supply, suit and lifejacket.
3. In the case of the rescue of a diver by a diver, it is absolutely essential that the weight-belt and aqualung of both parties can be jettisoned immediately and lifejackets inflated, should the need arise. Weight-belts and aqualung harnesses *must* have effective quick-releases which can be operated by a rescuer under the considerable difficulties of an open-water rescue of a struggling or insensible companion.
4. Whether or not an aqualung-equipped diver/rescuer should retain his breathing set depends largely on the circumstances: if his set contains an ample air supply and the distance to safety is not

great, he may well be advised to retain his Aqualung and will thus be assured of a continuous air supply even though he may be forced under water by the struggles of the subject. However, if a long tow is inevitable, or his air supply is low, the rescuer should jettison his Aqualung along with his weight-belt, and continue the rescue with mask, fins and snorkel, as practicable.

(*Note:* Despite any possible buoyancy of the cylinders, the water resistance and encumbrance of an Aqualung *does* create a burden during a tow and the rescuer should only retain his breathing set after due consideration of the advantages and disadvantages within a given situation.)

Making a Rescue

When a diver at the surface, or other person in the water struggles and treads water furiously, it is a sure sign that he is in distress and near panic. No time should be lost in giving him assistance.

To effect a surface rescue, the following requirements must be satisfied:

1. The subject must be approached as quickly as possible.
2. *Secure, Hold and Support:* The subject must not sink or break away, or otherwise be lost.
3. *Air:* If the subject is breathing, it is sufficient to keep his face out of the water. If not, then Expired Air Resuscitation must be administered.
4. *Transport:* The subject must be moved from hazard to safety.
5. *Safety:* The safety and survival of the rescuer is of the utmost importance.

Any real rescue is fraught with danger and unpleasantness for all concerned, but it may be possible to satisfy the above essentials without entering the water, or at least without swimming—which carries the greatest risk to the rescuer. When presented with an emergency, therefore, first check for the following alternatives in the order given:

1. *Reach:* Can you reach the subject without entering the water, perhaps by using a branch or oar?
2. *Throw:* Can you throw him a line or a rescue quoit, or something similar attached to a line, or any buoyant object to cling to?
3. *Wade:* Can you wade out to the subject, keeping your feet on the bottom; perhaps yourself hanging on to a line or another person?
4. *Row/Motor:* Is there a boat of any sort available? If so, can you handle it?

ONLY IF THE ANSWER TO ALL THESE QUESTIONS IS NEGATIVE should you consider SWIMMING out to the subject and towing him to safety, and even then you should do everything in your power to avoid contact with an unco-operative subject—remember, *your* safety is very important, too.

(By the way, can all your Branch Members, their wives or girlfriends REACH without overbalancing, or THROW a line with sufficient accuracy so that it can be grasped by someone in trouble in the water, or ROW a dinghy? If not, they should be taught!)

When swimming out to effect a rescue it is important to remember that time may decide the issue. *No time should be lost, compatible with arriving on the scene in a fit state to perform a rescue.* Thus, it is advisable to practise the fin crawl, which makes use of an overarm stroke in addition to that of finning. Using this stroke allows good visibility during the approach, and to some extent relieves the effort required of the leg muscles which alone will be used during the towing. Even as the rescuer approaches the subject, he should endeavour to calm him by giving reassurance and by taking his mind off his predicament by giving instructions, such as 'Inflate your lifejacket', or 'Swim on your back'. Often, the panicking diver/swimmer may forget to do these obvious self-help things.

Always avoid making contact with the subject from the front. Approach cautiously from the rear and grasp the subject from behind; hold him firmly and keep his head above water. There should be no need to take defensive action or to carry out a release as a clutch by the subject is generally due to a failure in technique by the rescuer. However, it is strongly recommended that all divers study and practise the techniques described in 'Defensive Methods' and 'Releases' in the RLSS Water Safety Handbook.

If the subject is struggling frantically to keep his head above water, he will probably calm down as soon as he realises that he is in capable hands. Only when he has quietened down is he ready for towing to shore or boat; the rescuer must conserve energy at all times.

In his panic the subject may have failed to inflate his lifejacket or dump his weight-belt. If necessary, the rescuer should do this for him, since the provision of buoyancy will give the subject confidence and he will become more passive. If EAR is required, a partially inflated lifejacket worn by the subject simplifies the application of resuscitation.

The application of EAR in the water, on a victim supported by a lifejacket or indeed by the rescuer, is quite feasible, as will be explained shortly. On the other hand, accurate location of a pulse is hampered by the use of wet suits, gloves, etc., and the application of effective ECM in the water is virtually impossible. The success of in-water resuscitation lies in catching the subject quickly, before cardiac arrest can occur. This presupposes vigilance and good 'buddy diving' practice by all.

If help is available which can approach the rescuer and subject (for example, a boat with other rescuers aboard) the rescuer should continue EAR until help arrives. Help should be hailed if necessary and the 'Distress at the Surface' signal given. When help cannot come to the rescuer he should commence towing the subject to the nearest point of safety where continuous resuscitation can be applied, and where additional help is available. The tow will obviously interrupt EAR which should be given at 20 second intervals.

Continuous EAR should be applied (with ECM if necessary and if possible) until either the victim reponds or is handed over to a doctor or ambulance crew.

In the section on *Resuscitation* it was explained that the subject may vomit or regurgitate swallowed water as he responds to resuscitation. If he is being supported in the water when this happens, it is difficult to tip his head forward so that the vomit drains from his mouth. The action of tipping the subject forward may well close the airway, preventing the escape of vomit. Evidence suggests that mouth-to-nose resuscitation is less likely to induce vomiting and this is one of the reasons why it is preferred for 'in water' rescues.

The above represents a brief summary of the actions which should be taken to effect a surface rescue. It is difficult to give advice other than in general terms, since the circumstances of every rescue situation will be different. The maxim proposed by the RLSS:

ASSESS—PLAN—ACT

sums up everything. It will be obvious that these steps should take no more than a few seconds, and that, during the rescue, the whole exercise should be continually reassessed so that the most effective approach, support, resuscitation and tow methods are being applied at all times.

Rescue Techniques for the Diver

Over the years several methods of surface rescue/lifesaving have been devised and recommended; yet few have been discarded. The result is a multiplicity of methods, some of which are, by modern standards, inefficient and complicated. This has led to confusion during training and, what is worse, when dealing with a real rescue situation. In the interests of diver safety, therefore, this edition of the BSAC Diving Manual will teach only one method of rescue incorporating EAR. The skills explained below are an amalgam of RLSS techniques and those developed by BSAC specialists, which take advantage of diving equipment as aids to the rescuer and the rescued. Simplicity and uniformity are the key words for the rescue techniques now advocated by the BSAC.

Recovering the Subject

The distressed diver is likely to be under water and the first action of the rescuer is to bring him to the surface. If the victim is in shallow water, this presents little difficulty, but an ascent from depth carrying an unconscious diver is a difficult procedure. The decreased buoyancy of the protective clothing renders both divers heavy and if, as in this case, only one diver is finning, a lot of leg power is needed to overcome the initial inertia unless additional buoyancy is obtained. The difficulty of formulating a set of rules for rescue ascent procedure is mainly caused by the diversity of diving equipment. The divers may be wearing adjustable buoyancy lifejackets, surface lifejackets or no jackets at all. Thus, the rules have to take into account these variations and tend to look unwieldy.

1. Assess the situation quickly (is the victim trapped by something?: be wary if he is struggling and approach from the rear).
2. Take hold of victim (from behind if he is struggling).
3. (a) If either diver is wearing an adjustable buoyancy lifejacket this should be inflated (only one, preferably the victim's).
   (b) If surface lifejackets, or no lifejackets, are worn, disregard these and slip victim's weight-belt. If this is difficult or does not supply enough buoyancy, slip own weight-belt (remember, if you slip your weight-belt and not his he will be heavy and you will be light. If you lose your grip on him he will sink and you will be unable to get back down). If buoyancy is still not adequate and surface lifejacket(s) are worn, inflate them (victim's first).
4. The victim's mouthpiece and mask should, if possible, be kept in position.
5. If the victim is not exhaling, press his diaphragm to ensure that he does.
6. The rescuer should not try to over-exert himself. This is important.
7. Nearing the surface, look out for surface obstructions.
8. In poor visibility hold one hand above head.
9. On reaching the surface, the rescuer should provide support to the subject by using one of the methods soon to be explained.

   A rescue from depth is a very arduous thing, and the possibilities of rescuer exhaustion are high. The following section explains 'Deep Rescue' procedures.

SUPPORT METHODS

Almost all divers wear some form of lifejacket or buoyancy aid, and this should be looked upon as an integral part of rescue equipment. The diver in distress may well have inflated his lifejacket, is thus supported and should soon relax. On the other hand, he may have failed to inflate it in his confused mental state; or the inflation mechanism may have failed. Either way, it is capable of supporting the subject if it were inflated, and this should be done at the earliest opportunity. There is no point in the rescuer supporting a victim, when by inflating the subject's lifejacket, by mouth if necessary, the victim can be rendered buoyant. The panicking conscious diver may be capable of obeying the rescuer's command 'Swim on your back and inflate your lifejacket'—('while I give you support'). If he is not, he is very close to unconsciousness. His struggles will be weak, and there is little danger of the rescuer being grasped while inflating the subject's lifejacket. *The lifejacket should not be fully inflated,* but filled about half to three-quarters full. If fully inflated, some air/gas should be vented before effective EAR can be applied. A half-full lifejacket will give about 8–10 kg of positive buoyancy—more than enough to support the subject.

It is recommended that, if the lifejacket can be quickly inflated to provide adequate buoyancy, the subject's weight-belt may be retained if not already jettisoned. The presence of the weight-belt will float the subject in a better position for resuscitation than would be the case if the belt were released. If the lifejacket cannot be inflated through its own system, dump the weight-belt before mouth-inflating the subject's lifejacket.

The second action is to clear the subject's natural airways by removing his face-mask and mouthpiece. This may already have been done, since in almost every case, the subject will tear off his mask and spit out his mouthpiece when in difficulty.

For the conscious subject, the actions of providing support and clearing the natural breathing airways may be sufficient to induce him to relax and become a co-operative subject. If the subject continues to struggle frantically, you may assume that he will not sink, and the rescuer is advised to keep clear until the victim tires or becomes co-operative. Reassure and give instructions to the subject while keeping out of his reach.

When providing support to a difficult subject who does not have a lifejacket, he should be grasped and held face-clear of the water by the RLSS Shoulder Restraint method which allows the rescuer to pinion the subject's arms so that he cannot struggle. Once his struggles have ceased, the rescuer can change his hold to that for the Extended Tow. The rescuer is advised to retain his aqualung mouthpiece and to partially inflate his lifejacket prior to applying this restraint. Where the subject has no buoyancy aid which can be inflated, the rescuer will have to rely on his lifejacket, or his own action of treading water to support himself and his subject.

So far we have dealt with conscious, breathing subjects, whose state of panic has been relieved by providing buoyancy or support. Let us now see what should be done for the victim whose struggles have ceased, and who is unconscious.

First and foremost, clear the mask and mouthpiece from the subject's face if present; then pull back on the chin from behind the subject to achieve the extended neck position and clear airway. If breathing efforts are present, this is frequently sufficient to cause resumption of normal breathing. The subject's lifejacket should be inflated if he has one—by mouth, by the rescuer, if necessary. Avoid over-inflation of the lifejacket which may prevent full neck extension. The subject should then be towed to safety by the Extended Arm Tow, which will ensure a clear airway during the tow. If the subject is not breathing resuscitation will be necessary.

RESUSCITATION IN THE WATER

If the action of extending the neck of the subject does not result almost immediately in spontaneous breathing, EAR should be applied without delay. Four quick breaths should be 'got in' before the lifejacket is inflated. (Having inflated the subject's lungs, it will take the same amount of time to put say, six breaths into the lifejacket, if this is required, and this added buoyancy will make things so much easier. Lifejacket inflation should be the second priority.)

The method of resuscitation advocated is Mouth-to-Nose in the manner described below.

Notes:
(a) The technique is explained for a right-handed person, approaching from the left side of the subject (the system is directly reversible) and not employing a lifejacket.
(b) The method works well with 'steam' swimmer rescuers, or those using diving apparatus; and may be used on any subject, including those supported by a *partially inflated* lifejacket. A fully inflated lifejacket may prevent full neck extension and impedes the 'arm lever' action of neck extension.
(c) For logical progression, item 1, which follows, refers to the approach and hold necessary when rescuing someone who does not have a lifejacket for support.
(d) The greatest difficulty would seem to centre around the rescuer's inability to rise sufficiently out of the water to make the necessary seal without submerging the unsupported subject. So long as the extended neck position is maintained, it is quite permissible to rock the entire subject's face and body towards the rescuer (after all, the head is both tilted back and turned to one side when an unconscious subject is placed in the Coma Position tion on land, and this causes no obstruction). Turning the body

as indicated reduces the amount by which the rescuer has to rise from the water.

1. The subject should be approached from behind and to his left side; the rescuer brings his left hand round to the subject's front and places it firmly under the subject's armpit, the thumb vertical on the front of the subject's left shoulder, the fingers gripping around the upper rear part of the subject's left arm. He then clamps the subject's elbow between his own arm and left side and leans slightly backwards, holding the subject as high in the water as he can (Fig. 75a). At this point, we are in the same situation as would be the subject supported by a partially inflated lifejacket, and the following actions apply equally to both types of subject.

2. Meanwhile, the rescuer's right palm is passed over the subject's head to the chin: the head is tipped backwards and snorkel and mask are removed by sweeping this hand up across the subject's face (Fig. 75b). The right hand is then used to grip the nape of the subject's neck (Fig. 75c), the back of the hand outwards and the right thumb on the left-hand side of the neck. Alternatively, support may be given by placing the right hand under the subject's right shoulder. With this support the subject is then held up in the water, the rescuer's left arm repositioned, with his left hand holding the subject's chin in a 'pistol grip', the thumb closing the lips.

3. The rescuer's left forearm should bear on the subject's left shoulder (Fig. 75d); this position provides the rescuer with a point of leverage against which he can now force the subject's chin backwards to straighten the throat and raise the body. The right hand, still supporting the subject, is pushed upwards, providing the reaction to the backward and downward motion of the left hand. In this position the subject is supported mainly by the water and little lift is required by the rescuer who only has to tread water gently.

4. The rescuer now spits out his mouthpiece, leaving his mask in position (though it may be removed if prefered); pulls back against the subject's chin and, with his forearm, levers outwards and slightly downwards on the subject's left shoulder, pushing upwards and rocking the subject towards him with his right hand, while maintaining the angle of approach to the subject's head (along a line from the subject's nose through the left ear). By applying this rocking action, he will find that the subject's right shoulder will rise in the water and the subject's nose will be presented to him (Fig. 75e).

5. With a stronger finning action the rescuer rises slightly, seals his mouth around the subject's nose and breathes into it. As soon as this is done he drops back into the water and allows the subject's

Fig. 71. RESUSCITATION IN THE WATER

The Support and Resuscitation method described in the text and illustrated here works well for all combinations of subject/rescuer, whether they are divers, snorkellers or swimmers. It is equally successful when the subject is supported by a partially inflated lifejacket. It can be reversed for the left-handed person, or if the rescuer finds himself approaching from the other side. The entire procedure can be carried out with the rescuers mask in place, but he may find it easier to remove it as in the last illustration.

(a)

The rescuer approaches from behind, and secures a hold, using his left hand to grip the subject's upper left arm at the arm-pit. The subject's left elbow is clamped between the rescuers left arm and body. At this stage, the subject's body is at right-angles to that of the rescuer. If the rescuer leans back, he will raise the subject slightly in the water.

(b)

The rescuer then uses his right hand to push the subject's chin up, thereby extending the airway. The hand continues upwards, removing the mouthpiece and facemask, and sweeps over the head to take a grip hold on the nape of the subject's neck.

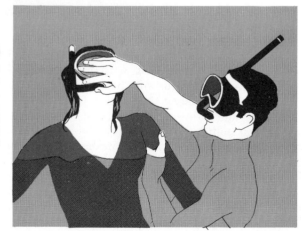

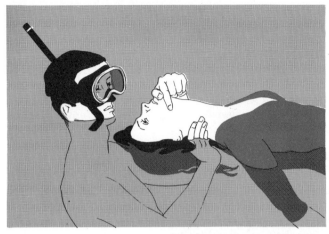

(c)

The rescuer briefly releases the hold with his left-hand, turns the subject round to the left so that he can take a "pistol-grip" hold on the subject's chin with the left hand. To do this, the rescuer reaches over the subject's left shoulder. The rescuer will now be behind and to the left of the subject.

(d)

The rescuer then levers the subject's head back, using his own left arm as a lever bearing on the subject's left shoulder. This closes the mouth; extends the airway, and lifts the subject's body high in the water. It also brings the subject's nose closer to the rescuer's mouth for resuscitation. The rescuer may then transfer his right hand to provide upward support beneath the subject's right shoulder, rather than continuing to grip the neck.

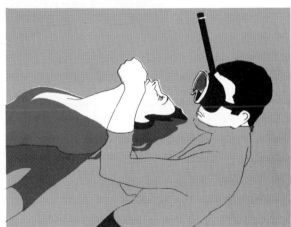

(e)

The rescuer rolls the subject over towards him by levering outward with his left hand, and pushing upwards with his right hand under the subject's shoulder. The subject's nose will now be very close to the rescuer's mouth. The rescuer treads water to lift himself slightly, seals his mouth over the subject's nose, and gives E.A.R. After doing so, he relaxes, sinks back into the water, "unwinding" the subject as he does so. The cycle is repeated for each breath of E.A.R. given to the subject.

right shoulder to fall again. The rescuer takes two quick breaths for himself and then repeats the cycle, continuing for four full breaths, after which he changes the towing position. Changing to a chin tow merely involves straightening the arm which is used to extend the neck. If the aqualung worn by the subject prevents full neck extension, it should be removed and jettisoned. Likewise, if the lifejacket is over-full, it too will prevent full neck extension. Vent off some air and try again.

At the risk of repeating what has been said before, the rescuer should initially give not less than four quick breaths into the subject, while assessing as best he can whether other help is on the way. If it is, he should apply continuous resuscitation at the normal breathing rate of 10–15 respirations per minute. If no other help is available, the rescuer should begin to tow the subject towards safety, interrupting the tow every 20 seconds or so to apply four good breaths of EAR.

TOW METHODS

The ideal tow method will allow:
1. Few changes of grip when interrupting the tow to apply resuscitation.
2. Unrestricted swimming/finning.
3. Firm control of the subject, and application of restraints.

The *Extended Tow* method approaches the ideal, and is the one which is recommended. It can be employed, in one of its variations, to tow both conscious and unconscious subjects, whether or not supported by a lifejacket. Fig. 76a shows the basic extended tow method.

The *Extended Chin Tow* requires a hand cupping the chin—as does the recommended method of EAR in the water, given above. Thus, only one hand has to move when changing from resuscitation to tow, and vice-versa. The relative positions of rescuer and subject gives the rescuer room to fin effectively. The rescuer may fin either on his back or on his side. Control is adequate for a passive subject. Since the extended tow requires only one hand, the other is available to apply restraints if necessary. Normally a rescuer would not be towing a subject who is not passive.

The extended chin tow should be used in a case where the subject is not breathing normally because:
(a) It maintains an extended neck and clear airway.
(b) It allows a speedy return to the resuscitation position.

An extended tow, holding the hair, or clothing if worn, would be suitable for the rescue of a swimmer, boating casualty, or wet-suited swimmer.

The *Closed-up Tow*

When using the Extended Tow in rough water conditions, it has been found that waves will sometimes wash over the victim's face. To avoid this, the subject may be towed in a 'Closed-up' position—as shown in Fig. 76b. While the rescuer's finning action may be somewhat restricted in this position, it is more comfortable for the subject.

A *Non-Contact Tow* (Fig. 77) employing a towing aid, may be used on a conscious and co-operative subject who is unable to propel himself. It is particularly suitable when towing someone supported by a lifejacket in rough water.

Other non-contact tows can be made by employing a buoyant aid such as a 'rescue quoit' or torpedo buoy. Anything buoyant which is handy can be used, the idea being to give the subject something to grasp—other than the rescuer! The rescuer approaches the subject and offers him one end of the towing aid, telling him to take hold of it. The subject may retain his mask and snorkel if he wishes, although he may subsequently find that it is more comfortable to be towed lying on his back and he will then wish to remove at least his snorkel. (As he will not wish to lose his equipment, he may well hold on to it with one hand, thus reducing the danger to the rescuer even more.) Should the subject 'climb' along the towing aid towards the rescuer, the rescuer should let go—the subject will soon get the message.

The rescuer usually removes his mask and snorkel to his forehead if swimming on his back. but may retain them in place if he intends to swim on his side. The aqualung diver rescuer should consider dumping his own set if it is hampering the rescue of an unconscious diver, who is obviously critically ill.

Note that the rescuer must keep watching the subject all the time, so he may only tow by finning on his side or back.

NOTE

In any rescue, the rescuer should be prepared to modify his actions to suit the circumstances. The rescue and tow methods which have been described should form the basis of the rescuer's technique—to which modifications can be made as necessary.

THE RLSS SUB-AQUA BRONZE MEDALLION

This chapter has explained that lifesaving is an arduous and exacting task, demanding a high degree of skill and above all, practice. While Club members may be able to meet the necessary standard of lifesaving ability to pass appropriate BSAC Tests, the skills can quickly be forgotten through lack of practice.

Some years ago, the Royal Life Saving Society introduced the Sub-Aqua Bronze Medallion so that divers could gain recognition

RESCUES

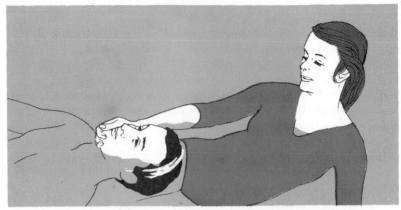

Fig. 76 **(a)** AN EXTENDED-ARM TOW OF A SWIMMER

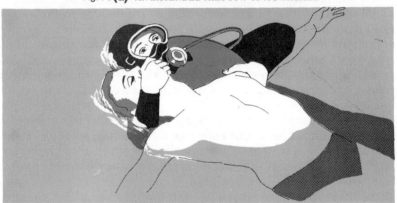

(b) A CLOSE-UP ARM TOW

Fig. 77 TOWING BY AN ABLJ STRAP OR HARNESS (NON-CONTACT TOW)

for the lifesaving skills. All divers are to be encouraged to gain the award by undergoing a course of training followed by an examination at some time after completing aqualung training (Tests E and F). Ideally, the award should be retaken at intervals so that skills are not forgotten and new techniques learned.

Each student should obtain a copy of the current RLSS Water Safety Handbook which not only gives full details of this and other awards, but also serves as a reference book for use during the training course. This publication may be obtained from RLSS Area Organisers or directly from the RLSS HQ at 14 Devonshire Street, London W1N 2AT.

SUMMARY:

1. This section covers lifesaving and surface rescue of divers. It outlines the essentials of transport, resuscitation, security and safety.

2. It is pointed out that the use of diving equipment when making a rescue requires new techniques. Also, bear in mind that lifesaving is physically hard work, and often has to be carried out by the unfit. It is also a highly emotional undertaking. Therefore, however efficient any method of lifesaving may be, it will be useless if the rescuer cannot remember it in times of stress; simplicity of technique must be the keynote. For this reason the SIMPLEST AND MOST EFFECTIVE METHOD of support, resuscitation and tow by a diver is presented.

3. Expired Air Resuscitation in the water is a life-saver and therefore, must be taught. It is not easy to carry out, but the essentials of support, tilt and seal are emphasised here.

4. With regard to buoyancy and struggling: no diver should be negatively buoyant on the surface. Indeed, by jettisoning weightbelts, etc., or inflating lifejackets, the rescuer can expect to be dealing with neutrally or positively buoyant subjects. In this situation, the subject who struggles need not be restrained at the expense of the rescuer's energy (although restraints are taught), but may be left alone until he stops struggling.

5. Rescues by non-divers, or those not wearing fins, etc., are taught by the Royal Life Saving Society, and divers are strongly recommended to take their Awards—particularly the Sub-Aqua Bronze Medallion.

Deep Rescue

In the past a number of accidents have occurred in which attempts by a rescuer to lift a victim from deep water have failed. These failures were generally due to the rescuer's lack of appreciation of the sheer effort required to lift a fully kitted diver from depth. Even after achieving neutral buoyancy at the surface, loss of buoyancy due to suit compression could render a diver as much as 10 kg overweight at 30 m. If both victim and rescuer happened to be this much overweight at depth it is easy to understand why rescue attempts failed.

The need for buoyancy compensation and the problems of Deep Diving are discussed elsewhere. Diving in accordance with the advice given in those sections will minimize both the chances of having to carry out a deep rescue and also improve the prospects of success when such a rescue is necessary. Deep Rescue is an exacting and strenuous activity—even for the most practised and active diver. Success requires forethought and practice and to this end the BSAC provides divers with the opportunity to learn the most suitable techniques for deep-water rescue through the Deep Rescue Exercise. During this exercise divers are given both theoretical and practical instruction in method of approaching the distressed subject; effecting a secure hold which permits control during the ascent; and surface lifesaving skills. The Deep Rescue Exercise is open to BSAC Third-Class divers who have logged not less than 20 dives and who have previously dived to 30 m, on more than one occasion. They should also hold the ABLJ Endorsement. Further particulars of Deep Rescue Exercise may be found in the BSAC Diving Officers Handbook. The exercise culminates with the simulated deep rescue by each student, who has to lift a victim from 30 m to 15 m, and after making a normal ascent to the surface, give support and resuscitation during the tow and on reaching land. The main purpose of the exercise is not necessarily to achieve a 'Pass' standard. While this is desirable the object of the Deep Rescue Exercise is to acquaint divers with the difficulties of carrying out such a rescue in extreme conditions. Those divers who find they are physically unable to lift a victim in full diving kit to 15 m at least appreciate that, in the real event, weightbelts must be jettisoned and possibly lifejackets inflated to bring both the subject and his rescuer to the surface.

Deep Rescue

It should be understood that the subject who gets into difficulties under water will normally make every effort to regain the surface (see chapter 2 *Apprehension and Panic*, and chapter 6 *Ascent Procedures*). Consequently the majority of deep rescue recoveries will be of those who have lapsed into unconsciousness under water —either because they are trapped or because an alternative ascent has failed. Generally (though by no means always) the subject will be unconscious and passive and it is his dead-weight which is the problem. The points made under *'Recovering the Subject'* in the previous section apply, and the subject has to be held and lifted in such a way that the following actions are achieved.

1. A good push off from the bottom.
2. Unobstructed finning by the rescuer.
3. Neck extension is maintained and the subject's mask and mouth-piece held in place if not already jettisoned.
4. Operation of the subject's weightbelt release and lifejacket by the rescuer.
5. The rescuer is not exposed to the struggles and clutches of the subject in the event of his regaining consciousness under water, and the rescuer should be able to apply restraints if necessary.
6. A quick change to the recommended support and resuscitation position at the surface.

It is not possible to recommend a single 'Hold and Lift' method which permits all these parameters to be met. However, an approach from the side or behind appears to be the most popular in-so-far as the subject can be held above the rescuer, allowing him to push off from the bottom and to fin powerfully without the subject's legs getting in the way. The rescuer can reach round the subject to get to the weightbelt and ABLJ, and is out of the way if the victim should struggle. A hold can be devised which keeps the subject's neck extended and retains the mask and mouthpiece. Another method is to approach from in front, again with the subject held above the rescuer, and this method permits continuous observation of the subject during ascent. However, the rescuer is more vulnerable if the victim should struggle and grasp at his rescuer. The BSAC is unwilling to recommend a single deep rescue hold and lift method, as it has done with surface support and resuscitation, because variables such as the diving equipment worn by the subject play a greater part in the effectiveness of the hold and lift method than they do in the surface lifesaving aspect of a rescue. Once again, the desirability of comparing and experiencing the various hold and lift methods currently used during a Deep Rescue Exercise is strongly recommended.

In the event of an actual emergency at depth the first essential is to make the subject positively buoyant by jettisoning his weightbelt and if this does not achieve the desired result, by inflating his ABLJ. The rescuer should stay with the subject at all times during the ascent and should remember that if he were to jettison his own weightbelt or inflate his own lifejacket before making the subject buoyant, then the rescuer might drift away from the subject and be unable to descend again to him. Only if insufficient buoyancy is gained by dumping the subject's weightbelt and inflating the sub-ject's lifejacket should the rescuer take steps to gain more buoyancy himself. In the event of a buoyant ascent (see chapter 6 *Ascent Procedures*) the rescuer should control the rate of ascent by venting lifejackets. He should also keep the subject's neck extended to maintain a clear airway and should exhale steadily himself.

Fig. 78 illustrates and summarizes the steps which should be taken when carrying out a rescue ascent. In the latter stages of any rescue ascent where weight-belts have been jettisoned or lifejackets inflated, buoyancy will increase rapidly during the last 10 m to the surface and the rescuer should slow things up at this stage if he can. During any rescue ascent, the rescuer should try not to over exert himself to the point where he will be too exhausted to apply further aid to the subject on the surface. A rescuer should not put his own life in jeopardy.

Fig. 78. RESCUE ASCENT PROCEDURE

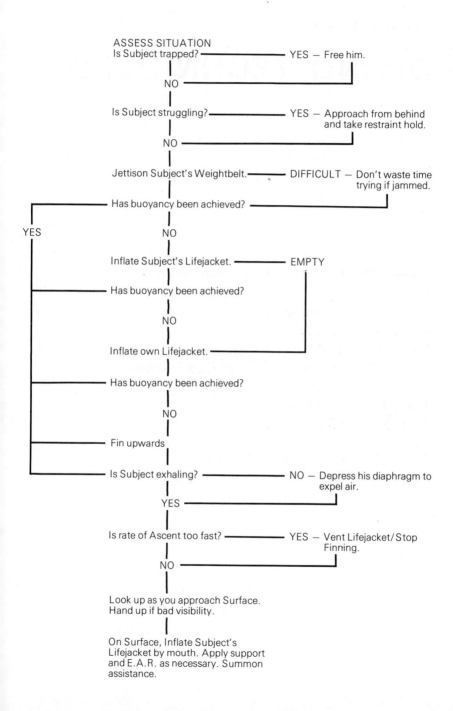

ASSESS SITUATION
Is Subject trapped? ——————————— YES — Free him.

NO

Is Subject struggling? ——————————— YES — Approach from behind
and take restraint hold.

NO

Jettison Subject's Weightbelt. ——————— DIFFICULT — Don't waste time
trying if jammed.

Has buoyancy been achieved? ————————————————

YES   NO

Inflate Subject's Lifejacket. ——————— EMPTY

Has buoyancy been achieved?

NO

Inflate own Lifejacket. ———————

Has buoyancy been achieved?

NO

Fin upwards

Is Subject exhaling? ——————————— NO — Depress his diaphragm to
expel air.

YES

Is rate of Ascent too fast? ——————— YES — Vent Lifejacket/Stop
Finning.

NO

Look up as you approach Surface.
Hand up if bad visibility.

On Surface, Inflate Subject's
Lifejacket by mouth. Apply support
and E.A.R. as necessary. Summon
assistance.

CHAPTER SIX
DIVING TECHNIQUES

Signals and Communications

The normal methods of communication between human beings on land are by voice, touch, gesture and writing, and whilst they also apply under water there are problems to be faced.

Vocal communication, for example, can be achieved, but the necessary equipment is expensive and at its best is still not ideal. A slate and pencil can be used for writing under water, but this has limited applications. Communication by touch is also not always practical.

The simple questions requiring simple answers, the urgent statements and the urgent orders are, therefore, usually dealt with by the remaining method—hand signals—and these have proved to be adequate in almost every situation. It must not be assumed that under-water visibility will be good enough to enable hand signals to be used all the time, but it is imperative for all divers to understand the basic signals, for this method of communication is standard and the most common.

This and other practical methods of signalling are dealt with here, and it should be noted that they are all sub-divided into the following categories:

VISUAL:
Under water   Diver to diver.
Surface   Diver on surface or boat, to boat or shore.

SOUND:
Under water   Diver to diver.
Surface   Surface to diver.

ROPE:
Under water   Diver to diver, diver to surface.
Surface   Surface to diver.

Visual Signals Under Water
The signals used by the BSAC are those adopted by the CMAS (World Under-water Federation) and consequently are widely used throughout the world. These signals are shown on the following pages with full meanings alongside. However, before carrying out a dive, divers should never assume that everyone will use the same set of signals, no matter what the rules of the Club may be. Always check in advance which signals are being used, and thus avoid confusion under water.

When giving signals under water, whether as a question, a request or an acknowledgement, the diver should remember the following points. The signals have been so devised that the diver does not need to wave his arms about like a bookmaker's tic-tac man at a racecourse, wasting energy and using up air. In other words, they should be given slowly, accurately and consciously exaggerated. Equally, the signals should each be acknowledged in the same manner, with, of course, the appropriate answer or reaction. If the signal is not understood the first time, the sequence is simple. The signaller repeats his signal until the other diver, or divers, acknowledge the signal with a correct reply, if not he takes appropriate action. It is also up to the diver at whom the signal is directed NOT to acknowledge the signal until he understands it. All these signals are officially approved by the BSAC. After studying them and what they mean, it is easy to understand how information can be exchanged under water between divers.

Visual Signals at the Surface

DIVER ON SURFACE/TO BOAT OR SHORE:

An analysis of diving accident reports indicates that the diver is most vulnerable at the surface and particularly so when he has returned to the surface after a dive. So that those responsible for his safety on the shore or in the boat from which he is diving are aware that he is OK or otherwise, other visual signals are employed and these must be clear to all concerned at fairly long range. Thus, a diver's 'OK, all is well' signal is unsuitable for use over long distances and something more obvious has to be employed. The following illustrations show the signals which are used to indicate 'OK, at the surface' and 'Distress at surface/Come and get me'. Divers swimming out on the surface to a dive site are expected to give the 'OK at the surface' signal just prior to their descent, to indicate to their surface or boat cover that all is well and that they are proceeding with the planned dive.

On their return to the surface after the dive they would immediately check amongst themselves, using the 'OK all is well' signal and if so, would then signal using the 'OK at the surface' signal to their cover, which is made simply by holding an arm straight above the head with the fingers in the OK position. This not only advises the shore or boat party that the divers are well but also lets them know the exact position of the group. As soon as the signal is received by the supporting party, it should be acknowledged by replying with the same signal.

If all is not well with the diving party when they return to the surface, they should give the 'Distress at surface' signal at the first possible moment. This is not acknowledged with another signal but is acted upon by rendering whatever assistance is needed quickly.

Other Visual Signals

The diver to diver and diver to surface signals which have just been given cover most of the normal diving eventualities which are likely to occur. However, it will probably be obvious to the reader that many other similar hand signals could be created and other books on diving may give examples of these. Divers who dive regularly together may wish to add to this normal essential range of signals by creating hand signals of their own to meet their particular interests or situations. As a simple example, numbers 1–10 can clearly be indicated by hand signals; the deaf and dumb language, once learned, would enable divers to communicate freely under water. While the scope and range of hand signals available to divers is limited only by their imagination and ingenuity, it should be repeated once more that it is essential for all people in a diving group to know all the signals which are likely to be used. Therefore, non-standard signals used by a pair of divers who habitually dive together should not be used when they are diving in company of others. If all divers involved know the meaning of the signals, then any hand signals can be used.

Sound Signals

DIVER TO DIVER:

When two divers are several metres apart in good visibility water, one may want to contact his partner without leaving the precise spot he is at. The easiest method is to hit one's tank with some hard, preferably metallic, object—a rock or stone found on the bottom, the handle of a knife, a torch if carried. Whatever is used the 'clang' carries some distance. For those divers who do not want to remove much paint from their cylinders, the alternative is to bang two stones together, or a stone against a rock. This, however, is not heard over such great distances. The diver may make a succession of short 'toots' into his mouthpiece, for this can be heard quite a long way under water. Sound signals are not effective with the beginner as he is inclined to confuse them with many other sounds in the so-called 'silent world'.

While the commercial diver enjoys the use of electronic communication devices, some of which work directly 'through water' without being relayed from the surface, the cost and complexity of these systems does not bring them within the reach of the average sports diver. Perhaps the future will see the development of underwater communication systems which will be suitable for, and within the financial reach of, sports divers.

Fig. 79 **VISUAL SIGNALS**

Stop stay where you are
Often followed by another signal explaining why – unless the reason is obvious.

OK all is well
This can be either a question from one diver to another, or an affirmative reply to this question. Keep the fingers straight.

Go up I am going up
An instruction to ascent. Upward hand movement adds emphasis.

Go down I am going down
An instruction to descend, normally made only at the start of a dive.

I am on reserve
Indicates that air supply is low and the dive should be terminated. Give 'ascend' signal in response.

You or me
Diver points to himself or another diver, indicating the person referred to in the signal which follows.

I cannot pull my reserve
Use in event of reserve valve failure. Buddy should check action of reserve and be ready to share if necessary.

Something wrong
Not an emergency, but an indication that all is not well. Usually followed by an indication of the source of trouble.

Distress
A signal which elicits immediate action to rescue the diver giving it.

DIVER TO DIVER

I have no more air
This signal, which is made by moving the arm with outstretched hand in and out from the throat, is now used internationally. On seeing this signal, close with diver making it and share from your aqualung.

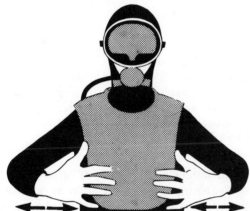

I am out of breath
Victim indicates his laboured breathing by to-and-fro movement of his hands. Stop, relax, and allow the victim to recover normal breathing.

ON THE SURFACE

Distress at surface – come and get me
Demands immediate action to assist the distressed diver. The more frantic the waving the greater the distress.

OK at surface
On surfacing, and if all is well, this signal must be given and maintained until it is acknowledged by the surface party.

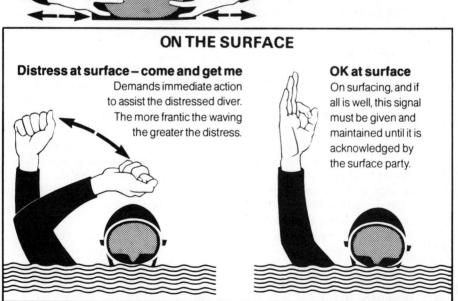

SURFACE TO DIVER:
No signals are laid down for this as many Clubs have their own system. If the diving boat has a metal ladder, this can be 'clanged' an agreed number of times. Alternatively, the boatman can reach into the water to 'clang' two metal bars together. Such sounds travel far. Also the motor can be started up and revved to a pre-arranged plan, and yet another system is to use waterproof thunder flashes which have an audible range of about 300 m. These are like large 'banger' fireworks which have their own built-in friction match lighter. Once ignited, there is a five-second delay during which the thunder flash should be dropped into the water. It is necessary to weight the thunder flash with a strip of lead or a large nail to ensure that it sinks beneath the surface. If it explodes on the surface, much of the sound will not penetrate the water. There is little risk of injuring a diver with one of these thunder flashes should it explode close to him. He would suffer injury only if he were physically in contact with the thunder flash at the moment of its explosion.

Though not a sound signal, the use by the diving group of a surface marker buoy (see *Safety Equipment*) is the simplest and most obvious means whereby the surface party may contact them. All the boatman has to do is to either haul in or give an agreed code of rope signals (see below) on the SMB line.

SURFACE TO SURFACE:
Most communication between divers on the surface or in boats is done by shouting, but other aids are available, such as whistles, loud-hailers, or signalling lamp. Again, everyone involved should know what the various signals mean.

LAMP SIGNALS:
When diving in dark water or at night, the code of diver to diver signals cannot be seen by the divers. The usual practice is for the diver to use his torch to illuminate his hand as he makes the signal. Care should be taken not to shine his torch into his partner's eyes. On the surface, a steady beam pointed in the direction of the boat or surface cover indicates 'OK at the surface' while a rapid swinging of the torch beam in a horizontal arc indicates 'Distress at surface'. A controlled horizontal movement of the torch by the diver after receiving his acknowledging 'OK at the surface' signal from the boat cover, indicates that the diver wishes to be picked up. (See also the section on *Night Diving*.)

When torches are carried and when diving in good visibility, a steady beam from the torch of diver A pointed towards another diver B indicates that A wishes B to close with him to communicate or for some other reason. Once again, any code of signals may be employed so long as it is known to all divers.

The morse code group $\cdots \,--- \,\cdots$ (SOS) is an internationally accepted method of indicating distress at sea and may be given by whistle or by torch. This signal could be employed by a diver or by a small boat in difficulties at night. Further information on methods of indicating distress at sea is given in the Appendix of this Diving Manual.

Rope Signals

The section of this chapter dealing with *Low Visibility and Roped Diving* explains that there are a number of situations when the diver should be in contact with his partner or with the surface by means of a rope along which signals can be transmitted by an agreed series of pulls. The rope may either be in the form of a buddy-line (see chapter 3, *Safety Equipment*) or may be a roped diver's life-line (see *Low Visibility and Roped Diving*). Signals may also be transmitted from the surface to a group of divers who have a surface marker buoy (see *Diving Accessories*).

The sports diver does not need a comprehensive range of life-line signals as does the commercial diver, and with this in mind the following five signals are those which should be known and understood by all sports divers. The interpretation of rope signals has to be made with care and thought on the part of both the sender and receiver of the signals. Varied shades of meaning may apply under different diving situations. For this reason, this short basic table has the simplest interpretations indicated; for amplified meanings reference should be made to the complete life-line signal code which is reproduced later on in this section and from which these five signals are taken.

BSAC Roped Diver Signals

Signal	Surface	Diver
ONE PULL	Are you OK?	I am OK.
TWO PULLS	Stay put.	I am stationary.
THREE PULLS*	Go on down.	Going down.
FOUR PULLS*	Come up.	Coming up.
CONTINUOUS PULLS	EMERGENCY. Bringing you to the surface.	EMERGENCY. Bring me to the surface.

If you wish to stop the diver before he reaches the surface, or closes with you if a buddy-line is used, give the TWO PULLS signal.

*When used in conjunction with a buddy-line, there is a slight variation in meaning:

THREE PULLS	MOVE AWAY FROM ME (to limit of line).
FOUR PULLS	COME TO ME.

The Attendant should always allow the diver sufficient time to make a reply or acknowledgement, because a diver at work might not be able to acknowledge a signal immediately. Therefore, after a slight pause, the signal should be repeated. If after a reasonable time has elapsed, the signal remains UNACKNOWLEDGED (the time allowed could be pre-determined) the Dive Marshal should be notified with a view to sending the Standby Diver down to investigate.

If signals are INCORRECTLY ACKNOWLEDGED, they should be repeated until the correct response is received. If, after repeating the signal, the correct acknowledgement is still not received, the Dive Marshal may take steps to surface the diver in order to clarify the situation.

While the BSAC Roped Diver Signals are sufficient for simple tasks and for the training requirements of 2nd Class Divers, it will be obvious to the reader that the more comprehensive range of signals is necessary in order for divers to effectively perform useful work under water when operating on a life-line. The Royal Navy and commercial diving companies have standardised on the following Single Life-line Signal Code which should be employed by all who require a more comprehensive range of life-line signals. The notes which followed the BSAC Roped Diver Signals Table concerning the manner in which signals should be made applies equally to the Single Life-line Signal Code.

It should be noted that these comprise either PULLS or BELLS or a combination of both. A PULL is a steady heave on the line, a BELL is a sharp, quick tug.

Example: For FIVE BELLS you give—TWO QUICK TUGS (pause), TWO QUICK TUGS (pause), ONE QUICK TUG.

All signals should be preceded by an 'ATTENTION' signal, which consists of ONE PULL. This should always be acknowledged with ONE PULL. The message should then follow.

Single Life-line Signal Code

General Signals:	Surface	Diver
ONE PULL	To call attention. Are you OK?	To call attention. Made bottom. Left bottom. Reached end of jackstay. I am well.
TWO PULLS	Am sending down a rope's end (or as pre-arranged).	Send me down a rope's end (or as pre-arranged).

THREE PULLS	You have come up too far. Go down slowly until we stop you.	I am going down.
FOUR PULLS	Come up.	May I come up?
FOUR PULLS followed by TWO BELLS	Come up—hurry up. Come up—surface decompression.	I want to come up. Assist me up.
FOUR PULLS followed by FIVE BELLS	Come up on your Safety Float.	May I come up on my Safety Float?
Succession of PULLS (Must be more than FOUR)		EMERGENCY SIGNAL Pull me up IMMEDIATELY.
Succession of TWO BELLS		Am foul and need the assistance of another diver.
Succession of THREE BELLS		Am foul but can clear myself if left alone.
FOUR PULLS followed by FOUR BELLS		Attend telephone/ DUCS.

Direction Signals:

Surface Attendant to Diver

ONE PULL	Search where you are.
TWO BELLS	Go to the end of distance line or jackstay.
THREE BELLS	Face shot, then go right.
FOUR BELLS	Face shot, then go left.
FIVE BELLS	Come into your shot, or turn back if on a jackstay.

Working Signals:

Diver to Surface Attendant

ONE PULL	Hold on/Stop.
TWO BELLS	Pull up.
THREE BELLS	Lower.
FOUR BELLS	Take up slack life-line/You are holding me too tight.
FIVE BELLS	Have found/started/completed work.

The section on *Low Visibility and Roped Diving* explains the organisation and conduct of dives made by divers in life-line communication to the surface.

Warnings to Surface Craft

The international regulations for preventing collisions at sea—1972 —requires in Rule 27 (e), 'Whenever the size of vessel engaged in diving operations makes it impracticable to exhibit the shapes prescribed in paragraph (d) of this Rule, a rigid replica of the international Code Flag A, not less than one metre in height, shall be exhibited. Measures shall be taken to ensure all-round visibility'.

The international Code Flag A has the meaning 'I have a diver down; keep well clear at slow speed'. This flag should be displayed by all craft engaged in diving activities including those used by sports diving clubs. The Marine Division of the Department of Trade and Industry has agreed that for sports diving boats a flag of half the size required by Rule 27 (e) may be used but it must be a rigid flag visible from all directions. The flag should be shown *only* whilst divers are in the water; it should be hoisted immediately before they enter the water and lowered as soon as the last diver is aboard the boat. To leave Flag A flying while the boat is not covering a group of divers may induce other water users to disregard it and this might ultimately cause an accident. The lowest point of the flag should be displayed at least one metre above sea level in small boats and as high as possible in larger craft.

The International Regulations for Preventing Collisions at Sea also require that vessels engaged in under-water operations shall exhibit during hours of darkness, 'Three all-round lights in a vertical line where they can best be seen. The highest and lowest of these lights shall be red, and the middle light shall be white', and by day, 'Three shapes in a vertical line where they can best be seen. The highest and lowest of these shapes shall be balls and the middle one a diamond'.

Every effort should be made to meet these international regulations but it may not be possible to do so when using small craft, such as inflatable boats. Where larger boats are used, and particularly if diving is taking place in or near shipping lanes, these regulations should be met.

There are two other flags which are used in some parts of the world to indicate diving operations, though they are not internationally recognised. One is the American Diving Flag—used widely in North and Central America, the Pacific and Australasia. It is a red flag with a white diagonal stripe. The other is the NATO Code Flag No. 4 —a red flag with a white diagonal cross—like the American flag, but with two crossing diagonal stripes. The NATO 4 flag is seldom used nowadays, but may be met in parts of Europe.

Initial Open-water Dives

Snorkelling
Snorkelling is the area of diving where no breathing apparatus is used and can be one of two things. It can be a very exciting and demanding sport in its own right or it can, as it is to those interested in aqualung diving, be a means to another end. As a sport snorkelling has many things to offer. Most obvious, perhaps, is that you do not need the support facilities which are required for aqualung diving. A small hold-all for your equipment and a companion to dive with is all that you need. No heavy aqualung sets, no compressor problems to worry about at all. Whilst this opens up many sites which are difficult to reach other than by boat for aqualung diving, there are of course, inherent restrictions of depth and duration. In various parts of the world, breath-holding diving is used for the collection of shell-fish, sponges and pearls, and it is not unknown for these divers to reach depths far in excess of 30 m with under-water durations of up to $2\frac{1}{2}$ minutes! The present world record for breath-holding diving stands at something in excess of 90 m, though the manner in which it is carried out hardly rates it as snorkel diving as we know it in most sports diving clubs.

Many unique films have been made by divers using snorkel equipment only. Because they are able to meet the fish on their own silent terms with no noisy exhaust bubbles to frighten them away, the under-water photographer frequently finds that he can approach fish more closely than he could whilst wearing an aqualung set. One marine scientist obtained unique pictures of whales in this way and our own grey seals are much more amenable to the snorkeller than to the noisy aqualung diver.

Cost is a major consideration with everybody these days and apart from the initial relatively low cost of basic equipment, snorkelling is the cheapest way to take part in diving. For the boy or girl at school, this can be particularly important and although the activity may lack the glamour of aqualung diving, it does present opportunities to make a start in the sport of under-water swimming, and what is more, makes useful contributions in the child's study of marine biology. The BSAC National Snorkellers Club exists to help young people take up this healthy and exciting sport.

In the past, spear-fishing has been a popular adjunct to snorkel diving but this aspect of the sport is now on the decline throughout the world as more people turn to hunting with a camera rather than with a spear.

FIRST SNORKEL DIVES:

After a full programme of basic snorkel diver training in the pool, the novice diver will be eager and ready to embark on open-water snorkelling activities. These snorkel dives should be looked upon as an opportunity to progress logically from the training pool to the open water in safety, and not treated as an unnecessary nuisance which has to be endured for the sake of the book. Diving experience should be progressive, not calamitous. Early snorkelling leads to watermanship and familiarity with equipment and the environment.

BSAC has no actual test requirement or training in the use of diving suits: early snorkelling experience provides the opportunity to experience use of a wet suit, lifejacket and weight-belt before the complications of the breathing set are introduced. The first open-water snorkel dive is likely to be the first time the wet suit, lifejacket and weight-belt are worn together and it is well worth getting into a distinct order or sequence when kitting up and this is the time to start.

Wet-suit trousers go on first and before you have the added restrictions of the jacket, put bootees and fin retainers on and secure the knife to your leg. You *can* put these on later but it is easier to bend down without the wet-suit top on. On with the jacket and then the lifejacket or ABLJ. Adjust the ABLJ harness crutch strap so that it is tight with the ABLJ fully inflated. The weight-belt goes on outside the ABLJ harness. Instruments can be worn on either wrist. All you need now is your mask, fins and snorkel tube and you are ready to go.

Normally your first open-water snorkel swim will commence from a safe beach, so enter the water up to your waist, prepare and fit your mask and snorkel tube and then put on your fins. The wet-suited snorkeller, just like the aqualung diver, should carry out a buoyancy check as explained in chapter 1. Once buoyancy is correctly adjusted, the first snorkel swim can begin. Launch yourself forward and commence fin swimming just as you would if you were in the training pool. If you are wearing a wet suit for the first time, you will find that the buoyant material of the suit effects the general trim of your body and this takes a little getting used to. For example, your lower legs will feel more buoyant than usual and extra effort has to be applied to keeping your fins under water whilst finning. You will quickly get use to it after a few minutes finning in shallow water.

When ready to do so, and at your instructor's invitation, progress into deeper water where you can commence snorkel dives and under-water swims. Compose yourself on the surface before making your dive, and if possible, spot where you intend to go. Lie on the surface and relax for a few seconds; take a couple of deep breaths and then a comfortable medium-sized inhalation. Make a neat surface dive with legs together and well out of the water so that their weight provides the initial thrust for your journey down. As you go, clear your ears as necessary and compensate for mask squeeze. Once on the bottom, fin and glide, fin and glide, and where possible, use your hands to pull yourself along; but at all times, make no more movement than necessary. Conservation of energy and effort is of prime importance for the breath-holding diver while under water. When ready to surface, push off from the bottom if you can and look upwards, letting your increasing buoyancy and the minimum amount of finning carry you back to the surface. Ensure that you are surfacing into unobstructed water and once on the surface, without taking your head out of the water, clear the snorkel tube, relax and recover your breathing rhythm. Once settled and composed, move off until you wish to dive again.

When snorkel diving with a companion, you should dive alternately so that one snorkeller can observe and cover the other while he is under water. Use of a surface marker buoy fitted with an under-water drogue to prevent its drifting away is a useful accessory which serves to warn surface craft and to provide something to hold on to at the surface should you need it. Check your position relative to land at regular intervals for many a pleasant snorkel dive has been spoiled because of an unscheduled long swim home at the end. The watch-word during snorkel diving is 'relaxation' and the avoidance of unnecessary effort. The body quickly becomes negatively buoyant under water and this factor should be largely responsible for your descent. Use strong finning actions to regain the surface rather than to achieve depth. When under water, relax and hold on to rocks or seaweed whilst observing marine life, rather than attempting to hold your position by finning or sculling actions of the hands.

Cold and fatigue are the main enemies of the snorkel diver. The activity of snorkel diving tends to cause more flushing through the wet suit than does aqualung diving, and during early snorkelling activities the novice diver will be physically unprepared for a long stay in the water. Learn to recognise when you have had enough and stop then.

The snorkel diver will have to demonstrate his ability to swim a distance of some 500 m and during that swim, carry out dives to 7 m. After two or three open-water snorkelling sessions, this should present few problems. Another aspect of the BSAC open-water snorkelling test is to perform a lifesaving tow with resuscitation in the open sea. This is performed in exactly the same way as carried out in the training pool but the victim's lifejacket may be used to provide support. Once this open-water snorkelling test and pool training tests in the use of aqualung breathing apparatus are completed, the snorkel diver is then ready for open-water aqualung diving.

Aqualung Diving

After pool training and open-water snorkelling the novice diver should have few worries about his first open-water aqualung dive. Ideally, his instructor will choose a safe but interesting site with plenty to see so that the novice's mind can be taken off any remaining doubts which might cause him concern. Early aqualung dives will be planned to give progressively more experience so that by the time the diver reaches 3rd Class grade, he is quite able to look after himself. This does not suggest that he should dive alone but rather that he should not be a cause for concern to his instructor or dive leader.

Dives should never be made without a reliable partner. Diving alone stacks up the odds against you to a considerable degree. It reduces safety margins, for there is no one to lend a hand when the unexpected happens, whether it is under water or at the surface. The 'buddy' system of diving in pairs (or more) is a BSAC diving rule, the only exception being that of the roped diver (see section, *Low Visibility and Roped Diving*).

Preparation

Divers should find out who is to be their Dive Leader and from him determine the time they should be ready to dive. Novices should allow plenty of time for kitting up, and should seek help if necessary. Make every effort not to be the last one ready to go.

Where the dive has a specific task or where each diver has a job to do, they should plan and prepare for this in advance before kitting up.

The preparation and kitting up order for the snorkel diver applies equally to the aqualung diver, except that he should fit the weight-belt over the aqualung harness as well as the ABLJ.

Briefings

All aqualung dives should begin with a pre-dive briefing so that everyone understands what is to be done, how, why, where, etc. In the case of an 'experience' dive, the briefing will be carried out by the Dive Leader (the diver in charge of a party of divers) and will cover such things as:

Discipline	The position each diver is to maintain during the dive/ specific duties/action if separated, etc.
Exercise	The purpose of the dive/what is to be done and how.
Equipment	Check air contents/lifejacket/instruments/quick-releases/buoyancy, etc.
Dangers	Barotrauma/decompression/effects of pressure/dangerous creatures or under-water hazards.
Signals	Signals to be used, including 'specials' for particular tasks.

The initials of each briefing point make up the word 'DEEDS'— a useful mnemonic for remembering what the briefing should cover.

If the diver has not already established his correct weighting for neutral buoyancy, the Dive Leader may insist that this be done before the dive really begins. There is nothing so disconcerting to the diver or his Dive Leader as being incorrectly weighted. It is inefficient diving practice.

The Dive

During the dive, the divers should keep close together, and if relative positions for each diver were established during the briefing, they should be adhered to. Signals should be received and clearly answered, and each diver should check his cylinder contents gauge periodically. The Dive Leader will also be checking this and will control the dive accordingly.

Loss of Contact

In the event of any diver becoming separated from his leader or other members of the party, the diver(s) should stop and look around in an effort to remake contact with the missing diver(s). If a look around reveals nothing—and it should only take 10 seconds or so—all divers should ascend and remake contact at the surface. They can then descend again and continue the dive. If one diver does not surface, the others can probably locate the exhaust bubbles at the surface (assisted by their boat or surface cover) and descend down the bubble stream to that diver. Use of a surface marker buoy can assist in regaining contact—if the diver towing the buoy is still below!

It may be possible to give sound signals by banging a knife handle against the cylinder to indicate one's whereabouts but in turbid water it is very difficult to home in on such sounds. Divers can retrace their 'steps' in the hope of regaining contact, but the missing diver may have ascended by then.

Surfacing

When cylinder contents fall to approximately $\frac{1}{4}$ full capacity, the party should ascend. The 'Ascend' signal should be given by the Dive Leader and acknowledged by all before they commence their ascent. Divers should keep together—do not streak off to the surface alone—and should cover each other by facing one another (or forming an inward-facing triangle if a threesome). If buoyancy aids have been inflated at depth, they should be vented during ascent.

On reaching the surface the Dive Leader will check that all are 'OK' and will give the appropriate signal to the boat or surface cover. The dive is concluded by a return to the shore or boat.

Debriefings

A debriefing is as necessary as a pre-dive briefing. It is the opportunity for questions to be asked and answered; criticism of technique made where necessary, and details and findings of the dive reported to the Dive Marshal.

The Under-water World

Many newcomers to the sport fail to appreciate the wonders of the undersea world. Especially under water, it is easy to look at something yet not to see it, or to see it yet not to understand its significance or recognise it because of the strangeness of its surroundings or its camouflage, and unless the diver makes a conscious effort to observe and identify, his dives will lack interest. The art of intelligent observation should be practised.

To set about this, look definitely at things as you come across them, and do not let your eye move idly from one thing to another as you fin along. Take deliberate note of the shape, size and colour of some facet of undersea life, plant or creature. Establish the circumstances surrounding it: whether it is among rocks, on sandy sea-bed, or in open water, hidden in dark holes or beneath overhanging ledges, its depth, environment and movement, or any other feature peculiar to it. Give it a name if you can as this is a sure method of fixing in your mind what you have seen. You can also discuss it afterwards with other people. If you do not know what it is you have seen, remember its characteristic features so that you can find out after the dive by asking your fellow divers or by using reference books—invaluable for such occasions.

There are so many new things to be seen under water that for the beginner it is an advantage to set out on a dive looking for only a few specific things (the amount of seaweed, the type of rocks or the number of crabs) to the exclusion of everything else. Thus, he will avoid being overwhelmed by too great a number and variety of facts. When diving in the same place a number of times, the diver can get to know not only the shape of the sea-bed, the location of rocks, gullies and patches of seaweed, but also the creatures living in the area—sea anemones, crabs and even individual fish. This way, he quickly builds up experience in knowing what to expect, and develops a keen awareness of anything unusual.

Do not forget a dive the moment you have finished it. Go over it in your mind at leisure when you have returned home. Picture the under-water scene; recall the significant things; try to account for the unexpected happenings. The more you ponder it the more you will be able to resolve and learn, and when you return to that diving site it will be with a friendly familiarity, just as you would when re-visiting fields, woods or village on a country walk.

Ecology is the study of creatures in their natural surroundings, and in this pursuit divers have one outstanding advantage over land-based marine biologists: only divers can see marine plants and creatures in their natural environment. Much can be learnt by careful study of fish in an aquarium—just as from animals in a zoo—but in both cases the environment is unnatural, and the creatures' actions and reactions are quite likely to be radically different from those in the wild state.

The greatest satisfaction can be derived from a dive by observing how plants and animals live, their interdependence, where they grow or are to be found, the effects of different types of sea-bed—rocks or flat bottoms—why some areas are devoid of life. The genuine explorer sets out from the humdrum world to record and bring back sights and experiences from an unknown or unfamiliar one. To seek for pleasures in under-water exploration is truly an end in itself.

The Seascape

The first time that a novice diver glances through a reference book on under-sea life he may well become confused at the wealth of different species and although these detailed books are invaluable later on, the beginner is advised to concentrate his attention on a few of the more common plants and animals that he may expect to see in his home waters.

The food chain of all living things commences with the absorption of energy from the sun's rays by the process of photosynthesis in plants. Plant life is thus limited to the depth to which the sun's light can penetrate. Much of this plant life is microscopic plankton drifting near to the surface, sometimes so numerous as to give a colour tint to the water. The diver, however, will see three main classes of seaweed: green coloured close to the surface and on rocks around the seashore; red in a little deeper water; but by far the most noticeable, the brown seaweeds that grow from a few feet below the surface down to about 10 m. The most significant of these is kelp, spreading its broad fronds outwards from the top of a thick stem as much as 2 m tall, which is attached by its holdfast to a rock—for seaweeds have no roots, but obtain their nourishment directly from the water.

It is often difficult for a diver to recognise the difference between animal and plant, as many animals give up the life of free movement and fix themselves—at least for some stage of their development—to a rock, seaweed or sea-bed. However, unlike seaweeds, animals are to be found in the sea at any depth because they feed either off the weed or off one another. Thus, anything below 15 m, although fixed to a rock and looking very much like a plant or flower, is more likely than not a member of the animal kingdom. Common amongst these are the many varieties of sea anemone that are found from the surface downwards, waving their tentacles in an attempt to catch the food which they pass to a mouth at their centre.

Other normally fixed creatures are the shellfish. A diver will see many of these, the type depending largely on the area in which he is diving. Periwinkles browse on weed-covered rocks, and empty shells of the common cockle may be often found on flat, sandy sea-beds.

Prominent among the legged animals are the many varieties of crab, including the edible one, the spider crab and the little hermit, scurrying over the sea-bed in the borrowed shell that he uses to protect his soft body. Also noticeable because of their distinctive features are the lobsters usually hiding in a well-chosen rock hole.

Starfish and sea urchins walk slowly on a multitude of tiny suckers. There are many varieties of each, but the starfish can be recognised by the radial arms, and the sea urchins by their hard shells, often spine covered.

From the diver's point of view there are three main categories of fish: the flat fish such as the plaice or ray, which are found on flat, sandy sea-beds; rock dwellers, like the grouper and wrasse, and those that swim in the open sea. The open sea fish are seen less frequently by the diver, and when seen they are usually timid and keep their distance.

Conservation

Marine creatures and plants are the diver's companions, and seeing them is one of the greatest pleasures of diving; a dive devoid of them lacks much interest, which is perhaps why diving in fresh water, where there is generally less under-water life than in the sea, is less popular. The balance of nature is sometimes very delicate, and the intrusion of man may easily disturb it. By disturbing the environment—by moving stones which provide shelter, by destroying seaweed patches on which animals feed, or in which they hide, or by hunting such fish as wrasse, or collecting creatures such as sea urchins—a whole area can be denuded of marine life.

It has long been known that thoughtless, destructive actions can damage and spoil the countryside, and laws and public opinion have succeeded in reducing much acts of vandalism to a minimum; however, it is sometimes not realised that considerations of this kind have equal validity under the sea. Divers should take particular care not to destroy any species of under-water life, for the sake of the creatures themselves, for the contribution they make to the life of the sea and for the pleasure their presence gives to other divers. The true under-water explorer looks and records; he does not destroy. This does not mean, of course, that the diver should never remove anything from the sea. Within limits, a trophy of some unusual or interesting specimen, or a lobster, crab or fish for the pot, is a legitimate prize and one which adds spice to the dive, gives a sense of achievement and provides pleasant memories afterwards.

By strange irony, ships that are lost at sea are often preserved long beyond their due time. Wrecks lying deeper than the pounding of tides or storm, or buried in sand or mud, can remain intact for long periods—even thousands of years—and the articles in them, protected from the ravages of men and decay, will hold the history of their peoples and times. Thoughtless souvenir or treasure hunting by divers can destroy their heritage. Ancient wrecks in particular should never be pillaged, but rather their site should be recorded for proper marine archaeological excavation.

The responsibility of divers does not end at avoidance of direct destruction, it also extends to observation of the effects of marine pollution such as that caused by oil spillage, sewage outfall and industrial effluent, and by drawing this to public attention unnecessary damage to the under-sea environment may be prevented.

Dangerous Creatures

In the cool waters of temperate climates there are no creatures that are a real danger to the diver, and none that can even cause him discomfort or harm providing he takes reasonable care. The injuries most frequently suffered by divers are cuts and abrasions caused by contact with barnacle or mussel-encrusted rocks or pier and jetty supports. The skin becomes soft and easily damaged by submersion in water and a cut which usually causes pain in the open air frequently does not do so when it occurs in water. In addition, because of the absorption of red light under water, blood diffusing from it into the water appears black. Consequently, the diver may be unaware of the danger, only to see the results of his actions when returned to the surface.

By comparison with the vast majority of sea creatures man is a large animal and few would attack him willingly; those that are able to do so usually prefer to keep their distance or retreat in flight. Moreover, he is new to their experience and sea creatures are ill-equipped to face such an intruder. However, should man attack or disturb any that are able to defend themselves, most will usually do so—sometimes to good effect.

A crab or lobster may make a tasty meal, but to take one the diver must be aware of its claws: a pinch can be not only painful but, also, from a large specimen, quite serious.

Even to thrust an enquiring hand into a rock hole or crevice may be inviting trouble. Other types of creature can inflict pain by stinging: those of the jellyfish, particularly the Portuguese Man-o'-War which floats along the surface trailing long thread-like tentacles, may be quite unpleasant. People with sensitive skins may even have a rash after contact with the small tentacles of the snake-locks anemone.

Unlike the relative safety of cool waters, in the tropics there are undoubtedly some creatures that must be treated with respect, such as the shark and stinging coral. Learn about these dangers beforehand.

If any harm befalls a diver from attack or contact with dangerous undersea creatures it is most probably caused mainly by his own folly. He should always take heed of local conditions and seek the advice of fellow divers experienced in the area, who are his surest guides to safe, enjoyable and interesting diving.

Air Endurance

A knowledge of air endurance is an important part of Dive Planning. How much air your breathing set contains and the ability to calculate how long it will last at your dive depth—and with what measure of safety reserve—can all be vital considerations on many dives.

The rate of breathing and volume of air used for respiration vary greatly from one diver to another, and from dive to dive depending primarily on the level of exertion. Apprehension, tension, state of fitness, cold and other factors can all affect the breathing rate, making it impossible to state a single firm air consumption figure. However, it has been assumed in the past that an experienced and relaxed diver under normal U.K. diving conditions will consume 25 litres of air per minute at atmospheric pressure.

Experienced divers have found that this figure is high—and beginners have found, occasionally to their embarrassment, that it is much too low. Bearing in mind the variability of air consumption, we can use breathing rates which correspond to experience and conditions. For instance, even an experienced diver would be wise to use a figure of 30 l/min for the cold first dives of the season, whereas for summer dives in warmer water, 20 l/min might be more accurate. For a beginner on his first sea dives, a higher figure of perhaps 50 l/min might be advisable, and a relaxed under-water photographer in tropical warm waters might use a figure of 15 l/min.

Having said this, it is vital that whatever breathing rate is assumed for calculating dive endurance, it must be applied in full consultation with the diver's buddy and with the Dive Marshal in charge, so that additional safety factors can be allowed for.

The first step in these calculations is to determine how much air a cylinder contains.

Steel cylinders made in the UK are still classified using Imperial units and are required to be stamped with their 'water capacity' which is the weight of water that fills the cylinder. They are also required to be stamped with their working and test pressures, as are all cylinders. So a UK steel cylinder might be stamped:

WC 28 lb 8 oz   WP 2250 psi   TP 3375 psi

(WC=Water Capacity, WP=Working Pressure, TP=Test Pressure)

The physical volume of this cylinder is:

$$\frac{\text{The water capacity}}{\text{Density of water}} = \frac{28.5 \text{ lb}}{2.2046 \text{ lb/l}} = 12.93 \text{ l}$$

EFFORT	on surface	DEPTH IN METRES				
		10	20	30	40	50
Light work	20 l/m.	40	60	80	100	120
Moderate work	30 l/m.	60	90	120	150	180

INCREASED AIR CONSUMPTION WITH WORK AT DEPTH

This cylinder might be described as a 12.9 l 'bottle' and the amount of air it will hold at its *working pressure* is:

Physical volume × Working pressure in bars (Atmospheres)

$$= 12.93 \times \frac{2250 \text{ psi}}{14.7 \text{ psi (Atmospheric pressure)}} = 1979 \text{ l of free air}$$

(*A similar calculation using the Imperial density of water (62·5 lb per cu ft) gives a capacity, when filled to working pressure, of 69.8 cu ft of free air—and this cylinder might still be described as a '70'.*)
    Aluminium cylinders and foreign steel cylinders are not yet required to be stamped with an expression of their physical volume, but foreign-made steel cylinders made to HSE specifications are marked with their capacity. It is necessary, therefore, to take the manufacturer's claim which may be expressed as the *physical* volume (in the 7–15 l range) or the *free air* capacity (in the 1100–2400 l range). Occasionally it might be listed in cubic metres of free air, so a 2.0 m³ cylinder will hold 2000 litres. The 'free air' rated capacity is always found by multiplying its physical volume by its working pressure in bars.

    Knowing how much air the cylinder should contain when full is all very well, but it is also necessary to measure how much is actually there at any other time. This is done by measuring the pressure of the air in the cylinder and comparing it with the cylinder's rated working pressure. If the cylinder is marked WP 200 bar and by fixing a pressure gauge to it and opening the tap, it is found that the actual pressure is 180 bar, then this cylinder is $\frac{180}{200}$ or 90% full; if the manufacturers claim 2000 l when full, in this case it has 1800 l of 'free air' in it.

As the petrol gauge in a car shows the state of fill of the petrol tank, so a pressure gauge, commonly mis-named a 'contents gauge', shows the state of fill of a diving cylinder. A pressure test gauge can be used on the cylinder before the dive, but nowadays most demand valves are fitted with a suitable pressure gauge on a flexible hose, enabling the diver to continuously monitor his cylinder pressure during the dive.

It is strongly recommended that all divers should use breathing sets fitted with a system which informs the diver when his set has only a limited volume of air remaining and he should surface. The most common system is to read the contents gauge and start to ascend when the gauge shows that pressure has dropped to the reserve level. Some cylinders are fitted with a special type of shut-off valve which curtails the air supply when cylinder pressure drops to a pre-set level. These valves are known as Reserve Valves (chapter 3, *Air Cylinders*). Pulling a lever by-passes the restriction, allowing the reserve air to be used for the ascent. More unusual reserve systems are:

(i) decanting between cylinders when using twin-cylinder sets, or
(ii) a sonic alarm in the demand valve which buzzes with each inhalation when cylinder pressure drops to reserve level.

In calculating air endurance, the pre-set reserve of air must be discounted; you must aim to have it intact at the start of the final ascent to the surface. It is a statistical fact that most diving accidents arise during the ascent, and every diver should have sufficient air left during this period to be able to carry out an under-water rescue if necessary.

Early aqualungs had a working pressure of 120 bar, and it was the recommended practice to start your ascent when your contents gauge fell to 30 bars; i.e. one-quarter of the cylinder capacity. Modern high-working pressure cylinders (200 bar or more) have made this 30 bar reserve level potentially dangerous. As the following table shows, older low-working pressure cylinders have more reserve air at 30 bar than their new high pressure counterparts, for the same free air capacities.

Rated capacity		Working pressure	Reserve air (litres)	
Litres	Cu. ft.	Bar	At 30 bar	At 50 bar
1700	60	120	425	708
1700	60	200	255	425
2040	72	150	408	680
2040	72	200	306	510

In the case of these 200 bar cylinders, the 30 bar reserve capacities may not be enough to reach the surface safely, particularly with a heavy breathing, nervous or novice diver. It is recommended that a diver should allow at least 350 l for reserve, which means using a 50 bar reserve for most cylinders with a working pressure of 200 bar or higher. As a general rule, use one quarter of the set's capacity as a reserve.

Having determined how much air the cylinder holds before the dive, and having allowed for a suitable reserve, it is possible now to calculate how much air may be consumed during the dive and how long it will last.

SOME EXAMPLES OF AIR-ENDURANCE CALCULATIONS:

1. A cylinder has a capacity of 1700 l of free air and a working pressure of 200 bar. A pressure gauge shows that it contains 175 bar. How much air is actually available?

$$\text{Total air available} = \frac{\text{Capacity} \times \text{actual pressure}}{\text{Working pressure}}$$

$$= \frac{1700 \text{ l} \times 175 \text{ bar}}{200 \text{ bar}}$$

$$= 1487.5 \text{ l}$$

2. The above cylinder is to be used for a dive to 25 m and a reserve level of 50 bars has been decided upon. What dive duration can be expected? (Assume breathing rate to be 25 l/min at 1 bar.)
Reserve air level of 50 bars represents:

$$\frac{1700 \times 50}{200} = 425 \text{ l}$$

Therefore, air available = Total air available — Reserve air for dive:

$$= 1487.5 - 425$$
$$= 1062.5 \text{ l}$$

Breathing rate at depth = Breathing rate at surface × Absolute pressure at depth
25 m depth is 3.5 bars absolute
$$= 25 \text{ l/min} \times 3.5 \text{ bar}$$
$$= 87.5 \text{ l/min}$$

$$\text{Dive duration} = \frac{\text{Air available for dive}}{\text{Breathing rate at depth}}$$
$$= \frac{1062.5 \text{ l}}{87.5 \text{ l/min}}$$
$$= 12 \text{ minutes (approx.)}$$

3. A diver wishes to remain at 30 m (4 bar) for 20 minutes, and to have an adequate reserve of air. What is the smallest size aqualung cylinder he can use? Breathing rate is 25 l/min at 1 bar.

Breathing rate at depth $= 25$ l/min $\times 4$ bar
$\qquad = 100$ l/min
$\qquad$ Duration of dive $= 20$ minutes
Therefore, Air available
for dive must be: $\qquad = $ Duration $\times$ Breathing Rate at depth
$\qquad = 20$ minutes $\times 100$ l/min
$\qquad = 2000$ l

Reserve air: An adequate reserve level is one-quarter of the total cylinder capacity. Thus 2000 l should be three-quarters of the cylinder capacity.

$$\text{Cylinder capacity required} = \frac{2000 \times 4}{3}$$
$$= 2666 \text{ l}$$

A cylinder of 2650 or 2700 l would be suitable.

4. A decompression dive of 60 minutes to 20 m is to be carried out. What quantity of air will be needed, including a safe reserve? (Assume breathing rate to be 25 l/min at 1 bar.)

In this question, the divers are to spend 60 minutes at 20 m (3 bars absolute) and—according to the RNPL/BSAC Table—will have to carry out a stop of 15 minutes at 5 m (1.5 bar absolute) during their ascent.

Breathing rate at depth $\qquad = 25$ l/min $\times 3$ bar
$\qquad = 75$ l/min

Duration of dive $\qquad = 60$ min
Therefore air required for
dive at maximum depth $\qquad = 75$ l/min $\times 60$ min
$\qquad = 4500$ l
Breathing rate during
Decompression Stop: $\qquad = 25$ l/min $\times 1.5$ bar $\times 15$ min
$\qquad = 562.5$ l
Total Air required
for dive: $\qquad = $ Requirement for depth
$\qquad$ + requirement for decompression
$\qquad = 4500$ l $+ 562.5$ l
$\qquad = 5062.5$ l

Reserve Air $=$ one-quarter of cylinder capacity, so Total air required represents three-quarters of cylinder capacity.
Therefore, Cylinder $\qquad = \dfrac{5062.5 \times 4}{3}$
Capacity required:
$\qquad = 6750$ l

Even the largest twin-set does not have this capacity. Divers would have to change sets at some time towards the end of their 60 minutes working period under water.

It is not worth trying to calculate exactly the air used during ascent and descent, but so long as a realistic reserve level and a sensible breathing rate is used, the slight differences in answers may be ignored. Remember though that such calculations are only as accurate as the one major assumption—the breathing rate at ambient pressure.

To keep to the assumed breathing rate, or even to improve upon it, development of proper breathing control is paramount. Activity and the level of exertion should be controlled to establish and maintain a slow yet free breathing rhythm. All demand valves offer some resistance to breathing and over-exerted or panicked divers may develop rapid, deep breathing, which this resistance compounds, leading to the possibility of over-breathing beyond the mechanical capabilities of the demand valve—'beating the lung'. Nowadays this is rare, due to the advancing design of demand valves, but should it arise it is imperative to regain normal breathing control as quickly as possible. Stop all activity, relax and regain composure. Concentrate on regulating exhalation, regular inhalation will rapidly follow.

It is foolhardy to attempt to extend air endurance by either holding the breath or by holding it between exhaling and inhaling (skip-breathing). Hypoxia and air embolism during upward movement are particular dangers of breath-holding, and there is a possibility of carbon dioxide build-up in skip-breathing at depth. A slow and steady breathing rhythm is essential at all times. The only way to extend air endurance is to overcome those factors which increase breathing rate, or to use larger-capacity cylinders, or twin-cylinder sets. Keeping warm represents the greatest air saving when diving in UK waters.

Ascent Procedures

Normal Ascent Procedure

1. The 'Go up' signal must be exchanged with your partner.
2. Fin upwards watching exhaust bubbles and partner.
3. Maintain speed or approximate speed of small bubbles (15 m per min).
4. Breathe normally all the time.
5. Look up and watch out for surface obstacles.
6. In poor visibility, hold hand above head—in this case your other hand should be holding your partner.
7. Immediately on surfacing, turn a complete circle in case a boat or other possible danger should be approaching. Be ready to take evasive action—by diving again if necessary.
8. Exchange OK signals with your partner.
9. Change over to snorkel breathing.
10. Signal OK or otherwise to look-out.

A diver's return to the surface will either be normal or will be the means of escaping from an under-water emergency. He may make an emergency ascent in a variety of ways:

1. *Assisted ascent,* which involves breathing air from his partner's aqualung during the return to the surface: both divers taking it in turns to take breaths.
2. *Free ascent,* during which the diver swims up to the surface exhaling as he does so, thus allowing expanding air within his chest to escape.
3. *Buoyant ascent,* achieved by inflating the ABLJ or buoyancy aid and ascending at speed under its influence. The diver has to exhale hard during such an ascent.

All emergency ascents are fraught with risk, particularly free ascent and buoyant ascent, which expose the diver to a real risk of lung damage.

Free and Buoyant Ascent

Practice must only be carried out under close supervision and with a recompression chamber at the immediate surface—a situation impossible for most sports divers. This creates an obvious problem because training to proficiency is usually achieved by constant practice, and proficiency is even more important in the case of emergency drills. When an emergency occurs under water an element of excitement, panic or fear is bound to appear, and under these conditions a person will react correctly only if able to perform emergency procedures automatically—virtually without thinking.

This is where the value of training comes in.

Although one should not practise free and buoyant ascents, there is much that can be practised or taught in the safety of a swimming pool or lecture room. Foolproof weight-belt release is one vital thing which should be stressed. Training should include practice in emergency weight-belt release—both on oneself and on another diver—*while fully equipped for diving.* It is no use practising in the pool in swimming trunks; the drill is only of value when you are fully equipped with bulky suits, snagable accessories and gloves.

Divers should be thoroughly acquainted with emergency ascent procedures, and should be able to quote the procedure for each type of ascent on demand. This is particularly important in view of the lack of practical training which can be given safely.

In the event of an air failure at depth, the recommended method by which a diver can return to the surface is known as 'assisted ascent'; its principle advantages being that the ascent rate is normal (15 m per minute), the technique may be practised beforehand, and decompression stops may be made if necessary.

Assisted ascent practice is encouraged at the shallower levels but —and although this is repeated elsewhere, it is well worth repeating —it should only be carried out on actual dives by divers who have practised regularly together. In the event of diving with virtual strangers, or divers who have not practised the technique with you, it might be better to carry out a free ascent. It is, unfortunately, something that your DO or instructor cannot decide for you, and you will only have a split second in which to make your decision. Far better to keep in practice, so that you will know exactly what to do should the event occur.

ASSISTED ASCENT PROCEDURE:

1. The 'distressed diver' attracts the attention of his companion by beckoning or banging on his cylinder. He makes the signal 'I need to share air'. He should then remain still and conserve any air that he has left.
2. The 'assisting diver' closes to him as quickly as possible. If using a twin-hose demand valve, he grips the 'distressed diver's' weight-belt or harness and pushes him up to a position slightly above him. If he has a single-hose valve, coming over his right shoulder, the 'assisting diver' takes up a position at the right-hand side of the victim and takes a secure hold on his aqualung harness. In this position, the 'assisting diver' is able to pass his mouthpiece horizontally across to the 'distressed diver' without putting undue strain on the demand valve hose.
3. The 'assisting diver' takes a breath and quickly removes his

mouthpiece passing it to his companion and turning the aperture to enable him to breathe as soon as he drops his own mouthpiece. Both divers should be resting vertically in the water. A difference of approximately 10–20 cm in their level ensures that the 'distressed diver' receives a bubbling (twin-hose) mouthpiece containing air and no water. This is essential as air failure is usually detected when trying to breathe in, and the diver in trouble may not have enough air to clear the tubes. The purge button may be used to expel water from single-hose valves if necessary.

4. After taking his two breaths, the 'distressed diver' returns the mouthpiece down to the 'assisting diver' who also receives only air as it is higher than his demand valve. He then in turn takes two breaths.

5. When a steady rhythm has been established, the 'assisting diver' signals, '(Let's) go up', and both divers start finning gently upwards, keeping the same relative position. During the ascent, each exhales slowly when not in possession of the mouthpiece to prevent any possibility of air embolism. The 'assisting diver' should check his rate of ascent, or at least that the small exhaust bubbles appear to remain stationary around his head, to make sure that the speed is not faster than 15 m/min.

It is especially important that as the surface approaches, the 'assisting diver' should look out for obstacles and watch for bubbles from the 'distressed diver' to check that he is breathing out between inhalations. Gentle pressure on his stomach will remind him. He should also check that increasing buoyancy is not accelerating the ascent unduly, and hold the 'distressed diver' back if necessary. Stopping finning and breathing out will help to do this. The 'assisting diver' should hold his companion's weight-belt or harness at all times.

In a real emergency, lack of air may give the 'distressed diver' a feeling of panic or breathlessness. The 'assisting diver' should then allow him to breathe three or four times to his own single breath on the bottom before indicating 'two breaths each' for the ascent. In extreme cases the mouthpiece may not be returned, and the 'assisting diver' will have to decide whether to forcefully retrieve it or to breathe out continually himself (see *Free Ascent* below) during their ascent.

Without doubt it is most important *to practise the technique regularly. This is ideally done by those who frequently dive together.* A diver cannot be expected to take the right actions in an emergency if he has never previously practised in open water.

Both divers should be well weighted for initial pool training. One sits on the bottom in the deep end and the other adopts a kneeling position facing him. The kneeling diver removes his mouthpiece and holds it against his chest. The sitting diver takes a deep breath, and then passes his mouthpiece up to his companion. Each in turn follows the breathing sequence: Fit and clear mouthpiece—Inhale—Exhale—Inhale—Remove and hand over mouthpiece—Exhale steadily. When sharing horizontally and using twin-hose valves, it should be remembered that the 'distressed diver' should swim on the side which keeps the exhaust tube below the inlet.

FREE ASCENT PROCEDURE:

Another way of regaining the surface quickly in emergency is by means of *Free Ascent*. This method may be used when a diver cannot contact his companion or when he is untrained in assisted ascent or unwilling to take part. The risk of pulmonary barotrauma (see *Burst Lung*) may now be greater and success is dependent on a calm and controlled technique.

Immediately the diver finds himself without air, he fins steadily upwards. If the lack of air was discovered when he tried to breathe in, he will have a feeling of air starvation. This may be overcome by holding his breath *briefly* until the residual air in his lungs expands with the fall in the surrounding pressure.

The diver must then remove his mouthpiece and commence to exhale gently and continually through pursed lips. The rate of finning should be slowed as he ascends and he should try not to overtake his bubbles. A maximum safe rate for free ascent is 30 m/min. In low visibility he should watch his depth gauge to make sure that he is ascending, and if difficulty is experienced the weight-belt should be jettisoned to lessen the load.

Most divers feel comfortable during this type of ascent and there is normally a desire to breathe out, rather than in. Enough partial pressure of O_2 exists, and CO_2 will be blown off as quickly as it is formed, providing little chance of CO_2 build up. The inexperienced diver has most to fear from panic and over-exertion, both of which may use up precious O_2.

As the surface approaches, the number and size of exhaled bubbles will increase and the diver should take the precaution of breathing out faster. If the diver does not get rid of the air continually during the ascent, he will suffer a serious accident through over-expansion or rupture of the lungs. Air embolism has occurred in trainees holding their breath when returning from a depth of as little as 3 m!

Current medical thinking is that free ascent should not be practised as a training drill in view of the dangers.

BUOYANT ASCENT:

Finally, an alternative to 'Free Ascent' is provided by the use of an ABLJ or buoyancy aid.

Most types of ABLJ (see *Lifejackets and Buoyancy Aids*) will bring a diver up at a rate of approximately 2 m/sec with a consequent risk of embolism or explosive decompression, especially if the dive has been near to the maximum 'no-stop' time. There is, however, a high degree of certainty of arriving at the surface.

This type of lifejacket is normally used by experienced divers who should be familiar with the mode of operation and the hazards.

The diver does not release his weight-belt before admitting air into his lifejacket as it will keep his body in the correct position on the surface should he lose consciousness.

The sequence of actions should be as follows:

1. Open tap of ABLJ bottle or direct feed.
2. As ascent commences, close tap.
3. Lean head back—breathe out—watch for surface.
4. Controlled venting of the buoyancy aid should be employed to prevent an excessively rapid ascent.

During the whole of the emergency buoyant ascent the diver breathes out forcefully, keeping the volume of air in the lungs near the minimum to avoid distension of the chest. He should remain as relaxed as possible. Buoyant ascent should only be carried out in a real emergency.

If any symptoms appear after free or buoyant ascents, the diver should be taken immediately to the nearest operational recompression chamber. Although there is a natural tendency to take solo action when suddenly deprived of air, there is little doubt that the slow return to the surface characteristic of assisted ascent, makes it often less hazardous than free or buoyant ascent, and decompression stops may even be completed while sharing. Its practice gives greater confidence at depth, greater appreciation of the importance of diving as a team, and makes a diver more use to others in a real emergency.

Under-water Navigation

A human being walking in dense fog loses his way in two dimensions. A free diver operating in conditions of poor, or nil, visibility and lacking firm ground under his feet is even more confused as he can easily lose his sense of direction in three dimensions. With no datum point for reference, and with no feeling of gravitational forces, he is often unable to distinguish up from down. The under-water environment is so different from the natural one that few of man's systems escape its influence and a close examination of these effects on the senses required for under-water navigation is, therefore, necessary.

Vision
Without the aid of artificial light, vision is dependent on the clarity of the water and the penetration of daylight which, in turn, is dependent on the depth and the time of day. At midday in clear water it is only just possible to see what one is doing as deep as 75 m. A considerable absorption of light by water is thus taking place. Even at the best times, under-water visibility is very greatly limited (in the clearest water to 30 m), but quite often suspended matter, such as stirred-up mud, may reduce it almost to zero.

Colours, too, are deceptive, for the light is unevenly absorbed so that objects on the bottom may have quite a different colour when removed from the water.

Hearing
Sound in water travels much faster than its speed in air. In air, man is able to locate the direction from which the sound is coming. He does this by turning his head until both ears are equidistant from the source and the sound is synchronised in each. The increased speed of sound under water makes this virtually impossible.

The Sense of Position
In water, no effort is required to maintain posture. Righting reflexes are not required and muscles which are normally responsible for posture and balance are relaxed. When blindfolded and still, the sense of position is soon lost and disorientation, not unlike that experienced in extremely high altitude flying, develops. The same situation can easily occur in water of poor visibility.

The fact is that the under-water swimmer is largely dependent upon visual sensations for his navigation. The lighter water above him indicates the position of the surface and ascending bubbles give him a vertical. Take away these and he is soon lost. He may swim around in circles and he may unwittingly increase his depth or even turn over. Many occasions have been reported where a swimmer, even an experienced one, presuming to be travelling along an even course at steady depth has found himself on the bottom very many metres below his intended depth. This happens especially in the dark. Loss of direction can occur vertically and horizontally. Such loss of direction in three dimensions can be very dangerous, and this can occur not only in shallow, low visibility conditions, but in clear water, at a point where the surface disappears and the bottom is not yet in view. The visual world of the diver then appears as a blue globe, which due to the light-scattering effects of water, and reflection from the unseen bottom, shows no difference in light intensity to indicate the surface. It can be extremely confusing to the beginner and can cause attacks of vertigo due to a sense of imbalance. The experienced diver turns to his bubbles as a guide to the surface. In dirty water it may not be possible to utilise these, or to read instruments clearly.

Such conditions, when first met, can cause panic, and sufferers from claustrophobia are badly affected. The proficiency test of swimming in a pool with a blacked-out mask was introduced to give pupils a foretaste of this experience and to guide instructors in detecting claustrophobic tendencies.

From the foregoing we see that the senses required for under-water navigation are seriously affected to different degrees according to the prevailing under-water conditions.

Under-water navigation can be broadly divided into two sections. (a) Pilotage, where direction is found by use of topographical features such as rocks or ripple marks in sand, etc., and (b) Navigation, where the use of instruments such as compass and depth gauge are employed. Quite often a combination of both arts is utilised.

Pilotage

We have seen that the senses required for direction are impaired under water and the first consideration should be to reduce the amount of direction-finding under water to the absolute minimum. Thus, if one has some specific object to locate, the maximum amount of available information should be obtained in order to commence the dive as near as possible to the object.

Having commenced the dive at the best possible position, the problem of navigating under water therefore entails (a) the steering of a fairly accurate course on the bottom, (b) the ability to return to the point of departure, and (c) the ability to define the direction of the surface and to stop at the proper depths for decompression if necessary. It is obvious that different techniques will be required according to the condition of the water with regard to visibility and currents.

The golden rule in acquiring a sense of direction under water is always to arrive on the bottom with a static reference point fixed clearly in the mind, be it the boat, the shore or another physical feature. If it is necessary to swim 'into the blue' to reach the bottom or if the water is dirty, then a tangible datum such as an anchor-chain, shot-line, or rope run out from the shore will have to be used. Once on the bottom with a sense of direction firmly established in the mind, it is then possible to swim over the floor picking out landmarks ahead, by which to steer a correct course, in the same way as a low-flying airman flies by picking out objects on the horizon. In limited visibility even large pebbles will suffice. It is both necessary to remember the landmarks, and to remember the turns made, and at each turn the diver must re-orientate himself with his home base.

Other guides can be the luminous patches overhead caused by the sun (for corroboration only), wave ripples in the sand, or even the current itself if there is no fear of an immediate change of tide or current. A flat, featureless sand or mud bottom can be very confusing. Marks made are obliterated by the water almost immediately, but in conditions of good visibility, if the texture of the bottom permits, a track in the form of a dust cloud can be beaten up by the fins when swimming close to the bottom, to be used as a guide on the return. This track can only be used in comparatively still water however, as otherwise the sand or mud haze is soon dispersed.

The worst type of sea floor to navigate over is one covered entirely by seaweed or similar vegetation, which soon causes confusion if no other reference is at hand. In shallow water, where the vegetation is being swung to and fro rhythmically by wave or current conditions, this can be a doubtful guide, and in this and similar conditions it is preferable to use a compass, or a guide line.

After some experience, a diver often develops a sixth sense with regard to direction under water. He is guided subconsciously and reacts automatically to such pointers as increasing pressure on the ears and mask, the sound of exhaust bubbles, the sag of his weight-belt or the gradient of a shelving sea-bed indicating the shore. The ascending exhaust bubbles or a slight amount of water in a face-mask will also indicate the surface direction.

Navigation

Under-water navigation, utilising instruments such as the compass and depth gauge, is again subject to the same conditions as pilotage in commencing the dive at the nearest possible surface position.

Magnetic Compass

Suitable compasses can be obtained for under-water use and these are described in the section on *Ancillary Equipment*. Being magnetic instruments, they are sensitive to the presence of iron and steel and to electrical circuitry. Consequently, if a compass is used close to a dive partner who has a steel cylinder, or in the vicinity of a shipwreck, deviation may cause it to become unreliable. Generally, the small compasses used by divers have to be pretty close to a large disturbing influence before they become unreliable. Check this for yourself by approaching someone wearing a steel aqualung cylinder, and note when the needle swings away from magnetic north and points towards the steel cylinder.

In the majority of cases the under-water swimmer uses his compass to navigate to objects whose bearing he has taken and set on the compass before he dived. The diver sights his destination or target along the 'direction of travel' line and then turns the bezel so that the lubber-line and the magnetic north-pointing needle coincide. He may then dive and so long as he holds the needle and lubber-line together, he is on course. He may return by rotating the lubber-line through 180°, thus setting a reciprocal course.

Alternatively, the diver may plan a course and determine compass headings which he should follow by using maps and charts. For example, if he wished to swim a triangular course, such as the one shown on page 356 he could use a chart to plot his headings in order to reach points B and C and subsequently to return to point A. He should align the chart and his compass to due North, then lay the 'direction of travel' line over the route he wishes to take between each point and read off from his compass his Magnetic heading for each leg of the course. When swimming from point B to point C the diver would be advised to follow the heading of 100° rather than 90°, thus ensuring that he did not pass outside the tip of headland C.

To use an under-water compass accurately requires practice, and the novice is advised to acquaint himself with his compass by using it in an open space on land before he starts using it under water. Any open space will do—a playing-field, car-park, or open country. Take a bearing on a prominent landmark not far away; set the compass up so that the 'direction of travel line' points towards this landmark and then, with head down watching the compass, walk steadily holding the compass bearing until you reach that landmark. If you do not reach it, or at least come very close to it, there is something radically wrong with your technique! Practise this two or three times until a satisfactory performance is achieved and then try walking in a square. To do this, mark a point on the ground with a small but conspicuous object, such as a coin, and then with the compass set at say 0°, walk forward twenty paces. At the

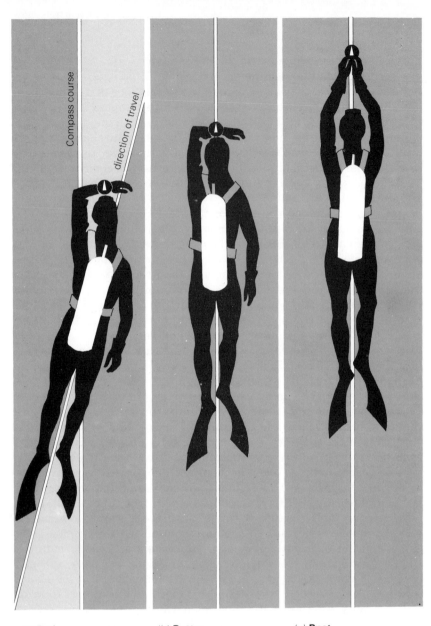

(a) **Bad**
The shoulder harness's drag makes it difficult to position the compass arm at a true right-angle to the body's line of travel

(b) **Better**
This shows the correct position but in practice it is difficult to fin like this for any length of time

(c) **Best**
A much better solution is to wear the compass on a lanyard and hold it in front with both arms

Fig. 80. MAINTAINING DIRECTION SWIMMING WITH A MAGNETIC COMPASS

twentieth pace, stop and turn through 90°. Let us assume that you have turned left. Once the compass has settled, walk forward again for a further twenty paces. Stop and turn left again through another 90° and allow the needle to settle. Once it has done so pace off a further twenty paces. Repeat this process until, on the twentieth pace on the fourth leg of the square, you should have returned to your original mark. At all times, watch the compass and do not look around for your mark. The effect of making a right-hand turn in error during this square compass exercise will be obvious. It is essential, therefore, that you are consistent in the direction to which you turn.

Once you have gained confidence in the use of your compass by carrying out these dry-land exercises, repeat them under water, using a sheltered site with a flat sea-bed. When practising a straight-line swim it is best to start from seaward and swim in towards the beach. If you started from the beach with the intention of navigating to a moored boat, for example, a slight inaccuracy could mean that you swim out past the boat, very much further than you intended. So, start from the boat and swim back to a mark on the shore. When swimming a straight-line course out to a headland, play safe by aiming inshore from the headland (Ref. Course BC on page 356).

When practising a compass square under water, the length of each leg of the square may be measured either by time or by a number of fin strokes. The procedure is just the same as the dry-land exercise, but it is vital that, when you have completed the final fin stroke or your time has run out on the final leg of the square, you stop and look around for your target. Do not swim on thinking that you have yet to reach the target for Murphy's Law will guarantee that you will be swimming away from it! Instead, ascend and you will probably find that you are within a metre or two of your target, which is just beyond the range of visibility under water. Triangular courses can be plotted and carried out in the same way. At all times, take great care to see that you *are* moving along the desired 'direction of travel' line.

Distance Travelled

Practice will quickly acquaint you with the correct use of a compass, but a greater problem for the under-water navigator is assessing accurately the distance travelled. In the limited visibility conditions usually met in British diving, your destination or target is seldom seen until you are on top of it and, therefore, some reasonably accurate method of calculating how far you have travelled is desirable. When carrying out a square or triangular course, you can measure the distance travelled either by time or by counting the number of breaths or fin strokes, and this will be accurate so long as your speed through the water is fairly constant and you are not affected by adverse tidal conditions when swimming in a particular direction. In order to ascertain how far they can travel within a certain period of time, divers are advised to practise swimming known distances at a normal swimming pace in order to see how quickly they do move through the water. This can be done by measuring off from a chart the distance between two conspicuous points (e.g. A to B on this page) and then swimming from one to the other to see how long it takes. With a fairly accurately known distance and time, the diver's average speed through the water in terms of metres per minute, or per second, can be determined. Knowing how fast the diver moves through the water, he can then calculate in advance how long it should take to swim any known distance. For example, when swimming from point B to point C in the diagram, he might calculate that it should take ten minutes. If after swimming for twelve minutes on the heading 090° he has still not reached the point C, he will be advised to surface, for it is most likely that he has overshot that particular headland. If he was not aware of his speed through the water, he might not realise that he has overshot and could swim on and place himself in a dangerous situation.

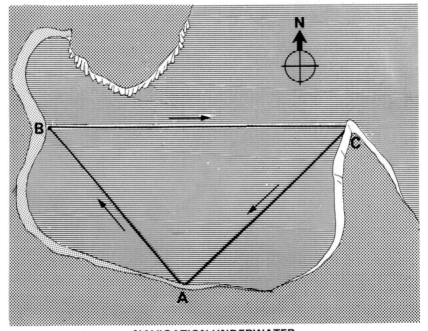

NAVIGATION UNDERWATER
Swimming along predetermined compass courses
A-B heading—320°, B-C—090° (100° for safety), C-A—220°

To summarise, navigation under water is something which requires practice, both for accurate pilotage and accurate use of instruments. It should be remembered that under-water navigation is three-dimensional and that a depth gauge should also be looked upon as a navigational instrument. The under-water navigator cannot perform adequately unless he has a compass, depth gauge and watch. In this section the effects of tidal movement on the diver swimming under water have been ignored for simplicity and the reader is referred to the section on *Basic Navigation,* sub section *Plotting a Course* in which the effects of tide and how it may be allowed for are explained. The principles of allowing for tide when plotting a course to steer for a vessel are exactly the same as those which would be applied by a diver under water. Do practise under-water navigation as often as you can. To know at all times where you are and to return directly to your starting point or nearest point of safety is not only sensible: it is also a safe and good diving practice. Finally, *do* trust your compass: it has a far more accurate sense of direction than you have!

Low Visibility and Roped Diving

The object of carefully organised diving is to keep all divers under observation so that in the event of one of them getting into difficulty, assistance can be rendered with sufficient speed to save life.

In calm clear water there is usually sufficient safety in divers swimming together—the 'buddy' system—with a safety boat in attendance following their Surface Marker Buoy.

It would be pleasant if it were possible to dive in such fair conditions all the time. However, in some waters the visibility varies from poor to non-existent, but diving may still be necessary—for search or recovery purposes; for training; or simply for the challenge. Also, as soon as a diver wishes to carry out a useful underwater task, he frequently finds he is unable to choose optimum diving conditions. Diving will have to take place by day or night in tidal streams; in wrecks or among wreckage; in caverns or narrow clefts; in zero visibility on soft muddy bottoms; in rough weather; or, perhaps, when it is just generally cold, wet and thoroughly miserable. This is to name but a few of the potentially hazardous conditions which exist.

When such conditions are experienced, a safety-line of one sort or another will usually HAVE to be used, with or without a surface marker, if the requirements of the first paragraph are to be met.

The decision to use a safety line is the sole responsibility of the Dive Marshal, for it is he who will be held responsible for any accident in the eyes of the law. The Marshal's decision will, of course, take into account the type of under-water task on hand; the prevailing under-water conditions; the present and anticipated weather and tides; boat availability and engine reliability; number and experience of divers; depth of water; availability of a recompression chamber, and any other relevant local factors.

The different types of safety-lines are as follows:

1. AS A BUDDY-LINE—from diver to diver.
2. AS A SURFACE MARKER FLOAT-LINE—from diver to surface float.
3. AS A LIFE-LINE—from diver to surface attendant.

These three methods may be combined as necessary and a common combination is divers on a buddy-line, with one of them on a float. The purpose of buddy-lines and SMB's was explained in chapter

4, *Safety Equipment.* The buddy-line is a useful aid when swimming in open, unobstructed water when visibility is other than good: the SMB should be employed on all open-water dives whatever the visibility. In this section, we are more concerned with diving in extremely poor conditions, using a roped diver operating on a life-line (or signal-line).

Some of the concepts of true free diving must be amended to meet the typical conditions of low visibility encountered in both inland and coastal waters.

Conditions envisaged are:
1. Very low or nil visibility.
2. Confined diving area.
3. Under-water obstacles of largely unknown position.

To counter such conditions several adaptations of normal free-diving techniques become necessary, viz:
1. In very low visibility, i.e. below 1 m, a diver is often very much better off diving alone. Two divers in such conditions are liable to get in each other's way, get tangled up and probably displace equipment.
2. There must be a positive and reliable link between the diver and a surface tender, i.e. a life-line or signal-line.
3. A pre-arranged code of diver–surface tender signals must always be used (see *Signals and Communications*).
4. The surface tender or attendant must be a responsible and experienced diver himself and in complete sympathy with his charge.
5. Provision should be made for under-water emergencies: a 'stand-by' diver must be available.

Roped Diver Operations

THE LIFE-LINE:

Material: 2.5 cm circumference manilla or sisal, 3 cm plaited hemp, or 1 cm nylon, terylene, polypropylene, or polyethylene (courlene), are all suitable and have a breaking strain in excess of 450 kg. The larger vegetable fibres are more bulky but are easier to handle. However, they tend to become slippery when wet.

As the man-made fibres tend to twist very easily—although they are very light and have very little resistance in a tideway—they are best kept on reels.

Length: 30 m is a manageable length for a life-line.

Fittings: No special fittings are required, but a life-line should be whipped at both ends.

Markings: There are no standard markings but, if required, the life-line may be marked at 2 m intervals.

The life-line should be passed under all other equipment and secured with a bowline

Fig. 81. SECURING A LIFE-LINE TO A DIVER

SECURING:

The ZERO end is taken around the diver underneath his arm-pits and all equipment in such a way that if weight-belt and set are jettisoned he is still held by the line. The line should then be tied with a bowline close to the body of the diver on the side of his useful arm (Fig. 81).

The inboard end of the life-line should always be securely tied to the diving platform; it cannot then be jerked from the attendant's hands.

LIFE-LINE SIGNALS:

A standard code of life-line signals exists and is widely used in commercial and military diving operations. An abbreviated code has been drawn up for Club diving use. Both codes are covered in the earlier section of this chapter, *Signals and Communications.*

THE ATTENDANT (OR TENDER) AND THE ART OF ATTENDING:

To the diver, groping along, blind, in mud and obstructions, it is a most comforting feeling to know that he is in the charge of an experienced and competent handler who appreciates his feelings.

The best attendant is another diver, for he will then be completely in sympathy with the diver and have an automatic knowledge of the diving signals.

His task is always to be aware of the diver's position and to keep the life-line free of obstruction so that signals may be passed quickly and easily. The inboard end of the line in particular should be kept clear for there is nothing more infuriating to a diver than being held up purely because the attendant has got himself in a mix-up.

The attendant should be very careful in a tideway that the drag on the line does not mislead him into paying out too much—it is easy for a diver to give a signal on a taut line, but very difficult for him if he first has to take up yards of slack.

At the first sign of any difficulty, the attendant should inform the Dive Marshal who in turn should not hesitate to send in the standby diver. Trouble down below can be indicated in a number of ways: no sign of bubbles, signals unanswered, life-line taut or slack, no movement felt when the diver should be working. Think twice, however, before hauling madly away on the life-line; it may well be caught on a bottom obstruction and if the line is heaved the diver may well be hauled down.

If it is necessary for the diver to swim to the end of his line or farther so that two lines have to be used, always make sure that the second line is either joined before the diver goes in or that it is readily available, again so that the diver is not held up by unnecessary delays.

At all costs the attendant must retain patience with the diver, giving him time to answer signals when working, repeating signals which are not understood. He should also always remember that the diver's safety and comfort are his responsibility; his full attention to his job is vital.

THE DIVER:

There are a few points that the diver himself must bear in mind when working on a line.

If the line becomes too taut or too slack he should not swim against it, nor should he coil it up. He should pause and give the relevant signal (four bells) to his attendant and wait until the requisite action has been taken. It is particularly important not to swim against a taut line; inexperienced divers have been known to exhaust themselves by doing just this.

Resist the temptation to overrun the safety-line when surfacing, as this will mean that signals will not get through, and an important one—perhaps ordering the diver to remain down because of the boat's movements or similar events—may be missed with subsequent embarrassment. Finally, have patience with the life-line and never hurry when you become mixed up with it. In an alien world of darkness and silence it is sometimes the only true friend.

PASSING LIFELINE SIGNALS:

A diver or attendant wishing to pass a signal should first give one pull to call attention, then wait for this to be answered. If the diver is engaged in a difficult task, the attendant must give him plenty of time to stop work, find his life-line and answer the signal. If there is no answer within a reasonable time, the signal should be repeated. Of course, if no reply can be obtained at all the standby diver must be sent in without delay. When the attention signal is answered the diver/attendant passes his signal. He must then ensure that it is answered correctly. If it is not, it must be repeated until it is.

It is NOT necessary to call attention before giving the first three working signals, or the EMERGENCY signal.

All signals should be positive and distinctive with good, long rope travel and should invariably be answered—with the exception of the 'Emergency' signal, which should be acted on immediately. The failure by the diver to answer any other signal should be considered an emergency.

THE STANDBY DIVER:

An experienced diver used to diving as a roped diver in low visibility should be available as a *Standby Diver*. He should be fully equipped, roped up, and ready to enter the water immediately should the diver signal that he is in difficulty. The standby diver should be standing by, not joking with friends, while thinking about kitting up. The diver should not be allowed to enter the water until the standby is ready.

The standby diver should have a good knowledge of what could go wrong and have worked out his procedure for dealing with emergencies. He should also know that if the diver gives the emergency signal he should go down the life-line, so that he is sure of getting straight to the man in difficulties.

A spare breathing set should be kept at hand for a dire emergency when, for instance, a diver may be trapped under water and needs to be kept supplied with air whilst he is being freed.

GENERAL HINTS:

Diving in really low visibilities can be thoroughly unnerving and must not be taken on lightly, or by inexperienced members. The possibilities of the development of claustrophobia are high, and the risk of sudden panic always present. Under-water movement should be slow, deliberate and exploratory.

With growing experience comes the ability to master the grave difficulties, and the technical ability to carry out quite comprehensive surveys and searches by touch alone or by the sight of only small sections of objects and surroundings.

An efficient knife must always be carried in an accessible place, and a torch is essential. It is probable that it will not be possible also to carry a snorkel tube, but it is reasonable to accept the risk of leaving it ashore, especially as the diver is roped, and can be hauled to the boat or bank on his back if exhausted.

Care must be taken to avoid fouling breathing tubes or other equipment on under-water obstructions. If such a thing does occur the diver should keep calm and try and disentangle himself in a slow and deliberate manner. He should always try to back out of such obstructions on the assumption that the way he went in was clear.

A diver surfacing in a confined area, e.g. between boats, pontoons, or other surface obstructions, should always be hauled to the surface so that his surfacing position is controlled by his tender. It is unlikely that this type of diving would be undertaken in depths where decompression stops need to be carried out, but should this be the case the diver should be hauled up at a rate of 15 metres per minute and the necessary decompression stops strictly observed.

The question of whether or not to use a shot-line (see *Underwater Search Methods*) in such conditions, in addition to the diver's life-line, is largely dependent on the type of diving being done. If a definite object is being sought or a particular area being worked on, a semi-permanent mark of this type—or a long-sounding pole—is definitely an asset. It provides a fixed datum point from which to work and saves much time in position fixing.

Divers should not discard their fins for this type of diving although they may be obliged to walk on the bottom rather than fin. The danger of diving without fins lies in the lack of positive control in free water and when on the surface. On the other hand, if work has to be carried out under water for which the diver needs to be heavy in order to achieve a 'purchase' on tools or the like, boots or hard-soled bootees and, perhaps, leg weights, may be employed.

Under-water Search Methods

Diving clubs are sometimes called upon to carry out under-water searches and recovery operations by other water uses, and from time to time by the police and other authorities.

Under-water searches are not difficult, requiring little more than average diving ability; good planning; common sense; and above all, patience and perseverance. Seldom is an under-water search satisfactorily concluded in a short time. If the area of search is large and the object sought small, a thorough search can take many hours of diving. If a Club or a diver is unwilling to do the job well, they should not take it on.

Any under-water search must be 'cost effective'; the cost being that of diver time. The area to be searched must be narrowed down: the search technique must be the one most likely to succeed under the circumstances; and the divers must know exactly what they are searching for.

The areas searched and still to be searched must be known and therefore it is vital that everything is plotted on a chart. The limits of each search sweep should be 'fixed' by position-fixing methods (chapter 8, *Position Fixing*) and the whole operation carefully planned, conducted and controlled.

The Area to be Searched

All too often the person who approaches a diving club requesting them to look for his lost outboard engine—or whatever—claims to know *exactly* where it is lying. And all too often the claim is wrong. Only if accurate 'marks' were taken at the moment of loss can such a position be expected to prove accurate. At best such claimed positions are a good spot to start from.

Among the factors to be considered when narrowing down the search area are:

1. Nature of the object lost. Is is heavy enough to sink immediately and not to be moved by the tide or current? Or is is something which would drift along with the tide before settling on the sea bed? Is it big or small?

2. Which way was the tide/current running at the moment of loss? The 'loser' may not know, but if he can tell you the approximate time of loss you can check back on charts and tide tables to see which way it is likely to have drifted.

3. The most likely position of the object. This will be based on the statement of position given to you, but subject to 1 and 2 above.

Of course, you may not be looking for something small. Perhaps you are looking for a wreck marked on the chart. To find it you have to carry out a search of sorts, but because it is so big, the search technique may differ. The answers may come in the form of transit bearings, given in exchange for pints of ale at the local fishermen's pub! A pleasant search procedure indeed!

Use all the means you can think of to narrow down the area to be searched. Do your homework: don't just flop into the water in the hope of stumbling across the object of the search. Time spent in planning is time saved, and time saved in searching means a satisfied 'customer'; and good publicity for the club.

Search Methods

Because there are so many methods of under-water search, it will be easier to describe them in relation to the size of the object being sought.

For large objects in a large area, such as a wreck, or reef, try the following:

(a) *Local Knowledge:* Ask for transit bearings or sextant angles. Sometimes the positions given on charts *are* accurate enough to put you straight on it.

(b) Searches from large boats using sonar, echo sounders or drag-lines.

(c) *Surface Indications:* Colour changes in the water indicating shallows or weed growth, or 'standing waves' at certain times of tidal flow. Colour changes are often best seen from a height. Is it worth an air search? You could take transits or compass bearings from a light aircraft.

(d) *Swim-line Search:* This is a diving search technique which requires quite a few dives and a lot of practice and perseverance! But, once the technique is mastered, acres of sea-bed can be searched in one sweep and in great detail. The Swimline Search is the subject of a special BSAC Publication—Technical Paper No. 2—'How to find', but will be described briefly.

A light *base-line*, weighted at intervals, is run out at speed from a fast boat which is following a distinct bearing which can be plotted on a chart. This base-line can be thousands of metres in length and is adequately weighted and buoyed at each end. Thus, by horizontal sextant angles (chapter 8, *Position Fixing*) the exact position of the line can be plotted on a chart. The base-line is laid out at speed to keep it straight and tight. If desired, a series of parallel base-lines can be laid out when a large area is to be searched.

A group of divers—up to 20 if they are versed in the skills of this search method—all wearing similar-size aqualungs (this is important) drop down on to the base-line, taking with them a *swim-line* whose length will depend on the number of divers and the visibility through the water. The divers run out the swim-line at right-angles to the base-line and at one end of it so that there are an equal number of divers on each side of the *swim-line controller* who is in the middle, over the base-line (Fig. 82). The distance between each diver is such that there is an overlap in each diver's range of visibility. All divers hold the swim-line in *both hands*.

Once the swim-line is deployed at right-angles to the base-line, the controller gives a 'two bells' signal with both hands to start the swim. Each diver repeats the signal to acknowledge it and to pass it on to the next diver. So the swim-line (let us say it is 50 m long with 10 divers at 5 m intervals) proceeds forward, the controller holding station over the base-line. Each diver scans the sea-bed and if he spots anything which is of interest—scattered wreckage for instance—he stops the line by giving a 'one bell' signal with both hands, which is the 'stop' signal. Again, all divers receive, acknowledge and pass on the stop signal as they receive it. The sighting is investigated and marked (with an SMB which each diver tows, or with small inflatable markers carried by the divers) and when ready to go on again, the 'go' signal is given and the swim-line proceeds.

When divers run low on air (see the need for similar size sets now?) an agreed signal is given to instruct the divers to close to the base-line, and ascend. The controller marks the point on the base-line which the group reached with his SMB. The next party of divers would commence their swim-line search from this point—or ideally, from a point a few metres back to give an overlap.

Once the whole distance of the base-line has been covered, the procedure is repeated on the next parallel base-line. The distance between base-lines should be such that there is an overlap on the sides of the areas searched. Failure to overlap means that some areas have not been searched, and therefore, the whole thing is a waste of time and effort: a search MUST be 100%.

There are variations on the swim-line search method described here. For example, the controller could be on the end of a swim-line while the man at the other end lays another base-line. On reaching the end of the first base-line, the whole group wheels round and goes back on the newly laid base-line, the diver who laid it now acting as controller.

Other variations use the principle in a smaller way—for searching up and down reef faces or sweeping along rivers or canals.

Fig. 82. A SWIMLINE SEARCH

The top illustration shows how divers are deployed along a swimline, which is wound onto a reel secured in the boat's bows.

The search area will have been marked out previously by jackstays suitably weighted and buoyed

For details of this method, consult the BSAC PAPER No. 2, 'HOW TO FIND'

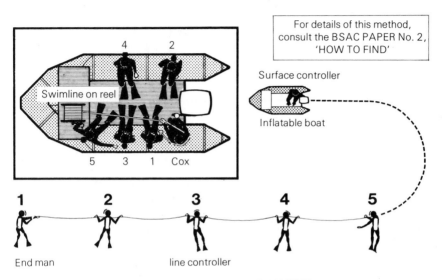

LAYING DIVERS ON THE SWIM-LINE

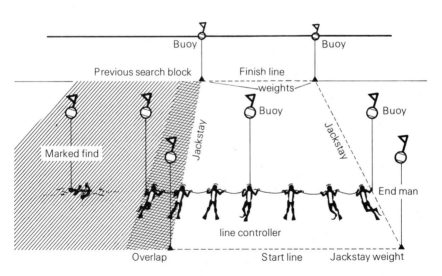

A SWIM-LINE SEARCH SYSTEM

The swimline search may be exploited in several modes; touch, dragline, snagline, or vision.

The important point is to adjust distance between divers to suit the prevailing visibility.

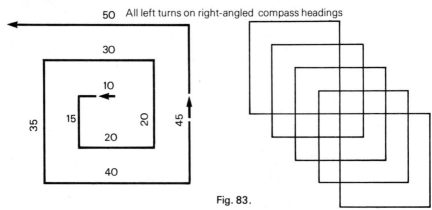

Fig. 83.

A SQUARE SPIRAL SEARCH   AN OVERLAPPING SQUARE SEARCH

The swim-line search is a very effective way of visually search-ing large areas, but requires quite a lot of rope, line, etc., several divers and plenty of practice. The method can be used when searching for relatively small items in a large area.

(e) *Compass Searches:* The section on *Under-water Navigation* ex-plained how a watch and compass can be used to swim square courses. Square courses of this sort can be extended or altered into a 'square spiral' or overlapping squares, thereby covering a large area of sea-bed. Some of the possibilities are illustrated in Fig. 83. The proposed compass course, distances and directions should be pre-plotted, and the start of each search pattern buoyed so that it can be 'fixed' by sextant angles or compass bear-ings, and plotted on the survey chart.

For small objects in small areas, such as an outboard engine, or lost aqualung, the following methods work well.

(f) *Grid or Jackstay Searches:* The Swim-line Search has to some extent superseded grid searches in open water, since the latter require much more in the way of grid ropes laid on the sea-bed. For a detailed search of a small area, however, the grid or jack-stay search has much to commend it.

The area to be searched is marked off by placing a *shot-line* in each corner and linking the corners with a perimeter of ground ropes (Fig. 84).

(*A shot-line is a weighted rope adequately buoyed at the sur-face, and used as a datum line for ascent and descent; as a datum or centre for a search; and as a means of controlling ascent during decompression. The weight on the bottom should be not less than 15 kg, and the float should have a buoyancy of not less than 50 kg.*)

The searching divers can swim along a jackstay—a single rope laid between opposite ends of the square/rectangular area to be searched, which can be moved along after each search sweep— or can follow a compass heading from end to end. On reaching the perimeter rope, they move across by a distance governed by under-water visibility, turn round, and swim back.

If a Grid Search is carried out on a flat sea-bed when looking for a large object, a snag-line search may work. This is clearly explained in Fig. 85.

Permanent grids are sometimes set up on sites where major investigation and excavation are taking place. Archaeological wreck sites are a good example. As finds are uncovered, their position can quickly be related to previous finds. The grid does not have to be ON the sea-bed: often it is easier to have it above the sea-bed, but clearly in visible range of it. Light chain can be used as a jackstay line when searching on undulating sea-bed.

(g) *Circular Searches:* The simplest type of search and one of the easiest to set up (Fig. 86). All that is needed is a shot-line placed in the centre of the area (circle or semi-circle) to be searched. A *distance line* is snap-hooked on to the shot-line just above the sinker weight and the divers swim in a circle, keeping the distance line tight. They should use a conspicuous object to mark the start of each circular sweep: on returning to it, they move in/out by a distance governed by visibility (allow some overlap), replace their marker and go round again. It does not take long to search the area of the entire circle, and it does not really matter whether they radiate outwards from the shot-line or inwards from the end of the distance line.

Rope drag prevents effective Circular Searches if the distance or sweep-line is longer than about 30 m. The sweep-line can also be used as a snag-line if desired. Semicircular sweep searches, made in exactly the same way, can be used when searching off a wall or river/canal bank.

The centre of each circular sweep should be plotted and care taken when covering an area with several circular sweeps, to allow sufficient overlap. Remember, compared with squares, circles do not overlap very well!

When searching a rocky sea-bed or in heavy weed, a grid/jackstay search is more effective. Divers must proceed carefully and methodically to ensure that nothing is missed. Leave no stone or kelp frond unturned!

Searches for very small items are obviously the hardest. Jackstay (or Circular Searches on a flat sea-bed) are the best.

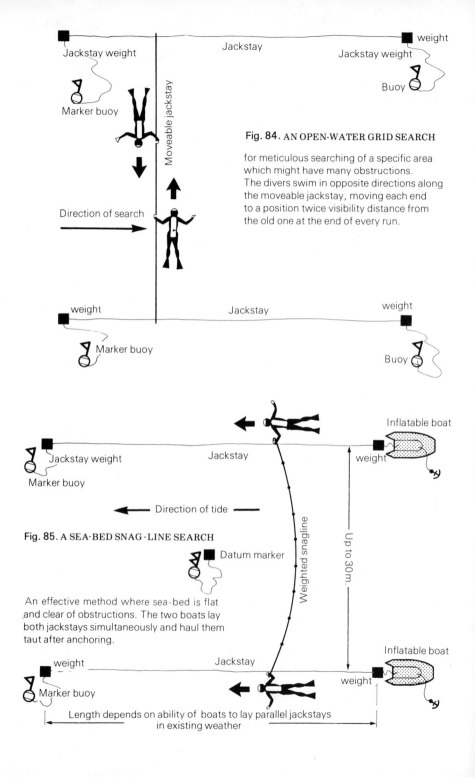

weight

Jackstay weight

Jackstay

Jackstay weight

weight

Buoy

Marker buoy

Moveable jackstay

Fig. 84. AN OPEN-WATER GRID SEARCH

for meticulous searching of a specific area which might have many obstructions. The divers swim in opposite directions along the moveable jackstay, moving each end to a position twice visibility distance from the old one at the end of every run.

Direction of search

weight

Marker buoy

Jackstay

weight

Buoy

Jackstay weight

Marker buoy

Jackstay

weight

Inflatable boat

Direction of tide

Fig. 85. A SEA-BED SNAG-LINE SEARCH

Weighted snagline

Up to 30m.

Datum marker

An effective method where sea-bed is flat and clear of obstructions. The two boats lay both jackstays simultaneously and haul them taut after anchoring.

weight

Marker buoy

Jackstay

weight

Inflatable boat

Length depends on ability of boats to lay parallel jackstays in existing weather

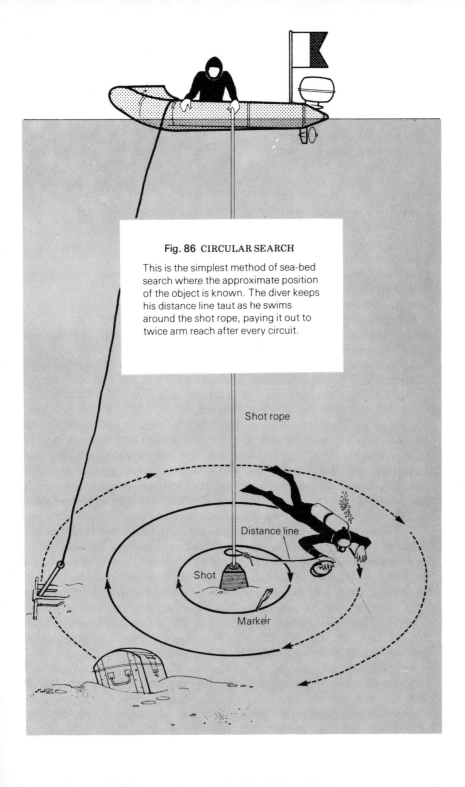

Fig. 86 CIRCULAR SEARCH

This is the simplest method of sea-bed search where the approximate position of the object is known. The diver keeps his distance line taut as he swims around the shot rope, paying it out to twice arm reach after every circuit.

Shot rope

Distance line

Shot

Marker

Deep Diving

What actually is a deep dive? Most divers would say, 'Over the ton' —the mystical 30 m, and this reply would be quite reasonable from the experienced diver. But to a trainee who has not yet been deeper than, say, 15 m, a dive to 25 m is a deep dive and should be approached with a greater degree of caution. The definition must be related to the diver's previous experience and deepest dive. It would be realistic to say that a dive to a depth twice as deep as the diver's previous maximum constitutes for him, if not for the dive leader, a deep dive. But for the diver who regularly frequents the 30 m plus zone, a dive to 50 m—close to the safe limits of air breathing—is much more than just another deep dive, and requires a correspondingly greater level of preparation and control of the dive itself.

However, most divers accept the 30 m mark as the threshold of deep diving, and for the purpose of this chapter we will do the same.

If 30 m is the start of deep diving, what is the safe maximum depth? Taking the advice of the Royal Navy and other learned authorities, it seems wise to accept 50 m as the safe limit for compressed air diving. It is not our intention to establish a Club rule by stating that the sports diver will not exceed this limit: it is hoped that common sense and the acceptance of advice given by such authorities will be enough. It will not be disputed that divers have safely gone deeper on air, and that the Royal Navy use air down to 75 m. What is so frequently overlooked by the eager sports diver is the colossal training, back-up, and surface support facilities employed by such teams—far more than could be provided by a diving club, however anxious they were to do the job properly.

The effects of nitrogen narcosis can be studied elsewhere in this Manual, and will be briefly mentioned later in this section. Nitrogen narcosis is among the great dangers to the deep diver, because it is unpredictable and cannot be controlled. By 50 m almost every air-breathing diver will be affected. Would you choose to perform any skill requiring quick reactions and coordination, and upon which your life depended, while breathing a gas mixture containing an increasing amount of anaesthetic? Of course you wouldn't. Yet when diving beyond 50 m, you would be doing just that!

As a final point in support of a limit of 50 m, a look at Decompression Tables will indicate that a dive to this depth comes so close to the 'No-Stop' limit (q.v.) that anyone doing even a 'bounce dive' would be strongly advised to carry out at least one decompression stop during the ascent. Any dive beyond 50 m must include decompression stops on the return. Stage decompression is not dangerous when it is planned and when provision is made for it; the danger lies in the diver who thinks 'with this set, I should just about make a bounce to 60 m, and there won't be much air left, but I shouldn't need to decompress'. And there are quite a few who do think that way.

Having defined a deep dive and suggested the safe limits that apply to the sports diver, it is necessary to consider some other problems which the deep diver must face and overcome.

Divers quickly discover that water clarity, and the visibility through water, play a very great part in influencing one's enjoyment of the dive. Clear water means a good dive: dark water means greater care and less enjoyment (though there may be more satisfaction in having overcome the problem). The deeper the diver goes, the more important it is for his safety that there should be adequate illumination. Those fortunate enough to dive regularly in more tropical waters or clear off-shore seas will find themselves facing fewer problems than their counterparts diving in deep, dark inland lakes and quarries (at least there seem to be fewer problems). Water temperature affects the diver in much the same way: the warmer it is, the fewer the problems. This theme will be developed later in the chapter.

What are the problems of deep diving? They can be broken down into four headings, each of which will be expanded upon later:
1. Psychological.
2. Physiological.
3. Physical.
4. Response and behaviour in an emergency.

It is the writer's opinion that psychological problems are reduced progressively as water clarity and temperature increase, though by no means to their total elimination. The other three are always present in any diving situation regardless of depth, but are often accentuated by an increase in depth.

1. PSYCHOLOGICAL PROBLEMS:
For anyone who has the slightest tendency to claustrophobia (this should have shown up by now in diver training!) the thought of all that water between himself and the surface, however clear it may be, is enough to bring on a state of mental concern. The true claustrophobe would not even get that far, but the most level-headed diver should not forget the fact that there is a lot of water. By the time the 30 m level is reached, few divers are likely to admit to feeling no degree of apprehension. The diver's mental concern for his well-being will be considerably increased if the water is dark and cold and if no tangible datum, such as a shot-line or the sea-bed, is visible.

Adding to this state of psychological stress may be a number of other factors—negative buoyancy, diminishing air supply, increased breathing resistance if faulty equipment is being used, and others which will be mentioned shortly. All these factors prey on the diver's mind to bring him close to the 'panic threshold', when he is a liability to both himself and his partner. In his state of mental stress, he might precipitate an incident, or react to one in such a way as to aggravate it. Apprehension—fear, if you prefer—can induce the onset of nitrogen narcosis. This is proven fact.

In the conduct of deeper dives (and of those not so deep) it is of vital importance, therefore, that every effort is made to eliminate or overcome all the stresses that might cause the diver to become apprehensive. The diver's training and experience should lead him steadily and safely to deep diving. To be launched into a 30 m plus dive after only two or three open-water dives would—in 99 out of 100 cases—be recklessness on the part of the dive leader. The diver should indulge in a series of 'work up' dives, each deeper than the previous one until the maximum depth is reached. This applies equally to the experienced diver who has not dived deep for some time. The number of 'work up' dives may vary according to the diving conditions—the diver in the tropics might progress from 20 m to 50 m in perhaps four dives, whereas the diver frequenting a cold dark quarry may need twice as many dives to reach the maximum depth in a relaxed mental state. The provision of a datum for the descent and ascent is to be recommended where a natural datum is not available. A shot-line, adequately weighted and very adequately buoyed (50 kg buoyancy minimum), should be used. This shot-line will help, not only by providing an up/down datum, but in overcoming initial buoyancy if weighted for depth; for the control of ascents; and to control decompression stops if they are to be made.

Sound training with regular practice of safety drills will help to ensure that the diver responds correctly in emergencies, and will help him to push back his own panic threshold.

2. PHYSIOLOGICAL PROBLEMS:

To the layman, the idea that the diver's body is subjected to an overall pressure of several tons when under water may be dramatic, but we know that the healthy diver is well able to withstand this pressure. However, in any diving situation, and particularly in deep diving, physical activity calls for a greater level of effort by body tissues which are already exerting themselves in their adaptation to increased ambient pressure. The diver must be fit, with a high level of exercise tolerance. But fitness is not just being able to run a mile in four minutes, or to do 50 press-ups. A fair degree of that sort of fitness is desirable, but the word is used to imply that the diver should be well-nourished and well-rested before the dive. Outside anxieties, weariness after a long drive to the dive site, a late night last night, recovering from a good party—each of these things is enough on its own, let alone combined, to render the diver 'unfit to dive'. To allow him to dive is putting an unnecessary load on his companions—more for them to worry about.

The section on nitrogen narcosis in this Manual clearly presents the causes and nature of the condition. Its effects upon individual members of a diving party are in no way predictable or consistent. Apprehension, fatigue and prior consumption of alcohol all speed up the onset of narcosis. Unless you dive deep regularly with the same buddy, there is no way of knowing how he will behave when at depth, or in an emergency.

Those responsible for leading deep dives should also take the students on their work-up dives—50 m is no place to get to know your new diving partner.

To the sports diver, the greatest practical danger of nitrogen narcosis is that of confusion: diver A acts in a manner which appears odd to diver B; B goes to assist A thinking that A is narcotised; A is thus provoked into thinking that B is under the influence . . . and so on, perhaps leading to an incident.

Confusion is close at hand, especially in cold dark water. Strict discipline, clear signals and adherence to an agreed dive plan are essential, even with groups who dive together regularly. It should always be realised that, while the narcotic effects of nitrogen disappear on the return to the surface, there is no guarantee that the narcotised diver will be able to make the ascent!

Nitrogen absorption is another fact of life, as far as the diver is concerned. Anyone who ventures beyond the 10 m level is exposing himself to a level of nitrogen absorption which, depending on the duration of his stay at pressure, may lead to decompression sickness (q.v.). Anyone contemplating deep dives beyond the 30 m mark MUST understand the problems of decompression and the conditions imposed by the Decompression Tables (see chapter 2 and Appendix 1). All divers should commit to memory the simple table of 'No-Stop Limits' for 20, 30, 40 and 50 m. Plotted on a graph, the 'No-Stop' curve appears to be quite a fine line. Experience shows, however, that it should be considered as a broad, woolly line. Any diver who comes close to the limit is advised to carry out a decompression stop for good measure: overstepping the line will definitely mean stops during the ascent. The fact that you have 'got away with it before' is no excuse for avoiding stops where they are indicated. It has been proved, beyond doubt, that decompression sickness is inconsistent. Why risk disablement for the sake of a few minutes doing stops?

N

There is nothing wrong with carrying out dives that necessitate decompression stops, as long as this was planned and provided for, and that the divers are clearly aware of the correct decompression procedure. But remember that it is quite easy to exceed the total 'No-Stop' marking time when repeat dives are made. One word of advice in this context: do not allow the total bottom time to exceed the limiting line shown in the Decompression Tables. This can be looked upon as a barrier between a reasonable and an unreasonable risk—for all decompression procedures involve some degree of risk. Without surface support facilities which include an adequate recompression chamber, to exceed the limiting line is most unwise.

It will be said again that when more than one dive is being carried out during a day's diving, the total dive time can rapidly tot up to exceed the 'No-Stop Limits'. This is the greatest danger of 'Repeat Dives' (q.v.). Observe the RNPL recommendations shown (Appendix 1) leaving a six-hour interval between dives if you can. Do the deep dive first, so that subsequent shallow dives are simply extended decompression for the first dive.

To avoid overstaying 'No-Stop' times, or to control decompression procedures, an accurate depth gauge and watch are essential. (When did you last check the accuracy of your depth gauge? Accidental dropping of a depth gauge could easily render it unreliable. We spend much time stressing that *bottom times* are important, but suppose your gauge is reading shallower than it should? Compare it with your buddy's gauge on the next dive, or in a recompression chamber—you might be alarmed at the discrepancy!)

Decompression meters are helpful, but are in no way consistent in their performance. Total reliance should never be placed upon them. They have their uses in variable bottom profile dives when they can be looked upon as a useful 'come up now' indicator.

An accurate record of dive times and depths should be kept for all dives. Knowing the whereabouts of the nearest operational recompression chamber and the quickest means of getting to it is a must.

The dangers of oxygen and carbon dioxide poisoning are virtually non-existent to the diver who does not go deeper than 50 m and who uses good equipment.

3. PHYSICAL PROBLEMS:

The most obvious physical problem of deeper diving is the loss of buoyancy of the diving suit due to compression. All types of suit are affected in this way. Dry suits, whether of traditional manufacture or the modern expanded neoprene type, are provided with means of inflation to overcome loss of buoyancy. Wet-suited divers may choose to partially inflate an ABLJ or other buoyancy aid to compensate for their apparent increase in weight. On the ascent, however, this air, whether in the suit or the ABLJ, will have to be vented off to prevent too rapid a return to the surface and the attendant problems after prolonged dives at depth.

Perhaps then, the best thing is to weight oneself for neutral buoyancy at working depth, and to use a shot-line to control descent and ascent. However, neutral buoyancy at depth presents problems near the surface should it be necessary to be free of shot-lines or the like. But if neutrally buoyant at the surface, the diver could be as much as 8 kg over-weight at 50 m from loss of wet-suit buoyancy; that is a lot of unnecessary weight (at that depth) and, unless the diver is pretty fit, there is a real risk that he might not be able to lift it. Furthermore, this excessive weight is going to prevent the diver from swimming normally through the water; he will be either walking or on hands and knees!

All points considered, the best advice would seem to be to ballast for neutral buoyancy at depth, and use a shot-line to assist and control the descent and ascent; OR have a means of suit inflation when using any type of dry suit, and use an ABLJ or buoyancy aid with 'direct feed' from the aqualung if diving with a wet suit—direct feed is preferred, since it leaves untapped the air in the emergency cylinder. Experience with either type of inflation system is essential before use on a deep dive. Orally inflating an ABLJ under water is acceptable for the diver who has mastered the technique, but the use of a direct-feed system is safer.

A close second to buoyancy problems is loss of insulation at depth. Deep water is always colder than shallow water, and frequently the deep-water temperature of fresh-water lakes and quarries is almost constant throughout the year. Add to this the fact that all wet suits and many dry suits are made of foam neoprene which loses its insulation when compressed, and cold becomes a major problem. Of course the dry-suited diver can wear extra undergarments, and with air inflation of the suit, can remain comfortable for hours at a time, so it is the wet-suited diver who suffers most. The only way to reduce the heat loss is, firstly, to have a well-fitting suit, and secondly, to wear extras such as an undervest, double hood, gloves and the like. Experience suggests that several thin layers are better than one thick one.

It is essential that the diver is himself warm within his suit before embarking on a deep dive or any dive in cold water. If he is not, there is almost no chance of becoming warm once the dive starts. Warm water may be poured into the suit when the diver has kitted-up, and this does help.

As depth, and therefore pressure, increases, so does the density or 'thickness' of the air breathed. The result is that at great depth noticeable effort has to be put into the normally relaxed cycle of respiration. Experiments in pressure chambers have revealed that at 4 bars pressure—equal to 30 m, the subject's maximum breathing capacity was reduced by 50%! Thus, the working diver, or the diver attempting to cope with an emergency, is, in effect, increasingly deprived of air as he goes deeper. Not a healthy state of affairs! Add to this the limitations of air flow through inferior or ill-maintained aqualung equipment . . . the moral is obvious.

The effects of contaminants in the air breathed will also increase with depth. Increasing total pressure will increase the partial pressure of any individual gas in the breathing mixture, proportionally enhancing its toxic effect. For instance, a cylinder containing 1% CO_2 would cause little bother if breathed at the surface: if breathed at 50 m it would rapidly cause distress, the effect on the diver being that of breathing 6% CO_2 at the surface.

Most insidious of all is carbon monoxide. An excess could, under the pressure of a deep dive, reduce the oxygen-carrying capacity of the blood haemoglobin to a dangerous level. While under pressure, sufficient oxygen is carried in solution to meet tissue requirements, but as pressure falls during the ascent, and if CO has poisoned the haemoglobin, there might come a time when there was insufficient oxygen in solution to support consciousness. The Coroner would report 'death by drowning', but in reality it would be by CO poisoning.

Diving in cold, deep water increases the effort required to breathe and the body's metabolic rate to such a degree that energy is used up at a massive rate. The term *Deep-Water Fatigue* has been coined, and sums up the situation very well. Deep diving is physically exhausting, and a fair degree of fitness is needed to meet the demands.

4. RESPONSE AND BEHAVIOUR IN EMERGENCIES:

Any emergency is serious: an emergency at depth is really something to contend with. At depth the ability to act swiftly and correctly is likely to be hampered by many of the points previously mentioned—cold, narcosis, breathing effort, over-weight, darkness, and so on. The deeper you are, the more extreme are the problems. Only the individual will know if he is ready to meet them.

At the risk of appearing repetitive, it must again be stressed that the only way to ensure that you, the diver, can cope in the event of some emergency at depth is through sound instruction and progressive experience. Practice and mastery of all safety drills in varied conditions and depths is vital. Divers should be practised at assisted ascent, and should know the procedure for free ascent.

Those who act as dive leaders for 30 m+ dives should be able to perform a rescue from depth. The BSAC Deep Rescue Test is by no means as easy as it might at first appear, but is well within the capability of the fit and practising deep diver. Your Coach will be pleased to assist you in gaining this award. But having gained the award, keep in practice with the rescue procedure.

So much for the problems: what about the pleasures of deep diving? These are the same thrills of exploration of an unknown world which all divers know, whether for wrecks, for the study of flora and fauna, or just spectacular scenery. Perhaps there is little enjoyment in stumbling, cold and over-weight, down the slopes of some dark flooded quarry on an ill-planned deep dive with panic only seconds away. However, the writer suggests that much of the fun of deep diving stems from the knowledge that, while you have tipped the scales in your favour by careful management, you are still challenging the unknown and exposing yourself to a degree of risk— which is what the sport is all about, isn't it?

The Conduct of Deep Dives

Having read this far, it is hoped that the reader will accept that deep diving DOES involve factors which do not face the diver in shallower waters. The planning and conduct of deep dives DOES need a greater degree of care and forethought. Since the risks of decompression sickness are perhaps the greatest problems facing the deep diver, it is of paramount importance that he should know exactly what these problems are, and how to avoid them by careful use of Tables. Dives should be planned and conducted within the scope of this knowledge.

It is not possible to draw up rules for deep diving because there are so many variables. However, certain principles of safe deep-diving practice can be suggested, and these are tabulated below:

1. All divers in a deep-diving party should be very fit, well-rested and free from external anxieties. They should hold a current medical certificate gained during the past twelve months.

2. All divers in a deep-diving party should be in deep-diving practice, gained by a series of progressively deeper work-up dives made during days preceding the deep dive.

3. There should be not less than four divers in a deep-dive group, on the other hand the party should not be so large as to be unmanageable.

4. Ideally, the Dive Marshal should be experienced in diving to the target depth. His appointment and authority should not be questioned by members of the diving team.

5. Avoid unnecessary 'hangers on'. Their presence is likely to impede and distract attention from the running of the operation.

6. The whereabouts of the nearest telephone and of recompression facilities should be determined in advance. Means of getting to the chamber in the event of an emergency must be considered; a car and driver (not one of the diving team) should be available.

7. Access to water: inland lakes and quarries or shore dive. Avoid sites which require an unduly arduous trek with heavy equipment to the point of entry. (Where this is unavoidable, rest before starting the dive.) Consider safety of access to and from the water, and suitability in the event of an emergency.

8. Access to water: open sea. Use an adequate boat, or a group of boats. All divers operating from one large boat is the best plan, but a party of, say six divers, could carry out a deep dive at sea from two or more inflatables. Each boat should be manned by a competent boatman who is not one of the diving team, and equipment should include means of contacting the shore base in the event of emergency.

9. The use of a shot-line is strongly recommended. It should be heavily weighted (15 kg) so that it will not be affected by tidal flow, and very adequately buoyed (50 kg minimum) so that it is capable of supporting the divers as they pull themselves to the surface.

10. If divers are to leave the shot-line, distance-lines or lines previously laid on the bottom should be followed. Where the use of shot- and distance-lines is impracticable, diving pairs should use buddy lines as well as a line attached to a Surface Marker Buoy.

11. In open-sea deep diving, great care should be taken in predicting tidal information accurately. Every effort should be made to be on-site ready to go before slack water; and to use tides to the best advantage.

12. One member of each diving party should be appointed as dive leader. The size of the party will largely depend on visibility: a pair of divers is the ideal, but in perfect conditions a group of four could be considered.

13. Standby divers should be available. While the second party can act as standby for the first, there will come a time when the final party require cover. The standby diver(s) should be experienced and used to diving to the target depth. They will have to accept that they will not be taking part in the deep dive that day except in an emergency: in fact they may not be able to dive at all. However, their presence is essential for safety, and it is hoped that the responsibility will be accepted willingly. Spare aqualung sets should be available.

14. All divers should wear ABLJ's and be fully trained in their use. All divers must wear a reliable depth gauge and watch: aqualungs should be fitted with contents gauges or a proven reserve system. All equipment should be in tip-top order. Air should be as pure as possible.

15. A thorough pre-dive briefing is essential: all divers should know the tasks they are to carry out on the bottom and any special action to be taken in emergencies. If the dive duration is to be strictly limited, all divers should know how long they are to be down; and any necessary decompression stops should be determined in advance and noted on an under-water slate. Where no dive duration is planned, a Decompression Table Slate must be carried.

16. The descent should be made by swimming or by means of the shot-line. Never use excess weight to speed the descent. Adjust for neutral buoyancy at depth, OR be prepared to compensate by ABLJ/suit inflation.

17. During the dive, stick closely to the dive plan. Keep a careful watch on elapsed time and cylinder contents; clear signals are vital.

18. Ascent should be made at a rate of 15 m/minute (the speed of small bubbles) to the first decompression stop, the divers keeping together at all times. Decompression should be carried out under relaxed conditions, and a shot-line is a great help at this stage of the operation. A spare breathing set should be provided at the depth (or deeper) of the first stop. Do not skimp on stops—ever.

19. Once the divers are ashore or aboard the boats, they should be de-kitted, changed and de-briefed. Make them comfortable and attend to creature comforts.

20. Any pain, discomfort or abnormality experienced by a diver after the event should be treated as decompression sickness. Do not delay in seeking recompression treatment—minor symptoms frequently develop into serious symptoms. If in doubt, recompress.

21. Remember that you dive for the enjoyment of it, so safety comes first. If things appear to be going wrong, abandon the dive.

Summary 1

THE PROBLEMS:

1. The greatest problem is within the mind of the diver! If you feel ill at ease, don't dive, or abandon the dive.
2. Nitrogen narcosis is an unavoidable condition. Stay above 50 m to avoid a dangerous degree of narcosis.
3. Every diver exposes himself to the risk of Decompression Sickness when diving below 9 m. Know the condition and the means of avoiding it.
4. Loss of buoyancy and insulation at depth require much thought; air density and purity also pose problems.
5. Deep diving is physically demanding. Be fit and fresh.
6. Sound training and regular practice at safety drills will help to overcome potential emergencies.

Summary 2

SOME SUGGESTIONS FOR SAFE AND ENJOYABLE DEEP DIVING:

1. Adopt the depth limit of 50 m. All things considered, is it really worth going deeper?
2. Deep diving IS something to get 'worked up' about!
3. Be fit, fresh and well-equipped; and master all the safety drills.
4. Reduce or eliminate problems by careful planning and conduct of deep dives.
5. For absolute safety, stay within the 'No-Stop Limits'; and if you do come close to them, make a precautionary five-minute stop at 5 m anyway.
6. Repeat dives quickly take you close to, or beyond, the 'No-Stop Limit'. Adhere to the recommendations shown in Appendix 1.
7. If, by accident or intent, you have to carry out decompression stops, do them thoroughly. Ensure that there is an adequate shot-line, and that reserve sets are placed *below* the level of the deepest stop.
8. Do not allow total bottom time to exceed the Limiting Line.

Night Diving

To the uninitiated it probably seems incredible that divers should wish to submerge themselves in an inky black sea at the dead of night. However, to those who have tasted the fruits of this facet of our sport, night diving presents a fascinating opportunity to observe the under-water world anew.

To the observant diver, the night-time scene is filled with activity, a number of normally timid creatures being mesmerised by the beam of torchlight. Crustacea and molluscs of all types are out and about searching for food and not holed-up as they are normally found during daylight hours. Also out of its daytime home is one of their predators, the conger, as well as many more creatures usually difficult to observe. To this scene the diver himself introduces a new dimension, that of colour.

The light found under water during the daytime is unnatural to our eyes in that most of the visible spectrum has been filtered out and we are left with a predominantly blue-green illumination which distorts our conception of the colour of under-water objects (see chapter 1, *Physics*). By introducing artificial light at close range, the diver can illuminate the under-water scene with a full spectrum and in this way reveal the riot of colour that truly exists: weeds and sponges which appear black by daylight are now bright scarlet, deep purple etc. Contrast and shadows are restored and the shape of objects can be seen more readily in the directional beam of light.

The diffuse daylight normally encountered hinders the recognition of objects, because of the lack of contrast and *directionality*, but the complete colour spectrum of the artificial light is a boon to the under-water photographer. The full benefit of colour film can now be exploited with the subject standing out clearly against a black background instead of framed in the normal luminescent blue-green water.

As with any form of sport, night diving is pointless in poor visibility conditions, but the visibility encountered at night can seem better than similar conditions by day. This is due to the limited range of the torch which causes the diver to study objects at a much closer range than usual (a similar apparent increase in visibility is experienced when diving under kelp).

If the diver turns off his torch for a while he will be surprised at just how much natural light exists under water. Apart from moonlight and starlight which will filter through from the surface, the diver can see many plants glowing quite strongly—once his eyes have become dark-adapted—and his every movement is accompanied by what appears to be a shower of sparks, in reality, phosphorescent-plankton giving off a bright luminous glow when agitated.

In short, night diving under good conditions can provide some of the most fascinating experiences in a diver's career. On the other hand, diving at night without adequate preparation and organisation and in conditions that are far from ideal can, in common with other forms of diving, turn out to be a nerve-racking and extremely hazardous undertaking.

Let us now consider the problems that are pertinent to night diving and how they can be overcome. On his first night dive, the diver will be under some psychological stress—anxiety of the unknown, the dark, and any other potential fears may well be at a peak as he enters the water, but if we can instil some well-founded confidence into this diver such anxieties will be minimised. He should be confident in his own, and his buddy's, ability, their equipment, and in the dive organisation. He must therefore have a fair amount of diving experience behind him, his buddy should have some previous experience of night diving, and the dive organisation must be meticulous.

It is becoming increasingly popular with Branches to incorporate a beach barbecue with a night dive, so let us study this type of occasion in some detail—one on which a number of divers would be in the water at the same time, so that they could all enjoy the hot food and a bonfire after the dive. The quality of this dive, in common with any large dive, would be in proportion to the organisation and prior preparation which had been put into it.

The chief hazard on a group night dive is that of a diver who might become separated from the main party and be swept out to sea —with no means of attracting attention. If this should happen, rescue would be very unlikely until the following morning, by which time the diver would reckon himself lucky to be alive. It is clear therefore that the organisation must, at all costs, prevent this type of situation occurring.

The Dive Marshal should choose his site very carefully: it should be well known to him under normal daylight diving conditions so that he can predict the type of bottom to be expected, and the currents, if any, that will be encountered. The water should be sheltered, preferably by a headland or reef, and the boundaries of the diving site should be clearly defined. Natural boundaries should, where they exist, be utilised and linked up with artificial boundaries in the form of under-water guide lines, and should also be buoyed so that it may be clearly identified by the surface cover. All diving should take place within this designated area, which may vary in size according to the natural conditions, the resources available and the number of divers being catered for, but must not exceed that which can be kept under constant surveillance.

The site of the barbecue bonfire is worth considering at this stage as it can be a useful homing beacon for the returning divers as well as possibly providing some illumination for the surface cover.

Divers should be paired off with buddy-lines of some 2–3 m in length; this minimises the danger of separation and aids communication between them. Each diver MUST have a torch and should be instructed that if one torch fails the pair should terminate the dive immediately, for if the second torch should fail the divers would have great difficulty in attracting the attention of the surface cover.

A careful pre-dive briefing should be given to ensure that the divers understand how the dive area has been defined and that they do not wander out of it. They should be logged in and out of the water by a member of the shore party so that the marshal knows immediately if anyone is overdue. Diver recall, if necessary, can be achieved by means of a weighted thunderflash or a bell struck under water.

Surface cover should be provided in the form of a boat (a 4–5 m inflatable is preferable) either anchored near to the down-tide marker buoy or rowed along the down-tide base line. The boat's motor should only be used in case of an emergency as the crew would have difficulty in hearing a call for assistance above the noise of the engine, and the revolving propeller would be very dangerous so close to the diving site. The divers may either snorkel to the dive area or be ferried there by boats other than the rescue boat mentioned above. If divers are ferried to the site they must be logged in and out of the water by a marshal who remains in a boat at the dive site throughout the operations. Only in this way can an account be kept on all the divers.

Divers in open boats should be discouraged from using their torches until they enter the water. In this way the eyesight of both the divers and particularly the boatman can become adapted to the darkness. Once their eyes have become accustomed to the low light level it is usually possible to see well enough to kit up and enter the water safely. If there is insufficient light for adequate pre-dive checks etc., a low intensity lamp should be rigged as high as possible shining down into the boat. What must be avoided is a number of divers each waving their torch about as they kit-up, etc. In this way everyone ends up dazzled and unable to see anything clearly for several minutes, just at the critical time when the divers are due to enter the water.

Diver to diver and diver to surface party signals should be agreed between the divers and their boat cover. Recommended Lamp Signals are given in the section *Signals and Communications*. Unnecessary torch waving on the surface should be discouraged. Under-water signals can be made in the normal way providing the diver shines his torch on to HIS OWN signal and not into his partner's face! This is a common fault and, of course, merely dazzles the partner who will be unable to see any signal for some considerable time afterwards.

Depths greater than 10–15 m would not be expected at the type of enclosed site described, but it is possible to dive to greater depths if a vertical cliff face is used as the dive area and guide-lines are run vertically down the cliff to define the horizontal limits of the site. This type of site usually provides very interesting diving and, given calm conditions, is relatively easy to monitor on the surface. However, the problems of deep diving (see previous section) must be avoided: a rescue from depth at night would prove extremely difficult and have little chance of success. Although suitable cliff sites do exist in a number of places around the British Isles, shelter from a sea swell is a prime requisite, and milder seas, e.g. the Mediterranean etc., would be preferable for this type of site.

Diving at night attached to a surface marker buoy is a further possibility, but only a very limited number of divers can be catered for as the hazards are greatly increased. This form of night diving is not recommended except in conditions of very low current since the range of vision is severely limited at night and the divers would see very little if they were continually moving.

The divers should be attached to a normal SMB, the cover boat also being firmly attached to the buoy with an extended painter. In this way the divers can drift in their desired direction and the boat can follow the buoy without the possibility of becoming separated from it. The boat should be rowed after the buoy or trouble will certainly be experienced with fouling the propeller on the long painter. Diver recall is easily accomplished, but is more likely to be required with this type of dive due to boat traffic.

If there are other vessels in the vicinity, the surface boat should carry recognition lights to warn them not to approach too close. These comprise two red lights in a vertical line with a white light between them. In very sheltered sites, a single white light displayed by the boat would suffice.

Drift diving at night is less likely to be as rewarding as a free dive in an enclosed area and carries a much greater risk if separation should occur. It is therefore not recommended except in exceptional circumstances.

As previously stated, each diver on a night dive must carry a torch; apart from the safety aspect he will derive little satisfaction from looking at areas illuminated by his buddy's torch—much like two people trying to read a book simultaneously. The range of a diver's vision is obviously linked to the power of the lamp he is using as well as to the prevailing visibility and, generally, the more powerful the lamp the better the diver is able to see. However, there is a limit to the power available to a free diver, unless he resorts to surface supply lines or under-water vehicles—this is around 50 watts, with about an hour's duration; anything more than this tends to be rather bulky and VERY expensive.

To conclude, a well-organised night dive on a calm and warm summer's night—with the promise of hot drinks and a large bonfire on shore afterwards—can be the ultimate in diving experiences! However, there are many snags, which, if not taken care of before the event, could mar the proceedings and even have tragic consequences. It is essential, therefore, that night dives be organised by experienced marshals on the lines explained above, and novices should gain confidence and experience with a number of day-time dives before attempting this fascinating aspect of our sport.

Suggested Form of Boundary Marker/Guide-line

The following pattern has been proved over a number of years and consists of a reel containing about 200 m of 8 mm diameter white polypropylene line, weighted at 2 m intervals with a piece of sheet lead wrapped around the line. At points midway between the weights, wooden floats about 5 cm long and 2 cm diameter covered with reflecting 'Scotch tape' are attached. The weighted line thus lays along the sea floor in a series of loops and is clearly marked by the reflection from the floats. In relatively open terrain it is impossible to miss this form of boundary marker if the divers stay on the bottom. If coloured reflector tape is used on the floats the divers can be made aware of their position within the marked area. This form of marker is of little use however in heavily weeded areas, e.g. kelp forests—this type of terrain is best avoided unless natural boundaries exist to prevent divers from wandering out of the designated area.

Diving Under Ice

Diving under ice is an unusual experience that offers the diver additional challenges, particularly in the sphere of dive organisation. In common with night diving, diving under ice needs more than the usual amount of pre-dive planning, since a diver lost under the ice has, literally, only minutes to live if not found.

Because of the risks inherent in such diving, sports divers should only undertake ice dives in the safest possible conditions—where the ice is a single, solid, stationary sheet. Such ice either occurs on lakes or in the sea with shore-fast ice.

Diving under dynamic ice fields of the sort found in the Arctic is more hazardous because of the danger from moving ice and the problem of keeping the entry or exit hole open. Such dives should only be contemplated when there is a definite need and never for sport.

Diving under loose pack ice floes can be undertaken without safety lines provided that an *accurate* assessment of ice and weather conditions can be made, but remember that a change in wind speed and direction can produce a very rapid change in ice packing.

Cold is always potentially dangerous and it is essential that appropriate protective clothing for both divers and surface support parties be used. Before commencing the dive the divers must be kept warm—a warmed vehicle or even a tent can be used for this purpose, and well-fitting (6 mm) cold-water wet suits or dry suits are needed. Using attendants to put on cylinders, fins, etc. also helps to prevent diver cooling. The surface team should consist of at least two experienced divers, plus a fully kitted-up standby diver. For the safety of the surface team, remember to check the strength of the ice carefully and, as an additional safety precaution, they should also wear lifejackets.

A reliable demand valve is a necessity; extreme cold can cause freezing-up of demand valves, and this generally results in a free-flow of air which, although not generally critical, necessitates the termination of the dive. Experience has shown that twin-hose valves are less likely to suffer from such freezing. However, it is possible to get a protective rubber cap for some single-hose models. This cap is filled with alcohol and may help to prevent first stage freeze-ups. To minimise the likelihood of freezing, the diver should ensure that his demand valve does not get wet when exposed to the cold surface conditions prior to his submerging.

The demand valve should be fitted with a contents gauge, and as an added safety feature a 'pony' cylinder a (a separate cylinder with a separate demand valve) can be used.

Before starting the dive, a hole should be cut in the ice as near to the site of diving as possible and the piece of ice slid under the ice edge. This hole should be sufficiently wide to allow two divers to surface or enter simultaneously (a width of about 2 m); remember that tools must be available to cut this and any other holes that might be necessary. Augers and ice axes are a likely choice of tools, although special power tools can be obtained for thick ice. Test the items 'on site' before the dive commences. For added safety, the site of the hole itself can be marked in a variety of ways: if the ice is covered with snow, an 'X' can be scored into the snow, with the hole at the centre; a brightly coloured bucket weighted with stones can be hung down from the dive hole to a depth of, say, 5 m as an effective marker (the depth depending on the planned depth of the dive and on the under-water visibility—generally good under ice). The holes can also be marked with lights.

When all diving is finished for the day, if possible the original piece of ice should be put back into the hole, and in any case, the hole should be clearly marked. This marking is for the safety of other persons who may be on the same patch of ice at a later date, as the new ice which re-covers the hole will be comparatively unsafe for some time.

The main emphasis on the procedure for ice diving should be on minimising the possibility of getting lost. Diving should, as usual, be in pairs, with each diver having a life-line attached to him and tended by a member of the experienced surface team (some divers use one line and a buddy-line—this is not recommended for, if the line were to be lost one could lose two divers instead of one). Careful tending is essential; a taut line should be maintained and regular signals should be exchanged between tender and diver.

Preferably, the line should be brightly coloured and buoyant, such as polypropylene. The secure attachment of this line to the diver is *essential*. It should encircle the chest, *under* all equipment, and be secured with a bowline knot (remember that polypropylene knots have a tendency to slip). Only a short length of line should be paid out to the diver, preferably not more than some 15 m; the free end should be secured.

There should never be more than two divers down one hole at any one time because of the risk of tangled lines, and if at all possible, the divers should remain within sight of the entry hole.

If a diver does get lost by losing his line in some way, an *established* rescue plan must be followed *in detail*. To avoid panic, a diver must know that he can depend on his colleagues to follow the rescue plan exactly. To ensure familiarity with the rescue procedure it should be practised under controlled conditions, each diver having experience of each position, i.e. tender, lost diver, buddy and stand-by diver.

The rescue procedure is outlined as follows:

1. The lost diver 'surfaces' immediately and remains stationary beneath the ice, perhaps helping himself to keep in position by driving his knife into the ice above and holding on to it, if the ice is firm enough to allow this. If at all possible the diver should penetrate the ice with his knife so that he will be able to use his snorkel (this is rarely possible in the colder parts of the world because the ice is invariably too thick, and may be covered by a deep layer of snow, but it should be noted that special pneumatic tools can be obtained for under-water use to be run off the compressed air from a cylinder).

2. The buddy returns to the entry/exit hole *immediately* to raise the alarm. He does not attempt to locate the diver other than by scanning around as he returns directly to the hole. On arrival at the surface he describes the general direction of his return to the standby diver.

3. The standby diver enters the water with a line attached to him that is *twice the length* of the diving lines originally used. He swims out under the surface of the ice to the extent of his line, and begins a rapid circular sweep search. If possible, the under-surface of the ice at the starting point of the sweep should be marked (perhaps by a spike). Remember that the under-surface of the ice can be very irregular and this may cause difficulties with the sweep.

4. When the line crosses him the lost diver should take hold of it and swim in either direction, thereby finding the surface exit or the standby diver.

5. After one revolution, the standby diver returns to the hole, after which a second revolution or a sweep on the bottom can be tried. If this fails, other methods of attracting a lost diver should be employed, i.e. under-water flares suspended on a line through the hole; hammering on the ice by the hole to attract the diver by sound. However, if the first sweep fails, a highly organised body search is usually the next step!

Remember that the standby diver is doing a solo dive and is himself vulnerable, and should not therefore be allowed to remain in the water for too long.

Training for ice diving is essential to ensure that a diver will not get lost. A rescue procedure must be available and should be practised. Having said this, let the author say that ice diving is an exciting experience and is well worth the effort if carried out with careful planning.

Diving in the Tropics

The tropical marine environment is characterised by mean sea temperatures of 28–30°C, and by the occurrence of coral reefs in generally clear water. Diving here is a little different from diving in the so-called Temperate Zone; on the whole, conditions are much more pleasant and diving easier.

The principal and obvious difference between the tropics and the rest of the world is that the sun is a good deal hotter! Even a few minutes of exposure can cause painful sunburn in a fair-skinned person, which can prevent him from wearing diving equipment for several days. So limit your daily exposure to the sun and increase it only gradually. Remember too that the damaging ultra-violet rays are absorbed in the passage of sunlight through the atmosphere, so that morning and evening sunshine is less potent than that of the midday sun. Protect your body with clothes or with a sun-tan lotion, but make sure that the lotion contains an ultra-violet-absorbing substance; some of the creams and oils that people commonly apply to themselves may make the skin feel better, but do nothing to prevent sunburn.

When snorkelling, it is advisable to wear a shirt to protect your back from the sun, and if it is very hot or a long exposure is contemplated, jeans should also be worn; it can be extremely painful to have the backs of ones knees and thighs burnt. A wet-suit jacket affords the best protection, indeed most people need one for a long dive because, despite the relative warmth of the water, it is still much cooler than the body.

Sunshine is not the only characteristic of a tropical climate: the existence of trade-wind belts, the doldrums, and the rarity of cold fronts results in more predictable weather patterns. Consult local knowledge.

Coral Reefs

Many different habitats may be found within the tropics, but most diving is carried out in the vicinity of coral reefs, as these and their fauna are one of the principal attractions.

The stony corals are mostly colonial anemone-like animals secreting beneath themselves an ever-growing calcareous skeleton, in the tissues of which live single-celled algae whose activities are essential to the proper growth of the coral. Like all green plants, these algae need sunlight, and so the corals themselves only grow in warm, sunlit waters. They form communities around the coasts of tropical land

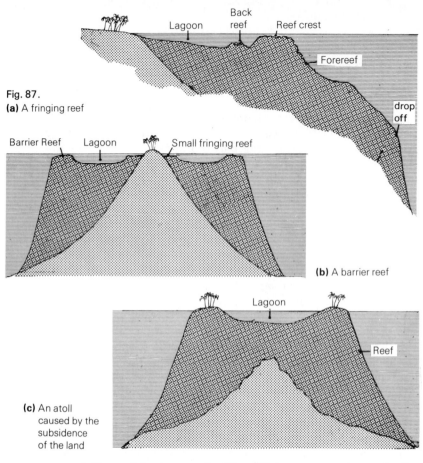

Fig. 87.
(a) A fringing reef

(b) A barrier reef

(c) An atoll
caused by the
subsidence
of the land

masses, and these fringing reefs (Fig. 87a) grow up towards the
light until they reach the surface, thus forming the reef crest. The
colonies nearest to the land are likely to be killed by fresh water, or
choked by sediment, so further reef growth occurs only in a seaward
direction. Behind the advancing reef crest and the immediate back-
reef area, is a shallow sandy zone, known as a lagoon, where little
coral growth occurs. Here, sea grasses may cover the bottom.

Seaward of the reef crest is the fore-reef, where corals and other
animals abound. The profiles of fore-reefs vary considerably, being
dependent on the geological structure and history of the region: the
reef may slope down gently, or a 'drop-off' may occur at any depth
from the surface to 60 m, and the vertical face may descend for only a
few metres—or for hundreds. Beyond the fore-reef there may be a
relatively shallow, sandy plain, a sandy slope, or inky depths.

The largest and oldest reefs occur in the Indo–Pacific where,
caused by further reef growth and land subsidence, barrier reefs and
atolls are formed (Figs. 87b and c).

The Lagoon

The lagoon and back-reef zone of a fringing reef may be up to a few hundred metres wide, and generally provides good snorkelling in 2–3 m of water, whereas the lagoon behind a barrier reef or within an atoll may be several miles across and over 60 m deep. Where the lagoon surrounds a 'high' island, run-off rainwater and sediment may reduce the visibility to British standards.

It is while swimming in the lagoon that one might first meet some of the nasty creatures for which the tropics are notorious; there are more of these dangerous animals in the Indo–Pacific than in the Caribbean, but simple precautious will reduce the likelihood of an accident:

(a) Never walk barefoot on the sea bottom; even when wearing shoes, slide and shuffle your feet on sandy bottoms.

(b) Do not touch or pick up anything unless you know what it is. There may be camouflaged fishes bearing poisonous spines, such as scorpion fish and sting-rays; cone-shells with poison-darts; sea-urchins with long sharp spines that can easily penetrate a shoe.

(c) Find out from local divers or fishermen what there is to worry about, if anything.

(d) Never swim alone out of sight of your friends.

The Reef Crest

The nature of reef crests varies according to their age, degree of exposure to breakers, and the tidal range. They form platforms that may be only several, or hundreds of metres across; the larger reefs may bear sandy islands. If there is a large tidal range, the reef may be left exposed for several hours so that one can walk about on it (wear shoes!).

Usually even the smallest reef crest presents a formidable obstacle to a swimmer, particularly on the seaward face, which is commonly hedged by thickets of tree-like corals. All coral exposed to currents or wave action should be treated with great respect. It is easy to be swept into a position from which one cannot retreat without attempting to push off from or step on the corals, only to find that they are brittle and give little support. Before getting free one has also discovered that their skeletons are hard and normally covered with a multitude of sharp edges; even a gentle brush can cause multiple cuts. This is another reason for wearing a wet-suit jacket and perhaps a pair of jeans. Not only can one be cut, but stung: mildly by most corals, more seriously by Fire Coral, which is abundant in areas of wave surge. This is easily recognisable by its tan-coloured and white-edged vertical plates, if not by its nettle-like sting!

The reef crest can usually be crossed through gaps and channels of varying size. In a well-developed Pacific reef such channels may be miles apart, but wide enough to be easily navigable in large boats. However, on the smaller scale of a young fringing reef, there may be channels through which a diver can swim, but it can be very dangerous to use and rely on these. To begin a dive via such a route may create a serious problem of finding the channel when returning from seaward, as often there are many blind re-entrants. To reduce this risk, use leading marks, or otherwise make sure that you can find the place again. Secondly, the weather may change for the worse, thus causing the sea to rise very rapidly, so the channel should be wide and deep enough for re-entry even when a sea is running. Thirdly, there is often a strong seaward current through these channels, especially if waves are breaking elsewhere over the reef, a wind is blowing along the shore, or the tide is falling. The fact that a wave-swept reef is so dangerous must affect one's assessment of the suitability of the sea conditions for diving purposes. Conditions which should be exciting but tolerable when returning to a rocky shore in Britain may easily rule out diving from the shore to seaward of a coral reef, unless there is a very wide channel through it. For all these reasons it is strongly recommended that a boat be used for all diving seaward of a reef crest.

The Fore-reef
The fore-reef is usually the most interesting area for diving. Here the corals are especially diverse and extensive, and the fish most spectacular. It is also here, outside the reef, that the clearest water is found, with visibility of up to 60 m.

The good visibility brings the danger of unplanned deeper diving, which can occur for two reasons. First, there is not the same feeling of depth as one experiences in the darker British waters, and a diver new to the tropics can therefore easily be at a greater depth than he thinks he is; he can probably stay down longer than usual because he may be using a 2000 l cylinder and because, through being warm and relaxed, his air consumption will probably be reduced. Thus it is easy to stray into decompression times if the diver does not make proper use of his depth gauge and watch. Secondly, even an experienced diver may be tempted by the vista of unexplored regions lying below him . . . but diving training teaches self-control, or it teaches nothing!

This said, it is a fact that tropical conditions are very good for deep diving. The good visibility, high illumination and warmth make the diver in the tropics much more at ease than he would be at equivalent depths in British waters. His low rate of air consumption and the probability of calm weather on the surface also help to make it a safer operation, provided of course that he is fit, experienced, and adheres to his depth and time schedule (see section on *Deep Diving*).

Sharks, etc.

It is on the fore-reef that most large fish are encountered, which may include sharks and barracuda. The latter are very curious fish and often follow divers, but are rarely known to attack, except in murky waters or when the diver is carrying speared fish. Do not draw your knife; they may attack shiny objects, mistaking them for injured fish. Although not considered a danger by most divers, they should be treated with respect, if only because of their large teeth and sinister expressions.

Moray eels may be seen poking their heads from beneath corals. They are very aggressive and will attack if provoked; their bite makes a nasty jagged tear. For this reason you should not put your hand into a hole to look for lobsters.

The likelihood of a shark attacking a diver is fairly remote; it is more likely to ignore him. However, swimmers and snorkellers *are* vulnerable. In any event, sharks are potentially very dangerous to anyone in the water, and all are unpredictable, so they should be regarded with suspicion. This applies even to nurse sharks which spend most of their time lying on the bottom and are generally considered harmless.

Sharks are attracted by blood, so a diver with a bleeding wound should leave the water. They are also attracted by erratic movements, surface splashing, noise, and, it is said, bright colours. Do not dangle your hands or feet from boats. If you spear fish, kill them quickly and get them out of the water as soon as possible. If you have to swim with dead fish, trail them on a line behind you so that a shark can take them if it wants; do not hold them in your hand or tuck them in your belt! Should you be investigated by a shark, it will probably circle warily before making a slow head-on approach. Do not attempt to wound it, but hit it, as hard as possible, preferably on the nose. It will probably go away.

Night Diving

Night diving in the tropics is generally very exciting for there is often abundant phosphorescence, and many animals, such as octopuses and basket-stars, that are not seen during the day are commonly observed. Because of the restricted visibility it is advisable to be fully clothed, i.e. wet-suit jacket or long-sleeved shirt and a pair of jeans; plankton is more abundant in near-surface waters at night and one might otherwise be stung by unseen jelly-fish such as sea-wasps (*Cubomedusae*). These are small cube-shaped jelly-fish with tentacles at the four corners, the stings from which have been known to be fatal. For further details see the section on *Night Diving*.

Treatment of Cuts and Stings
Coral cuts and stings should be rinsed with alcohol before being washed with fresh water; this will help prevent the discharge of loose stinging cells which would otherwise occur. Cuts should be treated with an antiseptic cream for, in the tropics, they can go septic easily. For more serious wounds medical treatment should be sought immediately.

Summary
Protect yourself against the sun.

Never dive without a watch and depth gauge.

Do not touch or pick up anything unless you know what it is.

Be careful of wave-swept coral.

Do not swim out through the reef crest unless you are sure that you will be able to swim back. Use a boat on the fore-reef if possible.

Do not provoke fish known to attack.

If badly cut while diving, leave the water.

Diving from Small Boats

Many diving clubs use small craft—particularly inflatables or runabouts—to transport divers to more distant and interesting sites offshore. The presence of a boat on any dive adds to the safety of the divers, so long as the craft is in capable hands.

Boat handling is a skill which comes through initial training and experience. If misused, boats can cause injury to divers so they should only be handled by experienced boatmen while covering or picking up divers.

Because of the limited amount of space available in small boats anyone diving from them should be acquainted with the generally accepted procedures of small-boat diving. To present this information we will consider the entire process of running a dive using an outboard-powered inflatable. Each step will be explained as it occurs.

First, the boat has to be prepared—possible assembled—and its engine and equipment checked and made ready for use. If the boat has to be assembled, this should be done under the direction of the boatman for the day. He will need help and will expect all who are going to take part in the boat dive to provide it. Give whatever help is asked of you in assembling and inflating. All can help since a 5 m inflatable takes about 500 'steps' on the bellows to inflate it.

Once the boat is inflated, some of its essential equipment (see chapter 8, *Seamanship*) can be stowed and secured, but heavier items are best not loaded until the boat is afloat. Help to carry the boat and its equipment to the water's edge: and to get it afloat and loaded if that is the plan. The boatman should see that everything is correctly stowed and test the engine.

Now is the time to get kitted-up. All being well you will have got all your gear ready to go—aqualung assembled, small items in your kit bag ready for the trip—so all you have to do is suit up and put on your ABLJ. Get your gear aboard the boat, putting it where the boatman wants it. If it is a short haul to the dive site, it may be worth kitting-up fully, except for mask and fins, before you leave the shore: if it is a long trip, stow the aqualung on the boat's floor. Carry fins, mask and other small items in a kit bag. This is an important thing which saves so much time and bother. Others grovel in the bottom of the boat for an odd fin or their snorkel while you are well organised by having it all together.

When stowing your gear DO NOT cover up any of the boat's equipment which might be needed: in particular the anchor and line. If anything goes wrong, the first thing to do is anchor. All too often

START OF THE DIVE, LAUNCHING AN INFLATABLE

the anchor tray invites the stowage of personal kit into it. Avoid the temptation.

With your kit aboard, await the boatman's instruction to climb aboard. He may ask you to wait, standing in thigh-deep water holding the boat while others get aboard—it's all part of the game. The boat's bow should be kept pointing into any waves which may be breaking and the boat must be kept afloat. Remember it will sink slightly as it is loaded, and if the tide is going out at the same time . . .!

Get aboard when the boatman asks you to, giving the boat a shove off if necessary. Sit down straight away on the hull tubes to keep the centre of gravity low—and to give the driver, who sits at the back near the engine, a clear view ahead.

Once under way, keep seated and hold on if it is a rough trip. Hand ropes are provided down the side of inflatables for this purpose. Help the boatman by keeping a watch ahead and do not hesitate to warn him of other craft or potential danger—he cannot spot everything. If the sea conditions are rough and there is a lot of spray about (inflatables are notoriously wet boats) turn your back to it. This is where you will appreciate that windproof jacket.

On arrival at the dive site, the first pair will kit up. Due to the cramped quarters, they will find little room to stand and will be glad of a hand or two in getting their aqualungs on and all the other gear together. Lend a hand as best you can: ask for help if you need it.

AT THE DIVE SITE, PREPARING TO DIVE

From inflatables, divers enter the water by rolling in backwards. Ideally this should be done with a diver on each side of the boat and the boatman giving a 'three, two, one, GO!' count-down. If the timing is right the boat will not roll an inch! (2.5 cm!) While the diving flag is being raised, cameras, tools, SMB's, etc. can be passed over to the divers and off they go. The boatman usually serves as 'Records Marshal' and will note their time of entry.

With the first pair away, the second pair have more room to move while kitting up. The boatman will give help where necessary. The second pair may go in as soon as they are ready or may wait for the first pair to finish their dive.

During any wait of this sort, keep warm and keep a look-out—for the divers and other surface craft in the vicinity. The boatman will drive the boat around quietly, following the divers' Marker Buoy and thereby remaining close to them. If surface craft are approaching the divers' position, the cautious boat handler will put himself between the divers and the threatening craft in such a way that the latter is obliged to alter course (maritime 'rules of the road').

When the divers surface the boat will close to them. Often it is a good idea for the second pair to go in before the first group come aboard. They will find the extra space welcome.

Weight-belts are removed and passed in first, then aqualung sets. Turn the cylinder valve off and remove the demand valve so that it

END OF THE DIVE, BEACHING AN INFLATABLE

does not get damaged. Small items—cameras, lobsters, face-masks, etc. are handed in and when directed by the boatman, the divers climb aboard. Getting into an inflatable is a quickly acquired knack, rather like climbing out over the edge of a swimming pool. Ask for help if you need it. Keep your fins on to help push you up when climbing aboard.

If you are getting back into an empty inflatable—not a wise or safe practice to leave it unattended—the easiest way is to use the outboard engine cavitation plate as a ladder and climb in over the transom. Use your 'Florida Dive Belt' (chapter 3, *Safety Equipment*) to hang your gear up with while doing so.

Stow the gear as neatly and safely as possible and put that windproof on again. Now is the time to pass the coffee flask around if you have one.

The trip home will be much the same as the outward journey. As you approach the shore, keep a sharp look-out for other craft, bathers and paddlers. Stand off till the landing place is clear if necessary. On the final approach, be ready to slip over the side to hold the boat or to beach it. Get all the heavy gear out and in an orderly pile on the beach or quay, then help to lift the boat clear of the water if this is necessary. Only when the boat is safe and secure are you free to deal with your own diving gear.

Finally, remember that the boat has to be packed away at the end of the day and your help will be needed then as well. The good club member is the one who helps, not the one who avoids helping. You will no doubt be asked to pay for the boat trip—petrol is expensive these days.

When diving from larger rigid launches, life is usually less cramped and not quite so bumpy as in an inflatable. Entry to the water is usually by stepping off the deck and entering feet first. Getting out is usually via a ladder (fins off) and you can take your set off once back on board. You might even be able to dry off and dress aboard the boat.

Boat diving is fun and gives access to many otherwise inaccessible offshore sites. In small boats, everyone has to muck in and do their share. But that is what it's all about! Practice at boat handling can be gained under the supervision of an experienced boatman, but attendance at a BSAC Boat Handling Course should be the first step.

END OF THE DIVE   CARRYING THE BOAT ASHORE

CHAPTER SEVEN

DIVING WITH A PURPOSE

Scientific Expeditions

Diving Expeditions, whether for pure fun, photography, science, or discovery, have become much more elaborate and professional in the last ten years. Most Branch DO's and Second and First Class divers have the experience today of organising diving trips of a weekend or a week, involving equipment checks, dive planning, organisation of boats—hired, loaned, or owned by the BSAC or Branch—and of planning the safe diving for perhaps 10–20 divers in open-sea conditions, perhaps several miles from shore. The essential point about scientific diving expeditions is that there are two goals:

1. Achievement of the scientific goals, and
2. Safe diving.

Good scientific diving maximises the first without jeopardising the second.

Scientific projects can be enormous fun, and individual divers and branches throughout the BSAC have enjoyed participating in various projects organised by the National Scientific Officer. If you want to find out about expeditions which are being planned, or to organise your own project, there are various approaches open to you. It is always useful to talk things over with people who have more experience. Firstly, watch *Diver* for news of scientific courses and projects; write to the Scientific Officer; contact the Universities' Federation of Sub-Aqua Clubs who may have useful contacts in research departments; contact the Under-water Association for Scientific Research, a group of professional university and research diving scientists; or contact the Committee for Nautical Archaeology, if your interests are in that field. All these groups may be able to help you.

If a scientific project is conducted as part of normal Branch diving, or is backed by the BSAC at national level, or is conducted from the Branch boat, then all the diving will be within normal Club Rules, and your insurance will be valid. If, however, you plan to work in a project not sponsored by the Club, or in cooperation with professional research organisations, or with foreign divers working abroad, and especially if you are in receipt of expenses paid or an actual salary or fee, then you may no longer be covered by the BSAC Third Party insurance. Scientific work often involves using equipment which is not usual sports diving equipment, or adapting techniques and safety regulations, so that they no longer conform to Club Rules, although additional measures may be introduced to maintain safety. Again, your BSAC Third Party insurance may not be valid. If you are in doubt about your insurance position, consult the Club's insurance adviser, or the Under-water Association for Scientific Research, which works closely with the BSAC, and has special policies for these situations.

Do NOT worry about your possible obligations to statutory government diving regulations. These regulations do not apply to amateur sports divers, and they do not apply to scientific, non-commercial diving, even if you are receiving expenses or payment of a salary or fees.

Having got some of the bureaucracy out of the way—it seems to hit everything—let us now look at the actual planning and conduct of a scientific expedition. We can use the following headings:

1. Defining aims, planning, flexibility.
2. Background literature, charts, special maps and books.
3. Time, place, season, weather, type of diving, special equipment.
4. Personal logistics, team selection, training, official bodies, banking, insurance.
5. Material logistics, boat, store, filling, fresh water, workshop, transport, accommodation.
6. Records, sonar, navigational fixing, dive-logging, photography, diary.
7. Special equipment.
8. Fitness, medicine, psychology, sleep, food, drink.
9. Written reports and publications.

1. The aim of a scientific diving project must arise naturally out of the existing knowledge in some area of science—geology, biology, fisheries studies, physiology, or archaeology, etc.—and the plans must be made entirely within the context of previous work in the field. Such an aim cannot be decided overnight, or fabricated after gathering a jolly team together and deciding a nice tropical diving site. This means making contacts as suggested above, and cultivating experts near your branch in institutions, such as university departments and technical colleges. From a rather practical viewpoint, it is seldom worth 'searching for something'. Search and recovery of lost war hardware can be fun, but is not science. Occasionally a really professional search such as that for the *Mary Rose* leads on to valuable scientific or archaeological work, but very few Branches will have the energy or determination to cope with such tedious searching. Most under-water features are first discovered by accident, and the discoverer is seldom qualified to take the work on to completion. Conversely, it is somewhat of a waste of effort to deploy an experienced diving team for many days or months, searching and searching, and then have no time to apply expertise to the

find. Moral: try to get your project clearly defined so that you can start work on it as soon as you arrive on site, or at least as soon as you are acclimatised and in diving trim.

A working scientific diving expedition will probably consist of between 4 and 10 experienced divers, and since diving efficiency increases rapidly during the settling-in period of about one week, it is hardly worth considering periods of less than two weeks. On the other hand, working periods of more than three months are unlikely because of variable seasonal conditions, and the necessity of working for a living. Planning period for an expedition varies from a minimum of six months for a four-man two-week job, to two years for a ten-man, three-month one. (Women not excluded, of course!)

Good planning involves calculating ahead to make allowances for bad weather, accidents, equipment breakdowns, or simply the failure of an idea to work out. Alternative targets, subsidiary plans, and alternative methods should be considered in advance so that something of value is obtained from the project, no matter what happens.

2. A scientific diving project is only a success if the science is a success as well as the diving. You may be able to recruit to your team a scientist who will take responsibility for the design of the experiment, observational techniques, etc., but if not, you will have to work these things out for yourselves, in discussion with experts before you start. The urge to be first—to discover things—leads many divers to neglect wilfully the search for other people who may have worked on the problem before them, and yet, only by doing this, and by basing your plans on other people's experience, can you hope to avoid duplication and the rediscovery of old facts.

The necessity is for thorough reading, plenty of contacts, and plenty of time. The popular and semi-popular diving and under-water books contain reading lists of a more specialised nature, and these in turn contain reference to original research papers, with the names of research workers, institutes, and manufacturers. All project leaders planning scientific diving expeditions are recommended to read Science Diving International, published by the BSAC, as well as the reports of the annual scientific symposia of the Under-water Association for Scientific Research. You might also attend specialist courses at Fort Bovisand, or at other centres and technical colleges, where you will meet experts who can advise you. In addition, the Scientific Committee of the World Under-water Federation has addresses of diving scientists from about 30 countries.

When the work site has been selected (see item 3) further research should be made into the special conditions of the area: geology, biology, weather, water movements, and so on. Admiralty charts, large-scale maps, and possibly geological survey maps should be purchased well in advance, possibly supported by aerial photographs. Always write in advance to local contacts, marine stations, coastguards, harbourmaster, boat owners, and any other officials you may have to deal with. Get from them information about local conditions, tides, weather, local diving regulations and laws.

3. Projects may be classified as *systematic* or *regional*. A *regional* project is concerned with a specific problem in a specific area: what species of nudibranchs occur off Jamaica? How fast does sand move down the La Jolla submarine canyon? Did stone-age man ever inhabit the submerged caves off the coast of Gibraltar? A *systematic* project is concerned with more general types of problems: what is the relation between waves on the surface and waves on thermocline? What is the relation between concentration of heavy minerals and wave pattern? What is the relation between light intensity, depth, and rate of growth of algae?

If you select a regional problem, your working site is obviously narrowly defined, and you have only to choose the exact harbour to work from, and the precise diving point. Nevertheless, it is often worth travelling to the site for a 'recce' and to make yourself known to the locals some months in advance. A pint of beer or a glass of wine will often work wonders with a contact who had previously not bothered to answer letters!

If your project is *systematic*, you should ask 'where in the world is the phenomenon most clearly manifested, and is it possible to visit the site within reasonable limits of time and money?' Because good diving conditions are an important consideration, the answer to this question (for those of us who live in the UK) is often the Mediterranean. But these good conditions are equivalent to stating that the Med does not display a wide range of problems which the diver might tackle; there is relatively little fauna and flora, no tides, few currents, little sediment transport, little mixing of waters.

Even though you have tentatively chosen the project area, you may still not feel inclined to launch the full-scale expedition. The solution to this is the pilot project: with about three members drawn from the final project team, plan a mini-expedition for a week or so, to test the feasibility of your plans and working methods, and modify your final project accordingly.

It is often convenient to stage the pilot project at about Easter, with a vew to launching the main project in the summer. During the pilot project you should test the methods and equipment you intend to use; estimate rate of work; daily air consumption; cost in terms of man-days. Special equipment may have to be developed; this is dealt with in section 7. If your study is *systematic*, the pilot project does not necessarily have to take place in the same area as the main project. But if your study is *regional*, one of the essential points at issue is that of suiting the methods to the precise study area. On the other hand, it may be worth staging a pilot project to test a new technique or run the team in, even if you cannot get to the final study area.

The time required for the project must be estimated: consider how much can be achieved by one man in one dive; calculate how many man-dives can be made in a day; estimate the number of man-dives required in the project, and assess the optimum balance of team size and time on-site to suit overall-budget and time available. In England between April and September, one can reckon on at least 30% of days lost through bad weather, but if planning has been flexible (see item 1) the work schedule can be compressed to allow for time lost and, conversely, if the weather is surprisingly good, secondary projects can be attempted without undue improvisation. It is worth noting that from May to August the visibility off many parts of the British coast is reduced by the bloom of plankton. Weather records and wind directions can be obtained from the Admiralty Pilot, with further details from the Meteorological Office. Tidal currents are indicated on charts, and times of tides in the Admiralty Almanac.

The rate of work will obviously depend on the type of work and the depth of water. Daily work rate slows down dramatically as depth increases, not just because of decompression, but because everything to do with the dive takes longer. In shallow water several divers can be working on different tasks at one time, whereas in deep water only one pair can be working while the rest of the team are fully involved in safety precautions.

You must assess what type of equipment is most suitable for the task: whether diving will be done in pairs or singly, roped or un-roped, swimming or with an electric tug, from a boat or from the shore. Estimate the amount of surface work connected with each dive, and from this arrive at your overall efficiency. Never underestimate the time required for paper-work, record-keeping, preserving samples, filling cylinders, charging batteries, and just plain thinking. In pre-planning, it is useful to divide the project up into parts involving spot or bounce dives, linear searches horizontally or vertically, and area searches horizontally or vertically. These factors, combined with the depth and distance from shore, determine the required equipment.

4. It is probable that a special team will have to be selected for the project, and the members should meet and work together many months before the main expedition. The project leader is ultimately responsible for everything, but his second in command should be of equivalent diving experience since, if the project leader is to dive, he

o

must leave somebody on the surface in charge. This rule will not apply so strongly when all diving is shallow and divers may work singly, but even here the project leader may wish to spend a day or two on administration. Depending on the type of project, the remaining members should have the special skills concerned with the object of the expedition, plus ability for engineering and maintenance, boat-handling, surveying, cooking, first-aid, and possibly languages.

The team should work together on the planning, each taking responsibility for an aspect of fund-raising, equipment, transport, and the separate research programmes. Where the project requires new or complex techniques, the proposed methods should be practised and snags ironed out in shallow water or during the pilot project. Team-work is vital, and the more the working methods are practised in advance, the less time will be wasted on the site.

Before going to work in a strange area, make sure that you have notified tactfully those official bodies who, at the very least, might be offended if you did not. For a foreign country get the necessary visas, and work permits if you are staying a long time; excavation permit if you are archaeological, and notify the official bodies concerned with the subject that you are studying. On site, get on good terms with the harbour-master, police, secretary of the nearest diving club, and the director of the local museum, etc. This may sound pompous and old-fashioned, but if you run into any trouble later, such as a breakdown of compressor or transport or illness, the goodwill of these officials will make the difference between a trivial inconvenience and disaster.

Make sure that you have plenty of cash or banking facilities close to the site. Although all your equipment must be specially insured and you should have full accident insurance, lost or damaged equipment will have to be replaced immediately if work is not to be held up, and you only get the money back later. Similarly with the costs of an accident.

5. We now consider the basic on-site logistics. The dive site, the boat loading point, equipment store and filling station, and the accommodation are the four fixed points in the work area. On a light mobile project they may be effectively united with a vehicle and trailer carrying gear, compressor, dinghy, and sleeping bags. On a large project the points must be chosen carefully. Since carrying heavy gear on land is the most tiresome activity the key step is to get the equipment store, the filling point, and the boat loading point as close together as possible—say within 150 metres of each other. This minimises the delay caused if people forget bits of gear. Ideally accommodation should be within 200 m of the loading point as this minimises the chore of working on the equipment late at night.

Depending on the local topography and the size of boat, the boat may be protected in rough weather by being pulled up on the shore, anchored offshore, berthed at a nearby jetty, or berthed some distance away in a sheltered bay, behind an island or in a harbour. The distance of the dive site from the loading point determines the type of boat required, and separation of the loading point from the accommodation determines the type of land transport. (It is assumed that the question of transport to the work area has been solved by buying a ticket—by far the quickest and often cheapest way.) A good boat and good land transport save time and boost morale. If you are working a 12-hour day six days a week (see item 8) a loss of two hours a day travelling is exactly equal to a lost day's work each week. The basic requirements of a boat are obvious, but it pays always to have plenty of deck space, to consider the difficulty and time taken in anchoring in the working depth, and to assess the loss of dive-site mobility if the boat is very large—over 20 m. In this case take an extra boat.

Accommodation must be good—again, don't make problems. It is possible to run a three-week trip on the assumption that everybody can afford to lose 5–10 kg and go without sleep, but diving efficiency drops rapidly during the second week and may become positively dangerous. If you are to work well for several weeks, this means at least air-beds and sleeping bags, and preferably accommodation with bed and breakfast, or renting an expedition house.

Remember that although a compressor is necessary in the wilds, a bank of supply cylinders is quicker, quieter, and more reliable: in most countries there are companies equivalent to BOC that will deliver air. Ensure that there is a supply of fresh water sufficient to wash all gear every day, especially in a hot climate, and find out in advance where the nearest workshop facilities are. If you are diving deep, below 30 m, lay on emergency decompression facilities.

6. Position fixing and mapping are fundamental to most projects, and, depending on the size of the area and distance from shore, you can use Decca Hi Fix, horizontal sextant angles, theodolite, or alidade, for surface plotting. When under water, use echo-ranging equipment, a compass, depth gauge, lines, tapes and a rule.

Anticipate the form in which you wish to record standard data, and prepare duplicated sheets with slots for each item of information. On shallow diving projects a record should be kept of the number of man-hours spent in the water each day, so that a watch can be kept on efficiency; if diving is regularly below 15 m, a detailed log of every dive should be kept. In any case, in addition to the special scientific reports, an overall diary should be maintained.

7. A random selection of the odd things which may be needed on

an expedition might include the following special items: electric tug, battery charger, distilled water, radios and acoustic communications, soldering iron, acoustic positioning equipment, sediment corers, hundreds of polythene bags and labels, fish-traps, floats, lifting bags, Dan-buoys, platform for use on stage decompression, derricks and winches, aquarium tanks, colour filters, stop-watch, books, duplicated forms, tape recorder, side-scan sonar, cameras, under-water lights, tools and spare parts, etc.

8. All members should be free of physical ailment, and in addition should be actively fit either as a result of frequent diving or from some other sport. Although an unfit person can dive, in regular diving, fitness prevents deterioration of efficiency and gets you out of emergencies.

During the project you will probably work a 12–14-hour day, but everybody must get at least 8 hours sleep a night, including the project leader. At least one day per week must be total rest without any diving or swimming at all. If any individual gets run down and starts making more mistakes than usual he should be given the day off; similarly if the whole team gets tired and inefficient a whole day's rest usually cures it.

On a scientific diving project there tend to be times of crisis, particularly towards the end, when the overriding desire to succeed with the goals of the expedition may conflict with safety. The expedition leader must be clear in his own mind of the relation between these two factors. He may have appointed a Diving Officer and a Chief Scientist for the expedition, in which case the conflict may take the form of these two men putting their demands to him very forcefully. In this situation the risks are clear for everybody to see, and can be resolved rationally. Where the expedition leader has taken upon himself the task of Chief Scientist, and particularly if he combines this with being Diving Officer as well, there is the danger that desire to succeed in scientific goals will be at the expense of safety. It is not impossible to combine the roles, but it requires very great experience to do so, and probably results in the expedition leader being over-worked.

Good food is as important as plenty of sleep. Try not to live out of tins; it is boring and not particularly nutritious—meat, milk, eggs, cheese, green vegetables and fruit are obtainable almost everywhere, even if it's called shashlik and yoghurt.

In many parts of the tropics, south and east Mediterranean and points east, it is advisable to treat water with chloride disinfectant tablets 24 hours before drinking it. The addition of fresh crushed lemons removes the chlorine taste and adds vitamins. If you must drink alcohol, indulge on the evening before your rest day.

Take plenty of sticking plaster, bandages, aspirin, codeine, enterovioform, kaolin, charcoal, mercurochrome, chloride tablets and tweezers. If you are going to be really isolated, include a doctor in the team, and take morphia.

An essential part of the pre-project training should be a personality shake-down. This does not mean that every man and woman must be a life-and-soul-of-the-party good mixer, but simply that people should get used to each other so that, under the stress of work and confined living space, personal idiosyncrasies do not seem intolerable. Although it takes all sorts to make a team, the obvious source of splinter groups, factions, rows, and recriminations must be dropped before the team is finalised.

9. The expedition has not been completed until every person or official body who helped the project has been thanked and provided with a brief report on results, and the full results have been published. This is liable to take at least six months, since different people require different sorts of reports. The simplest report is that which simply states that the project is completed successfully, and gives a brief idea of the results; this is sufficient to accompany thanks to a general sponsor, and the critical factor here is to get the report out quickly. Next come the specialised reports for those sponsors who are interested only in a limited part of the work. This might be a report on the performance of an outboard motor; usefulness of a type of medicine or first-aid; reliability of a flare after immersion to 50 m; or reliability of a new decompression table. Depending on the nature of the problem, these reports may vary from 'Yes, it worked', to 20 pages of closely typed A4.

The project leader may or may not be involved in writing up the scientific results of the expedition. In any case he should collect all the records of the expedition and prepare a general report on progress, diving efficiency, health, finances, usefulness of different methods, and such other matters. This document is of vital importance when planning future expeditions.

The last reports to see the light of day are usually the scientific or technical papers describing the complete results of the site work and subsequent analysis. Frequently, an expedition has to be followed by several months of laboratory or paper research, and this should never be skimped.

Remember that your sponsors never see how hard you work on the site, and probably never see the film and slides you shot. Their assessment of the value of your work is based solely on the written information they receive afterwards, and it is this which will influence their decision to support you again.

Nautical Archaeology

The purpose of archaeology under water is precisely the same as archaeology on land. It is a study of Man's past derived from what he has left behind. In the under-water world the diver will come across shipwrecks of all ages, cargoes from wrecks, the personal belongings of sailors and passengers and sometimes even the physical remains of these unfortunate people themselves. Then there are the odd articles that may have been accidentally lost, and because Man has tended to regard seas, lakes and rivers as fathomless litterbins, we find the sort of things that Man, for one reason or another, has tossed aside.

Under-water archaeology is a term known to most divers, but as there is much material that is restricted neither to land nor under water, such as harbours, anchorages and submerged sites, the terms nautical archaeology or marine archaeology have become more common. But of course the diver will be mostly concerned with the areas of discovery that he, and only he, can reach and therefore we shall concentrate on the under-water aspect.

One is familiar with the painstaking and systematic work of the land archaeologist and the diver would be seriously mistaken if he assumed that work under water is less exacting and demanding. Nevertheless the diver need not be put off by this, for as many have shown, the necessary skills are within his reach, and it is significant that every single recognised under-water archaeological project now under way in the UK is manned virtually 100% by BSAC divers.

First let us consider the whole archaeological process which in a simplified form can be split up as follows:
1. Survey
2. Excavation
3. Conservation
4. Conclusion and publication

Survey
The survey is the essential prerequisite of every 'dig'. The very act of excavation is destructive and therefore the importance of the 'predisturbance survey' cannot be overstressed. The diver must observe and commit his observations to paper in the form of drawings and photographs. Only after this can one consider excavation.

Excavation
The process of excavation is carried out generally with the aid of

specialist tools, and as it proceeds it is necessary to accurately record each stage of the excavation. Nothing is disturbed before it is fully recorded.

Conservation

As the excavation proceeds, so the material will be lifted to the surface. But much sunken material once lifted can, within a comparatively short period, perish. Therefore much of it will need careful treatment and in many cases this can only be carried out by skilled conservators in specialist laboratories.

Conclusions and Publications

Finally the archaeologist will gather together all the results of his project, prepare his report, drawings and photographs and have these published so that the knowledge and conclusions derived are available for all to read and study.

Training

How does the diver acquire the necessary skills to enable him to join an under-water archaeological team? In the U.K., regular courses for beginners are run by Fort Bovisand in conjunction with the BSAC, and the BSAC runs frequent regional courses. Courses and specialist symposiums are also arranged periodically by the following bodies:

The Council for Nautical Archaeology

The Nautical Archaeology Trust

St Andrews Institute of Maritime Archaeology

The Archaeological Research Centre, National Maritime Museum, Greenwich

In addition, there are many books to be studied and a selected bibliography is included at the end of this article.

The Law

It follows that wrecks of archaeological interest are part of our heritage and therefore they must be protected against vandalism. For this purpose the Protection of Wrecks Act 1973 provides for the 'designation' of wrecks of historic importance. If a wreck site is designated it will be marked by a buoy or other means and diving on the site other than by licence is prohibited. A diver may come across a wreck which is likely to be of historic importance: for example, more than 100 years old; and he will naturally wish to register his own interest and have the wreck considered for designation so that it may receive a degree of protection under the law. To do this he should apply to the Department of Trade, and in the first instance acquire from the Department a copy of 'Notes for the Guidance of Finders of Historic Wrecks'.

Unless a site is designated, there is nothing to prevent any diver from diving on a wreck as long as he does not lift anything. If however something is lifted from a wreck, then under the terms of the Merchant Shipping Act 1894 it must be reported to the Receiver of Wrecks at the nearest Custom House.

Official Bodies

The Government Committee that is involved in historic wrecks is the Department of Trade Advisory Committee on Historic Wreck Sites. This Committee, sometimes known as the Runciman Committee because it is under the Chairmanship of Lord Runciman, is responsible to the Secretary of State for the administering of the Protection of Wrecks Act 1973. Divers' interests are represented on the Committee by one of the BSAC Vice-Presidents.

Bodies Concerned with Nautical Archaeology

The Council for Nautical Archaeology acts as a voluntary advisory body and members of the BSAC are well represented on the Council. The CNA is available for consultation on ships, harbours, anchorages and submerged sites and its sister organisation, the Nautical Archaeology Trust, publishes the International Journal of Archaeology, Under-Water Exploration and a Newsletter called 'Natnews'.

The St Andrews Institute of Maritime Archaeology which is attached to the University of St Andrews is involved in research, training and the direction of and participation in archaeological research in the field. Its Director and staff are available to divers for consultation and it issues a regular Newsletter.

The Archaeological Research Centre at the National Maritime Museum in Greenwich is mainly concerned at present in research into the history of boat building in NW Europe from prehistoric to Medieval periods. It has facilities for conserving materials recovered from water and advice on conservation can be sought by writing to the Chief Archaeologist. Written applications may also be made to the Museum for several research facilities.

The Hydrographic Department of the Admiralty maintains files of wrecks. This Department is anxious to receive reports of unrecorded wrecks and of visits to known wrecks, and its files may be consulted for a modest fee.

Addresses

The Secretary, Council for Nautical Archaeology,
The Roman Palace,
Salthill Road, Fishbourne,
CHICHESTER, Sussex.   Tel.: 0243 85859

The Administration Secretary,
The Nautical Archaeology Trust Ltd.,
Meadow Bank, 26 Lucastes Road,
HAYWARDS HEATH, Sussex.

Fort Bovisand Under-water Centre,
PLYMOUTH PL9 0AB.   Tel.: 0752 42570

St Andrews Institute of Maritime Archaeology,
University of St Andrews, St Salvator's College,
ST ANDREWS, Fife KY16 9AJ.   Tel.: St Andrews 4343—Ext. 42

The Archaeological Research Centre,
National Maritime Museum,
GREENWICH SE10 9NF.   Tel.: 01–858 5265

The Secretary to the Committee,
Advisory Committee on Historic Wreck Sites,
Department of Trade and Industry,
Marine Division,
Sunley House, 90 High Holborn,
LONDON WC1V 6LP.   Tel.: 01–405 6911—Ext. 494

The Hydrographer of the Navy,
Wrecks Section, Ministry of Defence,
Beadon Road,
TAUNTON, Somerset.

Suggested reading on Marine Archaeology

BASS, GEORGE F. *Archaeology Under-water*. Thames and Hudson, 1966.
BASS, GEORGE F. *A History of Seafaring Based on Under-water Archaeology*.
    Thames and Hudson, 1972.
CRAWFORD, O. G. S. *Archaeology in the Field*. Phoenix House, 1953.
DU PLATT TAYLOR, JOAN. *Marine Archaeology*. Hutchinson, 1965.
FRANZEN, ANDERS. *The Warship Vasa*. Stockholm, 1960.
FROST, HONOR. *Under the Mediterranean*. Hutchinson, 1963.
MCKEE, ALEXANDER. *The Mary Rose*. Souvenir Press, 1973.
MCKEE, ALEXANDER. *History Under the Sea*. Hutchinson, 1968.
MAGNUSSON, MAGNUS. *Introducing Archaeology*. Bodley Head, 1972.
MARSDEN, PETER. *The Wreck of the Amsterdam*. Hutchinson, 1974.
MARTIN, COLIN. *Full Fathom Five: Wrecks of the Spanish Armada*. Chatto
    and Windus, 1975.
RULE, MARGARET. *Preservation of Artefacts*. BSAC Diving Officers' Con-
    ference Proceedings, 1973.
STENUIT, ROBERT. *Treasures of the Armada*. David and Charles, 1972.
THROCKMORTON, PETER. *Shipwrecks and Archaeology*. Gollanz, 1969.
WILKES, B. ST. JOHN. *Nautical Archaeology*. David and Charles, 1971.
WOOD, E. S. *Field Guide to Archaeology*. Collins, 1963.

Marine Biology

The object of this chapter is to provide a framework upon which to build a knowledge and understanding of life in the sea. In its widest sense marine biology is the ecology of marine organisms—a study of the plants and animals, the interdependence of various biological processes and the influence of the physical and chemical (*abiotic*) conditions in the sea upon these organisms and processes.

The marine environment is vast—71% of the Earth's surface is covered by sea-water: a total area of 360 million sq km (140 million square miles) and an average depth of around 3800 m. The most important abiotic features of this environment are light, salinity, temperature, water movement, pressure and the nature of the sea-bed.

All living organisms depend upon the production of organic matter by plants from water, carbon dioxide and inorganic nutrients. Sunlight energy drives the reaction—*photosynthesis*—which can only take place in the illuminated layers of the seas. Less than 1.5% of the total volume is sufficiently illuminated to support plant life. All the animals in the sea, at all depths, are dependent upon these productive surface layers.

The quality of the light that penetrates the sea-water is also important, particularly for the attached seaweeds. Different wavelengths of light are absorbed at different rates and the plants rely upon pigments in their tissues to trap the light-energy. In addition, light is essential to visual orientation in animals, and in many cases stimulates locomotion and various physiological rhythms.

Over three-quarters of the sea's salt is sodium chloride, but there are also quantities of magnesium, calcium and potassium salts, and small amounts of many others, their concentration in the water varying slightly around 35 parts per thousand. The significance of salinity to an organism lies in the balance between internal and external salt concentrations; each animal having a certain tolerance to salinity fluctuation.

The temperature of the sea-water is dependent upon the amount of incident sunlight and the water currents. In low latitudes the absorption of heat produces a permanent discontinuity layer or thermocline between warm surface water and cold, denser, deep layers. However, in polar regions heat passes from the sea and there is little difference between the temperature at the surface and at depth. In middle latitudes, for instance, around the British Isles, the surface water temperature varies with climatic changes: seasonal thermoclines are formed by surface heating during the summer and break down when the surface water cools in winter.

The biological significance of a thermocline lies in the prevention of exchange of gases and nutrients between the surface and deeper layers, and in the direct influence of the associated gradient in density upon the buoyancy of living organisms and dead particles. Water temperature greatly influences the distribution and activities of marine organisms generally, for, as with salinity, each species is adapted to a certain range of temperatures.

Pressure in the ocean increases by about one atmosphere for every ten metres in depth and ranges from one atmosphere at sea level to 1000 atmospheres in the deep trenches. Work in this field of research has been concerned with testing shallow-water animals for pressure tolerance, and on the sensitivity to small pressure changes (as low as 0.005 atm) displayed by many small marine animals, which may be the means by which a suitable vertical range is maintained.

The circulation of the seas and tidal currents is reflected both locally and generally in the biology of the sea. At all depths there are mainly horizontally moving currents which may vary in direction and rate, tidal currents being the movement of water associated with the periodic rises and falls of the sea surface. Both have important transporting roles. In addition, vertical movements of water, through cooling and sinking, or through turbulence, affect biological processes by transporting oxygen down, and by re-cycling mineral nutrients to the surface.

The flow of water has a major effect on sessile organisms—those attached to the sea-bed. The effects of strong currents range from dislodgement and interference with feeding processes, to the supply and removal of food, waste, oxygen and carbon dioxide, and the dispersal of offspring. In areas of weak currents, particles will not remain in suspension; feeding and respiratory mechanisms may become clogged, and oxygen and carbon dioxide concentrations will fluctuate and yet, on the favourable side, there will be an abundance of organic debris and bacteria for food.

The sea-bed provides, for different organisms, a resting place, a refuge, a spawning site, a substrate for attachment, a sediment to live in, and food for sediment feeders. There are at least 157,000 species living in and on the sea-bed and these are known as the *benthos*. There are approximately 3000 pelagic (swimming) species inhabiting the water mass above.

Benthic organisms can be sub-divided into the *infauna*—animals which live buried in sediments or which bore into the softer rocks; and the *epiflora* and *epifauna*—the animals and plants which live on the substrate. These include sponges, cnidarians, polyzoans,

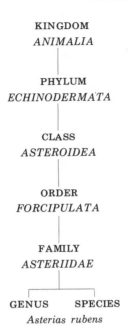

KINGDOM
ANIMALIA

PHYLUM
ECHINODERMATA

CLASS
ASTEROIDEA

ORDER
FORCIPULATA

FAMILY
ASTERIIDAE

GENUS   SPECIES
Asterias rubens

AN EXAMPLE OF CLASSIFICATION (*in this case the Common Starfish*)

barnacles and tunicates and, in shallow water where there is adequate light, numerous brown, red and green algae.

To survey as concisely as possible the diverse multitude of plants and animals which inhabit this environment, it is clearly essential to start by introducing a system of reference, to make order out of potential chaos, by grouping together organisms with similar basic characteristics. Taxonomy—the science of the classification of living things—takes into account many aspects of an organism's biology. A natural classification of organisms also functions as a short-hand method of describing species and groups and assists in the identification of specimens.

The basic unit, the *species,* is a collection of potentially naturally inter-breeding organisms. A *genus* consists of a number of species which closely resemble one another. The scientific name of a species consists of both the generic and specific names; in print both parts being italicised and the generic name having a capital letter: thus the common starfish of British coasts is *Asterias rubens.* Similar genera are grouped for convenience into *families* which take their names from one of the component genera. Families are grouped into *orders,* orders into *classes* and classes into *phyla.* The phyla are placed in either the plant or animal *kingdoms.* These are the essential categories of standard taxonomy.

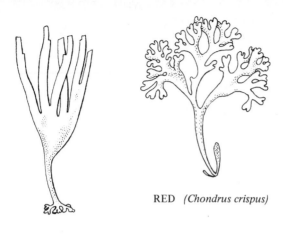

RED *(Chondrus crispus)*

BROWN *(Laminaria digitata)*

ALGAE

GREEN *(Ulva lactuca)*

The members of the two kingdoms can normally be distinguished by their methods of nutrition, and by the lack of cellulose cell walls in animals. Plants manufacture their own food from inorganic materials, whereas animals require a source of complex organic compounds. However, some simple forms cannot be assigned with confidence to either kingdom.

Nearly all the plants growing on the shallow sea-bed or drifting in the surface waters belong to the Algae; mostly photosynthetic, simple plants with chlorophyll and accessory light-trapping pigments. The three main classes are the Greens, the Browns and the Reds. In form the algae range from microscopic unicellular representatives to large and complex specimens. For example, in shallow, European waters, species of the genus *Laminaria* reach 5 m in length and form the dense kelp forests, whilst the American Pacific genus of brown alga, *Macrocystis*, may reach 60 m in length. A variety of microscopic drifting plants constitute the phytoplankton and form the basis of most food chains in the marine environment. The amount of phytoplankton produced annually has been estimated at around 15,000 million tons, compared with a total world catch of fish for example of about 50 million tons.

The majority of animals encountered in the sea will belong to one of the major groups of phyla which are considered below. These are the PORIFERA (sponges), CNIDARIA (hydroids, jelly-fishes, anemones, corals), ECTOPROCTA (sea-mats), ANNELIDA (segmented worms), MOLLUSCA (snails, slugs, bivalves, squids and octopus), ARTHROPODA (particularly the crustaceans and sea-spiders), ECHINODERMATA (feather-stars, starfishes, brittle-stars, sea-urchins, sea-cucumbers) and CHORDATA (particularly the tunicates and fishes).

PORIFERA

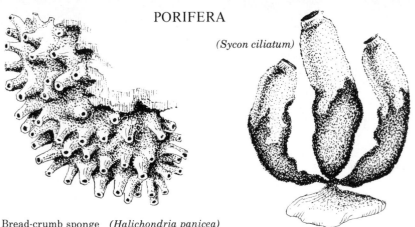

(Sycon ciliatum)

Bread-crumb sponge *(Halichondria panicea)*

PORIFERA:

Sponges are simple, sessile animals consisting of a loose mass of cells which act more or less independently. There are no sense organs, nervous or digestive systems. Specialised cells, each with a whip-like tail, line the maze of inner passages. The beating of these flagella draws in water and microscopic food particles through minute pores which cover the body surface. The particles are trapped and engulfed by the cells, and the water passes out of the sponge through larger openings, the oscula.

The sponges range in form from simple, small, vase-like structures to massive growths as high as 2 m and often provide refuge for small fish and crustacea. Some species bore into calcareous rock by a combination of acid secretion and mechanical action.

Reproduction is by the splitting-off and growth of fragments or buds and by sexual reproduction with the formation of small swimming larvae which eventually settle down and grow into the attached sponges.

CNIDARIA:

The fertilised egg of a typical cnidarian develops into a swimming larva which eventually settles on the sea-bed as a flower-like polyp. Through asexual reproduction many free-swimming medusae or jelly-fish stages are released by the polyp. These in turn produce fertilised eggs. Thus, the Cnidaria are radially symmetrical animals characterised by the occurrence of two types of individual during the life-cycle, the medusa and the polyp. Members of the class Hydrozoa display both polyp and medusa forms: in the Scyphozoa the medusa is dominant, whilst the Anthozoans are exclusively polypoid. The body is sac- or bell-like with a single opening surrounded by tentacles. Specialised stinging cells, the cnidoblasts, enable the capture of prey and repulsion of attackers.

CNIDARIA

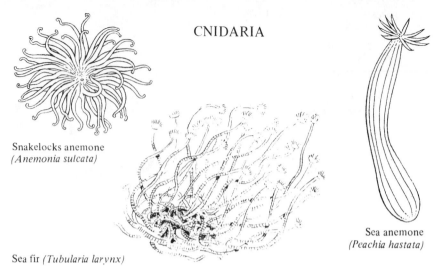

Snakelocks anemone
(Anemonia sulcata)

Sea anemone
(Peachia hastata)

Sea fir *(Tubularia larynx)*

The *Hydrozoa* includes the hydroids: branching colonies of small polyps protected by a tough outer covering. These inconspicuous 'sea-firs' are very common, attached to rock or weed surfaces. The second hydrozoan order, the Siphonophora, are complex floating colonies of highly modified individuals and include the Portuguese Man-o'-War (*Physalia physalis*) which floats over tropical and sub-tropical seas.

The 250-odd species of true jelly-fishes (class Scyphozoa) are mostly large, swimming medusae. With their feathery tentacles extended they sink slowly over plankton, fish or crustaceans. Their prey is stunned and transferred to the mouth.

The Anthozoa are either solitary or colonial polyps and include a diverse range of around 6000 species of sea-anemones, stony corals, soft corals and horny corals.

ANNELIDA:

Two-thirds of the 9000-odd species of segmented worms—the Annelida—belong to the class *Polychaeta,* the bristle worms, which are almost entirely marine, occurring in all seas at all depths. Each body segment typically has lateral outgrowths which bear numerous bristles or chaetae.

A few swimming species are pelagic, with flattened oar-like projections on each segment for swimming. But most are bottom-living, and are separated ecologically into the Errantia, which crawl, burrow or swim on or near the sea-floor, and the Sedentaria which construct and live in tubes or burrows. Whilst the errant polychaetes, such as ragworms and scale-worms, possess a protrusible, jaw-bearing proboscis and prey on small animals, some of the tube-dwellers display elaborate crowns of tentacles which filter food

ANNELIDA

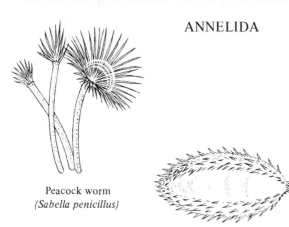

Peacock worm
(Sabella penicillus)

Ragworm (Neanthes
[Nereis] virens)

Sea mouse (Aphrodite aculeata)

particles from the water or which snake over the substrate collecting deposited material. Others produce a web of mucus through which water is strained. In turn the polychaetes are preyed upon by many other marine animals.

ECTOPROCTA:

The 'sea-mats', phylum Ectoprocta (Polyzoa or Bryozoa), are sedentary, colonial, polyp-like animals resembling small ferns or forming an encrusting layer over stone or weed. The calcareous or horny skeleton of the colony surrounds the microscopic individuals, each of which extends a funnel of delicate, ciliated tentacles. The beating hair-like cilia draw in water carrying oxygen and minute food particles. They are common in all seas, mainly in shallow water.

MOLLUSCA:

The abundant and widely ranging Mollusca form a major part of the terrestrial, fresh-water and marine communities, the great majority of the 31,000 marine species inhabiting the shore and shallow sea.

The three main classes are the Gastropoda—snails, slugs; the Bivalvia—clams, oysters; and the Cephalopoda—squids and octopus.

The gastropods have a well-developed head, bearing eyes and tentacles; a large flat foot and, typically, a coiled dorsal body hump with a single shell. Gastropods of the sub-class Prosobranchia, with the gills at the front, all have a shell which is cap-like (limpets), or coiled, whilst in the Opisthobranchia the shell is reduced, internal or absent. A diversity of feeding habits is displayed, some feeding exclusively on algae, e.g. limpets, winkles and the sea-hares (Opisthobranchia). Some cowries feed on sponges as well as algae and others on sea-squirts and soft corals,

MOLLUSCA

Lesser Octopus *(Eledone cirrosa)*

Great Scallop *(Pecten maximus)*

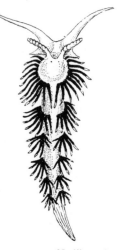

Common Whelk
(Buccinum undatum)

ECTOPROCTA

False Coral *(Myriozoum truncatum)*

Nudibranch
(Facelina auriculata)

Common Limpet
(Patella vulgata)

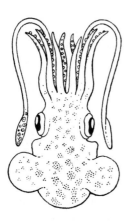

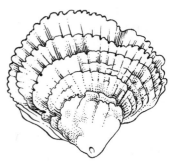

Little Cuttlefish *(Sepiola rondeleti)*

Native Oyster *(Ostrea edulis)*

whilst the whelks are important scavengers and carnivores, and the nudibranchs (Opisthobranchia) are highly specialised carnivores on sponges, hydroids, cnidarians, polyzoans or sea-squirts.

In bivalve molluscs the laterally compressed body is protected by two secreted calcareous valves, hinged and held above by a ligament and closed together by muscles. Many bivalves (razor-shells, cockles, tellins, clams) live buried in soft sand and mud, with siphons—one inhalant, one exhalant—as the only connection to the sea above. Others may be anchored to a hard substrate by secreted threads (mussels), or by one shell being firmly stuck to the bottom (oysters), whilst the scallops and file-shells can propel themselves forward and so escape predators (particularly starfish) by clapping the two valves together. Water carrying oxygen and food particles is swept past the large paired gills by ciliary beating; gas exchange takes place, and food particles are filtered off and sorted before being transferred to the mouth.

The highly developed cephalopod molluscs are entirely marine, occurring in all seas in large numbers. The 700-odd species include cuttlefish, squid and octopus. Ecologically the abundant squid are the most important as food for cetaceans (whales and dolphins), seals, fish and birds, and as the predators of many smaller animals. Ten arms, each complete with cutting toothed-rings or hooks, surround the head. Rapid forward or backward movement is achieved by a directional jet of water which is forced by the contraction of body muscles through a small siphon (the foot of other molluscs). The mid-ocean swimming species are torpedo-shaped, and buoyancy is adjusted by the retention of certain salts in the body fluids. The cuttlefish achieve neutral buoyancy by sucking water from cavities in the internal shell. Mid-water species of both groups display dazzling arrays of light-producing organs.

Octopuses have eight arms which are used for prey-catching and which are sensitive to touch and to certain chemicals. Although typically inshore animals, crawling and hiding on the bottom and possessing great powers of colour change and camouflage, there are also free-swimming mid- and deep-water species.

ARTHROPODA:

The success of the arthropods, as represented by over 800,000 living species, has been attributed to their locomotory equipment which is a series of jointed levers. The segmented body and paired limbs are covered by a hard chitinous exo-skeleton. To allow for growth, periodic moulting is necessary. The phylum includes the scorpions, spiders and mites, the insects (700,000 species) and the Crustacea (35,000 species).

The dominant arthropods in the sea in terms of range, diversity

ARTHROPODA

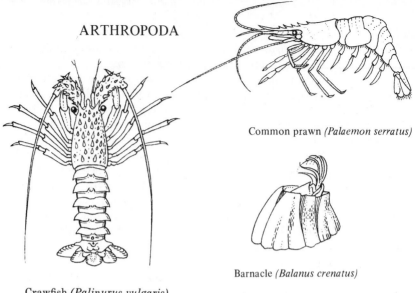

Common prawn *(Palaemon serratus)*

Barnacle *(Balanus crenatus)*

Crawfish *(Palinurus vulgaris)*

and abundance are the Crustacea, which include copepods, ostracods and cirripedes, as well as the higher forms: the crabs, shrimps, prawns and lobsters.

The copepods and ostracods are small but very common and prominent members of the zooplankton that drifts in the surface waters, representing the largest standing stock of protein in the world, and forming the main food of fish such as basking sharks, and whales. Most of the 12,000 or so species filter water for microscopic phytoplankton, others are predatory or scavenging or parasitic.

The Cirripedia are the barnacles. These unusual crustaceans start life as mobile larvae drifting in the water, but soon fix themselves head downwards on to a hard surface and secrete a series of calcareous plates for protection. Modified legs form a series of feathery appendages which are drawn through the water to catch detritus, plankton or larger particles of food. Some barnacles are parasitic. Others, the stalked barnacles, attach themselves to driftwood, ships and buoys, whilst the acorn barnacles are the commonest of all inter-tidal animals.

The sub-class Malacostraca includes all the other crustaceans— about 19,000 species—with the typical features of complex eyes, a hard shell-like carapace covering the thorax, main limbs for walking and swimming, and a tail-fan enabling rapid backward propulsion for escape. This group includes shrimps, prawns, the lobsters and crabs, together with the isopods and amphipods.

ECHINODERMATA

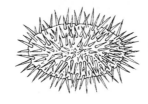

Rockboring sea urchin
(Paracentrotus lividus)

Feather star
(Antedon bifida)

Spiny starfish *(Marthasterias glacialis)*

ECHINODERMATA:

The Echinodermata are entirely marine animals showing radial symmetry on a five-rayed plan in the adult, and possessing a calcareous skeleton of plates or spicules, digestive and nervous systems, blood vessels and a remarkable system of vessels which hydrostatically operate rows of tube-feet.

The Crinoidea are the most primitive class: over 5000 fossil species but only 600 living representatives being identified. Of the latter a small number are stalked (sea-lilies) which anchor in deep-sea muddy sediments by means of discs or hooks. The remainder, the feather-stars (comatulids), are only stalked as juveniles; the free-moving adults cling and clamber over the sea-bed or swim by slowly beating their feathery arms. They are suspension feeders and intercept small food particles by waving their arms. The tube-feet pass food back along the arms to the mouth. They are found mainly on rocky substrates in coastal areas.

Most of the 1200 species of starfish (class Asteroidea) are bottom-dwellers in tropical and sub-tropical waters. The tube-feet on the wide arms have suction-tips which grip the substrate. The co-ordinated extension of the tube-feet enables the animal to move over the sea-bed. Whilst most asteroids are active predators, 'smelling out' prey—particularly bivalves, the shells of which are pulled apart by the tube-feet—a few feed on suspended particles or on deposits of organic detritus.

The brittle-stars (class Ophiuroidea) have a disc-shaped body and long agile arms. They have no suckers on the tube-feet and the arms pull the animal over the bottom. The group includes suspension feeders, which often occur in enormous numbers in current-swept areas, as well as predators of polychaetes, crustacea and molluscs and scavengers and detritus-feeders.

CHORDATA

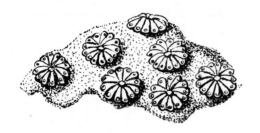

Star Sea-squirt *(Botryllus schlosseri)*   Tube Sea-squirt *(Ciona intestinalis)*

The 800-odd species of globe-shaped, oval or discoid sea-urchins, the Echinoidea, have a calcareous outer covering with long protective spines. The five-rayed plan is evident as five grooves containing long protrusible tube-feet. The irregular heart-urchins and sand-dollars are active burrowers in sand and extend long tube-feet from the burrows to pick up scraps from the sea-bottom, whilst the regular sea-urchins browse on encrusting animals and algae on hard substrates.

The Holothuroidea are the sluggish or sedentary sea-cucumbers with elongated cylindrical bodies, a leathery skin enclosing a skeleton of minute spicules, a mouth surrounded by a circle of modified tube-feet at one end, and an anus at the other. The mouth tube-feet gather suspended particles and deposited material as the animals crawls over the bottom or extends the tube-feet from a crevice.

CHORDATA

The phylum Chordata includes the Vertebrata but also other animals without backbones, notably the tunicates, or urochordates. This sub-phylum includes the sea-squirts (class Ascidiacea), bag-shaped animals enveloped in a jelly-like or leathery tunic and attached to the substrate, singly or in colonies; their resemblance to the vertebrates lies in the tadpole-like larval stage.

They have two openings or siphons, through one of which water containing food particles and oxygen enters to be strained through a fine meshwork. The waste products and the water are expelled through the second siphon, whilst the food is transferred to the gut. These simple animals are highly successful, occurring on hard substrates in all seas, from shallow to deep water. There are over 2000 species.

There are also pelagic tunicates, notably the salps, which are basically similar to the ascidians. The two siphons are at opposite ends and the water flow through the animal provides it with jet propulsion.

The members of the chordate sub-phylum Vertebrata, all of which possess a vertebral column of cartilage or bone and a highly organised brain housed within a skull, are divided between two super-classes: the jawless Agnatha, which includes the primitive hagfish and lampreys; and the Gnathostomata, the jawed vertebrates. The Gnathostomata is further divided into various classes, covering the fishes, amphibia, reptiles, birds and mammals.

In the elasmobranch fishes (class Chondrichthyes) the skeleton is cartilaginous. There is no operculum, the tail is usually hetero-cercal (i.e. asymmetrical), and the body is covered with hard skin 'teeth', the placoid scales. The class includes the sharks, rays, skate and dogfish—in all, about 500 species. Most of these are voracious carnivores, especially the fast-moving and powerful large sharks of the warm oceans, although some, including the largest, the whale shark (up to 20 m in length) and the basking shark (up to 15 m) feed on plankton and small fish with a sieve-like gill apparatus. The smaller forms, including the dogfish, live in temperate and tropical coastal seas, whilst the skates and rays lie or swim close to the sea-bed feeding on fishes, molluscs and crustaceans.

In the fish of the class Osteichthyes the skeleton is bony, an oper-culum covers the external opening of the slits, the tail is typically homocercal, i.e. with equal portions above and below the vertebral column, and the body surface is covered with overlapping scales. The majority of the present-day fishes, with well-developed and bony skull and vertebrae, are included in this class within the super-order Teleostei. This successful and diverse group of some 20000 species has representatives from the shallow to the deep seas. Their mobile fins and swim-bladder enable precise movement and energy-free flotation. Most species are good swimmers, and at one extreme there are some which can glide above the surface and some which can even climb on to land, whilst many live near the sea-bed and some bury themselves.

All these plants and animals react to their environments (to which each is completely adjusted) and to other organisms: there is con-tinual competition between individuals for the available resources of light, space, food, oxygen and so on; there are feeding interactions arising from the dependence of all animals on other living things for food; there are many fascinating, more intimate associations between individuals, including burrow-sharing, 'hitching' a ride, settling and living preferentially on the body surface of another animal or plant, cleaning associations, food-sharing, symbiosis (in which two orga-

SOME INTERTIDAL FISH

Sand Goby *(Pomatoschistus minutus)*

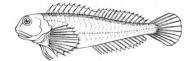

Shanny *(Lipophrys pholis)*

Lesser Sand-Eel *(Ammodytes lancea)*

Butterfly Blenny *(Blennius ocellaris)*

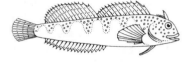

Montagu's Blenny *(Coryphoblennius galerita)*

Viviparous Blenny *(Zoarces viviparus)*

Rock Goby *(Gobius paganellus)*

Sprat *(Sprattus sprattus)*

Butterfish *(Pholis gunnellus)*

nisms are mutually dependent), and parasitism—in which the partnership is advantageous to one member but usually harmful to the other.

Now what can the average diver do with marine biology? How can he set about increasing his understanding of the marine environment? The process should not be rushed. Background reading and practical work should progress together. Two possible approaches, intended as guidelines, are outlined below.

An interested individual would be wise to concentrate his practical efforts on to one small group of organisms. In other words, start with *Laminaria* species, not Brown algae; or with starfish, not echinoderms. The first essential is positive identification of the species; firstly with laboratory confirmation but later underwater so that no interference with the organism is necessary. When you know exactly what you are looking at, you can record where it occurs and in what quantities, what sizes, at what times of the day or year, and you can try to find out what, when, where and how it eats, or whether it moves, and if it does, why, and again, how, where, and when.

If a group of divers is interested it would be profitable to concentrate its effort, perhaps, on to one under-water site, where the bottom conditions, depths, populations of animals, plants and so on can be surveyed and the results mapped. Particular species, or various influences on your under-water community, could then be studied in detail. What changes occur with time: daily, tidally, seasonally, or over a period of years? Do divers, or fishermen, or effluent have any effect? Could simple experiments be attempted under water, isolating and varying one factor, so that its influence may be assessed?

Other clubs, local scientists or organisations concerned with marine research, recreation or conservation, can be contacted with and for ideas for joint projects. In the past, the BSAC has itself, under the leadership of Dr. David Bellamy, the well-known botanist, conducted a number of marine surveys under the titles of 'Operation Kelp' and 'Operation Starfish'. Other groups visited the Shetland Islands to carry out pre-disturbance monitoring of various sites prior to their development as part of Great Britain's North Sea oil exploitation. It is almost certain that other similar projects, open to members of the BSAC with an interest in this field, will take place in the future. The Club already has a number of amateur specialists amongst its ranks and those with an interest in this subject are invited to contact HQ for further details of the 'Identikit' scheme.

For the would-be under-water naturalist, many excellent books are available, some of which are listed below. In addition, the BSAC Coaching Scheme offers basic introductory courses in Marine-life Identification, and there are many opportunities for British divers to attend regular field courses in Marine Biology or Ecology at centres such as the Dale Fort Field Centre in Dyfed or the Fort Bovisand Under-water Centre at Plymouth. Evening class courses are also available in most big cities.

Remember that you are trained to explore the shallow seas and to observe and to record scientifically and in safety. You have an essential role to play in the development of man's understanding of marine biological processes. Finally, remember that you must be aware of disturbing the objects of your interest, of disrupting the balance. Preserve under-water sites as places of interest and beauty for future divers by restricting your collection to a minimum—by taking photographs rather than souvenirs—and by discouraging spear-fishing and other activities that will scare away the more mobile fish and mammals.

Dive towards a better understanding of your alternative environment.

Whiting *(Merlangius merlangus)*

Lesser Weever *(Trachinus vipera)*

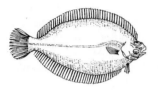

Lemon Sole *(Microstomus kitt)*

Mackerel *(Scomber scombrus)*

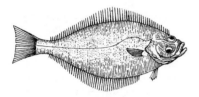

Halibut *(Hippoglossus hippoglossus)*

Cod *(Gadus morhua)*

Haddock *(Scophthalmus aeglefinus)*

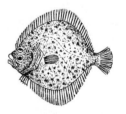

Turbot *(Rhombus maximus)*

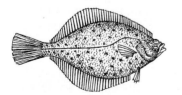

Flounder *(Platichthys flesus)*

Pollack *(Pollachius pollachius)*

Herring *(Clupea harengus)*

Sand Smelt *(Atherina presbyter)*

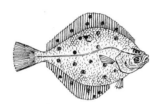

Plaice *(Pleuronectes platessa)*

Bass *(Dicentrarchus labrax)*

Conger Eel *(Conger conger)*

Spotted Catfish *(Anarrhichas lupus)*

Spur-dog *(Squalus acanthius)*

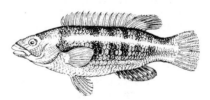

Ballan Wrasse *(Labrus bergylta)*

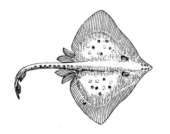

Skate *(Raja batis)*

Grey Mullet *(Chelon labrosus)*

Suggested reading on Marine Biology

BARRETT, J. H. & YONGE, C. M. *Collins Pocket Guide to the Sea Shore.*
BONEY, A. D. *A Biology of Marine Algae.*
BOWERBANK, J. S. *Monograph of the British Spongidae,* Volumes I, II, III and IV.
CAMPBELL, A. C. *Hamlyn Guide to the Seashore and Shallow Seas of Britain and Europe.*
CLARK, R. B. *Fauna of the Clyde Sea Area: Polychaeta with a key to the British Genera.*
DALES, R. P. *Annelids.*
DUDDINGTON, C. L. *Seaweeds and Other Algae.*
EALES, N. B. *Littoral Fauna of Great Britain.*
FORBES, E. *British Star Fishes.*
FRIEDRICH, H. *Marine Biology.*
GOTTO, R. V. *Marine Animals—Partnerships and Other Associations.*
GRAHAM, A. *British Prosobraachs.*
DE HAAS, W. & KNORR, F. *Marine Life—Young Specialist looks at.*
HARDY, SIR A. *Open Sea: I—The World of Plankton.*
HINCKS, T. *British Hydroid Zoophytes,* Volumes I and II.
HINCKS, T. *British Marine Polyzoa,* Volumes I and II.
HOLME, N. & MacINTYRE (Ed.) *Methods for Study of Marine Benthos.*
LEWIS, J. R. *The Ecology of Rocky Shores.*
LYTHGOE, J. & LYTHGOE, G. *Fishes of the Sea.*
MacGINITIE, G. & MacGINITIE, N. *The Natural History of Marine Animals.*
MACMILLAN, N. F. *British Shells.*
MARSHALL, N. & MARSHALL, O. *Ocean Life.*
MARSHALL, N. B. (Ed.). *Aspects of Deep Sea Biology.*
MARSHALL, S. M. & ORR, A. P. *Biology of a Marine Copepod.*
MILLAR, R. H. *Catalogue of Marine Fouling Organisms: IV. Ascidians.*
MILLAR, R. H. *British Ascidians.*
MOORE, H. B. *Marine Ecology.*
MORTENSEN, T. *Handbook of the Echinoderms of the British Isles.*
NAYLOR, E. *British Marine Isopods.*
NELSON-SMITH, A. *Catalogue of Marine Fouling Organisms: III. Serpulids.*
NICOL, D. *Echinoderms.*
NICOL, J. A. C. *The Biology of Marine Animals.*
RYLAND, J. S. *Catalogue of Marine Fouling Organisms: II. Polyzoa.*
SOUTHWARD, A. J. & CRISP, D. J. *Catalogue of Marine Fouling Organisms: I. Barnacles.*
STEPHENSON, T. A. *Sea Anemones,* Volumes I and II.
STREET, P., *The Crab and its Relatives.*
TAIT, R. V. *Elements of Marine Ecology.*
TEBBLE, N. *British Bivalve Seashells: A Handbook for Identification.*
WELLS, M. *Lower Animals.*
WHEELER, A. *The Fishes of the British Isles and North-West Europe.*
WOODS, J. P. & LYTHGOE, J. N. *Under-water Science.*
YOUNG, M. *The Sea Shore.*

Geology

There are three main subdivisions of the subject in which divers can play a useful part:
(i) Solid Geology—the study of rocks.
(ii) Sediment Geology.
(iii) The study of sea levels of the comparatively recent past.

SOLID GEOLOGY

The study of the rocks of the continental shelf in no way differs from the study of similar rocks of the adjacent continent, except that the raw materials, rock samples and observations of the way in which the rocks lie, are more difficult to obtain. The great advantage of this is that, unlike terrestrial biologists, who wish to study marine biology which is a whole new field of science, the terrestrial geologist who learns to dive can immediately apply his geological knowledge without additional study; likewise the non-geologist diver who wishes to take up the subject to give additional interest to his diving can acquire sufficient knowledge for the purpose by reading the books or attending the evening classes intended for the far more numerous dry-land students of the subject.

He can also get practice on land in examining the sort of rocks he expects to be dealing with under water; this is most important, since after all the bookwork is done, geology can only be learnt by examining large quantities of real rocks.

There is the further great advantage for those now going into the submarine branch of the study that until recently it just was not possible to obtain rock samples below the low tide mark except by the use of very inefficient grabs, and though the diver now has competition from corers and submersibles both manned and unmanned, these are all now scarce and expensive, so their use is best confined to those areas too deep or otherwise difficult, thus leaving a great part of the continental shelves as almost virgin territory for diving geologists.

Equipment

In addition to normal diving equipment, the equipment required by the diver-geologist is simple and similar to that used by his dry-land colleague: hammer, chisel, magnetic compass for orientation, collecting bag and something on which to take notes. However, being weightless, a diver cannot strike hard blows with a heavy hammer without propelling himself violently in the opposite direction, which usually results in his missing what he is aiming at. It is, therefore, better, where the nature of the rocks will allow it, to work a chisel into any natural crevices with a light hammer. Once the chisel is embedded one can secure oneself to it with one hand and strike it with the hammer in the other.

Observations

In making observations of the rocks and how the strata lie the diver often faces the problem of poor visibility which only allows him to see a very small section of the picture at a time, and in areas of complicated folding this can make things very confusing indeed. The only remedy is to take things calmly and methodically and, using a compass, carry out a series of observations, if possible at right-angles to the apparent strike; but if the current just will not allow this, in a straight line in some direction, carefully noting all changes in the nature and dip of the rocks. It is a help here if the diver has previously ascertained approximately how far he swims in full equipment with a certain number of fin beats.

At the end of the day and before memory fades, write up your notes and replace the scratches made under water to record the orientation of the rock samples by more visible marks. A small tin of quick drying enamel is excellent for this.

The sort of information which should accompany *each* sample is better if the sample or collection of samples is also accompanied by a fuller description of the type of bottom from which they were taken.

Using your information

As with all scientific work, there is little point in gathering samples and taking observations and then doing nothing with either, and it is just in this matter of directing work to the most useful project and seeing that the information gathered gets to the right quarters that the amateur most needs direction and advice from the established geologist. A group of divers who are thinking of taking up the subject should, therefore, make every effort to get a competent geologist, amateur or professional, to direct their work. If they know none, a visit to the local museum or college may produce the necessary introductions to the local learned society. With luck, one may even be able to find a geologist prepared to take up diving, but even without such a person, it should be possible to establish a sound working partnership between a group of divers who regularly dive in a certain area and a geologist interested in the adjacent coast who will usually jump at the chance to extend his knowledge outward from it, and in return can guide and direct the studies of the group.

Even in parts of the world where at present there is no higher education or learned society, divers may be able to find a geologist, since such areas are probably being explored geologically on land; English-speaking geologists are almost certain to be playing a part in this.

SEDIMENT GEOLOGY

'Sediment' here means any solid that is moving, being sorted or deposited on the bottoms of seas, lakes or rivers.

The fact that such movements take place has long been recognised; indeed, it forms the whole basis of the long-established science of Sedimentary Geology and plays a large part in the newer science of Coastal Morphology. Until the development of free diving, underwater television and submersibles, it was hardly possible to see these processes taking place, and, even now, we cannot see as much as we would like because sediment movement is often the cause of bad visibility. Despite this, enough has already been seen for us to be sure that, from now on, direct observation is going to play a considerable role. This is simply because Nature so often manages to surprise us, and the factor which the instruments were not set to detect or which was not allowed for in the wave-tank experiment turns out to be the vital one.

So, useful results should follow as more scientists learn to dive and as more divers, who see interesting movements taking place, report them to the experts either locally or at the Club's scientific congresses. With luck they may find that they are describing something unknown or largely ignored by science.

For example, one diver-geologist saw quite large stones being dragged across the sea-bed; seaweed was growing on them and acting as a sail, allowing tidal currents that would never move bare stones to move them quite easily; this factor had been previously overlooked and as a result of wave-tank experiments and short-term diver observations and on specially marked but weedless stones, various experts were flatly asserting that shingle did not move below the surf zone.

There were exceptions to this view. People in various parts of the world had seen weed-bearing stones come ashore and had guessed that this might be an important factor in beach supply, but it could not be proved so their guesses were largely overlooked and forgotten. When it was realised just how wrong this was, and the massive scale on which weed-dragging of shingle was taking place in certain areas such as Selsey Bill, in the south of England, where fresh supplies of weed-dragged shingle to the end of the Bill were the principal factor in maintaining its existence, it was obvious that the discovery had to be reported.

There followed three years of draft papers, discussions with various experts in coastal matters, more observations and redrafting, till finally contact was made with the one other person—in Britain at any rate—who seemed to be on the same track: Dr. I. P. Jolliffe at the Department of Geography, Bedford College, London, a scientist who had learnt to dive. The diver and Dr. Jolliffe decided to pool observations and produced a joint paper for the 1973 CMAS scientific symposium.

This example of studies made by an amateur diver/geologist points out two morals: that the amateur diver who sees something remarkable happening under water should do something about it, and that the marine or coastal scientist who takes up diving or makes the acquaintance of divers may well learn something to his advantage.

The subject of weed-dragged stones is one in which the observations of ordinary Club members can help, even if they don't want to go to the trouble of going into print themselves in the scientific journals. Detailed observations of this phenomena have been carried out only in quite restricted areas: the English Channel coast from Brighton to Selsey and from Swanage to Weymouth, and Summer observations on a small area in South Brittany. It is known that it occurs far more widely, and more information is needed. What weeds are involved and at what times of year? At what depth? Does shingle only come ashore in storms—as at Worthing, or almost all the time—as at Selsey? What sort of bottom were the weed-dragged stones moving on—sand, bare rock or a continuous blanket of other shingle? Amateur divers could provide this information.

PAST SEA LEVELS

From observation of wave-notches cut into cliffs overlooking the tideless Mediterranean, of regular terraces cut into hillsides in this country and others bordering the ocean, and the fact that these terraces are often covered by beach or river valley deposits according to whether they face the open sea or an inland valley, it has long been recognised that even in the comparatively recent past sea levels must have changed considerably and, geologically speaking, rapidly.

However, it is only the development of the science of glaciology and recent polar exploration that has led to an appreciation of the enormous quantities of water still locked up in the polar ice-caps—sufficient to raise sea levels by a hundred metres or so—and the converse realisation that when the ice-caps extended down to the Thames and the Great Lakes of America, the sea-level must have been lowered by hundreds of metres. The latter has been confirmed by reports from divers with submersibles on obvious submerged shorelines. This in turn has led to a deliberate attempt to determine the sea levels of the Pleistocene Ice Age—the last million years of the Earth's history, during which the glaciers have repeatedly advanced and retreated.

Knowledge on these matters is important both for a proper understanding of history and pre-history and also for predicting what is likely to happen in the future. It is also a matter of considerable practical importance as the proposed spending on vast sums of the flood defences of London and Venice demonstrates.

However, despite its importance, this whole subject is surrounded by a great deal of uncertainty, so although things have clarified considerably even in the last ten years, it is as well to read the latest works on the subject.

The major reason for the uncertainty is the fact that the Earth's crust is not static but heaves and buckles due both to the *Tectonic* forces originating in the interior of the Earth, forces which in the thousands of millions of years of the Earth's geological history have raised up and lowered whole continents; or to what is called *Isostatic* adjustment; the much shorter term but delayed adjustment of the crust to weight superimposed on it. An example of the latter is the fact that the whole of the British Isles is tilting like a flagstone, up in the north-west and down in the south-east by several centimetres a century as a result of the disappearance of the Scottish ice cap which occurred fifteen to twenty thousand years ago.

These Tectonic and Isostatic factors make it impossible to say anything definite from an examination of raised or submerged beaches at any one point about the world-wide or *Eustatic* changes in sea level. It can only be done by comparing similar terraces all over the world and by averaging the result. But this comparison is in itself a chancy business because the terraces are by no means continuous: they are only formed under certain conditions and, once formed, they are liable to be destroyed by later advances of the sea, or, if long above water, by the normal forces of sub-aerial erosion.

Despite these difficulties, progress has been made through careful correlation of evidence for past glacial advances and retreats in Scandinavia, the Alps and North America, with raised and submerged shorelines and with buried or submerged peat deposits. Peat that can be identified as having been formed in brackish estuarine conditions is especially valuable as an indicator of past sea levels, since it can be dated to within a century or two by carbon-14.

As a result of such calculations the rough magnitude and timing of the major sea-level fluctuations of the last million years is now broadly agreed. The timing of the recovery from the 100 m lower level at the peak of the last glaciation 20,000 years ago is also pretty clear up to the last 10 m and last 5000 years: then, just because the rise is so much slower, it is hard to separate it from local earth movements. So there is still argument as to whether the sea attained or nearly attained its present level 4000 or 5000 years ago and whether since then it has risen steadily or fluctuated, and by how much.

P

A brave attempt to resolve the uncertainty has been made by BSAC diver, Dr. N. C. Flemming (of Cambridge University, the National Institute of Oceanography and consultant to the office of Ocean Economics and Technology at the UN secretariat). Together with members of these institutions and other universities he has carried out observations at many hundreds of sites round the Mediterranean on both raised and submerged wave notches and on archaeological sites. (The advantage of using archaeological sites is that they can usually be dated, and the chief advantage of using the Mediterranean is that it is almost tideless so that closely spaced wave notches do not merge into one continuous slope, as is apt to happen elsewhere.)

A disadvantage of using the Mediterranean is that much of it is tectonically unstable, so observations were spread over both rising and subsiding areas and attempts made to determine just what these local movements were.

As a result of all this and research into work elsewhere, Dr. Flemming's present view is that the sea rose to its present level about 4000 years ago and has been fluctuating a metre or two above and below this ever since. It is too early yet to say that this view will be generally accepted; confirmation, as the result of equally detailed work in other parts of the world, would seem desirable.

The above 'history of the subject' is a necessary preliminary to considering what contribution divers, especially amateur divers, can hope to make, bear in mind that in the UK high-powered government institutions, the Institute of Geological Sciences and the National Institute of Oceanography are interested and are alive to the importance of using divers, they have diving scientists on their staffs, and are getting on with the job.

However, there is still plenty of work for all—amateur divers included—because for most areas local earth movements are more important than the eustatic level changes over the past 2000 years in predicting what is likely to happen in the next 200. For example, there is general agreement among most geologists on the fact, but not the extent, of the British tilt up in the north-west and down in the south-east. The archaeologists have pretty good evidence of a relative subsidence of about 5 m for the London area since early Roman times. But if one asks whether this has been a steady or intermittent movement and whether it applies to other sites in south-east England, one will get as many answers as there are experts; the supporting evidence is just not sufficient. Except for the Fens, the situation in most of the country is even more uncertain. In the Fens, archaeological work on old drainage sites and analysis of peat deposits suggests only slight up and down movements since early Roman times (which one would rather expect since this area lies close to the hinge line of isostatic tilt and is thus affected only by the slight eustatic fluctuations already mentioned). Divers can help remedy the situation by thorough reporting of chance finds, and by deliberate archaeological work on submerged sites.

The chance finds most likely to be met are the submerged terraces left by long standstills at lower sea levels, and peat beds. The term 'submerged terraces' instead of 'submerged beaches' is used deliberately because, to the layman, 'beach' is apt to suggest sand or shingle and in tidal waters such terraces are unlikely to have their original beach material still on them; any shingle that is present is likely to be the result of later weed-dragging. It is to be hoped that there is not too much weed-dragged shingle around, otherwise it will be difficult to check that the terrace is cut into the bedrock and is not just a sediment feature.

If you do come across a considerable length (about 100 m) of such a terrace running at a constant depth across the natural bedding plane of the rock, or if a number of offshore submerged pinnacles are all cut off at about the same level, though the rock of which they are composed is not horizontally bedded, it is worth running some deliberate echo-sounder profiles across them, noting the state of the tide and passing the results over to some interested geologist or geographer. If you know none, Dr. N. C. Flemming at the National Institute of Oceanography, or in Scotland, the Continental Shelf Survey Unit of the IGS, West Granton Road, Edinburgh, would be glad of the information.

If you come across submerged peat, first check that it is part of a continuous in-situ bed, because quite large slabs of peat can be washed a long way from where they were formed; then note the depth at which it was found, the state of tide and position; seal a pound or two in a plastic bag and ask the botany department of the nearest university whether they would like to receive it. The botanists come into the picture in the first instance since only they can determine the plants of which the peat is formed.

Deliberate Research on Past Sea Levels

A university branch that has decided to go on an expedition to a warmer climate could not do better than consult Dr. Flemming as to both where and how.

Those who live or dive in submerging areas such as southern and south-east England, or the mid-Atlantic coast of the USA, are advised to search the nearest, reasonably deserted and unpolluted estuary for abandoned quays, tidal mills, flood embankments and such like structures designed to operate at a particular high-tide level. Such a project is not glamorous diving but it does have the advantage that it can be indulged in when the weather is not suitable for going to sea, and divers with their wet suits, inflatables and knowledge of the tides are unusually well-equipped to attempt it.

Such work is very well worth while from the archaeological as well as the geological angle, since most of the Roman and some of the later abandoned ports of Britain remain to be located and mapped. Some have certainly gone over the edge of the cliff or lie under modern installations, but a great many remain up estuaries, usually, but not always, covered by a few metres of mud and just awaiting our attention.

At the time of writing this, the author is investigating what appears to be a Roman canal with the top of its banks and floors of the buildings which bordered it about 2.2 m below present high tide. He hopes to follow it down to the then sea level and shore.

Because such work is archaeology as well as geology, it is best undertaken in consultation with the local archaeologists; they may be able to advise on the best place to start looking. Once a site is located, do remember that it is most important that no excavation, or even clearing of mud beyond the minimum necessary to 'prove' it, should be undertaken unless expert archaeological advice and conservation facilities are available.

Suggested reading on Geology

FLEMMING, DR. N. C. *Cities in the Sea*. New English Library, 1972.
SHEPARD, F. P. *Submarine Geology*. A revised second edition. Harper & Row, 1963.
STEERS, J. A. *The Coastline of England and Wales*. A new and enlarged edition. Cambridge University Press, 1964.

PAPERS
BINNS, P. E. & WILLIS, S. K. *The Geology of Rockall and Helens Reef*. Science Diving, BSAC, 1973.
DILL, R. F. & SHUMWAY, G. *Geologic use of Self-contained Diving Apparatus*. American Association of Petroleum Geologists, Vol. 38, p. 148, 1954.
EDEN, R. A. & BINNS, P. E. *The Role of Divers and Submersibles in the Geological Mapping of the Continental Shelf around Scotland, 1967–72*. Science Diving, BSAC, 1973.
FLEMMING, N. C., CZARTORYSKA, N. M. & HUNTER, P. M. *Archaeological Evidence for Vertical Earth Movements in the Region of the Aegean Arc*. Science Diving, BSAC, 1973.

Under-water Photography

This section is intended to provide the basic information to set you on the road to getting good pictures in conditions ranging from the exotic clear waters of the Caribbean to the more challenging conditions around the British Isles.

The first thing you need, of course, is a camera. You can either put a standard, above-water camera in a housing, or you can buy an amphibious camera which is just as at home above or below water.

Cameras

Just as a group of divers will agree to differ on what is the best demand valve, so under-water photographers will argue as to which is the best camera for under-water photography.

The standard 35 mm format is popular because it yields 36 pictures from a single cassette, and the quality of this size is such that the slides are adequate for projection to large audiences. Good quality prints can also be obtained from black and white negatives. The transparencies which result from half-frame cameras cannot be illuminated with sufficient power to give large, bright pictures at Club showings. The even smaller format of 16 mm still cameras gives transparencies which are only really suitable for home viewing. Doubtless, as photographic technology advances, the results from these new miniature cameras will progress to the stage where they can be shown to large audiences.

At the other end of the scale, some photographers prefer the 6–6 cm ($2\frac{1}{4}$ in square) format. In the top photographic competitions the the resultant brilliant transparencies and pin-sharp, grain-free enlargements undoubtedly give this format an edge over 35 mm. However, the format is perhaps best reserved for the more experienced photographer.

In some respects the lens of a camera can be thought of as behaving like the lens of a human eye. When an unmasked diver swims under water he sees only blurred images. To use a camera with its lens in direct contact with the water would also lead to the production of blurred images. The diver puts on a face-mask to see clearly; housing a camera behind a flat glass porthole with air in contact with the lens has a similar effect and enables the lens to 'see' clearly and produce well-defined photographic images.

Housings

The number of different cameras on the market is huge and, like cars, some models go quickly out-of-date as new models are introduced. Producing under-water housings for such a range of cameras is not commercially viable and the result is that under-water housings are made for a number of the cheaper, very popular models, such as the Kodak Instamatic 35 mm cameras, and for the very expensive cameras such as the Hasselblad. In between these two extremes very few under-water cases for specific cameras are available. If you wish to house a camera it is worth enquiring of the camera manufacturers or importers whether or not they can fulfil your needs. It is also worth contacting large distributors of diving equipment as some of them carry good stocks of photographic equipment. However, many photographers who cannot obtain a 'ready-made' housing for their camera have a case 'tailor-made' by one of the small firms who specialise in this service. The addresses of such firms can usually be found in the diving journals.

Of course, you can build your own camera housing. Supplies of components are available for the DIY enthusiast. The camera controls are operated by control rods that pass through watertight glands in the walls of the box. Many ingenious mechanisms have been devised to translate the simple rotational movements of the control rods to the various movements of the camera controls. Perspex is a popular material for home construction as it is easily worked and has the advantage that the camera and its controls can be seen at all times. The pressures to which a rigid box is subjected when under water are staggering: thus a 15 cm cube has a total load of well over a ton on it at a depth of ten metres. Under-water camera housings must therefore be well constructed, of strong materials, if they are not to distort or collapse at depth.

The Siluro—an Amphibious Box Camera

Amphibious cameras are those that can be used above and below water. Unlike box cameras intended only for above-water use, which usually have objects between 3 m and infinity in sharpest focus, the Siluro produces its sharpest pictures when the subject is between 1 m and 3 m from the camera. This is a sensible arrangement because most under-water subjects are photographed when they are relatively close to the camera. However, this focus setting—which is fixed—does reduce the picture clarity of distant groups or views when the camera is used above water. The simple meniscus lens is sealed behind a clear flat porthole.

The Siluro takes twelve 6 × 6 cm pictures on a roll of 120 film. Unfortunately the black frame numbers on the red backing paper, which indicate the position of the film in the camera, are difficult to read under water, and this can lead to overlap of frames, or excessive gaps between shots on the film.

The Siluro has a single fixed shutter speed and aperture and therefore the exposure cannot be varied. Thus, correctly exposed film can only be obtained between specific depths under certain conditions.

With natural lighting, black and white or colour films with a speed in the region of 21 DIN or 100 ASA, are recommended for depths of less than 9 m in clear water. For greater depths, films in the 27 DIN or 400 ASA range are necessary. Flash is essential with medium-speed colour films except in very shallow water.

The Siluro is a box camera and it has the limitations of a box camera. It gives perfectly acceptable contact prints or small enlargements of subjects under good conditions, but will not usually produce pictures that will stand critical inspection at a high degree of enlargement.

The Anfibian—an Amphibious 35 mm Snapshot Camera

The Anfibian is an amphibious camera in the more modern 35 mm format. It is a camera for the under-water photographer who has not much knowledge of photography but who would like to take snapshots above and below the water.

The Anfibian has been designed for simplicity of construction and simplicity of operation. It takes standard cassettes (20 or 36 exposures) of 35 mm film. The film is loaded by passing the leader through the plastic frame (which defines the picture area) on to a take-up spool on to which the film is wound after each exposure. When the film has been loaded and the camera re-assembled a knurled disc is screwed up finger tight. This locks the three basic components together and compresses the rubber flanges that form watertight seals between them. For under-water use the flash-gun is then fitted. The connection to the lens barrel is made first and screwed up tight, before the universal head is slotted into the accessory shoe and locked into position. The film should be wound-on two frames before the first picture is taken. This clears film fogged during the loading operation and is allowed for by the film manufacturers.

After each picture has been taken, the film wind knob—which also serves as a frame counter—is rotated one revolution minus one small scale division, as indicated on the camera body. Although this method of winding on has the merit of simple construction, it lacks for the user the positive foolproof film advance action of a lever wind. The Anfibian is not fitted with a double exposure prevention device. When all of the film has been exposed, the film wind knob can no longer be rotated. The film must then be wound back into the cassette before the camera is opened.

The Anfibian is rendered amphibious by sealing a standard lens (35 mm focal length) behind a flat glass porthole. The shutter is

Fig. 89. THE ANFIBIAN 35 MM CAMERA

operated by a lever mounted on the lens barrel. The single shutter speed (1/60 sec) and single aperture f9.5 give the correct exposure for medium-speed films under sunny conditions. Kodacolor-X film (or its equivalent) is recommended for colour prints. For black and white prints use Kodak Panatomic-X under very bright conditions. Kodak Plus-X film is more widely available and should give reasonable results although the negatives may tend to be over exposed if the light intensity is high.

Except in shallow bright water the flash should always be used when the camera is taken beneath the surface. The flash-gun is designed to take bulbs with a bayonet fitting. Capless bulbs can be used in conjunction with the appropriate adaptor. Type 1 bulbs, e.g. Philips PF1B, will give the best results when the subject is about 1 m from the camera. The flash-gun can, of course, also be used to take indoor pictures.

If all you want is snapshot pictures with the minimum of fuss then the Anfibian camera should satisfy your needs. However, if you want to produce high-quality pictures and enter some of the major underwater photographic competitions, then you will need a more versatile camera.

Calypso-phot, Nikonos, Calypso/Nikkor—Calypso Cameras

The most popular 'still' camera for anyone taking up under-water photography seriously is the amphibious camera now made in Japan by Nikon. It started life in France in the late 1950's and was known as the Calypso-phot. Later, Nikon took over the manufacturing rights and introduced a new model which was sold in Britain as the Nikonos. Another version has since appeared and is available in the UK under the name Calypso/Nikkor. In the United States of America the latest model is still called the Nikonos. These changes of name can lead to confusion, but as all the models are very similar in basic design, they will be referred to collectively as Calypso cameras.

The Calypso cameras are truly amphibious and can be used above and below water without modification, thus they are ideal for taking on boats where cameras are likely to get covered in spray. They are no bigger than conventional 35 mm cameras yet they can be taken under water to a depth of 60 m.

The largest basic unit of Calypso cameras incorporates the film transport system and the focal plane shutter. This unit slots into a pressure-resistant alloy shell. The third and final unit comprises a lens assembly which is located by a bayonet fitting, and when introduced locks all three components together.

Cocking and firing the shutter is a simple operation: a lever on top of the camera is gently squeezed to trigger the shutter and when the lever is released it springs forward. Squeezing the lever again towards the body of the camera winds on the film and cocks the shutter. The entire operation can be carried out very rapidly. To prevent inadvertent firing of the shutter a safety catch can be flicked into position between the shutter lever and the camera body.

The standard Calypso camera has a lens of 35 mm focal length, that is sealed behind a flat, glass porthole. Over the years Nikon has introduced interchangeable lenses and other accessories and, as a result, the Calypso camera is now the basic unit in an under-water photographic system that provides the photographer with a means of getting good pictures in the very diverse conditions that are encountered under water. The Nikon lenses for Calypso cameras range from the very wide angle 15 mm to the 80 mm telephoto lens.

In addition to the accessories made by Nikon, other manufacturers market a range of equipment that extends this unique under-water system still further.

Reflex Cameras

One of the most popular types of camera used by serious photographers today for above-water work is the SLR—the single lens reflex—the great advantage of which is that the operator can see exactly what he is photographing before he releases the shutter.

Fig. 90. THE NIKONOS/CALYPSO III AMPHIBIOUS
CAMERA, fitted with an expendable flash-bulb
gun and a close-up lens with its special frame

(below) THE NIKONOS/ C III, shown about
half actual size

Rumours abound that somebody is going to produce an amphibious SLR camera, but at the time of writing under-water photographers are still waiting. When and if it comes it is sure to become very popular, but in the meantime, the photographer who wishes to use his SLR camera under water must go to the trouble of enclosing it in a housing. The most advanced designs of housings for SLR cameras have domed windows through which the photographs are taken. Such windows, also known as 'dome ports', have the advantage that the normal field of view of the lens is retained when the camera is taken under water. Any complications over focusing with this arrangement are negated by the fact that the photographer can focus using the focusing screen built into the camera.

The 6 × 6 cm camera most widely used under water is the Rolleiflex in a Rolleimarin housing. The Rolleiflex is a twin lens reflex camera. Although such cameras have been largely superseded by single lens reflex cameras, twin lens cameras still have their addicts. The Rolleimarin holds a unique position in under-water photography: despite the fact that it was one of the first professional housings on the market it is still sold in its near-original form. Certainly, a Rolleiflex camera in a Rolleimarin housing will give many years of faultless service if it is properly looked after, and those photographers who already own such a combination are unlikely to need to change it (although they may use other cameras for certain subjects or when diving from the shore when the sea is rough, because such a unit is both heavy and cumbersome out of the water, and walking through surf with it could be courting trouble).

The Hasselblad is the Rolls Royce of still cameras. The range of accessories is enormous and the manufacturers claim that the Hasselblad system is the world's most extensive 6 × 6 cm SLR camera system.

Hasselblad make waterproof cases for some of their camera range. The front section is common to all Hasselblad housings and has operating controls for shutter speed, diaphragm and shutter release. It also contains a battery unit, a contact for flash-bulb flash and a connection for electronic flash.

Knowledge and skill are required to use the Hasselblad efficiently: it is really a tool for the successful professional cameraman. For many aspiring amateurs its price will keep it that way.

Films

The sensitivity of films to light varies, and films with a high sensitivity are said to be 'fast'. Conversely, films with a low sensitivity are said to be 'slow'. A number of standards for measuring film speeds have been devised and two of the most widely used are DIN and ASA.

Fig. 91. A 6 X 6 CM TWIN LENS REFLEX IN A ROLLEIMARIN HOUSING

Fig. 92. A HOUSING AND BULB FLASH FOR A SINGLE LENS 35 MM REFLEX

SPEEDS OF SOME POPULAR FILMS				
Film speed			Colour	Black & White
Classification	DIN	ASA		
Slow	15	25	Kodachrome II	
	18	50	Agfa CT–18	
	18	50		Kodak Panatomic–X
	18	50		Ilford Pan F
Medium	19	64	Ektachrome–X	
	20	80	Kodacolor–X	
	21	100	Fujichrome	
	22	125		Kodak Plus–X
	22	125		Ilford FP4
	23	160	High Speed Ektachrome	
Fast	27	400		Kodak Tri–X
	27	400		Ilford HP4

The tonal range of a subject may be recorded differently by various photographic emulsions: those that produce strong differences between light and shaded areas are said to be 'hard'; those that produce a less intense image variation for the same subject are said to be 'soft'. As a general rule fast black and white films produce soft images and the slow films yield hard images.

Generally the under-water world is one of low contrasts and this would indicate the use of slow speed films to compensate, but unfortunately for the under-water photographer, the light intensity at depth is so diminished that the use of slow films is precluded. Kodak Tri-X film is popular for available light photography.

When mass-produced by commercial laboratories prints of under-water subjects taken on fast black and white film may be soft. However, considerable control over the quality of the final picture can be exercised in the darkroom: it is possible to produce bright pictures from fast film by selected development techniques and the use of hard printing paper. Thus the under-water photographer is advised to do his own developing and printing if he wishes to obtain optimum results.

Processing colour films necessitates more precise and elaborate techniques than does processing monochrome films. Far less control over the final product can be achieved by modification of darkroom technique. Most colour films are therefore processed commercially.

Colour films produced to yield colour transparencies for projection are called *reversal* films. Colour prints can be obtained from colour transparencies, but when these are printed by commercial processing laboratories they are not normally produced via an intermediate colour negative, and the results are therefore often insipid. Better prints can be obtained if colour negative film (which is designed specifically to yield colour prints) is used from the onset. However, as colour-printing techniques advance, so too will the quality of prints made direct from transparencies.

Slow reversal colour films tend to produce colour transparencies with vivid colours, whereas the very fast films yield transparencies with muted colours. Good results are obtained from a medium-slow speed film such as Agfa CT-18 or Ektachrome-X in bright conditions; resort to the medium-fast colour film, High Speed Ektachrome, when diving deeper.

Exposure

In order to get a good photographic image the amount of light falling on the film must lie within certain limits. The exposure variation between these two extremes is known as the *exposure latitude*. The photographer producing his own black and white prints can make good some of his exposure errors by control of the printing technique in the darkroom. This is not so if he is working in colour.

EXPOSURE GUIDE FOR FILM OF SPEED 64 ASA IN BRIGHT SUNSHINE WITH THE SUN OVERHEAD WITH A SHUTTER SPEED OF 1/125 SEC.

Depth (Metres)	Water visibility		
	Very clear (40 m)	Average clarity (10 m)	Poor clarity (5 m)
Above surface	f11	f11	f11
1	f8	f5.6	f4
5	f5.6	f4	f2.8
10	f4	f2.8	
20	f2.8		

It is essential therefore, that the photographer accurately exposes his film when taking colour shots.

In above-water photography it is possible to draw up a table of exposures for different conditions, and the exposure latitude for most films is such that reasonable results are assured if the table is followed. The same cannot be said of films taken under-water because of the tremendous variation in light intensity both with depth and the conditions of the water. It is not possible to draw up a simple comprehensive table of exposure for under-water conditions; the one given on page 452 should be regarded only as a general guide.

The best way of ensuring correct exposure is to use an exposure meter of the reflectance type, that is, one that measures the amount of light reflected from the subject.

With medium-speed colour films the sensitivity of the cheaper range of selenium cell activated light meters is sufficient to give a good indication of exposure if the light is bright enough to give a picture. When the light intensity under water is low, and a faster film is used, a meter with a higher sensitivity is required. Meters with a cadmium sulphide photocell (often referred to as CdS meters) powered by a small battery are the most sensitive and are recommended for the photographer who expects to work in low light conditions.

Provided there is room, and it can be operated and clearly seen, the meter may be conveniently placed inside the camera housing. However, most photographers have to resort to housing their meter in a separate watertight container. Housings are readily available for the popular Weston Master meters, and Nikon make a good plastic housing for the modestly priced Sekonic Auto-Lumi, with its high sensitivity selenium cell.

The Sekonic Marine Meter is of the CdS type. The switches are simple to operate under water and the clear bold figures on a luminous scale are easily read. The Marine Meter is negatively buoyant and when attached to the camera by a lanyard it tends to get knocked against the rocks. It is best mounted in a clamp and attached to the camera system.

Flash

Every diver is aware that light is absorbed by water: the deeper you go the darker it gets. But light is not uniformly absorbed—even pure 'gin clear' water absorbs the red component of white light more strongly than the other basic colours. Thus, if you have been fortunate enough to dive with a girl wearing a bright red (non-fluorescent) costume in the clear waters of the Caribbean you will no doubt have noticed that the colour of her costume apparently changed, and below 6–7 metres it took on a deep purple-grey tone. As an under-water camera 'sees' roughly what you as a diver see, a colour photograph of your diving buddy would also show her wearing a grey-purple swim suit at depth.

To get a picture of her showing all of the colours you would see on the surface she must be illuminated with light containing all of the colours of the visible spectrum. And the way to do this is to use flash.

There are two types of flash unit: one uses expendable flash-bulbs; the other, known as *strobe* or *electronic*, utilises the light from an electric discharge.

In expendable flash-bulbs (which must be discarded once used), the light is produced by rapidly burning a metal foil in an atmosphere of oxygen contained within the glass bulb.

Flash reflectors vary considerably in size, modern ones following the trend towards miniaturisation. The ultimate are those incorporated in the disposable flash cubes which consist of four individual miniature flash-bulbs, each with its own tiny reflector, built into a single compact unit. The cube is rotated in its socket after each bulb has been fired.

The light output from flash-bulbs varies and for the convenience of photographers it is correlated with film speed and exposure. Expressed in terms of *flash factors* it is usually indicated in a table on the bulb package. Assuming you are using a shutter speed of 1/30–1/60 and X-synchronisation, the correct aperture is determined by dividing the distance between camera and subject into the flash factor, thus, if the flash factor were 100, then for an above-water photograph in a room with a camera-to-subject distance of 3 m the correct diaphragm setting would be 100/9 i.e. about f11.

Under water, many influences combine to reduce the illuminating power, and therefore the flash factor, of a flash-bulb. As a general rule dividing the normal flash factor by 3 or 4 gives a reasonable correction. This reduction in lighting capacity is such as to preclude the illumination of big scenes even when large bulbs are used.

Flash-bulbs are used in direct contact with water and are changed by hand. The electrical components must, of course, be completely protected from water. They can either be contained in the camera housing, or in a separate watertight tube as in the Nikon flash-gun for the Calypso amphibious cameras.

As electronic flash-guns have become cheaper and more compact there has been a gradual move away from the use of expendable bulbs to the more convenient strobe flash for under-water use. In the past some very low power electronic flash-guns were put on the market for under-water use, but such guns are only of real value in ultra close-up photography or to 'fill-in' the colours in the foreground of a picture already well illuminated with natural light.

It is now possible to buy reasonably priced electronic flash-guns that are compact and have a usefully high light output. Such a model is the Sunpak GT32 which has a flash factor of about 80 for 64 ASA film. This flash unit can be readily housed in a plastic case with a watertight connection between the camera and the flash-gun. Unlike expendable bulbs, a flash tube can be fired thousands of times. Thus the entire unit (including tube and reflector) is enclosed in the watertight housing.

The duration of the flash from an electronic flash-gun is extremely short: usually in the region of 1/1000 second. It is therefore important to ensure that the shutter of the camera is fully open at the instant the flash fires. Thus, electronic flash should be used in conjunction with slow shutter speeds (1/30–1/60 sec) and X-synchronisation.

There are terminals in the flash socket in the base of Calypso amphibious cameras which give X- or FP-synchronisation. The FP setting enables high shutter speeds to be used with the special flash-bulbs for focal plane shutters and is satisfactory for conventional bulbs (such as the Philips PF1), provided the shutter speed does not exceed 1/60. In Calypso flash-guns the pins in the connector are set up to give FP-synchronisation: changing the terminal setting to X-synchronisation involves dismantling the watertight connector.

The Visibility Rule

When a camera is put in a housing with a flat glass porthole the acceptance angle of the lens is reduced. Visibility under water is seldom in excess of 30 m in most parts of the world and it is not surprising therefore that taking pictures under water has been likened to taking pictures on land in a thick fog with a telephoto lens. The diver-photographer should be prepared to recognise the limitations imposed by such a situation and work within them. Over the years a rule has been devised—the visibility rule—that can save a lot of wasted film.

The rule is based on the fact that the particles suspended in water that reduce the visibility also progressively degrade the quality of photographic image on a film until it is undetectable at the limit of visibility. Thus it is important to get as close to the subject as possible to reduce the loss in quality of the photographic image to a minimum.

The rule is: ALWAYS KEEP THE DISTANCE BETWEEN THE SUBJECT AND THE CAMERA TO LESS THAN ONE-THIRD OF THE VISIBILITY. If the subject-to-camera distance is greater than one-third of the visibility, the picture quality is so poor that it is not worth taking.

Close-ups

One of the obvious techniques that must be mastered when observing the visibility rule around the British Isles is that of close-up photography. As many cameras do not focus on subjects less than 1 metre away the use of supplementary lenses is essential. Indeed, using of such lenses opens up a treasure chest of beautiful and interesting photographic subjects.

The supplementary lens is located immediately in front of the camera lens. When used with amphibious cameras the supplementary lens must obviously get wet. Special 'wet' lenses that clip on to the front of Calypso cameras are available. The same lenses can also be used with a housed camera, provided the camera lens is close to the porthole.

The depth of field, which can be loosely defined as the distance between the boundaries of sharp focus, is very small for close-up shots. Accurate focusing is therefore essential.

For normal shots under water the visual or apparent distance of subject, which is shorter than the real distance, is the one to which the camera lens should be set. Thus the diver estimates the subject-camera distance as it appears to him, and focuses his camera lens accordingly. In close-up work, visually estimating distances is not sufficiently reliable and some device for accurately measuring the separation of the camera from the subject must be employed. The close-ups made by Nikon for the Calypso/Nikkor have a frame which is attached to the camera. This not only accurately sets the distance, it also defines the picture area.

Wide-angle Shots

If you want to take pictures of relatively large subjects, such as groups of divers, in low visibility conditions it is essential to use a wide-angle lens. The Nikon 15 mm wide-angle lens for Calypso amphibious cameras fits on to the camera in place of the normal lens. It is expensive and once in position it cannot be changed under water.

The ultimate in wide-angle lenses is the fish-eye lens that gives the camera a wider field of view than the diver can see through his face-mask. The fish-eye lens makes short distances close to the camera appear much greater, and straight objects appear curved when they are located at the edge of the picture. Such lenses enable surprisingly spectacular pictures to be obtained in conditions of very poor visibility.

The simplest way of getting fish-eye pictures with a Calypso/Nikkor camera is to use a fish-eye adaptor that is located in front of the normal lens. Such an adaptor is the Viz-Master fish-eye attachment that push-fits on to the standard lens and is easily fitted and removed under water. It is sold complete with the special viewfinder that enables the diver to see the extended field of view recorded by the camera.

Fig. 93. THE VIZ-MASTER FISH-EYE ATTACHMENT AND ITS
SPECIAL VIEWFINDER FITTED TO A NIKONOS CAMERA

People Pictures

Once you are under water it takes time to measure the light intensity
and to get your camera set up, so if you go in with a group of divers
you are likely to end up trailing behind them. This is bad. Not only
will they stir up the sediment, which will ruin the visibility from a
photographic standpoint, but you are also likely to finish with a
series of pictures of divers finning away from the camera. With fish-
eye lens shots, in which perspective is very exaggerated, this may
yield pictures in which the divers have huge fins and tiny heads. So
if you want to take pictures, give your diving buddies clear instructions BEFORE THE DIVE. Ask for their co-operation from the start.
Arrange to get shots of your partners swimming across the field of
view. Better still, if your group can actually carry out some activity
associated with the dive, such as measuring a cannon on an archaeological site, get them to pose for you. The final picture will be much
more interesting.

Fish Pictures

Fish pictures require a special approach and can only be obtained
with the co-operation of a patient diving partner. For the most part
fish are timid creatures: they can all swim faster than a diver—and
swimming after them is just a waste of time! Fish must be stalked
very carefully: at the first clumsy or hasty movement they are likely

to swim out of camera range or disappear into the rocks. So a cautious approach should always be made if you are after fish pictures.

Knowing the habits of the various species of fish is also an aid. Some fish—such as wrasse—are naturally curious; they will actually approach the camera and nibble at it if they are not frightened. So, with them the technique is to sit on the bottom and let them come to you. But bass are never so obliging (or foolish if spearfishermen are around), so pictures of these timid fish should be taken as soon as they are within camera range, for they are likely to disappear in an instant and not return—no matter how quiet you are.

Taking fish pictures is likely to impose a strain on the diving buddy system unless both partners have this common interest in fish. If you are carefully stalking a fish it is likely to take all your concentration. You cannot keep one eye on your quarry and one eye on your diving partner. So do not dive with a novice if taking pictures.

As far as diving technique is concerned, it is best to use an ABLJ and when photographing fish, go in slightly over-weight. Then, if necessary, the ABLJ can be vented, allowing the diver to settle firmly on the bottom. This allows the photographer to approach his subject with the minimum of disturbance. When you have got your pictures, the ABLJ is inflated until neutral buoyancy is regained and you can then swim away.

Film Making

How many divers first took up the sport as the result of seeing a film either in the cinema, or on television? Probably a great many.

In some ways making an under-water film is easier than getting good still pictures, particularly with the super 8 mm cameras now used by most amateurs. At present there are no truly amphibious 8 mm cameras on the market, so it is necessary to house a standard camera in an under-water case before you can embark on under-water movies. There are a number of features which should be taken into consideration when selecting a camera.

A number of cine cameras have a coupled exposure meter that automatically sets the iris diaphragm to give the correct exposure. The majority seem to work as well under water as they do on the surface, and the inclusion of this feature is to be recommended if you are buying a camera for under-water use.

Many modern cine cameras have a zoom lens which enables telephoto and wide-angle shots to be taken with the same lens. In virtually all conditions such a lens should be set to the widest angle if divers are to be the main subject of the film. For this and other reasons zoom lens should not be regarded as an essential feature for an under-water cine camera. Indeed as the definition from an

Fig. 94. AN UNDER-WATER HOUSING FOR AN 8 MM CINE CAMERA

inexpensive fixed focal length wide-angle lens is frequently far better than that from a cheap zoom lens, the former is to be preferred in most circumstances.

A cine camera with a clockwork motor always seems to need winding just when an exciting event occurs and you want to be filming. Thus, an electric drive, which allows long sequences and instant filming, is a feature to be advised.

A battery-powered super 8 mm camera with a fixed focus wide-angle lens and automatic exposure control is the camera recommended for the beginner. Once the film is loaded it has just one control for operation—the shutter release—making filming simple above and below water. And it can be accommodated in the simplest type of under-water housing.

The ambitious photographer who wants to show his films to large audiences and perhaps sell them for television must use a bigger film format. At present, 16 mm is the minimum size acceptable for television showing and films must be shot at 24 or 25 fr. per sec.

When most people watch a film they expect it to tell a story, so if you decide to make an under-water movie get at least a basic story line sorted out before you start shooting. It can always be changed later. And remember that you as a film maker are entitled to a large slice of 'artistic licence': the sequences do not have to be shot in the order they are finally screened. Almost any filming technique you adopt is acceptable provided that in the final blend the movie is convincing and entertaining.

A Final Word of Advice

An important point which cannot be emphasised too strongly is TRY OUT YOUR PHOTOGRAPHIC EQUIPMENT IN A POOL before going off on a holiday or major expedition. The try-out should include using a film, having it processed and carefully looking at the results. Under-water photographic equipment can often appear to be working in a satisfactory manner on the surface, but when it is taken under water a completely unforeseen shortcoming becomes apparent. It is obviously far better to identify and remedy such faults before you set off rather than suffer the anguish of discovering that what should have been a superb film or set of pictures is ruined when it is too late to go back and take it again.

Wreck Diving and Salvage

Wrecks provide some of the most interesting dives as there is usually an abundance of life to see as well as the excitement of diving on a sunken ship. However, wreck diving is not without risk for the unwary diver. The maritime law with regard to wrecks, by the way, is rather involved, but if the wreck is a modern one it usually belongs to someone, if only the insurance company, and permission may be required to dive on it.

How does one go about finding a shipwreck? There are many avenues to be explored, and obtaining information on wrecks usually involves a great deal of research and correspondence. A beginning can be made at any or all of the following sources:

1. By study of the charts for the area in question.

2. By consulting the growing number of books on the subject. In UK, the diver is very fortunate in having a wide range of books on wrecks lost on most parts of the British coastline; for example, 'Wrecks of Devon and Cornwall'.

3. The Admiralty Hydrographic Department, Beadon Road, Taunton, Somerset, maintains records of wrecks. This Department is anxious to receive reports of modern wrecks and aircraft lost at sea. Many of those lost during the war have never been identified, as well as others sunk without trace. Apart from inspecting wrecks for navigational hazards, they require data on how fast wrecks break up. This information must be available in many Branch logbooks, where the members dive regularly on known wrecks.

The Hydrographic Department's files carry information on many wrecks, ancient or modern, in British waters, and it is glad to receive reports of visits to known wrecks. Its files may be consulted for a modest fee. The Committee for Nautical Archaeology is also opening its own records for ships up to the 18th century, both at home and abroad, from which it hopes to build a solid foundation for research on ancient ships (see section on 'Nautical Archaeology').

4. Allied shipping losses during the World Wars were either wholly or partly underwritten by the Government, and information on those which may come into this category can be obtained from the Board of Trade (War Risks Insurance Office), Parliament Square House, 34/36 Parliament Street, London SW1.

5. If you have the name of the wreck and other information to assist identification, particularly the date of its sinking, the Shipping Editor, Corporation of Lloyds, Lime Street, London EC3, should have some information.

6. In the case of wrecks under the jurisdiction of Trinity House, write to The Secretary, Trinity House, Tower Hill, London EC3.

7. Local knowledge will also reveal information on wrecks. Try local museums, church records, Coastguard and Lifeboat Stations as well as fishermen and harbour masters.

Wreck Location

Except for those wrecks buoyed by Trinity House as a hazard to navigation, the location of wrecks can be a long, tedious and frustrating business so the various methods one can adopt must be considered.

The basic difficulties are time, opportunity and the facilities necessary to devote to searching for what is virtually a needle in a haystack, and the greatest single asset is probably the goodwill of local fishermen who can be of inestimable value. The thought to bear constantly in mind is that although you might be within a yard of your objective, a miss is as good as a mile. The section on *Underwater Search Methods* in chapter 6 gave information on some of the techniques available, and in particular, on diver search methods. Here we shall look more closely at locating wrecks without use of divers.

The simplest method of accurately pinpointing a position at sea assuming you are in sight of land is by the use of marks, i.e. geographical features, which are used to give transit bearings (see chapter 8, *Position Fixing*). These can be incredibly accurate, and a good set of marks can not only pinpoint the wreck but put you over a particular part of it, although for this sort of accuracy it is essential the bearings are as near to forming a right angle as possible. Good marks are usually known to local fishermen who may use them for laying crab and lobster pots, but it is also worth bearing in mind that so-called wreck marks used by trawlermen are often for trawling on a line in order to miss the wreck and may be of little use for actually locating it. Hiring the services of a local boatman is probably the best way of ensuring success as he may not only be able to locate the wreck quickly and accurately but his knowledge of local conditions is invaluable in ensuring a safe operation. An apparently calm and harmless looking stretch of water can be treacherous at certain states of the tide.

An extremely useful piece of equipment and a great help in finally pinpointing a wreck is a portable echo sounder, preferably the paper recording type. This is particularly the case when your marks may not be as accurate or as clear as you could wish, due perhaps to mist or summer heat haze. If you are working to a set of marks given verbally, it is even more important as often the phrase used is 'with such-and-such a landmark just open'. This rather vague phrase 'just open' can vary from person to person and can be very misleading if misinterpreted. A sketch can be of help in cases like this.

If you are working from a chart taking compass bearings from prominent landmarks, you will most certainly need an echo sounder as this method will only give a rough location.

When using either method you will be extremely lucky to pick up the wreck straight away and usually it will be necessary to search the area. This is invariably a waste of time unless tackled systematically and the easiest method is to drop a small buoy and sinker where you think the wreck should be, to use as a datum point, and using the echo sounder steam round the buoy in increasing circles or in parallel lines. In this way the whole area is covered thoroughly.

If you have no echo sounder available and the sea-bed is sand or shingle an alternative is to search the area by dragging a weighted anchor or *creep* astern on a length of chain or wire, tracing the same pattern as before in the hope of fouling the wreck. This is a slow business as the anchor will leave the bottom if towed too quickly. It is also possible to drag over a wreck without hooking into it, misleading you into continuing the search in the surrounding area without success. It is therefore, necessary to have someone holding or pressing on the towing line in order to 'feel' the progress of the anchor over the bottom. Should the anchor then come in contact with the wreck it will be felt and the skipper warned to ease up to prevent the line parting should the anchor foul as is hoped.

If you can persuade a fisherman with trawling gear to co-operate, a variation on this system is to put down trawl boards and the connecting ground chain but without the net attached. This enables a much broader path to be swept, but obviously it would be necessary to convince the trawlerman you will recover his gear or compensate him for any loss or damage, which could be expensive.

Decca Navigator equipment will give an accurate fix to within 15 m and used in conjunction with an echo meter is probably the ultimate in wreck location if you are fortunate enough to obtain the services of a skipper whose vessel is fitted with this equipment. If it is not possible to hire and dive from such a boat, it may be possible to persuade the skipper to drop a buoy supplied by you into the wreck during the course of his normal fishing activities. Generally speaking, most fishermen are not only willing but most interested to cooperate in the hope of learning more of their local hazards. Once the wreck is buoyed it is then only a matter of locating it at a later date, bearing in mind that even this can be difficult to find from a small boat in a choppy sea with a tide running. It is still necessary to have reliable marks to put you in the vicinity.

Another indication of a wreck's position in calm conditions with a tide running, particularly if the wreck is lying across the tidal stream, is a surface disturbance caused by the current being diverted over and around the obstruction.

The cooperation and goodwill of local fishermen is probably an amateur diver's greatest single asset in the location of wrecks in any particular area. Their knowledge may also include the many uncharted and, for the most part, unknown wrecks with which our coastline abounds, and knowing the area, they can also be invaluable in recommending the most favourable diving conditions. In any case, the amateur diving group is largely dependent upon such men for boat hire as vessels suitable for salvage operations, even on a small scale, are usually too costly to own and maintain for private purposes only.

ANCHORING IN POSITION:

If a wreck is in water unaffected by tide and wind, it is a simple matter of steaming ahead of the wreck, dropping the anchor and then, paying out the anchor rope, go astern until you are directly over the wreck again, when it is then possible to drop a shot line directly into the wreck. Unfortunately, most wrecks lie in tidal streams of varying strength and often the current is too strong to dive at most states of the tide. One is, therefore, obliged to wait until the tide slackens sufficiently to permit safe diving. Quite often the tide changes direction before the dive is completed or the wind may alter the lie of the boat so that if a shot rope is dropped in these conditions, it can easily be dragged out of the wreck or the line parted. Under these conditions, it is best to arrive at the site before slack tide and having located the wreck, steam against the tidal stream and drop the anchor, which should be on a stout wire or a sufficiently long length of chain so the anchor rope cannot chafe on the wreck. If the length of wire paid out is only a little more than the total depth of the water, this will prevent the anchor holding in the bottom and if the boat is then allowed to drift with the tide, with any luck the anchor will foul as it is dragged across the wreck by the boat. If unsuccessful the first time, the procedure can be repeated until the boat is firmly anchored in the wreck, when more wire should be paid out to ensure a good hold. The descent via the anchor rope is necessarily longer than by shot rope but it is the more practical method. The first two divers down should check the position of the anchor (and as a precaution, all subsequent divers) to ensure it cannot drag free from any position in which the boat may eventually lie. The anchor rope should be buoyed in case it becomes necessary to move the boat quickly and another buoy on as long a length of floating line as possible should be streamed out astern. Any tired diver surfacing away from the boat can then fin for the line and be hauled in.

Wrecks in deeper water unfortunately present the added difficulties of awkward currents and/or poor visibility. If a wreck is lying on a hard sand or gravel bottom which will give good light reflection and in an area subject to medium tidal streams, these conditions will give certain advantages. One can expect good visibility during slack water periods and the wreck to be relatively free from long weed and the sponge types of marine growth, with little fine silt to be stirred up except in confined spaces. On the other hand if the bottom is mud or very fine sand, even slight tidal streams stir this up to give poor visibility near the bottom from which there is little light reflection. The wreck is invariably covered in a thick layer of 'dust' which is easily disturbed when finning and is slow to clear. If the tidal streams are normally slight in the area, the wreck may well be covered by sponges and marine growth to such an extent it may be almost impossible to distinguish its shape apart from the main structure, and cutting away the growth immediately reduces the visibility.

An assessment of the strength and state of tidal streams and type of bottom taken from the Admiralty Chart for the area, together with prevailing weather conditions, will allow a fair appraisal of what you are likely to encounter at any particular site, but, ideally, diving is best undertaken during a calm weather spell at slack water, neap tides. High slack water generally gives better visibility than low, though low water may give a longer slack water period than high. Because of air endurance, decompression problems and lack of light, even under ideal conditions, 50 m is the maximum practical depth for this type of operation in British waters and then only for experienced divers.

Wreck Diving

Although normal safety precautions, dive planning and equipment are required, there are some points which should be stressed when diving on wrecks, being of particular importance and not encountered with other forms of diving.

A knife, of course, is essential, and no wreck diving should be undertaken without one. A torch is also a must and particularly useful for illuminating the confined spaces within the hull and attracting the attention of other divers. The hands more than anything can suffer a great deal of damage from rusting metal work, frayed wire hawsers, and so on, so gloves should be worn; a metal hook is also a useful tool for pulling yourself along and for general use in place of your hand. Tools, such as a pry-bar, hammer, chisel and hacksaw are useful for collecting small items. As diving will, of course, be conducted in pairs, the gear can be split between the two divers, a companion being one's greatest single safety factor. Diving on wrecks should never be attempted alone.

Although diving is best undertaken at slack water, it may be necessary to dive whilst there is still some tide in order to have the benefit of slack water when resurfacing. If this is the case it is important to ensure mask straps are secure and your mouthpiece in good condition as you will be descending the anchor rope against the tide and these items are under a much greater strain than normal due to the pressure of the water. Make sure, too, that your snorkel is secure and readily available.

It is also worth remembering that the tide is generally stronger on the surface than the bottom due to the surface drag of the sea-bed and in the lee of the wreck there is little, if any, tide at all.

Arriving on the wreck it is important first of all to orientate yourself. Some divers have a natural sense of direction whilst others move a dozen yards and have no idea where they are. If the type of vessel and something of its construction is known beforehand, a study of this before the dive will help you to recognise that part of the wreck into which you are anchored and what to expect as you investigate further. Unless a real effort is made to remember your point of departure in relation to the rest of the wreck, you may not be able to relocate the anchor rope, which may, of course, be lying in a different direction on your return, and this means surfacing free. This could entail a long surface swim against the current, perhaps at a time when you are tired. In any case, a controlled ascent up the anchor rope is infinitely preferable. For the preliminary survey and a quick overall impression, it is best to start on the lee side of the wreck, sheltering you from any tide, and in sight of the bottom. Working your way round will give an idea of its size, design and general condition and the disposition of any superstructure lying on the sea-bed. Particular care should be taken when rounding the extremities and when coming over the ship's side where tidal streams are strongest. It is easy to be taken off your guard and swept away, and in poor visibility you can lose sight of the wreck altogether.

Wrecks abound in sharp objects such as jagged steel plates, razor sharp shellfish and stranded wire ropes, and severe wounds can be incurred especially if any swell or sea movement is apparent on the wreck. The wreck diver is advised to wear a full diving suit including gloves for protection. He should constantly be aware that aqualung breathing tubes can easily snag on sharp projections and that a cylinder on the back is not ideal for squeezing through narrow openings. The danger of the collapse of corroded steel decks and rotten timber is ever present, especially if the diving boat is secured to some part of the wreck in a swell. Entering a wreck has its own special risks for a diver may lose himself and run out of air, or propped hatches may be closed by the movement of the sea.

When exploring the interior, extreme caution is of paramount importance. A guide line should be rigged and a torch carried as visibility can quickly be reduced to zero as you move in a confined space. It is in conditions such as these that panic can result very easily.

Inside the wreck it is best, where possible, to fin well clear of the deck as the fine silt which has settled inside is easily disturbed and, being sheltered, is slow to clear. Move with caution to avoid damage to gear and person; rusting plates are often reduced to paper thickness and will leave a bad gash in your suit, or you.

Many well-known wrecks are extensively fished by anglers whose tackle is frequently snagged and broken. Nylon line can be floating free, virtually invisible and can become entangled in your gear. Should this happen, do not attempt to break the line by pulling yourself free as this may result in the hook becoming embedded in you or your suit. Instead, use your knife or get your companion to free you.

Trawls lost by fishermen are also a very real hazard, particularly if diving is attempted in poor visibility. With the extensive use of man-made fibres, which are virtually unaffected by salt water, they are likely to be an increasing menace on wrecks in trawling areas. Caution, a sharp lookout with good visibility, a reliable companion, and a sharp knife are your safeguards.

It will be appreciated that wreck diving, particularly where salvage work is to be carried out, is a more hazardous form of diving than usual, so particular attention must be paid to dive planning, i.e. depth, time, cylinder contents, and where applicable, decompression stops. During the dive a regular check should be made on these points so that the return to the surface can be controlled and unhurried, with air and time in hand to allow for the unforeseen which could delay surfacing, resulting in the need to decompress. On the surface, divers should be timed in and out of the water and a shot rope with the decompression stops marked hung over the side with a spare aqualung(s) rigged ready for any diver surfacing short of air and requiring to decompress.

IDENTIFICATION

The positive identification of a wreck is often a most difficult task, so many of them being officially unknown so that it then becomes a matter of patient detective work and a great deal of luck. Quite often it is the apparently insignificant clue which builds up the picture and finally leads you to the answer. During exploration it is well worthwhile looking for items which might possibly bear manufacturers' names or the steamship company's crest. Crockery, cutlery, the ship's bell and various other non-ferrous fittings used in the ship construction are items well worth searching for.

The Law of Wreck and Salvage

The law on this subject is largely contained in Part 9 Merchant Shipping Act 1894, which enlarges upon the Old Common Law principles. The Act defines 'Wreck' and 'Salvage' and it clearly includes any vessel, part of a vessel, cargo, fittings or equipment, anchors and fishing gear—in fact, anything which might be found on a wrecked vessel or in tidal water. The law as applied to ships is now applied to aircraft by virtue of the Civil Aviation Act 1949.

Any object which comes within the definition of 'Wreck' remains the property of its lawful owner. Beware the object that apparently has no connection with ships or aircraft; any person who takes any such object commits a criminal offence. Any person who steals any object belonging to a wreck can be imprisoned for up to 14 years under Section 15 (3) Larceny Act (1916). There will be no offence if the owner has expressly given his permission to take the wreck or anything to do with it.

The Minister of Transport has appointed Receivers of Wreck around the coast of the UK, who are usually Customs Officers or Coastguards.

Summarising the law of Wreck and Salvage, any article which is brought into the UK shall be delivered to the Receiver of Wreck; if the article is unclaimed at the end of one year, it becomes Crown property and the Receiver sells the article deducting his fees and expenses and also the salvage claim upon the Ministry of Transport scale. There are instances where the Receiver may sell the article immediately, but he then retains the proceeds of sale for one year.

Where the owner or his agent brings the wreck or article into the UK, he need only declare it to the Receiver of Wreck. Customs Duty may be payable upon certain goods but that is another matter.

It is an offence to take any wreck which is within UK territorial waters to a foreign port; the offender is liable to imprisonment for three to five years. Anyone who fails to comply with the Merchant Shipping Act can be fined up to £100, and if he is not the owner of the wreck, he loses his right to claim salvage and will be liable to pay double the value of the article to its owner.

Wrecks which are of historic importance are covered by the Protection of Wrecks Act, 1973. This Act is explained further in the section, *Nautical Archaeology*.

Salvage

Although this Diving Manual is directed mainly towards the amateur diver and salvage, in the accepted sense, is usually beyond the scope of his normal diving activities, it is almost inevitable that sooner or later the opportunity to carry out some form of salvage will arise.

Divers wishing to enter the realms of salvage should make a serious attempt to discover the ownership of the wreck concerned, when he can either act as the owner's agent for the purposes of salvage, agreeing to accept a percentage of the value of the goods recovered. He might be able to purchase the wreck from the owner, thus being entitled to the full value of anything salvaged. The owner of a wreck is responsible to Trinity House for ensuring that the wreck does not become a hazard to navigation.

The basic problems of locating, raising and transporting salvage to shore, which is basically what all salvaging is about, will be considered here, bearing in mind the limitations of equipment and resources which would normally confront the average diver in these circumstances.

Although salvaging may be undertaken in a variety of circumstances, with each operation presenting its own particular problem, the sort of under-water work to come under the broad heading of salvage most likely to be encountered is as follows:

1. Small valuable items dropped into the sea, lost anchors, cables, moorings, etc.
2. Small boats sunk in relatively shallow water.
3. Non-ferrous metal, cargo and other items from wrecks going ashore and breaking up.
4. Non-ferrous metal, cargo and other items from wrecks in deeper water.

Group 1. Locating and Raising Small Objects
Although often a long and tedious business, the location of small objects in relatively shallow water in a restricted non-tidal area presents few problems, except that of time. When carried out properly, search techniques are usually successful. If a line with a small buoy is carried, it is a simple matter when the object of the search is located to attach the line and then surface, the buoy and line acting as a marker to which one can return directly with a heavier line and/or buoyancy bag for lifting purposes.

Points worth bearing in mind under these circumstances are:

(a) The object to be located is seldom where the loser imagines it to be and one should be prepared to search a relatively large area.
(b) A search, more often than not, is useless unless carried out systematically and thoroughly.
(c) In non-tidal waters, the longer the search the poorer the visibility becomes. Arrange the search so the ground is covered only once.

Group 2. Raising Small Boats:
As with any salvage operation, the raising of sunken craft will present particular problems with each case; for instance, whether it is on a hard or soft bottom, upright, upside down or on its side. The method adopted will also depend upon the design and size of the boat, whether it is open or partially decked, the number and position of its compartments, and so on.

In the case of small dinghies, it is usually possible to raise these by securing a line to the first thwart or the ring in the stem and then tow it, using a boat with sufficient power. If the line is kept as short as possible, the dinghy will come to the surface under tow and most of the water will be spilled out over the stern; the remaining water can then be baled out by hand. If the dinghy is holed, it will still come to the surface but it would be necessary to beach her in order to bale her out and effect repairs. If this is done at high water the falling tide will leave her high and dry for this to be done.

With larger boats, when lifting barges and/or block and tackle are not available, salvage may be carried out using buoyancy bags which can be installed inside compartments and inflated by air cylinders. In order to raise the craft on an even keel it may also be necessary to attach buoyancy bags externally but these should be secured by slinging lifting ropes under the keel in order to cradle the weight.

The amount of buoyancy required can be calculated and if the operation warrants the effort, it might also be worthwhile to construct a model in order to plan salvage procedure in a tank.

If the buoyancy method is adopted care should be taken to ensure the lift is equally balanced so the vessel is raised on an even keel and the bags are adequately vented so that any excess air is expelled during the lift. An alternative to bags for this sort of operation are large oil drums, which have the advantage of being both cheap and expendable. If the boat is lying on a soft bottom it may also be necessary to break the suction effect of the mud using high pressure hoses or 'rocking'.

Group 3. Wrecks Broken up in Shallow Water
Wrecks which have gone ashore and are lying in shallow water are quickly broken up and dispersed by gales, often in a matter of days. Even a wreck sheltered from heavy seas will disintegrate rapidly if lying in tidal waters from the wetting and drying action of the tide. They are also a relatively easy salvage proposition so there is usually little left after the sea and salvage have taken their toll.

Most of the older wrecks, however, have continued to break up and lie forgotten along the shore. The continuing sea action might well reveal material or cargo left because it was uneconomic to salvage or was unknown to the earlier salvors.

Enquiries from local sources, such as coastguards, local fishermen and in Lifeboat Institution records, will usually give a clue to wrecks lost in the area and then it is a matter of systematically searching that part of the coastline. These wrecks are not always easy to find as they quickly become encrusted with marine growth and are almost indistinguishable from their surrounding terrain. The secret is to look for regular shapes such as the straight lines and holes cast into the basic structure, ribs and ship's plates, these parts usually being too heavy to have moved from the original site of the disaster. It is then a matter of properly combing the area for anything that might be of value.

Group 4. Wrecks Sunk in Deeper Water

This last group offers the greatest scope for anyone considering serious salvage operations. Many are wartime casualties, others the result of collision or some unusual accident. Even though they may be charted they are often of unknown identity, lying forgotten on the sea-bed since disappearing beneath the waves.

PERMANENT BUOYING PRIOR TO SALVAGING

If a salvage operation on such a wreck is intended then it is obviously desirable to buoy the wreck permanently with at least one buoy. This will avoid the wasted effort of relocation with each visit and the descent via the buoy wire puts you on the same part of the wreck each time. Wire rather than rope should be used for this purpose, securely attached to a solid high point on the wreck with a small non-collapsible buoy fixed to the wire so as to be permanently under the water at all states of the tide and capable of supporting the lower end of the wire.

In this way, the wire below this supporting buoy is kept taut and clear of the wreck so preventing it becoming entangled at slack low water. In order to avoid trouble with HM Coastguards, the main buoy should not be of metal but preferably the inflatable orange plastic type or similar which is easy to see and will not damage a small craft should one hit the buoy in the dark.

If the salvage vessel is required to be moored directly over a particular part of the wreck then at least two buoys need to be positioned, preferably on the extremities of the wreck, so that by picking up both buoys and adjusting the length of the mooring lines at the bow and stern, the salvage vessel can take up any position between them. If a cross current or wind should affect this position-ing, then two further moorings would need to be placed to port and starboard, thereby mooring the salvage vessel between four positions. Mooring in this way allows the use of a shot rope for a direct descent to the working area.

Q

THE BOAT

The first essential is, of course, a boat which must be large enough to accommodate the divers and their gear and which is equipped with a well constructed diving ladder, a derrick and/or winch(es) for lifting purposes. Various ropes, buoys, shackles, wire, block and tackle, engineer's tools and the like will also be required, dependent upon the undertaking.

SALVAGE

It is not possible to lay down hard and fast methods of salvage since so much depends on the particular problems each operation presents together with the patience, skill, ingenuity and persistence of those involved. By comparison with the professional salvor, the amateur diver is limited in time, equipment and experience, and any success will depend entirely upon the best use that can be made of the resources available to him. On the other hand, the amateur diver can afford to attempt operations which would be uneconomic for a salvage company whose overheads are inevitably higher. Because of these considerations and the limitations of space, it is only possible here to outline the fundamental principles involved and give a brief description of materials and apparatus available and commonly used. For more detailed information it will be necessary to make reference to the various publications dealing specifically with under-water salvage techniques.

Several companies and diving schools offer courses of instruction in the use of under-water tools and salvage methods, and the Branch, or diver who intends to undertake wreck salvage is advised to learn from them.

Under-water Cutting Apparatus

If it is intended to salvage parts of a wreck, it will first be necessary to free the material before lifting. This can be done either by under-water cutting apparatus, by explosives or by hand. The oxy-hydrogen under-water gas cutting torch or oxy-arc electric cutter are in common use. Training and experience are essential to be successful.

Explosives

The selection of the type of explosive most suitable for a specific job, the amount required, its positioning and type of detonation are a matter of experience although the basic principles involved are covered by the pamphlet 'Under-water Blasting', published by the Nobel Division, ICI Ltd., Glasgow. It will be appreciated that there is also the problem of obtaining explosives, which require a police permit both to buy and use. With the exception of very small quantities, explosives must be stored in specially constructed buildings, but if the necessary experience is available and police permission is granted it may be possible to arrange storage with a local quarry where such facilities are usually available.

Other Under-water Cutting Appliances
Under-water wire-rope and chain cutting machines and various other pneumatic tools for drilling and cutting rock, wood and steel are available, but these tools are normally the province of the professional salvor and would not normally be readily available to the amateur diver.

RAISING AND TRANSPORTING SALVAGE TO SHORE
The basic methods here are either direct winching, buoyancy or tidal lift.

Winching
If the boat is equipped with a winch or derrick and the material to be lifted is within the capacity of the apparatus then direct lifting is possible either into the boat or an attendant barge. If the weight is beyond the capacity of the winch but the boat is capable of supporting the weight involved, then it may be possible to incorporate the use of block and tackle, preferably lifting on the bow. This would allow much greater weights to be raised and conveyed whilst slung under the lifting vessel.

Buoyancy
A submerged body in the sea displaces a mass of water equal to its cubic capacity. Therefore, if a hollow container of known capacity is filled with water, submerged and attached to the object to be lifted, the water can then be expelled, using compressed air, resulting in a lifting force being exerted equal to the amount of water displaced, less weight of the container in water. Points to bear in mind when using this method are:
1. The buoyancy container must be adequately vented to allow excess air to escape.
2. If the container is sufficiently buoyant to raise the object before all the water has been displaced, the air will expand, so increasing the speed of the ascent since more water is displaced by the expanding air as it approaches the surface due to lessening pressure.
3. The weight in water of the object to be raised is less than its weight in air by an amount equal to the mass of water it displaces. This difference can, therefore, be calculated if its volume is known.
4. If it is intended to use a buoyancy bag to assist in moving heavy

items from one point to another, e.g. to a central collecting point prior to lifting, it is virtually impossible to unfasten or spill out the air from a buoyancy bag under load unless prior provision is made for this purpose. Cutting it free will only send it straight to the surface.

Tidal Lift

This method also employs buoyancy but is that of the salvage vessel itself or a pontoon. Wires are slung under the salvage to be raised and attached to the lifting vessel or pontoon so that the load will be evenly distributed. Some means must also be arranged for the wires to be drawn as taut as possible at low water. As the tide rises the burden is also raised and it is then possible to steam to shallower water until grounding occurs. The process is then repeated with successive tides until the salvage can be dropped in the shallowest water, from whence it can be recovered by crane or other lifting tackle.

HARBOUR OR SHIP DIVING OR UNDER-WATER WORK

Diving Clubs may occasionally be requested to carry out some under-water task by a commercial organisation or local authority. The first point to be considered should be whether the dive comes within the jurisdiction of the appropriate legislation (see Appendix 6). Secondly, one should consider the question of insurance and whether one is still covered whilst carrying out the work.

In general, any under-water task should be commenced with the object of reducing the work under water to a minimum, which will obviously also reduce the hazards to the minimum. For example, in removing a wire from around a propellor shaft, hours may be spent under water with hacksaw, hammer and chisel. On the other hand, a thoughtful diver may spend a few minutes in the water securing a rope to the end of the wire which is taken to the barrel of a winch, and by turning the propellor in hand-turning gear and heaving at the winch the wire is unwound.

WORK ON SHIPS

The following safety precautions must be considered:

Inform all concerned of diving activities, especially engine room staff, if diving around propellors or inlets.

Shut off all dangerous inlets and outlets.

Fly the diving flag from the masthead and above the position where diving is taking place to keep other vessels away and their speed down. The wash from a fast boat can be dangerous.

Take adequate precautions to prevent the diver getting fouled by mooring the diving vessel in the best position, and rig bottom lines to guide the diver to his task and to facilitate hanging on.

Use life-lines where required. It is possible for a diver to lose himself under a large flat-bottomed vessel and run out of air before regaining the surface.

HARBOUR DIVING:
Appropriate lock and sluice gates, inlets, outlets and valves should be shut down as required.

If working around electricity cables, current should be switched off.

Diving near under-water submarine detection devices (Asdic and Sonar) can be hazardous to the diver.

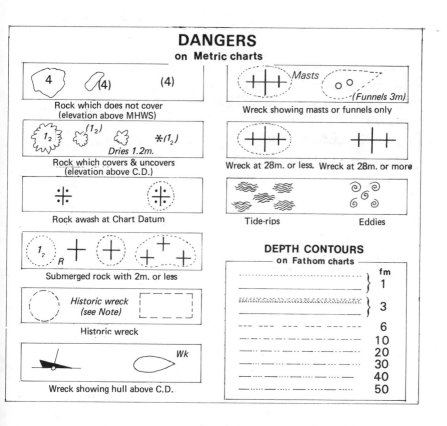

CHAPTER EIGHT
DIVE ORGANISATION AND SEAMANSHIP

Open-water Dives

This section deals mainly with the organisation and conduct of a day-long Branch dive, or a dive made by a small group of divers. The next section, *Branch Diving Expeditions*, considers aspects of organisation and management of longer expeditions, Branch holidays or projects. It will be understood that the two sections overlap to some extent.

In planning and organising any open-water diving, attention should be paid to far more than just the actual dives on the day. Successful open-water dives can only be achieved by thoughtful and detailed preparation prior to the event, and before reaching the site. This is the responsibility of the person in charge of the day's diving—the Expedition Leader or Dive Marshal.

PRELIMINARY PLANNING

The Expedition Leader or Diving Marshal

It is of primary importance that for all Branch diving outings, whether large or small, an Expedition Leader/Diving Marshal should be appointed by the Branch Diving Officer in order to comply with BSAC diving regulations. The purpose of this procedure is to ensure that there should be no risk of accident arising from any uncertainty as to who is in charge; confusion is certain to occur if several people give conflicting instructions at the same time. This regulation is also made to avoid complications about payment of insurance under the Club's policy in the event of an accident or claim for damages by a third party. So important is this matter that Club Rules stipulate that, as far as diving conduct is concerned, the Diving Marshal has authority to exclude a member from diving if he will not obey diving instructions given to him. (On Branch dives an 'Expedition Leader' will not be necessary, the appointed Diving Marshal being endowed through his appointment with the necessary powers of authority. Major Branch expeditions or holidays, projects, etc. do require a 'supremo' in the form of an Expedition Leader, who may appoint Diving Marshals on a day to day basis.)

Where and When to Dive

Some preliminary planning can be completed well in advance, such as the selection of the diving area and a decision as to the purpose of the dive—often the two points are correlated. For example, a dive to search for a sunken dinghy presupposes that its location is already fairly accurately known, but for a dive of general interest, the choice of dive site can make or mar the entire outing, so the selection should be made in the light of all available knowledge of previous dives in the area, of accounts by other divers, advice from local Branches, and other sources of local knowledge.

Selecting the date and time of the dive will frequently depend more on the availability of members than on ensuring ideal diving conditions, but the decision should be made as far in advance as possible, taking all factors into consideration. Do not forget that permission to dive in certain areas sometimes has to be obtained beforehand and failure to secure this may mean a refusal on the day. Similarly, the hire of diving boats, if required, should be arranged as early as possible, particularly if local facilities are unknown or if the area is popular for boating or diving.

If a sea dive is planned, the appropriate charts and coastal land maps should be studied for reefs and rocky outcrops, which make the most interesting dives, and for depths of water. Sandy sea-beds are seldom interesting. If it is necessary to dive at slack water, its time and duration should be established beforehand from Tide Tables. Under-water visibility will usually be better on the flood tide rather than the ebb tide or slack (especially if there is a river or estuary in the vicinity) and at Neap Tides rather than Spring Tides.

If shore dives, or diving after a short boat trip from a shore base are envisaged, it is preferable to choose a base where toilet facilities are available and where there is protection from inclement weather. If divers are accompanied by families, try to provide for their leisure too.

In selecting the diving site and obtaining access to it, care should be taken never to cause wilful or unnecessary damage to property, or to cause any inconvenience to the public. With this in mind, noisy compressors should not be run within earshot of the holiday public, and equipment should not be left lying around where it can be damaged or get in the way of other users of the beach, or be stolen. Leave the base site clean and tidy and respect the general public's interests at all times. In fact, always obey the Diver's Code of Conduct.

In recent years the phrase 'Diver Saturation' has been used to describe the problems which occur when too many divers use the same site: especially if that site is also one which is popular with the holiday-maker. This type of difficulty can often be avoided by liaison with someone having local knowledge—the local BSAC Branch, the Coach for the region, the BSAC Dive Site Information Centre, etc. Visiting divers can obtain advice about alternative dive sites or about behaviour on sites that will cause a minimum of annoyance to other beach users.

Sources of Information

The Diving Marshal or Expedition Leader needs to refer to a variety of publications, charts, maps, etc. when planning a dive. For the conduct of a dive, record sheets, both rough and fair, are necessary. So that all these references and materials are readily available, it is a good idea to have a 'Branch Dive/Expedition Kit' which is given to the Diving Marshal in advance. The sort of things included in this kit would be charts, maps, tide tables, Diving Manual, First-Aid handbook, Dive Record Sheets, check lists, rough paper, pens, pencils, chartwork instruments, clipboard, etc. There are no firm rules for what should be included—experience will dictate. If the kit can all fit into a briefcase, it can be managed very easily before and during the Branch dive.

Equipment

All equipment, whether owned privately or by the Branch should be checked adequately in advance of the expedition date. Preferably this should be done by whoever is going to use or be responsible for it. Cylinders should, of course, be fully charged a day or so in advance rather than leaving this until the day of the dive, lest unexpected delays occur. If cylinders need to be re-charged on or near the diving site, arrangements should be made either for the provision and discreet use of a portable compressor; or for the empty cylinders to be transported to the nearest cylinder filling station.

Charged cylinders should be protected from strong sun, if only by a towel or clothing, to prevent the heat causing a dangerous increase of pressure of air in the cylinder.

Each diver should be responsible for his own personal equipment. If all equipment is in the right place at the right time, and functioning properly, this will contribute considerably to the success of the dive and there will be less risk of failure or accident.

Safety

Apart from knowing in advance the location and telephone number of the nearest operational recompression chamber and such special services as the Coastguard, Doctor, etc., the Expedition Leader should also locate the nearest public or other telephone from which these services may be called. A simple first-aid kit should be available at the diving base.

One extremely important consideration is that the dive should be cancelled if conditions are obviously going to be unfavourable. The conditions at sea in any specific area can be obtained by telephone from the local Meteorological Office, which can also give a forecast for the next day. If the weather report is bad it may not be worth setting out for the diving site at all, and arrangements should be made to telephone those intending to dive and to advise them of cancellation or revised plans, i.e. change of dive site.

Deputy Marshals
Just as the amount and detail of advance planning depends on the complexity of the dive and the number of divers involved, so the degree of control and judgement that has to be exercised while diving is in progress will depend on conditions at the dive site and on the experience of the divers. Nevertheless, the Diving Marshal will find that supervising the overall conduct of the dive takes time, and he may wish to enjoy himself by participating in the diving. To this end he should appoint Deputy Marshals to whom he can delegate specific duties. The Marshals need not be the most experienced members of the party; in fact, less experienced divers should be given an opportunity to gain experience and competence in controlling the conduct of various aspects of a diving expedition. Such experience is required as part of Second Class Diver training.

Dive Procedures
Many a dive is necessarily cancelled because of the passing of slack water or the approach of evening, and frequently this is due to unnecessary delays caused by divers taking excessive time to kit-up. To ensure the smooth running of the dive the Dive Marshal should, therefore, tell all the divers in advance the diving order and who are to be the Dive Leaders. With this knowledge they should be able to kit-up and prepare in sufficient time to avoid delays or undue haste before their turn to enter the water.

Apart from checking his equipment thoroughly some days in advance of the expedition, the diver should also carry out a pre-dive check: to prove that his aqualung is functioning satisfactorily; that all his equipment is to hand—fins, mask, snorkel tube, weight-belt and harness (both correctly fitted with their quick-release in working order), lifejacket and any other special items being taken on the dive. Immediately before entering the water each group should also receive a pre-dive briefing from the Diving Marshal on the purpose and conditions of the dive, and giving special instructions relative to the dive.

The Dive Leader
Each dive made should be under the control of a Dive Leader whose instructions during the actual dive should be obeyed. The Dive Leader is, of course, responsible to the Diving Marshal. On dives involving training, the Diving Marshal may well appoint a novice as a Dive Leader, with an experienced diver as his companion, in order to give that novice experience and responsibility. In such

cases, the experienced diver should obey the instructions of the novice at all times short of actual emergency or danger—when his greater experience would clearly indicate that he should take charge.

The Dive Leader should confirm that his group has carried out their pre-dive checks and, if necessary, run over them himself. He should also give any last-minute instructions for the dive, including signals to be used.

The method of entry into the water will depend on whether it is a shore or boat dive, the ease of access to the water, the sea and weather conditions, and the experience of the divers, but whatever the method preferred, those already in the water should remain close to the point of entry until all those on the dive have come together and given an indication that they are ready to proceed, usually by means of an OK signal.

To proceed with a dive if incorrectly weighted is unpleasant, an annoyance to other divers and possibly a danger. If any doubt exists, buoyancy should be checked at the start and any necessary adjustments made by removing or taking on more weight. A member of the surface party—on shore or in the boat—should assist by passing the weights to the diver in the water.

When all the divers are ready the Dive Leader should signal to descend.

Conduct of the Dive

The conduct of the dive will depend entirely on under-water conditions; the Dive Leader should observe, assess and act in accordance with them and the objective of the dive. There are, however, five factors that influence every dive and which should be kept constantly in mind. These are:

1. The quantity of air remaining in the cylinders of each diver.
2. The diving party's whereabouts relative to the surface party or point of exit.
3. The necessity of remaining in constant contact with diving companions.
4. The depth of the dive and the possible effects of nitrogen narcosis.
5. The depth and duration of the dive relative to the need for decompression.

If the Dive Leader knows before entry the amount of air carried by each diver in his team, it should only be necessary to make a confirmatory check on reaching the bottom—just in case any diver has used an excessive amount of air while waiting at the surface, checking buoyancy or ear-clearing on the way down. Periodic checks should be made during the dive, particularly towards the end, to ensure that all divers surface in good time.

It is possible to travel considerable distances under water during a dive, particularly in shallow water when air consumption will be relatively low or if diving in a current. Usually it is best to complete the dive and to surface near to some predetermined point; shore, surface party or boat. If the divers lose their way, or are uncertain of their position, they should surface to determine their whereabouts, unless they are attached to a surface marker, which can be monitored at the surface.

Unless diving roped, diving should NOT be undertaken alone. Learning how to keep in constant contact with a companion diver without having to devote one's whole attention to this aspect of the dive is one of the first things to master. Visual contact will be more readily maintained if a pair of divers fin side by side sufficiently close that should one lag slightly behind his companion he is not at once lost from view, but always within the limits of under-water visibility. If one diver pauses to look at something, the other should remain close at hand. Before moving off again they should glance towards one another to check that their movements and intentions are understood. With divers unaccustomed to diving together, or with beginners, the Dive Leader may have to signal positively each change of direction or activity.

If a diver loses his companion he should set about finding him without delay. Firstly, by looking on either side, then by turning slowly round looking both up and down as well as on the level. If he or his bubbles cannot be seen do NOT fin off in a probable direction in the hope of finding him, but after a short time—rarely more than 15 seconds—start ascending, all the time circling slowly looking about for signs of the diver above, or of his bubbles rising from below.

Always surface if separated. If this is done, both divers should come to the surface within a short time and distance of each other, where they can come together again and recommence the dive.

Should a diver surface alone he should remain where he is and turn around for signs of his companion, looking into the water for rising bubbles as far as visibility will allow, and scanning the surface of the water for signs of bubbles. He should enlist the help of surface cover or look-out, who may help in the search and who, from a higher vantage point, can frequently see bubbles that are obscured from a diver's view. If the diver who is still under water has a Surface Marker Buoy, there will be no problem in establishing contact again.

If the surface cover is able to point out the direction of his companion's bubbles the diver should fin on the surface towards them looking below for the rising bubbles. Only if he sees them and is certain that he can make contact with his companion should he dive, otherwise it is likely that he will not be able to locate him due to changes in his companion's direction and the reduced visibility below water as compared with that at the surface.

The causes and effects of nitrogen narcosis and the precautions and procedures to be followed on dives or repeat dives necessitating special decompression stops are dealt with in chapter 2. In respect of these matters, the dive leader should always bear in mind the experience and ability of his companion divers, and preferably avoid dives at depths that might result in nitrogen narcosis and of durations that would necessitate decompression, particularly with novice divers.

When the Dive Leader decides to terminate the dive, he should signal to his companions to commence the ascent. The correct procedure for surfacing should be followed and signals given to the surface party. Particular care should be exercised to keep the divers together throughout the ascent and when returned to the surface. If finning back to base on the surface is necessary, care should be taken not to outstrip the companion diver. Fin close together so that each can see the other easily, but if visibility on the surface is hindered by rough water, or there is a strong current, it may be preferable to hold hands or to grasp the companion's harness.

Members of the surface party should always be ready to assist divers out of the water, particularly if the divers are likely to be cold or exhausted, have need to climb into a boat or to clamber over rocks. In such cases it is frequently advisable for the diver to take off his weights and aqualung in the water and pass them to the surface party before he attempts getting out himself. Once out, the aqualung and other kit should be stowed or placed so that they are not in the way, where they may become damaged, hinder other divers, or even be used by them in error for a subsequent dive. This error may be avoided by covering the air outlet of the cylinder tap with adhesive tape until it is taken into use, thus only used cylinders will have an unsealed pillar valve.

When the diving party are safely returned to base—whether shore or boat—the Dive Leader should report the maximum depth and bottom time of his dive to the Diving Marshal who will be keeping a record; and should carry out a debrief with his divers—answering their questions, giving advice and encouragement as necessary.

After the Dive

Apart from the actual diving there are matters of base organisation that require preparation and attention. Important among these is the provision of creature comforts for both divers and attendants. Diving makes demands on the body's heat and energy resources and food to replace these should be made available: hot drinks, soup and concentrated energy-giving foods such as chocolate, sugar or glucose sweets are preferable to a full meal some considerable time after a dive.

Persons who have finished their dive should not sit or stand around when other divers are getting ready to dive, or preparations are being made to leave the diving site. They should ensure their equipment is correctly stowed and make themselves ready to give any assistance required, particularly to other divers about to enter or leave the water.

Evaporation, which is accentuated by a wind, causes cooling and loss of heat, so divers should not sit about in wet clothing after a dive, but should change when practicable into dry ones. In the event of a long wait or boat journey back to base, a plastic mac or anorak worn over a wet suit will assist in keeping warm.

The First Dive

Anyone who has had a thorough training with the aqualung in a swimming pool and has been fully instructed in diving techniques will come to his first open-water dive adequately prepared. Nevertheless, special attention should be given to him because of the strangeness of his surroundings. His lack of experience in the new environment under water may induce fear or foolish behaviour unless he is accompanied by another diver who can reassure him and direct his actions, and in whom he is willing to place his trust.

Only an experienced diver should take a novice on his first dive. He should watch over him and give any necessary help whilst kitting-up. He should not order him about, but rather render assistance in a confident and kindly way.

The Dive Leader should enter the water first or with the novice, NEVER afterwards. He should check that the novice is correctly weighted and can clear his ears, then, giving frequent and precise indications and signals of what he should do, the Dive Leader should take him on an easy and gentle dive.

The first dive should never be in adverse conditions, even if the novice diver is roped, and it should be limited to a depth of not more than 10 m. At first it may be a comfort to the novice if he is led by the hand, and to divert his attention from a probable preoccupation with his equipment the Dive Leader should pause from time to time and point out some interesting plant, creature, or aspect of undersea life. This will also start the novice along the road to acute observation and intelligent diving.

Afterwards there should be a debriefing, during which the novice should be told of any interesting or significant aspects of the dive, instructed how to avoid any faults in his techniques or actions, but above all given encouragement and congratulations on his achievements.

The novice's subsequent open-water dives should give him progressively more experience and variety of diving. The wise Branch Diving Officer or Diving Marshal will arrange dives at different sites and in different conditions to ensure that progressive experience is gained. Such variety is required by BSAC Diving Qualifications.

Branch Diving Expeditions

This section, which could be sub-titled 'planning and organisation', is concerned with the general guidelines to be followed by those who may have the responsibility of running a Branch diving expedition of a longer duration than one day. Obviously, expeditions can vary in scope from a small group on a weekend's dive from a local beach, to a full-scale overseas holiday project lasting weeks or months. Yet, whilst the degree of planning, administration and organisation varies accordingly, the same basic problems have to be faced if a smooth, efficient operation is to be achieved—the hallmark of any successful expedition.

The particular problems of the larger scientific projects are dealt with elsewhere in this Manual, so this chapter will concentrate on the basic factors to be considered, whatever the scope of the operation, although we must assume by definition that 'expedition' is something a little more ambitious than a day's outing with no higher purpose than getting wet and perhaps getting something for the pot by way of a bonus.

Any success will depend entirely upon (a) pre-expedition organisation and (b) its efficient administration thereafter on-site. So, broadly speaking, we can split the problems to be considered into these two categories.

Pre-expedition Organisation

The purpose of and the decision to undertake any planned expedition will probably arise gradually from a great deal of informal discussion, as a result of some experience or knowledge of an individual or group. Although its purpose here is irrelevant, the expedition exists only to pursue a particular objective which must therefore be clearly defined and understood by all concerned, so that all planning is directed towards its success. It naturally follows therefore, that the Expedition Leader on whom the ultimate responsibility will fall, must fully understand the nature of the undertaking and appreciate the particular diving problems that may be encountered.

Having decided to organise an expedition with a specific objective in mind, the next logical step is to select a team, who should combine an enthusiasm for the stated aims of the project with a willingness to accept responsibility for other routine duties, and who have an ability to work as one of a group towards the common objective. Whatever other particular skills may be required, the expedition must be organised initially as a Diving Team, with the members accepting such duties as Dive Marshal, Dive Leader, Deputy and Equipment Marshals, Log and Record Keeper, Safety Cover, etc. Other essential duties may also be allocated to members of the Team for such matters as catering, accounting, transport, boats, compressor operation and cylinder filling. In some cases these will have to be duplicated or split up in order to spread the load of responsibility fairly throughout the group.

Having established the objective and selected the team, the pre-expedition planning can now go forward in more detail and can be considered under two headings:

1. The general logistics of any diving expedition.
2. The specific requirements of this particular project.

In the first category the prime objective will be to establish and organise the operational base. Here there must be suitable accommodation, with good food; facilities for washing, drying and maintaining diving gear; for filling aqualungs, a compressor and/or air bank—the latter being quicker, quieter and more reliable. There is nothing more tiring or frustrating at the end of a hard day's diving than lugging heavy gear unnecessarily, so, for maximum comfort, convenience and efficiency, the need to carry gear should be reduced to a minimum, either by setting up the base close to the boat or diving site, or by laying on transport (this also reduces the possibility of loss or breakage).

If possible a visit to the proposed base should be made some weeks before the event to check that provisional arrangements are satisfactory. This visit may reveal some unforeseen problems, and affords an opportunity of making personal contact with such local officials as the Harbourmaster, police, etc. and, last but not least, with members of the local Diving Club whose particular knowledge of the area and cooperation could be vital.

Accommodation, food and ancillary facilities should be as good and convenient as one can afford, but remember, it is one thing to 'rough it' for a weekend when there is nothing in particular at stake, and to follow this up with a week at work to recover, but it is entirely another matter to dive and work three or four times a day every day for a week or longer.

If a boat is to be hired it is vital that its essential facilities are checked and that the skipper is briefed on what is expected of him and his craft, and the selection of a suitable vessel for your intended purpose and the need for it to be adequately equipped cannot be stressed too strongly.

The final consideration in this category is the personal fitness of the team members, and the condition of their equipment. During an expedition the group must take full advantage of favourable conditions in order to achieve maximum effective bottom time, and this may well mean repeat dives over quite long periods, which can be extremely tiring. There is usually no time to get into 'diving trim' once the expedition is under way, so the weeks before should be devoted to building up a high standard of physical and diving fitness so that every member is in first-class shape before departure. To this end a medical check may also be considered desirable.

Similarly, personal diving gear should be thoroughly checked, overhauled and re-checked for maximum efficiency. A supply of repair materials, spares and duplicates of those items which are easily lost, damaged or liable to give trouble—such as demand valves, masks, fins, etc.—should also be taken by each member, or a pool of such items should be organised by the Equipment Marshal.

In the second category we are considering the means of achieving the purpose of the expedition, and this being the whole object of the exercise, considerable thought, planning and discussion, and—where possible—practise, is essential.

Sometimes the Expedition Leader becomes so personally involved in the project that he fails to keep the rest of the team fully informed. This tendency should be recognised and resisted: it is vital to the success of any expedition that as much basic research as possible—from every conceivable source and angle—should be undertaken, and the results analysed and discussed by *all* members of the group at regular meetings. Not only does this cultivate 'team spirit' and stimulate and maintain interest, but the significance of some seemingly irrelevant 'find' under water may well be appreciated by a member of the group who remembers some fact gleaned from the pre-expedition research.

With all the normal problems of open-water diving to contend with—tides, adverse weather, poor visibility, etc.—it must again be stated that maximum effective bottom time on site must be the aim of the pre-expedition planning, so with some knowledge of the sort of tasks likely to be undertaken, the necessary techniques should be practised and perfected as a group, in easy diving conditions in local waters, with the equipment that will be used. Some ancillary gear necessary for a specific task may have to be specially constructed and if this is the case, experiment and modification must be completed before departure. Ideas and equipment produced in theory do not necessarily work out in practice, so reduce your possible problems beforehand—there will be plenty of unexpected ones to contend with on-site!

On-site Administration

Assuming now that all the pre-expedition planning has gone ahead as arranged, the group will arrive on-site with everything ready to start operations. The timing of the expedition will have been planned to take advantage of tides, good weather, location, etc. and, although overall control will effectively be in his hands, the Expedition Leader on-site should concentrate on pursuing the main objective—assessing progress and varying the programme in the light of results obtained—while the actual diving organisation should be delegated to the appointed Dive Marshal for the day or duration, who will be responsible for the safe conduct of the diving operations which should be carried out in accordance with the Club's Code of Conduct.

A routine of briefing and debriefing each Dive Team should be developed; information and impressions should be recorded immediately on their return to the surface, and 'finds' should be labelled and stored in an orderly fashion. A blackboard ruled to show the day's diving routine and the results, based on the diving log, is a good method of recording basic information which can then be copied into a permanent log and individual logbooks, before erasure.

If the operational base is a boat, space will inevitably be at a premium, so orderly organisation—both as individuals and as a group—must be maintained. Team members not immediately involved should keep clear of the diving area, and all gear should be stowed safely out of the way when not in use. Cleanliness is also important: the decks should be regularly swilled and scrubbed down to prevent feet from being cut or slipping on the remains of some specimen.

Whilst continually stressing the need for effective organisation and planning, the possibility that factors beyond anyone's control could abort the objective must be faced, so an alternative project should be planned to offset such a contingency: this can also be of benefit if progress on the original project goes better than anticipated and extra diving time thus becomes available, in which case the extra time can be usefully employed to give the expedition an unexpected bonus.

Reports
The expedition can only be considered successful if the objective is achieved, and this may well include the provision of a written report —particularly if sponsors have been involved . So, to maintain interest to the end, such a report should be presented as soon as possible after completion of the expedition.

Both in planning and conducting the expedition it is likely that a great deal of help, advice and cooperation of one sort or another will have been sought and freely given, and to all those responsible, a letter of thanks with a copy of the results (if relevant), a personal visit or even a telephone call, will at least show that their efforts are appreciated. Apart from being common courtesy, it will also make it easier to ask again should the need arise!

In conclusion it must be stated that the organisation of a diving expedition should not be undertaken lightly, involving as it does a great deal of painstaking research and arduous work. But running a successful expedition is worth all the effort; it gives a real purpose to diving and a deep feeling of personal satisfaction to all those involved.

Small Boat Seamanship

Small boats are widely used by diving clubs to convey divers to off-shore sites and to provide safety cover while diving takes place. When chosen carefully, when properly equipped and handled, a small boat can be very seaworthy. Proper handling requires good seamanship. Seamanship can reasonably be defined as 'the Art and Science of conducting a vessel safely from one place to another', but this is not entirely true because only by experience can one determine the correct course of action to take in adverse conditions, despite all the sophisticated instruments that are available. When at sea it is necessary to follow a number of common-sense guidelines—just as you do when driving a car or running a dive. But more than this, remember that boats are traditionally referred to as 'she's'; their reactions in any given circumstances are not what you always quite expect . . . they need to be understood: caressed, not cuffed!

Naturally, in a car or on a dive, you place yourself in the hands of the driver or Dive Marshal; the same is true on a boat. Even in a voluntary group, the person appointed, elected or whatever, to 'drive' the boat—the boatman—is responsible for conducting the boat safely from one place to another and his decisions should be respected accordingly. Boats cannot be driven by committee any more than cars can.

Now let us consider some fundamentals which are of value to anyone who is going to work on a boat.

Ropework
First of all, to quote Jerome K. Jerome: 'There is something very strange and unaccountable about rope. You roll it up with as much patience and care as you would take to fold up a new pair of trousers, and five minutes afterwards, when you pick it up, it is one ghastly, soul-revolting tangle.'

MEASUREMENT:
Nowadays rope is generally described by its diameter in millimetres, although traditionally in Great Britain it has been measured by its circumference in inches, and references to this system may still be found—so beware!

COMPOSITION:
Spun or 'hawser laid' rope is the most commonly available and is composed of a number of thin 'yarns' spun into thicker 'strands',

which are in turn laid out together to form the rope. Most rope is three-stranded, and the strands are laid up right-handed, as shown in Fig. 96a. The majority of natural, nylon and terylene ropes are laid up in this way. Polyethylene and polypropylene ropes are too, but in these the yarns may be made up of either split fibres or mono-filaments. In the latter the yarns are extruded like thin wire; they have fewer yarns or filaments than the other types of natural rope and tend to be slippery, less strong, and difficult to handle because they kink more readily. A common factor among all polyethylene and poly-propylene ropes is that they float. Most materials can be 'plaited' which generally increases their flexibility, but reduces their strength; being difficult to splice, they are usually knotted and this results in a further reduction in strength.

STRENGTH

National standards are set for the various types of rope, and samples are tested to destruction at the factory. Manufacturers produce tables of breaking strength for size; examples are given in Fig. 95. It is obviously not sensible to work near this limit, and remember that the formulae are for unworn rope. Before using a rope you must find out what its Safe Working Load (SWL) is. This is found quite simply by dividing the Breaking Strength by a Safety Factor (SF) of 6 for natural, and 4 for man-made ropes.

A knot reduces the strength of a rope by about 50%, and a splice by 12%. It is also of note that a natural fibre rope loses almost 50% of its strength when saturated. Always be on the lookout and watch for chafe or fraying over the whole of a rope's length—like a chain, its strength is that of the weakest link.

	Breaking Strain kg/f	Recommended Safe Working Load kg/f	Stretch at Break	Mass in kg/30 m	Buoyancy
Manila Grade 1	543	90	18%	1.6	Sinks
Sisal	488	81	18%	1.6	Sinks
Nylon	1350	340	38%	1.3	Sinks
Prestretched Terylene	1015	254	7%	1.7	Sinks
Terylene	1015	290	28%	1.6	Sinks
Polypropylene	960	240	33%	1.0	Floats
Polyethylene	630	172	37%	1.07	Floats

Fig. 95   *Comparison of 8 mm diameter (1 inch circumference) rope.*

HANDLING

The golden rule when using rope is 'tidiness', particularly when we remember the quote of Jerome K. Jerome. Tidiness in this sense means coiling—either the whole of a rope when spare, or the end which is not in use.

Coiling should be thought about because that 'right hand lay' (Fig. 96b) is the cause of much twisting and tangling. Before coiling, tangled ropes are best laid out straight for their entire length on land, or streamed astern from a boat—even an inflatable. Once laid out on land, give them a good stretch; this helps to remove final kinks, particularly in new, natural fibre. Then work as in Fig. 96b starting with the end *which is secured* in the left hand, and drawing in and coiling CLOCKWISE with the right. The whole secret is to twist the rope, usually clockwise between thumb and forefinger of the right hand, before drawing it in to make each loop of the coil. This allows the rope to fall naturally, and neatly, on to the left hand. This 'twist' of the right hand will send the potentially tangly twists down the rope until they come out at the free end, though it may well prove necessary to shake the rope from time to time in order to clear them and prevent yet another tangle!

Having coiled them, stow. There are three methods: first, where, having coiled as in Fig. 96c, you are left with—hopefully!—a neat coil in the left hand. Take the free end in the right hand and wrap it round the coil about one-third from the top; then pass it through the top half and pull it tight. The coil may then be hung or thrown down with a reasonable chance of not tangling.

The second way is less often used, but has a great deal to commend it, especially for larger ropes or those you need to use quickly, like that for the anchor. Place the finished coil neatly on the ground —ropes too long or too heavy to be held in the hand may be coiled directly on to the ground. Simply take four short lengths of small, unwanted line and tie them at 90° intervals round the coil with a bow—shoelace type. The beauty of this method is that it provides an instant usable coil: just untie the bows—no knife required—and there it is.

Finally, there is one other method of stowing a rope. Just 'pour' it into a box or tub. As it goes in, so it should come out! And it works— providing you do not move or upset the box too much. If you do you will more than likely end up with a 'ghastly, soul-revolting tangle'.

Knots and Splices

So you leave shore on a nice, flat, sunny morning, carefully placing your team in the boat for best water entry. Slowly, as the dive progresses, the wind blows, the sea height increases until, by the time all the divers have scrambled back on board, it is really quite

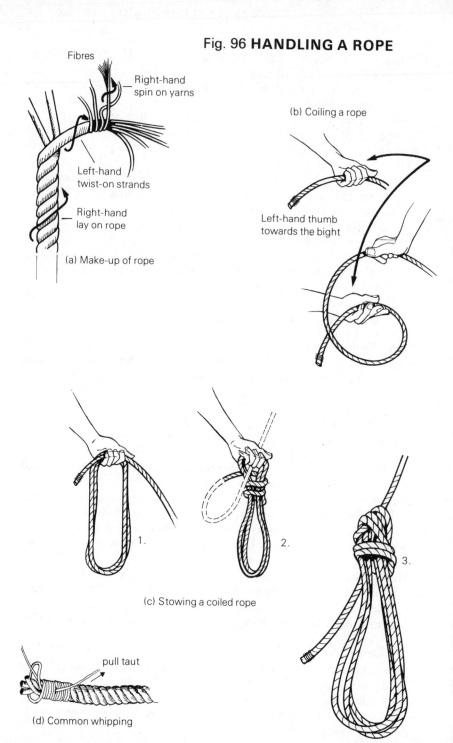

Fig. 96 **HANDLING A ROPE**

Fibres

Right-hand spin on yarns

(b) Coiling a rope

Left-hand twist-on strands

Right-hand lay on rope

Left-hand thumb towards the bight

(a) Make-up of rope

1.

2.

3.

(c) Stowing a coiled rope

pull taut

(d) Common whipping

'hilly'. On return, the previously calm water at the harbour steps is now moving up and down quite alarmingly. Bill jumps ashore—hopefully without injury, and holding the bow-line—and finds that he cannot hold the boat on his own, and in any case he must rush aft for the stern line in order to hold the boat so that someone else may leap out. Bill must tie a knot!

OK, so he may be able to wind the line round and round a handy projection until something jams—but remember the infallible law of the sea written by Murphy: 'You want a rope to jam? It won't!!' It is so much simpler to tie a knot than to try to jam it on purpose—it is also possible to untie it. Now here are five of the basic knots which are easily learnt (Fig. 97):

The Reef Knot	Join two ropes of equal thickness.
Bowline	A loop that will not slip.
Clove Hitch	For quickly securing a line.
Round Turn and 2 Half Hitches	For securing a line—it has the advantage over the clove hitch that it can be undone when under strain.
Sheet Bend	For joining ropes of unequal or equal thickness. A better knot than the reef.
Figure of Eight	A useful 'stopper' knot.

SPLICING:
This is a stronger and tidier method of permanently joining, or forming an eye in, either rope or wire, and a description of the method can be found in most manuals of seamanship.

To conclude this section on ropework, it is suggested that many knots would have less tendency to jam and would last longer if the ends were finished so that they would not fray. In natural rope, the answer is a whipping, as illustrated in Fig. 96d. In man-made fibres the same effect can be more simply obtained by wrapping the end in Sellotape, cutting through it, then melting the strands together against a hot surface or flame. It is not even vital to use Sellotape however: the ends may be sealed with a match and moulded together with the fingers.

Equipment to be Carried in a Small Boat

It helps if the equipment carried in a small diving boat is divided into three categories, thus:

Equipment essential for SAFETY   —which must be carried.
Equipment essential for FIRST-AID   —which should be carried.
Equipment essential for the EXPEDITION—which is essential for the dive.

Fig. 97. KNOTS AND BENDS

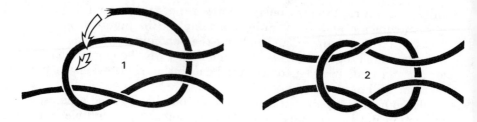

REEF KNOT For joining two ropes. May loosen if tension eases.

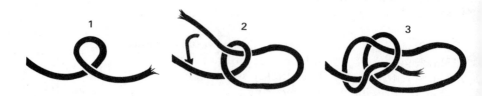

BOWLINE A jamming knot. Best for security and life lines. Can jam.

FIGURE OF EIGHT KNOT A self-jamming knot or as an end stopper

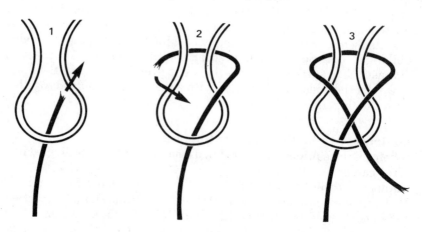

SHEET BEND For joining two ropes of unequal thickness. May loosen if tension eases.

HITCHES

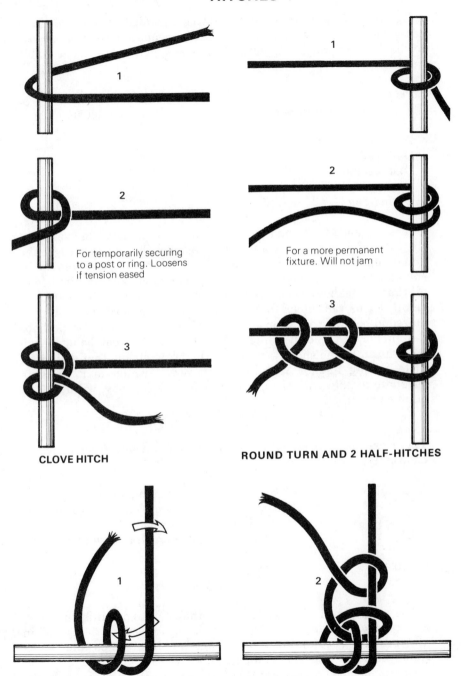

For temporarily securing to a post or ring. Loosens if tension eased

For a more permanent fixture. Will not jam

CLOVE HITCH

ROUND TURN AND 2 HALF-HITCHES

FISHERMAN'S BEND Very permanent self-jamming. Ideal for anchors

Opinions vary as to what should be included in each of these categories: therefore, the following recommendations do not propose to be in any way dogmatic, but are suggested as reasonable guide-lines.

Safety

The gear required is perhaps self-evident. However, let us make a list:

Anchor and line.
Oars/paddles.
Distress flares.
Diver recall signal.
Diving flag.

It is assumed that each person is carrying personal buoyancy in the form of a wet suit or a diver's lifejacket, but do not forget the non-diving boatman snugly wrapped in oilskins and seaboots: he or she also needs a lifejacket that is capable of supporting him/her in all that warm, heavy gear. Before we go on to discuss these items in detail, let us remember that safety items are almost inevitably required in bad weather. For instance, when the engine stops, perhaps the anchor is the only thing that will stop the boat being blown straight on to the shore. Viewed in this way, maybe that delightful little folding anchor weighing some 4 kg, which may be quite adequate to hold you for an hour or two on a fine day, will not look quite so good!

ANCHORS

There are three main types of small boat anchor from which to choose (Fig. 98):

Admiralty pattern	Suitable for sand and mud bottoms, fair on rock—not so good on shingle. Not readily available when stowed.
CQR	An excellent anchor. Not particularly good on rock.
Danforth	Suitable for most sea-beds; stows fairly well in all types of boat.

The most useful of these types are the CQR and Danforth which are immediately ready for use. A weight or large stone holds well in all types of sea-bed, in low tidal streams and light winds, and can be employed as an emergency anchor.

Having decided on the nature of equipment, the size should be determined by keeping in mind the maximum weight that can be

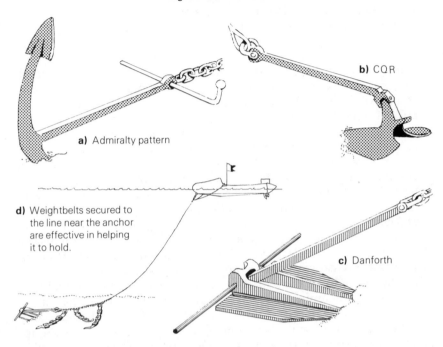

Fig. 98. **ANCHORS**

a) Admiralty pattern

b) CQR

c) Danforth

d) Weightbelts secured to the line near the anchor are effective in helping it to hold.

conveniently handled and stowed; i.e. in an inflatable it is often difficult for one man to work very conveniently, and a weight of perhaps 5 kg is enough, especially when it has to be stowed in a small space. On the other hand, in a 10 m launch there is usually room for two men to work easily, and weights of 15 kg can be considered. It may also be worth considering two anchors if there is space to stow them; one small, one large—for fair weather and foul.

As to line, a length of chain next to the anchor prevents chafe on the sea-bed: 4–5 m with links of, say, 5 mm diameter, are probably enough—again, not so much that it cannot be reasonably handled and stowed.

For the rest, nylon or terylene rope is a must, because of its strength, elasticity and durability. It also handles easily and will stow neatly. It is not worth considering a size less than 10 mm diameter, as it will be difficult to grasp with wet, cold, slippery hands.

The length of the line is another important consideration. It is necessary to decide how and why you are likely to anchor. There are two extremes for a small diving boat: the need to secure over a wreck in, say, 40 m, and the need to hold the boat in a few metres when the engine has failed and you are being blown onshore towards some rather unattractive rocks. You may read in various manuals that the length of line should be anything from 3–8 times the water depth. Applied to our 40 m depth, this obviously makes life in a small boat difficult, for 200-odd m of 10 mm line will leave very little room for passengers! There is, perhaps, a discrepancy and this is because most manuals are concerned with yachts and larger craft that cannot readily be beached above the high water line. Their owners wish to leave them—usually in poor holding ground, i.e. the mud and sand of a harbour or creek—*unattended*, and so it is necessary to put out several times the water depth to ensure a secure anchorage.

In our deep-water diving case, we seldom require an anchor to hold in the sea-bed; we usually hope that it will foul in some part of the wreck. We then want to hold the boat as close to the wreck as possible and, of course, the boat will always be manned—hopefully, by someone able to start and drive the engine! Our 10 mm terylene line is quite strong enough to take the snatch of a line (of only, say $1\frac{1}{2}$ times the water depth) which has nicely caught in the wreck. Diving-wise then, we are usually concerned with holding a manned boat close to a wreck by an anchor caught on it for a short period. The best advice would be to select the deepest depth at which you would normally expect to dive (that is, without some additional thought and planning), say, 30 m, and carry twice that length of line, i.e. 60 m. This amount of line, especially if tailed with chain as already mentioned, will also stand a reasonable chance of holding a boat in a heavy sea in shallow water, particularly if you remember that a diving boat is fortunate in carrying a number of weight-belts and that tying these to the line at, say, 3 m intervals from the chain will greatly increase the efficiency of the anchor (Fig. 98d). If you do want to anchor in poor holding ground then it will be necessary to carry additional line for the purpose.

Finally, do not forget to think about how the inboard end of the line will be secured; the little ring in the bows of many inflatable craft will hold them off the beach on a sunny day, but it is unlikely that they will hold under the conditions we have been discussing— and they are important ones. A yoke between the carrying handles or a special fitting on the keel or floor should be considered.

OARS/PADDLES

Whether to choose oars or paddles for when that engine breaks down (as it inevitably will): that is the next question. In a loaded boat, paddles are more easily used and do not require crutches (rowlocks), which somehow have a habit of getting lost! However, most new craft are supplied with oars, so perhaps the best advice is to use them —until one is broken or lost, and then consider their replacement with paddles—four rather than two. Controlling an inflatable under oars or paddles does take a little experience, but it is quite possible, and a little practice is as important as the many diving safety drills which are practised assiduously.

DISTRESS FLARES:

These fall fairly naturally into two categories: the rocket parachute type, which carries a red distress flare to high altitude and the hand-held type. Neither type is cheap, nor do they have an indefinite life, particularly when they spend long periods in a small wet boat. Which should you carry? The problem is much simplified if your diving organisation is such that a responsible person ashore is briefed to alert a form of rescue operation if you are overdue. Flares will then be needed to attract the attention of boats already on the lookout. Height is necessary and this is provided by the rocket parachute flare. This type is a must in the boat's kit, particularly if the vessel is likely to find itself adrift at night. A hand-held smoke flare is very good for use during the day in clear weather with light wind conditions for the orange smoke which it emits lingers for quite a while. Red hand flares are useful for pinpointing your position when rescue vessels or aircraft can be seen. For an inflatable boat a kit containing a rocket parachute flare, a hand smoke flare, and three red hand flares is a good compromise. Remember that the cardinal rule in an emergency situation is to refrain from using any of these devices until you are certain that someone will see the flare.

DIVER RECALL SIGNAL:

This is another item on our 'must' list. A 'thunderflash' firework is all that is needed, the latter being readily obtainable from the manufacturer or certain dive shops, and no form of certificate or licence is required. Again, divers should be given the opportunity of hearing this signal as an exercise so that they will recognise it when it is used in earnest. Do remember that for the sound of the explosion to carry its maximum distance (which is about 300 m) the thunderflash must detonate under water. As it is almost certainly buoyant, it must be weighted or secured to the end of an oar with a rubber band, and held under, or in some way kept beneath the surface.

DIVING FLAG:

As the leisure use of our waters increases it is not only essential that a diving flag be displayed from the cover craft and from the surface marker buoys used by the divers, but that this should be recognisable. Current regulations require the use of a rigid diving flag and the reader should refer to chapter 6, *Signals and Communications* for more details.

First-Aid

This may be defined as equipment not absolutely vital to the safety of the boat, but which may enable you to prevent an emergency situation from developing. For instance, one compartment of an inflatable may develop a slow puncture; the boat will still carry her load, but may not be able to proceed. She is quite safe, but an emergency situation may develop as the tidal stream carries her out to sea. The use of a pump may well maintain sufficient air in the punctured compartment to permit the boat to proceed and so prevent the emergency situation.

In this category then, include:

Air pump	Inflatables only.
Bailer	Whether or not the vessel has a hand- or engine-driven pump.

First-Aid gear for:

People	Simple materials for staunching blood flow and a large polythene bag to keep the wind off a patient.
Hull	Simple hull patching materials. Spare valve covers if appropriate for inflatables.
Engine	New sparking plugs of correct type. Split-pins and shear pins for the propellor drive. Spare starter cord. Any other items to cope with simple outboard defects. Tools to carry out basic repairs—a plug spanner, pliers and screwdriver are usually sufficient. Tools should be wrapped in a dry rag and spare parts stowed in a plastic bag.

The first-aid gear, and in fact, the distress flares, can usually be contained within the one box which should be water-tight—more difficult than it sounds—and opened only when the material that it contains is needed. This 'boat box' should be looked upon as an essential part of the boat's equipment. Make sure that the tools are kept in working order and that the box is checked and replenished after each expedition. The boat-box should also be strong enough to withstand a diver sitting on it by accident or intention without suffering damage. It is a good idea to have a check list on the outside of the boat-box so that everyone concerned knows exactly what it contains.

Expedition Gear:

This final category depends, of course, entirely on the expedition. Do make a list, and either make one person responsible for the lot, or each person responsible for the equipment he is to use. It is a total waste of time to provide yourself with every safety and first-aid device in the book, and then arrive at the dive site to find that a simple, yet vital, piece of equipment—be it a special tool, tape measure, camera or whatever—is sitting on the jetty back at base.

Boat Handling

Boat handling is an aspect of seamanship and is best learnt by experience. However, it is never too late, and always best, to start with some theoretical background; otherwise it can be a little expensive! As it is a practical activity, it is subject to opinion, and the aim of this section is to lay down some basic considerations which should be known by every boat handler and as many of his crew as possible.

There are, of course, an almost infinite number of different craft on the market, many of which would be suitable for diving purposes. Particularly useful are inflatable craft and open rigid boats which have the characteristics of stability and buoyancy which will be explained below, and whose length is in the range 3–6 m. Normally such craft would be powered by an outboard engine in the 20–60 hp range. Larger open launches also do sterling service as dive boats, though sometimes lacking the speed of the smaller outboard craft. Vessels in excess of 10 m in length are used for major expeditions and often the divers live aboard. The handling and management of vessels of this size normally requires a professional skipper.

Now, to some points on handling which apply to all types of craft in one way or another.

STABILITY AND BUOYANCY

A diving boat should be stable and buoyant, for it is essentially a work boat; these requirements do not necessarily preclude speed.

Stability is necessary so that fully kitted divers may enter the water or scramble back on board without causing the boat to heel so much that she is in danger of swamping. Buoyant, so that if for any reason the boat is swamped with a team of tired, cold divers on board, she will provide sufficient buoyancy to support them until the situation has been sorted out, either by baling or by rescue. An inflatable craft fulfils these requirements admirably, as well as being light enough to carry in and out of the water fairly easily.

Small rigid craft vary enormously and, on the whole, narrow shallow-draft craft are best avoided. Something of the *dory* type is probably best, with a blunt bow and plenty of beam, but again, make sure it has the necessary safe buoyancy. Features of an inflatable suitable for diving are shown in Fig. 99.

It is often necessary to fit buoyancy bags or expanded polystyrene foam on hulls of wood or GRP, although some craft of the latter type are being made of a 'sandwich' construction: the hull consisting of two hard shells, one within the other, leaving a gap of about 50 mm in between which is filled with a rigid buoyant foam.

R

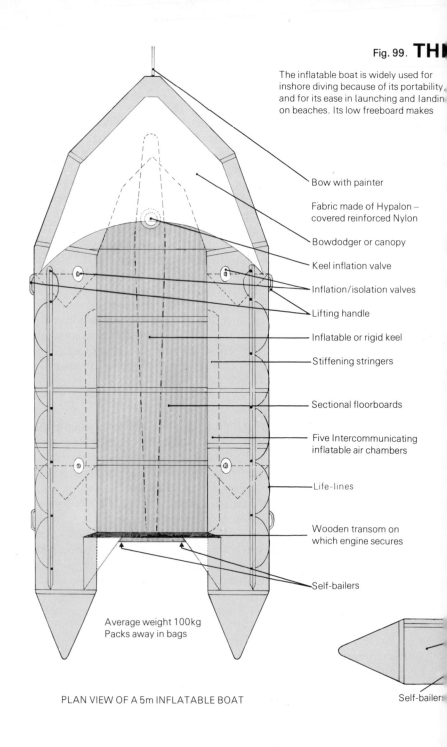

Fig. 99. **TH**

The inflatable boat is widely used for inshore diving because of its portability, and for its ease in launching and landing on beaches. Its low freeboard makes

Bow with painter

Fabric made of Hypalon – covered reinforced Nylon

Bowdodger or canopy

Keel inflation valve

Inflation/isolation valves

Lifting handle

Inflatable or rigid keel

Stiffening stringers

Sectional floorboards

Five Intercommunicating inflatable air chambers

Life-lines

Wooden transom on which engine secures

Self-bailers

Average weight 100kg
Packs away in bags

PLAN VIEW OF A 5m INFLATABLE BOAT

Self-bailers

INFLATABLE BOAT

getting into and out of the boat a
simple matter for divers. Its large reserve
buoyancy provides a big safety factor,
and makes it a virtually unsinkable boat.

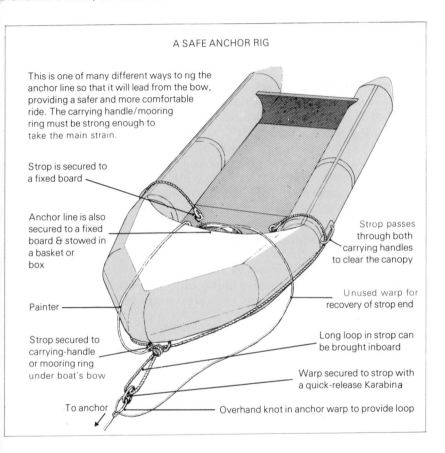

A SAFE ANCHOR RIG

This is one of many different ways to rig the
anchor line so that it will lead from the bow,
providing a safer and more comfortable
ride. The carrying handle/mooring
ring must be strong enough to
take the main strain.

Strop is secured to
a fixed board

Anchor line is also
secured to a fixed
board & stowed in
a basket or
box

Strop passes
through both
carrying handles
to clear the canopy

Unused warp for
recovery of strop end

Painter

Strop secured to
carrying-handle
or mooring ring
under boat's bow

Long loop in strop can
be brought inboard

Warp secured to strop with
a quick-release Karabina

To anchor

Overhand knot in anchor warp to provide loop

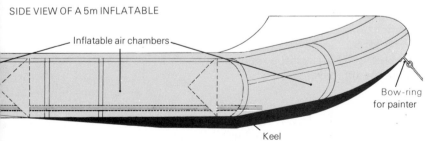

SIDE VIEW OF A 5m INFLATABLE

Inflatable air chambers

Bow-ring
for painter

Keel

As to larger vessels (say, over 6 m), again look for a broad beam, but not too shallow a draft, for such a boat must be seaworthy and requires the stability of a deepish keel.

WEATHER AND LOADING

Whatever the type of boat, it will have a maximum load in calm weather, which will be determined by its physical dimensions, i.e. just how many divers can actually get in with all their kit!

A safe boat is one which when full of water will either support the weight of the *maximum* number of people it is expected to carry, or, in the case of larger craft, carry life-rafts capable of supporting the same maximum. Stability also matters, for although a boat may be able to support a considerable weight, it might then be so unstable that it is no longer able to right itself, which means that although the boat appears perfectly safe at the steps of the jetty, out in the open water a violent helm movement will heel the boat such that she cannot recover, dip a gunwale and rapidly fill.

Now, having determined the maximum safe loading in calm water, what really matters is the sea state 'now' and, perhaps more important, what it is forecast to be at the end of the dive. A boat may be perfectly safe with her maximum load of fully kitted divers on board in calm weather, but the moment the sea begins to get up it is a very different matter. The load must be decreased to give manoeuvrability and to prevent too much water being shipped; in small craft there must also be room to move the crew around in order to allow the boat to ride comfortably.

Too little crew weight can be as dangerous as too much, for the weight of the crew may be necessary to stabilise the boat. An inflatable which will carry seven should have at least two aboard at any time, thereby giving the cox'n ballast which he may move around the boat as he wishes. In particular, it is possible for a strong wind to get under the bow of a light inflatable and turn it over. Ballast in the form of crew is needed to hold it down.

Before we go on to the practical aspects of boat handling, the effect of the weather needs to be looked at in a little more detail. It is the sea state—not wind force—which really matters and this is dependent on:

Wind force;
Surface and sub-surface topography;
Distance offshore;
Time;
Tidal streams.

Let us take the bay illustrated in Fig. 101, which is typical of many round the UK. A force 6 wind from the South East (winds are named as FROM a direction; tides are named as going TO a direction)

Fig. 100. **BOAT TRIM**

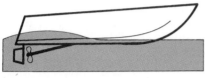

(a) A planing (high speed) hull

(b) A displacement (low speed) hull

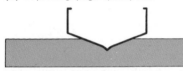

(a¹) At sufficiently high speed, it will ride on the surface of the water

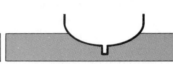

(b¹) Although more stable than (a) it has to push through the water

Engine Alignment | Load Distribution

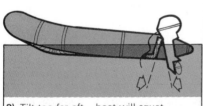

1) Forward tilt of engine — boat will plough

1) Crew too far for'ard — boat will plough

2) Tilt too far aft — boat will squat

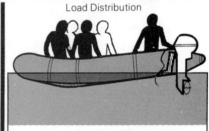

2) Crew huddled aft — boat will squat

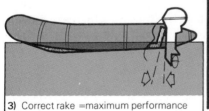

3) Correct rake =maximum performance

3) Balanced load =maximum performance.

is obviously ominous; the sea state will build up very quickly and diving will be impossible. However, if it is a force 3 it is a different matter. If it had only just started blowing, the chances are that the sea height will not be enough to stop the dive. However, if it has been blowing for a day or two the sea height may well have built up to such an extent that the dive is no longer possible. In other words, time is more significant than the wind force.

Let us now take a south-westerly wind. In this case topography matters. In the lighter winds the whole of Biscuit Bay may be nicely sheltered, whereas at X diving is impossible. However, as the wind increases in strength, the effect from the shelter from Heart Point diminishes and the sea at Flinders Bar may well be such that entry into harbour is impossible. There is an additional complication here in that waves break at a given relationship between their length and height, and the water depth; so that even if the wind force has produced only a relatively low sea in Biscuit Bay, at a certain tidal height this sea will break as it passes over the Bar and stop small craft entering or leaving the river. This effect will also occur on Smith's Shoal. At a given state of the tidal height, when the relationship of wave height to depth is right, the waves will literally stand up, walk across this shoal, and fall off the other side. This just might be dangerous in a gentle swell where conditions might otherwise appear almost perfect.

Finally, we are delighted when the wind blows northerly, as we may dive in Biscuit Bay in almost any wind force. Although, just a thought: north wind, ebb tide and engine failure might well bring an unexpected trip to distant shores! Do remember those distress flares—you never know, it might happen to you!

HANDLING

Whenever you handle a boat, you cannot escape the influences of wind, tidal stream, rudder and screw, sea state, hull shape and load —a formidable lot! Their effect can be predetermined, to a greater or lesser extent. That their effect cannot be totally predicted is the reason why boat handling can only be completely mastered through experience.

Hopefully, these few sentences give some idea of the measure of the problem. Let us now take a look at the factors which are reasonably consistent in each boat; but remember that they may vary from boat to boat even in the same class, because of minor variations in their construction.

SCREW

A screw is termed as being 'right' handed or 'left' handed according

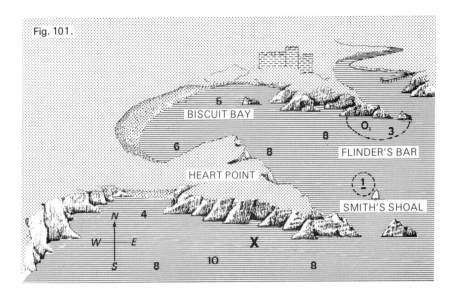

Fig. 101. **THE EFFECT OF WEATHER AND TIDE ON A DIVE SITE**

to which way it turns when viewed from astern. In an outboard, this is of little consequence as the screw is so small and turning so quickly that there is little differential water pressure between the top and the bottom. This is also true of smaller inboard engines. However, as screw size increases the pressure differential increases and the lower part of the blade, broadly speaking, bites the water more than the upper as the screw turns. This has the effect of 'walking' the stern in the direction of rotation.

Under way, this has little effect as it is overcome by the rudder. However, when moving off or going astern it must be taken into consideration. In the latter case, it may well dominate all other effects until the boat has reached a reasonable stern speed.

RUDDER

A rudder is only effective when there is a flow of water past it, either ahead or astern. Therefore, at slow speeds its effect will be dominated by the screw or one of the other effects, such as wind.

An outboard has no rudder, but the whole engine is turned, and so the stern will move as it is directed by the thrust of the propeller, either ahead or astern, irrespective of speed.

HULL SHAPE:

Above water, the shape of the hull will determine the effect of the wind, so that with a for'd cabin the wind will have a greater effect on the bow. Below water, the difference between inflatable and conventional craft is most marked. An inflatable has a very shallow draft, almost the same for'd as aft, and little or no keel; whereas a conventional hull has a keel and a greater draft aft.

The inflatable's direction of movement is determined by the direction in which the screw is pushing. The moment the screw stops the movement of the tiller has no effect, and the flat, shallow-draft hull has little directional stability and will only *tend* to continue in one direction, bow first; it will very easily skid sideways and will be blown off course by the slightest wind.

Conventional craft, on the other hand, have a fine under-water shape and a keel, which often means that once the screw stops they will continue in the same direction for some distance, and the rudder will be effective so long as there is a reasonable flow of water past it.

LOAD
Like a car free-wheeling down a hill, a loaded boat will continue much farther than a light one when the engine is stopped. Due allowance for this must be made when manoeuvring.

SEA STATE
Apart from rolling the boat and making life thoroughly uncomfortable, waves have the effect of slowing down a boat. When the engine is stopped in a craft heading into the sea, it will not 'free-wheel' as far as normal because of the waves smacking against the bow: another point to remember when manoeuvring.

Now let us consider the basic manoeuvres mentioned earlier in the light of these relatively consistent effects, coupled with those variables, wind and tide, though perhaps winds and tides are not so much variable as extremely difficult to assess accurately without instruments.

Let us now just take a look at what we mean by 'boat handling'. It means the ability to control a boat in at least seven basic manoeuvres—and any others which may crop up! The seven basic manoeuvres are as follows:

Picking up a man.
Anchoring.
Berthing and unberthing.
Open beach work.
Turning in a confined space.
Towing.
Securing to a buoy.

Fig. 102. PICKING UP DIVERS

PICKING UP A PERSON FROM THE SEA

As far as most fishermen, yachtsmen and boatmen are concerned, this is an emergency measure, whereas in diving it is an everyday occurrence. The diving boatman must, therefore, be very well versed in this procedure. The technique of picking up a man overboard or a diver are almost identical and the instructions which are about to be given apply equally to both situations. One or two fundamentals first: Your only concerns are the wind and waves; the tidal stream is quite irrelevant as both the subject and the boat are being moved in the same mass of water. It is the effect of the wind which is dominant together with the thought that we wish to avoid damaging the subject in the water with any part of the hull or the screw.

The essence of the manoeuvre is to stop the boat at right angles to, and up-wind of, the person in the water. In this position the boat presents a greater surface area to the wind than the person in the water and it will be blown down towards the subject. This makes it easy to stop the screw well clear of the person in the water, and the boat and subject make contact at minimum speed. (Because of their windage, inflatables should hold head to wind alongside the subject.) Even when the wind is light, it is remarkable how quickly the boat and subject separate if the boat is stopped downwind.

Should the boat be rolling uncomfortably, it may be worth stopping at 45° to the wind, but remember the boat will only hold this position for, say, half a minute; it will soon be blown broadside on to the wind. Finally, when this manoeuvre is a matter of emergency, there is one cardinal rule: one member of the crew MUST be detailed to WATCH THE SUBJECT and point at him until he is finally recovered. Preparations should also be made to help the subject inboard, and one of the crew should be ready WITH A SAFETY LINE to enter the water and provide assistance. These rules apply to all boats, although in small craft which are highly manoeuvrable and have low gunwales, it is unlikely that another person will be required to enter the water. Nevertheless, one should be ready.

ANCHORING

A relatively simple manoeuvre? Yes, but you have two concerns: that the anchor is dropped in the right place and that, once dropped, it stays put! It is probably best to drop the anchor when stopped, heading into the wind or tidal stream, whichever is dominant. Then go astern gently and lay out the anchor line on the sea-bed. A minimum of twice the water depth is necessary for the anchor line to hold a boat safely in good weather. This means quite a large coil when in, say, 30 m of water. To avoid a tangle in the anchor line, the lines must be laid out, not just tipped out.

Consider the tidal stream, i.e. will it run in the same direction throughout the dive? If so, it may be worth anchoring off site and allowing the boat to drop back over site. This will allow a nice, long safe anchor line and at the same time allow divers to reach the site quickly. It is also the only method if any form of lifting is to take place.

It is possible to anchor with a short anchor line, i.e. less than twice the water depth. If you do, remember that the line must be strong and preferably nylon (with its stretch capability), and the fittings on the boat must be equally strong to take the stress caused by the vertical movement of the boat.

Further, you MUST retain a competent boatman in the boat and have total faith in the engine starting without difficulty. If you have ANY thought of anchoring and leaving the boat unattended, you should ensure that the anchor line is at minimum, three times the water depth, and that the boatman never forgets the weather —actual and forecasted. It is bad seamanship to leave an anchored boat unattended. It also means that help cannot be rendered in an emergency.

BERTHING AND UNBERTHING

In this manoeuvre, all the various influences must be considered, for the shore—be it jetty, wall or whatever—is very solid and will not move, whereas the boat is subject to every whim of tidal stream and wind; it is also relatively flimsy and 'bends' rather easily!

The tidal stream, if it exists, is often the dominant factor and, whenever possible, berth heading into it. In fact, because it is necessary to keep the screw turning to hold the boat stopped over the ground, there is a flow of water past the rudder, and so a tidal stream is quite useful in that the boat may be steered until the very last moment. In all boats the safest method of berthing is to head slowly into the tidal stream, as near parallel to the jetty as possible, making due allowance for wind. Speed is often difficult to judge, and certainly in the larger conventional boats it is worth stopping short of the berth and then proceeding at slow speed up to it. Further, this manoeuvre will be much easier if bow and stern lines are made ready BEFORE arrival alongside. It is, to say the least, annoying when, after a 45-minute, cold, wet, miserable passage back from the diving area, the bowline is found to be buried under four sets of tanks, three weight-belts and two people!

With the wind blowing off an unsheltered berth, the approach cannot be quite parallel and the boat will 'crab', i.e. move slightly sideways (Fig. 103). The important thing in this case is to secure the bowline. Once this is done, even if the boat 'weathervanes' onto the wind, the stern line can be led ashore over the bow and the stern pulled bodily alongside.

UNBERTHING

An offshore wind (such as that just mentioned) presents no unberthing problems. However, an onshore wind is quite a different story. In an inflatable and the smaller outboard-engined boats, it may well be best to leave the berth stern first, as going out ahead means brushing along the side of the wall/jetty until the boat has attained sufficient speed to head up into the wind.

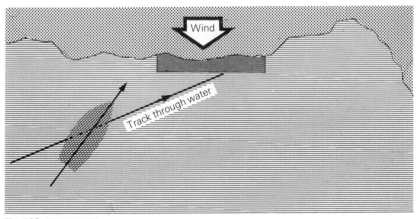

Fig. 103. BERTHING

Larger boats with inboard engines have even more of a problem, and here are two suggestions. First, lead or secure the bowline as far forward as possible in the boat, then secure it on the shore at least as far aft as the stern. Cushion the bow well, hold the tiller, or put the wheel over so as to head the boat into the jetty, then go ahead. Keep a careful eye on the bow and increase speed smoothly, and the stern will move out. When the boat has reached a minimum of a 45° angle with the wall, reverse the rudder, go full astern, and let go the bowline. The boat should move away from the jetty without damaging the bow. Now it may be that the effect of wind and tidal stream are such that the boat just will not reach 45° (Fig. 104). In this case, try laying out the anchor at right angles to the bow with a small boat. Then haul the bow off and go ahead; the tidal stream will help as soon as it is on the inner bow. In this situation, if an inflatable is available, it may well be worth using it as a mini-tug on either bow or stern.

OPEN BEACH WORK

Launch and recovery from an open beach is a means of berthing used more frequently by the diver than any other sea user these days. However, it should be appreciated that in anything but the lowest sea states this has never been and never will be a particularly simple or safe operation. Divers, however, have a bonus in that they are all wearing—or have available—a warm, buoyant wet suit and there should be no hesitation in entering the water.

As mentioned earlier, waves break at a given ratio between their height and the water depth—roughly 3:4. A steep shore may have only two or three rows of breakers, whereas on a shallow shore there may be a great many. It is the breaking waves which are the problem,

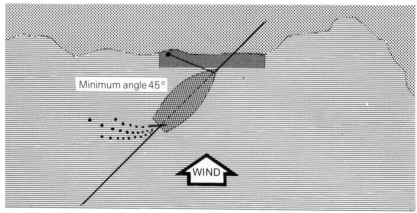

Fig. 104. UNBERTHING

as they break over and swamp a boat, rather than lift it up and down. Depending on the under-water terrain the situation may also be very different at high and low water. It is possible to leave shore at high water relatively simply only to return and find an impressive row of breakers, although wind and sea remain unchanged—beware!

Whether beaching or launching a boat in surf, the essential requirement is patience. Watch the breakers for some time, note that they are not all of the same height or character. There are periods of relative calm—but do not depend on the mythical seventh or eleventh wave being larger than the rest.

When launching, fit the engine and make the boat ready at the water's edge with enough men stationed round to lift it, and one ready to act as boatman. Wait quietly for the moment when one wave has broken and another is not hard on its heels. Lift the boat on to the water quickly, and push/swim it as fast as possible through the breakers. As soon as the boat floats the boatman must leap in, start up and motor off clear of the crew. He is then able to anchor and drop back just clear of the breakers and wait for the others to join him with the rest of the gear. It may be worth launching without starting the engine and relying on clearing the breakers by pushing or use of oars or paddles. So much depends on water depth, the number and rows of breakers and, not least, crew experience. Timing really is essential, and if there is any doubt—DON'T! Look for a more sheltered spot.

When landing, timing is equally important. Lie off and watch the waves for a while. In smaller breakers it may be possible to drive gently up to the beach—do not forget to unlock the outboard!—and for everyone to leap out the moment the bow touches and quickly lift the boat ashore clear of the waves. In larger breakers there is little choice but to anchor off clear of the breakers, unload the boat, and swim or walk ashore as much equipment as possible. Then, choosing the right moment of relative calm, pay out the anchor line rapidly until the crew can hold the boat, run it in stem first and lift it up the beach clear of the waves. If whilst doing this manoeuvre, a breaker threatens to overtake the boat DO NOT try to beat it ashore. Hold on to the anchor line, steady the boat, and wait for the wave or series of waves to pass.

TURNING IN A CONFINED SPACE

In the inflatable, outboard or twin-screwed conventional hull this presents little problem. However, in a single-screwed conventional hull it requires some thought.

At slow speeds with little movement of water past the rudder the effect of the screw dominates. To manoeuvre your boat it is then necessary to know whether your screw is right or left handed.

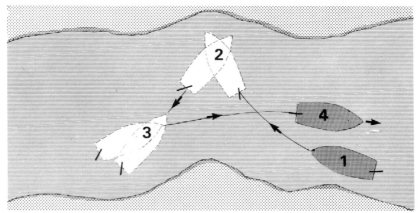

Fig. 105. TURNING IN A CONFINED SPACE (right-handed single screw boat)

Let us take a boat with a right-handed screw at rest in a channel—position in Fig. 105.

1. Put the rudder to starboard; go half-ahead for a few seconds, making sure the boat does not gather way. The stream of water past the rudder will kick the stern to port.

2. As soon as the boat is on the point of moving ahead, go half astern and put the rudder hard to port. The rudder is ineffective, and the screw turning left-handed astern will continue to 'walk' the stern to port.

3. As soon as the boat is on the point of moving astern, put the rudder hard-to-starboard and go half-ahead. The stream of water past the rudder makes it effective and the stern will continue to port.

4. Repeat actions 2 and 3 until the boat points in the required direction.

Theoretically, this is a beautifully simple manoeuvre. However, in practice remember that the tidal stream may be moving the boat bodily towards a hazard although the manoeuvre appears to be going well. Further, the wind may distort the manoeuvre and if strong enough may well make it impossible, especially in boats with high superstructure forward.

TOWING

This sounds a simple manoeuvre, and certainly is in small boats and calm weather. However, as the sea state increases so do the problems. These guide-lines are recommended:

1. Tow with your longest, strongest rope. It is then possible to adjust the length of tow until the boat being towed rides com-

fortably. Avoid using your anchor line, though it may fit the bill perfectly.

2. TOWING POINTS

Boat Towed —Must be strong. The ring on the bow of an inflatable is probably not strong enough; consider the use of a yoke from the lifting handles. The thwarts of an open launch may well be stronger than the fittings on the bow. If towing a sailing dinghy, secure the line around the foot of the mast.

Towing Boat—In an inflatable, consider a yoke from the transom either side of the engine, or the bottom boards or keel structure. If the construction of the boat permits, the best point of tow is as near the pivoting point as possible—about one-third from the bow.

3. If you are towing, use 'his' anchor line or painter—if he has one! Then, should your engine fail your anchor will be the best remaining safety measure.

4. Towing alongside (Fig. 106). Good control possible, but very wet in small craft and of course, there is the possibility of damage in any sea. The simplest method is to rig one line from bow to bow, another from stern to stern, and a third from the bow of the towing boat to the stern of the vessel being towed. Try to adjust these so that the stern of the towing boat is behind that of the boat towed. This leaves the stern clear and permits greater manoeuvrability. This method is probably best used in sheltered waters or when manoeuvring the boat alongside after a sea tow, and is applicable to all craft from inflatables upwards.

SECURING TO A BUOY

This is a fairly simple operation, especially when the buoy is small

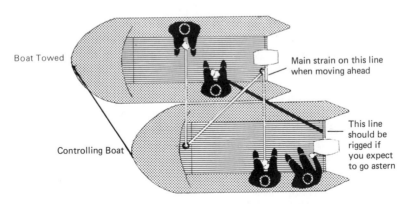

Boat Towed

Main strain on this line when moving ahead

This line should be rigged if you expect to go astern

Controlling Boat

Fig. 106. TOWING ALONGSIDE

and the freeboard of the boat is low, but tide and wind may change the situation since the buoy is fixed to the sea-bed. In the larger boats the cox'n may well be unable to see the buoy in the final stages of the approach; do help by placing someone forward in the boat to point it out to him. The cox'n in turn might well be advised to make his approach from the direction in which other boats are lying—a simple method of observing if wind or tide has the major effect.

ROUGH WEATHER

The best answer to rough weather in small open boats is to avoid it! As we have discussed already, most of these craft are limited to working by day and over relatively short distances, which means that we are concerned with very small areas.

Weather forecasts in the United Kingdom relate to very large areas (Appendix 8) and although shipping forecasts are given regularly for each of these, they are made for large vessels and concern the maximum wind strengths to be expected. As the areas covered are so large, this can be very misleading, as other parts of the area may be undergoing very different weather. As an example, take the Plymouth area. A gale in the southern part certainly does not necessarily mean a gale on the south coast of England some hundred miles away. What then are our best courses of action? There are two obvious ones. First, at a time which will allow you to contact the remainder of your team in the event of adverse weather, ring the nearest Meteorological Office to the dive area. These Offices are geared to provide a telephone information service and will tailor it as best they can to cover the particular activity and area with which you are concerned. Their advice is given against the background of experience and an increasing number of sophisticated instruments. However, the weather, certainly around the British Isles, is fickle, to say the least, and can often change unexpectedly— particularly near the coast and estuaries, i.e. the normal diving areas.

A second line of attack, therefore, is to ring the Meteorological Office as before, but only cancel the dive if the forecaster is quite sure of the situation, i.e. it has been blowing a gale on shore for the last two days and shows absolutely no signs of letting up. Otherwise take the chance and go down to the area but have two dive plans— one for reasonable weather, one for bad. There are very few of us who cannot do with practice in low visibility and roped searches, compass swims and all manner of other ideas which can be practised in sheltered areas.

Another problem experienced by many groups coming from inland is the pressure put on them to dive anyway in marginal weather conditions because they have travelled a long way and at some expense.

If the plan is to dive offshore and there is no alternative, then this pressure is very difficult to resist, and can often lead to an incident or accident. If divers know that there is an interesting alternative to their offshore dive the whole atmosphere of the dive can be more relaxed and the correct decision made in view of the prevailing weather.

Now what happens if the weather changes after you have left shore—in the worst case when the dive is actually in progress? First, you will have had some idea that this was likely to happen because the forecaster was aware that the weather might change, i.e. that the wind strength would increase or that sea fog was likely to form. His difficulty is usually in predicting just when this change may occur.

The fundamental rule in these conditions is that your diving organisation must permit recall of divers at the first sign of deterioration, whether it be an increase in the wind strength or a decrease in the visibility. The first worry in these circumstances is that you may lose sight of a diver who has surfaced, or have difficulty in picking him up. Sea fog creeps up remarkably quickly, especially when you are not expecting it, and seeing divers on the surface—whether wearing fluorescent hoods or not—can be very difficult.

Having recovered all the team there are now two things that may prevent your returning home easily: an increasing sea state and/or the fact that you can no longer see the shore. Let us take the problem of setting course for home first. Hopefully someone in your group has a diving compass—perhaps this is something that should be checked when the forecaster has indicated that the visibility may deteriorate. Before anchoring on the dive it would be prudent to aim the boat at your base or some known point on shore and note the compass heading—remembering the problem of masses of ferrous metal near the compass. This compass heading then provides a guide to the course you should steer when the shore is no longer visible—allowance being made for the tidal stream and leeway.

When the wind strength increases there will be a different problem (unless of course, the visibility decreases at the same time), the most important factor being speed. Let us consider it in two ways. First, when the wind is ahead, and second, when it is astern of you. The waves will, of course, be coming from the same direction. With the wind ahead speed should be adjusted so that the amount of water shipped is kept to a minimum and boat does not slam. In other words, if the boat, whatever type, is crashing into waves so frequently that it feels as though something will break—it probably will! SLOW DOWN. In this situation it is reassuring to know that your craft has a good reserve of buoyancy and that you have a bailer and/or an efficient pump.

If the craft has an adequate engine, it should be able to punch its way steadily into a head sea even though it means a slow, wet ride home. The bow should be pointed directly into breaking waves even though this may take you slightly off course. It may be necessary to dash at speed along the troughs between wave crests, turning the bow into the wave crest at the last moment. This is the best way of making progress in a sea approaching diagonally to your course.

When the seas are approaching from behind you, the greatest danger when running with the sea is that of burying the bow of your boat into the trough of the wave in front of you. As the bow digs in, the wave coming up behind you can lift the stern and suddenly swing the boat round causing it to broach and possibly roll over. Somersaulting is not unknown in this situation! If the distance between wave crests is large (4 or 5 times the length of the boat) the safest place to be is pointing down hill on the face of a wave and running at such a speed that you maintain your position on the wave. In effect, the boat is surf-riding. The temptation to increase your speed should be avoided as this is likely to cause the bow to dig in. Even in very rough seas there are moments when the waves are lower than usual and the boatman must adjust his speed to take maximum advantage of these flatter areas. He cannot relax at all but must be constantly varying the speed and direction of the boat so that he gains the most ground with the minimum of discomfort and risk. Sudden manoeuvring may be necessary so the crew should hold tight at all times (particularly when the boat is going 'uphill' into a wave crest!) and should carry out the boatman's instructions immediately and without question. After all he is in charge of the boat.

Another point to bear in mind is that the combination of rugged bottom topography and increased tidal streams off many of our headlands causes unusually short steep seas even in relatively calm weather. These conditions are aggravated as the wind strength increases. The areas are shown on tidal stream atlases and indicated on charts and you will see that their position and size varies with the strength and direction of the tidal stream. Talking of tidal streams, remember that they do tend to change the character of the seas so that relatively shorter steeper waves can be expected when the wind is against the stream.

The responsibilities of a boatman (or coxswain, to give him his correct title) are many, but the satisfaction of doing the job well far outweighs the burden of responsibility. The BSAC offers Boat Handling Courses through its Coaching Scheme and these represent an ideal opportunity for members to gain experience and knowledge which will put them well on their way to becoming competent boat handlers.

Fig. 107. **AN OUTBOARD ENGINE**

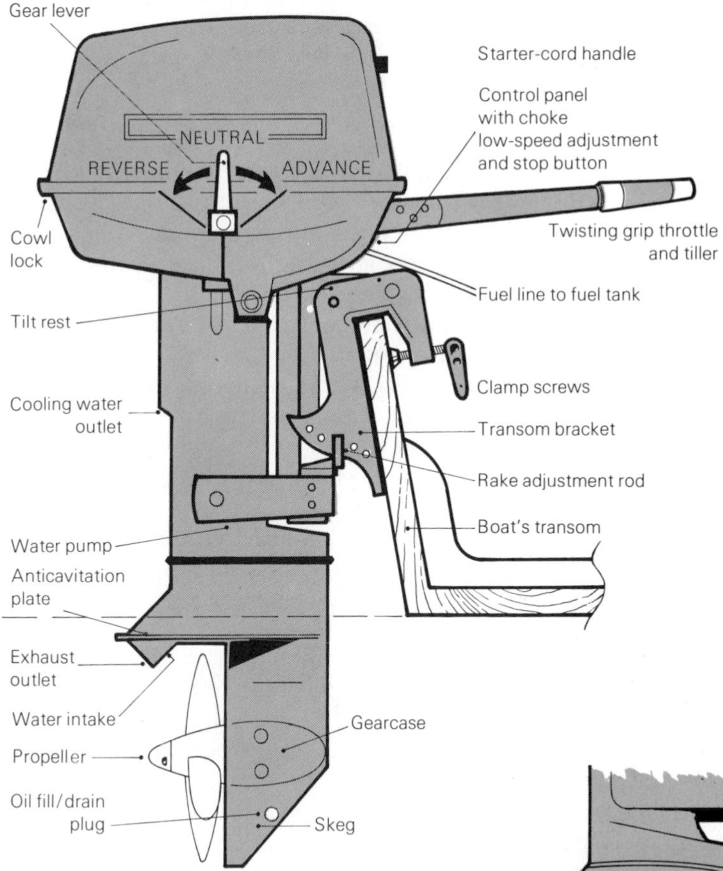

Gear lever

Starter-cord handle

Control panel
with choke
low-speed adjustment
and stop button

NEUTRAL

REVERSE   ADVANCE

Cowl
lock

Twisting grip throttle
and tiller

Tilt rest

Fuel line to fuel tank

Clamp screws

Cooling water
outlet

Transom bracket

Rake adjustment rod

Boat's transom

Water pump

Anticavitation
plate

Exhaust
outlet

Water intake

Gearcase

Propeller

Oil fill/drain
plug

Skeg

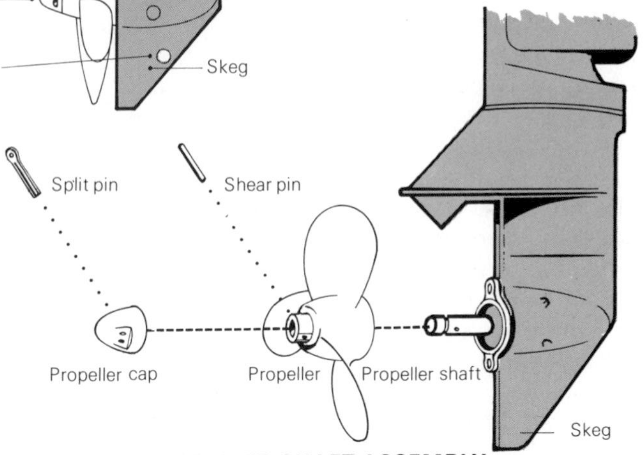

Split pin   Shear pin

Propeller cap   Propeller   Propeller shaft

Skeg

A TYPICAL PROPELLER SHAFT ASSEMBLY

Charts and Tide Tables

Charts

First, let us sort out why we need to understand a chart at all, for many of the boatmen who take us on a dive do not use one. Equally, there seems little need when we dive from our own small boat, for we usually stay within sight of recognisable landmarks, and stand little chance of running aground wherever we go.

There really is not much need of a chart in these cases, *provided* we accept two fundamental limitations:

either (i) we wish to dive on a site where someone else has been before and has observed the 'transits' or 'marks' (see Fig. 114, page 538) for us:

or (ii) we shall not know where we have dived.

These limitations do not matter when we are diving purely for the enjoyment and thrill of being under water, provided we understand and follow the common sense guidelines of seamanship that we have already discussed.

However, the chances are that we shall soon wish that we could find our way around the sea even if only to obtain a particular depth of water for a training dive—quickly! Our thoughts might then develop, and we might consider that our group tends to dive in one area a few times a year. These dives are sometimes interesting, sometimes not. Wouldn't it be useful if the position of each dive were recorded and plotted so that a picture of the under-water terrain was developed and an interesting dive assured? Once thoughts like these have taken root, then it is not a big step to consider following our land interests in biology, archaeology, photography, etc, under water. In all these cases and in activities like straightforward wreck salvage, knowledge of 'position' becomes essential and we need to be able to find our way around, using a chart.

Now, as divers, the understanding we need of these maps is different from the understanding needed by the average yachtsman, for two main reasons:

(a) We are most often concerned with small, open craft less than 6 m long, which have limited range and speed (certainly when loaded). This means that we tend to launch from a coastal position as near the dive site as possible. So, we are usually travelling across the tidal stream, by day, in a craft which can carry only elementary navigational equipment.

(b) Most important of all, we need to know our position with considerably greater accuracy than any yachtsman: even if we are looking for a wreck 100 m long, our need for accuracy is much greater than that of a yacht travelling along the coast, whose skipper will be more than happy if he knows where he is to within the nearest 300–400 m. It is interesting to note that if we wish to find a site, the evidence of which is spread over an area of less than 100 m, then our need for accuracy begins to approach that of the surveyors who made the chart!

Although some organisations own large boats, their diving trips are limited by the fact that, as very few such boats carry a compressor or have accommodation, they must return to harbour each day to refill cylinders and sleep. However, once your boat is fitted with sufficient equipment to make overnight passages, knowledge of Coastal Navigation *IS* required. This is best gained by acquiring one of the national qualifications in this subject (in Great Britain, these are available through the Royal Yachting Association), and/or by gaining experience with a qualified skipper.

Now let us have a look at the charts themselves. In most countries with an appreciable coastline, there is a Hydrographic Office or Bureau run by the Government, which is responsible for making charts. The UK was among the first to set up a HO, which was established in the late 18th century to provide charts on a world-wide basis for both civil and military purposes. Nowadays, hydrography has a truly international basis and most countries belong to the International Hydrographic Commission. They have agreed areas of responsibility and, perhaps more important for us, are beginning to agree standard units, and methods of presentation.

In most countries there are several companies which reproduce, often very inexpensively, charts which were originally surveyed by the Governmental authority, and this is of course, an attractive proposition. They are usually designed for specialised markets, the most common being for the yachtsman. Which should we buy? Indeed, come to think of it, what on earth is the good of a paper chart in a small, very wet boat? It would be best to solve this problem first, because it is really rather pointless finding out about a chart if we don't believe we shall be able to use it in practice.

One answer is to cut a piece of board—say, marine-ply—into a square of a size that can be reasonably handled on your knee (about 60 cm square). It needs to be thick enough not to bend when you lean on it and, of course, it should be varnished or painted to repel water. Having selected your chart, you can either cover it with matt plastic paper, so making it waterproof, or trace significant points and the coastline onto the plastic paper direct with drawing ink. Either can then be fixed to the board. This produces a chart that is totally waterproof and virtually indestructible. It can be used in rain and spray, stowed on the bottom boards under all that diving gear when not in use, and more, it will float if dropped over the side.

Having shown that a chart can be used in a small boat, the question now is: which one to choose? The answer is quite simple: the one that shows the dive area and the point of departure on the largest possible scale. The choice can be made by consulting the catalogue of charts provided by the chart makers, which should be available for consultation at any chart seller or 'agent' or which can be bought fairly cheaply.

LATITUDE AND LONGITUDE—POSITION:

Let us say that we have written to the wreck section of the Admiralty Hydrographic Department at Taunton, Somerset, and they have given us a list of the wrecks in the area covered by, say, Chart 1900. An area in which we dive frequently. The position of each wreck will be listed by *latitude* and *longitude* in the following way:

Latitude 50° 19·5′ N
Longitude 4° 14·7′ W

We need to be able to interpret these figures so that we can plot the position of the wreck on our chart. This is a fairly simple matter because centuries ago, the problem was solved by assuming that the world was covered with a grid so that positions would be plotted relative to one another on a global basis. Like any grid, it consists of horizontal and vertical lines at right angles to one another. In this case, the vertical lines are aligned to the axis of rotation of the earth and the horizontal parallel to the equator. Each set of lines includes a zero degree line as a basis for reference. For the vertical lines known as *longitude*, which run from Pole to Pole, it is the one which passes through Greenwich, London. For the horizontal lines known as *latitude*, it is the one passing exactly round the waist of the earth, i.e. the equator. Angular measurement is then used to specify any particular position—imagine you are standing in the centre of the earth looking outwards, then the latitude is the vertical angle between the equator and the chosen position measured North or South as appropriate. Equally, the longitude is the horizontal angle between Greenwich and the position measured East or West (Fig. 108).

The chartmakers are able to draw the grid on the chart and so we can conveniently plot positions anywhere in the world using the system.

In practice the simplest way to plot a given position is to align a parallel ruler to the horizontal latitude lines and move one blade so that it just overlaps the appropriate graduation on the vertical

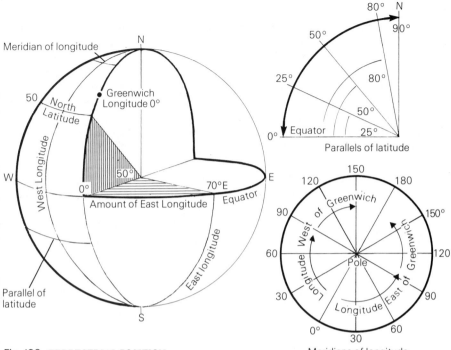

Fig. 108. TERRESTRIAL POSITION

Meridians of longitude

edge of the chart. Then with a pair of dividers measure off the longitude on one of the horizontal edges from one of the lines actually shown on the chart. Then transfer the dividers to the parallel rule and the position is easily determined.

The next thing we need to sort out if we are to use a chart is its scale. You will find that on the larger scale charts it is shown in much the same way as a land map, and can be used just as simply. On the smaller scale charts this is not so, and we must make use of the fact that our ancestors decided that a convenient unit of distance was that subtended on the earth's surface by one minute of latitude. This distance has become known as a *Nautical Mile,* and for all practical purposes it can be taken as 2000 yards or 1850 metres. (This was established in the heyday of Imperial measure, and does not 'metricate' into a convenient figure.) With charts on which there is no normal scale, therefore, we can use the latitude grid notations on the left- and right-hand sides to calculate distance.

At this point, it is worth having one or two more thoughts on the subject of plotting a position, so take another look at the Chart 1900. The scale of the chart when it is full-size is about 9 cm to a nautical mile, which seems fairly reasonable except that when we plot a position, a thick pencil line can be getting on for 1 mm, or, to scale, 20 m thick! This may not sound much, but coupled with slightly inaccurate plotting, it can mean that the position we mark on the chart is 100 m out. Now, 100 m is rather more significant; it will not be too easy, as we shall see in the next section, to find an instrument capable of guiding us to within 100 m of a position. So the net result of these inaccuracies can be an error of over 200 m—which is quite a long way if we are using divers, or a search instrument with limited range. Our search will take that much longer if we have to allow for this inaccuracy. Agreed, our plotting error and instrument error may compensate each other and we may land in the right spot; but remember 'Murphy's Law'! And so, in order to keep the errors to a minimum, we need to use the largest possible scale chart, so that our pencil represents the smallest possible distance, and we also need to plot with the greatest care.

Choosing the largest scale chart is best done from the catalogues published by the chartmaker and available at the stores which sell the charts. While we are at the store there is another publication which is extremely useful: the catalogue of 'Signs, Symbols and Abbreviations' used on charts. In UK this is known as Admiralty Hydrographic Department Publication 5011. With this you will be able to make a thorough interpretation of the chart, and now that there is international agreement over chart symbols and abbreviations, the work is particularly useful.

DIRECTION:

Having sorted out how position and distance are determined, we must now turn our attention to 'direction'. How do we actually get from our launching point to the chosen position?

First, let us take a look at the lines of latitude and longitude which are drawn on the chart, and at the same time remember Fig. 108. We can see that all the lines of longitude finish at two points: the North and South Poles. In other words, all the vertical lines on our chart in effect point in the same direction, and so provide us with a reference. If we then take a 360° protractor and place it so that the centre is in our present position and the zero is pointing up the chart towards the North Pole, in line with the lines of longitude, we can describe the direction of any position to which we want to go, or past which we must go by simply reading off the protractor. Equally, by aligning a parallel ruler between any two points on the chart, it is possible to transfer the line between them on to the same protractor and so determine the direction from one to another.

This gives us a simple method of determining any direction on a chart, but what happens when we are at sea? Where do we steer? Ideally, we should like to be able to point the bow of the boat in the direction we have read off the chart. One way of doing this would be to arrange that our protractor was stabilised in some magic way so that the zero always pointed North, then to have it placed in a bowl fixed to the hull and marked with a line which represented the bow (Lubber Line, or 'direction of travel' line). As the boat altered course, the bowl would move with it and our heading in relation to the protractor could easily be seen by looking at the mark on the bowl. In most large ships today this is exactly what happens. The protractor is known as the 'compass card' and is stabilised by a gyroscope and determining direction is very simple. Regrettably, in smaller vessels there is just not room for the gyro and its associated electrical supplies, so some other method of stabilising the card is needed. Fortunately, our ancestors developed such a method several hundred years ago. They found that a small strip of magnetised iron/steel always tended to point in the same direction if pivoted or hung at its point of balance, and that its direction was quite near the North Star, which mariners from classical times had used as a guide. Being almost directly above the northern end of the earth's axis of spin, the star does not appear to move in the sky and so provides a reference for direction. Thus, was the magnetic compass created.

The magnetised strip of ferrous material was easily attached to a protractor or compass card and placed in a bowl, just like the gyro compass. However, having done this, snags began to crop up and as the years went by scientists and mariners found that the magnetic compass's North was not the same as *True North* (the 'top' end of the earth's axis of spin). What is more, they found that there was every indication that the direction varied from year to year and from place to place . . . They were right: the piece of magnetised iron or steel—compass needle—aligns itself to the earth's magnetic field, which is formed as though there is an enormous bar magnet in the centre of the earth which is slowly moving as the earth orbits in space. As it moves, so apparently does the bar magnet, and *Magnetic North* with it.

By using a magnetic compass, we have a reference direction we can use at sea; the problem now is how to show it on a chart—for it is not the same as True North and varies from place to place with time. The answer is that the angle between True North and Magnetic North (generally known as *Variation*) and its rate of change can be predicted for any part of the world. It is, therefore, shown on every chart and is printed in the form of a 'Magnetic Compass Rose' with the 'True Compass Rose'.

Generally speaking, for the purposes of our diving navigation problem, the simple answer to using a magnetic compass is to buy an up-to-date chart. For instance, one printed in 1973 shows the magnetic compass rose aligned to the direction of Magnetic North expected in 1974. If we wish to know the course, we must steer from one

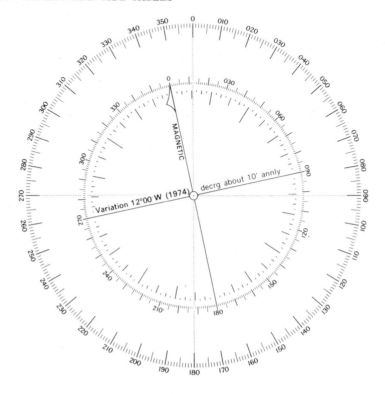

A COMPASS ROSE

A compass rose as found on Admiralty charts showing both Magnetic and True North.

point to another; we have only to line up our parallel ruler to a line joining those points, then transfer it to the inner compass rose and read off the *course* or *heading*. However, be careful: it is quite easy to make the error of using the outer, 'true' ring! Remember, the inner one is marked 'magnetic' on the vertical axis, and the amount of variation and its annual rate of change are shown on the horizontal one. It is also possible for the variation to alter between one side and another of a small scale chart and so the rose nearest your position should always be used. Navigation using the 'magnetic' ring of the compass rose is quite accurate enough for the sort of thing we shall be doing: if you plan to 'go foreign', use the 'true' ring and take into account the need to correct various errors!

Now we might hope that finding our way about on the chart or at sea was just as simple as so far described. Regrettably not! There is one additional problem which could upset us. You will remember that the magnetic needle of our compass aligns itself to the earth's magnetic field; now, the lines of magnetic force which make up this field have an affinity for ferrous metals and will alter their path to pass through them rather than travel through air or other materials. When we travel on a course parallel to the lines of force, there is very little effect. However, as we alter our course across them, the effect increases until, when we are travelling at right angles to the lines of force, the compass needle is aligned to lines of force that may not indicate anything like the real direction of Magnetic North. This direction is known as *Compass North* and it obviously varies with the heading of the boat, its position and the amount of ferrous material in it. The angle between Compass North and Magnetic North is known as *deviation*.

This is as far as we will go with 'direction' for the moment; when we go on to talk of determining position, in the next section, we will also discuss how to avoid errors due to deviation.

Tides

Now, let us consider one of the factors that must always be taken into account when in the waters of the UK and many other parts of the world: the tides. The manner in which gravitational attraction of the sun and moon produce tides was explained in chapter 1, *The Sea*, and if the reader has not already studied that section, this should be done before proceeding with this one.

Although the land masses complicate the tidal cycles, they do follow a fairly regular pattern and it is possible to compile Tide Tables that predict the height of tides in any place at any time. However, it would be difficult to show the predictions for each little port or harbour, so the Institute of Oceanographic Sciences in the UK publishes one volume of tables for major ports in Europe, and two others which cover the remainder of the world. By applying corrections to the figures for the major ports, heights can be calculated for any of the minor ones. In most ports it is also possible to buy little booklets which give the prediction for that port only.

Fine, so we understand why the height of the sea changes regularly, and we can look up the times and amount of this variation in sea level in a table. But the heights must refer to something! What do we do with them now we've got them?

Let us take a look at the Chart 1900. It is covered with a number of figures and what are obviously depth contours, which must refer to some datum—and indeed they do. In all major ports there is a mark set into the harbour wall at a point below the level of the lowest tide there has ever been. The mark is known as *Chart Datum* and all depths on the chart and heights of tide refer to it. In other words, a chart is drawn in the safest possible way so that we can always

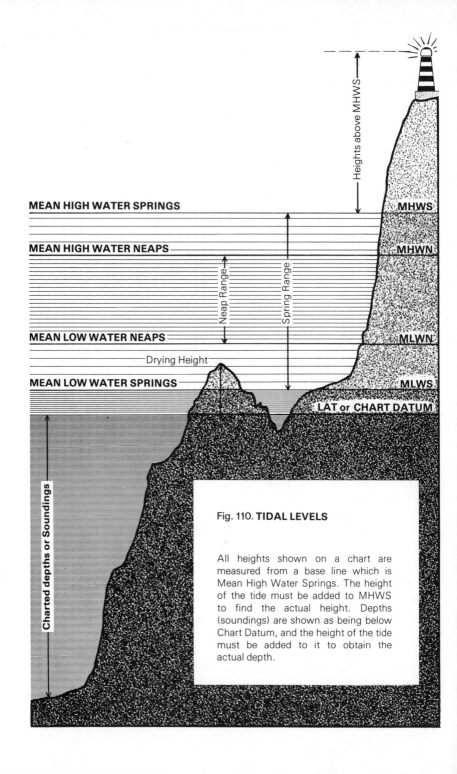

MEAN HIGH WATER SPRINGS — **MHWS**

MEAN HIGH WATER NEAPS — **MHWN**

Heights above MHWS

Neap Range

Spring Range

MEAN LOW WATER NEAPS — **MLWN**

Drying Height

MEAN LOW WATER SPRINGS — **MLWS**

LAT or CHART DATUM

Charted depths or Soundings

Fig. 110. **TIDAL LEVELS**

All heights shown on a chart are measured from a base line which is Mean High Water Springs. The height of the tide must be added to MHWS to find the actual height. Depths (soundings) are shown as being below Chart Datum, and the height of the tide must be added to it to obtain the actual depth.

expect to find the depths it shows—the *Charted Depths*—the tide is then a bonus.

The depth of water is something we are frequently concerned with in dive planning. If we just use the figure on the chart then we shall be wildly wrong at High Water when it is another 6 or 7 m deeper—a difference which will affect decompression times and air endurance significantly. Back ashore, the depth of water may make all the difference to our being able to use a short slip, or to bringing our deep-draught launch alongside; or on a shallow, sandy beach, to having to carry our boat several hundred metres to launch it!

We also need to sort out the tidal heights, because they tell us what tidal streams or horizontal movement of the water can be expected.

To find the depth of water we can expect in a particular position, we obtain the depth of water from the chart and the height of tide from the Tide Tables, and add them together.

This sounds fine, but then we stumble into the problem that the Tide Tables only show the heights of tide at High or Low Water, and of course, we always seem to want to know the height at some time in between them. Fortunately, there is a simple answer to this problem. It is called the *Rule of Twelfths*, which states that: 'A Tide may be assumed to rise or fall, as appropriate, by—

1/12 of its range in the	first	sixth of its duration,
2/12 ,, ,, ,, ,, ,,	second	,, ,, ,, ,,
3/12 ,, ,, ,, ,, ,,	third	,, ,, ,, ,,
3/12 ,, ,, ,, ,, ,,	fourth	,, ,, ,, ,,
2/12 ,, ,, ,, ,, ,,	fifth	,, ,, ,, ,,
1/12 ,, ,, ,, ,, ,,	final	,, ,, ,, ,,

The *Range* of a tide is the difference in height between High and Low Water: the *Duration* is the time difference between High and Low Water. It is very convenient, if small errors are acceptable, to take the duration as six hours rather than the usual period of approximately six and a half hours.

Suppose we want to dive between 0930 and 1030 on a particular day, at a site where the Charted Depth is 8.2 m. We want to determine the actual depth at the time of the dive. The first step is to find out the times of High and Low Water which bracket the time of the dive, and the heights of High and Low Water. In this case, let's say the Tide Tables gave these figures:

High Water 0730. Height 5.7 m. Low Water 1403. Height 1.1 m.

The Tidal Range is (5.7 m − 1.1 m) = 4.6 m. 1/12th of the range is 0.38 m. The Duration is 6 hours 33 minutes. If we take it as 6 hours dead, it will simplify the working at the expense of a few centimetres accuracy.

To determine the depth of water at the start of the dive, and at the end of it, the Rule of Twelfths can now be applied. We are working from High Water to Low Water, so the increments must be subtracted. (If we were going from Low to High Water, they would be added.)

0730 (High Water)   Height of Tide   =5.70 m
0830: 1st Hour, subtract 1/12 (0.38 m) 5.70 m−0.38 m=5.32 m
0930: 2nd   ,,   ,,   2/12 (0.76 m) 5.32 m−0.76 m=4.55 m
1030: 3rd   ,,   ,,   3/12 (1.15 m) 4.56 m−1.14 m=3.40 m
1130: 4th   ,,   ,,   3/12 (1.15 m) 3.42 m−1.14 m=2.25 m
1230: 5th   ,,   ,,   2/12 (0.76 m) 2.28 m−0.76 m=1.48 m
1330: 6th   ,,   ,,   1/12 (0.38 m) 1.52 m−0.38 m=1.10 m

The final figure approximates to the height of Low Water. Had we worked it out to the minute rather than shortening the duration, it would have been spot on. However, for our needs, the results of a quick approximation are good enough. If more accuracy is required, Admiralty Tide Tables should be employed.

Having calculated the height of tide at a particular time, the actual depth of water is quickly determined by adding together the charted depth and the height of tide you have calculated.

Depth at start of dive=8.2 m (charted)+4.56 m (height of tide)
                                                              =12.76 m
   ,,   ,, end   ,,   ,, =8.2 m   +3.42 m   =11.62 m

Heights of tide at intermediate times can quickly be interpolated.

We have now sorted out the vertical water movement, so now let us move on to the horizontal movement, or the *tidal stream* as it is commonly called. We are certainly very concerned with this for, if we are wreck diving or want to stay in one spot for any particular reason, we need to dive at times when the tidal stream is less than ½-knot. (A *knot* is a speed of 1 nautical mile per hour.) Fortunately, the most accurate way of ascertaining this information is also simple. Refer to the Chart 1900. Dotted over it are a number of diamonds, each containing a different letter; each one refers to one of the tables on the chart. For simplicity, a blown-up version of the tables are shown in Fig. 111, and we can see that they show the true direction of the tidal stream as well as its speed in knots at Springs and Neaps for each hour of the tidal cycle relative to High Water (HW) Devonport. The direction is given as the true bearing *towards* which the stream is running as opposed to the description of wind direction. Remember: tides to, winds from. All

Admiralty Charts contain these tables, the data being based on the nearest major port, and the most accurate way of sorting out the tidal stream is to use the largest scale chart—which hopefully you are using anyway—and refer to the table for the *tidal diamond* nearest to the diving area. If we are diving midway between two diamonds, then we will need to look up both tables and take the mean. Equally, if we are diving between Springs and Neaps, we will need to assess how far we are towards one or the other and adjust the rate accordingly.

There are, of course, various other ways of determining the tidal stream, mainly by using a Tidal Stream Atlas of one sort or other, which gives a pictorial representation of what is happening: again, for each hour of the tidal cycle relative to High Water at the nearest standard port. It is then fairly easy to find out what tidal streams can be expected.

Surface winds and weather conditions can also upset the predictions for tidal heights: great masses of water can be held against the land with a resultant increase in the heights of both High and Low Waters; in prolonged gales from one direction, this increase can amount to a metre or two, and sometimes more.

		A 50°18·3N 4 07·7W			B 50°18·4N 4 10·8W			C 50°20·0N 4 07·9W			D 50°20·2N 4 09·7W		
Hours		Dir.	Rate *(kn)* Sp.	Np.	Dir.	Rate *(kn)* Sp.	Np.	Dir.	Rate *(kn)* Sp.	Np.	Dir.	Rate *(kn)* Sp.	Np.
Before HW	6	297	0.8	0.4	236	0.7	0.4	276	0.2	0.1	156	0.2	0.1
	5	306	0.7	0.3	264	0.6	0.3	328	0.7	0.3	051	0.6	0.3
	4	307	0.6	0.3	316	0.6	0.3	342	1.2	0.6	046	1.3	0.6
	3	304	0.3	0.2	031	0.5	0.2	350	1.1	0.6	035	1.3	0.6
	2	098	0.3	0.1	047	0.7	0.4	358	0.8	0.4	038	0.9	0.4
	1	109	0.7	0.3	053	1.0	0.5	014	0.5	0.2	048	0.5	0.3
HW		110	0.9	0.4	081	1.0	0.5	061	0.2	0.1	054	0.1	0.0
After HW	1	111	0.8	0.4	111	0.8	0.4	145	0.3	0.2	232	0.4	0.2
	2	121	0.6	0.3	129	0.3	0.2	168	0.7	0.3	228	0.8	0.4
	3	156	0.3	0.2	235	0.3	0.1	171	0.9	0.4	226	1.1	0.5
	4	265	0.4	0.2	242	0.8	0.4	174	1.0	0.5	225	1.1	0.5
	5	294	0.7	0.4	236	0.8	0.4	174	0.7	0.3	213	0.8	0.4
	6	296	0.8	0.4	232	0.9	0.5	221	0.2	0.1	190	0.3	0.1

Fig. 111. A TABLE OF TIDAL STREAMS

Note:
To ascertain the direction and rate of the tidal stream for a particular locality, it is necessary to look at the general area on the appropriate Admiralty Chart and find the nearest purple lozenge symbol to your own position. Few symbols mean the tidal stream pattern is much the same all over the area: many symbols

indicate the likelihood of variable and sometimes contrary streams.

With the letter indicated in the nearest lozenge, consult the table of tidal streams usually found around the edge of the chart.

Look down the column under the corresponding symbol. The left-hand column shows the Interval, the hours before or after High Water at the standard port printed at the top of the table. The tide tables will indicate the time of HW for that particular day.

Reading across to the right, we find first the direction of the stream in degrees, and then two columns showing the rate in knots, one for Springs and the other for Neaps. To determine which, refer to the tade tables again; the greatest range will indicate Springs, the least Neaps.

Example

Chart No. 1900 Approaches to Plymouth.

The table shown above is that for the standard port of Devonport and shows that the tidal stream for position [B] (off Penlee Pt.) at 2 hrs. before HW at Devonport will be 047° (True) and 0.7 kts. at Springs or 0.4 kts. at Neaps.

In diving we usually require to know the time of slack water. By inspection of the table it will be found that at position [A] (off Mewstone Ledges) slack water occurs at 2 hrs. before HW when the direction of the stream changes from the NW to E; and again 3 hrs. after HW when the stream has gone round from the SE to W.

Slack water is not really necessarily at High or Low Water.

Position Fixing

Having taken a look at our sea map—the chart— and thought about the problems imposed on us by the tides, we are now ready to find our way about at sea.

Over the centuries various instruments have been devised to help solve this problem and of course, better and more sophisticated ones are still being produced each year.

Those instruments which can be used in a small boat are designed to provide either a *position line* or a *position circle* which are defined as follows:

A position line (Fig. 112a) is a line of infinite length through an object on the shore marked on the chart. Its direction can be obtained in a number of ways and the important thing about it is that we know we were somewhere on that line at a given moment in time.

A position circle (Fig. 112b) has a radius of a given distance from a charted mark, again obtained in a number of ways. This time we know that we were somewhere on the circle at a specific time, but do not know the direction of the mark.

Two or more position lines or circles, or a combination of both taken at the same time, will give us our position at that time. This is generally known as a *Position Fix*. Fig. 112 (c, d, e, f) illustrates some ways in which position lines and circles may be used.

The simplest method of finding our way about at sea or 'navigating' is to use the appropriate instrument or instruments to obtain 'fixes' at time intervals which suit our speed, purpose and the weather conditions.

Fig. 113 shows a simple example of finding the way from a river out to a wreck site. We first determine the theoretical Magnetic course we should steer in order to travel from the harbour entrance over the wreck. Then fix our position from time to time and adjust our course as necessary to cope with wind, tidal stream, and errors in the compass and the helmsman's steering. It is never quite as simple as this in practice, but it is important at this stage to have an idea of what we are trying to do.

Now let us take a look at the instruments which we can use in small craft to obtain position lines or circles. These are:

Our eyes.
The sextant.
Magnetic compass.
Echo sounder.

S

Fig. 112. **POSITION FIXES**

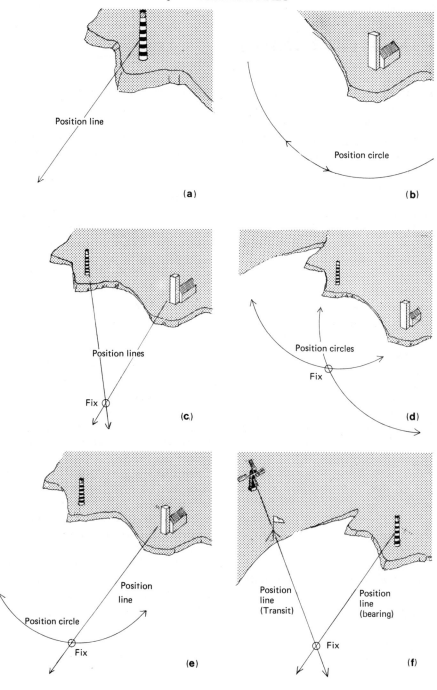

Position line

(a)

Position circle

(b)

Position lines

Fix

(c.)

Position circles

Fix

(d)

Position
line

Position circle

Fix

(e)

Position
line
(Transit)

Position
line
(bearing)

Fix

(f)

Our Eyes

By far the cheapest instrument available to us, and they can of course, be supplemented with binoculars. Their main navigational use is to observe what are known as transits or fisherman's marks.

A transit is obtained, or marks are noted by observing two reasonably conspicuous objects in line on shore (Fig. 114). IF these marks are charted then a position line can be drawn through them on the chart, and we know that we were somewhere on that line at the time of the observation.

In practice, the problem is usually that marks which are quite conspicuous from the sea seldom seem to be on the chart. So as a means of navigating when we are moving, a transit is only of occasional use. It really comes into its own when we have already found an interesting position. We can then look to the shore and choose any two sets of marks which give us two position lines (Fig. 114) and so a fix. If the marks are on the chart we can plot the position. If not, they can be noted, drawn or even photographed, and this means that we shall always be able to return to that position, although we shall not know where it is geographically.

To return to the position, simply steer a course along one set of marks, preferably towards them, then when the other two come in line you are 'on top'. To give reasonable accuracy the two position lines should cross at an angle somewhere between 60° and 120°.

It is also worth remembering that the marks should be aligned with the greatest care. Try to use conspicuous marks which:

(i) Have sharp vertical edges which can be aligned accurately.
(ii) Are not too far apart in height—preferably so that the top of the nearer lower mark is just touching the bottom of the upper.
(iii) Are separated horizontally such that the distance between the nearer mark and your position is less than the distance between the two marks.

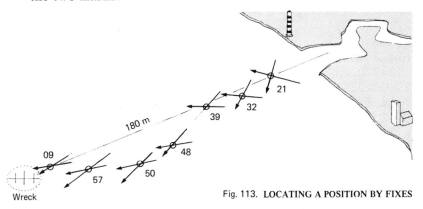

Fig. 113. LOCATING A POSITION BY FIXES

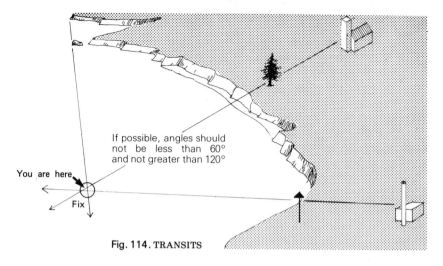

If possible, angles should not be less than 60° and not greater than 120°

You are here

Fix

Fig. 114. TRANSITS

When a tidal stream is running or the wind is blowing, a shot-line or the anchor must be dropped immediately both sets of marks are in line—perhaps even a short distance up tide or wind—or keep the engine running and hold the boat on the marks. It may also help to lower the anchor at least half the water depth, before the position is reached so that the time for it to reach the bottom is kept to a minimum. In haze, drizzle or where the marks are not clearly defined, be prepared for a search on the bottom, for even a small misalignment will mean that you are some tens of metres off position. This is a long way under water in low visibility, and a time-consuming search may be necessary.

The Sextant

This instrument is much misunderstood. It is simply a device for measuring angles accurately. There are generally three types which might be of interest to us:

(i) The conventional steel and brass model used by navigators.

(ii) A robust version of the navigator's model termed a 'boat sextant'.

(iii) A simple version made from plastic. Much cheaper to buy than (i) and (ii).

Fortunately for us as divers using very small boats, a plastic sextant is both accurate enough to cope with our navigational needs, and also robust enough to stand the rough handling and salt spray which it is liable to suffer in our care. A sextant can be used to measure either the horizontal angle between two charted marks or the vertical angle between the top and bottom of a tall object, giving a 'distance off' or range circle.

The horizontal angle can be converted into a position circle be-

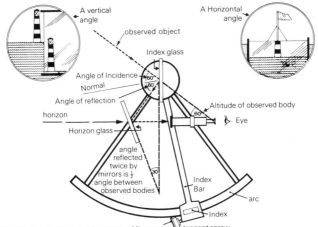

Fig. 115. PRINCIPLES OF THE SEXTANT

cause of a simple geometric principle. Take a circle and draw across it a straight line—AB in Fig. 116a—then the angles at any point of the circumference on the same side of the line are identical. In the smaller sector the angles will be greater than 90° and in the larger, less than 90°.

We can see from this principle that an angle can represent a circle, and so if we use our sextant to measure the angle between two charted marks, that angle represents a circle—in fact, a position circle on which we must have been in order to measure the angle!

The problem now is to draw the position circle on our chart. Fortunately this is simply solved and the method is as follows:

Measured angle greater than 90°
This means that the centre of the circle lies on the opposite side of the short AB to the boat.
Method:
(i) Join AB (that is, the two charted marks).
(ii) Subtract 90° from the measured angle.
(iii) Lay off lines from A and B respectively as on Fig. 116a.
(iv) Where they cross is the centre of the circle.
(v) The radius of the circle is the distance from this cross to A or B.
(vi) Draw the circle. For the measured angle our boat must be somewhere on its circumference to seaward of A and B.

Measured angle less than 90°
This means that the centre of the circle is on the same side of the chord AB as the boat.
Method:
(i) Join AB (that is, the two charted marks).
(ii) Subtract the measured angle from 90°.

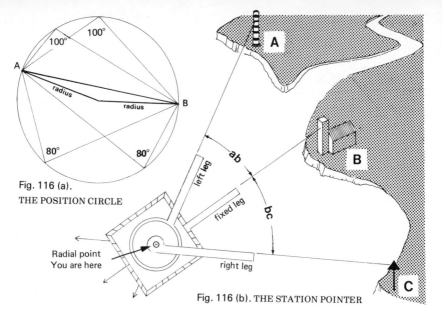

Fig. 116 (a).
THE POSITION CIRCLE

Fig. 116 (b). THE STATION POINTER

(iii) Lay off lines from A and B respectively as in Fig. 116a. Then continue as in the previous case.

But one position circle is not enough to give us a 'fix'. We must establish either another position line or position circle to do this. If there are three landmarks A–B–C, it is a simple matter to take sextant angles between A and B, and B and C, and using the geometric construction above, to plot two position circles. Where these cross each other is our position fix.

It is fairly obvious that drawing position circles on our chart in this way when we are bobbing about in a small wet boat is not terribly practical. Fortunately for us it is very simple to plot the position given by the two angles needed for a fix. We use an instrument called a *station pointer*—again there is a relatively cheap plastic version which is quite suitable for small-boat work.

To obtain the fix we take three charted marks and measure the two angles between them (Fig. 116b) then set them on our station pointer which has two movable arms for just this purpose. We then place the station pointer on our chart, and after some 'jiggling' which becomes simpler with practice, we can adjust it so that the three arms pass through the three marks. Our position is then straight under the centre of the instrument's hub, through which a hole is provided so you can plot the point on the chart.

Obtaining a position circle from a vertical angle is a simpler proposition. This time the angle is converted directly to a distance which is the radius of the circle. Just measure the angle between the top and bottom of a mark whose height is known. Tables are available in most nautical almanacs which lay out the distances for various heights and angles. With low objects or at a great distance from a tall object, a very small change in angle represents a significant change in distance. To be of value to us as divers the angle must, therefore, be measured very carefully. There is a further pitfall in that heights on a chart are given from the HAT (Highest Astronomical Tide), which means that when measuring an angle at any time other than High Water, it is necessary either to make sure that you measure from the high water mark—usually visible as a dark rim at the base of the object, cliff or whatever—or that you add the height of tide to the height of the object when entering the tables.

Magnetic Compass

As we have already discussed the compass needle is set in a circular card marked clockwise in 360° with zero at North. If a sighting device containing a prism is placed over the top of the compass it is possible to look along a line from the centre of the needle to any chosen mark. By looking down through the prism the angle between this sighting line and North may be read. This angle is known as the magnetic bearing—90° in Fig. 117. The compass we use which is fitted with a sighting device is known as a *Hand Bearing Compass.*

The sighting line may be reproduced on the chart of the area by adjusting a parallel ruler on the representation of the compass rose until it lines up to the magnetic bearing. The ruler is then run over the chart until it passes through the mark, and a pencil line drawn along its edge.

The pencil line is our position line for we know that at the time of the sight we were somewhere on it. Bearings from two objects

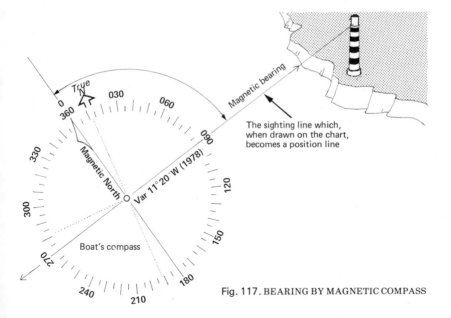

Fig. 117. BEARING BY MAGNETIC COMPASS

will give us two position lines and so a fix. Beware of two bearing fixes however, for although they can be taken quickly and very simply it is not at all easy to assess their accuracy. There are several reasons for error apart from the problems of deviation and variation which we will discuss more fully in a moment. Observer error is probably the most important, for when using the hand bearing compass from a small boat which is moving on even a slight sea, the compass card will swing with the movement and so make the observation difficult and inaccurate. The spacing of the divisions on the compass card, the quality of the prism used to read the card, and the strength of the magnets under the card all affect accuracy, and generally you get what you pay for—the more expensive the instrument the more accurate it is.

The error of a two bearing fix can be illustrated fairly simply. Anchor or secure your boat in a stable position. Then take three bearings and plot them. It is almost certain they will produce a *cocked hat*. The correct position is probably, but not necessarily, somewhere in the triangle or cocked hat, but whatever, it is easy to see that any two of the bearings would have been accurate. Even so, the hand bearing compass has a number of advantages over the sextant in certain conditions. A fix may be obtained from only two objects and at somewhat greater distances than can be obtained with a sextant. It is also usable in worse conditions of rain or spray, as it is possible to see through and clean the prism of the compass more easily than the two mirrors of the sextant. It is fairly obvious that the fixes taken under these conditions will not be accurate: however they may be better than none!

The compass can never be as accurate as the sextant even under ideal conditions, because apart from the errors we have discussed, it is susceptible to errors of deviation and variation. (Variation has been explained in the previous section: *Deviation* is another variable compass error induced by the proximity to the compass of ferrous metals or active electrical circuitry, which give out a magnetic field. The strength of this field may be greater than that of the earth, and the compass needle is deviated towards this 'local' magnetic field.)

There is one way of overcoming these errors completely, leaving only the errors of the observer. It is to use it exactly as a sextant and measure the two angles between three objects. This is done quite simply by taking the bearings of the three objects (Fig. 118).

Angle A = Bearing b − Bearing a.
Angle B = Bearing c − Bearing b.

and it is easy to see that the two angles will be the same wherever the compass needle is pointing. The position can then be fixed using the station pointer just as it is used with the sextant.

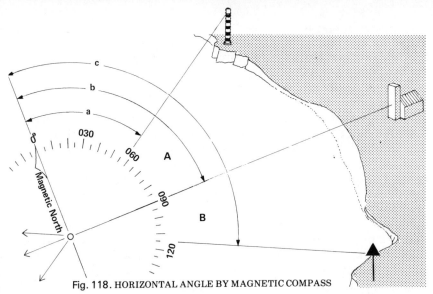

Fig. 118. HORIZONTAL ANGLE BY MAGNETIC COMPASS

There are occasions when there are only two charted marks available and we will have to make the best of compass bearings. In this case we must do our best to allow for the effects of deviation and variation, for they bother us just as much when taking a bearing as they do when we are steering and if not taken into consideration will make our position line wildly inaccurate. We have already sorted out in the previous section that we can avoid the problem of variation by using an up-to-date chart. Deviation is a somewhat different matter, and again our best way out is to avoid it.

This may or may not be possible and it will depend on whether or not we are able to find a position in our boat which is free from the influences of ferrous materials. If we can then there will be no deviation and no problem. If we cannot then something must be done— more of that in a moment. Our first need is to find a method which will allow us to sort out whether or not there is a deviation-free position in our boat. Briefly one of the simplest methods is to find a convenient transit shown on the chart so that we can measure its magnetic bearing. Then run across it on various headings checking the bearing each time with our hand bearing compass until we find a position in the boat where there is no difference on any heading between the magnetic and known compass bearings. Having done this once we need not repeat it unless we alter the magnetic material in the boat radically. In the sort of craft we are most likely to be using, it should be simple to find a place where there is no deviation. If such a place cannot be found, then it is necessary to produce a 'Deviation Table', and make the appropriate allowances when taking bearings. The means of producing a Deviation Table is beyond the scope of this Manual, and specialist publications on the subject, available from good marine bookshops, should be consulted.

T

Some Practical Notes on Fixing

Perhaps these notes should start with a word of warning. Navigation from a very small open craft is quite possible, but not necessarily easy the first time you ever try. If you go straight to the open sea the chances are that you will be tempted to give up the whole idea in the first half hour! The boat will never be still, the eyepiece of the instrument difficult if not impossible to look through—let alone line up on a small inconspicuous mark which seemed so large on the chart. Equally if you are with a team of divers they may well become somewhat impatient as you try madly to put your theory into practice!

Experience is as necessary in navigating as in anything else. Practise first on land, then in calm water and finally at sea, making sure that these first attempts are not sidetracked by any other activity and are solely for practice. In a Club it is possible to develop simple practice exercises. For instance, one team might go out and drop a very small buoy—take readings preferably with the sextant for maximum accuracy. Then a second team go out armed with the readings and try to find the buoy. Finding such a container which can only be seen from a few metres away helps to build up confidence.

NAVIGATIONAL INSTRUMENTS:

Try to buy the best you can afford. The card of a cheap compass will not steady on North very quickly after it has been moved suddenly, which means that it is difficult to know quite when to take the bearing of an object and quite large errors are possible. Equally the card of cheaper compasses may only be graduated every 5°, which means great accuracy is quite impossible.

As we have already discussed, it is best to take three bearings whenever possible. They should be taken as quickly as possible, and the angle between each pair should be between 25 and 75 degrees. The time of the fix is the time of the last bearing. If you have any chance it is always better to use the most conspicuous marks at the same height on the same piece of land, and with clear vertical edges. Going back to the time between the first and third bearings, at just 1 knot the boat will travel 30 m in 1 minute. Quite clearly the accuracy of the fix can never be better than the distance travelled in this time. It is essential to keep the boat's speed to a minimum during the fix.

Accuracy can be increased considerably if two sextants are used simultaneously; a simple drill will allow both angles to be measured at exactly the same time and so any error due to the boat's travel during the fix can be ruled out.

To sum it all up, 'Practice makes perfect'.

Appendices

Appendix 1—Decompression Tables—General Notes

These Tables are based on the RNPL Air Diving Table 1972 which is reproduced in full as part 2 of this appendix. The explanatory notes and instructions for using the Table therefore, apply to both the RNPL/BSAC Table and the RNPL 1972 Table. The only significant difference is that the RNPL 1972 Table has 5 m depth increments, whereas the RNPL/BSAC Table employs 2 m increments, this being considered more suitable for sports diving.

The RNPL 1972 Table has been extensively proved and an 'incidence factor' of less than 0.05% is claimed, making it safer than any other table so far published.

The Table allows for arduous activity such as fin swimming, which in earlier tables, required additional time/depth increments for safety.

In adopting this Table the BSAC National Diving Committee have not been influenced by the 'best buy' idea of bottom time plus decompression stops, but purely by the concept of safety, plus the fact that for the first time ever, we have a safe, sensible method of calculating repeat dives.

Using the RNPL/BSAC Table

1. The 'Bottom Time' is taken as the time between leaving the surface and leaving the bottom (commencing the ascent).
2. All descents to depth are to be made not faster than 30 m/minute.
3. All ascents are to be made at 15 m/minute.
4. All time spent ascending from one stop to another—including from depth to the first stop—is included in the stop time. The final ascent from a 5 m stop to the surface, which takes 20 seconds, is also included in the final stop time.

Study the Table carefully. The left-hand column shows depths in 2 m increments to a maximum of 50 m. (This level is recommended as the absolute limit for sports divers and should only be approached with great caution and after careful preparation.)

The second column shows 'No-Stop' limits. Dives with Bottom Times up to this time limit for any chosen depth require no decompression.

The remaining columns show Bottom Times for which decompression stops are required. Should the actual Bottom Time fall between figures along the line, the right-hand higher figure should be taken. For example if, on a 12 m dive, the actual Bottom Time were 143 minutes, the column for 159 minutes should be used.

The purpose of the two horizontal columns showing 'stops at . . .' should by now be obvious. Note that decompression dives not exceeding 20 m require only a single 5 m stop, whereas deeper decompression dives require stops at 2 levels.

The times shown in the right-hand column can be looked upon as a 'limiting line'. Dives with a longer Bottom Time could be made, but would carry a much greater risk of contracting decompression sickness. Also, the total duration of decompression stops for longer dives is very protracted. It is the Club's strong advice that members do not allow their diving to take them 'off the table'. However, if this does occur (and it should be anticipated before the dive, not discovered while trying to figure out decompression requirements during an ascent), the RNPL 1972 Table in part 2 of this appendix should be used to determine decompression requirements.

In the left-hand column of the Table find the figure which represents the greatest depth reached during the dive. If doubt exists, take the next greater depth.

Enter the Table horizontally along that line until the figure equal to, or next greater than the Bottom Time, is found.

RNPL/BSAC AIR DIVING DECOMPRESSION TABLE

Max. Depth metres	No. Stop mins.	Bottom Time					
9		NO LIMIT					
10	232	431	—	—	—	—	—
12	137	140	159	179	201	229	270
14	96	98	106	116	125	134	144
16	72	73	81	88	94	99	105
18	57	59	66	71	76	80	84
20	46	49	55	60	63	67	70
stops at 5 m		5	10	15	20	25	30
22	38	42	47	51	55	58	
24	32	37	41	45	48	51	
26	27	32	37	40	43	45	
28	23	29	33	36	39	41	
30	20	25	30	33	35	37	
32	18	23	27	30	32	34	
34	16	21	25	28	30	31	
36.	14	20	23	26	27	29	
38	12	18	21	24	26	27	
40	11	17	20	22	24	25	
42	10	16	19	21	22	24	
44	9	15	18	20	21		
46	8	14	17	18	20		
48	8	13	16	17			
50	7	12	15	17			
stops at 10 m		5	5	5	5	5	
5 m		5	10	15	20	25	

Ascent Rate 15 m/min. Descent Rate Max. 30 m/min. No more than 8 hrs. in 24 hrs. spend under pressure (submerged).

DOUBLE DIVES (A, B)

Decompress for the deepest depth	
1st dive Bottom Time A mins 2nd dive Bottom Time B mins B < 9 metres—No stop	
Both dives less than 40 m Interval Bottom Time	Either dive more than 40 m Interval Bottom Time
Up to 2 hrs. $A+B$	Up to 2 hrs. $A+B$
2–4 hrs. $\frac{A}{2}+B$	2–4 hrs. $\frac{A}{2}+B$
4–6 hrs. $\frac{A}{4}+B$	4–8 hrs. $\frac{A}{4}+B$
6+hrs. B	8–16 hrs. $\frac{A}{8}+B$
	16+hrs. B

Descend to the 'stops at . . .' line below to read off the depth and duration of stops. *Example 1.* Dive to 16 m for 75 minutes.

Enter horizontally on 'Maximum Depth—16 m' line. Bottom Time of 75 minutes falls between figures of 73 and 81 minutes, so take longer time for safety, i.e. 81 minutes. Descend to 'stops at' line where a 10 minute stop at 5 m is called for. *Example 2.* Dive to 30 m for 17 minutes.

This dive is within the 'No-Stop' limit (second column from left). No decompression stops are needed for Bottom Times up to this point. *Example 3.* Dive to 39 m for 25 minutes.

There is no information for 39 metres, so take the next greater depth of 40 m. Enter horizontally to 25 minutes. Read down to see that two stops are required—5 minutes at 10 m: 25 minutes at 5 m.

Repeat Dives

For a second dive (B) following a previous first dive (A) the computation of decompression depends upon the interval of time between the two dives and the depths concerned. For instance:

BOTH DIVES ARE TO LESS THAN 40 METRES

(a) If the time interval is up to 2 hours, add the two dive times.
(b) If the time interval is 2–4 hours, add half the first dive (A) time to the second (B).
(c) If the time interval is 4–6 hours, add a quarter of the first dive (A) time to the second (B).
(d) If the time interval is over 6 hours, treat as a separate dive.

EITHER DIVE IS TO MORE THAN 40 METRES

(a) If the interval is up to 2 hours, add the two dive times.
(b) If the time interval is 2–4 hours, add half the first dive (A) to the second (B).
(c) If the time interval is 4–8 hours, add a quarter of the first dive (A) to the second (B).
(d) If the time interval is 8–16 hours, add on eighth of the first dive (A) to the second (B).
(e) If the time interval is over 16 hours, treat as a separate dive.

In all cases, the depth for determining the decompression for the repeat dive is the deeper of the two dives.

If the second dive does not exceed 9 m (B < 9 m), it is safe to surface from this dive without stops.

Time spent on decompression stops following the first dive does NOT have to be included in the Bottom Time of A minutes when calculating Repeat Dive times.

Example 4.
Dive A: 20 m for 30 minutes. (No stops required).
Interval: 45 minutes.
Dive B: 20 m for 25 minutes.
Interval is less than 2 hours, so combine dive times.
Decompress for 20 m for 55 minutes.
Stops required: 10 minutes at 5 m.

Example 5.
Dive A: 27 m for 25 minutes. (Stops required).
Interval: 5 hours.
Dive B: 18 m for 30 minutes.
Dive A requires decompression stops of 5 minutes each at 10 m and 5 m. Decompression requirements after dive B are as follows:

$$\left(\frac{25}{4}+30\right) = 36\tfrac{1}{4} \text{ minutes at maximum depth of 27 m.}$$

Using 28 m Table and 39 minute Bottom Time, stops required are 5 minutes at 10 m: 20 minutes at 5 m.

Example 6.
Dive A: 42 m for 15 minutes. (Stops required).
Interval: 9 hours.
Dive B: 36 m for 30 minutes.
Dive A requires decompression stops of 5 minutes each at 10 m and 5 m. Decompression requirements after Dive B are as follows:

$$\left(\frac{15}{8}+30\right) = \text{approximately 32 minutes at a maximum depth of 42 m.}$$

THIS IS OFF THE TABLE! To find the decompression requirements, the full RNPL Air Diving Table 1972 should be consulted. This combination of dives takes the diver beyond the 'limiting line' and thus involves unreasonable risk as well as prolonged decompression. This dive sequence underlines the need to determine decompression requirements *before* the dive, not afterwards.

Diving at Altitude

Diving at altitude, perhaps in mountain lakes, needs adjustments to be made to compensate for surface pressure being less than one bar.

Altitude	Adjustment to get Dive Depth.
100 to 300 m	Add one quarter of measured depth.
300 to 2000 m	Add one third of measured depth.
2000 to 3000 m	Add one half of measured depth.

Do not allow for the fact that most lakes will be fresh water.

Example 7.

A 30 m dive of 22 minutes Bottom Time is made in a lake 550 m above sea level. Adjustment increment—add ⅓ of measured depth, i.e. decompress for a 40 m dive of 22 minutes Bottom Time.

Stops required are: 5 minutes at 10 m; 15 minutes at 5 m.

Flying Restrictions

To avoid the risk of decompression sickness being brought on by flying after having dived the following rules apply to flights in normal commercial cabin altitudes of 1500–3000 m.

Type of Dive	Period before Flying
No-Stop	2 hours
Dive needing stops	24 hours

RNPL Air Diving Tables 1972

The same Notes, Repeat Dive procedures, Diving at Altitude and Flying Restrictions given for the abbreviated RNPL/BSAC Table, apply to this full Table.

Normally, the Table recommends the use of Oxygen during decompression for dives requiring more than 30 minutes of stops, i.e. beyond the limiting line. This is obviously impractical for sports divers as well as being contrary to BSAC Rules so air stops only have been given.

Note that depths are in 5 m increments. The layout of the Table is self explanatory. If doubts exist over maximum depth or Bottom Time, use the next greater increment of depth or time.

RNPL Air Diving Table 1972—Air Stops only

Depth not Exceeding (metres)	Bottom Time not exceeding (min)	Stoppages at Different Depths (metres)					Total Time for Decompression (min)
		25 m	20 m	15 m	10 m	5 m	
9	No limit						—
10	230	—	—	—	—	—	1
	420	—	—	—	—	5	5
	480	—	—	—	—	10	10
15	80	—	—	—	—	—	1
	85	—	—	—	—	5	5
	90	—	—	—	—	10	10
	100	—	—	—	—	15	15
	110	—	—	—	—	25	25
Limiting	120	—	—	—	—	30	30
Line	150	—	—	—	—	50	50
	180	—	—	—	—	60	60
	240	—	—	—	—	80	80

Depth not Exceeding (metres)	Bottom Time not exceeding (min)	Stoppages at Different Depths (metres)					Total Time for Decompression (min)
		25 m	20 m	15 m	10 m	5 m	
20	45	—	—	—	—	—	1½
	50	—	—	—	—	5	5
	55	—	—	—	—	10	10
	60	—	—	—	—	15	15
	65	—	—	—	—	25	25
	Limiting 70	—	—	—	—	30	30
	Line 75	—	—	—	—	40	40
	90	—	—	—	—	60	60
	120	—	—	—	—	90	90
	150	—	—	—	—	110	110
	180	—	—	—	10	110	120
	240	—	—	—	10	120	130
25	25	—	—	—	—	—	2
	30	—	—	—	5	5	10
	35	—	—	—	5	10	15
	40	—	—	—	5	15	20
	Limiting 45	—	—	—	5	20	25
	Line 50	—	—	—	10	30	40
	55	—	—	—	10	40	50
	60	—	—	—	10	60	70
	75	—	—	5	—	80	85
	90	—	—	5	10	100	115
	105	—	—	5	10	120	135
	120	—	—	5	20	120	145
	150	—	—	5	30	120	155
	180	—	5	—	40	125	170
30	20	—	—	—	—	—	2
	25	—	—	—	5	5	10
	30	—	—	—	5	10	15
	Limiting 35	—	—	—	5	20	25
	Line 40	—	—	—	10	40	50
	45	—	—	—	10	50	60
	50	—	—	5	—	70	75
	55	—	—	5	10	80	95
	60	—	—	5	10	90	105
	75	—	—	5	10	110	125
	90	—	—	5	20	120	145
	120	—	—	5	50	125	180
35	15	—	—	—	—	—	2½
	20	—	—	—	5	5	10
	25	—	—	—	5	15	20
	Limiting 30	—	—	—	5	25	30
	Line 35	—	—	—	10	40	50
	40	—	—	5	10	60	75
	45	—	—	5	10	80	95

Depth not Exceeding (metres)	Bottom Time not exceeding (min)		Stoppages at Different Depths (metres)					Total Time for Decompression (min)
			25 m	20 m	15 m	10 m	5 m	
		50	—	—	5	10	90	105
		55	—	—	5	10	100	115
		60	—	—	5	10	110	125
		75	—	5	—	30	120	155
		11	—	—	—	—	—	3
		15	—	—	—	5	5	10
		20	—	—	—	5	10	15
	Limiting	25	—	—	—	5	25	30
40	*Line*	30	—	—	5	—	50	55
		35	—	—	5	10	70	85
		40	—	—	5	10	90	105
		45	—	—	5	10	100	115
		50	—	5	—	20	110	135
		55	—	5	—	20	120	145
		60	—	5	—	30	120	155
		9	—	—	—	—	—	3
		15	—	—	—	5	10	15
	Limiting	20	—	—	—	5	20	25
45	*Line*	25	—	—	5	10	40	55
		30	—	—	5	10	70	85
		35	—	—	5	10	90	105
		40	—	5	—	10	100	115
		45	—	5	—	20	110	135
		50	—	5	5	30	120	160
		55	—	5	5	40	125	175
		7	—	—	—	—	—	$3\frac{1}{2}$
		10	—	—	—	5	5	10
	Limiting	15	—	—	—	5	10	15
50	*Line*	20	—	—	5	10	30	45
		25	—	—	5	10	60	75
		30	—	—	5	10	80	95
		35	—	5	—	10	100	115
		40	—	5	5	20	120	150
		45	—	5	5	30	120	160
		50	5	—	5	40	125	175
		6	—	—	—	—	—	4
		10	—	—	—	5	5	10
	Limiting	15	—	—	5	—	15	20
55	*Line*	20	—	—	5	10	40	55
		25	—	—	5	10	70	85
		30	—	5	—	10	100	115
		35	—	5	5	20	120	150
		40	—	5	5	30	120	160
		45	5	—	5	45	125	180

Depth not Exceeding (metres)	Bottom Time not exceeding (min)	Stoppages at Different Depths (metres)					Total Time for Decompression (min)
		25 m	20 m	15 m	10 m	5 m	
	5	—	—	—	—	—	4
	10	—	—	—	5	10	15
	Limiting 15	—	—	5	5	20	30
	Line 20	—	—	5	10	50	65
60	25	—	—	5	10	90	105
	30	—	5	5	20	110	140
	35	5	—	5	30	120	160
	40	5	—	5	45	125	180
	45	5	—	10	60	125	200
65	10	—	—	—	5	10	15
	15	—	—	5	10	30	45
70	10	—	—	5	5	10	20
	15	—	—	5	10	40	55
75	10	—	—	5	5	15	25
	15	—	5	—	10	50	65

Appendix 2—Recompression Treatment

The only effective treatment for suspected air embolism or decompression sickness is prompt recompression under medical supervision. This can only be carried out successfully in a two-compartment recompression chamber under the guidance of a specialist medical adviser.

There are a number of suitable recompression chambers around the British Isles; some operated by commercial diving companies, others by the Royal Navy or by certain hospitals. In the UK, the Royal Navy Diving Establishment at HMS _Vernon_, Portsmouth maintains a record of the state of readiness of RN Recompression chambers and those in hospitals, but not of those operated by commercial diving companies. HMS _Vernon_ can also locate specialist medical advisers who can assist and advise local doctors or hospitals in the provision of care and treatment of a casualty requiring recompression.

Recompression chambers operated by other bodies may or may not be able to provide treatment, and this fact should be determined before a patient is conveyed to what may seem to be the nearest chamber. Check in advance of the dive whether the local facility is likely to be available should the need arise. Don't just turn up expecting it all to happen! Unless you know, by checking before the dive, that a chamber is available, contact HMS _Vernon_ first from any address in the UK. (Overseas divers should locate their nearest operational chamber before diving.)

Unless alternative arrangements have been confirmed, anyone seeking recompression treatment in the UK should in the first instance seek medical help and then contact HMS _Vernon_ by telephoning:

(a) Business Hours—Portsmouth (0705) 22351, Extension 872375, and ask for 'the Superintendent of Diving'.

(b) At other times—Portsmouth (0705) 822351, Extension 872413/4/5, and ask for 'the Duty Lieutenant Commander'.

Once in touch with the Officer, give the following information:
1. Your name, telephone number (so *Vernon* can phone you back if necessary) and exact location.
2. Name of patient, and symptoms exhibited.
3. Name, address and phone number of local doctor or hospital caring for the patient.
4. Details of the dive(s) made prior to the onset of symptoms. Be honest about them— someone's future fitness is at stake.
5. Any other information which may be asked of you.

HMS *Vernon* will then alert specialists and facilities as required to provide treatment. If you do use a local commercially operated recompression chamber, specialist medical advice from HMS *Vernon* is still available to you.

Except in cases of acute and obvious air embolism, one-man chambers should not be used. Once pressurised, the subject cannot be given the additional medical care which is normally part of the treatment.

Police and Ambulance services may be able to assist in transporting cases to recompression facilities. These are best called upon by a doctor or hospital.

Appendix 3—BSAC Training and Tests

The tests detailed in this appendix may change from time to time. Information about what changes, if any, have been made should be available from the Secretary or Diving Officer of your Branch. Alternatively, it may be obtained from the Principal National Coach, 16 Upper Woburn Place, London WC1H 0QW.

In addition, it is a BSAC rule that prospective members should have a medical examination on entry to the Club. Further medicals should be taken at five-yearly intervals up to the age of thirty, every three years to the age of fifty and every year after attaining this age.

It must be stressed that *no Branch has the right to add, or subtract, from the current standards.* This is to ensure uniformity.

Snorkel Diver

In the following tests the various groups must be taken in sequence, and the tests in each group taken at one time in the sequence specified. Diving suits may be worn—in which case buoyancy correction is made before commencing the tests.

Tests in the following Groups B and C call for the use of basic equipment, i.e. fins, mask and snorkel. Nose clips should not be worn, and the snorkel tube should be of the single bend, open-end type.

SWIMMING TEST:
All tests in this group to be completed without equipment.
Group A
1. Swim 200 m freestyle (except backstroke) without a stop.
2. Swim 100 m backstroke without a stop.
3. Swim 50 m wearing a 5 kg weight-belt.
4. Float on back for 5 minutes (hand and leg movement permitted).
5. Tread water with hands above head for one minute.
6. Recover 6 objects from deep end of training pool (one dive per object).
N.B.—Item 3—Weight may be reduced for junior or female members, or for those with a low buoyancy index.

PRIMARY TESTS:
Before commencing training for these tests, the pupil must satisfy the Branch Diving Officer that he is aware of the dangers of hypoxia and of eardrum rupture and is in fact able to 'clear ears' by pressure equalisation through the eustachian tubes.

It is recommended that ALL training be completed before the tests are taken, and that Groups B and C tests should, whenever possible, be taken together.

Group B
1. Sink basic equipment in deep end of training pool: dive for each item in turn and fit on the surface.
2. Fin 200 m, surface diving every 25 m.
3. Tow an adult 50 m by BSAC method incorporating EAR in the water: give at least three effective breaths in this distance. Land 'body' and continue EAR.
4. Perform three rolls forward and three rolls backward (breath may be taken between rolls).
5. Fin 15 m under water.
6. Hold breath for 30 seconds under water.

Group C
1. Fin 50 m wearing 5 kg weight-belt.
2. Release weight-belt in deep end of pool. Remove mask.
3. Fin 50 m, face submerged, using snorkel but no mask.
4. Complete at deep end, replace mask, surface dive, recover and re-fit weight-belt. Give signal 'I am OK, proceeding'.
5. Fin an additional 50 m wearing 5 kg weight-belt.

On completion of Groups A, B and C, the pupils may, at the discretion of the Branch Diving Officer, progress to pool aqualung training. Concurrently with this training they should gain practical open-water experience of using basic equipment by taking the Open-Water Snorkel Diving Test.

OPEN-WATER SNORKEL DIVING TEST:
Before commencing training for the test, the pupil must satisfy the Branch Diving Officer that he knows and thoroughly understands the hazards of doing any form of diving when suffering from a cold, ear or sinus infection, respiratory or heart weakness. If any doubt as to fitness exists, a medical certificate should be obtained.

Group D
1. Confirm physical fitness.
2. Fin 500 m in open water wearing basic equipment and, at some time during this swim, surface dive to a depth of 7 m and also perform a rescue and 50 m tow of a Snorkel Diver, using a BSAC method.
3. Attend at least three open-water meetings, using basic equipment.

LECTURES:
Sinuses; Circulation and Respiration; Hypoxia, Anoxia and Drowning; Rescue and Resuscitation; Signals and Surfacing Drill; Exhaustion and Exposure; Diving Suits and Protective Clothing; Ancillary Equipment; Snorkelling Activities.

On completion of Groups A–D inclusive and on passing an appropriate examination by the Branch Diving Officer, the pupil may be rated by the Branch Committee as a SNORKEL DIVER.

3rd Class Diver

This grade is recognised by the World Under-water Federation (CMAS) as equivalent to a Two-Star Diver. A BSAC 3rd Class Diver is a diver who is proficient in the basic open-water use of an aqualung, wet suit and ancillary equipment; in related safety and rescue procedures; and having a good basic knowledge of diving theory. Although still regarded as a diver under training, diving with another diver of the same standard is permitted but not normally with a diver of a lower standard.

To qualify as a 3rd Class Diver, the Snorkel Diver must complete a course of theory and practical training, on completion of which, the following qualifying tests are taken. The test groups must be taken in sequence and the individual parts of the group taken in the sequence specified.

Groups E and F tests should, whenever possible, be taken together.

INTERMEDIATE AQUALUNG TEST:

Before commencing aqualung training, the pupil must satisfy the Branch Diving Officer of his/her knowledge of the elementary diving hazards, i.e. pressure effects, burst lung and exhaustion, and a familiarity with the diver-to-surface-party signals.

The following group of tests should be carried out in a training pool or in other safe water where continuous observation and control of the pupil is possible. Diving suits may be worn when taking these tests.

GROUP E

1. Fit harness and demand valve to cylinder. Test and adjust aqualung.
2. Sink all equipment in the deep end. Dive and fit without surfacing.
3. Remove mouthpiece under water, replace and clear. Repeat twice more.
4. Remove mask under water, replace and clear. Repeat twice more.
5. Demonstrate mobility with aqualung by completing three forward and three backward rolls.
6. Demonstrate buoyancy control by adjusting diving level by depth of respiration. Breathe out hard, relax and lie on bottom. Lift off bottom by controlled inspiration.
7. Remove aqualung at surface in deep end, fit snorkel and fin 50 m towing aqualung.
8. Dismantle, clean and dry aqualung, and stow away to instructor's satisfaction.

GROUP F

1. Fin 100 m on the surface as follows:
   (a) 50 m alternating between snorkel and aqualung;
   (b) 50 m on back wearing aqualung and carrying snorkel, but using neither.
2. Surfacing drill. From deep end, surface, remove mouthpiece, fit snorkel and give OK signal. Repeat twice more.
3. Share aqualung with companion at a depth not greater than 3 m. Establish breathing exchange, then fin 25 m providing air and 25 m receiving air.
4. Fin 50 m under water with mask blacked out, led by a companion or following a rope.
5. Fin 50 m submerged at speed. Complete in deep end where companion is simulating insensibility. Release both weight-belts, bring 'body' to the surface and tow for 25 m by BSAC method incorporating EAR while towing.
6. Remove both sets of equipment in the water, land 'body' (assistance permitted) and carry out EAR.

OPEN-WATER AQUALUNG TEST

On completion of Groups E and F tests, the pupil may, at the discretion of the Branch Diving Officer, progress to open-water aqualung training.

GROUP G

1. Demonstrate in open water with aqualung the surfacing drill and code of diver-to-surface-party signals.
2. Demonstrate in open water with aqualung, correct adjustment of buoyancy when wearing a diving suit.
3. Enter the water in full equipment, from a height of not less than 1 m above water level in a depth of water of not less than 2 m. Repeat twice more. Take care to ensure unobstructed water.
4. At a depth of 7 m, remove, replace and clear mouthpiece, then remove, replace and clear mask.
5. Establish a breathing and exchange rhythm when sharing mouthpiece as recipient while stationary at a depth of 7 m. Maintain rhythm while finning horizontally for 20 m. Repeat, acting as donor.
6. On one open-water dive, rescue an aqualung diver. Tow 50 m using BSAC method incorporating EAR (another diver may assist).

7. *Qualifying Dives*—Carry out 10 open-water qualifying dives from at least five different sites and on at least five different dates. These dives should each have a submerged duration of not less than 15 minutes and should show experience of five of the following conditions:

(a) Shore dive along shelving bottom;
(b) Dive from a boat;
(c) Dive in fresh water;
(d) Dive in moving water (1 knot maximum);
(e) Dive in sea water;
(f) Low visibility dive (less than 2 m);
(g) Dive in cold water (10°C or less);
(h) Dive to 25 m.

LECTURES

Physics of Diving; Principles of the Aqualung; Aqualung Use and Buoyancy Control; The ABLJ—its use and application; Burst Lung and Emergency Ascent; Air Cylinders and Air Endurance; Underwater Navigation; Open-Water Diving; Diving from Small Boats; Decompression Sickness—avoidance; Nitrogen Narcosis; CO Poisoning; Oxygen Poisoning; Deep Diving and its Problems.

On completion of all theory and practical training, and on passing an appropriate theory test to the satisfaction of the Branch Diving Officer, the candidate may be rated by the Branch Committee as a THIRD CLASS DIVER.

2nd Class Diver

To qualify for the rating of 2nd Class Diver, the 3rd Class Diver must log a minimum of 20 additional open-water dives under the direct supervision of the Branch Diving Officer or a Diving Marshal. Each of these dives are to be of a submerged duration of not less than fifteen minutes.

The dives should be from at least 10 different sites and on at least 10 different dates, and should show experience in at least five of the following conditions:

(a) Large boat dive;
(b) Wreck dive;
(c) Night dive;
(d) Simulated stage decompression dive;
(e) Dive with task of work (other than (l) and (m)):
(f) Dive to 30 m;
(g) Drift dive;
(h) Zero visibility dive;
(i) Cold weather dive;
(j) Dive under ice;
(k) Dive into under-water cavern;
(l) Recovery exercise;
(m) Survey.

These qualifying dives are not to be regarded solely as 'experience' dives, but are part of the continuous training programme. Thus, during the course of this further training, the candidate should, to the satisfaction of the Branch Diving Officer, demonstrate his or her ability on open-water dives in the following manner:

1. Having first established a breathing and exchange rhythm, carry out two assisted ascents from 20 m to the surface: first receiving air from companion, and on the second occasion, providing air for companion.
2. Act as a tender to a roped diver: act as a roped diver. Give and receive satisfactory signals for a period of not less than fifteen minutes on both occasions.
3. Demonstrate ability to find the way under water—use of compass for straight line and square navigation exercises.
4. Plan and execute a rope search at a depth of not less than 7 m.

5. Plan and execute a search in very low visibility water.
6. Swim 500 m wearing full aqualung equipment but using a snorkel; and at some time during the swim, tow a 'body' for 50 m by BSAC method incorporating EAR. Neutral buoyancy should be demonstrated both before and after the swim.

The candidate for 2nd Class Diver should act as Dive Leader on at least four occasions: and, under the supervision of the Branch Diving Officer, should act as deputy to a qualified Dive Marshal on two occasions—one of which should be a boat dive, and then act as a Dive Marshal on two occasions—one of which should be a boat dive in a tide or current.

LECTURES:
Decompression Sickness—the condition and its treatment; Compressors and Recharging; Under-water Search Methods; Roped Diver Operations; Low Visibility and Night Diving; Basic Seamanship; Charts and Tide Tables; Basic Navigation and Position Fixing; Expeditions; Advance Planning and On-site Conduct; Safety and Emergency Actions.

On completion of all theory and practical training, and on passing an appropriate theory test to the satisfaction of the Branch Diving Officer, the candidate may be rated by the Branch Committee as a SECOND CLASS DIVER.

First Class Diver

This is the highest diving qualification in the BSAC. It is a national qualification which cannot be given at Branch level. Despite this, it is the Branch's duty to see that facilities for attaining First Class grade are available to all members. This means that provision for taking the Deep Rescue Test and Sub-Aqua Bronze Medallion are just as important as the tests of lower grades, and should be provided if possible.

Apart from the personal satisfaction of attaining First Class, the study and work involved leading up to the examination cannot fail to make the candidate a better diver.

The First Class Diver is the person the Club calls upon when representation is required in a particular area—and the National Diving Committee consists largely of First Class Divers.

To qualify for a 1st Class Diver's Certificate the candidate must satisfy the following conditions:
1. Be rated Second Class Diver in the age group 20–50.
2. Provide evidence of current BSAC membership, having been a member continuously for the past three years.
3. Submit properly certified Logbooks showing a minimum of 100 water dives under varying conditions. A proportion of these dives should show reasonable experience of depths greater than 30 m.
4. Submit a current BSAC Medical Certificate.
5. Submit a Royal Life Saving Society Sub-Aqua Bronze Medallion, or equivalent qualification, obtained not more than three years prior to the examination.
6. Submit evidence of having successfully carried out the Deep Rescue Test.
7. Submit a letter of recommendation from his Branch Committee.
8. Satisfactorily complete a written examination.
9. Pass a practical diving test.

On completion of the above conditions, the member may, at the discretion of the Council of the British Sub-Aqua Club, be awarded a certificate of competency as FIRST CLASS DIVER. Up-to-date details of the examination syllabus may be obtained from the First Class Diver Examination Organiser, c/o BSAC Headquarters.

Club Instructor

This is the first of the three grades of BSAC Instructor qualifications. To attain this rating which equates to the CMAS One-Star Instructor rating, it is necessary to attend a day-long examination. Members wishing to apply for the Club Instructor Examination should meet the following qualifying conditions:

1. Hold BSAC 2nd Class Diver qualification.
2. Provide evidence of current BSAC Membership, having been a member for not less than one year.
3. Submit a current Medical Certificate of fitness, and written proof of a satisfactory current chest X-ray.
4. Be not less than 18 years of age.
5. Submit a letter from the candidate's Branch Committee, confirming that the candidate has experience as an Instructor at Branch level.
6. Have previously attended an Instructor Training Course.
7. Complete an Entry Form and submit it, together with the Examination fee and items listed above, to the Examination Organiser.

Advanced Instructor

This is the next grade up from Club Instructor and equates with the CMAS Two-Star Instructor rating. The course/examination is held over a weekend and is open to Club Instructors only who should meet the following qualifying conditions:
1. Hold BSAC Club Instructor qualification.
2. Provide evidence of current BSAC Membership.
3. Submit a current Medical Certificate of fitness, and written proof of satisfactory current chest X-ray.
4. Be not less than 19 years of age.
5. Submit a letter from the candidate's Branch Committee, confirming that the member has at least one year's experience of instructing since qualifying as a Club Instructor.
6. Complete an Entry Form and submit it, together with the Examination Fee and items listed above, to the Examination Organiser.

National Instructor

This grade equates with the CMAS Three-Star Instructor rating and members wishing to apply for the examination should meet the following qualifying conditions:
1. Hold BSAC Advanced Instructor qualification.
2. Provide evidence of current BSAC Membership.
3. Submit a current Medical Certificate of fitness, and written proof of a satisfactory current chest X-ray.
4. Be not less than 20 years of age.
5. Submit a letter from the candidate's Branch Committee confirming that the member has had at least one year's experience of instructing since qualifying as an Advanced Instructor.
6. Submit two passport-size photographs.
7. Complete an Entry Form and submit it, together with the Examination Fee and items listed above, to the Examination Organiser.

Logbook Endorsements

A number of optional awards/qualifications are available, in subjects such as Boat Handling; Chartwork/Navigation; RLSS Sub-Aqua Bronze Medallion; Deep Rescue; Marine Biology; First Aid; etc. Some of these are required for BSAC First Class Diver grade. For further details, see the BSAC Diving Officers Handbook; discuss with your Branch Diving Officer, or seek information from the Director of Coaching at BSAC HQ.

Appendix 4—Pool Discipline

Behaviour at 'wet' meetings is most important: if it isn't good, you may lose the best swimming pools in your area. It has happened to others, don't let it happen in your Branch.

Pool Regulations

1. Members are to observe and obey the rules and regulations of the swimming pool as laid down by the owners, the pool superintendent or relevant authority.
2. While responsibility for the organisation of instruction and direct training discipline is in the hands of the relevant Branch Diving Officer of the British Sub-Aqua Club, and his assistants, the swimming pools are at all times in the charge of the pool superintendent, whose ultimate authority must be unquestioned.
3. Payment for the use of the swimming pools must be made to the relevant authority, as arranged and stipulated in the terms of hire.
4. Where necessary, arrangements must be made for the collection of payments from the members present at the training sessions, preferably at the door, by a responsible member of the British Sub-Aqua Club properly appointed for that duty.
5. The swimming pool must be vacated at the time stipulated and on the instruction of the pool superintendent.
6. Any mishap resulting in physical injury to any person, whether a member of the British Sub-Aqua Club or not, or any damage to any property of the swimming pool authorities must be reported immediately to the instructor in charge, and, by him, to the pool superintendent.

British Sub-Aqua Club Regulations

1. All instruction in swimming pools must be under the authority of the Branch Diving Officer, who may delegate his authority to pool marshals, suitably qualified to take charge of training sessions.
2. Such pool marshals are to be responsible for the enforcement of pool rules and regulations, the maintenance of pool discipline and for the proper conduct of training.
3. No 'mixed' swimming may take place, i.e. some members with and others without under-water swimming equipment, unless in separate sections of the pool.
4. It is recommended that pool marshals wear red skull caps, armbands, or other distinguishing marks when on duty at training sessions.

Pool Discipline

1. No interference with other swimmers using the pool.
2. No jumping or diving into the water. *You run the risk of hurting others and damaging equipment.*
3. No overarm strokes except when taking swimming tests, in approved free swimming sessions, or in parts of the pool distinctively set aside for free swimming only. *You might impede others, and you are wasting vital energy.*
4. Move quietly and calmly in the water. *That is good diving.*
5. No splashing with fins. *That is bad diving.*
6. No racing or under-water endurance contests. *Exhaustion and hypoxia can kill.*
7. Always look down before diving, up before surfacing. *Remember the other pool users.*
8. All equipment must be in sound condition and of high standard. *Faulty and shoddy equipment is inefficient and dangerous.*
9. Never drop heavy equipment either in the pool or on the surrounds. *It can cause considerable damage.*
10. Equipment is always to be worn in the water, except under certain circumstances of controlled instruction.
11. No running round pool sides in equipment. *Fins can easily trip you and others: masks fall off.*
12. No shouting or rowdyism. *You might divert attention from an emergency.*
13. It is recommended that skull caps or helmets be worn. *For identification, hygiene and prevention of heat loss.*
14. Never enter the water with a cold, catarrh or other infection. *It is dangerous to swim in such circumstances.*

15. Never enter the water with an open wound, or when wearing a bandage or plaster. *It is unhygienic and inconsiderate.*
16. Obey the instructions of the pool marshals. *Non-compliance may result in exclusion from pool training sessions.*

(Approved in principle by the Institute of Baths Management.)

Appendix 5—The Divers' Codes of Conduct

As an island nation, it is not surprising that a great number of people indulge in sporting and leisure pursuits which are water based.

This means, of course, that some recognised form of conduct is essential in order that the best use is made of our inland and coastal water areas.

The British Sub-Aqua Club, and also the National Snorkellers Club both have a Code of Conduct which members should observe. By so doing, members will not only demonstrate their consideration for other water users, but will also avoid alienating the general public who could be inconvenienced by thoughtless conduct.

Members should observe the Codes at all times.

The Snorkel Diver Code

1. Before Snorkel Diving within harbour limits or in private water, or where access is over private land, obtain permission.
2. Preferably consult the local diving Branch about diving conditions, particularly before using a new site. Avoid overcrowding.
3. Do not let your vehicles obstruct highways or damage land or verges.
4. Pick up litter, close gates, guard against fire risk. Do not damage land or crops.
5. Avoid Snorkel Diving in fairways or areas of heavy surface traffic. Remember that large ships cannot alter course or speed quickly and must keep to recognised channels.
6. Select a point of easy access and exit from the water. Arrange for a boat or shore cover. Only use a boat that is suitable and is in competent hands.
7. Do not interfere with fishermen's lines, nets or pots, or with activities of other users in the area.
8. Do not take fish or shellfish below the minimum permitted sizes. Do not sell shellfish.
9. Do not remove articles from wrecks without permission. Avoid damage, pillage or disturbance to under-water plants and creatures, or to the sea-bed.
10. Remember the reputation of the Club depends on your snorkel diving efficiency and good conduct.

The Divers' Code

Before leaving home:

Contact the nearest British Sub-Aqua Club Branch to the dive site for their advice. Ask the National Coach for the Region about local conditions and regulations.

ON THE BEACH

1. Obtain permission before diving in harbour or estuary or in private waters. Thank those responsible when you leave. Pay harbour dues.
2. Try to avoid overcrowding one site.
3. Park sensibly. Avoid obstructing narrow approach roads. Keep off verges. Pay parking fees and use proper car parks.
4. Don't spread yourselves and your equipment so that you upset others. Keep launching ramps and slipways clear.
5. Please keep the peace. Don't operate a compressor within earshot of other people —especially at night.
6. Pick up litter. Close gates. Be careful about fires. Avoid any damage to land or crops.

7. Obey special instructions such as National Trust rules, local bye-laws and regulations about camping and caravanning.
8. Remember divers in wet suits are conspicuous and bad behaviour will ban us from beaches.

IN AND ON THE WATER

1. Ask the harbour-master, local officials or fishermen where to launch your boat—and do as they say. Tell the Coastguard or responsible person where you're going. And tell them when you're back.
2. Stay away from buoys, pots and pot markers. Ask local fishermen where not to dive. Offer to help them recover lost gear.
3. Remember ships have not got brakes. So avoid diving in fairways or areas of heavy surface traffic.
4. Never use a speargun with an aqualung. Never use a speargun in fresh water.
5. Always fly the diving flag when diving. Not when on the way to or from the dive site.
6. Only take mature fish or shellfish and then only what you need to eat yourself. Never sell your catch or clean it above the high water mark. Don't display your trophies.
7. Be conservation-conscious. Avoid damage to weeds and the sea-bed. Do not bring up sea fans, corals, starfish or sea-urchins—in one moment you can destroy years of growth.
8. Do not come in under power to bathing beaches. Use any special approach lanes. Do not disturb seal or bird colonies with your boat. Watch your wash in crowded anchorages.

ON WRECKS

1. Do not dive on a designated wreck site. These are marked by buoys. Historic wreck buoys are green and yellow with vertical stripes unless they are spar buoys when the green and yellow markings will be in horizontal bands. Some sites may not be marked by buoys but yellow and green wreck warning notices about them are displayed at lighthouse stations.
2. Do not lift anything which appears to be of historical importance. Carefully pinpoint the site, do a rough survey and report it to the BSAC Archaeological Adviser and the local representative of the Committee for Nautical Archaeology who will advise you.
3. If you discover a wreck, do not talk about it. Await CNA and BSAC advice.
4. If you do not lift anything from the wreck, it is not necessary to report your discovery to the Receiver of Wreck. If you do lift, you must report.
5. Start conservation treatment immediately on any item recovered.
6. If your find is really historic, it may well become a designated or protected wreck site. Then you can build up a well-qualified team with the right credentials and apply for a licence to work on the site.
7. Don't be a wreck robber. Don't use explosives.

Appendix 6—Legislation Relating to Diving

The British Sub-Aqua Club is a club for sports divers, and it is a happy fact that there are no mandatory government regulations or laws about the way the sport is conducted, except with regard to the standards and testing of air cylinders. In all other matters, the BSAC, as the governing body for the sport, is trusted to make sensible regulations for the safe conduct of instruction and diving, not only by BSAC members but all other UK sports divers with due regard for the welfare of other water users.

However there may be times when Club members may be asked to dive for reward—for example, cleaning the hull of a yacht, or they may participate in scientific expeditions, or simple search and recovery tasks. At some point, not always easy to define, the diving activity ceases to be classed as sports diving. The BSAC Third Party insurance cover then ceases to apply.

If you take commercial diving employment, the legal situation is clear—you must be qualified as a commercial diver and your diving activities (in UK territorial waters) must be carried out in accordance with the Health and Safety at Work Act—*Diving Operations at Work Regulations—1981*. These Regulations came into force in July 1981, and superseded all other earlier legislation.

It would occupy far too much space to print these Regulations in full in this Manual, but they apply to anybody who earns part or all of their livelihood by diving. For example, the Regulations apply to professional Instructors of sports diving: underwater Cine and Still Photographers; Journalists; Scientists; Archaeologists; Inspectors, etc., as well as to the more obvious cases of North Sea Rig diver, harbour or river work diver.

Exemptions from some of the Regulations have been negotiated by certain groups representing Diving Schools, Scientists and Archaeologists, Photo-journalists, etc., but the exemptions are mainly concerned with the conduct of diving operations. In every case, the diver must undergo a Commercial Diver Medical Examination annually and has to maintain a detailed record of dives.

While amateur divers may still carry out 'good works' for donations to charities or branch funds; and in certain circumstances may dive with commercial divers in the course of their activities, the net cast by the Diving Operations at Work Regulations is very broad. It can be said that if you can earn any money by diving, the Regulations apply.

For more information, study a copy of the Health and Safety series booklet *HS(R) 8—A Guide to the Diving Operations at Work Regulations 1981* obtainable from HMSO. BSAC HQ is able to give further particulars about diving activities where Exemption Certificates may apply and advice on where to receive training as a Commercial Diver. At the time of preparing this text, the HSE have indicated that a BSAC Second Class Diver should be able to qualify as a 'Part IV' diver through a short training course and assessment. Members who are not Second Class or who seek HSE Part III or Part I Commercial Diver standards will have to undergo a full course at an HSE Approved Commercial Diver Training School.

Appendix 7—Fish Law

There are laws about practically everything found in or taken from the sea. Fish and shellfish are not exceptions and here is a guide to those laws. *There may be local restrictions as well and this should be checked.*

MINIMUM SIZES FOR FISH AND SHELLFISH:

Under the Sea-Fishing Industry (Immature Sea-Fish) Order, 1968, legal minimum sizes are specified for the under-mentioned sea-fish, measured from the tip of the snout to the end of the tail fin.

Brill	30 cm	11.8 in	Lemon Soles	25 cm	9.8 in
Cod	30 cm	11.8 in	Megrims	25 cm	9.8 in
Common Soles	24 cm	9.4 in	Plaice	25 cm	9.8 in
Dabs	15 cm	5.9 in	Turbot	30 cm	11.8 in
Haddock	27 cm	10.6 in	Witches	28 cm	11.0 in
Hake	30 cm	11.8 in	Whiting	25 cm	9.8 in

Under the Immature Crabs and Lobsters Order, 1976, the following sizes for shellfish are prescribed:

(a) in relation to crabs of the species *Cancer pagurus*, a width of 115 mm across the broadest part of the back:

(b) in relation to lobsters, a carapace of 83 mm, being measured from the rear of either eye socket to the rear end of the body shell along a line parallel to the centre line of the body shell.

The landing, sale or possession for sale in Great Britain of 'berried' lobsters and 'berried' or soft crabs (i.e. lobsters or crabs in spawn) is also prohibited.

FRESHWATER FISH:

Under the Salmon and Freshwater Fisheries Act 1923 (Section 1), the use of a spear or like instrument for the purpose of taking salmon, trout or freshwater fish is prohibited.

There are laws, too, that govern the spearfisherman through his possession of a harpoon gun, and the following should be noted:
The spearfisherman may be affected by both the Gun Licence Act of 1870 and the Firearms Act of 1937. An inquiry about previous confusion over whether or not spearguns came under these Acts brought the following reply from Scotland Yard:
'All types of spearguns need a gun licence, that is a licence obtained from the Post Office as for shotguns, etc.
'But certain of the types of spearguns require a firearms licence which must be obtained from the Police as for revolvers, etc.
'It is suggested that the owner of such a weapon should ask the advice of the police locally about his particular speargun.'

Appendix 8—Weather

Gales and weather can wipe out a dive—so can a light wind from the wrong direction. Too many checks on the weather cannot be made before a dive.
Details of weather services in the British Isles via Press, Radio, Television, Coastal Stations and Telephones are given in MO Leaflet No. 1, obtainable free of charge from the Senior Meteorological Officer, London Weather Centre, 284 High Holborn, London WC1. Telephone 01-836 4311.
BBC Shipping Forecasts are given on Radio 2. 200 kHz (1500 m). As the times may vary they are not listed here. Full details of current times are given in the Radio Times.

Sea and Swell

Sea is defined as the waves caused by wind at a given place.
Swell is caused by waves formed by past wind, or wind at a distance.
Short swell: where the length or distance between each successive top of the swell is small.
Long swell: where the length or distance as above is large.
Low swell: where the height between the lowest and highest part of the swell is small.
Heavy swell: where the height as above is great.

International Swell Scale

Code Figure	State of the swell in the open sea	
0	None	
1	Short or average length	Low
2	Long	
3	Short	
4	Average length	Moderate height
5	Long	
6	Short	
7	Average length	Heavy
8	Long	
9	Confused	

Fog and Visibility Scale for Ships at Sea

Code No.	Description	Definition	
0	Dense fog	Objects not visible at	5 metres
1	Thick fog	,, ,, ,, ,,	200 metres
2	Fog	,, ,, ,, ,,	400 metres
3	Moderate fog	,, ,, ,, ,,	$\frac{1}{4}$ mile
4	Mist or haze or very poor visibility	,, ,, ,, ,,	1 mile
5	Poor visibility	,, ,, ,, ,,	2 miles
6	Moderate visibility	,, ,, ,, ,,	5 miles
7	Good visibility	,, ,, ,, ,,	10 miles
8	Very good visibility	,, ,, ,, ,,	30 miles
9	Excellent visibility	Objects visible more than	30 miles

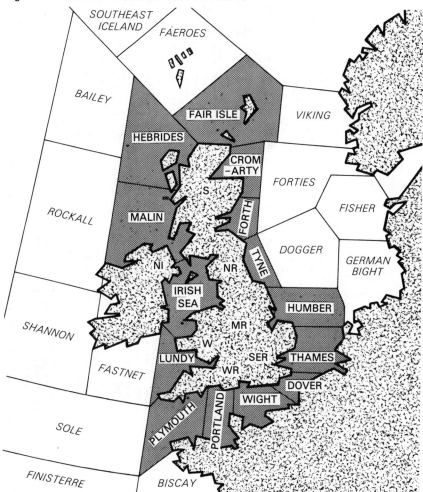

Fig. 119. BBC & GPO WEATHER FORECAST AREAS

Boundaries of Sea Areas as used in BBC and GPO Weather Forecasts
Weather within an estuary, and particularly the visibility there, may often be expected to differ from that forecast for the coastal sea area in which the estuary lies, though this will not necessarily be mentioned in the forecast.

The tinted sea areas are those for which visual gale warnings are displayed.

Appendix 9—When is it High Tide?

Table of Tidal Constants Relative to High Water at London Bridge

Add+, or Subtract−, to time at London Bridge. The places given in the table are listed anticlockwise, starting from the Thames Estuary.

Place	hr. min	Place	hr. min
Southend	−1.25	Aldeburgh	−3.23
Clacton	−2.11	Lowestoft	−4.26
Felixstowe	−2.18	Gt. Yarmouth	−4.55

The Beaufort Wind Scale

Beaufort International Number	As used by Mariners				As used by Landsmen		
	Wind	Nautical miles per hours (knots)	Feet per second	Indications at sea	Wind	Statute m.p.h. recorded at 33 ft. above ground level	Indications on land
0	Calm	Less than 1	Less than 2	Sea mirror smooth	Calm	Less than 1	Smoke rises vertically.
1	Light air	1–3	2–5	Small wavelets like scales, no foam crests	Light air	1–3	Direction shown by smoke but not by wind vanes.
2	Light breeze	4–6	6–11	Waves short and more pronounced; crests begin to break; foam has glassy appearance—not yet white	Light breeze	4–7	Wind felt on face; leaves rustle, ordinary vanes moved by wind.
3	Gentle breeze	7–10	12–18		Gentle breeze	8–12	Leaves and small twigs in constant motion; wind extends light flag.
4	Moderate breeze	11–16	19–27	Waves are longer; many white horses	Moderate breeze	13–18	Raises dust and waste paper; small branches are moved.
5	Fresh breeze	17–21	28–36	Waves now pronounced and long; white foam crests everywhere	Fresh breeze	19–24	Small trees in leaf begin to sway; crested wavelets form on inland waters.
6	Strong breeze	22–27	37–46	Larger waves form; white foam crests more extensive	Strong breeze	25–31	Large branches in motion; whistling heard in telegraph wires; umbrellas used with difficulty.
7	Strong wind	28–33	47–56	Sea heaps up; wind starts to blow the foam in streaks	Moderate gale (see note)	32–38	Whole trees in motion; inconvenience felt when walking against wind.
8	Fresh gale	34–40	57–68	Height of waves increases visibly; also height of crests; much foam is blown in dense streaks	Fresh gale	39–46	Breaks twigs off trees; greatly impedes progress.
9	Strong gale	41–47	69–80		Strong gale	47–54	Slight structural damage occurs (chimney pots and slates removed)
10	Whole gale	48–55	81–93	High waves with long overhanging crests; great foam patches	Whole gale	55–63	Seldom experienced inland; trees uprooted; considerable structural damage occurs.
11	Storm	56–65	94–110	Waves so high that ships within sight are hidden in the troughs; sea covered with streaky foam; air filled with spray.	Storm	64–75	Very rarely experienced; accompanied by widespread damage.
12	Hurricane	Above 65	Above 110		Hurricane	Above 75	—

Note: Mariners never use the term 'Gale' for winds of less than Force 8. Gale warnings are only issued and cones hoisted for winds of Force 8 upwards.

Place	hr. min	Place	hr. min
Wells-next-the-sea	+5.11	Falmouth	+3.36
Skegness	+4.25	Plymouth	+3.54
Grimsby	+4.2	Salcombe	+4.6
Bridlington	+3.11	Torquay	+4.39
Scarborough	+2.43	Lyme Regis	+4.46
Whitby	+2.19	Weymouth	+5.5
W. Hartlepool	+2.5	Swanage	−3.23
Sunderland	+2.0	Cowes	−2.30
Alnmouth	+1.22	Ventnor	−2.50
Berwick-upon-Tweed	+0.55	Southsea	−2.28
Dunbar	+0.33	Bognor Regis	−2.28
Leith	+0.41	Brighton	−2.38
Kirkcaldy	+0.38	Hastings	−2.47
Fife Ness	+0.20	Dover	−2.42
Dundee	+1.11	Margate	−2.1
Montrose	+0.30	Sheerness	−1.19
Aberdeen	−0.20	Portpatrick	−2.38
Fraserburgh	−1.25	Balcary Point	−2.12
Lossiemouth	−2.0	Annan	−2.2
Inverness	−1.38	Whitehaven	−2.35
Dornoch	−1.40	Barrow-in-Furness	−2.46
Golspie	−2.14	Morecambe	−2.36
Wick	−2.28	Blackpool	−2.41
Thurso	−5.31	Wallasey	−2.37
Tongue	−6.6	Llandudno	−3.18
Kylesku	+5.39	Holyhead	−3.32
Ullapool	+5.29	Nefyn	−4.30
Portree	+4.59	Barmouth	−5.47
Plockton	+5.9	Aberystwyth	−6.12
Mallaig	+4.26	Cardigan	+5.40
Tobermory	+4.23	Skomer	+4.28
Oban	+4.13	Tenby	+4.28
Crinan	+3.33	Llanelly	+4.32
Greenock	−1.32	Swansea	+4.33
Ayr	−1.52	Porthcawl	+4.40
Padstow	+4.8	Barry	+5.13
St Ives	+3.43	Clevedon	+5.18
Lizard	+3.20	Burnham-on-Sea	+5.17
		Ilfracombe	+4.28

Printed by permission of the
Liverpool Observatory and Tidal Institute.

N.B.—The times of High Water at London Bridge or Dover may be obtained from the newspapers each day, and from various almanacs and other publications.

Appendix 10—In Trouble at Sea

The following are internationally-recognised signals for indicating distress at sea:
1. A rocket parachute flare, or a hand flare showing a red light.
2. Rockets throwing red stars at short intervals.
3. A smoke signal giving off a volume of orange-coloured smoke.
4. A signal made by whistle, torch or radio consisting of the Morse Code group S O S (· · · − − − · · ·), or the spoken word MAYDAY.
5. Slowly raising and lowering outstretched arms repeatedly.
6. The continuous sounding of a whistle or siren.
7. Flames on the vessel—as from burning oily rags.

8. The International Code Flag Signal of distress indicated by the flags N C.
9. A signal consisting of a square flag having above or below it a ball or anything resembling a ball.
10. An ensign hoisted upside down.
11. An ensign made fast high in the rigging.
12. A coat or article of clothing on an oar or mast.

Note—Signals 1, 2, 3, 4 (except by radio), 5, 6 and 12 are most suitable for small craft.

Appendix 11—Coastguard Stations

Here is a list of HM Coastguard and Maritime Rescue Co-ordination Centres (MRCCs) and Maritime Rescue Sub-Centres (MRSCs) with their telephone numbers. The centres are listed alphabetically in each country.

ENGLAND
Brixham MRSC, Devon *(08045) 2156*.
Dover MRCC, Kent *(0304) 210008*.
Falmouth MRCC, Cornwall *(0326) 317575*.
Great Yarmouth MRCC, Norfolk *(0493) 51338*.
Hartland MRSC, Devon *(02374) 235*.
Humber MRSC, N. Humberside *(09646) 351*.
Liverpool MRSC, Merseyside *(07048) 72903*.
Portland MRSC, Dorset *(0305) 820441*.
Ramsey MRSC, Isle of Man *(0624) 813255*.
Shoreham MRSC, West Sussex *(07917) 2226*.
Solent MRSC, Isle of Wight *(0983) 752265*.
Tees MRSC, Cleveland *(0642) 474639*.
Thames MRSC, Essex *(02556) 5518*.
Tyne MRSC, Tyne & Wear *(0632) 572691*.

WALES
Holyhead MRSC, Gwynedd *(0407) 2051*.
Milford Haven MRSC, Dyfed *(06465) 218*.
Swansea MRCC, West Glamorgan *(0792) 66534*.

SCOTLAND
Aberdeen MRCC, Aberdeenshire *(0224) 52334*.
Clyde MRCC, Renfrew *(0475) 29988*.
Forth MRSC, Fife *(03335) 666*.
Moray MRSC, Aberdeenshire *(0779) 4278*.
Oban MRSC, Argyllshire *(0631) 63720*.
Orkney MRSC, Orkney *(0856) 3268*.
Shetland MRSC, Shetlands *(0595) 2976*.
Stornoway MRSC, Isle of Lewis *(0851) 2013*.
Wick MRSC, Caithness *(0955) 2332*.

NORTHERN IRELAND
Belfast MRSC *(0247) 84284*.

In an emergency for coastal or sea rescue, dial 999 and ask for 'Coastguard'.

Appendix 12—Conversions

At some time or other, divers may find themselves having to convert from metric to imperial measure or vice-versa. The following conversion figures should prove helpful.

TEMPERATURE
To convert degrees Centigrade to degrees Fahrenheit: multiply by 9/5 and add 32.
To convert degrees Fahrenheit to degrees Centigrade: subtract 32 and multiply by 5/9.

LENGTH

1 centimetre	= 0.394 inches
1 metre	= 3.281 feet
1 metre	= 1.094 yards
1 metre	= 0.547 fathoms
1 kilometre	= 0.621 statute miles
1 kilometre	= 0.540 nautical miles
1 inch	= 2.54 centimetres
1 foot	= 0.305 metres
1 yard	= 0.914 metres
1 fathom	= 1.829 metres
1 statute mile (5280 feet)	= 1.609 kilometres
1 nautical mile (6080 feet)	= 1.853 kilometres

CAPACITY/VOLUME

1 cubic centimetre	= 0.061 cubic inches
1 cubic metre	=35.315 cubic feet
1 cubic metre	= 1.308 cubic yards
1 litre (1000 cc)	= 0.035 cubic feet
1 litre	= 0.220 gallons
1 litre	= 1.760 pints
1 cubic inch	=16.387 cubic centimetres
1 cubic foot	= 0.028 cubic metres
1 cubic foot	=28.316 litres
1 cubic yard	= 0.765 cubic metres
1 pint	= 0.568 litres
1 gallon	= 4.546 litres

WEIGHT

1 kilogram	= 2.205 pounds
1 metric tonne	= 0.984 long tons (2205 pounds)
1 lb	= 0.454 kilograms
1 long ton	= 1.016 metric tonnes (1016 kilograms)

PRESSURE

1 kilogram per square centimetre=14.223 pounds per square inch
1 pound per square inch = 0.0703 kilograms per square centimetre

WATER

1 litre of fresh water weighs 1 kilogram.
1 cubic foot of fresh water weighs 62.5 pounds (approx.).
1 cubic foot of sea water weighs 64 pounds (approx.).

APPROXIMATE CONVERSIONS:

Miles to kilometres	multiply by 8/5
Kilometres to miles	multiply by 5/8
Statute miles to nautical miles	deduct 1/8
Nautical miles to statute miles	add 1/7
Pounds per square inch (psi) to atmospheres ...	divide by 14.7
Atmospheres or bars to kilos per square centimetre	nearly the same
Water depth (feet) to bars absolute	divide by 33 and add 1 bar
Water depth (metres) to bars absolute	divide by 10 and add 1 bar
Bars absolute to feet of water depth	subtract 1 bar and multiply by 33
Bars absolute to metres of water depth	subtract 1 bar and multiply by 10

EPTH CONVERSION TABLE:

Metres	Feet	Fathoms	Metres	Feet	Fathoms
1	3.2808	0.5468	20	65.6	10.9
2	6.5616	1.0936	30	98.4	16.4
3	9.8424	1.6404	40	131.2	21.9
4	13.1	2.2	50	164.0	27.3
5	16.4	2.7	60	196.8	32.8
6	19.6	3.3	70	229.7	38.3
7	23.0	3.8	80	262.5	43.7
8	26.2	4.4	90	295.3	49.2
9	29.5	4.9	100	328.1	54.7
10	32.8	5.5	110	360.9	60.1
11	36.1	6.0	120	393.7	65.6
12	39.4	6.6	130	426.5	71.1
13	42.7	7.1	140	459.3	76.6
14	45.9	7.7	150	492.1	82.0
15	49.2	8.2	160	524.9	87.5
16	52.5	8.7	170	557.7	93.0
17	55.8	9.3	180	590.6	98.4
18	59.1	9.8	190	623.4	103.9
19	62.3	10.4	200	656.2	109.4

Comparison of Cylinder Capacities and Mass of Air Contained

CAPACITY OF CYLINDER			MASS OF AIR	
Cubic Feet	Litres	Cubic Metres	Pounds	Kilogrammes
40	1133	1.133	3.1	1.39
45	1274	1.274	3.4	1.56
50	1416	1.416	3.8	1.74
55	1557	1.557	4.2	1.91
60	1699	1.699	4.6	2.08
65	1841	1.841	5.0	2.26
70	1982	1.982	5.4	2.43
75	2124	2.124	5.7	2.60
80	2265	2.265	6.1	2.78

Comparison of Cylinder Pressures

lbf/in^2	MN/m^2	ats	bar
1800	12.4	122	124
2000	13.8	136	138
2250	15.5	153	155
2500	17.2	170	172
2650	18.2	180	183
3000	20.7	204	207

Index